PAGE
52

ON THE ROAD

YOUR COMPLETE DESTINATION GUIDE
In-depth reviews, detailed listings
and insider tips

Trekking Routes >p266

Biking, Rafting & Kayaking >p292

Pokhara
p191

The Terai & Mahabharat
Range p216

Kathmandu to
Pokhara p182

Kathmandu
p54

Around the Kathmandu
Valley p112

Health

Recommended
Vaccinations

D1040378

THIS EDITION WRITTEN AND RESEARCHED BY

Bradley Mayhew,
Lindsay Brown, Trent Holden

welcome to Nepal

Mountain Adventures

Ever since Nepal first opened its borders to outsiders in the 1950s, this tiny mountain nation has had an irresistible mystical allure for travellers. Today, legions of trekkers are drawn to the Himalaya's most iconic and accessible hiking, some of the world's best, with rugged trails to Everest, the Annapurnas and beyond. Nowhere else can you trek for days or even weeks in incredible mountain scenery, secure in the knowledge that a hot meal, cosy lodge and warm slice of apple pie await you at the end of the day. Nepal is nirvana for mountain lovers.

Other travellers are drawn here by the adrenaline rush of rafting down a roaring Nepali river or bungee jumping into a bottomless Himalayan gorge. Canyoning, climbing, kayaking, paragliding and mountain biking all offer a rush against the backdrop of some of the world's most dramatic landscapes.

Temples & Tigers

Other travellers prefer to see Nepal at a more gentle pace, admiring the peaks over a gin and tonic from a Himalayan viewpoint, strolling through the temple-lined medieval city squares of Kathmandu, Patan and Bhaktapur, and joining Buddhist pilgrims on a spiritual stroll around the centuries-old stupas and temples that lie scattered across the Kathmandu Valley.

Wedged between the high wall of the Himalaya and the steamy jungles of the Indian plains, Nepal is a land of snow peaks and Sherpas, yaks and yetis, monasteries and mantras.

(left) The majestic Annapurna Range, viewed from the Annapurna Circuit Trek (p274)
(below) Gurung women (p330) performing a traditional dance

Further south lie Nepal's wild and woolly national parks, where nature buffs scan the treetops for exotic bird species and comb the jungles for rhinos and tigers from the backs of lumbering Indian elephants. Whether you cross the country by mountain bike, motorbike, raft or tourist bus, Nepal offers an astonishingly diverse array of attractions and landscapes.

Travel Heaven

There are few countries in the world that are as well set up for independent travel as Nepal. Wandering the trekking shops, bakeries and pizzerias of Thamel and Pokhara, it's easy to feel that you have somehow landed in a kind of backpacker Disneyland. Out in the countryside lies a quite different Nepal, where traditional mountain life continues stoically and at a slower pace, and a million potential adventures glimmer on the mountain horizons.

The biggest problem faced by visitors to Nepal is how to fit everything in. Many people have spent a lifetime exploring the mountain trails of the Himalaya and the atmospheric temple towns of the Middle Hills, and they still keep coming back for more. Our advice is to pick a handful of essential experiences for your first visit and save the rest for trips two, three and four...

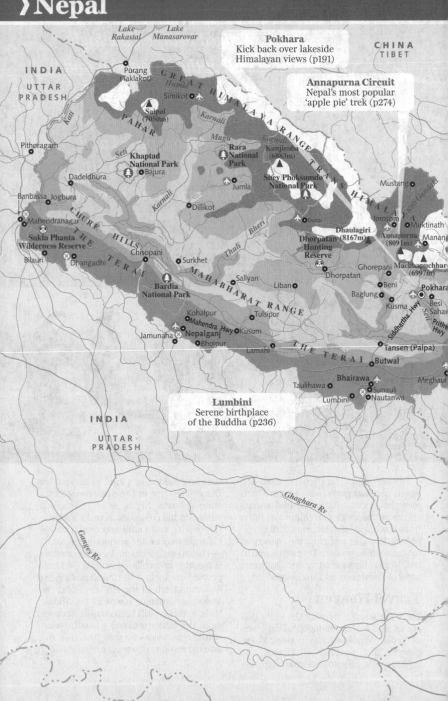

Pokhara
Kick back over lakeside
Himalayan views (p191)

Annapurna Circuit
Nepal's most popular
'apple pie' trek (p274)

Lumbini
Serene birthplace
of the Buddha (p236)

Top Experiences ›

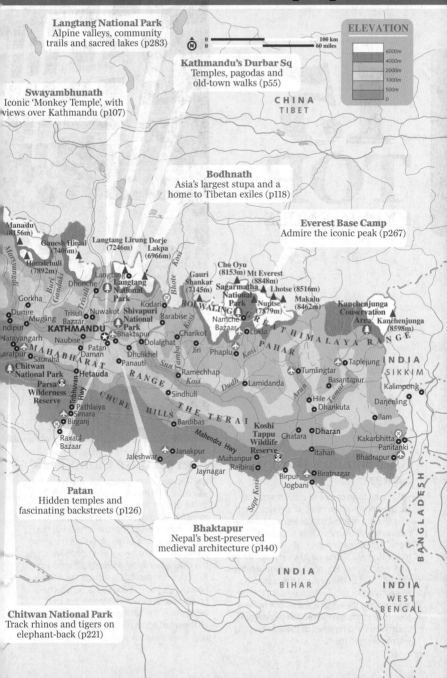

Langtang National Park
Alpine valleys, community trails and sacred lakes (p283)

Kathmandu's Durbar Sq
Temples, pagodas and old-town walks (p55)

Swayambhunath
Iconic 'Monkey Temple', with views over Kathmandu (p107)

Bodhnath
Asia's largest stupa and a home to Tibetan exiles (p118)

Everest Base Camp
Admire the iconic peak (p267)

Patan
Hidden temples and fascinating backstreets (p126)

Bhaktapur
Nepal's best-preserved medieval architecture (p140)

Chitwan National Park
Track rhinos and tigers on elephant-back (p221)

ELEVATION

6000m
4000m
2000m
1000m
500m
0

100 km
60 miles

CHINA
TIBET

Manaslu (8156m)
Ganesh Himal (7406m)
Himalchuli (7892m)
Langtang Lirung (7246m)
Dorje Lakpa (6966m)
Gauri Shankar (7145m)
Cho Oyu (8153m)
Mt Everest (8848m)
Lhotse (8516m)
Nuptse (7879m)
Makalu (8462m)
Kanchenjunga Conservation Area
Kanchenjunga (8598m)

Marsyangdi
Buri Gandaki
Trisuli
Bhote Kosi
Kosi
Tamba Kosi
Sun Kosi
Kosi
Dudh Kosi
Arun
Tamur
Sapt Kosi

Gorkha
Dumre
Mugling
Dhunche
Langtang
Langtang National Park
Shivapuri National Park
Nuwakot
Kodari
Barabise
ndipur
Trisuli
KATHMANDU
Naubise
Patan
Bhaktapur
Dolalghat
Charikot
Namche Bazaar
Lukla
Sagarmatha National Park
Phaplu
Narayangarh
Sauraha
Daman
Dhulikhel
Panauti
Jiri
Ramechhap
Lamidanda
Tumlingtar
Taplejung
Basantapur
Chitwan National Park
Hetauda
Sindhuli
Hile
Dhankuta
Darjeeling
Ilam
Parsa Wilderness Reserve
Simara
Pathlaiya
Bardibas
Koshi Tappu Wildlife Reserve
Chatara
Dharan
Kakarbhitta
Panitanki
Birganj
Raxaul Bazaar
Jaleshwar
Janakpur
Mahanpur
Rajbiraj
Itahari
Bhadrapur
Birpur
Jogbani
Biratnagar
Jaynagar

ROLWALING
SAGARMATHA
PAHAR
GREAT HIMALAYA RANGE
MAHABHARAT RANGE
CHURE HILLS
THE TERAI
Mahendra Hwy
Tribhuvan Hwy

INDIA
SIKKIM
Kalimpong

INDIA
BIHAR

INDIA
WEST BENGAL

BANGLADESH

15 TOP EXPERIENCES

Kathmandu's Durbar Square

1 The historic centre of old Kathmandu is an open-air architectural museum of magnificent medieval temples, pagodas, pavilions and shrines. Once occupied by Nepal's cloistered royal family and still home to the Kumari, Kathmandu's very own living goddess, Durbar Sq (p55) is very much the sacred heart of the city and the backdrop to several spectacular festivals. For the best approach to the square, follow our walking tour (p72) through the hidden backstreet courtyards and temples of the surrounding warren-like old town.

Everest Base Camp Trek

2 Topping many people's travel bucket list is this two-week-long trek (p267) to the base of the world's highest, and most hyped, mountain. The actual views of the mountain are partial at best but the surrounding Himalayan peaks are truly awesome, and the half-hour you spend watching the alpenglow ascend beautiful Pumori or Ama Dablam peaks is worth all the altitude headaches you will doubtless suffer. The crowds can be thick in October but the welcome at the Sherpa lodges is as warm as the fresh apple pie that is served. Nuptse with Everest in background

Annapurna Circuit Trek

3 This 19-day hike (p274) around the 8091m Annapurna massif is Nepal's most popular trek, and it's easy to see why. The lodges are comfortable, the mountain scenery is superb, the crossing of the 5416m Thorung La provides a physical challenge and the sense of journey from lowland to Trans-Himalayan plateau is immensely satisfying. Our best tip is to take your time and explore the spectacular side trips, particularly around Manang. Road construction may have eaten away at the western sections around Jomsom, but some spectacular alternative footpaths continue to avoid the road.

Bhaktapur & the Kathmandu Valley

4 The Kathmandu Valley boasts the world's densest collection of World Heritage Sites. Of the valley's three former cities, all Unesco sites, medieval Bhaktapur (p140) is easily the most intact and is bursting with temples, pagodas and ornate pools. Winding backstreets of traditional red-brick buildings lead onto squares used by locals for drying corn and making pottery. The traffic-free streets offer fabulous scope for exploration on foot. For the full experience, stay overnight in a guesthouse or attend one of the city's fantastic festivals.

PAUL A SOUDERS/CORBIS ©

BRUNO MORANDI/HEMIS/CORBIS ©

Elephant Safari, Chitwan National Park

5 In the 'other Nepal', down in the humid plains, Chitwan is one of Asia's best wildlife-viewing spots and the place to don your safari togs, clamber atop a lumbering elephant (p226) and head into the dawn mist in search of rhinos and tigers. There's plenty to keep you busy here, from joining the elephants at bath time to visiting local Tharu villages, and the brave can even take a guided walk through the jungle, surrounded by the hoots and roars of the forest.

Bodhnath Stupa

6 The village of Bodhnath is the centre of Nepal's Tibetan community and home to Asia's largest stupa (p120), a spectacular white dome and spire that draws pilgrims from hundreds of kilometres away. Equally fascinating are the surrounding streets, bustling with monks with shaved heads and maroon robes, and lined with Tibetan monasteries and shops selling prayer wheels and incense. Come at dusk and join the Tibetan pilgrims as they light butter lamps and walk around the stupa on their daily kora (ritual circumambulation).

Views from Pokhara

7 Nepal's second-biggest tourist town (p191) may lack the historical depth of Kathmandu, but it more than makes up for this with a seductively laid-back vibe and one of the country's most spectacular locations. The dawn views of Machhapuchhare and Annapurna, mirrored in the calm waters of Phewa Tal or seen from the town's hilltop viewpoints, are simply unforgettable. Take them in on a trek, from the saddle of a mountain bike or, best of all, dangling from a paraglider high above the valley floor.

Lumbini – Birthplace of the Buddha

8 A pilgrimage to the birthplace of the Buddha (p236) ranks as one of the subcontinent's great spiritual journeys. You can visit the exact spot where Siddhartha Gautama was born 2500 years ago, rediscovered only a century or so ago, and then tour the multinational collection of temples built by neighbouring Buddhist nations. But perhaps the most powerful thing to do is simply find a quiet spot, and a book on Buddhism, and meditate on the nature of existence. Travel experiences don't get much more profound than that.

CHRIS KLEP/LONELY PLANET IMAGES ©

JANE SWEENEY/LONELY PLANET IMAGES ©

RICHARD I'ANSON/LONELY PLANET IMAGES ©

Langtang Trekking

9 If you have only a week but want to get a taste of Nepali-style trekking, it's hard to beat the Langtang region (p283), which borders Tibet. The scenery ranges from steep hillsides of bamboo and rhododendrons to sprawling yak pastures and finally an alpine cul de sac framed by 7000m peaks. You can even get fresh yak-cheese toasted sandwiches along the way. There are also plenty of trekking add-ons here, including walks to the sacred lakes of Gosainkund and through the charming traditional villages of the Tamang Heritage Trail.

White-Water Rafting

10 Nepal is one of the world's best rafting and kayaking destinations. Fuelled by water rushing down from the Himalayan peaks, day runs on the Bhote Kosi offer thrilling white water that comes straight from Tibet. Even better are the longer multiday adventures – liquid journeys that take you down the Karnali, Tamur and Sun Kosi Rivers through some of Nepal's remotest corners. Sections switch from roller-coaster white water to serene floats through jungle wilderness, with nights spent camping on pristine sand beaches. See p297 for more.

Nepal's Fantastic Festivals

11 Nepal has so many spectacular festivals that any visit is almost certain to coincide with at least one. Celebrations range from masked dances designed to exorcise bad demons to epic bouts of tug-of-war between rival sides of a town. For a full-on medieval experience, time your travel with one of the slightly mad chariot processions, when hundreds of enthusiastic devotees drag tottering 20m-tall chariots through the crowded city streets of Kathmandu and Patan. Indra Jatra (p20)

Swayambhunath

12 The iconic whitewashed stupa of Swayambhunath (p107) is both a Unesco World Heritage Site and one of Nepal's most sacred Buddhist shrines. Beneath the iconic, all-seeing eyes of the stupa lies an eclectic mishmash of prayer flags, Buddha statues and Tibetan chapels. Pilgrims wander the shrines, spinning prayer wheels and murmuring mantras, while nearby astrologers read palms, and shopkeepers sell magic amulets and sacred beads. Come at dusk for spectacular views over the city lights of Kathmandu.

Patan

13 Kathmandu's sister city (p126) doesn't get the attention it deserves. The best way to explore the city's interconnected Buddhist courtyards and hidden temples is on foot. Wander the fascinating backstreets, the magnificent central Durbar Sq and the Patan Museum, easily the best in the country. Throw in four ancient stupas and the valley's best collection of international restaurants and it's clear you need a couple of trips to take it all in. Best of all, spend the night here and you'll likely have the backstreets all to yourself.

RICHARD I'ANSON/LONELY PLANET IMAGES ©

RICHARD I'ANSON/LONELY PLANET IMAGES ©

14

RICHARD I'ANSON/LONELY PLANET IMAGES ©

15

Momos

14 These little meat- or vegetable-filled dumplings are Nepal's unofficial national dish. Enjoy them in one of Kathmandu's grandiose traditional Nepali restaurants, at a shared table with monks in a backstreet Tibetan kitchen or in a trekking lodge overlooking the Annapurnas – they are the quintessential taste of the Himalayas. Join a cooking class to learn how to make these deceptively simple morsels that are savoured from China to Central Asia. Kathmandu's restaurants also fill them with apple and cinnamon, and serve them with ice cream. Yum!

Nepal's People

15 It is often said that while you first come to Nepal for the mountains, you return here for the people. From quietly protective Sherpa guides to welcoming Tibetan hotel owners and Newari shopkeepers, all Nepalis receive guests with respect and a *namaste* greeting. They're quick to smile in the most trying circumstances, and you'll rarely hear a raised voice or an angry word anywhere you go. It's one of the great joys of travelling here. See p326 for more about Nepal's people.

Musicians performing at the Holi festival (p19)

need to know

When to Go

Subtropical warm winters, hot wet summers
Cool winters, warm wet summers
High altitude freezing winters, cool summers

Jomsom
GO Jun–Nov

Everest Base Camp
GO Mar–May
Oct–Nov

Pokhara
GO Oct–Apr

Chitwan
National Park
GO Oct–Mar

Kathmandu
GO Sep–Apr

High Season
(Oct–Nov)
» Clear skies and warm days make autumn the peak season. Thousands of people hit the trails in the Everest and Annapurna regions and accommodation in Kathmandu gets booked up as prices peak.

Shoulder
(Mar–Apr)
» The second-best time to visit brings warm weather and spectacular springtime rhododendron blooms.

Low Season
(Jun–Sep)
» The monsoon rains bring landslides and clouds obscure mountain views, though hefty hotel discounts are common. Rain and leeches deter most trekkers, but this is a popular time to travel overland to Tibet.

Your Daily Budget

Budget less than
US$40
» Budget hotel room in Kathmandu: US$5–20

» Dinner & breakfast in a trekking lodge: US$10–12

» Trekking porter/guide: US$13/20 per day

Midrange
US$40–100
» Organised camping trek: US$50–80 per person per day

» Midrange meal in Kathmandu: US$7–10

» Midrange hotel: US$20–80

Top End over
US$100
» Top-end hotel in Kathmandu or lodge in Chitwan: US$150–250

» Mountain flight: US$171

» Mustang trekking permit: US$500 per week

Money

» Easy to change cash and access ATMs in Kathmandu, Pokhara and other cities but almost impossible in rural areas or on treks

Visas

» Tourist visas available on arrival; bring two photos and cash in US dollars

Mobile Phones

» Buy SIM cards at Kathmandu airport on arrival or at Ncell offices across the country

Driving/ Transport

» Buses are slow and cramped, especially on mountain roads; tourist buses are more comfortable. Taxis are good value for shorter trips.

Websites

» **Explore Nepal** (www.explorenepal. com) Useful Nepal portal; try also www. nepalhomepage.com or www.nepaltourism.info.

» **Nepal Tourism Board** (www. welcomenepal.com) Government site.

» **Nepal Travel Blogs** (http:// nepaltravelblogs.com) Interesting collection of travel tips.

» **Visit Nepal** (www. visitnepal.com) Comprehensive private website with detailed travel tips.

» **Lonely Planet** (www. lonelyplanet.com/nepal) Hotel bookings, traveller forum and more.

Exchange Rates

Australia	A$1	Rs 77
Canada	C$1	Rs 75
China	Y1	Rs 12
Europe	€1	Rs 106
Japan	¥10	Rs 10
UK	£1	Rs 122
US	US$1	Rs 80
India	₹1	Rs 1.60

For current exchange rates see www.xe.com.

Important Numbers

Country code	☑977
International access code	☑00
Police	☑100
Tourist police	☑4247041
Tourism hotline	☑4225709

Arriving in Nepal

» **Kathmandu's Tribhuvan Airport** Prepaid taxis are available inside the terminal. Many midrange hotels offer useful free pick-ups from the airport. Long queues at immigration can slow things up if you are getting your visa on arrival.

» **Sunauli (Indian border)** For Kathmandu and Pokhara take a direct bus from the border. Golden Travels (p105) offers the most comfortable service. For other destinations take a jeep or rickshaw to Bhairawa and change there.

Don't Leave Home Without

» A face mask against Kathmandu's air pollution if you plan to rent a motorcycle or bike

» Earplugs for travel on noisy turboprop planes and local buses, plus noisy hotel rooms

» Lip balm and sunscreen for mountain hikes

» Hiking boots or shoes – buying footwear in Nepal is a shortcut to blisters

» A good padlock for locking your bag to bus baggage racks

» An LED torch for inevitable power cuts, and night-time toilet trips while trekking

» Insect repellent for the Terai (plus anti-leech oil for monsoon travel)

» A swimming costume for rafting, kayaking, canyoning, elephant washing (yes, elephant washing; see boxed text p227) and, well, swimming!

» A reusable water bottle and iodine tablets to purify your own water

if you like...

Temples

Nepal's Hindu and Buddhist temples are masterworks in oiled brick, stone and carved wood. Awe-inspiring statuary, incredibly ornate toranas (lintels) and erotic carvings still inspire the desired amount of wonder.

Kathmandu's Durbar Square Take a perch on one of the tiered temples in this magical medieval square and watch traditional city life pass below you (p55)

Bhaktapur Nepal's best-preserved medieval town offers the tallest temple in the country, a royal palace and even some carved elephant erotica (p141)

Golden Temple, Patan This 15th-century courtyard is centred on a beautiful Buddha statue and fine Tibetan frescoes, fiercely guarded by slow-moving tortoises (p131)

Changu Narayan Temple The 1500-year-old Licchavi statues and carvings at this World Heritage Site rank it as a treasure-house of Himalayan art (p156)

Trekking

There are few places in the world where you can walk for days through incredible mountain scenery, safe in the knowledge that you'll find a hot dinner and a place to stay at the end of each day. You simply can't say you've seen Nepal until you've done some trekking there.

Everest Region Astounding high mountain scenery and cosy Sherpa lodges, but try to visit outside of October (p267)

Annapurna Circuit Nepal's most popular trek has lots of variety, passing Tibetan-style villages, fabulous mountain views and a challenging 5500m pass (p274)

Langtang Quieter trails, alpine valleys and lots of route combinations make this a good low-key option (p283)

Annapurna Sanctuary A straight shot past Gurung villages and bamboo groves into an incredible amphitheatre of frozen Himalayan peaks (p281)

Villages & Day Hikes

Nepal's ridges and valleys are laced with a network of footpaths travelled for centuries by traders and holy men. Bring your daypack to the following for a fine taste of rural Nepali life.

Tansen Wander ancient trade routes, visit a potters' village or explore the eerie ruins of a riverside palace, once the home of an exiled politician (p243)

Jomsom Plane and now minibus connections mean you can use this hub as a base to visit fabulous nearby Himalayan villages like Kagbeni and Marpha (see the boxed text on p209)

Bandipur Base yourself in comfortable digs at this charming medieval village and day hike out to temples, viewpoints and caves (p187)

Pokhara There are loads of options here, from a day's stroll around Phewa Tal to cardio hikes up to Sarangkot or the Peace Pagoda, all offering superb views (p193)

GARRY WEARE/LONELY PLANET IMAGES ©

» Porter team ascending a ridge in the Annapurna Range (p281)

Wildlife Watching

Nepal's subtropical plains hide an array of wildlife worthy of the *The Jungle Book*. Enthusiasts should visit between February and March and bring their own binoculars.

Chitwan National Park Lumber through this World Heritage Site on elephant-back to spot rhinos, gharial (crocodiles) and maybe one of the park's majestic Bengal tigers (p221)

Bardia National Park Track wildlife on elephant-back, 4WD, raft or foot, well away from the crowds in the far west of the country (p249)

Koshi Tappu A birdwatcher's paradise with 450 species, best spotted from guided canoe trips on the Sapt Kosi river (p259)

Sagarmatha National Park Look for Himalayan tahr, yaks and maybe the odd yeti on a trek through this World Heritage Site in the Everest region (p267)

An Adrenaline Rush

Despite what Kiwis might tell you, Nepal is the ultimate outdoor-sports destination. From climbing and mountaineering to mountain biking and ziplining, Nepal does it all – and at a fraction of the cost of other countries.

Bungee Jumping Follow Asia's highest bungee jump with a giant Tarzan-style swing (see the boxed text on p178)

Canyoning Abseil down and through a series of rushing waterfalls and pools near the Tibetan border (see the boxed text on p178)

Rafting From a white-water rush on the raging Bhote Kosi to a weeklong expedition on the Sun Kosi (p41)

Paragliding Glide tandem above Pokhara, savouring incredible views of Machhapuchhare and the Annapurnas (p195)

Climb a trekking peak Learn the basics of ropework and crampons before summiting a 6000m Himalayan peak (see the boxed text on p272)

The Sacred & the Spiritual

The fascinating blend of Indian Hinduism and Tibetan Buddhism is one of Nepal's great draws. From holy lakes to marigold-laden crossroad shrines, the sacred imbues every aspect of Nepali life.

Lumbini Meditate on the nature of suffering at the birthplace of the Buddha (p236)

Bodhnath Light a butter lamp at the subcontinent's largest stupa, focal point of Nepal's Tibetan community (p118)

Kopan Monastery One of the best places in Asia to learn about Tibetan Buddhism and meditation, or take a short retreat (p123)

Learn yoga Kathmandu and Pokhara are both good places to practise and learn yoga, with classes from an hour to a week (p77 and p195)

Pashupatinath Nepal's holiest Hindu shrine, on the cremation ghats of the sacred Bagmati River, draws holy men from across the subcontinent (p115)

RICHARD I'ANSON/LONELY PLANET IMAGES ©

» Nagarkot (p167) backed by the Himalaya

Getting Off the Beaten Track

It's easy to find your own private corner of Nepal. You'll likely have the following towns all to yourself, especially if you visit outside of October.

Gorkha Historically important town huddled 1500 steps below the ridgetop former palace of the Shah dynasty (p185)

Nuwakot You'll find Newari palace architecture in this charming village that offers a great stopover en route to a Langtang trek (p180)

Sankhu Crumbling temples and weathered traditional architecture just 30km from Kathmandu. With just one hotel room in town, you're guaranteed the place to yourself (p159)

Ilam Darjeeling's quiet younger brother offers strolls through cultivated tea estates and some adventurous DIY trips (p263)

Panauti Overnight at this sacred confluence to visit the many temples and shrines at dawn and dusk (p175)

Himalayan Views

Mountain panoramas are not hard to come by in Nepal. That said, the following stand out for their stirring views. Come at dawn for a spectacular light show.

Daman Billed as Nepal's widest mountain panorama, revealing a 300km-long chain of peaks from the Annapurnas to Everest (p246)

Nagarkot The best mountain views close to Kathmandu, on the edge of the valley rim and visible from your hotel bed (p167)

Pokhara Machhapuchhare's Fish Tail peak lies reflected in the calm waters of Phewa Tal (p193)

Mountain flight Pray for clear weather on this dawn flight along the spine of the Himalaya, offering face-to-face views of Everest (p76)

Kala Pattar Breathless views of Everest and the Khumbu Glacier from 5545m on the Everest Base Camp trek (p267)

A Life of Luxury

There's no need to rough it in Nepal. Top-end accommodation includes luxury jungle lodges, converted traditional mansions and wonderful rural retreats, all offering organic food and spa treatments.

Dwarika's Kathmandu's most romantic hotel is all oiled brick and carved woods, linked by lovely traditional pools (p90)

Tiger Tops Chitwan's first and finest jungle lodge offers the height of luxury and even comes with its own resident elephants (p221)

Top-end Trekking Prefer your hiking days to end with a cosy lodge and cocktails rather than a campsite latrine? Several companies offer luxury lodges in the Everest and Annapurna regions (see the boxed text on p268)

Baithak Get a taste of the royal life in this lush restaurant housed in the converted former palace courtyards of the Babar Mahal (see the boxed text, p96)

month by month

Top Events

1 **Dasain**, October

2 **Bisket Jatra**, April

3 **Indra Jatra**, September

4 **Mani Rimdu**, November

5 **Holi**, February/March

February

The end of winter is an especially good time for a low-altitude trek or to visit the national parks of the Terai without the crowds. Pokhara is warmer than chilly Kathmandu.

Losar

Tibetan peoples from Dolpo to the Khumbu celebrate their New Year with parades, pujas (religious offerings or prayers) and prayer flags. Find celebrations in the Kathmandu Valley at Bodhnath, Swayambhunath and Jawalakhel, near Patan.

Maha Shivaratri

Shiva's birthday heralds festivities at all Shiva temples, but particularly at Pashupatinath, and hundreds of sadhus flock here from all over Nepal and India. The crowds bathing in the Bagmati's holy waters are a colourful and wonderful sight.

March

The trekking season kicks in as the weather gets warmer. The spring trails are less crowded than in autumn but cloud is more likely to roll in and obscure the views.

Holi

Known as the Festival of Colours, when coloured powder and water are riotously dispensed as a reminder of the cooling monsoon days to come. Foreigners get special attention, so keep your camera protected and wear old clothes. Can be in February.

Seto Machhendranath

Kicking off in the wake of the sacrificial festival of Chaitra Dasain, crowds drag an image of Seto Machhendranath from its temple at Kel Tole in Kathmandu on a towering, tottering *rath* (chariot), through the backstreets of the old town, for four days (see p70).

April

It's getting uncomfortably hot in the lowlands and Terai, but the rhododendrons are in full technicolour bloom at higher elevations, making this the third most popular month for trekking.

Bisket Jatra

Nepalis celebrate their New Year as huge crowds drag tottering chariots through the winding backstreets of Bhaktapur, pausing for a quick tug-of-war (see p145).

Balkumari Jatra

Thimi celebrates New Year by hosting palanquins from 32 nearby villages at the town's Balkumari Temple, for three days of festivities. Nearby Bode holds a grisly tongue-boring ceremony at the same time.

Balaju Jatra

Thousands of pilgrims keep an all-night vigil at the Swayambhunath temple during the full moon of Baisakh. The following day they trek to the Baise Dhara (22 waterspouts) at Balaju in northern Kathmandu for a ritual bath.

May

The dusty run-up to the monsoon pushes the mercury over 30°C in the Terai and Kathmandu Valley, and the coming rains hang over the country like a threat.

This is the key month for Everest expeditions.

⭐ Rato Machhendranath

Patan's biggest festival involves the spectacular month-long procession of a temple chariot, culminating in the showing of the sacred vest of the god Machhendranath (see p134).

⭐ Buddha Jayanti

A great full-moon fair at Lumbini (the birthplace of the Buddha) marks the Buddha's birth, enlightenment and passing into nirvana, and there are celebrations in Swayambhunath, Bodhnath and Patan. Swayambhunath displays a collection of rare thangkas (Tibetan religious paintings) for one day only.

August

The monsoon rains lash Nepal from mid-June to September, bringing swollen rivers, muddy trails, landslides and leeches. Tourist levels are at a low, though high Trans-Himalayan valleys such as Mustang and upper Dolpo enjoy perfect weather.

⭐ Ghanta Karna

This festival celebrates the destruction of the demon 'bell ears' when a god, disguised as a frog, lured him into a deep well. Ghanta Karna is burnt in effigy on this night throughout Newari villages to cleanse evil from the land for another year.

⭐ Naga Panchami

On this day, nagas (serpent deities) are honoured all over the country for their magical powers over the monsoon rains. Protective pictures of the nagas are hung over doorways of houses, and food is put out for snakes, including a bowl of rice (see p149).

⭐ Janai Purnima

On the full moon, all high-caste men (Chhetri and Brahmin) change the janai (sacred thread), which they wear looped over their left shoulder. Janai Purnima also brings crowds of Hindu pilgrims to sacred Gosainkund lakes (p287) and the Kumbeshwar Temple in Patan (p135).

⭐ Gai Jatra

Newars believe that, after death, cows will guide them to Yama, the god of the underworld, and this 'Cow Festival' is dedicated to those who died during the preceding year. Cows are led through towns and small boys dress up as cows (especially in Bhaktapur).

⭐ Krishna Jayanta (Krishna's Birthday)

The birthday (also known as Krishnasthami) of the popular Hindu god Krishna is celebrated with an all-night vigil at the Krishna Mandir in Patan: oil lamps light the temple and singing continues through the night.

⭐ Teej

The Festival of Women starts with a sumptuous meal and party; at midnight, women commence a 24-hour fast. On the second day women dress in their red wedding saris and head to Shiva temples across the country to pray for a happy marriage.

September

The end of the monsoon brings unpredictable weather but warm temperatures, and the land is beautifully lush and green. High water levels make for especially exciting rafting.

⭐ Indra Jatra

This colourful autumn festival combines homage to Indra with an annual appearance by Kathmandu's Kumari (living goddess), who parades through the packed streets of the old town in a palanquin (p79). It also marks the end of the monsoon.

October

Crystal-clear Himalayan views and comfortable temperatures means peak season and competition for airline seats, hotels and trekking lodges, so book ahead. The Dasain festival brings disruptions to some services.

⭐ Pachali Bhairab Jatra

The fearsome form of Bhairab, Pachali Bhairab, is honoured on the fourth day of the bright fortnight in early October or September. Bhairab's bloodthirsty nature means that there are numerous animal sacrifices.

⭐ Dasain

Nepal's biggest festival lasts for 15 days. It celebrates the victory of the goddess Durga over the forces of evil (personified by the buffalo demon Mahisasura): across the country hundreds of thousands of animals are sacrificed and bamboo swings are erected at the entrances to villages.

⭐⭐ Fulpati (Phulpati)

Fulpati ('Sacred Flowers') is the first really important day of Dasain. A jar of flowers symbolising the goddess Taleju is carried from Gorkha to Kathmandu and presented to the president at the Tundikhel parade ground before being transported on a palanquin to Durbar Sq.

⭐⭐ Maha Astami

The 'Great Eighth Day' and Kala Ratri, the 'Black Night', mark the start of the sacrifices and offerings to Durga. At midnight, in a temple courtyard near Durbar Sq, eight buffaloes and 108 goats are beheaded, each with a single stroke of a sword or knife.

⭐⭐ Navami

The sacrifices continue on Kathmandu's Kot Sq the next day: visitors can witness the bloodshed but you'll need to arrive early to secure a place. Blood is sprinkled on the wheels of cars (and Nepal Airlines' aircraft) and goat is on almost everyone's menu.

⭐⭐ Vijaya Dashami

The 10th day of the Dasain festival is a family affair: cards and greetings are exchanged and parents place a *tika* (sandalwood-paste spot) on their children's foreheads, while evening processions and masked dances celebrate the victory of Lord Rama over the evil demon-king Ravana in the Ramayana.

(above) Monks sounding horns at the Mani Rimdu festival (p22)
(below) Deepawali (p22) preparations in Bhaktapur's Potters' Sq

Kartika Purnima

The full-moon day in September/October marks the end of Dasain. It is celebrated with gambling in many households: you will see even small children avidly putting a few coins down on various local games of chance.

Tihar

Tihar (also called Diwali or Deepawali on the third day of celebrations) is the second most important Hindu festival in Nepal. The festival honours certain animals, starting with offerings of rice to the crows ('messengers of death' sent by the god Yama), followed by dogs (who guide departed souls across the river of the dead), cows and bullocks on consecutive days.

Deepawali (Festival of Lights)

The third day of Tihar is when Lakshmi, the goddess of wealth, comes to visit every home that has been suitably lit for her presence. No one likes to turn down a visit from the goddess of wealth and so homes throughout the country are brightly lit with candles and lamps.

Newari New Year

The fourth day of Tihar is also the start of the New Year for the Newari people of the Kathmandu Valley. The following day marks Bhai Tika, when brothers and sisters meet to offer gifts of sweets and money and place *tikas* on each other's foreheads.

Haribodhini Ekadashi

On the 11th day after the new moon the god Vishnu awakens from his four-month monsoonal slumber. The best place to see the festivities is at the temple of the Sleeping Vishnu in Budhanilkantha, north of Kathmandu.

November

The continued good weather makes this the second most popular month to visit Nepal, perfect for outdoor activities and trekking, though tourist numbers start to drop off at the end of the month.

Kartik Dances

Patan's Durbar Sq fills with music and dancers for this festival that traces its origins back to choreographed human sacrifices ordered during the 17th-century rule of King Siddhinarsingh Malla. Dancers wear masks to represent the god Narsingha and demon Hiranyakashipu. Dates can fall in late October.

Mani Rimdu

This popular Sherpa festival takes place at Tengboche Monastery in the Solu Khumbu region and features masked dances and dramas. For dates see www.tengboche.org. Another Mani Rimdu festival takes place six months later at nearby Thame Gompa.

December

Winter brings chilly nights to Kathmandu, and morning mist sometimes delays flight schedules. Snowfall can close passes on high trekking routes, while visiting Everest Base Camp can be a real feat of endurance.

Bala Chaturdashi

On the new-moon day in late November or early December, pilgrims flock to Pashupatinath, burning oil lamps at night, scattering grain for the dead and bathing in the holy Bagmati River (see p118).

Sita Bibaha Panchami

Tens of thousands of pilgrims from all over the subcontinent flock to Janakpur (the birthplace of Sita) to celebrate the marriage of Sita to Rama. The wedding is re-enacted with a procession carrying Rama's image to Sita's temple by elephant (see p257).

World Elephant Polo Championships

Connoisseurs of the absurd flock to this annual five-day elephant polo tournament, held on the airstrip at Meghauli near Tiger Tops. Referees watch for such pachyderm fouls as laying down in front of the goal or eating the ball. The current world champion is... Switzerland.

Pokhara street festival

Around half a million visitors flock to Pokhara to enjoy street food, parades and cultural performances in the run-up to New Year's Day. Book your accommodation well in advance.

itineraries

Whether you've got six days or 60, these itineraries provide a starting point for the trip of a lifetime. Want more inspiration? Head online to lonelyplanet. com/thorntree to chat with other travellers.

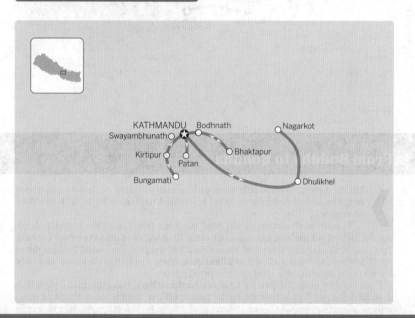

One Week
The Kathmandu Valley

A week gives you time to see the great cultural highlights of the Kathmandu Valley, including no less than six Unesco World Heritage Sites.

Start off in **Kathmandu** with the walking tour south from Thamel to the stunning medieval temples and palaces of Durbar Sq. On day two, walk to the towering stupa of **Swayambhunath** and the quirky National Museum. You can fill the afternoon with a walk around the famous stupa at the Tibetan centre of **Bodhnath**.

Make time for a day trip to **Patan** for its spectacular Durbar Sq and Patan Museum, combined with another great backstreet walking tour and dinner in Jawalakhel. Complete the trilogy of former royal kingdoms with a full-day visit to **Bhaktapur**, ideally with an overnight stay.

Next get your Himalayan kick with dawn mountain views at **Nagarkot** or **Dhulikhel** before returning to Kathmandu on foot via temples at Changu Narayan or Sankhu. Fill another day by mountain biking to the southern valley towns of **Kirtipur** and **Bungamati**.

On your last day, take time for some serious shopping in Kathmandu or the fair-trade shops of Patan.

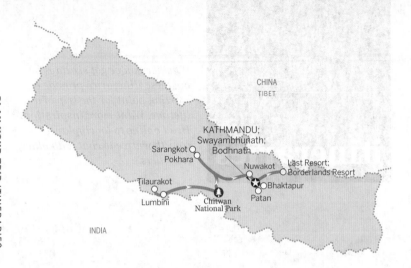

Two Weeks
From Buddha to Boudha

Mixing contemplative temple tours with a healthy dose of wilderness and adventure, this 500km route across Nepal is one part meditation mixed with two parts adrenaline.

To catch some culture as you head northeast from the Indian border to Kathmandu, kick off at **Lumbini**, the birthplace of the Buddha, 20km from the border crossing. Take your time exploring this world map of Buddhist temples, then spend the next day at the little-visited archaeological site of **Tilaurakot**, where Siddhartha Gautama, later to be known as the Buddha, once ruled as a pampered prince.

From Lumbini make a beeline for **Chitwan National Park**, budgeting two or three days to make dawn and dusk safaris among the prolific wildlife. Even if you don't spot a rhino, you can still get up close and personal with the wildlife by helping out at elephant bath time.

From Chitwan take the day-long tourist bus to **Pokhara** for your first proper peek at the mountains. While enjoying the shops and cocktail bars of Lakeside, take a few days to hike up to the World Peace Pagoda, enjoy the views at lofty **Sarangkot** or glide past the peaks at eye-level on a tandem paraglide.

Another long bus trip will take you to **Kathmandu**, where you can fill up three or four days with the pick of the Kathmandu Valley itinerary. If you want to break the trip, consider an overnight stay at either Bandipur or the charming and little-visited historic hill town of **Nuwakot**.

Once in the valley, make time to explore the backstreets of **Bhaktapur** on a walking tour, gain a deeper understanding of Buddhist art at Patan Museum in **Patan** and enjoy the views over the city at dusk from **Swayambhunath**.

Figure on three or four nights in Kathmandu or, better still, base yourself in Bodhnath, Bhaktapur or Patan to escape the traffic and pollution.

There should just be time for a two-day adrenaline rush near the Tibetan border, combining some white-water rafting and canyoning at the **Last Resort** or **Borderlands Resort**, both a half-day drive from the capital.

On your last day, give thanks for a head-spinning trip at **Bodhnath** (Boudha), where you can hit the shops and pick up a Buddha statue or a bundle of prayer flags to take home.

» (above) Street scene, Bhaktapur
(p140)
» (left) One-horned Indian rhinoceros,
Chitwan National Park (p225)

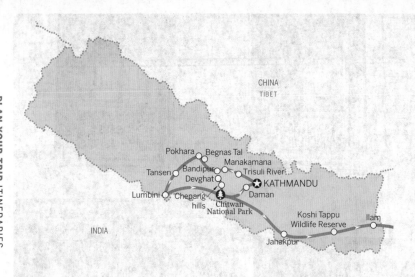

Three to Four Weeks
Once Around the Middle

> Many of Nepal's most interesting and seldom-visited attractions are scattered like pearls around the dense hills of central Nepal. This off-the-beaten-track, 400km-loop route combines the best of the hills and the plains and offers lots of opportunities for great day hikes.

Start with a few days visiting the temples and stupas of **Kathmandu**, then book a rafting trip or kayak clinic on the **Trisuli River**, staying in one of the riverside adventure camps. After a day or two churning on the rapids or canyoning down rushing waterfalls, enjoy a smoother ride on the **Manakamana** cable car to experience the medieval atmosphere of this blood-soaked Tantric temple.

Next stop is **Bandipur**, a little-visited gem of a village where you can stroll to eerie caverns and relax among some wonderfully preserved traditional Newari architecture. From here, roll on to **Pokhara** for a row-boat ride around the lake and a quick jaunt across to **Begnas Tal**.

Take the winding Siddhartha Hwy southwest to charming **Tansen**, the base for some great day hikes. Continue south to peaceful **Lumbini** in the sultry Terai plains to amble around the Buddhist monasteries by bicycle.

Having come this far, it would be a shame to miss **Chitwan National Park**. If your budget allows, stay at one of the lodges deep inside the park for the most atmospheric digs. You might also consider a guided uphill tramp to the **Chepang hills** or a reflective stroll to the village of **Devghat**, at the sacred confluence of the Trisuli and Kali Gandaki Rivers.

The logical return route to Kathmandu would be to follow the snaking Tribhuvan Hwy north to **Daman**, one of Nepal's most impressive viewpoints, and rise at dawn for a 300km-wide panorama of majestic Himalayan peaks.

Alternatively, if your ultimate destination is India you could dive off the beaten track, heading east to the temple town of **Janakpur** (especially during the Sita Bibaha Panchami festival in November or December) and then on to **Koshi Tappu Wildlife Reserve** for some fine birdwatching opportunities. Continue east to the tranquil tea fields of **Ilam** for some off-map adventure before continuing to the border and the delights of Darjeeling and Sikkim, beyond, in India.

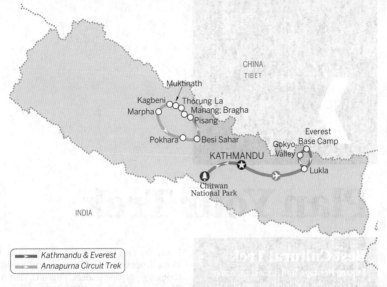

CHINA
TIBET

Muktinath
Kagbeni · Thorung La
Marpha · Manang; Bragha
Pisang
Pokhara · Besi Sahar
Everest
Base Camp
Gokyo
Valley
KATHMANDU · Lukla
Chitwan
National Park
INDIA

Kathmandu & Everest
Annapurna Circuit Trek

One Month
Kathmandu & Everest

> With a month to spare, you can explore the Kathmandu Valley and fit in a trek into the mighty Himalaya.

From Kathmandu, fly east to **Lukla** (book return flights from Lukla to Kathmandu before arriving in Nepal) to start the **Everest Base Camp** trek. This is perhaps the definitive Himalayan trek, climbing from teahouse to teahouse among snow peaks to the base of the tallest mountain on earth. The trek takes at least two weeks because of the gain in altitude.

With an extra week to play with, consider doing an Everest loop, detouring to the spectacular glaciers and lakes of the **Gokyo Valley** en route to Base Camp for a total trek of about 21 days.

Because of the changeable weather in Nepal, it's wise to leave yourself a buffer at the end of the trip in case flights are cancelled. Finish off by exploring the highlights of the Kathmandu Valley itinerary, but do your sightseeing *after* the trek, not before.

After the thrills and chills of the mountains, finish off with a four-day excursion to steamy **Chitwan National Park**, where you can scan the jungle for rhinos and tigers.

One Month
Annapurna Circuit Trek

> The most popular alternative to Everest is the Annapurna region. From **Pokhara** (or Kathmandu) take the morning bus to **Besi Sahar** or Bhulbule to set off on the Annapurna Circuit. The full circuit takes about 20 days but you can shorten it to 12 days by flying to Pokhara from Jomsom, or taking the bus back from Tatopani (16 days).

The highlights of the trek are around **Manang**, and it's worth tacking on a few extra days to walk the high route between **Pisang** and Mungji and visit the lovely village of **Bragha**. The trek's major physical challenge is crossing the high pass of **Thorung La**, and it's vital that you acclimatise sufficiently between Manang and the pass.

Muktinath on the other side of the pass is a major Hindu pilgrimage site and there are some fine short walks to the nearby Tibetan-style villages of Jhong and Purang. The medieval village of **Kagbeni** is another highlight, as is the charming village of **Marpha** and nearby Chhairo Gompa.

Back in Pokhara it's worth taking it easy for a couple of days. Get clean clothes, enjoy a hearty yak steak and have a shave and/or head massage at the barbers.

Plan Your Trek

Best Cultural Trek

Tamang Heritage Trail Homestays, community lodges and traditional villages bring you closer to the locals.

Best Mountain Scenery

Everest Base Camp & Gokyo Lakes Walk into the heart of the world's highest mountains, following in the footsteps of mountaineers and Sherpas.

Best Overall Trek

Annapurna Circuit A huge variety of landscapes, charming villages and great lodges make this one of the world's classic walks.

Best Short Trek

Langtang Valley Hike past bamboo groves, rhododendron forests and yak pastures, before gazing at glaciers and 7000m peaks.

Best Medium Trek

Annapurna Sanctuary A relatively short trek with a powerful punch that leads you into a breathtaking amphitheatre of peaks and glaciers.

Best Winter Trek

Ghorepani to Ghandruk Loop Gurung villages, superb Annapurna views and great lodges, all in just six days.

Easily the best way to see Nepal is on foot along a network of trails trodden for centuries by porters, traders, pilgrims, mountaineers and locals travelling from village to town, plains to hills, Nepal to Tibet. Nothing beats strolling from teahouse to teahouse under crystal-clear Himalayan skies as an 8000m peak towers over you.

Trekking in Nepal is not wilderness walking. You'll meet Sherpas, Gurungs, Rai and Thakali people and pass by monasteries, temples and sacred lakes, experiencing the friendliness, outgoing nature and good humour that characterises almost all Nepalis.

This chapter outlines the basic requirements for safe trekking in Nepal's mountains and gives an overview of the major teahouse trekking routes. For detailed coverage and treks to more remote regions see Lonely Planet's *Trekking in the Nepal Himalaya*.

Officials of all embassies in Nepal stress the benefits of registering with them, telling them where you are trekking, and reporting in again when you return. The offices of KEEP (Kathmadu Environmental Education Project) and the Himalayan Rescue Association stock registration forms from most embassies. You can also register online with embassies of the following countries:

Australia (www.orao.dfat.gov.au)

Britain (www.britishembassy.gov.uk/nepal, https://www.locate.fco.gov.uk/locateportal)

Canada (www.voyage.gc.ca/register)

New Zealand (www.kiwisoverseas.govt.nz)

USA (https://travelregistration.state.gov)

When to Trek

In general the best trekking time is the dry season from October to May; the worst time is the monsoon period from June to September. However, this generalisation doesn't allow for the peculiarities of individual treks.

Several festivals enliven the main trekking trails. November's Mani Rimdu festival brings particularly colourful masked dances at the Everest region's Tengboche Monastery.

October to November The first two months of the dry season offer the best weather for trekking and the main trails are heaving with trekkers at this time, for good reason. The air is crystal clear, the mountain scenery is superb and the weather is still comfortably warm.

December to February Good months for trekking, but the cold can be bitter and dangerous at high altitudes. Getting up to the Everest Base Camp can be a real endurance test, and the Thorung La (Annapurna Circuit) and Laurebina La (Gosainkund trek) are often blocked by snow.

March to April Dry weather and dust means poorer Himalayan views but the compensations are several: fewer crowds, warm weather and spectacular rhododendron blooms. By May it starts to get very hot, dusty and humid in lower altitudes.

June to September Monsoon rains bring landslides, slippery trails and hordes of *jukha* (leeches). Raging rivers often wash away bridges and stretches of trail. Trekking is difficult but still possible and there are hardly any trekkers on the trails. Good for regions like Mustang, Dolpo and around Jomsom.

What Kind of Trek?

There are many different styles of trekking to suit your budget, fitness level and available time. Most independent trekkers plan to sleep and eat in lodges every night and forego the complications of camping. You can carry your own pack and rely on your own navigation skills and research; or you might find it makes sense to hire a local porter to carry your heavy backpack so that you can enjoy walking with only a daypack. A good guide will certainly enhance the trekking experience, though a bad one will just make life more complicated. Most of the trails in this chapter are not hard to follow in good weather, so you don't strictly need a porter or guide for route-finding alone.

To save time, many people organise a trek through a trekking agency, either in Kathmandu or in their home country. Such organised treks can be simple lodge-to-lodge affairs or extravagant expeditions with the full regalia of porters, guides, portable kitchens, dining tents and even toilet tents.

Trekking is physically demanding. Some preparation is recommended, even for shorter treks. You will need stamina and a certain fitness level to tackle the steep ascents and descents that come with trekking in the highest mountain range in the world. It makes sense to start on some kind of fitness program at least a month or two before your trek. That said, Nepal's treks are well within the range of most active people.

On the trail you will begin to realise just how far you are from medical help and the simple comforts that you usually take for granted. For most people this is part of the appeal of trekking, but for some it is a shock to realise just how responsible you are for your own wellbeing. A simple stumble can have catastrophic results. Even a twisted ankle or sore knee can become a serious inconvenience if you are several days away from help and your companions need to keep moving.

Independent Trekking

Independent trekking does not mean solo trekking; in fact we advise trekkers not to walk alone. It simply means that you are not part of an organised tour. The trekking trails described in this chapter have accommodation and food along their entire length, often every hour or two, so there's no need to pack a tent, stove or mat.

There are many factors that will influence how much you spend on an independent trek. Accommodation often costs around Rs 200. A simple, filling meal of daal bhaat (rice, lentils and vegetables) costs around Rs 250 at the start of the trek but can rise to Rs 500 just before a high pass. You can double your bill by having a cold beer or slice of apple pie at the end of a long hiking day. A reasonable daily budget in the Annapurna and Everest regions is US$15 to US$20 per person per day, which should cover the occasional luxury but not a guide or porter. You can sometimes negotiate a cheaper room if you promise to eat your meals at your lodge.

Food prices are standardised and fixed across most lodges in a particular region and rates are reasonable considering the effort it takes to carry the food up there.

Guides & Porters

If you can't (or don't want to) carry a large pack, if you have children or elderly people in your party, or if you plan to walk in regions where you have to carry in food, fuel and tents, you should consider hiring a porter to carry your heavy baggage.

There is a distinct difference between a guide and a porter. A guide should speak English, know the terrain and the trails, and supervise porters, but probably won't carry a load or do menial tasks such as cooking or putting up tents. Porters are generally only hired for load-carrying, although an increasing number speak some English and know the trails well enough to act as porter-guides.

Professional porters employed by camping groups usually carry their loads in a bamboo basket known as a *doko*. Porter-guides used to dealing with independent trekkers normally prefer to carry your backpack on their shoulders. They will likely carry a daypack for their own gear, packed on top of your pack or worn on their front.

If you make arrangements with one of the small trekking agencies in Kathmandu, expect to pay around US$20 to US$25 per day for a guide and US$10 to US$15 for a porter. These prices generally include your guide/porter's food and lodging.

Finding Guides & Porters

To hire a guide, look on bulletin boards, check out forums, such as www.lonelyplanet.com/thorntree or www.trekinfo.com, hire someone through a trekking agency, or check with the office of the KEEP (see p33). It's not difficult to find guides and porters, but it is hard to be certain of their honesty and ability. Don't hire a porter or guide you meet on the street in Kathmandu or Pokhara.

If during a trek you decide you need help, either because of illness, problems with altitude, blisters or weariness, it will generally be possible to find a porter. Most lodges can arrange a porter, particularly in large villages or near an airstrip or roadhead, where there are often porters who have just finished working for a trekking party and are looking for another load to carry.

Whether you're making the arrangements yourself or dealing with an agency, make sure you clearly establish your itinerary (write it down and go through it day by day), how long you will take, how much you are going to pay and whether that includes your porter's food and accommodation. It's always easier to agree on a fixed daily inclusive rate for your guide and porter's food and accommodation rather than pay their bills as you go. Note that you will have to pay your porter/guide's transportation to and from the trailhead and will have to pay their daily rate for the time spent travelling.

Chhetri Sisters Trekking (☎061-462066; www.3sistersadventure.com) at Lakeside North, Pokhara, organises women porters and guides for women trekkers.

Obligations to Guides & Porters

An important thing to consider when you decide to trek with a guide or porter is that you become an employer. This means that you may have to deal with disagreements over trekking routes and pace, money negotiations and all the other aspects of being a boss. Be as thorough as you can when hiring people and make it clear from the beginning what the requirements and limitations are.

Porters often come from the lowland valleys, are poor and poorly educated, and are sometimes unaware of the potential dangers of the areas they are being employed to work in. Stories abound of porters being left to fend for themselves, wearing thin cotton clothes and sandals when traversing high mountain passes in blizzard conditions.

When hiring a porter you are responsible (morally if not legally) for the welfare of those you employ. Many porters die or are injured each year and it's important that you don't contribute to the problem. If you hire a porter or guide through a trekking agency, the agency will naturally pocket a percentage of the fee but it should provide insurance for the porter (check with the agency).

There are some trekking companies in Nepal, especially at the budget end of the scale, who simply don't look after the porters they hire.

The following are the main points to bear in mind when hiring and trekking with a porter:

» Ensure that adequate clothing is provided for any staff you hire. Clothing needs to be suitable for the altitudes you intend to trek to and should protect against bad weather. Equipment should include adequate footwear, headwear, gloves, windproof jacket, trousers and sunglasses.

» Ensure that whatever provision you have made for yourself for emergency medical treatment is available to porters working for you.

MOUNTAIN LITERATURE

Trekking offers plenty of time to catch up on your reading. Pack the following titles for those long teahouse evenings:

» *Annapurna* by Maurice Herzog – a controversial mountaineering classic from 1950

» *Into Thin Air* by Jon Krakauer – the gripping story of the 1996 Everest disaster

» *The Ascent of Rum Doodle* by WE Bowman – a highly enjoyable spoof of all those serious mountaineering tomes

» *The Snow Leopard* by Peter Matthiessen – profound metaphysical description of a trek through Dolpo in the company of grumpy naturalist George Schaller

» *Nepal Himalaya* by WH Tilman – British wit from the 1950s trekking pioneer

» *Everest* by Walt Unsworth – the ultimate but hefty Everest reference, if you have a porter to carry it

» *Himalaya* by Michael Palin – tales of adventure on Annapurna and Everest by the charming ex-Python

» *Chomolungma Sings the Blues* by Ed Douglas – A thought-provoking 'state-of-the-mountain' address detailing the dirtier side of Everest mountaineering

» Ensure that porters who fall ill are not simply paid off and left to fend for themselves (it happens!).

» Ensure that porters who fall ill, and are taken down and out in order to access medical treatment, are accompanied by someone who speaks the porter's language and also understands the medical problem.

» If you are trekking with an organised group using porters, be sure to ask the company how they ensure the wellbeing of porters hired by them.

In order to prevent the abuse of porters, the **International Porter Protection Group** (IPPG; www.ippg.net) was established in 1997 to improve health and safety for porters at work, to reduce the incidence of avoidable illness, injury and death, and to educate trekkers and travel companies about porter welfare.

You can learn a lot about the hardships of life as a porter by watching the excellent BBC documentary *Carrying the Burden,* shown daily at 2pm at KEEP (see p33).

If you're hiring your own porters, contact the porter clothing bank at KEEP, a scheme that allows you to rent protective gear for your porter. A similar clothing bank operates at Lukla. If you've got gear left over at the end of your Everest trek, consider donating it there (it is well signed and just off the main drag in Lukla).

It's common practice to offer your guide and porter a decent tip at the end of the trek for a job well done. Figure on about one day's wages per week, or about 15% to 20% of the total fee. Always give the tip directly to your porters rather than the guide or trek company.

Organised Trekking

There are more than 300 trekking agencies in Nepal, ranging from those connected to international travel companies down to small agencies that specialise in handling independent trekkers. Organised treks can vary greatly in standards and costs so it's important you understand exactly what you are getting for your money.

Organised treks generally charge solo travellers a supplement if you don't want to share a tent or room.

International Trekking Agencies

At the top of the price range are foreign adventure-travel companies with seductive brochures. The trek cost will probably include accommodation in Kathmandu before and after the trek, tours and other activities, as well as the trek itself. A fully organised trek provides virtually everything: tents, sleeping bags, food, porters, as well as an experienced English-speaking *sirdar* (trail boss), Sherpa guides and sometimes a Western trek leader. You'll trek in real comfort with tables, chairs, dining tents, toilet tents and other luxuries. All you need worry about is a daypack and camera.

Although the trek leaders may be experienced Western walkers from the international company, the on-the-ground organisation in Nepal will most probably be carried out by a reputable local trekking company.

Foreign-run companies that are based in Nepal include the excellent **Project Himalaya** (www.project-himalaya.com).

Local Trekking Agencies

It's quite possible (and it can save a lot of money) to arrange a fully organised trip when you get to Nepal. Many trekking companies in Nepal can put together a fully equipped trek if you give them a few days' notice. Organised treks normally cost US$50 to US$100 per person per day for a fully equipped camping trek, or US$30 to US$50 for a teahouse trek, depending on the itinerary, group size and level of service.

Smaller agencies are generally happy to fix you up with individual porters or guides. You can either just pay a daily rate for these and then pay your own food and lodging costs or you can pay a package rate that includes your food, accommodation and transport to and from the trailheads. You gain a measure of protection by booking with an agency that is a member of the Trekking Agencies Association of Nepal (TAAN).

Several agencies run specialist treks: **Nature Treks** (www.nature-treks.com) focuses on wildlife, birdwatching and community ecolodge treks, while **Purana Yoga & Treks** (www.nepalyogatrek.com) is one of several agencies that run yoga treks on all the main trails.

Some trekking agencies that have been recommended include the following (all are Kathmandu-based unless noted):

Adventure Pilgrims Trekking (☎01-4424635; www.trekinnepal.com)

Adventure Treks Nepal (☎01-2266534; www.adventurenepaltreks.com)

Alpine Adventure Club Treks (☎01-4260765; www.alpineadventureclub.com)

Ama Dablam Trekking (☎01-4415372; www.amadablamadventures.com)

Asian Trekking (☎01-4424249; www.asian-trekking.com)

Crystal Mountain Treks (☎01-4428013; www.crystalmountaintreks.com)

Dharma Adventures (☎01-4430499; www.dharmaadventures.com)

Earthbound Expeditions (☎01-4701051; www.enepaltrekking.com)

Explore Himalaya (☎01-4418100; www.explorehimalaya.com)

Explore Nepal (☎01-4226130; www.xplorenepal-group.com.np)

Firante Treks & Expeditions (☎01-4414381; www.firante.com)

Friends in High Places (☎01-5533258; www.fihp.com)

High Spirit Treks (☎01-4701084; www.allnepaltreks.com)

Himalaya Journey (☎01-4383184; www.himalayajourneys.com)

Himalayan Encounters (☎4700426; www.himalayanencounters.com)

Himalaya Glacier (☎4411387; www.himalayanglacier.com)

International Trekkers (☎01-4371397; www.intrekasia.com)

Journeys International (☎01-4414662; www.journeys-nepal.com)

Langtang Ri Trekking (☎01-4423586; www.langtang.com)

Mountain Travel Nepal (☎01-4361500; www.tigermountain.com)

Multi Adventure (☎01-4257791; www.multiadventure.com)

Nepal Social Treks (☎01-4701573; www.nepalsocialtreks.com)

Sherpa Shangrila Treks (☎01-4810373; www.trekandclimb.com)

Sherpa Society (☎01-4249233; www.sherpasocietytrekking.com)

Sherpa Trekking Service (☎01-4421551; www.sts.com.np)

Sisne Rover Trekking (☎061- 461893; www.sisnerover.com) In Pokhara.

Thamserku Trekking (☎01-4354491; www.thamserkutrekking.com)

Three Sisters Adventure Trekking (☎061-462066; www.3sistersadventure.com) In Pokhara.

Trek Nepal International (☎01-4701001; www.treknepal.com)

What to Pack

Clothing & Footwear

The clothing you require depends on where and when you are trekking. If you're going to Everest Base Camp in the middle of winter you must take down gear, mittens and thermals. If you're doing a short, low-altitude trek early or late in the season the weather is likely to be fine enough for T-shirts and a fleece to pull on in the evenings.

Apart from ensuring you have adequate clothing to keep you warm, it's essential that your feet are comfortable and will stay dry if it rains or snows. Uncomfortable shoes and blistered feet are the worst possible trekking discomforts. Make sure your shoes are broken in, fit well and are comfortable for long periods. Running shoes are adequate for low-altitude (below 3000m), warm-weather treks where you won't encounter snow, otherwise the minimum standard of footwear is lightweight trekking boots. Don't even think about buying boots in Kathmandu and then heading on a trek.

If you are going on an organised trek, check what equipment is supplied by the company you sign up with.

Buying or Renting in Nepal

It's always best to have your own equipment since you will be familiar with it and know for certain that it works. That said, you can buy almost anything you need these days from Kathmandu's trekking gear stores (see p100). Much of what's for sale is fake; the backpacks won't quite fit comfortably, the seams on the Gore-Tex jackets will leak and stitching will start to fray eventually. Even so, most items are well made and will stand up to the rigours of at least one major trek.

The best buys are probably down jackets, fleeces and other jackets.

It's possible to rent sleeping bags (four-season) for Rs 60 or a down jacket for Rs 40 to 50 in Kathmandu, Pokhara and even Namche Bazaar. Tents are harder to find; hire costs around Rs 250. Large deposits are often required (never leave your passport). You can purchase sundries, such as sunblock, shampoo and woolly hats on the main trails in places like Chame and Namche Bazaar.

Bhutane gas canisters are available in Kathmandu for between Rs 350 and 450.

Information

The following organisations in Kathmandu offer free, up-to-date information on trekking conditions, health risks and minimising your environmental impact. They are also excellent places to visit and advertise for trekking companions.

Himalayan Rescue Association (HRA; Map p80; ☎01-4701223; www.himalayanrescue.org; 1st fl, Mandala St, Thamel; ☻10am-1pm & 2-5pm Sun-Fri) Runs health posts at Pheriche, Macchhermo (with a porters' shelter) and Manang and hopes to eventually run a post at Thorung Phedi on the Annapurna Circuit. Free lectures on altitude sickness are held at the Thamel office upstairs at 3pm Monday to Friday. There are also embassy registration forms.

EQUIPMENT CHECKLIST FOR TEAHOUSE TREKKING

Clothing
☐ spare socks (minimum three pairs)
☐ hiking trousers
☐ quick-drying T-shirts (not cotton)
☐ down vest or jacket
☐ fleece
☐ rain shell or poncho
☐ fleece hat
☐ sun hat

Equipment
☐ sleeping bag (three- or four- season)

☐ daypack
☐ head torch and spare batteries
☐ trekking poles
☐ polarised sunglasses
☐ sunscreen (SPF 30+)
☐ water bottle
☐ water purification (see p387)
☐ camera, batteries and memory cards

Miscellaneous
☐ pocket knife (optional)
☐ lip balm
☐ toiletries

☐ toilet paper and lighter
☐ camp towel (quick-drying)
☐ laundry soap (biodegradable)
☐ hand sanitiser
☐ medical kit (see the boxed text p383)
☐ blister kit with moleskin, scissors and strong tape
☐ book, cards
☐ stuff sacks and plastic bags
☐ padlock
☐ emergency whistle

KEEP (Map p80; ☎01-44100952; www.keep nepal.org; Thamel; ⊙10am-5pm Sun-Fri) Has a library, some useful notebooks with up-to-date information from other trekkers, an excellent noticeboard and embassy registration forms for most countries. It also sells iodine tablets (Rs 500), biodegradable soap, trekking garbage bags and other environmentally friendly equipment. It's a good place to find a trek partner or donate clothes to the Porter's Clothing Bank. It shifts location frequently, so check before heading out.

Trekking Agencies' Association of Nepal (TAAN; ☎01-4427473; www.taan.org. np; Maligaun Ganeshthan, Kathmandu) Details trekking regulations, can mediate in disputes, and issues TIMS cards (p34).

The slideshows by **Chris Beall** (www.chris beallphoto.com), a British freelance photographer, writer and trek leader, are another good source of up-to-date information in Kathmandu for independent trekking. The shows cost Rs 1000 (including dinner) and you get plenty of time to ask questions at the end. They are currently held in the Courtyard Hotel. You'll see posters up around town or check the website.

Maps

Most trekkers are content to get one of the trekking route maps produced locally by **Himalayan Map House** (www.himalayan-map house.com), Nepa Maps or **Shangri-La Maps** (www.shangrilamaps.com). They are relatively inexpensive (Rs 400 to 800) and are adequate for the popular trails, though not for off-route travel. They are found everywhere in map and bookshops in Thamel. Be aware that there is a great deal of repackaging going on; don't buy two maps with different covers and names assuming you are getting significantly different maps.

The best series of maps of Nepal is the 1:50,000 series produced by Erwin Schneider and now published by Nelles Verlag. They cover the Kathmandu Valley and the Everest region from Jiri to the Hongu Valley. There are also 1:100,000 Schneider maps of Annapurna and Langtang available.

National Geographic produces 1:125,000 trekking maps to the Khumbu, Everest Base Camp, Annapurna and Langtang areas, as part of its Trails Illustrated series.

All of these maps are available at bookshops in Kathmandu and the following speciality map shops overseas:

Stanfords (www.stanfords.co.uk; United Kingdom)

Omni Resources (www.omnimap.com; USA)

Melbourne Map Centre (www.melbmap. com.au; Australia)

Useful Websites

Great Himalaya Trail (www.thegreathimalaya trail.com) Excellent website detailing different sections of the epic trail, with articles, practical advice and a forum board

Lonely Planet Thorn Tree (www.lonely planet.com/thorntree) Both the Nepal and Trekking branches of this forum are good places to get the latest trail information and track down trekking partners.

Nepal Mountaineering Association (www.nepalmountaineering.org) Everything you need to know about climbing and trekking to the top of Nepal's mountains.

TAAN (www.taan.org.np) The Trekking Agencies' Association of Nepal website details current trekking regulations.

Trekinfo.com (www.trekinfo.com) Some of the information is dated but there's a cracking forum board.

Yeti Zone (www.yetizone.com) An excellent day-by-day description of the big treks.

Documents & Fees

TIMS Card

All trekkers are required to register their trek by obtaining a **Trekking Information Management System** (TIMS; www.timsnepal. com) card. The card costs Rs 1610 (US$20) for individual trekkers or Rs 800 (US$10) if you are part of a group. The best place to get a TIMS card is from the **Tourist Service Centre** (Map p80; ☎01-4256909 ext 244; www.welcomenepal.com; Bhrikuti Mandap, Kathmandu; ⊙10am-1pm & 2-4pm Sun-Fri), mainly because you can also get conservation-area and national-park tickets in this building. Bring a photocopy of your passport and two passport photos. The card is issued on the spot; green for individuals and blue for group trekkers.

You need to show the TIMS card at the start of the Annapurna, Langtang and Everest treks.

PRACTICALITIES

» Rechargeable batteries can be charged at many trekking lodges for a fee of Rs 100 to 300 per hour. To charge batteries or an iPod off the beaten track, consider a solar charger like the iSun or Solio (www.solio.com).

» Tip: batteries lose their juice quickly in cold temperatures so keep them in your sleeping bag overnight at higher elevations.

» You can change cash in Namche Bazaar, Chame and at some trailheads, and access ATMs in Jomsom and Namche Bazaar, but you should generally bring all the cash rupees you need with you, plus a stash of US dollars in case you need to buy an emergency flight home.

» Bring water purification – either chemical tablets, liquid iodine, a filter or a UV steriliser like a Steripen (see p387).

National Park & Conservation Fees

If your trek enters a national park such as Langtang or Sagarmatha (Everest), you will need to pay a national-park fee. You can pay the fee at the entry to the parks, or in advance from the **national parks office** (🖉42224406; ⏲9am-2pm Sun-Fri), which is located at the Tourist Service Centre, a 20-minute walk from Thamel in Kathmandu. The fee is Rs 1000 for each park. No photo is required.

If you are trekking in the Annapurna, Manaslu or Gauri Shankar (Rolwaling) regions you must pay a conservation-area fee to the **Annapurna Conservation Area Project** (ACAP; 🖉01-4222406; www.ntnc.org.np; Bhrikuti Mandap; ⏲9am-4pm daily), which is also at the Tourist Service Centre. Bring Rs 2000 and two photographs. The permit is issued on the spot and isn't a hassle unless there is a long queue. Note that if you arrive at an ACAP checkpoint without a permit you will be charged double for the permit.

Conservation fees for the Annapurna area are also payable in Pokhara at the **ACAP** (Map p191; 🖉061-463376; ⏲10am-5pm, to 4pm winter), at Damside inside the Nepal Tourism Board (NTB) office.

Trekking Permits

Trekking permits are not required for treks in the Everest, Annapurna and Langtang regions described in this book.

The following treks require trekking permits, which can only be obtained through registered trekking agencies:

AREA	TREKKING FEE
Kanchenjunga & lower Dolpo	US$10 per week
upper Mustang & upper Dolpo	US$500 for 1st 10 days, then US$50 per day
Nar-Phu	US$90 per week Sep-Nov, US$75 per week Dec-Aug
Manaslu	US$70 for 1st week, then US$10 per day Sep-Nov, US$50 per week then US$7 per day Dec-Aug
Humla	US$50 for 1st week, then US$10 per day
Tsum Valley	US$35 per week

Responsible Trekking

Nepal faces several environmental problems as a result of, or at least compounded by, tourists' actions and expectations. These include the depletion of forests for firewood; the build-up of nonbiodegradable waste, especially plastic bottles; and the pollution of waterways. You can help by choosing an environmentally and socially responsible company and heeding the following advice.

KEEP is a good resource for tips on responsible trekking. For general information on travelling sustainably in Nepal see p351.

Firewood & Forest Depletion

» Minimise the use of firewood by staying in lodges that use kerosene or fuel-efficient wood stoves and solar-heated hot water. Avoid using large open fires for warmth – wear additional clothing instead. Keep showers to a minimum and spurn showers altogether if wood is burnt to produce the hot water.

» Consolidate cooking time by ordering the same items at the same time as other trekkers. Daal bhaat (rice and lentils) is usually readily available for large numbers of people, does not require lengthy cooking time, and is nutritious and inexpensive. Local meals are usually prepared between 10am and 11am, so eating then will usually not require lighting an additional fire.

» Treat your drinking water with iodine rather than boiling it.

» Those travelling with organised groups should ensure that kerosene is used for cooking, including by porters. In alpine areas ensure that all members are outfitted with enough clothing so that fires are not a necessity for warmth.

Garbage & Waste

» Purify your own water instead of buying mineral water in nonbiodegradable plastic bottles.

» Bring a couple of spare stuff sacks and use them to compact litter that you find on mountain trails to be disposed of down in Kathmandu.

» Independent trekkers should always carry their garbage out or dispose of it properly. You can burn it, but you should remember that the fireplace in a Nepali home is sacred and throwing rubbish into it would be a great insult. Don't bury your rubbish.

» Take away all your batteries, as they will eventually leak toxins.

» Toilet paper is a particularly unpleasant sight along trails; if you must use it, carry it in a plastic bag until you can burn it. Those travelling with organised groups should ensure that toilet tents are properly organised, that everyone uses them (including porters) and that rubbish is carried out. Check on a company's policies before you sign up.

Water

» Don't soap up your clothes and wash them in streams. Instead, use a bowl or bucket and discard the dirty water away from watercourses.

» On the Annapurna Circuit, the ACAP has introduced the Safe Drinking Water Scheme – a chain of 16 outlets selling purified water to trekkers. Its aim is to minimise the estimated one million plastic bottles that are brought into the Annapurna Conservation Area each year and are creating a serious litter problem. A litre of water costs between Rs 35 and 60, which is a fraction of the cost of bottled water.

Health & Safety

For the majority of trekkers health problems are likely to be minor, such as stomach upsets and blisters, and commonsense precautions are all that are required to avoid illness. See p382 for more detailed information on staying healthy while in Nepal.

Make sure you and your teeth are in good health before departing, as there is very little medical or dental attention along the trails. See p269 for more information on medical assistance on the Everest trek, and p284 for Langtang.

Trekking Safely

Fired up by the gung-ho stories of adventurous travellers, it is also easy to forget that mountainous terrain carries an inherent risk. There are posters plastered around Kathmandu with the faces of missing trekkers and travellers – several of whom go missing every year on Nepal's trekking trails.

In rural areas of Nepal rescue services are limited and medical facilities are primitive or nonexistent. Helicopter evacuations are possible but the costs run into the thousands of US dollars.

Only a tiny minority of trekkers end up in trouble, but accidents can often be avoided or risks minimised if people have a realistic understanding of trekking requirements. Don't take on a Himalayan trek lightly; the end of the first week is not the time to discover that you're not that keen on walking.

Several basic rules should be followed: don't trek alone, don't make ostentatious displays of valuable possessions and don't leave lodge doors unlocked or valuables unattended.

Choosing Companions

» Never trek alone. You'll appreciate having someone around when you're lost, sick or suffering from altitude sickness. It's useful to have someone to occasionally watch your pack or valuables when you visit the bathroom or take a shower.

» Solo women travellers should choose trekking companions and guides particularly carefully.

» To find a fellow trekking companion, check the bulletin board at KEEP or post a message on www.trekinfo.com, www.trekkingpartners.com, www.yetizone.com or www.lonelyplanet.com/thorntree, or just chat with travellers you meet and perhaps your schedules and ambitions will match.

HEALTH ON THE TRAIL

AMS (Altitude Sickness)

AMS, or altitude sickness, is the major concern on all high-altitude treks – be ever-alert to the symptoms of AMS (see p385).

Diarrhoea

This is a fairly minor problem but it can ruin a trek, so watch what you eat and ensure your medical kit contains antidiarrhoeal medicine such as Lomotil or Imodium (for emergencies only) and a broad-spectrum antibiotic like Azithromycin or Norfloxacin, available without a prescription at pharmacies in Kathmandu and Pokhara. Always treat your water.

Trekker's Knee

Many people suffer from knee and ankle strains, particularly if they're carrying their own pack. Elastic supports or bandages can help, as can anti-inflammatories such as Ibuprofen tablets and analgesic cream, and using collapsible trekking poles.

Blisters

Always carry moleskin, plasters (Band-Aids) and tape in your daypack in case of blisters. Investigate any hot spot as soon as you feel it. Wear clean socks.

Sunburn & Snowblindness

The high-altitude Himalayan sun is incredibly strong. Bring plenty of high-factor suncreen, a brimmed hat and a good pair of sunglasses for pass crossings.

» Unless you are an experienced trekker or have a friend to trek with, you should at least take a porter or guide.

Trail Conditions

» Walking at high altitudes on rough trails can be dangerous. Watch your footing on narrow, slippery trails and never underestimate the changeability of the weather – at any time of the year.

» If you are crossing high passes where snow is a possibility, never walk with less than three people.

» Carry a supply of emergency rations, have a map and compass (and know how to use them), and have sufficient clothing and equipment to deal with cold, wet, blizzard conditions.

» You will be sharing the trail with porters, mules and yaks, all usually carrying heavy loads, so give them the right of way. If a mule or yak train approaches, always move to the high side of the trail to avoid being knocked over the edge.

Rescue Insurance

» Check that your travel-insurance policy does not exclude mountaineering or 'alpinism'. Although you will not be engaging in these activities on a trek, you may have trouble convincing the insurance company of this fact. Check what insurance is available through your trekking company, if using one.

» Rescue insurance will need to cover an emergency helicopter evacuation or a charter flight from a remote airstrip, as well as international medical evacuation. A helicopter evacuation from 4000m near Mt Everest will cost you US$2500 to US$10,000 and payment must be cleared in advance. Your embassy can help with this if you have registered with it.

Altitude

Walking the trails of Nepal often entails a great deal of altitude gain and loss; even the base camps of Nepal's great peaks can be very high. Most treks that go through populated areas stick to between 1000m and 3000m, although the Everest Base Camp Trek and the Annapurna Circuit Trek both reach over 5000m. On high treks like these ensure adequate acclimatisation by limiting altitude gain above 3000m to 500m per day. The maxim of 'walking high, sleeping low' is good advice; your night halt should be at a lower level than the highest point reached in the day.

Make a point to catch the free altitude lectures given by the Himalayan Rescue Association (p33) in Kathmandu, or at their Manang and Pheriche aid posts on the Annapurna and Everest treks respectively.

Bike Tracks & White Water

Best Wilderness Rafting Trip

Sun Kosi or Tamur Exciting expedition-style trips that last for a week and traverse a huge range of remote terrain.

Best Place for a Kayak Clinic

Trisuli River Base yourself at one of several comfortable riverside camps and take a few days to learn about Eskimo rolls and eddies.

Best White-Water Trip

Bhote Kosi The biggest bang for your buck, best done as an overnight trip and combined with some canyoning.

Best Mountain-Biking Trip

Jomsom to Pokhara Downhill trail that follows jeep tracks down the western half of the spectacular Annapurna Circuit.

Best Mountain-Biking Day Trip

Scar Rd from Kathmandu Tough, uphill off-road sections that reward with great valley views and forested trails.

Nepal offers some of the best mountain biking and rafting trips in the world. Both offer the opportunity to get way off the beaten track and to see the country at a slower pace and from a different perspective than from the window of a speeding tourist bus. There's a huge variety of adventures on offer, from village day rides in the Kathmandu Valley to challenging mountain trails, and from family-friendly warm-water floats to full-on white-water trips through some of the remotest corners of the country.

Exploring Nepal's trails and rivers on your own is possible but most people sign up for organised trips, which generally leave every few days in high season. Kathmandu alone has dozens of adventure companies specialising in both fixed group departures and customised private trips. All you have to do is come with enough time to pack it all in.

This chapter deals with background information for planning your biking, rafting or kayaking in Nepal. For specific route information see the separate Biking, Rafting & Kayaking chapter.

Mountain Biking

Fat tyres, a soft padded seat and 17 more gears than the average Nepali bike – the mountain bike is an ideal, go anywhere, versatile machine for exploring Nepal. These attributes make it possible to escape sealed roads, and to ride tracks and ancient walking trails to remote, rarely visited areas of the country. Importantly, they allow a liberating freedom of travel – you can stop whenever you like – and they free you from crowded buses and claustrophobic taxis.

The Kathmandu Valley offers the best and most consistent biking in Nepal, with a dense network of tracks, trails and backroads. A mountain bike really allows you to get off the beaten track and discover idyllic Newari villages that have preserved their traditional lifestyle. Each year more roads are developing, opening trails to destinations that were previously accessible only on foot.

Many trails are narrow, century-old walkways that are not shown on maps, so you need a good sense of direction when venturing out without a guide. To go unguided entails some risks, and you should learn a few important words of Nepali to assist in seeking directions.

Nepa Maps and Himalayan Maphouse produce the useful maps *Mountain Biking the Kathmandu Valley* and *Biking around Annapurna,* though they aren't to be relied on completely.

For a description of some of the best biking routes, see p292.

Guided Tours

A booming number of Nepali companies offer guided mountain-bike trips. They provide high-quality bicycles, local and Western guides, helmets and all the necessary equipment. There is usually a minimum of four bicyclists per trip, although for shorter tours two is often sufficient. For the shorter tours (two to three days) vehicle support is not required, while for longer tours vehicles are provided at an extra cost.

Local group tours range from US$25 to US$35 for a simple day trip, such as the loop routes north from Kathmandu to Tinpiple, Tokha and Budhanilkantha; or south to the traditional village of Bungamati. Expect to pay around US$25 a day if you just want a mountain-bike guide.

A downhill day trip with vehicle support costs around US$55 per person. Options include driving to Nagarkot and riding down to Sankhu and Bodhnath or Bhaktapur, or driving to Kakani and taking the Scar Rd down. Dawn Till Dusk offers exhilarating downhill runs from the top of Phulchowki and Nagarjun peaks.

Multiday trips around the Kathmandu Valley cost around US$45 per day without vehicle backup, or US$65 with vehicle support and range from two to 10 days. Prices include bike hire, a guide, hotel accommodation and meals.

The following routes rank among the most popular organised itineraries:

» Budhanilkantha-Chisopani-Nagarkot and back (three to four days)

» Budhanilkantha-Nagi Gompa-Mulkharkha-Gokarna (day trip)

» Nagarkot-Kathmandu downhill (day trip or overnight) via Sankhu or Changu Narayan Temple

» Kathmandu to Chitwan National Park via Daman and Hetauda; the most interesting route leads via the back roads west of Dakshinkali.

» Bhaktapur-Dhulikhel-Namobuddha-Panauti (three days)

» Nagarkot-Dhulikhel-Panauti-Lakuri Bhanjyang-Sisneri (three days) – see p295

» Tibet border (four days)

A few companies have recently started operating trips down the Kali Gandaki Valley, along the new unpaved road (and former trek route). Tours take around a week, with overnights in Ghasa, Tatopani, Beni and Pokhara, plus two days in Muktinath and Jomsom. An all-inclusive tour with flights and guide costs around US$1000, or you can organise a guide and bike only for around US$400. A few diehards even attempt the full Annapurna Circuit (see p274), though even the hardiest biker ends up carrying their bike 70% of the time on the Manang side.

Tour Companies

The following companies have good-quality imported mountain bikes that can also be hired independently of a tour.

Alternative Nepal (Map p80; ☎01-4700170; www.alternativenepal.com) Bike hire US$10 per day, day/overnight trips to Kakani and Shivapuri US$30/50 with bike hire and guide.

Biking First (Map p80; ☎01-4701771; www.bikingfirst.com; Z St) Small operation with day trips in the valley costing US$35 with guide, bike and tea. Bike hire costs Rs 500 to 750.

Dawn Till Dusk (Map p80; ☎01-4700286; www.nepalbiking.com; JP School Rd, Thamel, Kathmandu) Local tours and rentals at the Kathmandu Guest House office; for bike repairs and servicing see the workshop a five-minute walk east, near Kilroy's restaurant.

Himalayan Mountain Bikes (HMB; Map p80; ☎01-4212860; www.bikingnepal.com, www.bikeasia.info) Kathmandu Valley multiday tours US$45 to US$65 per day, plus full service and repairs and bike hire US$12 to US$15 per day.

Himalayan Single Track (Map p80; ☎01-4700909; www.himalayansingletrack.com; Saatgumthi) Six-day Kathmandu Valley and also lower and upper Mustang tours, plus daily early morning outings from Kathmandu (US$20).

Path Finder Cycling (Map p80; ☎01-4700468; www.pathfindercycling.com, www.tibetbiking.com; Thamel, Kathmandu) Offers day and multiday tours, Tibet rides, bike rental, repairs and accessories. Located across from La Dolce Vita Restaurant.

Transporting Your Own Bicycle

If you plan to do a mountain-biking trip of more than a day or two, it may be a good idea to bring your own bicycle from home. Your bicycle can be carried as part of your baggage allowance on international flights. You are required to deflate the tyres, turn the handlebars parallel with the frame and remove the pedals. Passage through Nepali customs is quite simple once you reassure airport officers that it is 'your' bicycle and it will also be returning with you, though this requirement is never enforced.

On most domestic flights if you pack your bicycle correctly, removing wheels and pedals, it is possible to load it in the cargo hold. Check with the airline first.

Local buses are useful if you wish to avoid some of the routes that carry heavy traffic. You can place your bicycle on the roof for an additional charge (Rs 50 to 100 depending on the length of the journey and the bus company). If you're lucky, rope may be available and someone will be there to assist you. Make sure the bicycle is held securely, to cope with the rough roads, and that it's lying as flat as possible to prevent it catching low wires or tree branches. Unless you travel with foam padding it's hard to avoid getting scratches to the frame. Supervise its loading and protect the rear derailleur from being damaged. Keep in mind that more baggage is likely to be loaded on top once you're inside. A lock and chain is a wise investment.

Equipment

Most of the bicycles for rent in Nepal are low-quality, Indian mountain bikes, not suitable for the rigours of trail riding. The better operators, such as Himalayan Mountain Bikes or Dawn Till Dusk rent high-quality front-shock, 18-gear mountain bikes for around US$8 to US$12 per day, with discounts for a week's hire. Cheaper companies offer battered front-suspension bikes for Rs 450, with discounts for a week's hire. The better rental shops can supply helmets and other equipment.

If you bring your own bicycle, it is essential to bring tools and spare parts, as these are largely unavailable outside of Kathmandu. Established mountain-bike tour operators have mechanics, workshops and a full range of bicycle tools at their offices in Kathmandu. Dawn Till Dusk also has a separate repair workshop near Kilroy's restaurant in Thamel (see Map p80).

Road Conditions

Nepali roads carry a vast array of vehicles: buses, motorcycles, cars, trucks, tractors, holy cows, wheelbarrows, dogs, wandering children and chickens, all moving at different speeds and in different directions. Traffic generally travels on the left-hand side, though it's not uncommon to find a vehicle approaching you head-on or even on the wrong side of the road. In practice, smaller vehicles give way to larger ones, and bicycles are definitely at the bottom of the heap.

The centre of Kathmandu is a particularly unpleasant place to ride because of pollution, heavy traffic and the increasingly reckless behaviour of young motorcyclists.

A few intrepid mountain bikers have taken bicycles into trekking areas hoping to find great riding but these areas are generally not suitable for mountain biking and you have to carry your bicycle for at least 80% of the time. In addition, there are always trekkers, porters and local people clogging up the trails. Sagarmatha National Park doesn't allow mountain bikes. Courtesy and care on the trails should be a high priority when biking.

Trail Etiquette
Clothing

Tight-fitting lycra bicycle clothing might be functional, but is a shock to locals, who maintain a very modest approach to dressing. Such clothing is embarrassing and also offensive to Nepalis.

A simple way to overcome this is by wearing a pair of comfortable shorts and a T-shirt over your bicycle gear. This is especially applicable to female bicyclists, as women in Nepal generally dress conservatively.

Safety

Trails are often filled with locals going about their daily work. A small bell attached to your handlebars and used as a warning of your approach, reducing your speed, and a friendly call or two of '*cycle ioh!*' (cycle coming!) go a long way in keeping everyone on the trails happy and safe. Children love the novelty of the bicycles, the fancy helmets, the colours and the strange clothing, and will come running from all directions to greet you. They also love to grab hold of the back of your bicycle and run with you. You need to maintain a watchful eye so no one gets hurt.

Rafting & Kayaking

Nepal has a reputation for being one of the best places in the world for rafting and kayaking, with outstanding river journeys ranging from steep, adrenaline-charged mountain streams to classic big-volume wilderness expeditions. Warm water, a subtropical climate (with no bugs!) and huge white sandy beaches that are ideal for camping just add to the appeal.

There has been a continuous increase in the number of kayakers coming to Nepal over the last few years, and it is justifiably recognised as a mecca for paddlers. Several companies offer trips that cater specifically to kayakers, where you get to explore the river with rafts carrying all your gear and food, and often camp near choice play spots.

When to Go

In general the best times for rafting and kayaking are September to early December, and March to early June.

March to May The summer season has long, hot days and lower water flows, which generally means the rapids are a grade lower than they are from September to November. The rivers rise again in May with the pre-monsoon storms and some snowmelt.

June to August Monsoon rains mean the rivers carry 10 times their low-water flows, and can flood with 60 to 80 times the low-water levels, making most rivers insanely difficult. Only parts of the Seti, Upper Sun Kosi and Trisuli are commercially run during the monsoon.

September to early October & May to June Rivers can be extremely high with monsoon runoff. Any expeditions attempted at this time require a very experienced rafting company with an intimate knowledge of the river and strong teams, as times of high flows are potentially the most dangerous times to be on a river.

Mid-October to November One of the most popular times to raft or kayak, with warm, settled weather and exciting runs.

December Many of the rivers become too cold to enjoy unless you have a wetsuit, and the days are short with the start of winter – the time to consider shorter trips.

What to Bring

If you go on an organised rafting or kayaking trip, all specialised equipment is supplied, as well as tents. Roll-top dry bags keep your gear dry even if the vessel flips.

Usually you will only need light clothing, with a warmer change for cool nights. A swimsuit, a towel, a sunhat, insect repellent, sunscreen and light tennis shoes or sandals (that will stay on your feet) are all necessary, but can be bought in Kathmandu. Overnight trips require a sleeping bag, but these can be hired. In winter you will need thermal clothing, especially on rivers like the Bhote Kosi. Check if companies provide paddle jackets and wetsuits.

Waterproof camera containers are useful to take photos along the river – ask your company if they have any for rent or, better, bring your own.

Information

Anyone who is seriously interested in rafting and kayaking should get *White Water Nepal* by Peter Knowles. It has very detailed information on river trips, with 60 maps, river profiles and hydrographs, plus advice on equipment and health. Check out www.riverspublishing.co.uk or get a copy of the book in Kathmandu.

Himalayan Maphouse and Peter Knowles have produced three river maps for kayakers and rafters: *Whitewater Rafting and Kayaking for Western Nepal, Central Nepal* and *Eastern Nepal.*

The website of the **Nepal Association of Rafting Agents** (www.raftingassociation.org.np) has listings of rafting companies, overviews of river routes and information on the annual Himalayan Whitewater Challenge.

Whitewater Adventures – Nepal (www. raftnepal.org/Raft-Nepal-Index.html) offers an excellent overview of rafting options across Nepal, as well as advice about other extreme sports.

Choosing a River

Before you decide on a river, you need to decide what it is that you want out of your trip. There are trips available from two to 12 days on different rivers, all offering dramatically different experiences.

First, don't believe that just because it's a river it's going to be wet 'n' wild. Some rivers, such as the Sun Kosi, which is a full-on white-water trip in September and October, are basically flat in the low water of early spring. On the flip side, early spring can be a superb time to raft rivers such as the Marsyangdi or Bhote Kosi, which would be suicidal during high flows. The Karnali is probably the only river that offers continually challenging white water at all flows, though during the high-water months of September and May it's significantly more challenging than in the low-water months.

Longer trips such as the Sun Kosi (in the autumn), the Karnali and the Tamur offer some real heart-thumping white water with the sense of journey inherent in a long river trip. With more time on the river, things are more relaxed, relationships progress at a more natural pace, and memories become entrenched for a lifetime. River trips are much more than gravity-powered roller-coaster rides; they're liquid journeys traversed on very special highways.

If a long trip is simply impossible because of financial or time constraints, don't undervalue the shorter ones. Anyone who has ever taken a raft or kayak down the Bhote Kosi (at any flow) would be hard pressed to find anything better to do with two days in Nepal.

For a shorter float combined with some premier wildlife-watching consider also the two- to three-day raft from Mugling to Chitwan National Park (p234) and a day raft on the Geruwa River near Bardia National Park (p250).

Organised Trips

There are dozens of companies in Kathmandu claiming to be rafting and kayaking operators. A few are well-established companies with good reputations, and the rest are newer companies, often formed by guides breaking away and starting their own operations. Although these new companies can be enthusiastic and good, they can also be shoestring operations that may

RIVER TRIPS IN NEPAL

Note that in the 'Season/Grade' column, the number in brackets refers to the grade when the high river flows, which is normally at the beginning and end of the season.

RIVER	TRIP DURATION (DAYS)	APPROX COST	TRANSPORT
Bhote Kosi	2	US$90-110	3hr from Kathmandu
Upper Sun Kosi	2	US$100-120	2hr from Kathmandu
Trisuli	2	US$90-100	2hr from Kathmandu
Seti	2-3	US$100-130	1½hr from Pokhara
Kali Gandaki	3	US$150-165	2hr from Pokhara
Marsyangdi	4	US$200-250	5hr from Kathmandu
Sun Kosi	8-9	US$440-600	3hr from Kathmandu then 16hr bus back to Kathmandu or fly from Biratnagar
Karnali	10	US$550-700	16hr bus ride or flight and 4hr bus ride
Tamur	12	US$700-800	18hr bus or flight, then 3-day trek; flight or 16hr bus back (6 days of rafting in total)

not have adequate equipment and staff. Most of the small travel agencies simply sell trips on commission; often they have no real idea about the details of what they are selling and are only interested in getting bums on seats.

If a group has recently returned from a trip, speak to its members. This will give you reliable information about the quality of equipment, the guides, the food and the transportation. Question the company about things such as how groups get to and from the river, the number of hours spent paddling or rowing, where the camps are set up, food provided (rafting promotes a very healthy appetite), who does the cooking and work around the camp, the cooking fuel used (wood isn't convenient or responsible), what happens to rubbish, hygiene precautions and night-time activities. Check how many people have booked and paid for a trip, as well as the maximum number that will be taken.

Shorter trips depart every few days but the longer rafting trips only depart every week or so, so it's worth contacting a company in advance to see when they are planning a trip. The best companies will refer you to a friendly competitor if they don't have any suitable dates.

Generally you'll be rafting or kayaking for around five to six hours a day, and you can expect to be running rapids about 30% of the time depending on the river. The first and last days will most likely be half days. Longer trips of a week or more will probably have one rest day when you can relax or explore the surroundings.

Trips booked in Nepal range in price from US$50 to US$80 a day, depending on the standard of service, number of people on the trip, and the river. Generally you get what you pay for. It is better to pay a bit more and have a good, safe trip than to save US$100 and have a lousy, dangerous trip. As one rafting company says, 'saving you a little can cost you a lot'.

With the constant change in rafting and kayaking companies it's difficult to make individual recommendations; the fact that a company is not recommended here does not necessarily mean it will not deliver an excellent trip. Nonetheless, the following Kathmandu companies have been recommended for their professionalism. For contact details of Pokhara-based operations see p195.

Adventure Aves (Map p80; ☎01-4700230; www.adventureaves.com; Saat Gumti) Nepali-British operation focused on rafting and kayaking.

SEASON/GRADE	ADD-ONS
late Oct-May/4 (5-)	bungee jump, canyoning, kayak clinics, day trips possible (US$45)
Oct-May/3 (4), Jun-Sep/4 (4+)	
Oct-May/3 (4), Jun-Sep/4 (4+)	excursions to Bandipur or Pokhara, day trips possible (US$45)
Sep-May/2 (3+)	kayak clinics are popular here
late Sep-May/3 (4)	Chitwan National Park
late Oct-Apr/4 (5-)	Annapurna Circuit Trek
Sep-Nov/3+ (4+), Dec-Apr/3 (4)	Koshi Tappu Wildlife Reserve or continue on to Darjeeling in India
late Sep-May/3 (4+)	Bardia National Park
Oct-Dec/4 (5-)	trek to Kanchenjunga

Adrenaline Rush (Map p80; ☎01-4700961; www.adrenalinenepal.com; Thamel) Trisuli rafting and kayaking trips, including tubing and 'ducky' (inflatable kayak) trips, from a simple camp at Kuringhat on the Trisuli. It also offers a canyoning and kayaking combo day trip (US$65).

Drift Nepal (Map p80; ☎01-4700797; www.driftnepal.com) Contact Samir Thapa. All the major rivers are represented, as well as kayak clinics and treks.

Equator Expeditions (Map p80; ☎01-4700782; www.equatorexpeditionsnepal.com, www.nepalgate.com; Thamel, Kathmandu) This company specialises in long participatory rafting/kayaking trips and kayak instruction.

GRG Adventure Kayaking (Map p80; ☎01-4700928; www.grgadventurekayaking.com) Run by Nepal's best kayaker, operates rafting and kayaking trips and a four-day kayak clinic (US$300) at a tented camp close to Fishling, near Kuringhat. Also rents kayaks.

Himalayan Encounters (Map p80; ☎01-4700426; www.himalayanencounters.com; Kathmandu Guest House courtyard, Thamel, Kathmandu) This company has a solid reputation. Its Trisuli trips (one/two days US$55/95) stay at the Trisuli Center camp, near Big Fig beach, while its Seti trips hike in from Bandipur.

Ultimate Descents Nepal (Map p80; ☎01-4701295; www.udnepal.com) Near Northfield Cafe and part of the Borderlands group; it also has an office in Pokhara. Specialises in long participatory rafting trips as well as kayak instruction and clinics on the Seti River.

Ultimate Rivers (Map p80; ☎/fax 01-4700526; info@urnepal.wlink.com.np; Mandala St, Thamel, Kathmandu) Associated with the New Zealand company Ultimate Descents International (www.ultimatedescents.com). The Kathmandu office is shared with The Last Resort.

Safety

Safety is the most important part of any river trip. Unfortunately, there are no minimum safety conditions enforced by any official body in Nepal. This makes it very important to choose a professional rafting and kayaking company. Your guide should give you a comprehensive safety talk and paddle training before you launch off downstream. If you don't get this, it is probably cause for concern.

» Modern self-bailing rafts, good life jackets and helmets are essential.

» There should be a minimum of two rafts per trip. In higher water three rafts are safer than two.

» Good safety kayakers are invaluable on steeper rivers where they can often get to swimmers in places no other craft could manage.

» If possible, speak with the guide who will lead the trip to get an impression of the people you will be spending time with and the type of trip they run.

» All guides should have a current first-aid certificate and be trained in cardiopulmonary resuscitation. International accreditation such as the Swiftwater Rescue Technician (SRT) qualification is a bonus.

» Always wear your life jacket in rapids. Wear your helmet whenever your guide tells you, and make sure that both the helmet and jacket are properly adjusted and fitted.

» Keep your feet and arms inside the raft. If the raft hits a rock or wall and you are in the way, the best you'll escape with is a laceration.

» If you do swim in a rapid, get into the 'whitewater swimming position'. You should be on your back, with your feet downstream and up where you can see them. Hold on to your paddle as this will make you more visible. Relax and breathe when you aren't going through waves. Then turn over and swim at the end of the rapid when the water becomes calmer. Self-rescue is the best rescue.

Kayaking

The opportunities for kayak expeditions are exceptional. Apart from the rivers discussed later in this chapter, of note at the right flows are the Mardi Khola, Tamba Kosi, Karnali headwaters, Thuli Bheri, Balephi Khola and tributaries of the Tamur.

The upper Modhi Khola is also good for experienced kayakers. The side creek of the Bhurungdi Khola, by Birethani village, hides several waterfalls that are runnable by experienced kayakers.

Kayak Clinics

Nepal is an ideal place to learn to kayak and several companies offer learner kayak clinics. Due to the high levels of communication required to teach, the best instruction clinics tend to be staffed with both Western and Nepali instructors. Kayak clinics normally take about four days, which gives you time to get a good grounding in the basics of kayaking, safety and river dynamics.

The clinics are a pretty laid-back introduction to kayaking, with around four to six hours of paddling a day. On day one you'll learn self-rescue, T-rescue and Eskimo roll, which will help you to right yourself when you capsize. Day two sees you on the river, learning to ferry glide (cross the river), eddy in and eddy out (entering and leaving currents) and perfecting your paddling strokes. Day three is when you start really having fun on the river, running small (class 2) rapids and journeying down the river, learning how to read the rapids. The key is to relax your upper body to move with the kayak, and not to panic if you tip over. Physical flexibility is a real plus. Expect one instructor for every three people.

Equator Expeditions and Ultimate Rivers (see Organised Trips, p44) operate clinics on the upper Sun Kosi. Equator runs the Sukute Beach Resort, just north of Sukute village between kilometre markers 69 and 70. It's fairly comfortable but with squat toilets and cold showers, it isn't as luxurious as Borderlands or the Last Resort. Still, it has a great spot on the river, with a private beach, a bar area with pool tables and a lovely stretch of river nearby. It also has a pool, which is a real bonus when learning Eskimo rolls.

Ultimate Rivers uses the Riverside Camp, between kilometre markers 83 and 84, which is a similarly basic camp. Both companies charge around US$200 for a four-day clinic, though you can often negotiate a cheaper price if you take the local bus. For both trips check what kind of transportation is included. You may find yourself flagging down local buses and putting your kayak on the roof for short rides after a trip down the river.

The **Royal Beach Camp** (Map p80; ☎01-4700531; www.royalbeachnepal.com) offers two- to seven-day kayak clinics from its fixed camp and swimming pool at Kataudi on the Trisuli River, 85km from Kathmandu. Packages include two-day kayak clinics (US$99), and three-day rafting, kayaking and canyoning (US$155). Contact Royal Beach Camp at its office in Kathmandu, just north of the Kathmandu Guest House. See also p185.

Ultimate Descents Nepal operates its four-day clinics on the gentle Seti River, for around US$250, from Pokhara to Pokhara. The first day's training takes place on Phewa Tal and the remaining three days are on the Seti, with two nights' riverside camping. The advantage to learning on the Seti is that you get to journey down a wilderness river. Upper Sun Kosi kayak clinics can be structured for instruction from one to four days. Kayaking specialists like GRG Adventure kayaking can often arrange kayaking tuition during the quieter sections of a Sun Kosi rafting run.

Nose plugs are useful for those practice Eskimo rolls and you should bring a warm change of clothes as you are going to get wet. The bulk of kayak clinics operate in late October, November, March and April. December to February clinics are still possible, but with shorter days, and there's a lot less sunlight to warm you up at the beginning and end of the day.

Volunteering

Choosing an Organisation

Consider honestly how your skill set may best benefit an organisation and community, choose a cause that you are passionate about and do some research to ensure your potential organisation is reputable and transparent.

Time Required

Think realistically about how much time you can devote to the project. You are unlikely to be of lasting help if you stay for less than a couple of months.

Money

It may surprise you to have to pay to volunteer but many companies charge substantial placement fees and ask you to cover your own costs, including accommodation, food and transport.

Resources

www.lonelyplanet.com/volunteer/index.cfm Our online advice.
www.ethicalvolunteering.org Useful tips on selecting an ethical volunteer agency.
Volunteer: A Traveller's Guide By Lonely Planet; invaluable one-stop information and directory.

Hundreds of travellers volunteer in Nepal every year, working on an incredible range of development and conservation projects, covering everything from volunteering with street children in Kathmandu to counting the tracks of endangered animals in the high Himalaya. The rewards for the traveller can certainly be high. The potential for personal growth and the opportunity to forge a deeper connection with a local community can give a profoundly deeper aspect to the notion of travel.

However, it is important to remember the principles of ethical volunteering – good volunteer agencies match a volunteer's skill sets to suitable projects that result in real and lasting benefit to local communities, rather than simply offering travellers the chance to feel better about themselves during a fleeting two-week placement.

As 'voluntourism' has grown in popularity, dozens of organisations have sprung up to take advantage of a new potential source of revenue, muddying an already murky issue. You'll need to do some serious research to ensure that your time and money are genuinely going to help the cause you are trying to advance. Do it right though, and an extended time spent volunteering in Nepal will bring you much closer to the country. Dare we say it, it may even change your life.

Voluntrekking

A number of trekking and tour agencies use the proceeds from their trips to support charitable projects around Nepal, and many travellers also undertake sponsored treks and climbing expeditions in Nepal to raise money for specific charities and projects.

Organisations that set up expeditions of this kind include the following:

Community Action Treks (www.catreks. com) Offers various treks that contribute to the work of Community Action Nepal.

Crooked Trails (www.crookedtrails.com) Runs fundraising treks and volunteer programs that can be combined with treks.

Exodus (www.exodus.co.uk/responsible-travel) UK agency offering various treks; proceeds help fund tree-planting in Mustang and an orphanage in Patan.

Explore Nepal (www.xplorenepal.com.np) Trek and tour agency with commendable ethical policies; money from trips helps to fund litter clearing and other environmental projects.

Nepal Trust (www.nepaltrust.org) Runs fundraising treks to Humla that focus on construction, medical and cultural projects.

Restoration Works International (www. restorationworksinternational.org) Paid volunteer treks to Mustang to help with the restoration of Chairro Gompa.

Social Tours (www.socialtours.com) Runs charity and yoga treks where profits go to Save the Children or orphans' homes and can organise volunteer placements.

Summit Climb (www.summitclimb.com, www. servicetreknews.org) Runs an annual service trek providing health care in remote parts of Solu Khumbu.

Several trekking routes offer community-based tourism initiatives. You can stay in a community lodge in Gotlang on the Tamang Heritage Trail (p285), or travel and trekking agencies can arrange overnight stays on a village homestay program in the Gurung village of Sirubari, about 56km from Pokhara.

Volunteer Work

In recent years 'voluntourism' has become a booming business in Nepal, with travel companies co-opting the idea as a branch of their for-profit enterprises. To avoid the bulk of your placement fees going into the pockets of disinterested third-party agencies, it's important to do your research on the hundreds of organisations that now offer volunteer work and find a suitable one that supports your skills.

Although you give your time for free, you will be expected to pay for food and lodging, and you may also be asked to pay a placement fee. Volunteers should try to find out exactly how much of their placement fees is going into Nepal, and how much is going towards company profit and administrative costs. Fees paid to local agencies tend to be much lower than the large fees charged by some international volunteer agencies.

The better organisations offer support throughout the volunteering period, with in-country staff who can give a great deal of advice, training and direction and, most importantly, help to maintain the projects that you are involved in once you've returned home. To maximise the benefit to your host organisation, it's essential to be honest in evaluating what specific skills and experience you have to offer.

Nepal's orphanages in particular have come under a critical spotlight in recent years, with several operations linked to child trafficking and adoption scandals. Conor Grennan's book *Little Princes* is an inspiring account of time volunteering in a Nepali orphanage that touches on the corruption and murky moral dilemmas inherent in trying to do the right thing in Nepal.

For a more sobering perspective on the volunteering industry, see www.just-one. org/your-chance/volunteering. See also the boxed text 'When Giving is Selfish' in the Kathmandu chapter (p85).

When looking for a volunteer placement, a good place to start is the Kathmandu office of **Kathmandu Environmental Education Project** (KEEP; www.keepnepal.org). This well-regarded organisation places volunteers with a variety of local NGOs and offers one-month placements in Kathmandu teaching English and other skills to porters and guides in December/January and July/August. A minimum two-month time commitment is preferred and there's a US$50 administration fee.

Organisations that arrange volunteer placements and volunteer treks:

Butterfly Foundation (www.butterflyfounda tion.org) Accepts volunteers to help with administration and child care at its orphanage in Pokhara; linked to Butterfly Lodge (p199).

Child Environment Nepal (www.cennepal. org.np) Takes child-care volunteers in its orphanage at Naya Bazaar in Kathmandu.

Community Action Nepal (www.canepal. org.uk) Development project established by British climber Doug Scott.

Cultural Destination Nepal (www.volun teernepal.org.np) A cultural immersion package, combining a homestay and Nepali language course with a one- to three-month volunteer placement.

Esther Benjamins Trust (www.ebtrust.org. uk) Can arrange placements working to improve the lives of trafficked and abandoned children.

Ford Foundation (www.fordnepal.org) Arranges volunteer work focusing on teaching and child care; accommodation is provided by a host family.

Global Vision International (www.gvi. co.uk, www.gviusa.com) Offers both short- and long-term internships on teaching and volunteer placements on teaching and childcare projects, some combined with trekking in the Everest region. Volunteers are also able to obtain a BTEC award in leadership. The GVI Charitable Trust raises funds to support local projects and the community.

Global Volunteer Network (www.global volunteernetwork.org/nepal) A Kiwi organisation offering placements in health care, education, child care and social development.

Helping Hands (www.helpinghandsusa.org) Places medical volunteers at clinics around Nepal.

Himalayan Children Care Home (www. hchmustang.org) Accepts volunteers to help with the care and education of kids from remote Mustang who are attending schools in Pokhara.

Himalayan Healthcare (www.himalayan -healthcare.org) Arranges medical and dental treks around Nepal.

Hope & Home (www.hopenhome.org) Nepali NGO placing volunteers on health, teaching and child-care programs.

Insight Nepal (www.insightnepal.org.np) Combines a cultural and education program near Pokhara with a volunteer placement and a trek in the Annapurna region; the package lasts seven weeks or three months.

Kanchenjunga School Project (www. kangchenjunga.org) Arranges treks with volunteer placements in health and education at villages in the Kanchenjunga region.

Mamata Volunteers (www.mamatavolun teers.org) Wide range of fee-paying volunteer work.

Mountain Fund (www.mountainfund.org) Offers fairly pricey volunteer opportunities in Kathmandu.

Mountain Trust Nepal (www.mountain-trust. org) British NGO that can arrange volunteer placements in social projects around Pokhara.

Nepal Sathi (www.nepalsathi.ws) Places volunteers on projects at villages near the Arniko Hwy in central Nepal.

Nepal Trust (www.nepaltrust.org) A focus on Humla in western Nepal.

Nepali Children's Trust (www.nepalichild renstrust.com) Runs an annual trek for volunteers and disabled Nepali children from the Annapurna region.

Prison Assist Nepal (www.panepal.org) Kathmandu-based organisation that needs volunteers to help look after children whose parents are in prison.

Rokpa (www.rokpa.org) Swiss-Tibetan organisation that needs volunteers for its soup kitchen and medical tent at Bodhnath for six or more weeks (December to March).

Rural Assistance Nepal (www.rannepal.org) UK-based charity that places volunteers in education and healthcare.

Rural Community Development Programme (www.rcdpnepal.org) Arranges placements on volunteer projects that can be combined with organised treks.

Sustainable Agriculture Development Programme (www.sadpnepal.org) Arranges placements in sustainable and organic agriculture and other social programs near Pokhara.

Vajrayana School (www.vajrayanaschool.org. np) Teach Tibetan refugees in Bodhnath.

Volunteer Nepal (http://volunteernepal.net) Wide range of volunteer placements, connected with Nepal Orphan's Home (www.nepalorphans home.org).

Volunteer Nepal National Group (www. volnepal.np.org) Places volunteers on a variety of teaching, conservation and development programs.

Volunteers Initiative Nepal (www.volun teeringnepal.org) Wide range of opportunities; see also www.friendsofvin.nl.

regions at a glance

Like the Hindu deities guarding its temples, Nepal has many aspects and incarnations. If you like your beauty man-made, then it doesn't get better than the sublime golden temples, red-brick pagodas and medieval public squares that dominate the historic cities of the Kathmandu Valley. Framing the northern horizon of these cities is the high Himalaya, an almost limitless smorgasbord of alpine splendour criss-crossed by trekking routes.

Lesser known to visitors are the Middle Hills, a collection of hill towns that offer fine mountain viewpoints, traditional architecture and plenty of scope to get off the beaten track. Furthest south lie the steamy southern plains and their impressive wildlife reserves and easy access to India.

Kathmandu

Temples ✓✓✓
Food ✓✓
Shopping ✓✓

Temples
Kathmandu's old town is stuffed with ancient stupas and sculptures at every crossroad, while its central Durbar Sq is a masterpiece of medieval Malla architecture.

Food
The Thamel district is a global mash-up of Tibetan, Japanese, Thai and Italian restaurants, separated only by bakeries offering espresso drinks and lemon cheesecake. The city's Newari restaurants offer the more refined tastes of the Rana court.

Shopping
Where to start? World-class outdoor gear, Asia's best bookshops, bargain-priced pashminas, thangkas (Tibetan religious paintings) and prayer flags...the list is endless. Bring a spare bag – you'll need it.

p54

Around the Kathmandu Valley

Temples ✓✓✓
Outdoor Activities ✓✓
Traditional Towns ✓✓✓

Temples
Offering the world's densest collection of World Heritage Sites, almost every town in the valley is blessed with stunning temples and exquisite statuary.

Outdoor Activities
The valley's web of fine hiking and mountain-biking trails offers the best way to explore this area. To up the ante, head for the Tibetan border for some wild rafting and canyoning.

Traditional Towns
Bhaktapur wins the prize here but there are dozens of other charming villages to explore, from Kirtipur and Bungamati in the south to sleepy Nuwakot in the north. All offer fine traditional architecture and village squares that seem lifted from the 15th century.

p112

Kathmandu to Pokhara

Temples ✓
Outdoor Activities ✓✓
Traditional Towns ✓✓

Temples
Blood sacrifices at the hilltop temple at Manakamana are a macabre draw, especially on Saturdays, while Nepal's first capital at Gorkha boasts a historically important and impressive royal fort palace, with dozens of local temples littering the backstreets.

Outdoor Activities
Rafting and kayaking on the warm waters of the Trisuli River are the most popular excursions, and there are some exciting canyoning add-ons at the Royal Beach Camp.

Traditional Towns
Bandipur's Newari-style old town is one of the most atmospheric of Nepal's Middle Hills villages, with outdoor teahouses, good accommodation options and excellent day hikes.

p182

Pokhara

The Easy Life ✓✓
Mountain Views ✓✓✓
Trekking ✓✓✓

The Easy Life
With a warm climate, little pollution, and backpacker comforts, Pokhara is the perfect place to take a break, preferably over a leisurely lakeshore breakfast or an ambitious round of yoga and massage.

Mountain Views
It's all about Machhapuchhare and the Annapurnas, with spectacular dawn views from atop Sarangkot ridge, the World Peace Pagoda or while paddling a dhunga rowboat around serene Phewa Tal.

Trekking
A superb range of treks kick off from Pokhara, from short teahouse treks into the foothills around Ghorepani and Ghandruk to the alpine splendour of the Annapurna Sanctuary, Tibet-style Trans-Himalayan deserts around Jomsom or the full monty: the Annapurna Circuit.

p191

The Terai & Mahabharat Range

Temples ✓
Wildlife ✓✓✓
Outdoor Activities ✓

Temples

There are two major religious sites in the Terai. Buddhists celebrate the birthplace of the Buddha at Lumbini, while Hindus flock to the colourful temple complex at Janakpur to commemorate the marriage of Rama to Sita.

Wildlife

Fabulous Chitwan and remote Bardia National Parks both offer big-game wildlife watching in sultry river deltas and grasslands, while Koshi Tappu Wildlife Reserve is ground central for birdwatchers.

Outdoor Activities

Scanning for wildlife on a lumbering elephant's back or by boat are the major activities in the Terai, though there's also some good off-the-beaten-track walking around Ilam and nontouristy Tansen.

p216

Every listing is recommended by our authors, and their favourite places are listed first

Look out for these icons:

 Our author's top recommendation

 A green or sustainable option

 No payment required

See the Index for a full list of destinations covered in this book.

On the Road

Kathmandu

Includes »

Best Places to Eat

» Or2K (p91)

» Third Eye (p91)

» K-Too Steakhouse (p91)

» Delices de France (p91)

» Kaiser Cafe (p95)

Best Places to Stay

» Hotel Ganesh Himal (p88)

» Dwarika's (p90)

» Kantipur Temple House (p87)

» International Guest House (p86)

» Hotel Tibet (p89)

Why Go?

For many, stepping off a plane into Kathmandu is a pupil-dilating experience, a riot of sights, sounds and smells that can quickly lead to sensory overload. Whether you're barrelling through the traffic-jammed alleyways of the old town in a rickshaw, marvelling at the medieval temples of Durbar Sq or dodging trekking touts in the backpacker district of Thamel, Kathmandu can be an intoxicating, amazing and exhausting place.

To really glimpse the soul of the city, take a walk through the backstreets, and the capital's timeless cultural and artistic heritage reveals itself in hidden temples overflowing with marigolds, courtyards full of drying chillies and rice, and tiny hobbit-sized workshops.

This endlessly fascinating, sometimes infuriating, city has enough sights to keep you busy for a week but be sure to leave its backpacker comforts and explore the 'real Nepal' before your time runs out.

When to Go
Kathmandu

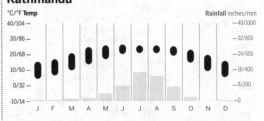

Oct–Dec Fine mountain views and warm days until December, with high-season crowds.

Mar–May March brings the Seto Machhendranath festival. Days can be hot in May.

Jun–Sep Monsoon months bring hot days and frequent showers but also spectacular Indra Jatra.

History

The history of Kathmandu is really a history of the Newars, the main inhabitants of the Kathmandu Valley. While the documented history of the valley goes back to the Kiratis, around the 7th century BC, the foundation of Kathmandu itself dates from the 12th century AD, during the time of the Malla dynasty.

The original settlements of Yambu and Yangala, at the confluence of the Bagmati and Vishnumati Rivers in what is now the southern half of the old town, grew up around the trade route to Tibet. Traders and pilgrims stayed at rest houses such as the Kasthamandap, which later lent its name to the city.

Originally known as Kantipur, the city flourished during the Malla era, and the bulk of its superb temples, buildings and other monuments date from this time. Initially, Kathmandu was an independent city within the valley, but in the 14th century the valley was united under the rule of the Malla king of Bhaktapur. The 15th century saw division once more, this time into three independent kingdoms: Kathmandu, Patan and Bhaktapur. Rivalry between the three city-states led to a series of wars that left each state weakened and vulnerable to the 1768 invasion of the valley by Prithvi Narayan Shah.

The ensuing Shah dynasty unified Nepal and made the expanded city of Kathmandu its new capital – a position the city has held ever since.

A massive earthquake in 1934 destroyed much of the city, creating a network of modern boulevards such as New Rd. Kathmandu escaped the worst of the Maoist uprising (1996–2005), though the city was frequently crippled by demonstrations and strikes. Tens of thousands of Nepalis flooded into the rapidly expanding city to escape the political violence, and the city infrastructure is still struggling to cope.

◉ Sights

Most of the interesting things to see in Kathmandu are clustered in the old part of town, focused around the majestic Durbar Sq and its surrounding backstreets.

DURBAR SQUARE

Kathmandu's **Durbar Square** (Map p64; foreigner/SAARC Rs 300/100, no student tickets) was where the city's kings were once crowned and legitimised, and from where they ruled ('durbar' means palace). As such, the square

---

KATHMANDU & AROUND IN...

Two Days

Start off the day with our two-hour walking tour on p72. Grab lunch overlooking **Basantapur Sq** or in nearby **Freak St** and then spend the afternoon soaking up the architectural grandeur of **Durbar Sq**. Finish the day with a cold beer and dinner in the Thamel area.

Next day cycle out to **Swayambhunath** in the morning and spend the afternoon shopping in **Thamel**. For your final meal splurge at one of the blowout Newari restaurants such as **Bhojan Griha** or **Thamel House**.

Four Days

If you have an extra couple of days, take a short taxi ride out to **Patan** (p126) for a full day exploring its Durbar Sq, Patan Museum (the best in the country) and another fascinating backstreet walking tour. Take your dinner in one of Jhamsikhel's excellent restaurants.

On day four take a taxi to **Pashupatinath** (p115) and then make the short walk out to **Bodhnath** (p118) to soak up some Tibetan culture as the pilgrims gather at dusk.

One Week

With a week up your sleeve you can spend a day (and preferably a night) at **Bhaktapur** (p140). When stress levels build, fit in some quiet time at the delightful **Garden of Dreams**.

Seven days gives you the chance to gorge on Thai (Yin Yang), Indian (Third Eye), Korean (Hankook Sarang), buff steak (K-Too), falafel (Or2k) and maybe even some Nepali food! Don't get us started on lunch...

Kathmandu Highlights

1 Follow our walking tour through the labyrinthine backstreets of the **old town** (p71), bursting with hidden courtyards and little-known temples

2 Soak up the amazing architectural monuments of **Durbar Square** (p55), an artistic and architectural tradition that rivals the great cities of Europe

3 Dine on momos (dumplings) and wild boar to the beat of *madal* (drums) and *bansari* (flutes) at one of the city's superb **Newari restaurants** (see the boxed text, p96)

4 Ensure the enduring love of friends and family by snapping up the bargains in Thamel's excellent **shops** (p100)

5 Chill out in one of Thamel's rooftop garden **restaurants** (p91) with a good book, a pot of masala tea and a slice of chocolate cake

6 Take a day trip to the nearby Unesco World Heritage Site of **Swayambhunath** (p107)

7 Escape the traffic in the peaceful and beautifully restored Rana-era **Garden of Dreams** (see the boxed text, p69)

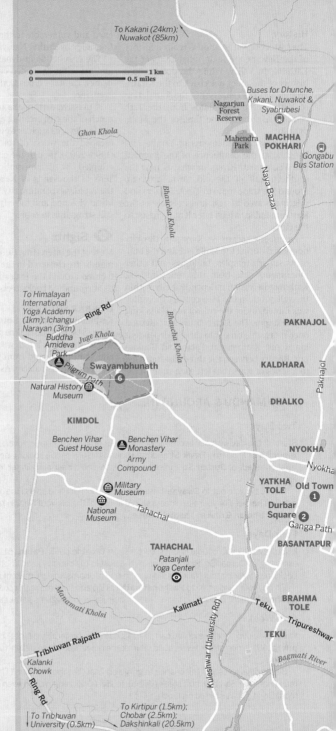

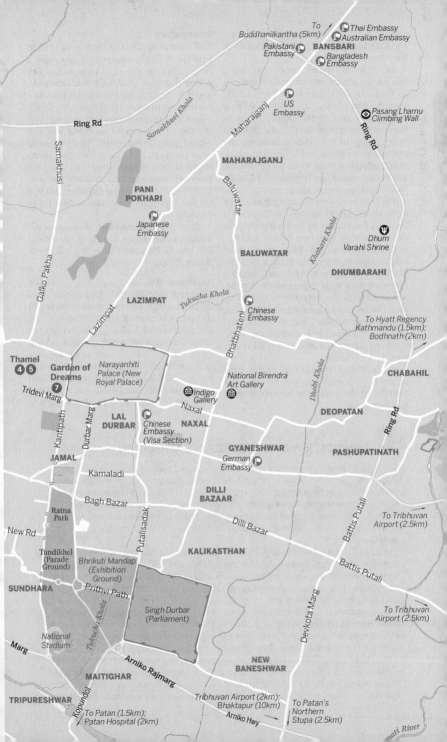

remains the traditional heart of the old town and Kathmandu's most spectacular legacy of traditional architecture.

It's easy to spend hours wandering around the square and watching the world go by from the terraced platforms of the towering Maju Deval; it's a wonderful way to get a feel for the city. Although most of the square dates from the 17th and 18th centuries (many of the original buildings are much older), a great deal of rebuilding happened after the great earthquake of 1934. The entire square was designated a Unesco World Heritage Site in 1979.

The Durbar Sq area is actually made up of three loosely linked squares. To the south is the open Basantapur Sq area, a former royal elephant stables that now houses souvenir stalls and off which runs Freak St. The main Durbar Sq area, with its popular watch-the-world-go-by temples, is to the west. Running northeast is a second part of Durbar Sq, which contains the entrance to the Hanuman Dhoka and an assortment of temples. From this open area Makhan Tole, at one time the main road in Kathmandu and still the most interesting street to walk down, continues northeast.

A good place to start an exploration of the square is with what may well be the oldest building in the valley, the unprepossessing Kasthamandap.

Information

The admission ticket to Durbar Sq is valid only for the date stamped. If you want a longer duration you need to go to the **site office** (Map p64; ☎4268969; www.kathmandu.gov.np; ☺7am-6pm), on the south side of Basantapur Sq, to get a free visitor pass, which allows you access for as long as your visa is valid (if you extend your visa you can extend your visitor pass). You will need your passport and one photo (no photo required for less than three days) and the process takes about two minutes. You generally need to show your ticket even if you are just transiting the square to New Rd or Freak St.

There are tentative plans to combine admission to the square and Hanuman Dhoka into one Rs 750 ticket. There is a toilet near the site office.

Kasthamandap   PAVILION

(Pavilion of Wood; Map p64) Kathmandu owes its name to this ancient building. Although its history is uncertain, local tradition says the three-roofed building was constructed around the 12th century from the wood of a single sal tree. It first served as a community centre where visitors gathered before major ceremonies (a *mandap* is a 16-pillared pilgrim shelter), but later it was converted to a temple dedicated to Gorakhnath, a

---

ORIENTATION & ADDRESSES IN KATHMANDU

The most interesting part of Kathmandu is the crowded backstreets of the rectangular-shaped old town. This is bordered to the east by the sprawling modern new town and to the north by the main tourist and backpacker district of Thamel (pronounced tha-*mel*). With over 2500 tourist-related companies jammed into half a dozen narrow streets, Thamel boasts a collection of hotels, restaurants, trekking agencies, bakeries and shops that is rivalled only by Bangkok's Khao San Rd. Thamel is 15 to 20 minutes' walk north from Durbar Sq.

East of Thamel is Durbar Marg, a wide street flanked by airline offices, restaurants and expensive hotels. Further north are the embassy and NGO districts of Lazimpat and Maharajganj. To the south of town is Patan (see p126), a historically distinct city, which has now partially merged with Kathmandu's southern sprawl. Both Kathmandu and Patan are encircled by the Ring Rd.

In old Kathmandu, streets are only named after their district, or *tole*. The names of these districts, squares and other landmarks (perhaps a monastery or temple) form the closest thing to an address. For example, the address for everyone living within a 100m radius of Thahiti Tole is Thahiti Tole. 'Thamel' is now used to describe a sprawling area with at least a dozen roads and several hundred hotels and restaurants.

Given this anarchic approach it is amazing that any mail gets delivered – it does, but slowly. If you're trying to find a particular house, shop or business, make sure you get detailed directions. Otherwise, the interactive online map at www.mapmandu.com can sometimes help.

13th-century ascetic who was subsequently linked to the royal family.

A central wooden enclosure houses the image of the god, which is noteworthy since Gorakhnath is usually represented only by his footprints. In the corners of the building are four images of Ganesh.

The squat, medieval-looking building is especially busy in the early morning hours when the valley's vegetable sellers set up shop and porters sit awaiting customers. Piles of smoked fish, banana leaves and marigolds spill into the surrounding alleyways.

Across the square is the **Kabindrapur Temple** (Dhansa Dega), an ornate 17th-century performance pavilion that houses the god of music.

Singh Sattal   PAVILION

(Map p64) Built with wood left over from the Kasthamandap Temple, this squat building was originally called the Silengu Sattal (*silengu* means 'left over wood' and a *sattal* is a pilgrim hostel) until the addition of the golden-winged *singh* (lions) that guard each corner of the upper floor. The building has some fascinating stalls and curd shops on the ground floor and is a popular place for *bhajan* (devotional music) in the mornings and evenings.

Ashok Binayak   SHRINE

(Maru Ganesh; Map p64) On the northern side of Kasthamandap, at the top of Maru Tole, stands this tiny golden shrine. Its small size belies its importance, as this is one of the four most important Ganesh shrines in the valley. Ganesh is a much-loved god and there is a constant stream of visitors, helping themselves to the self-serve *tika* dispenser and then ringing the bells at the back. A visit to this shrine is thought to ensure safety on a forthcoming journey, so you might choose to make an offering here if you are headed on a trek.

It's uncertain how old the temple is, although its gilded roof was added in the 19th century. Look for the golden shrew (Ganesh's vehicle) opposite the temple.

Maru Tole   STREET

This *tole* (street) leads you away from Durbar Sq down to the Vishnumati River, where a footbridge continues the pathway to Swayambhunath. This was a busy street in the hippie era but the famous pastry shops that gave it the nickname 'Pie Alley' have long gone. Just 30m from Durbar Sq down

Maru Tole is **Maru Hiti** (off Map p64), one of the finest sunken water conduits in the city.

Maju Deval   HINDU TEMPLE

(Map p64) A pleasant half-hour can easily be spent soaking up the atmosphere on the steps of this Shiva temple, especially at dawn and dusk. In fact, the nine-stage ochre platform of the Maju Deval is probably the most popular meeting place in the city. From here you can watch the constant activity of fruit and vegetable hawkers, the comings and goings of taxis and rickshaws, and the flute and other souvenir sellers importuning tourists. The large, triple-roofed temple has erotic carvings on its roof struts and offers great views over the square and across the roofs of the city. Marigold sellers set up shop on the ground level.

The temple dates from 1690 and was built by the mother of Bhaktapur's king Bhupatindra Malla. The temple has a Shiva lingam (phallic symbol) inside.

At the bottom of the temple stairway on the east side is a small white temple to Kam Dev, the Hindu god of love and desire. It was built in the Indian shikhara style, with a tall corn cob–like spire.

Trailokya Mohan Narayan Temple   HINDU TEMPLE

(Map p64) The other temple standing in the open area of the square is this small five-roofed temple, just to the south. Dating from 1680, it is easily identified as a temple to Narayan/Vishnu by the fine Garuda kneeling before it. This powerful stone figure was a later addition, erected by King Prithvibendra Malla's widow soon after his death.

Look for the Vaishnavite images on the carved roof struts and the window screens with their decoratively carved medallions. Dances depicting the 10 incarnations of Vishnu are performed on the platforms to the east of the temple during the Indra Jatra festival.

Shiva-Parvati Temple   HINDU TEMPLE

(Nawa Jogini Temple; Map p64) From the steps of the Maju Deval you can look north across to this temple, where a pair of much-photographed white images of Shiva and his consort look out from the upstairs window onto the chaos below them. The temple was built in the late 1700s by Bahadur Shah, the son of Prithvi Narayan Shah. Although the temple is not very old by Kathmandu standards, it stands on a two-stage platform that may have been an open dancing stage hundreds

Central Kathmandu

500 m
0.25 miles

Bhatbhateni

GYANESHWAR

To Pashupatinath (2km);
Tribuvan Airport (5km);
Bodhnath (6km)

NAXAL

Gairidhara

Naxal

Kamal Pokhari

Tukucha Khola

LAZIMPAT

Narayanhiti
Palace Museum

Kamaladi

To Hotel Shangri-La
(120m)

LAL
DURBAR

Indian
Embassy

Narayanhiti Palace
(New Royal Palace)

JAMAL

LAINCHHAUR

To Balaju (3km);
Kathmandu Bus
Station (3km)

Galko Pakha

Lekhnath Marg Lainchhaur

THAMEL
BHAGWAN
BAHAL

Kaiser
Mahal

Tridevi Marg

Kantipath

PAKNAJOL

Naya Bazar

See Greater Thamel Map (p80)

Jyatha Rd

Commission

JYATHA

ASAN
TOLE

Asan Tole

Paknajol

Thamel
Chowk

Teuda

Jyatha

KALDHARA

DHALKO

JP School

CHHETRAPATI

Chhetrapati
Chowk

Rha
Pokhari

Nyokha

Kilagal

Dhobichaur

To National
Museum (1km);
Swayambhunath (2km)

BIJESHWARI

To Swayambhunath
(2km)

Vishnumati River

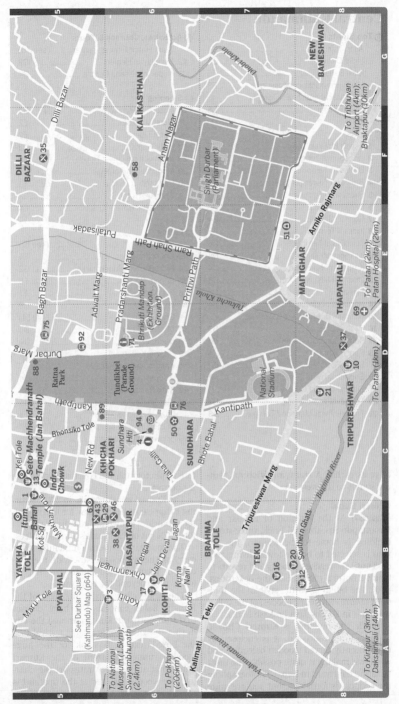

Central Kathmandu

of years earlier. A **Narayan (Vishnu) temple** stands to the west side.

Kumari Bahal COURTYARD
(Map p64) At the junction of Durbar and Basantapur Sqs, this red brick, three-storey building is home to the Kumari, the girl who is selected to be the town's living goddess until she reaches puberty and reverts to being a normal mortal (see the boxed text, p66). The building, in the style of the Buddhist *viharas* (monastic abodes) of the valley, was built in 1757 by Jaya Prakash Malla.

Inside the building is **Kumari Chowk**, a three-storey courtyard. It is enclosed by magnificently carved wooden balconies and windows, making it quite possibly the most beautiful courtyard in Nepal. Photographing the goddess is forbidden, but you are quite free to photograph the courtyard when she is not present.

The Kumari went on strike in 2005, refusing to appear at her window for tourists, after authorities denied her guardians' request for a 10% cut of the square's admission fees!

The courtyard contains a miniature stupa carrying the symbols of Saraswati, the goddess of learning. Non-Hindus are not allowed to go beyond the courtyard.

The large yellow gate to the right of the Kumari Bahal conceals the huge chariot that transports the Kumari around the city during the annual Indra Jatra festival (see the boxed text, p79). Look for the huge wooden runners in front of the Kumari Bahal that are used to transport the chariot. The wood is painted at the tips and is considered sacred. You can see part of the chariot from the top of the nearby Trailokya Mohan Narayan Temple steps.

Gaddhi Baithak
PALACE

(Map p64) The eastern side of Durbar Sq is framed by this white neoclassical building. With its imported European style, it was built as part of the Hanuman Dhoka palace in 1908 during the Rana period and makes a strange contrast to the traditional Nepali architecture that dominates the square. It is said to have been modelled on London's National Gallery following Prime Minister Jung Bahadur's visit to Europe.

Bhagwati Temple
HINDU TEMPLE

(Map p64) On the northwest corner of the Gaddhi Baithak, this triple-storey, triple-roofed temple is easily missed since it sur-mounts the building below it, which is lined with shops selling thangkas (Tibetan religious paintings) and their Newari equivalents, called *paubhas*.

The temple is actually part of the Hanuman Dhoka palace courtyard. The best view of the temple and its golden roofs is probably from the Maju Deval, across the square.

The temple was built by King Jagat Jaya Malla and originally had an image of Narayan. This image was stolen in 1766; when Prithvi Narayan Shah conquered the valley two years later, he simply substituted it with an image of the goddess Bhagwati. In April each year the image of the goddess is conveyed to the village of Nuwakot, 65km to the north, then returned a few days later.

Durbar Square (Kathmandu)

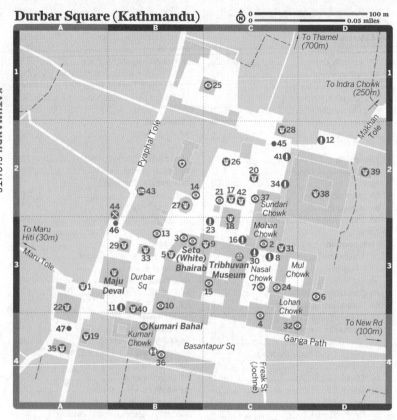

Great Bell
MONUMENT

(Map p64) On your left as you leave the main square along Makhan Tole is the Great Bell, elevated atop a white building erected by Rana Bahadur Shah (son of Prithvi Narayan Shah) in 1797. The bell's ring drives off evil spirits, but it is only rung during puja (worship) at the nearby Degutaleju Temple.

Across from the Great Bell is a very ornate corner **balcony**, decorated in gorgeous copper and ivory, from where members of the royal court could view the festival action taking place in Durbar Sq.

Krishna Temple
HINDU TEMPLE

(Chyasin Dega; Map p64) The history of the octagonal Krishna Temple is well documented. It was built in 1648–49 by Pratap Malla, perhaps as a response to rival Siddhinarsingh's magnificent Krishna Temple in Patan. Inside there are images of Krishna and two goddesses, which, according to a Sanskrit inscription, are modelled on the king and his two wives.

The temple's Newari inscription neglects to mention the king's little act of vanity. The temple is a favourite of sadhus who pose (and expect to be paid) for photos here.

Great Drums & Kot Square
MONUMENT

(Map p64) Just beyond the temple are the Great Drums, to which a goat and a buffalo must be sacrificed twice a year. In front of these is the police headquarters building. Beyond here is the closed-off Kot Sq, where Jung Bahadur Rana perpetrated the famous 1846 massacre that led to a hundred years of Rana rule (see p311). Kot means 'armoury' or 'fort'. During the Dasain festival each year, blood again flows in Kot Sq as hundreds of buffaloes and goats are sacrificed. Young soldiers are supposed to lop off each head with a single blow.

King Pratap Malla's Column
MONUMENT

(Map p64) Across from the Krishna Temple is a host of smaller temples and other

Durbar Square (Kathmandu)

structures, all standing on a slightly raised platform in front of the Hanuman Dhoka and the towering Taleju Temple behind. The square stone pillar, known as the Pratap Dhvaja, is topped by a statue of the famous King Pratap Malla (1641–74), seated with folded hands and surrounded by his two wives and his five (including an infant) sons. He looks towards his private prayer room on the 3rd floor of the Degutaleju Temple. The column was erected in 1670 by Pratap Malla and preceded the similar columns in Patan and Bhaktapur.

This area and its monuments are usually covered in hundreds if not thousands of pigeons; you can buy packets of grain to feed them.

Seto (White) Bhairab   CARVING
(Map p64) Seto (White) Bhairab's horrible face is hidden away behind a grille opposite King Pratap Malla's Column. The huge mask dates from 1794, during the reign of Rana Bahadur Shah, the third Shah-dynasty king. Each September during the Indra Jatra festival the gates are opened to reveal the mask for a few days. At that time the face is covered in flowers and rice; at the start of the festivities beer is poured through the horrific mouth as crowds of men fight to get a drink of the blessed brew. At other times of the year you can peek through the lattice to see the mask, which is used as the symbol of Nepal Airlines.

Jagannath Temple   HINDU TEMPLE
(Map p64) This temple, noted for the erotic carvings on its roof struts, is the oldest structure in this part of the square. Pratap Malla claimed to have constructed the temple during his reign, but it may actually date back to 1563, during the rule of Mahendra Malla. The temple has a three-tiered platform and two storeys. There are three doors on each side of the temple, but only the centre door opens.

KUMARI DEVI

Not only does Nepal have hundreds of gods, goddesses, deities, bodhisattvas, Buddhas, avatars (incarnations of deities) and manifestations – which are worshipped and revered as statues, images, paintings and symbols – but it also has a real, living goddess. The Kumari Devi is a young girl who lives in the building known as the Kumari Bahal, right beside Kathmandu's Durbar Sq.

The practice of having a living goddess probably came about during the reign of the last of the Malla kings of Kathmandu, and although there are actually a number of living goddesses around the Kathmandu Valley, the Kumari Devi of Kathmandu is the most important. The Kumari is selected from a particular caste of Newari gold- and silver-smiths. Customarily, she is somewhere between four years old and puberty, and must meet 32 strict physical requirements ranging from the colour of her eyes and shape of her teeth to the sound of her voice. Her horoscope must also be appropriate, of course.

Once suitable candidates have been found they are gathered together in a darkened room where terrifying noises are made, while men dance by in horrific masks and 108 gruesome buffalo heads are on display. These goings-on are presumed unlikely to frighten an incarnation of Durga, so the young girl who remains calm and collected throughout this ordeal is clearly the new Kumari. In a process similar to the selection of the Dalai Lama, as a final test the Kumari then chooses items of clothing and decoration worn by her predecessor.

Once chosen as the Kumari Devi, the young girl moves into the Kumari Bahal with her family and makes only a half-dozen ceremonial forays into the outside world each year, mainly during the September Indra Jatra festival, when she travels through the city on a huge temple chariot.

The Kumari's reign ends with her first period, or any serious accidental loss of blood. Once this first sign of puberty is reached she reverts to the status of a normal mortal, and the search must start for a new Kumari. On retirement the old Kumari is paid a handsome dowry but readjusting to normal life can be hard. It is said that marrying an ex-Kumari is unlucky, but it's believed more likely that taking on a spoilt ex-goddess is likely to be too much hard work!

Degutaleju Temple
HINDU TEMPLE

(Map p64) This triple-roofed temple is actually part of the darker, red-brick Hanuman Dhoka, surmounting the buildings below it, but it is most easily seen from outside the palace walls. The painted roof struts are particularly fine. Degutaleju is another manifestation of the Malla's personal goddess Taleju.

Kala (Black) Bhairab
MONUMENT

(Map p64) North of the Jagannath Temple is the figure of Kala (Black) Bhairab. Bhairab is Shiva in his most fearsome aspect, and this huge stone image of the terrifying Kala Bhairab has six arms, wears a garland of skulls and tramples a corpse, which is symbolic of human ignorance. The figure is said to have been brought here by Pratap Malla, having been found in a field to the north of the city. The image was originally cut from a single stone but the upper left-hand corner has since been repaired. It is said that telling a lie while standing before Kala Bhairab will

bring instant death and it was once used as a form of trial by ordeal.

Indrapur Temple
HINDU TEMPLE

(Map p64) Immediately east of the horrific Bhairab stands the mysterious Indrapur Temple. This puzzling temple may be of great antiquity but has been renovated recently and little is known of its history. Even the god to which it is dedicated is controversial – the lingam inside indicates that it is a Shiva temple but the Garuda image half-buried on the southern side indicates that it is dedicated to Vishnu. To compound the puzzle, however, the temple's name clearly indicates it is dedicated to Indra! The temple's unadorned design and plain roof struts, together with the lack of an identifying torana (pediment above the temple doors), offer no further clues.

Kakeshwar Temple
HINDU TEMPLE

(Map p64) This temple just to the northeast was originally built in 1681 but, like so many other structures, was rebuilt after it was badly damaged in the 1934 earthquake. It may have been considerably altered at that time as the temple is a strange combination of styles. It starts with a Newari-style floor, above which is an Indian shikhara-style upper storey, topped by a spire shaped like a *kalasa* (water vase), indicative of a female deity.

Stone Inscription   CARVING

(Map p64) On the outside of the white palace wall, opposite the Vishnu Temple, is a long, low stone inscription to the goddess Kalika written in 15 languages, including one word of French. King Pratap Malla, renowned for his linguistic abilities, set up this inscription in 1664 and a Nepali legend tells that milk will flow from the spout in the middle if somebody is able to decipher all 15 languages!

Kotilingeshwar Mahadev Temple   HINDU TEMPLE

(Map p64) This distinctive early stone Malla temple dates from the reign of Mahendra Malla in the 16th century. The three-stage plinth is topped by a temple in the *gumbhaj* style, which basically means a square structure topped by a bell-shaped dome. The bull facing the temple on the west side indicates that it is dedicated to Shiva.

Mahendreshwar Temple   HINDU TEMPLE

(Map p64) At the extreme northern end of the square, this popular temple dates from 1561, during the reign of Mahendra Malla, and is always bustling with pilgrims. The temple was clumsily restored with marble in 1963 and is dedicated to Shiva. At the northeastern corner there is an image of Kam Dev. The temple has a wide, two-level plinth and a spire topped by a golden umbrella.

Taleju Temple   HINDU TEMPLE

(Map p64) The square's most magnificent temple stands at its northeastern extremity but is not open to the public. Even for Hindus admission is restricted; they can only visit it briefly during the annual Dasain festival.

The temple was built in 1564 by Mahendra Malla. Taleju Bhawani was originally a goddess from the south of India, but she became the titular deity, or royal goddess, of the Malla kings in the 14th century, after which Taleju temples were erected in her honour in Patan and Bhaktapur, as well as in Kathmandu.

The temple stands on a 12-stage plinth and reaches more than 35m high, dominating the Durbar Sq area. The eighth stage of the plinth forms a wall around the temple, in front of which are 12 miniature temples. Four more miniature temples stand inside the wall, which has four beautifully carved wide gates. If entry to the temple were permitted it could be reached from within the Hanuman Dhoka or from the **Singh Dhoka** (Lion Gate) facing Durbar Sq.

On the west side of the compound wall look for the small **shrine** that has been crushed by the tree that sprouted from its roof decades ago, looking like something out of Cambodia's Angkor Wat.

Tana Deval Temple & Makhan Tole   HINDU TEMPLE

(Map p64) Directly north of the Taleju Temple is a 10th-century kneeling **Garuda statue** facing a small Vishnu Temple.

To the east, in a walled courtyard just past the long row of stalls, is the neglected Tana Deval Temple, with three carved doorways and multiple struts, the latter of which show the multi-armed Ashta Matrikas (Mother Goddesses). It's possible to enter the temple.

Crowded and fascinating Makhan Tole (*makhan* is the Nepali word for butter, *tole* means street) starts from here and runs towards the busy marketplace of Indra Chowk. Makhan Tole was at one time the main street in Kathmandu and the start of the main caravan route to Tibet.

From here you can either head south to visit the Hanuman Dhoka, continue northeast up Makhan Tole, or follow our walking tour on p72 in reverse order to get to Thamel.

Hanuman Dhoka   PALACE MUSEUM

(Map p64; admission Rs 250; ⊙10.30am-4pm Tue-Sat Feb-Oct, to 3pm Tue-Sat Nov-Jan, to 2pm Sun) The inner palace complex of the Hanuman Dhoka was originally founded during the Licchavi period (4th to 8th centuries AD) but, as it stands today, most of it was constructed by King Pratap Malla in the 17th century. The royal palace has been renovated many times over the years. The oldest parts are the smaller Sundari Chowk and Mohan Chowk at the northern part of the palace (both closed). The complex originally housed 35 courtyards and spread as far as New Rd, but the 1934 earthquake reduced the palace to today's 10 chowks (courtyards). Cameras are allowed only in the courtyards, not inside the buildings of the complex.

Hanuman's assistance to the noble Rama during the exciting events of the Ramay-

EROTIC ART (OR HOW THEY DID IT IN ANCIENT TIMES)

The most eye-catching decorations on Nepali temples are the erotic scenes, often quite explicit, that decorate the *tunala* (roof struts). These scenes are rarely the central carving on the strut; they're usually the smaller carving at the bottom of the strut, like a footnote to the larger image and in a crude, even cartoonlike style.

The purpose of the images is unclear. Are they simply a celebration of an important part of the life cycle? Are they a more explicit reference to Shiva's and Parvati's creative roles than the enigmatic lingams (phallic symbols) and yonis (female sexual symbols) scattered around so many temples? Or are they supposed to play some sort of protective role for the temple? It's popularly rumoured that the goddess of lightning is a shy virgin who wouldn't dream of striking a temple with such goings-on, although that's probably more a tourist-guide tale than anything else.

Whatever the reason for their existence, these Tantric elements can be found on temples throughout the valley. Some temples reveal just the odd sly image, while others are plastered with the 16th-century equivalent of hard-core pornography, ranging from impressively athletic acts of intercourse to medieval *ménages à trois*, scenes of oral or anal intercourse or couplings with demons or animals.

The temples you may want to avoid showing your kids include Kathmandu's Jagannath Temple, Basantapur (Kathmandu) Tower and Ram Chandra Temple; Patan's Jagannarayan Temple; and Bhaktapur's Erotic Elephants and Pashupatinath Temples.

ana has led to the monkey god's appearance guarding many important entrances. Here, cloaked in red and sheltered by an umbrella, a **Hanuman statue** marks the *dhoka* (entrance) to the Hanuman Dhoka and has even given the palace its name. The statue dates from 1672; the god's face has long disappeared under a coating of orange vermillion paste applied by generations of devotees.

Standards bearing the double-triangle flag of Nepal flank the statue, while on each side of the palace gate are stone lions, one ridden by Shiva, the other by his wife Parvati. Above the gate a brightly painted niche is illustrated with a central figure of a ferocious Tantric version of Krishna. On the left side is the gentler Hindu Krishna in his traditional blue colour accompanied by two of his comely gopi (milkmaids). On the other side are King Pratap Malla and his queen.

Nasal Chowk

From the entrance gate of the Hanuman Dhoka you immediately enter its most famous chowk. Although the courtyard was constructed in the Malla period, many of the buildings around the square are later Rana constructions. During that time Nasal Chowk was used for coronations, a practice that continued until as recently as 2001 with the crowning of King Gyanendra. The **coronation platform** is in the centre of the courtyard, while the Basantapur (Kathmandu) Tower looms over the southern end of the courtyard.

The rectangular courtyard is aligned north–south and the entrance is at the northwestern corner. Just by the entrance there is a surprisingly small but beautifully carved doorway, which once led to the Malla kings' private quarters.

Beyond the door is the large **Narsingha Statue**, Vishnu in his man-lion incarnation, in the act of disembowelling a demon. The stone image was erected by Pratap Malla in 1673 and the inscription on the pedestal explains that he placed it here for fear that he had offended Vishnu by dancing in a Narsingha costume. The Kabindrapur Temple in Durbar Sq was built for the same reason.

Next is the Sisha Baithak, or **Audience Chamber**, of the Malla kings. The open verandah houses the Malla throne and contains portraits of the Shah kings.

At the northeastern corner of Nasal Chowk stands the **Panch Mukhi Hanuman Temple**, with its five circular roofs. Each of the valley towns has a five-storey temple, although it is the great Nyatapola Temple of Bhaktapur that is by far the best known. Hanuman is worshipped in the temple in Kathmandu, but only the priests may enter.

In Nepali *nasal* means 'dancing one', and Nasal Chowk takes its name from the **Dancing Shiva statue** hidden in the white-washed chamber on the northeasternside of the square.

Tribhuvan Museum

The part of the palace west of Nasal Chowk, overlooking the main Durbar Sq area, was constructed by the Ranas in the middle to late part of the 19th century. Ironically, it is now home to a **museum** that celebrates King Tribhuvan (r 1911–55) and his successful revolt against their regime, along with memorials to Kings Mahendra (1955–72) and Birendra (1972–2001).

Exhibits with names such as the 'Royal Babyhood' include some fascinating recreations of the foppish king's bedroom and study, with genuine personal effects that give quite an eerie insight into his life. Some of the exhibits, such as the king's favourite stuffed bird (looking a bit worse for wear these days!), his boxing gloves, the walking stick with a spring-loaded sword hidden inside and his dusty, drained aquarium, add some surreal moments. There are several magnificent thrones, plenty of hunting photos and the obligatory coin collection.

Halfway through the museum you descend before ascending the steep stairways of the nine-storey **Basantapur (Kathmandu) Tower** (1770), which was extensively restored prior to King Birendra's coronation. There are superb views over the palace and the city from the top. The struts along the facade of the Basantapur (Kathmandu) Tower, particularly those facing out to Basantapur Sq, are decorated with erotic carvings.

It's hard not to rush through the second half of the museum, full of dull press clippings about the rather Peter Sellers–looking King Mahendra, before conveniently glossing over the massacre of King Birendra by his son in 2001 (see the boxed text, p317). The museum exits into Lohan Chowk.

Lohan Chowk & Other Chowks

King Prithvi Narayan Shah was involved in the construction of the four red-coloured towers around **Lohan Chowk**. The towers represent the four ancient cities of the valley: the Basantapur (Kathmandu) Tower, the Kirtipur Tower, the Bhaktapur Tower (Lakshmi Bilas) and the Patan (Lalitpur) Tower (known more evocatively as the Bilas Mandir, or House of Pleasure).

The palace's other courtyards are currently closed to visitors, but you can get glimpses of them from the Tribhuvan Museum, and they might reopen at a future date.

North of Lohan Chowk, **Mul Chowk** was completely dedicated to religious functions within the palace and is configured like a *vihara,* with a two-storey building surrounding the courtyard. Mul Chowk is dedicated to Taleju Bhawani, the royal goddess of the Mallas, and sacrifices are made to her in the centre of the courtyard during the Dasain festival.

A smaller Taleju temple stands in the southern wing of the square and the image of the goddess is moved here from the main temple during the Dasain festival.

KATHMANDU SIGHTS

DON'T MISS

GARDEN OF DREAMS

Just two minutes' walk, but a million miles from Thamel, is the beautifully restored **Garden of Dreams** (Swapna Bagaicha; Map p80; ✒4425340; www.asianart.com/gardenofdreams; adult/child Rs 160/40; ☻9am-10pm), one of the most serene and beautiful enclaves in Kathmandu.

Field marshal Kaiser Shamser (1892–1964), whose palace the gardens complement, built the Garden of Dreams in the 1920s after a visit to several Edwardian estates in England, using funds won from his father (the prime minister) in an epic Rs 100,000 game of cowrie shells. The gardens and its pavilions suffered neglect to the point of collapse before they were lovingly brought back to life over a six-year period by the same Austrian-financed team that created the Patan Museum.

There are dozens of gorgeous details in the small garden, including the original gate, a marble inscription from Omar Khayam's *Rubaiyat,* the new fountains and ponds, and a quirky 'hidden garden' to the south. Of the original 1.6 hectares and six pavilions (named after the six Nepali seasons), only half a hectare and three pavilions remain. To truly savour the serenity, come armed with a book or picnic to distract you from the overly amorous Nepali couples and relax on one of the supplied lawn mats. Wi-fi is available (Rs 250 for five hours). Dwarika's operates the serene Kaiser Cafe here (see p95) and there are occasional cultural events and exhibitions.

North of Nasal Chowk is **Mohan Chowk**, a residential courtyard used by the Malla kings. It dates from 1649 and, at one time, a Malla king had to be born here to be eligible to wear the crown. (The last Malla king, Jaya Prakash Malla, had great difficulties during his reign, even though he was the legitimate heir, because he was born elsewhere.) The golden waterspout, known as Sundhara, in the centre of the courtyard delivers water from Budhanilkantha in the north of the valley. The Malla kings would ritually bathe here each morning.

NORTH OF DURBAR SQUARE

Hidden in the fascinating backstreets north of Durbar Sq is a dense sprinkling of colourful temples, courtyards and shrines. The best way to get a feel for this area is on our walking tour (p72).

Kathesimbhu Stupa   STUPA

(Map p60) The most popular Tibetan pilgrimage site in the old town is this lovely stupa, a small copy dating from around 1650 of the great Swayambhunath complex. Just as at Swayambhunath, there is a two-storey pagoda to Hariti, the goddess of smallpox, behind and to the right of the main stupa. The courtyard entrance is flanked by metal lions atop red ochre concrete pillars. It's just a couple of minutes' walk south of Thamel.

Asan Tole   SQUARE

(Map p72) From dawn until dusk the junction of Asan Tole is jammed with vegetable and spice vendors selling everything from yak tails to coconuts. It's the busiest square in the city. Every day, produce is carried to this popular marketplace from all over the valley, so it is fitting that the three-storey **Annapurna Temple** in the southeast corner is dedicated to the goddess of abundance; Annapurna is represented by a *purana* (bowl) full of grain. At most times, but especially Sundays, you'll see locals walk around the shrine, touch a coin to their heads, throw it into the temple and ring the bell above them.

Nearby the two-storey **Ganesh shrine** is coated in bathroom tiles. On the south side of the square is the **Yita Chapal** (Southern Pavilion), which was once used for festival dances (the dance platform out front is just visible underneath several stalls). Cat Stevens wrote his hippie-era song *Kathmandu* in a smoky teahouse in Asan Tole, penning the lines: 'Kathmandu I'll soon be seeing you, and your strong bewildering time will hold me down.'

On the western side of the square are spice shops. Near the centre of the square, between two potted trees, is a small **Narayan shrine** (Narayan is a form of Vishnu).

Seto Machhendranath Temple
(Jan Bahal)   TEMPLE

(Map p60) Southwest of Asan Tole at the junction known as Kel Tole, this temple attracts both Buddhists and Hindus – Buddhists consider Seto (White) Machhendranath to be a form of Avalokiteshvara, while to Hindus he is a rain-bringing incarnation of Shiva. The temple's age is not known but it was restored during the 17th century. The arched entrance to the temple is marked by a small Buddha figure on a high stone pillar in front of two metal lions.

In the courtyard there are lots of small shrines, chaitya (stupas) and statues, including a mysteriously European-looking female figure surrounded by candles who faces the temple. It may well have been an import from Europe that has simply been accepted into the pantheon of gods. Facing the other way, just in front of the temple, are two graceful bronze figures of the Taras seated atop tall pillars. Buy some grain to feed the pigeons and boost your karma.

Inside the temple you can see the white-faced image of the god covered in flowers.

SETO MACHHENDRANATH FESTIVAL

Kathmandu's Seto (White) Machhendranath festival kicks off a month prior to the much larger and more important Rato (Red) Machhendranath festival in Patan (see the boxed text, p135). The festival starts with removing the white-faced image of Seto Machhendranath from the temple at Kel Tole and placing it on a towering and creaky wooden temple chariot known as a *rath*. For the next four evenings, the chariot totters slowly from one historic location to another, eventually arriving at Lagan in the south of Kathmandu's old town, where the chariot is hauled three times around the square. The image is taken down from the chariot and carried back to its starting point in a palanquin while the chariot is disassembled and put away until next year.

WALKING TOURS

Kathmandu's backstreets are dense with beautiful temples, shrines and sculptures, especially in the crowded maze of streets and courtyards in the area north of Durbar Sq, and exploring these half-hidden sights is a real highlight.

Both walking tours described in this chapter (see p72 and p75) will take you to traditional markets, temples, *toles* (streets), bahals (Buddhist monastery courtyards), *bahils* (residential courtyards) and chowks (intersections), which remain the focus of traditional Nepali life. You only really appreciate Kathmandu's museumlike quality when you come across a 1000-year-old statue – something that would be a prized possession in many Western museums – being used as a plaything or a washing line in some communal courtyard.

The walks can be made as individual strolls or linked together into one longer walk. The 'South from Thamel to Durbar Square' tour gives you a taste of the crowded and fascinating shopping streets in the oldest part of Kathmandu and takes you to some of the city's most important temples. The 'South from Durbar Square' tour takes you to a lesser-known section of southern Kathmandu, without spectacular sights but where the everyday life of city dwellers goes on and tourists are few and far between.

If these walking tours leave you wanting more, pick up Annick Holle's book *Kathmandu the Hidden City* (Rs 250), which details dozens of backstreet courtyards across town.

The image is taken out during the Seto Machhendranath festival in March/April each year and paraded around the city in a chariot. You can follow the interior path that circles the central building.

In the courtyard you may see men standing around holding what looks like a bizarre string instrument. This tool is used to separate and fluff up the downlike cotton padding that is sold in bulk nearby. The string is plucked with a twang by a wooden double-headed implement that looks like a cross between a dumb-bell and a rolling pin.

As you leave the temple, to the left you'll see the small, triple-roofed **Lunchun Lunbun Ajima**, a Tantric temple that's red-tiled around the lower level and has some erotic carvings at the base of the struts at the back.

Indra Chowk SQUARE
(Map p72) The busy street of Makhan Tole spills into Indra Chowk, the courtyard named after the ancient Vedic deity, Indra. Locals crowd around the square's newspaper sellers, scanning the day's news.

On the west side of the square is the facade of the **Akash Bhairab Temple**, or Bhairab of the Sky Temple. From the balcony four metal lions rear out over the street. The temple's entrance is at the right-hand side of the building, guarded by two more brass lions, but non-Hindus cannot enter. The silver image inside is visible through the open windows from out in the street, and during important festivals the image is displayed in

the square. In a small niche just to the left of the Akash Bhairab Temple is a very small but much-visited brass Ganesh shrine.

Indra Chowk is traditionally a centre for the sale of blankets and cloth, and merchants cover the platforms of the **Mahadev Temple** to the north. The next-door **Shiva Temple** to the northeast is a smaller and simplified version of Patan's Krishna Temple (see p127).

Itum Bahal COURTYARD
(Map p72) The long, rectangular courtyard of the Itum Bahal is the largest bahal (Buddhist monastery courtyard) in the old town and remains a haven of tranquillity in the chaotic surroundings. A small, white-painted stupa stands in the centre of the courtyard. On the western side of the courtyard is the **Kichandra Bahal**, or 'Keshchandra Paravarta Mahar Bihar', one of the oldest bahals in the city, dating from 1381 and renovated in 2007. A chaitya in front of the entrance has been completely shattered by a Bodhi tree, which has grown right up through its centre. In autumn and winter the square is decorated with ornate swirling patterns of drying grain.

Inside the Kichandra Bahal is a central pagodalike sanctuary, and to the south is a small chaitya decorated with graceful standing bodhisattvas. On the northern side of the courtyard are four brass plaques mounted on the upper-storey wall. The one on the extreme left shows a demon known as Guru Mapa taking a misbehaving child from a woman and stuffing it greedily into his

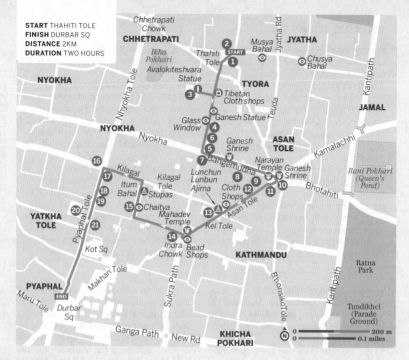

START THAHITI TOLE
FINISH DURBAR SQ
DISTANCE 2KM
DURATION TWO HOURS

Chhetrapati
Chowk
CHHETRAPATI
Jyatha Rd
JYATHA
Musya
Bahal
Chusya
Bahal
Ilkha
Pokhari
Thahiti
Tole
START
Kantipath
NYOKHA
Avalokiteshvara
Statue
TYORA
Tibetan
Cloth shops
JAMAL
Nhyokha Tole
Glass
Window
Ganesh Statue
Teuda
Nyokha
NYOKHA
Ganesh
Shrine
ASAN
TOLE
Kamalachhi
Bangemudha
Narayan
Temple Ganesh
Shrine
Rani Pokhari
(Queen's
Pond)
Kilagal
Lunchun
Lunbun
Ajima
Kilagal
16
Itum
Bahal
Tole
Stupas
Cloth
Shops
Bhotahiti
17
18
19
Chaitya
Mahadev
Temple
Asan Tole
15
YATKHA
TOLE
Pyaphal Tole
20
21
Kel Tole
Kot Sq
Indra
Chowk
Bead
Shops
KATHMANDU
Ratna
Park
Makhan Tole
PYAPHAL
END
Maru Tole
Durbar
Sq
Sukra Path
Bhonsiko Tole
Kantipath
Tundikhel
(Parade
Ground)
Ganga Path
New Rd
KHICHA
POKHARI
N
0   200 m
0   0.1 miles

Walking Tour
South from Thamel to Durbar Square

❭ This walk is best made en route from Thamel to Durbar Sq, or vice versa. To get to Thahiti Tole, walk south from Thamel on the road from the main Thamel Chowk; the first square you come to is Thahiti.

Thahiti Tole wraps around a 15th-century ❶ stupa. The ❷ **Nateshwar Temple**, on the northern side of the square, is dedicated to a form of Shiva that doubles as the local Newari god of music; the brass doorway depicts creatures busily playing a variety of musical instruments.

Take the road heading south past shops selling prayer flags, *khata* (ritual scarves) and Buddhist brocade, then bear west to the impressive ❸ **Kathesimbhu Stupa** (p70), radiating colourful prayer flags. There are thangka (Tibetan religious paintings) and *mala* (prayer beads) stalls in the square, as well as a little teahouse if energies are already flagging.

Further down on the left, past a Ganesh statue, is a small recessed area and a dark grilled doorway marking a small but intricate central ❹ **stone relief** dating from the 9th century. It shows Shiva sitting with Parvati on Mt Kailash, her hand resting proprietarily on his knee in the pose known as Uma Maheshwar. Various deities and creatures, including Shiva's bull Nandi, stand around them. To the right of the door is an almost unrecognisable orange-coloured Ganesh head. Incidentally, the impressive wooden balcony across the road is said to have had the first glass windows in Kathmandu (it looks like it's the same glass!).

Continue south past a string of dentists' shops (the reason will soon become clear), advertised by signs showing a grinning mouthful of teeth. When you hit a square you'll see the small, double-roofed ❺ **Sikha Narayan Temple**, easily identified by the kneeling Garuda figure and the modern clock on the wall. The temple houses a beautiful 10th- or 11th-century four-armed Vishnu figure that you might be able to see through the two grills and garlands of marigolds.

In the middle of the nondescript northern frontage, directly beneath the 'Raj Dental Clinic' sign, is a standing ⑥ **Buddha statue** framed by modern blue and white tilework. The image is only about 60cm high but dates from the 5th or 6th century. It's a reminder of how casually artistic treasures lie strewn around Kathmandu.

At the southern end of the area, just across the crossroads on the corner, you will see a lump of ⑦ **wood with coins** into which thousands of coins have been nailed. The coins are offerings to the toothache god, which is represented by a tiny image in the grotesque lump of wood. The square at the junction is known as Bangemudha, which means 'Twisted Wood'.

Head east to the triple-roofed ⑧ **Ugratara Temple** by a small square known as Nhhakantalla; a prayer at the half-sunken shrine is said to work wonders for the eyes. Just further on your right you will pass the Krishna Music Emporium (maker and repairer of harmoniums), before spotting a gated entrance on the right that leads into ⑨ **Haku Bahal**. Look for the sign that advertises 'Opera Eye Wear'. This tiny bahal has a finely carved wooden window overlooking the courtyard, which doubles as motorbike parking.

You'll soon come to the bustling chowk of ⑩ **Asan Tole** (p70), old Kathmandu's busiest junction and an utterly fascinating place to linger. The diagonal southwest-to-northeast main road was for centuries the main commercial street in Kathmandu, and the start of the caravan route to Tibet. The main shrine here is the three-storey ⑪ **Annapurna Temple**.

The street continues southwest past the octagonal ⑫ **Krishna Temple**, jammed between gleaming brass shops. It looks decrepit, but the woodcarvings on this temple are very elaborate, depicting beaked monsters and a tiny Tibetan protector, holding a tiger on a chain like he's taking the dog for a walk. Look for the turn-of-the-century plaques depicting marching troops on the building to the left.

The next square is Kel Tole, where you'll find one of the most important and ornate temples in Kathmandu, the ⑬ **Seto Machhendranath Temple** (p70). Just to the north of the temple on the side street known as Bhedasingh is a collection of shops selling *topi* (cloth hats) and the Nepali traditional dress known as a *daura suruwal* (a long shirt over tapered drainpipe trousers), including adorable miniature versions for children.

The busy shopping street spills into Indra Chowk (p71), marked by the stepped Mahadev Temple and ⑭ **Akash Bhairab Temple**. Before you leave Indra Chowk, look for the market hidden in the alleyways to the east, crowded with stalls selling the lurid beads that are so popular with married Nepali women.

Take the quiet alleyway west from Indra Chowk, past *tika* (sandalwood paste) shops and bangle stalls, and after 200m or so, by a small square, look for a tiny entryway to the right, by a triple shrine and under the sign for 'Jenisha Beauty Parlour'. The entryway leads into the long, rectangular courtyard of Itum Bahal, one of the oldest and largest bahals in the city, with some lovely architecture and stupas. See p71 for more on this and the ⑮ **Kichandra Bahal**.

Exit the courtyard at the north end and turn left (west). On your right at the next junction is the ⑯ **Nara Devi Temple** (p74). On the south side of the ⑰ **dance platform** is a small shop occupied by one of Kathmandu's many marching bands, mainly used for weddings – look for gleaming tubas, red uniforms and tuneless trumpeting.

At the Nara Devi corner, turn left (south); after 30m or so you come to a corner photocopy/magazine shop on your left with an utterly magnificent ⑱ **wooden window** above it. It has been called *deshay madu* in Nepali, which means 'there is not another one like it'. Next door in a small courtyard is the recently restored triple-roofed ⑲ **Bhulukha Dega Temple**, dedicated to Shiva.

Further south, on the right is the entrance to the ⑳ **Yatkha Bahal**, a huge open courtyard with a central stupa that looks like a mini-Swayambhunath. Directly behind it is an old building, whose upper storey is supported by four superb carved-wood struts. Dating from the 12th to 13th century, they are carved in the form of *yakshas* (attendant deities or nymphs), one of them gracefully balancing a baby on her hip. The struts were restored in 2002.

Back on the road you'll see the deep redbrick ㉑ **temple** to Chaumanda, a Newari mother goddess that features a six-pointed star in the upper window frame. Head south again, past the drum and marching-band shops on the right, to Durbar Sq, your final destination for this walk.

mouth. Eventually the demon was bought off with the promise of an annual feast of buffalo meat, and the plaque to the right shows him sitting down and dipping into a pot of food. With such a clear message on juvenile misbehaviour it is fitting that the courtyard houses a primary school – right under the Guru Mapa plaques!

To this day, every year during the festival of Holi the inhabitants of Itum Bahal sacrifice a buffalo to Guru Mapa on the banks of the Vishnumati River, cook it in the afternoon in the courtyard and in the middle of the night carry it in huge cauldrons to a tree in the Tundikhel parade ground where the demon is said to live.

Nara Devi Temple HINDU TEMPLE
(Map p60) Halfway between Chhetrapati and Durbar Sq, the Nara Devi Temple is dedicated to Kali, Shiva's destructive consort. It's also known as the Seto (White) Kali Temple. It is said that Kali's powers protected the temple from the 1934 earthquake, which destroyed so many other temples in the valley. A Malla king once stipulated that a dancing ceremony should be held for the goddess every 12 years, and dances are still performed on the small dance platform that is across the road from the temple.

EAST OF THAMEL

Three Goddesses Temples TEMPLES
(Map p80) Next to the modern Sanchaya Kosh Bhawan Shopping Centre in Thamel are the often ignored Three Goddesses Temples. The street on which the temples are located is Tridevi Marg – *tri* means 'three' and *devi* means 'goddesses'. The goddesses are Dakshinkali, Manakamana and Jawalamai, and the roof struts have some creative erotic carvings.

Narayanhiti Palace Museum MUSEUM
(Map p60; ✆4227844; admission Rs 500; ◷11am-4pm Thu-Mon) Few things speak clearer to the political changes that have transformed Nepal over the last decade than this walled palace at the northern end of Durbar Marg. King Gyanendra was given 15 days to vacate the property in 2007 and within two years the building was opened as a people's museum by then prime minister Prachandra, the very Maoist guerrilla leader who had been largely responsible for the king's spectacular fall from grace.

Full of chintzy meeting rooms and faded 1970s glamour, the palace interior is more gaudy than opulent. The highlights are the impressive throne and banquet halls and the modest royal bedrooms (check out the great armchair with built-in speakers). Stuffed gharial, tigers and rhino heads line the halls next to towering portraits of earlier Shahs and photos of the royal family taken with other doomed leaders – Yugoslavia's Tito, Romania's Ceauşescu and Pakistan's Zia ul-Haq.

The locations where Prince Dipendra massacred his family in 2001 are rather morbidly marked, though the actual building was rather suspiciously levelled after the crime. Bullet holes are still visible on some of the walls. Just as interesting as the building are the locals' reactions to it, as they peek at a regal lifestyle that for centuries they could only have dreamed about. Photography is not allowed.

Rani Pokhari POND
(Map p60) This large fenced tank just off Kantipath is said to have been built by King Pratap Malla in 1667 to console his queen over the death of their son (who was trampled by an elephant). The pool (*pokhari* means pool or small lake) was apparently used during the Malla era for trials by ordeal and later became a favourite suicide spot.

The tank and its central Shiva Temple is unlocked only one day each year, on the fifth day of the Tihar festival. At other times you can get the best views from the footbridge over the nearby chowk (the chowk has rather optimistically been declared a no-horn zone!).

Siddhartha Art Gallery GALLERY
(Map p60; ✆4218048; www.siddharthaartgallery. com; Babar Mahal Revisited; ◷11am-6pm) This is the city's best gallery for contemporary Nepali art, with a wide range of top-notch exhibitions, and worth a visit if you're shopping at Babar Mahal Revisited.

National Birendra Art Gallery GALLERY
(Map p60; ✆4411729; admission Rs 75; ◷9am-5pm Sun-Fri) The offbeat location of this gallery in a crumbling old Rana palace at the Nepal Academy of Fine Arts is probably more interesting than the dusty collection of Nepali oils and watercolours.

SOUTH OF DURBAR SQUARE
Easily the best way to explore this part of town is on our walking tour (opposite).

Bhimsen Temple BUDDHIST TEMPLE
(Map p75) The Newari deity Bhimsen is said to watch over traders and artisans, so it's quite appropriate that the ground floor of

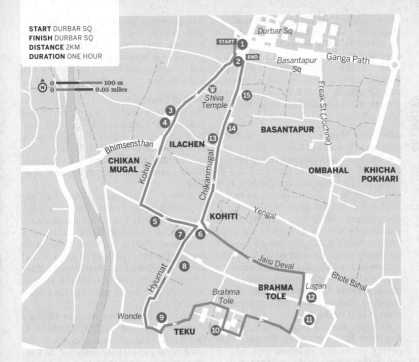

START DURBAR SQ
FINISH DURBAR SQ
DISTANCE 2KM
DURATION ONE HOUR

Walking Tour
South from Durbar Square

Starting from the ❶ **Kasthamandap** in the southwestern corner of Durbar Sq, fork right at the ❷ **Singh Sattal**, and follow the road past a Shiva temple with a finely carved pilgrim shelter. Soon you come to a large sunken ❸ **hiti**, or water tank, beside the highly decorated ❹ **Bhimsen Temple** (p74).

Continue south beyond the Bhimsen Temple, then continue straight at the junction, instantly losing the traffic as you swing left and pass the deep and ornate ❺ **Kohiti water tank**. At the top of the hill you'll come out by the tall, triple-roofed, 17th-century ❻ **Jaisi Deval Temple** (p76), which stands on a seven-level base. Nearby is the ❼ **Ram Chandra Temple** (p76).

Heading southwest you pass through the small and lived-in courtyard of ❽ **Tukan Bahal**. The Swayambhunath-style 14th-century stupa in the centre is surprisingly impressive.

The road continues with a few bends, then turns sharply left (east) at Wonde junction, which is marked by several temples, including a tall, white ❾ **shikhara temple**.

Our walk continues past Brahma Tole to the ❿ **Musum Bahal**, with its phallic-shaped Licchavi-style chaityas, an enclosed well and surrounding interconnecting bahals. Take a right when you get back to the main road and then a sharp left (north) at the next main junction. After 25m look out for the spacious and sunny ⓫ **Ta Bahal**, with its lovely chaityas, hidden down an alley on the right.

The road turns into an open square, known as Lagan, featuring the white, 5m-high ⓬ **Machhendranath Temple**, as well as the occasional neighbourhood cricket match.

Continue straight out of Lagan, swinging left back to the Jaisi Deval Temple, then turn right (northeast) back towards Durbar Sq. Pass the slender ⓭ **Hari Shankar Temple** (1637) and continue north past a ⓮ **Vishnu (Narayan) Temple** to a second, larger Vishnu temple, the ⓯ **Adko Narayan Temple**, one of the four most important Vishnu temples in Kathmandu. There's a particularly ornate *path* (pilgrim's shelter) on the street corner. Just 50m beyond the temple lies Durbar Sq.

this well-kept temple should be devoted to shop stalls. An image of Bhimsen used to be carried to Lhasa in Tibet every 12 years to protect those vital trade routes, until the route was closed by the flight of the Dalai Lama in 1959. Tourists are not allowed inside the temple, which is fronted by a brass lion on a pedestal, ducking under the electric wires.

Jaisi Deval Temple
HINDU TEMPLE

(Map p60) The south of Kathmandu's old city was the heart of the ancient city in the Licchavi period (4th to 8th centuries) and its major temple is the tall, triple-roofed Jaisi Deval Temple, built just two years before Durbar Sq's famous Maju Deval (which is one platform higher). It's a Shiva temple, as indicated by the bull on the first few steps and the mildly erotic carvings on some of the temple struts. Right across the road from the temple is a natural stone lingam rising a good 2m from a yoni (female equivalent of a phallic symbol). The monolith is definitely a god-sized phallic symbol and a prayer here is said to aid fertility.

In its procession around the town during the Indra Jatra festival, the Kumari Devi's chariot pauses here and dances are held on the small platform across from the temple.

Ram Chandra Temple
HINDU TEMPLE

(Map p60) West of the Jaisi Deval Temple is this courtyard named after Ram, an incarnation of Vishnu and the hero of the Hindu epic, the Ramayana. This small temple is notable for the tiny erotic scenes on its roof struts; it looks as if the carver set out to illustrate 16 different positions, starting with the missionary position, and just about made it before running out of ideas (there's one particularly ambitious, back-bending position). The north side of the courtyard is used as a cow stable, highlighting the wonderful mix of the sacred and profane in Nepal!

Bhimsen Tower (Dharahara)
MONUMENT

(Map p60; ☑4215616; foreigner/SAARC Rs 299/160, over 65yr & child under 5yr Rs 160; ☺8am-8pm) Towering like a lighthouse over the labyrinthine old town, this white, minaret-like tower near the post office is a useful landmark. The views from 62m up – 213 steps above the city – are the best you can get. There is a small Shiva shrine right at the very top.

The tower was originally built in 1826 by the Rana prime minister, Bhimsen Thapa, for Queen Lalit as part of the city's first European-style palace. It was rebuilt with nine storeys, two less than the original building, after it was severely damaged in the 1934 earthquake. The nearby Sundhara water tank is the largest in the city and lends its name to the district.

Pachali Bhairab & the Southern Ghats
HINDU TEMPLES

(Map p60) The northern banks of the Bagmati River south of the old town are home to little-visited temples and shrines, as well as the worst urban poverty in Kathmandu; rarely do such splendour and squalor sit so close.

Between Tripureshwar Marg and the Bagmati River at Pachali Bhairab a huge, ancient pipal tree forms a natural sanctuary for an image of Bhairab Pachali, surrounded by tridents (Pachali is a form of Shiva). To the side lies the brass body of Baital, one of Shiva's manifestations. Worshippers gather here on Tuesday and Saturday. It is particularly busy here during the festival of Pachali Bhairab Jatra.

From the temple head south to the ghats (riverside steps) on the holy riverbank to find a collection of lovely statuary. To the south is the Newari-style pagoda of the Lakshmi Mishwar Mahadev; to the southeast is the interesting Tin Deval Temple, easily recognisable by its three shikhara-style spires.

From here you can continue west along footpaths to cremation ghats and a temple at the holy junction of the Bagmati and Vishnumati Rivers; or east past some of Kathmandu's poorest and lowest-caste communities to the triple-roofed Tripureshwar Mahadev Temple, currently a museum of Nepali folk musical instruments. Further east is the Mughal-style Kalmochan Temple, built in 1873.

🏃 Activities

For golfing near the capital, see the Gokarna Forest Resort (p158).

Mountain Flight
SCENIC FLIGHTS

A popular activity from Kathmandu is to take an early morning scenic mountain flight along the spine of the Himalaya for close-up views of Mt Everest and other peaks from a distance of just 5 nautical miles. All major airlines offer the hour-long flights (US$171) and each passenger on the six- to 30-seat turbo props is guaranteed a window seat. The quality of the views depends on weather conditions. If the flight is cancelled due to bad weather, airlines offer a full refund or a seat on a later flight.

Seeing Hands   MASSAGE
(Map p80; ☑4253513; www.seeinghandsnepal.org; massage 60/90min Rs 1200/1800; ☺10am-6pm) Branch of the Pokhara-based organisation that offers massage from blind masseurs, providing employment to some of Nepal's 600,000 blind. Choose between a relaxing Swedish massage or remedial sports therapy for specific issues.

Himalayan Healers   MASSAGE
(Map p60; ☑2090641; www.himalayanhealers.org; Hotel Ambassador, Lazimpat; ☺10.30am-6.30pm) This impressive operation trains war widows and victims of human trafficking or domestic violence in 500 hours of massage therapy and then organises a placement. Treatments are a flat rate of Rs 850/1350/1650 for 30/60/90 minutes, for massage (Swedish, Nepali), reflexology, body wraps or scrubs. Branches are planned for Club Himalaya in Nagarkot and in Borderlands.

Ananda Yoga Center   YOGA
(☑4311048; www.anandayogacenter.blogspot.com; Kathmandu Valley) On the edge of the valley at Satungal, overlooking Matatirtha Village, 8km west of Kathmandu, this is a nonprofit yoga retreat offering courses in hatha yoga and teacher training.

Pranamaya Yoga   YOGA
(Map p80; ☑9851002920; www.pranamaya-yoga.com; classes Rs 600) Faced with one too many hairy male yoga teachers displaying contortive poses in their underpants, the owners of this centre decided to set up a modern, comfortable environment for drop-in practitioners. Classes take place in the restaurant 1905 near Thamel, and in Patan opposite Moksh Live, mornings and evenings and range from power yoga and pilates to teacher training courses.

Pasang Lhamu Climbing Wall   CLIMBING
(Map p56; ☑4370742; www.pasanglhamu.org; ☺10am-5.30pm) If you need to polish your climbing skills before heading to the big peaks, try this wall on the Ring Rd on the city's northeastern edge. A day's membership costs Rs 350 and equipment rental costs Rs 100. Week-long climbing courses (Rs 4800) and private tuition are available. The centre is named after the first Nepali woman to summit Everest, in 1993.

KATHMANDU FOR CHILDREN

Pilgrims Book House (see p100) has a fine collection of kids' books, including colouring books.

Away from the tourist areas highchairs are virtually nonexistent but finding nonspicy food that children will eat isn't a problem.

Kids will probably enjoy the zoo in nearby Patan (see p134) and older kids will get a thrill from spotting the monkeys at Swayambhunath (p107).

Clark Hatch Fitness Center   GYM
(Map p60; ☑4411818) This gym at the Radisson charges Rs 1200 for a day pass, while the Hyatt Regency charges a similar amount for its gym, pool, sauna, steam room and Jacuzzi.

Hash House Harriers   RUNNING
(www.aponarch.com/hhhh) The Nepal branch of these 'drinkers with a running problem' meets for a run every Saturday afternoon. Check the website for details.

ADVENTURE SPORTS
See p39 and p42 for a list of adventure operators offering mountain biking, rafting and kayaking trips from Kathmandu.

Alternative Nepal   ADVENTURE SPORTS
(Map p80; ☑4700170; www.alternativenepal.com; Mandala St, Thamel) Rafting, trekking, climbing and biking trips.

Borderlands   ADVENTURE SPORTS
(Map p80; ☑4701295; www.borderlandresorts.com; by Northfield Cafe, Thamel) Rafting, canyoning and trekking based at the resort near the Tibetan border (see p178), together with Ultimate Descents Nepal.

Chhango   CANYONING
(Map p80; ☑4701251; www.canyoninginnepal.com; Thamel) Canyoning in Sundarijal.

Hardcore Nepal   ROCK CLIMBING
(Map p80; ☑9813463599; www.hardcorenepal.com; Bhagwati St, Thamel) Rock-climbing courses and caving excursions from Kathmandu, including to Nagarjun and Siddha Gufa.

Himalayan Encounters   ADVENTURE SPORTS
(Map p80; ☑4700426; www.himalayanencounters.com; Kathmandu Guest House courtyard, Thamel) Rafting, trekking, tours and booking for lodges in Bandipur and Nuwakot.

Last Resort ADVENTURE SPORTS
(Map p80; ☑4700525; www.thelastresort.com.np;
Mandala St, Thamel) Rafting, canyoning, bungee jumping and accommodation near Borderlands (see p178), together with Ultimate Rivers.

⚡ Courses

Nepal is a particularly popular place for people to take up spiritual pursuits. Check the noticeboards in Thamel for up-to-date information about yoga and Buddhism courses and shop around before you commit yourself.

Social Tours COOKING
(Map p80; ☑4412508; www.socialtours.com;
⊙10.30am-2pm) This excellent company runs a half-day Nepali cookery course that involves a trip to a local market to get ingredients for momos and daal bhaat, including spinach curry, alu gobi (potato and cauliflower), tomato achar (pickle) and alu paratha (fried chapatti with potato). The cost is Rs 750 per person, minimum of two, including ingredients. The company also runs a pottery tour to Bhaktapur to learn how to throw pots, in addition to walks through Kathmandu's old town.

**Himalayan International
Yoga Academy** YOGA
(HiYA; ☑2021259; www.yogainnepal.com; 2 days
s/d US$45/70, bungalows s/d US$60/90) In a peaceful location between Swayambhunath and Nagarjun hill, HiYA offers residential yoga and meditation courses to help you decompress. Rates include tented or bungalow accommodation, vegetarian meals, a morning yoga and evening guided meditation lesson and one massage or alternative medicine treatment.

**Gandharba Culture and
Art Organisation** MUSIC
(Map p80; http://gandharbas.nyima.org; Thamel) Offers lessons in the *sarangi* (four-stringed instrument played with a bow) and it can probably find teachers for other instruments such as the *madal* (drum), *bansari* (flute) and *arbaj* (four-string guitar). Expect to pay around Rs 250 per hour.

Healing Hands Centre MASSAGE
(☑4371470; www.ancientmassage.com; Maharajganj) Various monthly courses in Thai massage. The five-day course (20 hours, US$200) teaches you how to give a full-body massage; there are also 10-day courses and one-month professional courses for US$900. Accommodation is available. The office is hard to find, so call or email in advance.

Nepal Vipassana Centre MEDITATION
(Map p60; ☑4250581; www.dhamma.org.np; Jyoti Bhawan Bldg, Kantipath; ⊙10am-5pm Sun-Fri) Ten-day retreats are held twice a month (starting on the 1st and 14th of the month) at its centre northeast of Kathmandu, just north of Budhanilkantha, and there are also occasional shorter courses for intermediate students. These are serious meditation courses that involve rising at 4am every morning, not talking or making eye contact with anyone over 10 days, and not eating after midday. The fee is donation only.

✨ Festivals & Events

Kathmandu has many festivals, of which the most outrageous is probably Indra Jatra in September, closely followed by the Seto Machhendranath chariot festival in March/April, Dasain in October, and the Pachali Bhairab Jatra, also in October. See p19 for other festivals that are celebrated nationwide.

**Kathmandu International
Marathon** SPORTS
(www.kathmandumarathon.com) This annual road race attracts over 6000 runners in October, with courses ranging from 5km to 42km. Registration costs US$30 for foreigners. Amazingly, the police hold back Kathmandu's revving traffic for a full five hours to let the race take place.

Jazzmandu Festival MUSIC
(www.jazzmandu.org; tickets around Rs 900) This annual music event is a week-long program of local and international jazz, fusion and world music acts that is staged in venues across town in late October/early November. See the website for details.

🛏 Sleeping

Kathmandu has a huge range of places to stay, from luxurious international-style hotels to cheap and cheerful lodges, and although prices have risen considerably in recent years, almost all offer competitive prices.

It's difficult to recommend hotels in the budget and middle brackets, as rooms in each hotel can vary widely. Many of these hotels have multiple wings and, while some

KATHMANDU'S INDRA JATRA FESTIVAL

Indra, the ancient Aryan god of rain, was once captured in the Kathmandu Valley while stealing a flower for his mother, Dagini. He was imprisoned until Dagini revealed his identity and his captors gladly released him. The festival celebrates this remarkable achievement (villagers don't capture a real god every day of the week). In return for his release Dagini promised to spread dew over the crops for the coming months and to take back with her to heaven all those who had died in the past year.

The Indra Jatra festival thus honours the recently deceased and pays homage to Indra and Dagini for the coming harvests. It begins when a huge wooden pole, carried via the Tundikhel, is erected outside the Hanuman Dhoka. At the same time images and representations of Indra, usually as a captive, are displayed and sacrifices of goats and roosters are made; the screened doors obscuring the horrific face of Seto (White) Bhairab are also opened and for the next three days his gruesome visage will stare out at the proceedings.

The day before all this activity, three golden temple chariots are assembled in Basantapur Sq, outside the home of the Kumari living goddess. In the afternoon the Kumari appears to a packed crowd, either walking on a rolled-out carpet or carried by attendants so that her feet do not touch the ground. The Kumari mounts the central chariot, flanked by two boys also in chariots, playing the roles of Ganesh and Bhairab.

The chariots move off and the Kumari is greeted from the balcony of the old palace by the president. The procession then continues out of Durbar Sq towards Hanuman Dhoka, where it stops in front of the huge Seto (White) Bhairab mask. The Kumari greets the image of Bhairab and then, with loud musical accompaniment, beer starts to pour from Bhairab's mouth! Getting a sip of this beer is guaranteed to bring good fortune, but one lucky individual will also get the small fish that has been put to swim in the beer – this brings especially good luck (though probably not for the fish).

Numerous other processions also take place around the town until the final day, when the great pole is lowered and carried down to the river. A similar pole is erected in Bhaktapur as part of the Bisket Jatra festival, celebrating the Nepali New Year.

rooms may be very gloomy and run-down, others (generally the upper floors) might be bright and pleasant. In general, roadside rooms are brighter but noisier than interior rooms, and top-floor rooms are the best as you stand a chance of getting a view and have easy access to the roof garden.

Budget places generally don't have heating so in winter you'll want the warmer south-facing rooms and garden access, as it's always pleasant to sit outside during the cool, but sunny, autumn and winter days.

Quite a few hotels bridge the budget and midrange categories by having a range of room standards – these places have been grouped according to their lowest price.

Normal high-season rates are listed here, but it's always worth asking for a discount, particularly during low season when most places offer discounts of between 20% and 40%. If you email a reservation in advance you can get a free airport pick-up in many places. Midrange and top-end places add on

an extra 23% tax but most budget places offer inclusive rates.

Most budget and some midrange places are found in the bustling Thamel district. Midrange and top-end places are widely scattered around Kathmandu, some quite a way from the centre.

Some travellers base themselves further afield, outside Kathmandu in Patan or Bodhnath, to escape the increasingly unpleasant traffic, pollution and commercialism of Thamel, and this isn't a bad idea. For something quieter still, an increasing number of midrange and top-end resorts around the Kathmandu Valley offer a peaceful rural atmosphere less than an hour from the centre of Kathmandu.

THAMEL

For budget and midrange places, the tourist ghetto of Thamel is the main locale. It's a convenient area to stay for a short time, especially to meet fellow travellers or indulge in some last-minute shopping, but you are

Greater Thamel

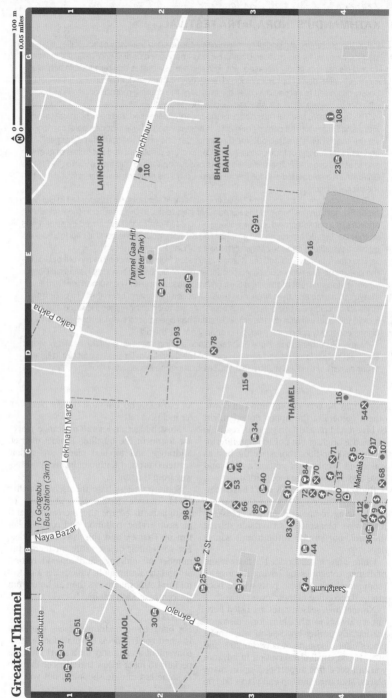

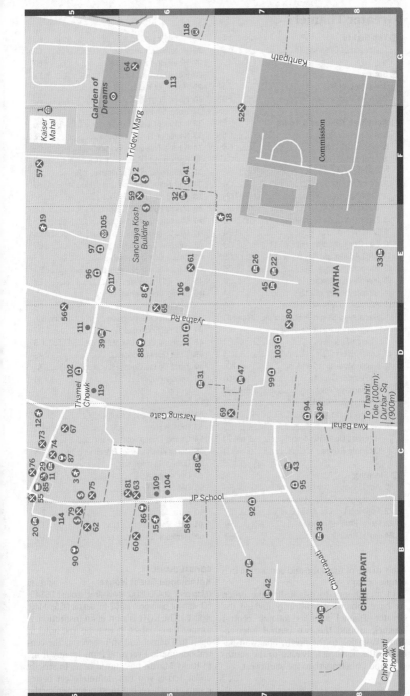

Greater Thamel

likely to tire of the noise and congestion in a couple of days.

In an attempt to establish some order, we have somewhat arbitrarily divided the Greater Thamel area as follows: central Thamel, around the two central intersections; Paknajol, to the north; Bhagwan Bahal, to the northeast; Jyatha, to the southeast; and Chhetrapati, to the southwest.

CENTRAL THAMEL

Kathmandu Guest House   HOTEL **$$**
(Map p80; ☎4700800; www.ktmgh.com; r US$40-60, without bathroom US$2-16, deluxe US$80-140; ❄@☎) The KGH is a bit of an institution. A former Rana palace, it was the first hotel to open in Thamel and still serves as the central landmark. Everyone from Jeremy Irons to Ricky Martin has stayed here. In strictly dollar terms you can definitely get better rooms elsewhere, but most people enjoy the

atmosphere here and it's often booked out weeks in advance. The particularly pleasant rear garden acts as a much-needed haven from the Thamel mayhem.

A vast range of rooms is available. The cheapest rooms without bathroom form part of the original 13-room guesthouse and are very basic – you can get better value elsewhere. In the newer wing, the best-value rooms are probably the garden-facing rooms

(single/double US$50/60). Rooms come with breakfast.

Hotel Courtyard BOUTIQUE HOTEL **$$**
(Map p80; ☎4700648; www.hotelcourtyard.com; Z St; s/d US$50/56, deluxe US$75/81, ste US$112/118) For something more stylish, this well-run hotel is one of the few boutique options in Thamel. Built in a traditional style with oil bricks, Newari-style carved wooden lintels and stone waterspouts, brought up to

date with dramatic orange walls and black trim, the rooms are big enough to tango in and there are pleasant seating areas that seem a world away from the Thamel madness. A small massage room, cosy library and bar enhance the lush, romantic mood. The hotel's sociable owners have made the courtyard a popular hang-out for local volunteers, mountaineers and other interesting folks, especially during the popular barbecue nights; great if you want to plug into the Kathmandu scene but bad if you want to go to bed early. Rates include breakfast and taxes.

Hotel Horizon HOTEL $

(Map p80; ☎4220904; www.hotelhorizon.com; economy s/d US$8/10, standard US$12/15, deluxe US$20/25; ✴@☎) The Horizon is a good choice down an alley off the main street in southern Thamel, making it a quiet and central option. All rooms have a bathroom and most are bright and spacious, if a little old fashioned, plus there are some nice communal seating areas, including around the newly designed courtyard. The midpriced rooms are the best value; more than this and you are just paying for air-con and a bath tub.

Karma Travellers Home GUESTHOUSE $

(Map p80; ☎4417897; www.karmatravellershome.com, www.hotelkarma.com; s/d US$10/14, deluxe US$18/25; ✴☎) This popular central place has decent rooms, several nice terrace sitting areas and helpful owners. The air-con deluxe rooms are more spacious and some rooms come with a balcony. You can get a 20% discount online and a free airport pick-up.

Student Guest House GUESTHOUSE $

(Map p80; ☎4251448; krishna@student.wlink.com.np; s/d Rs 500/800; @) With a convenient location on the eastern edge of Thamel, near traffic-soaked Tridevi Marg, this budget place is quiet and clean but the buildings are so crammed in that there's little natural light and no views. The neat and spacious rooms out the back on higher floors are best and solo travellers can often get these double rooms for a single price, which makes this one of the better cheapies in Thamel.

Marco Polo Guest House GUESTHOUSE $

(Map p80; ☎4251914; marcopolo@wlink.com.np; r Rs 400-700) Right next door to the Student Guest House and a similar deal, down to the boarding-school feel. The rooms at the top and back are surprisingly quiet and bright,

especially the larger deluxe rooms; others are noisier and darker.

Hotel Silver Home GUESTHOUSE $

(Map p80; ☎4262986; www.hotelsilverhome.com; dm/s/d/tr US$2/9/12/16; @☎) Plus points here include a central, quiet location, a friendly, helpful manager, one free airport pick-up and one of the only dorms in Thamel. The rooms are simple but come with hot water in the bathroom, and the hotel shares a little garden with two other good budget places, including the Pokhara Peace Hotel (which has good corner deluxe rooms for Rs 800).

Thorong Peak Guest House GUESTHOUSE $

(Map p80; ☎4253458; www.thorongpeak.com; s/d US$14/18, without bathroom US$8/12, deluxe US$20/24, superior US$26/30; @☎) A clean and well-looked-after place, off the main street in a small cul de sac. Most rooms are spacious, light and airy, if a little bland, and have super-clean bathrooms. Plus points include nice communal balconies, bike rental and a decent courtyard restaurant, though without the standard discount of 20% it's a bit overpriced. Deluxe rooms probably offer the best value, with large bathrooms.

Ambassador Garden Home BOUTIQUE HOTEL $$

(Map p80; ☎4701133; www.aghhotel.com; s/d US$45/55, deluxe US$72/91; ✴) Right in the eye of the Thamel storm but surprisingly peaceful, this place has splashes of style in the rooms and a nice garden and lobby reading area. Avoid the noisy east-facing rooms above the pub. Standard rooms are a bit small; deluxe rooms come with air-con and minibar and are more spacious. What you are paying for is the location.

Hotel Potala GUESTHOUSE $

(Map p80; ☎4700159; www.potalahotel.com; s/d US$8/12, without bathroom US$5/8, deluxe US$10/15; @) Bang in the beating heart of Thamel, this small backpacker place is a good option, and has free internet, a nice rooftop area and a convenient restaurant overlooking Thamel's main drag. Rooms are simple but clean and decent, with sunny corner deluxe rooms the best. It's down an alleyway near the Maya Cocktail Bar. Rates include taxes. Don't confuse it with Potala Guest House.

Prince Guest House GUESTHOUSE $

(Map p80; ☎4700456; princeguesthouse@hotmail.com; s/d US$12/15) The Prince Guest

LOCAL KNOWLEDGE

THE PROBLEM WITH GIVING

We chatted with Dhan Saru, the director of an NGO working with disadvantaged children in Nepal, about the problem of street children in Kathmandu and how, or even if, travellers should help.

What drives children onto the streets of Kathmandu?

Many children on the streets of Kathmandu are there because of poverty and domestic violence. Although illegal, child labour is commonly accepted in Nepal and is often seen as a good escape from poverty – both for the children themselves and for the families that send them away. Kids often come to the streets of Kathmandu in search of better fortune, either of their own accord or under the influence of friends or family.

Perhaps a more important question is what 'keeps' these children on the street? Bizarrely, kindness is often the answer. Consider the following scenario: a child is sent by poor and uneducated parents to Kathmandu to work and discovers that the 'boss' is unkind, uncaring and often quite cruel. Seeing how other children seem able to survive on the street, the child decides to try their luck and falls under the influence of older street kids – kids who've learnt that begging can be a lucrative game, who know the escape of solvent abuse, who no longer have the tension of living with impoverished and overstressed parents, and who are prepared to put up with various hardships in return for what they see as a life of total freedom.

What can travellers do to help?

More often than not, doing nothing probably won't make the traveller feel better about a particular situation, but that should never be their reason for wanting to help. Often the best thing travellers can do to help is to do nothing. There are many organisations working to help Nepal's street children lead a 'normal' life of school, learning, family, routine, structure and rules. Handing out food, money and other gifts in the street will not provide a lasting solution to the child's problems. What it will do is give the child a reason to stay on the street – at home, parents rarely give them any of the gifts that travellers bestow on them.

What is your advice for travellers who are interested in donating or volunteering in Nepal?

While there are thousands of organisations in Nepal, and many welcome volunteers and donations, travellers on tourist visas are prohibited from working in Nepal. Also, the volunteering industry is unregulated – travellers should look very carefully at any organisation that they donate time or money to. When volunteering, think about your own skills and experience and look for an organisation that can use those skills in its work.

(For more on volunteering in Nepal, see p46)

House, situated across the road from Down Town, is a passable budget place cheered up by potted plants as well as a pleasant rooftop. Plain, carpeted rooms are on the small side but they come with small, hot-water bathrooms. The upper-floor rooms are much brighter.

Mustang Guest House GUESTHOUSE $
(Map p80; ☑ 4700053; www.mothersland.com; r with/without bathroom Rs 700/500; ☎) Another acceptable cheapie, this place is tucked away down an inconspicuous laneway. It has neat, well-maintained carpeted rooms

and clean bathrooms but a dearth of natural light, no TVs and no real sitting areas or rooftop.

Hotel Florid GUESTHOUSE $
(Map p80; ☑ 4701055; www.hotelflorid.com.np; s/d US$10/12, without bathroom US$5/6.50, deluxe r US$15; @) This is one of several small guesthouses just north of central Thamel down Z St. There is a pleasant garden restaurant at the rear and no buildings behind, so there's a feeling of space that is often lacking in Thamel. The suitelike deluxe rooms overlooking the garden are

sunny and spacious. Doubles overlooking the road are noisier but come with a shared balcony. You'll need to negotiate a discount to get good value here.

Thamel Eco Resort
HOTEL $$

(Map p80; ☑4263810; www.thamelecoresort.com; economy s/d US$35/40, standard US$55/60, deluxe US$70/80; ☏) A new complex set back off the road, it has fresh modern rooms set around a pleasant central stupa courtyard decorated with carved wood and traditional touches. Good breakfast buffet, central location and rooftop yoga classes are a bonus. Noisy dance clubs on the weekend and unreliable hot water are occasionally an issue, depending on the room. This place is popular with trekking groups. Discounts of 20% are possible.

PAKNAJOL (NORTHERN THAMEL)

This area lies to the north of central Thamel and can be reached by continuing north from the Kathmandu Guest House, or by approaching from Lekhnath Marg to the north.

Not far from the steep Paknajol intersection with Lekhnath Marg (northwest of Thamel) are a few pleasant guesthouses grouped together in a district known as Sorakhutte. They're away from traffic, a short walk from Thamel (but it could be a million miles), and they have fine views across the valley towards Balaju and Swayambhunath.

International Guest House
HOTEL $$

(Map p80; ☑4252299; www.ighouse.com; s/d US$24/28, deluxe US$34/38, superior deluxe US$44/48, ste US$60) West from the Saatghumti (Seven Bends St) in an area known as Kaldhara, this is a recommended and quietly stylish place that boasts century-old carved woodwork, terraced sitting areas, a spacious garden and one of the best rooftop views in the city, which you can enjoy in the sun loungers. Though not exactly luxurious, the superior deluxe rooms in the renovated wing are generally bright, spacious and well decorated, while the best deluxe rooms in the old building come with a garden view. The plainer standard rooms vary. This area is quieter and much less of a scene than Thamel but still close to plenty of restaurants. Rates include breakfast, wi-fi and airport pick-up. Keep an eye out for the stuffed yak...

Tibet Peace Guest House
GUESTHOUSE $

(Map p80; ☑4381026; www.tibetpeace.com; Sorakhutte; r Rs 800-1200, s/d without bathroom Rs 300/400) Friendly and family-run, this is a quiet and mellow hang-out with a very nice back garden and a small restaurant. There's a wide range of rooms, some ramshackle and others with private balconies, so have a dig around before committing.

Yellow House
GUESTHOUSE $

(Map p80; ☑4381186; theyellowhouse2007@gmail. com; Sorakhutte; r Rs 800-1200, without bathroom Rs 400) This friendly place across the road from Tibet Peace Guest House is an excellent addition to the expanding budget Paknajol scene. The 20 rooms are bright, there's lots of garden space and the house restaurant dishes up decent Thai food.

Kathmandu Peace Guest House
GUESTHOUSE $

(Map p80; ☑4380369; www.peaceguesthouse. com; Sorakhutte; s US$12-16, d US$16-21, s/d without bathroom US$8/12; @☏) Situated along the road from the Tibet Peace Guest House, this is a little more upmarket, offering rooms with satellite TV in either the slightly ramshackle old wing or the fresher pine-clad new block. The ground floor and rooftop garden are pleasant. Rates here include taxes.

Kathmandu Garden House
GUESTHOUSE $

(Map p80; ☑4381239; www.hotel-in-nepal.com; Sorakhutte; s/d Rs 900/1200, r without bathroom Rs 400) This is a small and intimate guesthouse that is cosy and deservedly popular. The views from the roof are excellent and there are nice sitting areas and a lovely garden where you can sit back and marvel at the staff cutting the grass by hand (literally!).

Shree Tibet Family Guest House
GUESTHOUSE $

(Map p80; ☑4700902; www.hotelshreetibet.com; s/d US$12/16, deluxe US$15/20; @☏) It's easy to miss this budget, Tibetan-run place and most people do (it's often deserted). It's a clean, quiet and friendly place with cosy rooms, although some are dark and smallish due to the buildings being very close together. As always, the back rooms on the higher floors are best. The small restaurant serves decent Tibetan food and breakfasts. Prayer wheels mark the entrance.

Hotel Premium
HOTEL $

(Map p80; ☑4383102; www.hotelpremium.com. np; Paknajol; s/d Rs 700/900; ☎) Friendly management, a pleasant rooftop cafe as well as thoughtful touches such as cold drinks in the lobby make this a good budget option, even if the road outside the hotel is a bit of a horror. You'll find that road-facing rooms are noisy and lower-floor options can be dingy but all come with bathroom and satellite TV.

BHAGWAN BAHAL (NORTHEASTERN THAMEL)

Hotel Blue Horizon
HOTEL $

(Map p80; ☑4421971; www.hotelbluehorizon.com; Tridevi Marg; s/d US$15/20, deluxe US$25/30, super deluxe US$35/40, ste US$40/45; ✳@☎) Renovations have revitalised this old favourite, adding a spacious garden and a new block of midrange rooms. The deluxe and new block rooms are bright and fresh and offer the best value (suites are great for families), though perhaps best is the quiet neighbourhood and secluded location down an alleyway off Tridevi Marg, which makes it super easy for transport around the city. Discounts of 30% and free airport pick-up are available for online bookings, making this a good deal.

Hotel Norbu Linka
HOTEL $$

(Map p80; ☑4410630; www.hotelnorbulinka.com; s/d US$31/35, deluxe US$42/55) This modern, secluded place, central but quiet, is down an alley opposite the colourful Thamel Gaa Hiti (water tank). The spacious modern rooms aren't as Tibetan as you'd think from the name but they are clean and comfortable, and there are a couple of rooms on the rooftop garden area. The deluxe rooms are great for families and the restaurant is open 24 hours, so if you are jetlagged and with kids, look no further.

Annapurna Guest House
GUESTHOUSE $

(Map p80; ☑4420159; www.annapurnaguesthouse.com; s/d US$10/14, without bathroom US$7/9, deluxe US$15/20, incl tax; ☎) The rooms at this somewhat dour family guesthouse are smallish but clean and most come with a private bathroom, though some are dark. Down a side alley near the Hotel Norbu Linka, this area is quieter than Thamel proper and has not yet been completely taken over by restaurants, souvenir shops and travel agencies. The rooftop restaurant is pleasant.

JYATHA (SOUTHEASTERN THAMEL)

The neighbourhood southeast of Thamel is traditionally known as Jyatha, but the word is also used to describe the main north–south road that runs into the western end of Tridevi Marg.

Turn east a short way down Jyatha Rd, and a couple of twists and turns will bring you to a neat little cluster of modern guesthouses, whose central but quiet location feels a million miles from the Thamel hustle.

Kantipur Temple House
BOUTIQUE HOTEL $$

(Map p80; ☑4250131; www.kantipurtemplehouse. com; s/d US$60/70, deluxe US$100/140) Hidden down an alley on the edge of the old town, at the southern end of Jyatha, this Newari temple-style hotel has been built with meticulous attention to detail. The spacious rooms are tastefully decorated, with traditional carved wood, window seats and specially commissioned fair-trade dhaka (hand-woven) cloth bedspreads. Due to the traditional nature of the building, rooms tend to be a little dark. This place is doing its best to be eco-friendly – guests are given cloth bags to use when shopping and bulk mineral water is available free of charge in bronze pitchers (in fact, there's no plastic anywhere in the hotel). The new block encircles a traditional brick courtyard and there's garden and rooftop seating. The old-town location is close to almost anywhere in town, but taxi drivers might have a hard time finding it.

Sacred Valley Inn
HOTEL $$

(Map p80; ☑4251063; www.sacredvalleyinn.com; r US$25-30, deluxe r US$35-45; @☎) This branch of the popular Pokhara hotel is a good upper budget choice. The carpeted rooms are clean, modern and fresh and have sunny balconies, though there are no single rates for solo travellers. The excellent rooftop garden is the place to hang out and the ground-floor lounge and library are welcome, as is the quiet but central location, tucked away in a lane behind Hotel Utse. Rates include tax.

Hotel Holy Himalaya
HOTEL $$

(Map p80; ☑4263172; www.holyhimalaya.com; s/d US$35/40, deluxe US$45/55, ste US$75/85; ✳@☎) Just across from the Sacred Valley Inn, this is a good midrange find that is frequented by small in-the-know tour groups. It's a modern, well-run place that feels like a 'real' hotel, down to the marbly lobby and lift. The rooms are bland but reassuring and some come with a balcony. The spacious deluxe rooms in the new building are the best value. Perks include organic coffee, a nice rooftop garden and free guided meditation in the mornings.

Fuji Hotel
HOTEL **$$**

(Map p80; ☑4250435; www.fujiguesthouse.com; s/d from US$15/25, deluxe US$30/40, ste US$70; ✲@🖥🛜) The well-run Fuji is popular with Japanese travellers and rooms are neat, quiet and spotlessly clean. Some rooms have a balcony and the sunny rooms on the rooftop are particularly spacious. Rooms with a bath tub cost an extra US$5. Online bookings get a 15% discount.

Imperial Guest House
GUESTHOUSE **$**

(Map p80; ☑4249339; www.imperial.idia.ru; s/d US$12/15; 🛜) Across from the Mustang Holiday Inn, this cheap and plain guesthouse has a boarding-school feel, with threadbare but functional rooms and narrow beds with elephant-grey blankets. There's a rooftop sitting area that overlooks a small shrine.

Mustang Holiday Inn
HOTEL **$**

(Map p80; ☑4249041; www.mustangholiday.com; s/d US$15/20, deluxe US$20/25, super deluxe US$30/35; 🛜) Once owned by the king of Mustang, the dimly lit rooms here are looking a bit neglected these days, with bedside speakers that date from around 1962, but rooms are spacious and some come with a balcony. It's quiet, and has a restaurant and nice terrace seating. Discounts of 25% are standard.

CHHETRAPATI (SOUTHWEST THAMEL)

This area is named after the important five-way intersection (notable by its distinctive bandstand) to the southwest of Thamel. The further you get from Thamel, the more traditional the surroundings become.

⟨TOP CHOICE⟩ Hotel Ganesh Himal
HOTEL **$**

(Map p60; ☑4263598; www.ganeshhimal.com; standard s/d US$15/20, deluxe US$20/27, super deluxe r US$35; ✲@🛜) Our pick for comfort on a budget is this well-run and friendly place, located a 10-minute walk southwest of Thamel – far enough to be out of range of the tiger-balm salesmen but close enough to restaurants for dinner. The rooms are among the best value in Kathmandu, with endless hot water, satellite TV and lots of balcony and garden seating, plus a sunny

rooftop. The deluxe rooms are more spacious and a little quieter and the new super-deluxe rooms have brick floors. The best standard rooms are in the new block. Throw in free internet access, a good-value garden restaurant and free airport pick-up and this place is hard to beat, even if the reception gets a bit overwhelmed at times. Here's a tip: bring earplugs, as the residential neighbourhood can be noisy.

Tibet Guest House
HOTEL **$$**

(Map p80; ☑4251763; www.tibetguesthouse.com; s/d US$16/20, standard US$30/35, deluxe US$40/50, superior US$60/65, ste US$80/90; ✲@🛜) This well-run and popular hotel gets heavy use and things are looking a bit worn in places but it's a good choice, so book in advance. All the rooms here are comfortable, though lower floors can be dark; the superior rooms have a lot more space. There's a lovely breakfast patio, a lobby espresso bar and the superb views of Swayambhunath from the rooftop garden and library just cry out to be appreciated at sunset with a cold beer. Some of the standard rooms are located in a separate block across the street and come with a balcony. Discounts of 20% to 30% are standard.

Khangsar Guest House
HOTEL **$**

(Map p80; ☑4260788; www.khangsarguesthouse.com; s/d US$10/12; 🛜) This is a friendly and central option, though there are few bells and whistles. The threadbare rooms come with an anorexically thin but clean bathroom with (generally) hot water, plus there's a pleasant rooftop bar for cold beers under the stars. The upper-floor rooms are best. Rates include tax.

Nirvana Garden Hotel
HOTEL **$$**

(Map p80; ☑4256200; www.nirvanagarden.com; s/d US$40/50, deluxe US$50/60, ste US$80; @🛜) The relaxing garden here isn't quite nirvana but it is a real oasis, making this hotel a decent choice close to the centre. The deluxe rooms with sunny balcony and garden view are the ones to opt for, though all are getting a bit tired and overpriced these days.

Potala Guest House
HOTEL **$$**

(Map p80; ☑4220467; www.potalaguesthouse.com; budget s US$12, s/d US$20/25, deluxe r US$35-45; ✲) Located at the quiet southern end of Thamel is this large, fairly popular Tibetan-owned hotel. The garden is small but pleasant, with a lovely terrace and a rooftop garden. The quiet and spacious deluxe rooms with air-con and wooden floors at the back are the best bet; the other rooms are older and much plainer, especially the cheapest singles, which are worth avoiding.

FREAK STREET (JOCHNE) & DURBAR SQUARE

Although Freak St's glory days have passed, a few determined budget restaurants and lodges have clung on. Staying here offers three pluses – you won't find much cheaper, there are fewer crowds and you're right in the heart of the fascinating old city. On the downside, the pickings are slimmer and the lodges are generally grungier than in Thamel.

Monumental Paradise   HOTEL $
(Map p60; ✆4240876; mparadise52@hotmail.com; s/d/ste Rs 500/700/1500) A newish place that's a lot more modern than the rest of Freak St. Rooms are generally clean, fresh and spacious and have a tiled bathroom, and the upper-floor back rooms come with a private balcony and lots of natural light. There's an excellent rooftop bar/restaurant and one suite in the crow's nest has its own private balcony with views towards Durbar Sq. A good choice.

Dwarika's Chhen   BOUTIQUE HOTEL $$
(Map p64; ✆4261862; www.dwarikaschhen.com; House 30, Maru Pyaphal; s US$35-55, d US$60-95) Well away from the Thamel bustle, this new traditional-style apartment hotel is a splash of class just a stone's throw from the splendours of Durbar Sq. The five rooms have lots of potential and are decked out in stone and wood, with ikat bedspreads, window seats and kitchenettes. Rooms are spacious but a little dark. Hopefully the problems with hot water and wi-fi will iron themselves out...

CENTRAL KATHMANDU

These hotels are within walking distance of Durbar Marg and the Thamel area, and fall into the top-end price range.

Yak & Yeti Hotel   HOTEL $$$
(Map p60; ✆4248999; www.yakandyeti.com; Newari/Durbar wing d US$205/225, executive US$275; ❄️🛜🏊) This hotel is probably the best known in Nepal, due to its connections with the near-legendary Boris Lissanevitch, its original owner. The oldest section of the hotel is part of the Lal Durbar, a Rana palace that houses restaurants and a casino; these are worth a look for traces of an over-blown but spectacular baroque decor and some excellent old black-and-white photos of Rana royalty. The actual rooms are in two modern wings: the older Newari wing incorporates Newari woodcarvings, oil brick walls and local textiles, while the Durbar wing is modern and stylish and has better bathroom facilities. Request a garden-facing room. There's also a beautiful garden, two pools, tennis courts and a fitness centre. The borscht at the hotel's famous Chimney Restaurant remains a tenuous link with its Russian past. Discounts of 20% are standard.

Shanker Hotel   HISTORIC HOTEL $$
(Map p60; ✆4410151; www.shankerhotel.com.np; s/d US$105/125; ❄️🛜🏊) There's nowhere in town quite like this creaky former Rana palace – the kind of place where you expect some whiskered old Rana prince to come shuffling around one of the wooden corridors. The palace conversion means that rooms are idiosyncratic, with some rooms split over two floors and featuring hobbit-sized half-windows, but all are comfortable. For real grandeur you'll have to track down the dining halls and Durbar Hall conference space. The entry columns of neoclassical whipped cream overlook a palatial manicured garden and swimming pool. Rates include breakfast.

LAZIMPAT

North of central Kathmandu is the Lazimpat embassy area, popular with NGO staff, repeat visitors and business people.

Hotel Tibet   HOTEL $$
(Map p60; ✆4429085; www.hotel-tibet.com; s/d US$80/90, ste US$110/120; ❄️🛜) Tibetophiles and tour groups headed to or from Tibet like this recommended midrange choice, run by a friendly Tibetan family and with a very Tibetan vibe. The 56 quiet and comfortable rooms are plain compared to the opulent lobby, but many of the larger front-facing rooms have a balcony. Breakfast is included. There's also a great rooftop terrace, a side garden and even a top-floor meditation chapel. It's just in front of the Radisson. The next-door Shambhala Spa offers a 'trekkers' recovery massage' alongside hot stone therapy.

Hotel Manaslu   HOTEL $$
(Map p60; ✆4410071; www.hotelmanaslu.com; standard s/d US$45/50, deluxe US$55/60; ❄️🏊) Just beyond Hotel Tibet, the big draw at this

nice modern hotel is the pleasant garden and pool fed by Newari-style fountains. The glorious carved windows in the restaurant were brought in from Bhaktapur. After this initial splendour, the unglamorous rooms themselves are ho-hum. Rooms vary considerably; try to get a room in the back block overlooking the garden. Rates include breakfast and are generally discounted by 15%.

Radisson HOTEL **$$$**
(Map p60; ☎4423888; www.radisson.com/kathmandune; superior/deluxe/club r US$185/205/250; ❊❖❄) A favourite of embassy staff and business travellers, the Radisson is a modern, fresh and well-maintained five-star choice, with a 5th-floor pool and a good gym operated by Clark Hatch. The instant coffee supplied with the coffee maker doesn't exactly scream five stars, but several good cafes and bars loiter outside the main gates.

Hotel Shangri-La HOTEL **$$$**
(off Map p60; ☎4412999; www.hotelshangrila.com; s/d incl breakfast US$200/220, executive US$225/250; @❖❄) The real draw at this alleged five-star place is the large relaxing garden, with a small but nice pool; the rooms themselves are well overpriced unless you get a good deal. Try a High Lama cocktail at the cosy Lost Horizon Bar.

ELSEWHERE

TOP CHOICE Dwarika's BOUTIQUE HOTEL **$$$**
(☎4470770; www.dwarikas.com; Battis Putali; s/d US$270/280, ste US$400-470; ❖❄) For stylish design and sheer romance, this outstanding hotel is unbeatable; if you're on honeymoon, look no further. Over 40 years the owners have rescued thousands of woodcarvings from around the valley (from buildings facing demolition or collapse) and incorporated them into the hotel design, which consists of clusters of traditional Newari buildings separated by brick-paved courtyards. The end result is a beautiful hybrid – a cross between a museum and a boutique hotel, with a lush, pampering ambience. Each room is unique and some have sexy open-plan granite bathrooms. The location on a busy street east of town, a short walk southwest of Pashupatinath, is a pain, but finding a taxi is never a problem.

Hyatt Regency Kathmandu LUXURY HOTEL **$$$**
(☎4491234; www.kathmandu.regency.hyatt.com; d from US$165; ❖❄) No expense has been spared on this superb palace-style building, from the dramatic entrance of Newari water tanks to the modern Malla-style architecture. It's worth popping in en route to Bodhnath to admire the gorgeous stupas in the foyer (there's a lamp-lighting ceremony at dusk). As you'd expect, the rooms are furnished tastefully and many have views over nearby Bodhnath stupa. The large swimming pool, good restaurants and Sunday brunch make this the perfect spot for a splurge: after a tough day's sightseeing unwind with a *shirodhara* (oil pouring) ayurvedic treatment at the spa. The Hyatt is a couple of kilometres outside Kathmandu, on the road to Bodhnath.

Hotel Vajra BOUTIQUE HOTEL **$$**
(Map p60; ☎4271545; www.hotelvajra.com; s/d from US$33/38, without bathroom US$14/16, ste US$85/90) Across the Vishnumati River in the Bijeshwari district, this is one of Kathmandu's most interesting hotels in any price category. The brick complex feels more like an artists' retreat than a hotel, with lush gardens, a library of books on Tibet and Buddhism, a fine rooftop bar and an ayurvedic massage room. All the rooms in the old wing are unique (the cheapest share bathrooms), so take a look at more than one. If you are in the new wing (single/double US$53/61), try to score a balcony. The only catch is the location, which, though peaceful, makes it tricky for getting a taxi. Rates include breakfast.

Benchen Vihar Guest House GUESTHOUSE **$**
(☎4284204; www.benchen.org; r Rs 400-600; @) If you've ever fancied staying in a Tibetan monastery, try this comfortable guesthouse attached to the Benchen Phuntsok Dargyeling Monastery, 10 minutes' walk from Swayambhunath. It's surprisingly comfortable and well run, with en suite bathrooms and fine views from the upper floors, and there are plenty of opportunities for meditation (prayers are held at 6am and 4pm) or learning some Tibetan from the local monks. There's a cheap cafe on-site.

Soaltee Crowne Plaza LUXURY HOTEL **$$$**
(☎4273999; s/d US$190/200, club r US$240; ❄) Space and tranquillity are precious commodities in Kathmandu but the Soaltee has acres of both; 11 acres, to be precise, so take a map if you go for a stroll. Spread around the palatial grounds (the hotel is connected to former King Gyanendra) are some excellent restaurants, a lovely poolside area, a casino and even a bowling alley. The price you

pay is the crummy location on the western edge of town, a 15-minute taxi ride from the centre.

✕ Eating

Kathmandu has an astounding array of restaurants. Indeed, with the possible exception of the canteen at the UN building, there are few places where you have the choice of Indian, Chinese, Japanese, Mexican, Korean, Middle Eastern, Italian or Irish cuisines, all within a five-minute walk. After weeks trekking in the mountains, Kathmandu feels like a culinary paradise.

Many restaurants in Kathmandu try to serve something from everywhere – pizzas, momos, Indian curries, a bit of Thai here, some Mexican tacos there. Predictably, the ones that specialise generally serve the finest food.

Thamel's restaurant scene has been sliding upmarket for a few years now, with most places now charging US$5 per main course, plus 24% tax. A bottle of beer will double your bill in most places. Finding a budget meal is still possible but it involves some hunting.

THAMEL

The junction outside the Kathmandu Guest House is the epicentre of Thamel dining and you'll find dozens of excellent restaurants within a minute's walk in either direction.

TOP CHOICE **Or2k**　　　　　MIDDLE EASTERN **$**
(Map p80; www.or2k.org; mains Rs 200-350; ☑) This bright, buzzy and popular Israeli-run vegetarian restaurant is our favourite for fresh and light Middle Eastern dishes. The menu spreads to crêpes, soups, zucchini pie, coconut tofu and *ziva* (pastry fingers filled with cheese), as well as a great meze sampler of hummus, felafel and *labane* (sour cream cheese) served in neat little brass bowls. The fresh mint lemonade is a lifesaver on a hot day. All seating is on cushions on the floor; you have to take your shoes off so make sure you're wearing your clean pair of socks. A small stand at street level serves takeaway felafel wraps (Rs 155).

Third Eye　　　　　INDIAN **$$**
(Map p80; ☑4260160; www.thirdeyerestaurant. com; mains Rs 340-450) Next door to Yin Yang, and run by the same people, this is another long-running favourite, popular with well-heeled tourists. Book a window seat at the sit-down section at the front or try the more informal section at the back with low tables and cushions at the back; both are candlelit to create an intimate vibe. Indian food is the speciality and the tandoori dishes are especially good, even if the portions are a bit small. Spice levels are set at 'tourist' so let the efficient (if not friendly) suited waiters know if you'd like extra heat.

K-Too Steakhouse　　　　STEAKHOUSE **$$**
(Map p80; ☑4700043; www.kilroygroup.com; mains Rs 400-500) Run by the same people who run Kilroy's, the food and warm and buzzy atmosphere are excellent. Dishes range from chip butties to spinach salad with honey mustard dressing, but it's all about the steaks. The pepper steak sizzler (Rs 510) followed by fried apple momos and an Everest Beer is already a post-trekking classic, even if it now costs close to US$20! Live European football is broadcast on the TV. For a quieter vibe head for the garden.

Delices de France　　　　FRENCH **$$$**
(Map p80; ☑4260326; www.restaurantnepal. com; mains Rs 400-800, fixed menus Rs 650-1100; ⊙closed Mon) For Provençal-influenced French food done right, this place is unbeatable. The recommended Mediterranean platter is packed with intense flavours (olive tapenade, Parma ham, goat's cheese and chicken-liver pâté) and the dessert tasting plate includes the wonderfully zesty lemon crêpe cake. The fixed menus offer particularly good value. With the introduction of weekly live music, a weekend brunch and cookery classes, the energetic owner Christine has single-handedly created a cultural magnet for Francophiles and Francophones. Check the current location, as there are plans to move to Lazimpat.

Northfield Cafe　　　　INTERNATIONAL **$$**
(Map p80; breakfast Rs 115-220, mains Rs 300-440; 🍴) Next door to Pilgrims, this reliable and pleasant open-air spot is the place for serious breakfast devotees (huevos rancheros included), with the option of half or full portions. The Mexican and Indian tandoori dishes (dinner only) are excellent and the comfort food spreads to good burgers, nachos and even chilli fries. The sunny garden and outdoor firepit is a real plus in winter and there's traditional Nepali music in the evenings. It's also one of the few places to offer kids' meals.

La Dolce Vita ITALIAN $$
(Map p80; ☎4700612; pastas Rs 310-385, mains Rs 430-850, house wine per glass Rs 340) Life is indeed sweet at Thamel's best Italian bistro, offering up delights such as parmesan gnocchi; excellent antipasti; goat's cheese, spinach and walnut ravioli; sinfully rich chocolate torte; gelato; and wines by the glass. The pastas are better than the pizzas. Choose between the rustic red-and-white tablecloths and terracotta tiles of the main restaurant, a rooftop garden, the yummy-smelling espresso bar or sunny lounge space; either way the atmosphere and food are excellent. It's right on the corner opposite Kathmandu Guest House.

Yin Yang Restaurant THAI $$
(Map p80; ☎4425510; www.yinyangrestaurantbar.com; curries Rs 450) Just south of the intersection, this is one of Thamel's most highly regarded restaurants. It serves authentic Thai food cooked by a Thai chef, and there is either garden or floor seating. It's not cheap but the food is a definite cut above the imitation Thai food found elsewhere. The green curry is authentically spicy, and the massaman curry (with onion, peanut and potato) is sweeter. There's a good range of vegetable choices.

Roadhouse Cafe PIZZERIA $$
(Map p80; ☎4267885; Arcadia Bldg; pizzas Rs 350-475) The big attraction here is the pizzas from the wood-fired oven. The pizzas are pretty darn good, and the decor, especially the courtyard located out the back, is warm and intimate. The salads, soups (tomato coconut), sandwiches, desserts (sizzling brownie with ice cream) and espresso coffees are all top-notch and there are some good Newari snacks, including smoked chicken *sandekho* (marinated with spices). Credit cards are accepted.

Utse Restaurant TIBETAN $
(Map p80; mains Rs 130-290) In the hotel of the same name, this is one of the longest-running restaurants in Thamel and it turns out excellent Tibetan dishes, including unusual Tibetan desserts such as *dhayshi* (sweet rice, curd and raisins) that you won't find anywhere else. The traditional decor feels lifted straight from an old Lhasa backstreet. For a group blowout, *gacok* (also spelt *gyakok*) is a form of hotpot named after the brass tureen that is heated at the table (Rs 780 for two). The set meals are a worthy extravagance.

New Orleans Cafe INTERNATIONAL $$
(Map p80; ☎4700736; mains Rs 250-380; ✎) Hidden down an alley opposite Pilgrims Book House, New Orleans boasts a relaxed and intimate candlelit vibe and a great selection of music, live on Wednesdays. It's a popular spot for a drink but the menu also ranges far and wide, from Thai curries and good burgers to Creole jambalaya and oven-roasted vegies, plus good breakfasts.

Gaia Restaurant INTERNATIONAL $$
(Map p80; mains Rs 250-360; 🛜) This popular place combines good breakfasts, salads, sandwiches and organic coffee in a pleasant garden courtyard with global music and reasonable prices. The Indian dishes are a bit tame but you're bound to find something good in a menu that ranges from daal bhaat to carrot cake.

Yangling Tibetan Restaurant MOMOS $
(Map p80; Saatghumti Chowk; momos Rs 90-140; ⏲closed Sat) Both locals and tourists flock to this unpretentious family-run place for possibly the best momos in town (try the chicken ones). The kitchen here is a non-stop momo production line. You can also get soupy Tibetan butter tea and tasty *thenthuk* (noodle soup).

Yak Restaurant TIBETAN $
(Map p80; mains Rs 100-250) We always find ourselves returning to this unpretentious and reliable Tibetan-run place at the southern end of Thamel. The booths give it a 'Tibetan diner' vibe and the clientele is a mix of trekkers, Sherpa guides and local Tibetans who come to shoot the breeze over a tube of *tongba* (hot millet beer). The menu includes Tibetan dishes, with good *kothey* (fried momos), and some Indian dishes, at unbeatable prices. It feels just like a trekking lodge, down to that familiar electronic sound of a chicken being strangled every time a dish leaves the kitchen.

Hankook Sarang KOREAN $
(Map p80; www.hankooksarang.com; mains incl tax Rs 250-450) The Hankook is that rare combination of authentic taste and good value. Korean staples such as *bibimbap* come with crunchy kimchi, salad, soup, dried fish, sweet beans and green tea (*bibimbap* is rice and vegetables in a stone pot, to which you add the egg and sweet chilli sauce and mix it all together). Alternatively, fire up the barbecue for some *bulgogi* (barbecued beef cooked at your table and eaten with lettuce)

or try the good-value vegetarian sushi. The service is friendly and there's a pleasant alfresco garden. It's down an alley near Tamas Spa Lounge.

Furusato
JAPANESE $

(Map p80; set meals Rs 200-400) A Japanese restaurant that is full of Japanese travellers is almost always a good sign. Dishes include udon noodles, cold soba noodles, rice bowls, bento boxes and *gyoza* dumplings (the Japanese version of a momo) but most people opt for one of the set meals, which come with salad, miso soup and pickles. Bright and calming, with traditional sitting area and tables, it's perfect for a light dinner, though there are more reliable places for sushi. It's hidden down an alley opposite Weizen Bakery.

Krua Thai
THAI $$

(Map p80; www.kruathainepal.com; curries Rs 320-380) North of Sam's Bar, this is another good open-air Thai place, though it's not quite up to Yin Yang's standards. The food is reasonably authentic (ie spicy), with good curries (our favourite is the chicken Penang), *tom yam* soup and *som tam thai* (green papaya salad), although some dishes taste more Chinese than Thai.

Nargila Restaurant
MIDDLE EASTERN $

(Map p80; mains Rs 150-250; 1-10pm) Across from the Northfield Cafe, on the 1st floor, this somewhat dour budget favourite is a quiet place to just take a break from the bustle outside. Try a *lafa shwarma* (grilled meat, salad and fries in a pita) or hummus served with pita, washed down by fresh mint tea. The hot waffle with fruit and yoghurt is probably the best in Kathmandu. Don't be offended if the staff seem unfriendly; they're like that to everyone.

Dechenling
TIBETAN, BHUTANESE $

(Map p80; mains Rs 150-260, set meals Rs 550-600) Quality Himalayan food and one of the most relaxing courtyards are the draw of this attractive beer garden. It's one of the few places in town to offer interesting Bhutanese dishes such as *kewa dhatsi* (potatoes and cheese curry) and the *thukpa* (Tibetan noodle soup) is the best in town. If you can't decide, opt for one of the grand Tibetan or Bhutanese set meals.

Fire & Ice Pizzeria
PIZZERIA $$

(Map p80; 4250210; www.fireandicepizzeria. com; Sanchaya Kosh Bhawan, Tridevi Marg; pizzas Rs 350-480; 8am-11pm) This is an excellent and informal Italian place, serving some of the best pizzas in Kathmandu (wholewheat crusts available), as well as breakfasts, smoothies, seriously good Illy espresso and rousing opera – Italian, of course. It's very popular so make a reservation and expect to share one of the tavern-style tables.

Kilroy's
INTERNATIONAL $$$

(Map p80; 4250441; www.kilroygroup.com; mains Rs 400-700; 9am-10pm) It may not be quite as good as it thinks it is (the eponymous founding chef left Nepal years ago), but this place is still a definite cut above the average Thamel restaurant. The menu ranges from Balti chicken (Rs 430) to Irish stew (Rs 605), via such interesting hybrids as seafood *thukpa* with lemongrass (Rs 480). The desserts are worth leaving space for, especially the bread-and-butter pudding, or try the dessert platter for a taste of all five. You can sit in the cosy interior, or outside in the spacious shady garden, complete with waterfall.

Thakali Kitchen
NEPALI $

(Map p80; veg/nonveg daal bhaat Rs 130/190; 10am-10pm) If, after having travelled all the way to Nepal, you actually fancy some Nepali food (!), this upstairs restaurant is a modern place popular with local Thamel workers on their lunch break. Most opt for the daal bhaat (rice, curry and lentil soup) but there's also a range of Thakali snacks such as *bandel* (wild boar) and *aa lang kho,* a dried meat, cheese and radish soup. For the full-on local experience, replace the rice with *dhido,* a doughy buckwheat paste eaten daily by millions of Nepalis.

Pumpernickel Bakery
BAKERY $

(Map p80; mains Rs 80-250; 7am-7pm) Bleary-eyed tourists crowd in here every morning for fresh croissants, yak-cheese sandwiches, pastries and filter coffee in the pleasant garden area at the back. The cafeteria-style restaurant is self-service.

Chang Cheng Restaurant
CHINESE $$

(Map p80; Centre Point Hotel; veg dishes Rs 120-200, meat dishes Rs 420-480) The 'Great Wall' is the real deal for Chinese food, and is normally full of visiting Chinese businesspeople and Chinese Tibetans who shout, smoke, slurp and burp their way through large portions of wonderfully spicy Sichuanese food.

Dahua Restaurant
CHINESE $

(Map p80; dishes Rs 110-220) In contrast, this definitely isn't 'real' China – sticky sweet-and-sours and greasy egg foo yong are the rule here – but it's quiet, cosy and tasty, and the price is right. On the eastern edge of Thamel.

Tashi Delek Restaurant
TIBETAN $

(Map p80; mains Rs 110-180) This place, a long-time favourite, feels like a trekking lodge that's been transplanted from Everest into a Thamel time warp. Prices are decent and the spinach mushroom enchilada (Rs 170) is surprisingly good for Tibetan-Mexican food (Tib-Mex?). Consult the pictures of the dishes before you order. It's located down a quiet corridor, slap bang in the centre of the Thamel action, but can be a bit gloomy during the day.

Helena's
INTERNATIONAL $$

(Map p80; mains Rs 200-450; ☺7am-10pm; 🛜) Helena's is deservedly popular for its set breakfasts, one of the highest rooftops in Thamel, its cosy interior and super-friendly service. It has a wide range of kebabs, good cakes, tandoori dishes, steaks and even Bengali-style *kathi* rolls. If you are heading off trekking, consider breakfast on the 8th floor a form of high-altitude training.

Pilgrims Feed 'N Read
VEGETARIAN $$

(Map p80; mains Rs 220-340, set meals Rs 375; 🖉) Keep walking past the self-help section of Pilgrims Book House and you'll end up in this quiet and classy cafe, with indoor and garden seating. The focus is on herbal teas (Rs 65 per pot) and vegetarian Indian food (including dosas), but there are also good breakfasts and there's no shortage of reading material.

Mustang Thakal
NEPALI $

(Map p80; daal bhaat Rs 160) Located on the 2nd floor, this is a good option for local Thakali daal bhaat and is popular with local Manangis.

BK's Place
SNACKS $

(Map p80; chips Rs 140-200) This place has a well-deserved reputation for good old-fashioned chips (French fries), with a variety of sauces (try the house sauce of mayo, ketchup and onions), as well as good momos.

FREAK STREET (JOCHNE) & DURBAR SQUARE

Freak St has a number of budget restaurants where you can find good food at lower prices than Thamel. Even if you're staying in other areas of the city, it's nice to know there are some good places for lunch if you're sightseeing around Durbar Sq.

Snowman Restaurant
BAKERY $

(Map p60; Freak St; cakes Rs 60-70) A long-running and mellow, if slightly dingy, place, this is one of those rare Kathmandu hangouts that attracts both locals and nostalgic former hippies. The chocolate cake has been drawing overland travellers for close to 40 years now. When Lennon starts singing 'I am the Walrus' on the eight-track it suddenly feels like 1967 all over again...

Cosmo de Café Restaurant
INTERNATIONAL $

(Map p64; Durbar Sq; mains Rs 190-290) This is the best value of the several rooftop tourist restaurants that overlook Durbar Sq. The views over the tiered Maju Deval temple are nice, the range of food is good and prices are reasonable.

FREAK STREET – THE END OF THE ROAD

Running south from Basantapur Sq, Freak St dates from the overland days of the late 1960s and early 1970s, when it was one of the great gathering places on 'the road east'. In its hippie prime, this was the place for cheap hotels (Rs 3 a room!), colourful restaurants, hash and 'pie' (pastry) shops, the sounds of Jimi and Janis blasting from eight-track players and, of course, the weird and wonderful foreign 'freaks' who gave the street its name. Along with Bodhnath and Swayambhunath, Freak St was a magnet for those in search of spiritual enlightenment, cheap dope and a place where the normal boundaries no longer applied.

Times change and Freak St (better known these days by its real name, Jochne) is today only a pale shadow of its former funky self. While there are still cheap hotels and restaurants, it's the Thamel area in the north of the city that is the main gathering place for a new generation of travellers. However, for those people who find Thamel too slick and commercialised, Freak St retains a faint echo of those mellower days.

Diyalo RestaurantINTERNATIONAL $
(Map p60; Freak St; mains Rs 120-260) At the Annapurna Lodge, this is a cosy little garden restaurant with a large menu, including tasty crêpes, burgers and a few Chinese, Mexican and Indian dishes, most for less than Rs 180.

Kumari RestaurantINTERNATIONAL $
(Map p60; Freak St; mains Rs 130-225, set Nepali meals Rs 195-260) Next to the Century Lodge, this friendly hang-out is one of few places that seems to have hung onto some of the mellowness of times past. Grab a seat outside if the interior is too glum. All the travellers' favourites are here at basement prices.

CENTRAL KATHMANDU
The restaurants in the Kantipath and Durbar Marg areas are generally more expensive than around Thamel but there are several worthwhile splurges.

Kaiser CafeINTERNATIONAL, AUSTRIAN $$$
(Map p80; Garden of Dreams, Tridevi Marg; mains Rs 400-950; ◉9am-10pm) This cafe/restaurant in the Garden of Dreams is run by Dwarika's (see p90) so quality is high. It's a fine place for a light meal (such as savoury crêpes or build-your-own sandwiches), a quiet breakfast or to linger over a pot of tea or something stiffer at the stylish Barkha Bar. Austrian-inspired dishes such as Wiener schnitzel and Sachertorte are a nod to the country that financed and oversaw the garden's restoration. You have to pay the garden's admission fee to eat here.

1905INTERNATIONAL $$$
(Map p80; ☑4215068; www.1905restaurant.com; Kantipath; lunch mains Rs 250-400, dinner Rs 600-800) You can dine with ambassadors and ministers in this classy top-end restaurant set in a charming former Rana summer palace. The tables on a bridge over a wonderful lily pond add a vaguely colonial Burmese feel, so it's fitting that there are several Southeast Asian dishes on offer. Lunch is light and casual, with wraps, paninis and salads. Dinner is a more serious affair, so dress up for dishes such as beef Wellington (Rs 780), Goan chicken or salmon mousse. If nothing else, it's a very romantic place for drinks or a dessert sampler plate for two.

Dudh SagarINDIAN $
(Map p60; Kantipath; dosas Rs 85; ◉8am-8pm) This local sweet house is the place to reacquaint yourself with South Indian vegetarian snacks such as dosas and *idly* (pounded rice cakes), topped off with Indian sweets such as *barfi* (fudge) and *gulab jamun* (deep-fried milk balls in rose-flavoured syrup). A *masala* dosa followed by *dudh malai* (cream-cheese balls in chilled pistachio milk) makes a great meal for less than Rs 140 and you won't find another tourist here.

Koto RestaurantJAPANESE $$
(Map p60; ☑4226025; Durbar Marg; dishes Rs 360-450, set menus Rs 730; ◉11.30am-3pm & 6-10pm) There are now two branches of long-running Koto next to each other on Durbar Marg; the southern one has the larger selection of sushi and sashimi, if that's what you are after. Both branches have a wide range of Japanese dishes, from cold soba noodles and mackerel dishes to sukiyaki, plus several set menus.

Ghar-e-KebabNORTH INDIAN $$$
(Map p60; Durbar Marg; dishes Rs 500-600; ◉6.30-11pm) Located inside the Hotel de l'Annapurna on Durbar Marg, this has some of the best north Indian and tandoori food in the city. Indian miniatures hang on the walls underneath an ornate carved-wood ceiling and in the evenings classical Indian music is played and traditional Urdu *ghazals* (love songs) are sung. Try the pistachio sherbet for dessert.

ELSEWHERE
Dwarika's (p90) has a candlelit Friday-night poolside barbecue and dance show that makes for a great splurge.

There are also several excellent midrange and top-end dining options in Patan (see p135), a short taxi ride away.

Lazimpat Gallery CafeBRITISH $
(Map p60; Lazimpat; mains Rs 100-250; ◉9am-8pm Sun-Fri; ☎) This friendly and good-value place occupies a unique niche, somewhere between a greasy spoon and an art cafe, with a menu boasting both beans on toast and fresh carrot and coriander soup. Everything from the cakes to the juices is made fresh on the spot. It's great for a cheap, light lunch, especially if you're out in Lazimpat and suddenly need a cheese-and-ham toastie.

Mike's BreakfastBREAKFAST, AMERICAN $$
(Map p60; ☑4424303; www.mikesbreakfast.yolasite.com; breakfasts Rs 330-435, mains Rs 430; ◉7am-9pm) As the name suggests, this place specialises in big American-style breakfasts

NEPALI & NEWARI RESTAURANTS

A growing number of restaurants around town specialise in Nepali (mostly Newari) food. Most are in converted Rana-era palaces that offer a set meal, either veg or nonveg, and you dine on cushions at low tables. All offer a cultural show that consists of musicians and dancers performing 'traditional' song and dance routines. The whole thing is a bit touristy but it's a classy night out nonetheless. At most places it's a good idea to make a reservation during the high season.

The food stretches to half a dozen courses that generally include a starter of momos and such main dishes as *alu tareko* (fried potato with cumin and tumeric), *bandhel* (wild boar), *chicken sekuwa* (barbecued or smoked meat), *alu tama kho jhol* (bamboo shoot stew) and *gundruk* (sour soup with dried greens), finished off with *shikarni* (sweet yoghurt with dried fruit and cinnamon) and a masala tea. Look out also for *kwati,* a soup consisting of a dozen types of sprouted beans that is prepared during Newari festivals.

Thamel House (Map p80; ☑4410388; www.thamelhouse.com.np; dishes Rs 225, veg/nonveg set meals Rs 800/950) This place is set in a traditional old Newari building and has bags of atmosphere, as well as a dance show at 7pm. Choose between the downstairs courtyard or upper-floor traditional seating. The food is traditional Nepali and Newari, and there are à la carte options. It's particularly convenient for Thamel.

Baithak (Map p60; ☑4267346; www.baithak.com.np; snacks Rs 200, 12-course set menus veg/nonveg Rs 1200/1500; ⊙10am-10pm) At Babar Mahal Revisited (p100), southeast of the centre, this restaurant has a dramatic and regal, almost Victorian, setting, with crystal and linens, and diners are attended by waiters dressed in royal costume and watched over by looming portraits of various disapproving Ranas. The authentic menu features 'Rana cuisine', a courtly cuisine created by Nepali Brahmin chefs and heavily influenced by north Indian Mughal cuisine. The setting is probably the most memorable part of the restaurant. The attached terrace bar is delightful for a predinner drink. A *baithak* is a royal suite or state room.

Bhojan Griha (Map p60; ☑4416423; www.bhojangriha.com; Dilli Bazaar; set menus Rs 997) In the same vein as Bhanchha Ghar, but perhaps more ambitious, Bhojan Griha is located in an imaginatively restored 150-year-old mansion that was once the residence of a caste of royal priests. Most of the seating is traditional (ie on cushions on the floor), although these are actually legless chairs, which saves your back and knees. In an effort to reduce waste, plastic is not used in the restaurant and mineral water is bought in bulk and sold by the glass.

Bhanchha Ghar (Map p60; ☑4225172; per person Rs 1100; ⊙10am-10pm) You'll find Bhanchha Ghar in a traditional three-storey Newari house in Kamaladi, just east of Durbar Marg, next to a Ganesh Temple. There is an upstairs loft bar where you can stretch out on carpets and cushions for a drink, snacks and the obligatory cultural show (try to arrive before 7pm). You can then move downstairs to take advantage of an excellent set menu of traditional Nepali dishes and delicacies, from *chiura* (beaten rice) to *kukhura ko ledo* (chicken in gravy).

(Mike was a former Peace Corps worker), served up to a mix of expats and well-heeled locals. The breakfast menu includes excellent waffles, fresh juices and great eggs Florentine, and an order of organic Nepali coffee from Palpa gets you three refills. Lunch extends to Mexican quesadillas, pizza, wraps and daily specials. The restaurant looks set to move from its leafy but inconvenient location in an old Rana house in Naxal, so check the website for the new location.

Koketsu JAPANESE $$$
(☑6218513; Panipokhari; teppanyaki Rs 200-400, sushi Rs 300-1000; ⊙noon-3pm & 5-10pm) It takes a brave person to order sushi in the Himalaya but raw-fish experts (afishionados?) generally rate Koketsu as the best Japanese place in town. The seafood here is flown in fresh from Thailand, as are the *takosu* (marinated octopus), squid and roe. The focal point of the restaurant is definitely the central teppanyaki grill. It's at the north-

ern end of Lazimpat, right across from the Japanese embassy, which is no coincidence.

Chez Caroline
FRENCH $$$

(Map p60; ☑4263070; mains Rs 500-1300; ☺9.30am-10pm) In the Babar Mahal Revisited complex (p100), Caroline's is a sophisticated outdoor bistro popular with expat foodies. It offers French-influenced main courses such as wild-mushroom tart with walnut sauce, Roquefort salad, and crêpes Suzette with passionfruit sorbet, plus fine quiches and pastries, daily specials and a lazy weekend brunch (Rs 825), all with a wide range of desserts, teas and wines. Try a swift glass of pastis (liquorice-flavoured liqueur) with mint syrup: it's the perfect aperitif to an afternoon's shopping.

Krishnarpan Restaurant
NEPALI $$$

(☑4470770; www.dwarikas.com; set meals US$24-37; ☺dinner only) One of the best places for Nepali food is this impressive place at Dwarika's hotel. The atmosphere is superb and the food gets consistent praise from diners. If you are coming on Friday, arrive in time for the 6pm dance show in the hotel courtyard and take advantage of happy hour. Reservations required.

Self-Catering
For trekking food such as noodles, nuts, dried fruit and cheese, there are several extensive supermarkets grouped around central Thamel Chowk. For more supermarkets try the **Bluebird Mart** (Map p60; ☺10am-9pm) by the main bridge across the Bagmati River to Patan; **Big Mart** (Map p60) in Lazimpat, near the French embassy; **Kasthamandap Bazaar Supermarket** (Map p60), just off the southern end of Durbar Marg; and **Bhat Bhateni Supermarket** (Map p60), south of the Chinese embassy.

Weizen Bakery
BAKERY $

(Map p80; www.weizenrestaurant.com; mains Rs 150-280) Down from the Yin Yang, this bakery restaurant has decent cakes, breads and pastries, with bakery goods (but not cakes) discounted by 50% after 8pm. The pleasant attached garden is a nice quiet place for breakfast.

Curry Kitchen/Hot Bread
BAKERY $

(Map p80; pastries Rs 40-70) This bakery on the main Thamel junction does a roaring trade in sandwiches, bread rolls, pizza slices and pastries. Add an espresso and head upstairs to the sunny terrace for a leisurely breakfast or pack a ham-and-veg roll for lunch on the run. Bakery items are discounted by 50% after 9.30pm.

Organic Farmer's Market
MARKET $

(Map p80; 1905 restaurant, Kantipath; ☺9am-noon Sat) On Saturday morning local expats and foodies head to 1905 restaurant to stock up on local cheeses, organic produce and other freshly made goodies. The market shifts to Patan's New Orleans restaurant on Sunday.

Drinking

There are a few bars scattered around Thamel, all within a short walk of each other. Just poke your nose in to see which has the crowd and style that appeals. Most places have a happy hour between 5pm and 8pm, with two-for-one cocktails. Most bars in Thamel close by 11pm, though there are moves to extend hours. A beer costs between Rs 300 and Rs 350 in most places.

The noisy 'dance bars' that litter Thamel are generally worth avoiding. Most are aimed at locals or Indian tourists and while pretty tame at first look they are essentially fronts for prostitution.

Himalayan Java
CAFE

(Map p80; ☑4422519; Tridevi Marg; coffee Rs 85-150, snacks Rs 200; ☺8am-9pm) The various branches of this modern and buzzing coffeehouse are the place to lose yourself in a sofa, a laptop and a pulse-reviving Americano. There are also breakfasts, paninis and cakes. The main Tridevi Marg branch has a balcony, lots of sofas and big-screen TV for the football but feels a bit like a hotel foyer, whereas the smaller central Thamel branch suffers from road noise.

Rum Doodle Restaurant & Bar
BAR

(Map p80; ☑4227068; www.rumdoodlebar.com; ☺10am-10pm) Named after the world's highest mountain, the 40,000½ft Mt Rum Doodle (according to WE Bowman, author of *The Ascent of Rum Doodle,* a spoof of serious mountaineering books), the original Rum Doodle was a favourite meeting place for mountaineering expeditions – Edmund Hillary, Reinhold Messner, Ang Rita Sherpa and Rob Hall left their mark on the walls. The new location doesn't have the history but it's a pleasant place with a fine terrace and sunny rooftop, and trekking groups can add their own yeti footprint trek report to the dozens plastered on the walls. The restaurant (mains Rs 440 to Rs 530) serves up decent steaks, pasta and pizza.

Maya Cocktail Bar COCKTAIL BAR

(Map p80; cocktails Rs 280; ⊘4-11pm) A long-running favourite; the two-for-one cocktails between 4pm and 7pm are a guaranteed jump-start to a good evening. The nearby Pub Maya is somewhat more boisterous.

Tom & Jerry Pub BAR

(Map p80) Close to Nargila Restaurant, this is a long-running, rowdy upstairs place that has pool tables and a dance floor. Thursday is ladies' night.

Jatra LOUNGE

(Map p80; ☑4211010; ⊚) A quiet, intimate and pretty cool venue for a beer or dinner (mains Rs 250 to Rs 350), with spacious indoor and outdoor seating, global music and candle-light. Friday nights bring live music jams; on Wednesdays ladies get a free cocktail.

Tamas Spa Lounge LOUNGE

(Map p80; ☑4275658; drinks Rs 300; ⊘10am-midnight) *Sex and the City* fans will enjoy this glam lounge bar, decked out in sofas and satin in a lush palette of cool creams. Take a seat in the courtyard or the old Rana house and indulge your inner princess with a sparkling Bellini or espresso martini. Live music livens things up on Saturday and Wednesday, and a basement club pumps out the bass on Friday and Saturday after 10pm. The entrance is suitably low-key, hidden down an alleyway just south of Yin Yang Restaurant.

J-Bar LOUNGE

(Map p80; ☑4418209; drinks Rs 250-300; ⊘6pm-midnight) At the back of Himalayan Java, the J-Bar is more like a New York club than a Nepal bar, decked out in leather sofas and satins; it's a place to rub shoulders with Nepal's beautiful set. Expect a cover charge on Fridays. After 10pm access is via the side alley.

Sam's Bar BAR

(Map p80; ⊘4-11pm) A long-time favourite with trek leaders, mountain guides and other Kathmandu regulars. There's reggae every Saturday.

Full Moon LOUNGE

(Map p80; beer Rs 175; ⊘6-11pm) A tiny chill-out bar and den of iniquity that draws a mixed Nepali-foreign clientele.

☆ Entertainment

Nepal is an early-to-bed country and even in Kathmandu you'll find few people on the streets after 10pm, especially when the capital's political situation is tense. Most bars

close their doors by 11pm, though a few keep serving those inside.

Duelling cover bands compete for aural supremacy at various Thamel restaurants on Friday and Saturday nights in the high season – just follow the sounds of Bryan Adams and Coldplay covers.

Beyond this, you could take in a Bollywood blockbuster or try to earn back your flight money at one of half a dozen casinos. Major sporting events such as Premier League football and the Formula 1 grand prix are televised in all the major bars.

There are also several cultural performances, which generally involve local youths wearing a variety of dress over their jeans and performing traditional dances from Nepal's various ethnic groups, accompanied by a live band that includes a tabla, harmonium and singer.

Casinos

Kathmandu's casinos are all attached to up-market hotels and are open 24 hours. New casinos have opened recently at the Shangri-La and Malla hotels.

At all casinos you can play in either Indian rupees or US dollars, and winnings (in the same currency) can be taken out of the country when you leave. The main games offered are roulette and blackjack. Most clients are Indian; Nepalis are officially forbidden from entering.

Casino Royale CASINO

(Map p60; ☑4271244; ⊘24hr) Pull your tuxedo out of your backpack, polish up your best Sean Connery impersonation ('Aaah, Mish Moneypenny...') and make a beeline for this former Rana palace at the Yak & Yeti Hotel. Hang around the tables (not the slots) long enough and staff will ply you with free drinks and a dinner buffet, though sadly the Russian dancing girls have gone back to Moscow.

Music & Dance

There are a few performances of Nepali music and dancing in the restaurants of the top-end hotels but little is scheduled.

Be wary of Thamel's numerous sleazy 'shower dance' bars. At first glance many seem quite tame, but most are simply fronts for prostitution, and the majority of customers are Indian or local Nepalis.

Jazz Upstairs LIVE MUSIC

(Map p60; ☑4410436; cover Rs 200; ⊘noon-11pm Sun-Fri, 7-11pm Sat) It's worth schlepping out

QUIRKY KATHMANDU

Kathmandu has more than its fair share of quirk and, as with most places in the subcontinent, a 10-minute walk in any direction will throw up numerous curiosities.

The corridors of the **Natural History Museum** (p110) are full of bizarre moth-eaten animals and jars that lie somewhere between a school science experiment and *The Texas Chainsaw Massacre*. The 20ft python skin and nine-month-old baby rhino in a jar are guaranteed to give you nightmares. The other exhibits are a bit slapdash, including the line of stuffed birds nailed carelessly to a bit of wood to indicate their distribution, or the big pile of elephant dung deposited randomly in the front corner.

The nearby **National Museum** (p111) also houses more than its fair share of weirdness, including the skin of a two-headed calf, a portrait of King Prithvi Narayan Shah giving everyone the finger (apparently symbolising the unity of the nation...), and a man poking a fox in the backside with a stick, the significance of which passed us by completely.

For items of personal quirkiness, the **Tribhuvan Museum** (p69) in Hanuman Dhoka offers up such gems as the king's personal parachuting uniform, his film projector and his walking stick with a spring-loaded sword inside – very '007'.

Kathmandu's **Kaiser Library** (Map p80; Ministry of Education & Sports compound, cnr Kantipath & Tridevi Marg; ⊙10am-5pm Sun-Thu, to 3pm Fri) is definitely worth a visit, partly for its remarkable collection of antique travel books but also for the main reading room, which has antique globes, a stuffed tiger and suits of armour that you expect to spring to life at any moment.

Compared to all this funkiness, Kathmandu's old town is pretty docile. Look for the antique **fire engines** (Map p60) hidden behind a grille just west of the junction of New Rd and Sukra Path.

If you get a toothache during your trip, be sure to visit the old town's **toothache god** (see stop number seven on the walking tour on p72) – a raggedy old stump of wood covered with hundreds of nails and coins.

---

to Lazimpat on a Wednesday and Saturday night (from 8pm) to catch the live jazz in this tiny upstairs bar. The stage is snug and intimate, the vibe is friendly and the clientele is an interesting mix of locals and expats. Monday brings live blues.

House of Music   LIVE MUSIC
(Map p80; ☑9841904105; cover around Rs 200; ⊙2pm-midnight Tue-Sun) This beery bar is the best place in Kathmandu to listen to original Nepali rock, reggae and R'n'B music, mostly Friday and Saturday nights. It's in northern Thamel but miles away from the cover bands of the centre. Upcoming concerts are posted on the venue's Facebook page. It's part-owned by the drummer of 1974AD, one of Nepal's biggest bands.

**Gandharba Culture and Art
Organisation**   LIVE MUSIC
(Map p80; ☑4700292; http://gandharbas.nyima.org) This organisation represents the city's musician caste and often has informal music jams between 5pm and 7pm at its offices, which are located on the 3rd floor above Equator Expeditions (tourists are welcome).

It also plays in local restaurants such as the Northfield Cafe and individual musicians offer music lessons.

**Kalamandapa Institute of Classical
Nepalese Performing Arts**   TRADITIONAL DANCE
(Map p60; ☑4271545; admission Rs 500) Nepali classical dance (and occasional theatre) is performed at Hotel Vajra most Tuesdays at 7pm. Phone ahead to check schedules.

Cinemas
Sadly, the video cafes made famous by the title of Pico Iyer's book *Video Night in Kathmandu* have disappeared, replaced by fake DVD stores.

Jai Nepal Cinema   CINEMA
(Map p60; ☑4442220; www.jainepal.com; Narayanhiti Marg; stalls Rs 100-150, balcony Rs 200) This and the branch **Kumari Cinema** (Map p60) are good places to catch the latest Bollywood-style Hindi or Nepali hit. Not understanding the dialogue is really only a minor hindrance to enjoying these comedy-musical 'masala movies'.

QFX Civil Mall CINEMA

(Map p60; ☑4442220; www.qfxcinemas.com; 7th fl, Civil Mall, Sundhara; tickets Rs 250-550) The main cinema for English-language Hollywood blockbusters, with morning and matinee discounts.

🛍 Shopping

Kathmandu offers the best shopping in the country. Everything that is turned out in the various centres around the valley can be found here, although you can often find a better choice, or more unusual items, in the centres that produce the items – Jawalakhel (southern Patan) for Tibetan carpets, Patan for cast-metal statues, Bhaktapur for wood-carvings, and Thimi for masks. For the best range of fair trade handicrafts and interior design, see p139.

Thamel has some excellent trekking gear for sale, but don't think that you are getting the genuine article. Most of the 'Columbia' fleeces and 'North Face' jackets are Chinese knock-offs or made locally but with imported fleece and Gore-Tex. See p33 for details on hiring trekking gear.

Kathmandu has dozens of excellent bookshops with a great selection of Himalaya titles, including books that are not usually available outside the country. Most dealers will buy back books for 50% of what you paid.

An endless supply of curios, art pieces and plain old junk is churned out for the tourist trade. Most does not come from Tibet but from the local Tamang community. Prayer flags and prayer wheels are a popular buy in Durbar Sq, Bodhnath and Swayambhunath but be prepared to bargain.

Remember that antiques (over 100 years old) cannot be taken out of the country. Get a receipt and a description of any major purchase from the shop where you bought it. See p360 for more information on taking antiques through customs.

Thamel in particular can be a pretty stressful place to shop, what with all the tiger-balm sellers, rickshaw drivers and high-speed motorbikers. Dive into a side street or garden haven when stress levels start to rise.

Pilgrims Book House BOOKS

(Map p80; ☑4424942; www.pilgrimsbooks.com, www.pilgrimsonlineshop.com) The best bookstore in town is so good that it's an attraction in its own right. It's particularly strong on antiquarian travelogues and there's a good teahouse and vegetarian restaurant in the back. It's a couple of doors north of the Kathmandu Guest House.

Amrita Craft Collection HANDICRAFTS

(Map p80; ☑4240757; www.amritacraft.com) This broad collection of crafts and clothing is a good place to start your Thamel shopping. Quality isn't top-notch but subtract 20% from its fixed prices and you get a good benchmark for what you should aim to pay on the street if you don't mind haggling. The upstairs branch across the road has a larger selection.

Aroma Garden INCENSE

(Map p80; ☑4420724) As the name suggests, this is Thamel's sweetest-smelling shop. It's a good one-stop shop for *dhoop* (incense), essential oils, soaps and almost anything else that smells great.

Paper Park PAPER PRODUCTS

(Map p80; ☑4700475; www.handmadepaperpark. com) One of the best of several shops in Thamel that sell handmade paper products, from photo albums to paper lamps. It's next to the Hotel Marshyangdi. The paper comes from the *lokta* (daphne) plant, whose bark is boiled and beaten with wooden mallets and the pulp is spread over a frame to dry. The finished product folds without creasing and is used for all official Nepali documents. You can see the manufacturing process in Bhaktapur.

Babar Mahal Revisited ARTS & CRAFTS

(Map p60) Originally built in 1919, this unique complex of old Rana palace outbuildings has been redeveloped to house a warren of chic clothes shops, designer galleries and handicraft shops, as well as a couple of top-end restaurants and bars. It's aimed squarely at expats and wealthy locals so prices are as high as the quality. It's southeast of the city near the Singh Durbar government offices.

Curio Arts ARTS & CRAFTS

(Map p60; ☑4224871; www.devasarts.com) Durbar Marg has several top-end showrooms concentrating on statues, Tibetan furniture and other crafts. Curio Arts is a good place to start.

Mahaguthi FAIR TRADE, HOMEWARES

(Map p60; ☑4438760; www.mahaguthi.org; ⊙10am-6.30pm Sun-Fri, to 5pm Sat) Good range of crafts and home furnishings, much of it made by disadvantaged or minority groups, with nice batiks made by paralysed women. There's a larger outlet and collection of other fair-trade stores in Kopundol in Patan. Nearby fair-trade stores a couple of minutes' walk south include Folk Nepal (www.folkne pal.org) and Third World Craft (www.third worldcraft.com).

Phaba Chengreshi Thangka Art School THANGKAS
(Map p80; ☏4220428) You can see thangkas being painted on the spot at this school in Thamel.

Dharmapala Thangka Center THANGKAS
(Map p60; ☏4223715; www.thangka.de) Down an arcade, off Durbar Marg, and upstairs is this workshop for a local school of thangka painting. The showroom is in the nearby Annapurna Hotel.

Shona's Alpine Rental OUTDOOR EQUIPMENT
(Map p80; ☏4265120) Reliable rentals and gear shop that makes its own sleeping bags and offers advice on the best trek gear for

THE ESSENTIAL THAMEL SHOPPING GUIDE

From Kashmiri carpets and fake CDs to trekking poles and yak-milk soap, Thamel offers the best collection of shops in the country. Bring an extra bag and stock up on next year's Christmas presents.

» **Spices** Plenty of shops and supermarkets in Thamel sell small packets of spices, from momo mixes to chai spices, or head to Asan Tole (see p70), where the locals buy their freshly ground masalas.

» **Embroidery** Sewing machines around Thamel whir away late into the night adding logos and Tibetan symbols to jackets, hats and T-shirts. Trekkers can commission badges and T-shirts commemorating their successful trek or even get a business logo made.

» **Jewellery** Kathmandu is a great place for jewellery, particularly silver. Buy it ready-made, ask the jeweller to create a design for you or bring in something you would like copied. The price of silver is quoted per *tola* (11.7g) in the daily newspaper.

» **Puppets** Puppets make good gifts for children and are made in Bhaktapur as well as other centres. They're often of multiarmed deities clutching little wooden weapons in each hand. The puppet heads may be made of easily broken clay or more durable papier mâché.

» **Pashminas** A shawl or scarf made from fine pashmina (the underhair of a mountain goat) is a popular buy. The cost of a shawl depends on the percentage of pashmina in the mix and from which part of the goat's body the hair originated, starting from the cheapest back wool and rising through the belly and chest to neck hair, which is about five times more expensive than back hair. The cheapest shawls are a 70/30% cotton/pashmina blend, silk-pashmina blends cost around 30% more and pure pashmina shawls range from around US$50 to US$275 for a top-end ring shawl (named because they are fine enough to be pulled through a finger ring; also known as a water shawl).

» **Tea** Ilam, Ontu, Kanyan and Mai Valley teas are the best Nepali teas, from the east of the country near Darjeeling. Expect to pay anything from Rs 600 (in Ilam) to Rs 3000 (in Thamel) per kilogram for good Ilam tea. The excellently named 'super fine tipi golden flower orange pekoe' tea is about as good as it gets. Connoisseurs choose the first (March) or second (May) flush, rather than the substandard monsoon flush. Lemon tea flavoured with lemongrass is another favourite, as is pre-spiced masala tea (Rs 100 to Rs 150 per 100g).

» **Clothes** There are lots of funky wool hats, felt bags, embroidered T-shirts (our favourite has 'Same Same...' on the front and '...But Different' on the back!), jumpers etc, particularly on the twisting road known as Saatghumti. Always try clothes on before handing over the cash. Impossibly cute baby-sized North Face fleeces and down jackets are hard to pass by.

» **Prayer flags** The best place to buy is the street in front of the Kathesimbhu Stupa south of Thamel. Choose between cheaper polyester and better-quality cotton flags and remember, this is your karma that we are talking about.

your trip. Get a season warmer than they recommend. Sleeping bags and down jackets cost Rs 50 to Rs 60 each per day to rent. You can make a deposit in any combination of currencies.

Holyland Hiking Shop OUTDOOR EQUIPMENT
(Map p80) The better trekking gear shops are at the southern end of Thamel. Both this and the nearby **Everest Adventure Mountaineering** (Map p80) have been recommended.

North Face OUTDOOR EQUIPMENT
(Map p80) Tridevi Marg is home to a collection of *pukka* (not fake) gear shops, including North Face, Mountain Hard Wear, Marmot and other brands, offering imported gear at foreign prices. These shops sell everything from Black Diamond climbing gear to US Thermarests.

New Tibet Book Store BOOKS
(Map p80; Tridevi Marg) The best collection of Tibet-related titles but few discounts.

United Books BOOKS
(Map p80; Thamel) A well-chosen selection and sensible prices, run by Danish Lars.

Vajra Books BOOKS
(Map p80; www.vajrabooks.com.np; Jyatha) This knowledgeable local publisher offers an excellent selection of academic books and will post books internationally. There's a branch across the road.

Tara Oriental WOMEN'S CLOTHING
(Map p60; 4436315; www.taraoriental.com; Lazimpat) This designer's studio is the best place for top-end designer pashmina throws, scarves and sweaters, retailing at around US$160. Yes, it's expensive but it's top-end stuff.

Indigo Gallery ART GALLERY
(4424303; Naxal; 8.30am-5pm) An upmarket gallery set in a lovely old Rana building, with excellent exhibits of modern thangkas, photography and prints for sale. It's set to move location in 2012.

ℹ Information

Emergency
Ambulance service (4521048) Provided by Patan Hospital.
Fire Brigade (101, 4221177)
Police (Map p64; 100, 4223011; www.nepal police.gov.np; Durbar Sq)
Red Cross Ambulance (4228094)

Tourist Police Bhrikuti Mandap (4247041); Thamel (4700750)

Internet Access
Cybercafes are everywhere in Thamel. The best have scanners and printers plus, importantly, power backup. Connection speeds are generally fast and the rates hover between Rs 50 and Rs 70 per hour. Most cafes, restaurants and hotels offer free wi-fi.

Laundry
Several laundries across Thamel will machine wash laundry for Rs 50 per kilo. Get it back the next day or pay double for a three-hour service. Amazingly, it all comes back relatively clean, even after a three-week trek. Power cuts can delay wash times so don't cut it too fine by handing in your laundry the day before your flight.

Medical Services
Dozens of pharmacies on the fringes of Thamel offer all the cheap antibiotics you can pronounce.

CIWEC Clinic Travel Medicine Center (Map p60; 4424111; www.ciwec-clinic.com; 9am-noon & 1-4pm Mon-Fri) Just across from the British embassy, to the northeast of Thamel and used by many foreign residents. It has operated since 1982 and has developed an international reputation for research into travellers' medical problems. The clinic is staffed mostly by foreigners and a doctor is on call around the clock. A consultation costs around US$65. Credit cards are accepted and the centre is used to dealing with insurance claims.

CIWEC Dental Clinic (Map p60; 4440100; emergency 4424111; ciwecdental@subisu.net. np) US dentist on the top floor of CIWEC Clinic.

Healthy Smiles (Map p60; 4420800; www. smilenepal.com) UK-trained dentist, opposite the Hotel Ambassador.

Nepal International Clinic (Map p60; 4434642, 4435357; www.nepalinternation alclinic.com; 9am-1pm & 2-5pm) Just south of the New Royal Palace, east of Thamel. It has an excellent reputation and is slightly cheaper than the CIWEC Clinic. Credit cards accepted.

NORVIC International Hospital (Map p60; 4258554; www.norvichospital.com; Thapathali) Private Nepali hospital with a good reputation for cardiology.

Patan Hospital (Map p128; 5522295; www. patanhospital.org.np) Probably the best hospital in the Kathmandu Valley, in the Lagankhel district of Patan. Partly staffed by Western missionaries.

Money
There are dozens of licensed moneychangers in Thamel. Their hours are longer than those of

DANGERS & ANNOYANCES

Electricity cuts ('load shedding') are a fact of life in Kathmandu; they last for up to 16 hours a day in winter when hydro power levels are at their lowest. Electricity is currently rationed across the city, shifting from district to district every eight hours or so. Most hotels post a schedule of planned electricity cuts. Try to choose a hotel with a generator and make sure your room is far away from it.

The combination of ancient vehicles, low-quality fuel and lack of emission controls makes the streets of Kathmandu particularly dirty, noisy and unpleasant. Bear in mind the following:

» Traffic rules exist, but are rarely enforced; be especially careful when crossing streets or riding a bicycle.

» Traffic is supposed to travel on the left side of the road, but many drivers simply choose the most convenient side, which can make walking in Kathmandu a deeply stressful experience.

» Remember that pedestrians account for over 40% of all traffic fatalities in Nepal.

» Consider bringing a face mask to filter out dust and emission particles, especially if you plan to ride a bicycle or motorcycle in Kathmandu. After a few days in the city you will likely feel the onset of a throat infection.

Other annoyances in Thamel are the crazy motorcyclists, and the barrage of irritating flute sellers, tiger-balm hawkers, chess-set sellers, musical-instrument vendors, travel-agency touts, hashish suppliers, freelance trekking guides and rickshaw drivers.

Note that the colourful sadhus (itinerant holy men) who frequent Durbar Sq and Pashuputinath will expect *baksheesh* (a tip) if you take a photo, as will the Thamel 'holy men' who anoint you with a *tika* on your forehead.

Kathmandu is occasionally the focus of political demonstrations and bandhs (strikes), which close shops and shut down transport. See p368 for more.

the banks (generally until 8pm or so) and rates are pretty consistent, though slightly lower than the banks. See p365 for information on commissions and transfers.

Useful ATMs in the Thamel area are located beside Yin Yang Restaurant, Ganesh Man Singh Bldg and Himalayan Java.

Himalayan Bank (Map p80; ☎4250208; www. himalayanbank.com; Tridevi Marg; ☺10am-8pm Sun-Fri, 9am-noon Sat) The most convenient bank for travellers in Thamel. The kiosk on Tridevi Marg changes cash (no commission) and travellers cheques (commission of 0.75%, minimum Rs 150) until 3pm; after this head to the main branch in the basement of the nearby Sanchaya Kosh Bhawan shopping centre (counter 12). Cash advances on a Visa card are possible and there's a prominent ATM next to the kiosk, in front of the Three Goddesses Temples.

Standard Chartered Bank (Map p60; ☎4418456; Lazimpat; ☺9.45am-7pm Sun-Thu, 9.45am-4.30pm Fri, 9.30am-12.30pm Sat & holidays) Has well-located ATMs – opposite the Third Eye restaurant and in the compound of the Kathmandu Guest House – and others around town. The main branch in Lazimpat charges 1.5% (minimum Rs 300) to change

travellers cheques and Rs 200 per transaction for cash. There's no charge for a rupee cash advance on a credit card but you pay 2% to get the cash in US dollars.

Post

Most bookshops in Thamel, including Pilgrims Book House (p100), sell stamps and deliver postcards to the post office, which is much easier than making a special trip to the post office yourself. Pilgrims charges a 10% commission for this service.

Everest Postal Care (Map p80; Tridevi Marg; ☺10am-5.30pm Sun-Fri) Convenient private post office near Thamel that posts letters and parcels at the same rates as the post office.

Foreign post office (Map p60; Sundhara; ☺10am-5pm Sun-Fri) Parcels can be sent from here, in a separate building just north of the main post office. Parcels have to be examined and sealed by a customs officer. Start the process before 2pm.

Main post office (Map p60; Sundhara; ☺7am-6pm Sun-Thu, to 3pm Fri) Close to the Bhimsen Tower. Stalls in the courtyard sell airmail and padded envelopes. Get stamps at counter 12. You can post packages up to 2kg at counter

16; beyond that you need to go to the foreign post office.

Sending parcels from the foreign post office is something of an ordeal so, if you're short of time, you're best off using a cargo agency such as **Diki Continental Exports** (Map p80; ☑4256919; www.dikiexports.com; JP School, Thamel).

Courier agencies include the following:

DHL (Map p60; ☑4481303; www.dhl.com.np; Kamaladi) With a branch in Lazimpat.

FedEx (Map p60; ☑4269248; www.fedex.com/np; Kantipath; ⏰9am-6pm Sun-Fri, to 1pm Sat)

Telephone

You can make international telephone calls from any of the dozens of 'communication centres' for around Rs 20 per minute. A public-telephone rank below Or2k offers international calls for Rs 10 per minute to the US or UK. Most internet cafes offer Skype.

Ncell (Map p60; ☑9805554338; www.ncell.com.np; Sherpa Mall, Durbar Marg; ⏰9.30am-7.30pm) is the most convenient central office to get an Ncell SIM card.

Tourist Information

There are a number of good noticeboards in Thamel that are worth checking for information on apartments, travel and trekking partners, courses and cultural events. The Kathmandu Guest House has a good noticeboard, as do the Pumpernickel Bakery and Fire & Ice Pizzeria.

For Kathmandu-based offices that offer trekking-related information, see p33.

Tourist Service Centre (Map p60; ☑4256909, ext 223, 24hr tourism hotline 4225709; www.welcomenepal.com; Bhrikuti Mandap; ⏰10am-1pm & 2-5pm Sun-Fri), on the eastern side of the Tundikhel parade ground, has an inconvenient location but is the place to get trekking permits and a TIMS card (see p34) and pay national park fees.

Travel Agencies

Kathmandu has a great number of travel agencies, particularly along Durbar Marg, Kantipath and in Thamel. See p32 for details of trekking agencies. Reliable places include the following:

Flight Connection International (Map p80; ☑4250782; www.flightconnectionintl.com; Jyatha, Thamel) Good for flight tickets. The international department is in Gaia Restaurant.

President Travel & Tours (Map p60; ☑4220245; www.pttnepal.com; Durbar Marg) Professional agency favoured by expats and wealthy Nepalis; particularly good at getting seats on heavily booked fights.

Wayfarers (Map p80; ☑4266010; www.wayfarers.com.np; Thamel; ⏰9am-6pm Mon-Fri, to 5pm Sat & Sun) For straight-talking ticketing, bespoke tours and Kathmandu Valley walking trips (see p114).

Visa Extensions

Visa extensions of 30 to 60 days are fairly painless at the **Central Immigration Office** (Map p60; ☑4429659; www.immi.gov.np; Kalikasthan, Dilli Bazaar; ⏰10am-4pm Sun-Thu, 10am-3pm Fri, 11am-1pm Sat). Get a form, join the queue, supply one photo and then join a separate queue to pay the fee. If you apply before 2pm you should get your passport back the same day at 3.30pm. See p371 for more on visa extensions.

ⓘ Getting There & Away

See p373 for details on getting to/from Kathmandu both by air and by land from neighbouring countries, including package tours to Tibet.

Air

It's a good idea to double-check the departure time of your return flight before flying. This goes double for the notoriously unreliable Nepal Airlines; at peak times you should reconfirm when you first arrive in Nepal and reconfirm again towards the end of your stay. Even this may not guarantee you a seat – make sure you get to the airport early as people at the end of the queue can still be left behind.

DOMESTIC AIRLINES

Kathmandu is the main hub for domestic flights, including to Pokhara (US$98), Lukla (US$120), Bharatpur (US$88; for Chitwan) and Bhairawa (US$116). The various domestic airlines have sales offices around the city but locations and phone numbers seem to change with the weather. It's far less hassle to buy tickets through a travel agency, and you'll probably get a better deal this way. See p378 for an overview of domestic airlines and their Kathmandu contact details.

Nepal Airlines domestic office (Map p60; ☑4227133; ⏰9.30am-1pm & 2-5pm) has computerised booking on five routes: Pokhara, Jomsom, Lukla, Bharatpur and Manang. Other domestic flights are booked in a much more haphazard manner at an office to the side of the main international booking centre. A special tourist counter here avoids the bulk of the booking chaos. The other domestic carriers are much more reliable.

Bus

LONG-DISTANCE BUSES

The **Gongabu bus station** (Map p56; Ring Rd, Balaju) is north of the city centre. It is also called the Kathmandu Bus Terminal, or simply 'new bus park'. This bus station is basically for all long-distance buses, including to Pokhara and destinations in the Terai. It's a huge and confusing place and there are very few signs in English, but most of the ticket sellers are very helpful. There's often more than one reservation counter for each destination. Bookings for long trips should be made a day in advance – Thamel travel agents will do this for a fee and this will save you both time and the taxi fare.

Bus 23 (Rs 15) runs to the bus station from Lekhnath Marg on the northern edge of Thamel but takes an age. A taxi from Thamel costs around Rs 150.

Buses to Dhunche and Syabrubesi (see p284), and also Nuwakot (Rs 160, 7.15am, 9.15am and 1pm) and Kakani (Rs 50, every 30 minutes), run from the Machha Pokhari (Fish Pond) stand, diagonally across the Ring Rd from Gongabu bus station.

The main exceptions to these are the popular tourist buses to Pokhara (Rs 450 to 500, seven hours) that depart daily at 7am from a far more convenient location at the Thamel end of Kantipath. Buses are comfortable and you get a fixed seat number with your ticket. For more details, see p211.

There are also tourist buses from here to Sauraha for Chitwan National Park (Rs 400 to Rs 500, five to seven hours). For details, see p233.

Greenline (Map p80; ☑4257544; www.greenline.com.np; Tridevi Marg; ⏰7am-5.30pm) offers air-con deluxe services that are considerably more expensive than the tourist buses (but include lunch). There are daily morning buses at 7.30am to Pokhara (US$18, seven hours) and Chitwan (US$15, six hours), with a lunch break and bus change in Kurintar. You should book a day in advance. Ask about its good-value fly-drive packages, which combine a bus trip with a one-way flight.

Golden Travels (Map p60; ☑4220036; Woodlands Complex, Durbar Marg) runs similar services, departing at 7am from Kantipath to Pokhara (US$15 with lunch). Golden and similar transport companies Baba Bhairav and Buddha Darshan run a daily service at 7.30am to Sunauli (US$14), inconveniently departing from Kalanki on the southwestern corner of the Ring Rd. All three companies offer a free transfer to Kalanki from the general post office at Sundhara, departing around 6.45am.

A similar service runs to Lumbini (Rs 900, nine hours), leaving Kakani at 8am. Buy tickets at any travel agency.

TO/FROM THE KATHMANDU VALLEY

Buses for most destinations within the Kathmandu Valley, and for those on or accessed from the Arniko Hwy (for Jiri, Barabise and Kodari on the Tibetan border), operate from the **Ratna Park bus station** (Map p60), also known as the old or city bus stand, in the centre of the city on the eastern edge of Tundikhel parade ground. The station is a bit of a horror, drenched in diesel fumes, with no English signs and not much English spoken. Keep shouting out your destination and someone will eventually direct you to the right bus.

As with anything in Nepal, however, there are exceptions to the rule. Buses to Bhaktapur (Rs 50,

KATHMANDU GETTING THERE & AWAY

BUSES FROM GONGABU BUS STATION

DESTINATION	KM	DEPARTURES	DURATION (HR)	COST (RS)	TICKET WINDOW
Besi Sahar	150	6.30-10am	6	330	25
Bhairawa/Sunauli	282	5am-noon, 4-8pm	8	465	23, 24, 29
Bharatpur	150	hourly	5	260-300	17, 16
Biratnagar	540	4.30pm	14	810-860	11
Birganj	300	6.30-8.30am, 6.15pm	8	400-450	16
Butwal	237	every 30min 4-8pm	7-9	430	28, 29
Gorkha	140	5.45am, 6.15am, 6.30am, 6.45am, 11am	5	250	24
Hile	635	3pm	14	1060	11
Kakarbhitta	610	4.30am, 4-5pm	14	980	26 & others
Lumbini	260	7.30pm	9-10	505	28, 29
Nepalganj	530	7am, every 30min 3-7.30pm	12	850-1350	24, 25
Pokhara	200	every 30min until 1pm	6-8	360	25
Tansen (Palpa)	300	6.20am, 7.20am, 5.30pm	10	525	28, 29

BUSES FROM RATNA PARK BUS STATION

DESTINATION	DEPARTURES	DURATION	COST (RS)
Banepa		2hr	35
Barabise	last bus 4pm	4hr	175-220
Dhulikhel		2hr	46
Kodari	7am, 2pm	4½hr	220
Panauti		1½-2hr	45-53
Patan		20min	13

Unless otherwise noted, buses depart when full.

one hour) run from a stand (Map p60) on Bagh Bazar. Drivers often try to charge foreigners double on this route.

Buses to Pharping (Rs 21, two hours) and Dakshinkali (Rs 32, 2½ hours) leave from Shahid Gate (Martyrs' Memorial) at the southern end of the Tundikhel parade ground (Map p60), as well as the Ratna Park station.

Buses heading to Bungamati, Godavari and Chapagaon in the southern valley leave from Patan – see p140.

A daily direct tourist minibus runs to Nagarkot (Rs 250, two hours) at 1.30pm in front of the Hotel Malla in Lainchhaur, though it's not the most reliable service and you may have to ask around to find it.

Car

Although you cannot rent cars on a drive-yourself basis, they can be readily rented with a driver from a number of operators. The rental cost is high, both in terms of the initial hiring charge and fuel. Charges are as high as US$50 per day, although they can be lower, especially if you are not covering a huge distance.

Wayfarers (see p104) can arrange car hire for a one-way drop to Pokhara (Rs 6875) or Chitwan (Rs 6200). Sightseeing around the Kathmandu Valley costs around Rs 1100/2100 for a half/full day, depending on the itinerary.

Taxi

A better option than hiring a car is to hire a taxi for the day. Between several people, longer taxi trips around the valley, or even outside it, are affordable. A half-/full-day sightseeing trip within the valley costs around Rs 800/1500.

For longer journeys outside the valley count on about Rs 2500 per day plus fuel, which is generally cheaper than hiring a car through a travel agency.

ⓘ Getting Around

The best way to see Kathmandu and the valley is to walk or ride a bicycle. Most of the sights in Kathmandu itself can easily be covered on foot, and this is by far the best way to appreciate the city, even if the traffic is atrocious. If and when you run out of steam, there are plenty of reasonably priced taxis available.

To/From the Airport

Kathmandu's international airport is called **Tribhuvan Airport** (off Map p56; ☑4472256) after the late king; the area's former name of Gaucher (literally 'cow pasture') speaks volumes about Kathmandu's rapid urban expansion. See p373 for details of arrival and departure procedures.

Getting into town is quite straightforward. Both the international and domestic terminals offer a fixed-price prepaid taxi service, currently Rs 500/550 to Thamel/Patan.

Once outside the international terminal you will be confronted by hotel touts, who are often taxi drivers making commission on taking you to a particular hotel. Many hold up a signboard of the particular hotel they are connected with and, if the one you want is there, you can get a free lift. The drawback with the taxis is that the hotel is then much less likely to offer you a discount, as it will be paying a hefty commission (up to 50% of the room) to the taxi driver.

If you book a room in advance, many hotels will pick you up for free and without commission.

Public buses leave from the main road – about 300m from the terminal – but they're only really practical if you have very little luggage and know exactly how to get to where you want to go.

From Kathmandu to the airport you should be able to get a taxi for Rs 300 during daylight hours, a bit more for a late or early flight.

Bicycle

Once you get away from the crowded streets of Kathmandu, cycling is a pleasure and, if you're in reasonable shape, this is the ideal way to explore the valley. See p38 for general information on biking, and p292 for some route ideas.

Mountain bikes cost around Rs 300 to Rs 500 per day for simple models. For longer trips around the valley, the major mountain-bike companies such as Dawn Till Dusk, Himalayan Mountain Bikes and Pathfinder Cycling hire out high-quality bikes with front suspension for around US$10 to US$12 per day. See p39 for company details.

If you want to make an early start, most places are happy to give you the bike the evening before. For all bikes, negotiate discounts for rentals of more than a day. Check the brakes before committing and be certain to lock the bike whenever you leave it.

Cycle-Rickshaw

Cycle-rickshaws cost around Rs 50 for short rides around Thamel or the old town but you can expect to have to haggle hard. It's essential to agree on a price before you start.

Motorcycle

There are a number of motorcycle rental operators in Thamel. You will have to leave your passport as deposit. For Rs 600 per day you'll get a 150cc Indian-made Hero Honda or Pulsar road bike, which is generally fine for road trips in the Kathmandu Valley.

Officially, you need an international driving licence to ride a motorbike in Nepal. This regulation hasn't been enforced for years but recent reports suggest traffic police are targeting foreigners on this and other hitherto disregarded traffic violations in an attempt to raise funds. A traffic fine will set you back around Rs 1000.

Motorcycles can be great fun outside the town, once you master the traffic. The main problem is getting out of Kathmandu, which can be a stressful, choking and dangerous experience. You will need a pair of goggles and some kind of face mask (available in most pharmacies).

Fuel currently costs Rs 110 (and rising) per litre; you'll only need a couple of litres for a day trip. Beyond the ring road petrol stations are few and far between.

Singh Motorbike Centre (Map p80; ☑9851040595; ☺8am-7pm) is a reliable place for bike hire. Indian-made Pulsar 150/200cc (Rs 600/800) motorbikes are most commonly available, though you might find a cheaper Hero Honda or Yamaha.

Pheasant Transportation Service (Map p80; ☑4701090; biketournepal@yahoo.com), in a side street off the central Thamel junction, has somewhat more elastic prices, ranging from Rs 500 for an older model Pulsar to Rs 1200 for an Enfield Bullet.

Taxi

Taxis are quite reasonably priced, though few taxi drivers use the meters in these days of rising fuel prices. Shorter rides around town (including to the bus station) cost around Rs 150. Night-time rates (between 10pm and 6am) cost 50% more.

Most taxis are tiny Suzuki Marutis, which can just about fit two backpackers and their luggage.

The closest taxi stand to Thamel is on Tridevi Marg, close to the junction with Jyatha Rd (Map p80). Taxis can be booked in advance on ☑4420987; at night call ☑4224374.

Other approximate taxi fares from Thamel:
Bhaktapur Rs 700 to Rs 800
Bodhnath Rs 300
Budhanilkantha Rs 500
Changu Narayan Rs 1500
Nagarkot Rs 2500
Pashupatinath Rs 250
Patan Rs 250
Swayambhunath Rs 250

AROUND KATHMANDU

There are several outlying attractions inside the ring road that surrounds Kathmandu. All can be reached by taxi or rickshaw, by rented bicycle or motorcycle, or on foot. For sights and spectacles outside the ring road, see p115.

Swayambhunath

A journey up to the Buddhist temple and Unesco World Heritage Site of **Swayambhunath** (foreigner/SAARC Rs 200/50) is one of the definitive experiences of Kathmandu. Mobbed by monkeys and soaring above the city on a lofty hilltop, the 'Monkey Temple' is a fascinating, chaotic jumble of Buddhist and Hindu iconography.

The compound is centred on a gleaming white stupa, topped by a gilded spire painted with the eyes of the Buddha. Depictions of these eyes appear all over the Kathmandu Valley.

Coming to Swayambhunath is an intoxicating experience, with ancient carvings jammed into every spare inch of space and the smell of incense and butter lamps hanging heavy in the air. The mystical atmosphere is heightened in the morning and evening by local devotees who make a ritual circumnavigation of the stupa, spinning the prayer wheels set into its base. It is a great place to watch the sun set over Kathmandu.

According to legend, the Kathmandu Valley was once a lake – geological evidence supports this – and the hill now topped by Swayambhunath rose spontaneously from the waters, hence the name *swayambhu*, meaning 'self-arisen'.

The emperor Ashoka allegedly visited 2000 years ago, but the earliest confirmed activity here was in AD 460. During the 14th century, Mughal invaders from Bengal broke open the stupa in the search for gold, but the stupa was restored and expanded over the following centuries.

◉ Sights

Eastern Stairway   MONUMENT

There are two ways to approach Swayambhunath temple, but by far the most atmospheric is the stone pilgrim stairway that climbs the eastern end of the hill. Constructed by King Pratap Malla in the 17th century, this steep stone staircase is mobbed by troops of rhesus macaques, teenage skater punks who have made an artform of sliding down the steep handrails. A word of advice: keep foodstuffs out of sight of these simian hoodlums!

From a collection of brightly painted Buddha statues at the bottom of the hill, the steps climb past a series of chaityas and bas-reliefs, including a stone showing the birth of the Buddha, with his mother Maya Devi grasping a tree branch. You can often see Tibetan astrologers reading fortunes here. At the top, the steps are lined with pairs of Garudas, lions, elephants, horses and peacocks, the 'vehicles' of the Dhyani Buddhas.

> ### ⓘ DAY TRIPS FROM KATHMANDU
>
> The great thing about Kathmandu is that there are so many fantastic sights just a couple of kilometres outside the city centre. You can check out any of the following sites and still be back in Thamel for the start of happy hour:
>
> » **Bhaktapur** – see p140
>
> » **Patan** – see p126
>
> » **Bodhnath** – see p118
>
> » **Budhanilkantha** – see p124

Near the end of the climb is the ticket office (there's another one at the western entrance, near the tourist bus park). When you reach the top, remember to walk around the stupa in a clockwise direction.

Great Thunderbolt   MONUMENT

At the top of the eastern stairway is an enormous, brass-plated dorje (thunderbolt), one of the core symbols of Tibetan Buddhism. Known as the *vajra* in Sanskrit, the thunderbolt is a symbol of the power of enlightenment, which destroys ignorance, but is itself indestructible. In rituals the dorje is used to indicate male power, while female power is represented by a ceremonial bell.

Around the pedestal supporting the symbol are the animals of the Tibetan calendar; flanking the plinth are the **Anantapura** and **Pratapura** temples, two slender, Indian-style shikharas built by King Pratap Malla in the 17th century. Nearby is a viewpoint and a raised area with telescopes for hire.

Swayambhunath Stupa   STUPA

The Swayambhunath stupa is one of the crowning glories of Kathmandu Valley architecture. This perfectly proportioned monument seems to hint at some celestial perfection with its gleaming, gilded spire and whitewashed dome. From the spire, four faces of the Buddha stare out across the valley in the cardinal directions. The nose-like squiggle below the piercing eyes is actually the Nepali number *ek* (one), signifying unity, and above is a third eye signifying the insight of the Buddha. The entire structure of the stupa is symbolic – the white dome represents the earth, while the 13-tiered, beehivelike structure at the top symbolises the 13 stages that humans must pass through to achieve nirvana.

The base of the central stupa is ringed by prayer wheels embossed with the sacred mantra *om mani padme hum* ('hail to the jewel in the lotus'). Pilgrims circuiting the stupa spin each one as they pass by. Fluttering above the stupa are thousands of prayer flags, with similar mantras, which are said to be carried to heaven by the winds. Set in ornate plinths around the base of the stupa are statues representing the Dhyani Buddhas – Vairocana, Ratnasambhava, Amitabha, Amocha Siddhi (Amoghasiddhi) and Aksobhya – and their shaktis (consorts). These deities represent the five qualities of Buddhist wisdom.

Swayambhunath

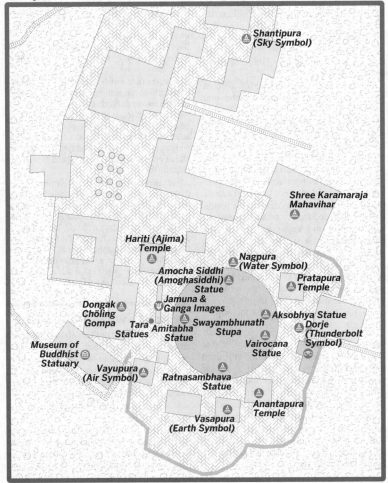

Stupa Platform   MONUMENT

The great stupa is surrounded on all sides by a veritable sculpture garden of religious monuments. At the rear of the stupa, next to a small, poorly lit **museum** of Buddhist statuary, is the Kargyud-school **Dongak Chöling gompa**, set above a brick *path*. Take your shoes off to view the murals inside.

North of the pilgrim shelter is the pagoda-style **Hariti (Ajima) Temple**, with a beautiful image of Hariti, the goddess of smallpox. This Hindu goddess, who is also responsible for fertility, illustrates the seamless interweaving of Hindu and Buddhist beliefs in Nepal.

Mounted on pillars near the Hariti Temple are figures of **Tara** making the gesture of charity, with an upturned palm. In fact, there are two Taras – Green Tara and White Tara – said to be the Chinese and Nepali wives of King Songtsen Gampo, the first royal patron of Buddhism in Tibet. The Taras are also female consorts to two of the Dhyani Buddhas.

Nearby, bronze images of the river goddesses **Jamuna** and **Ganga** guard an eternal flame in a cage. Northwest of these statues is a garden of ancient chaityas, and at the back of this group is a slick black statue of **Dipankara**, carved in the 7th century. Also known as the 'Buddha of Light', Dipankara is one of the 'past Buddhas' who achieved enlightenment before the time of Siddhartha Gautama, the historical Buddha. Also note the **black chaitya** at the north end of the courtyard, set atop a yoni – a clear demonstration of the mingling of Hindu and Buddhist symbology.

Back at the northeast corner of the complex is the **Shree Karmaraja Mahavihar**, a Buddhist temple enshrining a 6m-high figure of Sakyamuni, the historical Buddha. A prayer service takes place every day at around 4pm, accompanied by a cacophony of crashing cymbals, honking horns and the rumbling chanting of Sutras (Buddhist texts).

Symbols of the five elements – earth, air, water, fire and ether – can be found around the hilltop. Behind the Anantapura temple are shrines dedicated to **Vasupura**, the earth symbol, and **Vayupura**, the air symbol. **Nagpura**, the symbol for water, is a stone set in a muddy pool just north of the stupa, while **Agnipura**, the symbol for fire, is the red-faced god on a polished boulder on the northwestern side of the platform. **Shantipura**, the symbol for the sky, is north of the platform, in front of the Shantipura building.

Western Stupa   SHRINE

If you follow either path leading west from the main stupa, you will reach a smaller **stupa** near the car park for tourist buses. Just behind is a **gompa** surrounded by rest houses for pilgrims and an important **shrine** to Saraswati, the goddess of learning. At exam time, many scholars come here to improve their chances, and school children fill the place during Basanta Panchami, the Festival of Knowledge.

ℹ Getting There & Away

You can approach Swayambhunath by taxi (Rs 250), by bicycle or as part of an easy stroll from Kathmandu. Taxis can drop you at the tourist bus park at the western end of the hill or the steep pilgrim stairway at the eastern end of the hill.

Safa (electric) tempo 20 (Rs 13) shuttles between Swayambhunath's eastern stairway and Kathmandu's Sundhara district (near the main post office).

Walking & Cycling

There are two possible walking or bicycle routes to Swayambhunath – using both offers a useful circuit, either in the direction described or in reverse, though traffic can make walking hard work.

Starting at the Chhetrapati Tole junction near Thamel, the road runs west to the Vishnumati River (with Swayambhunath clearly visible in the distance), passing the pagoda-style Indrani Temple, which is surrounded by ghats used for cremations.

Cross the river and detour right to the Shobabaghwati Temple, with its gaudy painted statues of Shiva and other Hindu deities. Return to the bridge and follow the steps uphill past the courtyard-style Bijeshwari Temple, following an arcade of shops selling *malas* (prayer beads) and *gau* (Tibetan-style amulets) that lead to the statue-lined stairway at the east end of Swayambhunath hill.

You can return to the centre of Kathmandu via the National Museum. From the bottom of the eastern stairway, go west around the base of the hill and turn left at the first major junction, past the Benchen monastery and cafe, then left again at the large T-junction to reach the museum. Continue southeast along this road to reach Tankeshwor, then turn left again and cross the Vishnumati River. On the other side, it's a short walk north to the bottom of Durbar Sq.

Around Swayambhunath

There are several other sights scattered around Swayambhunath. Before moving on, get a taste of Tibet by joining the old pilgrims on a clockwise kora (pilgrim circuit) around the base of the hill, passing a series of gigantic chörtens (reliquary shrines), *mani dungkhor* (giant prayer wheels) and Buddhist chapels.

Starting from the eastern gateway to Swayambhunath, walk around the southwest side of the hill, passing the turn-off to the tourist bus park and the Natural History Museum. The path meets the Ring Rd at **Buddha Amideva Park** (Map p56), a compound containing three enormous shining golden statues of Sakyamuni Buddha, four-armed Chenresig and Guru Rinpoche, constructed in 2003. Return past the string of chörtens and chapels along the north side of the hill.

◉ Sights

Natural History Museum   MUSEUM
(Map p56; foreigner/SAARC Rs 50/20; ⊙10am-5pm Sun-Fri) Below Swayambhunath, on the road to the tourist bus park, this neglected museum offers a faded but quirky collection of exhibits, including varnished crocodiles,

model dinosaurs and mounted animal heads that look suspiciously like hunting trophies.

National Museum   MUSEUM
(Map p56; ☑4271504; www.nationalmuseum.gov.
np; Tahachal; foreigner/SAARC Rs 100/40, camera/
video Rs 50/200; ☉10.30am-4.30pm Wed-Sun,
to 2.30pm Mon Apr-Oct, to 3.30pm Wed-Sun, to
2pm Mon Nov-Mar) Around 800m south of
Swayambhunath at Chhauni, the walled
compound here looks a little moth-eaten
and overgrown, but there are some interesting treasures on display and the museum is
never crowded.

As you enter the compound, turn left to
reach the **Judda Art Gallery**, which contains
some exquisite stone, metal and terracotta
statues of Nepali deities and fabulous *paubha*
cloth paintings. Look out for the 1800-year-
old life-sized statue of standing Jayavarma,
only discovered in 1992, as well as the statue
of buffalo-headed Sukhavara Samvara with
34 arms, 16 feet and 10 faces! You can climb
to the top of the mandala-shaped building for
great views of Swayambhunath, but watch
your footing as there are no guard rails.

At the back of the compound is the temple-style **Buddhist Art Gallery**. As well as
Buddhist statues, votive objects, thangkas
and manuscripts as big as coffee tables, there
are some informative displays on mandalas
(geometric Buddhist diagrams). A highlight
here is the eighth-century stone depiction of
the birth of Buddha, showing Queen Maya
holding onto the branch of a tree.

To the north of the main compound,
housed in a handsome Rana-era palace, is
the **Historical Museum**, which displays a
blood-thirsty collection of weapons, including the personal *kukris* (daggers), *katars*
(punch-daggers), *tulwars* (curved swords)
and *khandas* (hatchet swords) of such national heroes as Prithvi Narayan Shah, the
founder of Nepal. Note the leather cannon
seized in the 1792 Nepal-Tibet War.

In the same building, the **Natural History Museum** displays stuffed animals and
old bones, including, bizarrely for this landlocked location, the jaws of a whale. Upstairs
are the rather matter-of-fact Numismatic
and Philatelic Museums.

Ticket sales stop an hour before closing
time; bags must be left in the free lockers
at the gate. See p110 for directions to the
museum.

Military Museum   MUSEUM
(Map p56;☑4271504; Tahachal; foreigner/SAARC
Rs 100/40, camera/video Rs 50/200; ☉10.30am-
4.30pm Wed-Sun, to 2.30pm Mon Apr-Oct, to
3.30pm Wed-Sun, to 2pm Mon Nov-Mar) Opposite
the National Museum in an army compound,
this will likely appeal only to fans of military
history. Highlights lined up in parade outside the museum include Nepal's first ever
Rolls-Royce, gifted by Queen Elizabeth II in
1961, and a Skyvan transport plane.

The interior displays lead past endless
paintings of death and mayhem depicting
Nepali battles over the centuries, including
several against British and Tibetans, as well
as an armoury (including a fine bazooka)
and the beds used by 'Mr Phillip' (Prince
Phillip) and his wife Liz during their state
visit in 1961. Look for the portrait of the
intriguing 18th-century queen Rajendra
Laxmi Devi Shah, who trained as a soldier
and led her army on three campaigns.

Around the Kathmandu Valley

Best Hikes

» Nagarkot to Dhulikhel (see boxed text, p170)

» Dhulikhel to Panauti via Namobuddha (p173)

» Gokarna Mahadev Temple to Bodhnath, via Kopan Monastery (see boxed text, p160)

Best Places to Stay

» Shivapuri Heights (p125)

» Famous Farm (p180)

» Traditional Homes Patan Durbar Square (p135)

» Last Resort (p178)

Why Go?

In many ways the Kathmandu Valley *is* Nepal. Created by the sword of the Buddhist deity Manjushri, the natural basin is a patchwork of terraced fields and sacred temple towns that showcase the glory of the architects and artisans of Nepal. The valley is literally full of medieval villages, centuries-old temples and sacred sites, while just beyond the valley rims lie Himalayan viewpoints and two adventurous roads to Tibet.

Aside from the great Unesco World Heritage Sites of Patan, Bodhnath and Bhaktapur, try to visit one or two of the smaller Newari villages off the mainstream tourist circuit. All of the attractions in this chapter can be explored by frequent minibuses, taxi, mountain bike, motorcycle, or even on foot, following a web of ancient trails. You'll likely see fewer tourists just 10km outside Kathmandu than you will if you trek for days through the Himalaya.

When to Go
Nagarkot

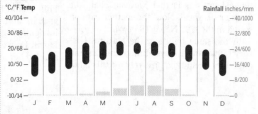

Mar–Apr Warm weather, green farmland and some spectacular chariot festivals.

Oct–Jan Clear views and sunny days but chilly nights at Nagarkot and Dhulikhel.

May–Sep Hot and humid, with regular rainfall and temperatures over 30°C, but the valley is green.

To Kakani (11km);
Trisuli Bazaar (66km);
Nuwakot (70km)
Dhunche (117km)

To Chisopani (4km)

Shivapuri Nagarjaun
National Park

Shivapuri
(2725m)

Nagi Gompa

Bhotichaur

Chule

Nagle

Shivapuri
Heights

Tinpiple

Budhanilkantha

Chowki
Bhanjyang

Nagarjun Hill
Nagarjun
Forest Reserve
Jamacho
(2095m)

Phulbari

Tokha
Village

Park Village
Resort

Mulkarkha

Sundarijal

Nagarkot to
Sundarijal trail

Bagdhara

Jarsingpouwa

Kopan
Monastery

Gokarna
Mahadev
Temple

Vajrayogini
Temple

Ichangu
Narayan

Balaju

Gokarna Mahadev
to Kopan &
Bodhnath trail

Kattike

Halchok

Gokarna Forest
Resort

Sankhu

Nagarkot to
Sankhu trail

Nagarkot

Ring

Rd

Bramhakhel

Chabahil

Jorpati

Mulpani

Changu
Narayan
Temple

Tharkot

KATHMANDU

Bodhnath

Bagmati River

Tribhuvan
Airport

Pashupatinath
Temple

Nagarkot to
Changu
Narayan trail

Lookout
Tower

Bode

Manohara River

Ghimiregaon

Nagadesh

Nagarkot to Nala
& Banepa trail

Kirtipur

Jawalakhel

Patan

Thimi

Balkumari
Temple

Bhaktapur

Nala

Panga

Chobar

Hanumante

Suriya
Binayak
Temple

Jal Binayak Temple
Taudaha Pond
Hattiban
Resort

Khokana

Karya
Binayak

Harisiddhi

Lubbhu

Sanga

Banepa

Champa
Devi
(2249m)

Dollu

Bungamati

Bandegaon

Vajra
Varahi

Bishankhu
Narayan

To Dhulikhel (3km);
Barabise (80km);
Kodari (100km);
Namobuddha

Neyndo Tashi
Choling

Pharping

Chapagaon

Godavari

Royal
Botanical
Gardens

Riyale

Dakshinkali

Godavari Kunda

Kushadevi

Panauti

Naudhara Kunda

Tika Bhairab

Lele

Godavari
Village
Resort

Pulchowki
(2760m)

To Borderlands (107km);
Last Resort (107km)

Bagmati River

Nakhu Khola

N   0   4 km
     0   2 miles

Around the Kathmandu Valley Highlights

1 Lose yourself in **Patan's** (p126) courtyards on a walking tour, soak in the glorious Newari architecture of its Durbar Sq and visit Patan Museum, the best in the country

2 Explore the fascinating backstreets of **Bhaktapur** (p140), Nepal's best-preserved medieval town

3 Join the Tibetan exiles on the kora (clockwise circuit) around the enormous **Bodhnath Stupa** (p120)

4 Have a hiking or biking mini-adventure in the little-visited towns of the Southern Valley – **Kirtipur** (p160), **Bungamati** (p164) and **Chobar** (p161)

5 Get the pulse racing on a bungee, canyoning or rafting trip at the adventure resorts of **Borderlands** (p178) or the **Last Resort** (p178), just a stone's throw from the Tibet border

6 Escape the crowds and relax at little-visited **Nuwakot** (p180), a historically important village with fine architecture

History

The legend that the Kathmandu Valley was formed from a vanished lake is in fact quite true. The uprising of the Himalaya trapped rivers draining south from Tibet, creating a vast lake that eventually burst its banks and drained away around 10,000 years ago.

As people settled the valley from the north and south, it became the biggest clearinghouse on the trade route from India to Tibet. Himalayan missionaries and saints transferred Buddhism across the Himalaya into Tibet and centuries later migrating Tibeto-Burman tribes carried Buddhism back into Nepal, fusing Tantric Indian beliefs with the ancient Bön religion of Tibet. This has resulted in a fascinating hybrid culture, where Hindu and Buddhist beliefs jointly infuse Nepali life.

Historically, the Kathmandu Valley has been the homeland of the Newars, great traders and craftspeople, of mixed Indian and Tibeto-Burman origin. Much of the iconography, architecture and culture associated with Nepal today is actually based on Newari culture. For more on the customs and traditions of the Newars, see p330.

The first formal records of Newari history come from the Licchavi era (AD 400 to 750), but the golden age of the Newars came in the 17th century when the valley was dominated by three rival city-states – Kantipur (Kathmandu), Lalitpur (Patan) and Bhadgaon (Bhaktapur) – all competing to outshine each other with architectural brilliance. The reign of the Malla kings (see p308) saw the construction of many of Nepal's most iconic palaces, temples and monuments.

The unification of Nepal in 1768–69 by Prithvi Narayan Shah signalled the end of this three-way struggle for supremacy. Nepali, an Indo-European language spoken by the Khas of western Nepal, replaced Newari as the country's language of administration and Kathmandu became the undisputed capital of the nation.

Dangers & Annoyances

If you explore the Kathmandu Valley on a rented motorcycle, be wary of the traffic police, particularly after dark. Locals are routinely stung with fines for trumped-up traffic offences and foreigners are being increasingly targeted.

Women in particular should avoid hiking alone in remote corners of the valley. Pulchowki Mountain south of Godavari has seen several robberies in recent years. For general security advice see p36.

ⓘ Getting Around

If you intend to do any biking, hiking or motorcycling, it's worth investing in Nepa Maps' rather useful 1:50,000 *Around the Kathmandu Valley* or Himalayan Maphouse's *Biking Around Kathmandu Valley*. Both are available from bookstores in Kathmandu.

BICYCLE & MOTORBIKE

By far the easiest and most economical way of getting around the valley is by rented bicycle or motorbike – see p39 for mountainbike rental companies. On day trips, give yourself time to get back to Kathmandu by nightfall – you really don't want to ride these roads after dark.

Once you get beyond the Kathmandu Ring Rd, there is surprisingly little traffic and the valley offers some spectacular riding country. However, take corners slowly as buses and trucks will not give way. Be sure to securely lock your bike or motorcycle when you stop, and carry plenty of petrol from Kathmandu as rural petrol stations regularly run dry.

See p292 and p295 for two ambitious but excellent cycling routes around the Kathmandu Valley.

BUS & TAXI

From Kathmandu's Ratna Park bus station, inexpensive public buses run to every town in the valley, though you may need to change in Patan or Bhaktapur. However, the buses can be incredibly crowded, and ye gods are they slow. As a more comfortable alternative, consider hiring a car or taxi – as a guide, a day hire to Bodhnath, Pashupatinath and Bhaktapur or to Dakshinkali, Chobar and Kirtipur costs around Rs 2900.

HIKING

A web of footpaths around the valley links its villages and towns and there are many interesting day hikes and overnight treks around the valley, allowing you to take shortcuts that are not accessible by bicycle or motorcycle. You can easily link several towns on foot and could even put together a multiday hike linking Kakani to Budhanilkantha, Chisopani, Nagarkot, Namobuddha and Panauti.

ORGANISED TOURS

Many of the travel agents in Thamel, in Kathmandu, can arrange day trips around the valley, but standards vary. See p39 for information on organised mountain-biking trips around the valley.

If you prefer a guided walk, **Wayfarers** (Map p80; ☑4266010; www.wayfarers.com.np; Thamel, Kathmandu) offers guided day hikes through Kirtipur, Khokana, Bungamati and Chapagaon (US$35 per person) on Wednesday and Saturday, which include lunch and transport. Three-day minitreks to Panauti, Namobuddha, Dhulikhel, Nagarkot and Sankhu (US$175 per person with accommodation) leave on Thursday and Sunday.

AROUND THE RING ROAD

There are several interesting sights just outside the Kathmandu Ring Rd, all accessible by public transport, on foot or by rented bike or motorcycle.

Pashupatinath

Nepal's most important Hindu temple stands on the banks of the holy Bagmati River, surrounded by a bustling market of religious stalls selling marigolds, prasad (offerings), incense, rudraksha beads, conch shells, pictures of Hindu deities and temples, *tika* powder in rainbow colours, glass lingams, models of Mt Meru and other essential religious paraphernalia.

At first glance, Pashupatinath might not look that sacred – the temple is just a few hundred metres from the end of the runway at Tribhuvan Airport, overlooking a particularly polluted stretch of the Bagmati. However, in religious terms, this is a powerhouse of Hindu spiritual power. Elsewhere in Nepal, Shiva is worshipped in his wrathful form as the destructive Bhairab, but at Pashupatinath he is celebrated as Pashupati, Lord of the Beasts.

Sadhus and devotees of Shiva flock to Pashupatinath from across the subcontinent and many Nepalis choose to be cremated on the banks of the holy river. Even the kings of Nepal used to come here to ask for a blessing from Pashupati before commencing any important journey. Nepal's Dalit ('untouchable') community was only allowed access to the shrine in 2001.

Non-Hindus cannot enter the main temple, but the surrounding complex of Shaivite shrines, lingams and ghats (stone steps) is fascinating and highly photogenic. Groups of 'photo me' sadhus loiter around in out-

TOP FIVE TEMPLES IN THE KATHMANDU VALLEY

The following are our five favourite temples in the valley:

» **Changu Narayan** (p156) A treasure house of sculpture at this Unesco World Heritage Site.

» **Gokarna Mahadev Temple** (p157) A visual A to Z of Hindu iconography.

» **Indreshwar Mahadev Temple** (p176) A perfect temple by a mystical river confluence south of the highway to Tibet.

» **Budhanilkantha** (p124) Impressive monolithic stone carving of a sleeping Vishnu.

» **Dakshinkali** (p164) Spooky place of blood sacrifices and wrathful goddesses.

landish paraphernalia hoping to make a little money posing for tourist photos. Be respectful with your camera at the funeral ghats – you wouldn't take snaps of bereaved relatives at a funeral back home, so don't do it here.

You can visit Pashupatinath as a half-day trip from central Kathmandu and walk on easily to Bodhnath. There are ticket booths near the southern entrance to the main Pashupatinath temple and next to the Guhyeshwari Temple, where foreigners must pay the entrance fee. Guides can be hired from the office of the **Guide Association of Pashupatinath** (1½hr tours Rs 500; ⊙9am-5pm) close to the main temple.

The best times to visit are early in the morning or around 6pm during evening prayers.

◉ Sights

Pashupatinath Temple   HINDU TEMPLE
(admission Rs 500, child under 10yr free; ⊙24hr) Only Hindus are allowed to enter the compound of the famous main temple here, but you can catch tantalising glimpses of what is going on inside from several points around the perimeter wall. From the main gate on the west side of the compound, you can view the mighty golden behind of an enormous brass statue of **Nandi**, Shiva's bull. Inside

Pashupatinath

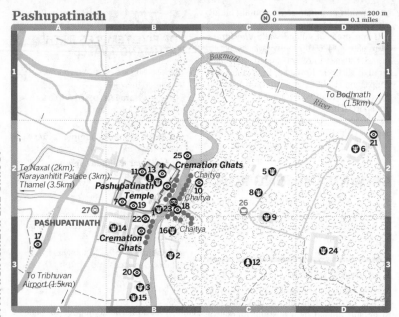

the shrine, hidden from view, is a black, four-headed image of Pashupati.

The pagoda-style temple was constructed in 1696 but Pashupatinath has been a site of Hindu and Buddhist worship for far longer. If you climb the terraces to the west of the temple, you can look down on the gilded rooftop. There are more views from the top of the terraces on the east side of the Bagmati, inside the temple complex.

If you follow the road running south from the side entrance to the temple, you will pass the **Panch Deval** (Five Temples), a former temple complex that now acts as a social welfare centre for destitute old people. A donation box offers a way for visitors to directly contribute.

Riverbanks of the Bagmati   RELIGIOUS
Despite being clogged with garbage and black with pollution, the fetid Bagmati is actually an extremely sacred river and Pashupatinath is the Nepali equivalent of Varanasi on the sacred River Ganges. The **cremation ghats** along the Bagmati are used for open-air cremations, but only members of the royal family can be cremated immediately in front of Pashupatinath Temple. The funerals of 10 members of the Nepali royal family took place here after the massacre in 2001 (see the boxed text, p317).

Funerals of ordinary Nepalis take place daily on the ghats to the south of the temple. Bodies are wrapped in shrouds and laid out along the riverbank, then cremated on a wooden pyre in a surprisingly businesslike way. It's a powerful place to contemplate notions of death and mortality. Needless to say, this is a private time for relatives to grieve and tourists intruding with cameras is not appropriate.

At the north end of the ghats, best viewed from across the river, are a series of **yogis' caves** used as shelters in medieval times.

If you walk south along the west bank, you will pass a huge uprooted **lingam** and a small 7th-century **standing Buddha image**, next to the **Raj Rajeshwari Temple**, with its unusual rounded stucco outbuildings.

Bachhareshwari Temple   HINDU TEMPLE
Between the two groups of ghats on the west bank of the Bagmati is this small, 6th-century temple, decorated with Tantric figures, skeletons and erotic scenes. It is said that human sacrifices were once made at this temple as part of the Maha Shivaratri Festival (p118).

East Bank   HINDU TEMPLES
Two footbridges cross the Bagmati in front of the Pashupatinath Temple, entering a

Pashupatinath

garden of stone terraces covered in dozens of small **Shiva shrines**. These one-room temples are often used as lodgings by wandering sadhus and each contains a central Shiva lingam. Although the shrines are built in many styles, all share certain design features – note the mask of Bhairab, Shiva's fearsome incarnation, on the south wall, and the Nandi statue and animal-head water spout to the north. Look for the interesting **lingam with the Shiva face** at the northern end of the group.

Two flights of steps lead up the hillside between the shrines, passing the elaborately frescoed **Ram Temple**, which is often thronged by visiting sadhus, especially during the Maha Shivaratri Festival. At the top, where the path enters the forest, a side track leads north along the top of the terraces to an excellent **viewpoint** over the Pashupatinath Temple. Look for the enormous **golden trident** on the northern side of the temple and the golden figure of the king kneeling in prayer under a protective hood of nagas (serpent deities) to the south.

On the ghats below this terrace, devotees ritually bathe in the dubious-looking waters of the Bagmati and holy men perform rituals on the stone steps. Look out for children retrieving coins from the murky river using a magnet on the end of a string.

Vishwarup Temple   HINDU TEMPLE
The steps continue up the hill from the terraces to a convenient cafe and another huge complex of **Shiva shrines** on the edge of the forest that is well worth exploring. There are more than 50 shrines here and the variety of architectural forms is quite stunning. If you bear right at the top of the hill, you will reach the courtyard-style Vishwarup Temple, topped by a Mughal-style onion dome. You can peek through the gates but only Hindus may enter.

Gorakhnath Temple   HINDU TEMPLE
Turning left at the top of the hill will take you to the towering red-and-white shikhara (temple with tall corn cob–like spire) of the Gorakhnath Temple, dedicated to the 11th-century yogi who founded the Shaivite monastic tradition and invented Hatha yoga. Past the Gorakhnath Temple, the path drops down through the forest, passing the **Mrigasthali Deer Park**, a fitting blend of nature and religion, as Shiva is said to have frolicked here once in the shape of a golden deer.

Guhyeshwari Temple   HINDU TEMPLE
The path drops out of the forest to the side of the large, courtyard-style Guhyeshwari Temple, built by King Pratap Malla in 1653 and dedicated to Parvati (the wife of Shiva) in her terrible manifestation as Kali. Entry is banned to non-Hindus, but you can peek into the compound from the path to see the four huge gilded snakes that support the roof finial.

The riverbank in front of the temple is lined with Shiva shrines and octagonal plinths for ritual bathing.

The temple's curious name comes from the Nepali words *guhya* (vagina) and *ish-wari* (goddess) – literally, it's the temple of the goddess' vagina! According to legend, the father of Parvati insulted Shiva and the goddess became so incensed that she burst into flames, providing the inspiration for the practice of *sati,* where widows were burned alive on the funeral pyres of their husbands. The grieving Shiva wandered the earth with the disintegrating corpse of Parvati and her genitals fell at Guhyeshwari. However, Indian Hindus make the same claim for the Kamakhya Temple at Guwahati in Assam.

✥✥ Festivals & Events

Pashupatinath is generally busiest (with genuine pilgrims rather than tourists) from 6am to 10am and again from 6pm to 7.30pm, especially on *ekadashi,* which falls 11 days after the full and new moon each month. As night falls, pilgrims release butter lamps on boats made of leaves onto the Bagmati as part of the *arati* (light) ceremony.

Maha Shivaratri Festival   RELIGIOUS
In the Nepali month of Falgun (in February or March), pilgrims throng to Pashupatinath from all over Nepal and India to celebrate Shiva's birthday. It's an incredible spectacle, and a chance to see members of some of the more austere Shaivite sects performing rituals through the night.

Bala Chaturdashi   RELIGIOUS
During the new moon of November/December, pilgrims hold a lamplit vigil and bathe in the holy Bagmati the following morning. Pilgrims then scatter sweets and seeds around the compound for their deceased relatives to enjoy in the afterlife.

❶ Getting There & Away

From Kathmandu, the most convenient way to Pashupatinath is by taxi (Rs 250 to Rs 300 from Thamel) – taxis usually drop you off by the police station at Gaushala, but you can ask to be dropped off closer to the temples.

If you are walking or cycling, head east from the Narayanhitit Palace through Naxal, meeting the Ring Rd near the Jayabageshwari Temple, with its fine painting of Bhairab. To reach Pashupatinath Temple, cross the Ring Rd and follow the winding lanes lined with religious stalls towards the Bagmati.

If you want to walk on from Pashupatinath to Bodhnath, it's a pleasant 20-minute walk through villages and farmland, offering a window onto ordinary life in the Kathmandu 'burbs. Take the footbridge across the river in front of the Guhyeshwari Temple and head north for five minutes, then turn right by a temple surrounding a large pipal tree. At the next junction follow the Buddha's example and take the middle (straight) path, which eventually emerges on the main Bodhnath road, right across from the stupa.

Chabahil

East of the centre of Kathmandu, on the way to Bodhnath, the suburb of Chabahil has a number of historic temples and shrines. Right on the Ring Rd is the imposing **Chabahil Stupa** (admission free), the fourth largest stupa in the Kathmandu area after Bodhnath, Swayambhunath and the Kathesimbhu Stupa near Thahiti Chowk. According to legend, the stupa was constructed by Charumati, the daughter of Ashoka, but it has been patched up numerous times, most recently in 2002, when the tower cracked because of vibrations from passing traffic.

If you take the lane just north of the stupa, and turn left, you will reach the **Charamuti Vihar**, a medieval Buddhist monastery that used to house the monks who tended the stupa. Continuing past this turning will take you to the revered **Chandra Binayak Ganesh Temple**, enshrining a tiny silver image of Ganesh. The courtyard is full of *tika*-powder-covered statues – note the Budhanilkantha-style statue of Narayan reclining on his serpent bed, next to a human figure made of beaten brass panels.

Bodhnath (Boudha)
🎵 01

There is nowhere quite like Bodhnath. Asia's largest stupa pulses with life as thousands of pilgrims gather daily to make a ritual circumnavigation of the dome, beneath the watchful eyes of the Buddha, which gaze out from the gilded central tower. Tibetan monks in maroon robes and shaved heads wander the prayer flag–decked streets while pilgrims spin prayer wheels and stock up on yak butter and *tsampa* (roasted barley flour). This is one of the few places in the world where Tibetan Buddhist culture is accessible and unfettered, and the lanes around the stupa are crammed with monasteries and workshops producing butter lamps, ceremo-

Bodhnath (Boudha)

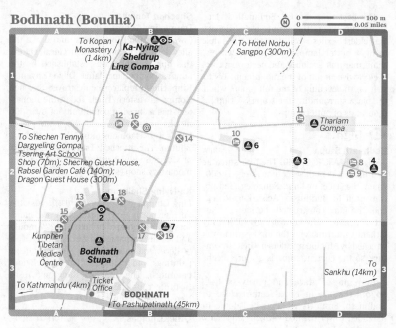

Bodhnath (Boudha)

◎ **Top Sights**

Bodhnath Stupa....................................A3
Ka-Nying Sheldrup Ling Gompa............B1

◎ **Sights**

1 Guru Lhakhang Gompa B2
2 Hariti (Ajima) Shrine A2
3 Pal Dilyak Gompa.................................D2
4 Pal Nye Gompa D2
5 Rangjung Yeshe Institute.....................B1
6 Sakya Tharig Gompa............................C2
7 Samtenling Gompa...............................B3

◎ **Sleeping**

8 Lotus Guest House..............................D2
9 Pema Guest House...............................D2

10 PRK Guest House.................................C2
11 Tharlam Guest House........................... D1
12 Valley Guest House..............................B1

✕ **Eating**

13 Café du Temple A2
14 Double Dorjee Restaurant....................B2
15 Flavor's Café A2
16 Garden Kitchen.....................................B1
17 Saturday Café.......................................B3
18 Stupa View Restaurant.........................B2
19 White Dzambala Tibetan
     Restaurant..B3

nial horns, Tibetan drums, monks' headgear and the other paraphernalia essential for Tibetan Buddhist life.

Historically, the stupa was an important staging post on the trade route between Lhasa and Kathmandu, and Tibetan traders would pray here for a safe journey before driving their yaks on to the high passes of the Himalaya. Today, most of the Tibetans living in the village of Boudha (pronounced *boe*-da) are refugees who fled China after 1959, but the stupa also attracts many Sherpas, descendants of Tibetan tribal people who migrated to Nepal in the 16th century. Many of the monasteries around the stupa have opened their doors to foreign students, so you'll see plenty of Western dharma students in maroon robes as you stroll around the backstreets.

The best time to visit Bodhnath is late afternoon, when the group tours depart and elderly exiles stroll down to the stupa to light butter lamps, spin prayer wheels, chant mantras, socialise and perform a ritual clockwise circuit of the monument. Try to visit on the evening of the full moon, when the plaza surrounding the stupa is lit up by thousands of butter lamps.

Sights

Bodhnath Stupa
STUPA

(foreigner/SAARC Rs 150/40) The first stupa at Bodhnath was built sometime after AD 600, when the Tibetan king, Songtsen Gampo, converted to Buddhism. According to legend, the king constructed the stupa as an act of penance after unwittingly killing his father. Unfortunately, the first stupa was wrecked by Mughal invaders in the 14th century, so the current stupa is a more recent construction.

In terms of grace and purity of line, no other stupa in Nepal comes close to Bodhnath. From its whitewashed dome to its gilded tower painted with the all-seeing eyes of the Buddha, the monument is perfectly proportioned and highly symbolic, serving as a three-dimensional reminder of the Buddha's path towards enlightenment.

The plinth represents earth, the *kumbha* (dome) is water, the harmika (square tower) is fire, the spire is air and the umbrella at the top is the void or ether beyond space. The 13 levels of the spire represent the stages that a human being must pass through to achieve nirvana.

Stupas were originally built to house holy relics and some claim that Bodhnath contains the relics of the past Buddha, Kashyapa, while others say it contains a piece of bone from the skeleton of Siddhartha Gautama, the historical Buddha. Around the base of the stupa are 108 small images of the Dhyani Buddha Amitabha (108 is an auspicious number in Tibetan culture) and a ring of prayer wheels, set in groups of four or five into 147 niches.

To reach the top of the plinth, look for the gateway at the north end of the stupa, beside a **small shrine** dedicated to Hariti (Ajima), the goddess of smallpox. The plinth is open from 5am to 6pm (till 7pm in summer), offering a raised viewpoint over the tide of pilgrims surging around the stupa. Note the committed devotees prostrating themselves full-length on the ground in the courtyard on the east side of the stupa.

Shechen Tennyi Dargyeling Gompa
TIBETAN MONASTERY

(www.shechen.org) To the west and down the alley leading to the Dragon Guest House, this huge complex was established by the famous Nyingmapa lama Dilgo Khyentse Rinpoche to replace the destroyed Shechen Gompa in eastern Tibet. Today, the monastery has a thriving community of over 300 monks and novices and the main prayer hall features fabulous murals by artists from Bhutan. The attached **Tsering Art School** produces Buddhist crafts that are sold in the monastery shop (see p123).

Ka-Nying Sheldrup Ling Gompa
TIBETAN MONASTERY

Further north, down a side alley, the handsome 'white gompa' is home to 225 monks and features ornamental gardens and a richly decorated interior with some exquisite paintings and thangkas (Tibetan religious paintings). The attached Rangjung Yeshe Institute runs classes in Tibetan, Sanskrit, Nepali and Buddhist studies.

Other Gompas
TIBETAN MONASTERIES

Since the Chinese sent thousands of troops to enforce their claim on Tibet in the 1950s, dozens of new monasteries have been constructed at Bodhnath by refugees. All welcome visitors but many close their doors in the middle of the day.

The main monasteries worth visiting are the **Guru Lhakhang Gompa**, **Samtenling Gompa**, **Sakya Tharig Gompa**, **Pal Dilyak Gompa** and **Pal Nye Gompa**. There's little to choose between them, so follow the sounds of booming trumpets and crashing cymbals to see which are open.

Most places have prayer sessions around 4am and 3pm.

Courses

Rangjung Yeshe Institute
BUDDHISM, LANGUAGES

(4483575; www.shedra.org) Located at Ka-Nying Sheldrup Ling Gompa, the institute offers a fairly advanced 10-day course ('Vajrayana empowerment') on Tibetan Buddhist teachings, practice and meditation, led by the monastery's abbot Chokyi Nyima Rinpoche. The course is held in mid-November and costs US$100. The institute also offers a university-accredited summer course in Buddhist theory and meditation (US$1760) in June/July, as well as eight-week summer Tibetan and Nepali language

VISITING TIBETAN MONASTERIES

Most Tibetan Buddhist monasteries welcome visitors and entering these atmospheric buildings can be a powerful and evocative experience. During the morning and evening prayers, the lamas (Tibetan Buddhist monks or priests) and novices gather to chant Buddhist texts, normally accompanied by a cacophony of crashing cymbals, thumping drums and booming Tibetan horns.

Tibetan gompas (monasteries) follow a remarkably consistent layout. The main prayer hall is invariably decorated with intricate murals depicting various Buddhas, bodhisattvas and protectors, who also appear on dangling thangkas (Tibetan religious paintings) edged with brocade and in statue form behind the main altar. Pick up the booklet *Short Description of Gods, Goddesses and Ritual Objects of Buddhism and Hinduism in Nepal* (available in Nepali bookshops) for a guide to the myriad Buddhist deities.

Many gompas also have a library of cloth-wrapped, loose-leafed Buddhist manuscripts set into alcoves around the altar, which is frequently covered in offerings, including butter lamps and seven bowls of water. The throne of the abbot is often surrounded by pictures of past abbots and the Dalai Lama, the spiritual leader of Tibetan Buddhism and the representation on earth of Chenresig (Avalokiteshvara), the deity of compassion.

As you enter a monastery you will see murals of the four guardian protectors – fearsome-looking deities who scare away ignorance – and the Wheel of Life, a highly complex diagram representing the Buddha's insights into the way humans are chained by desire to the endless cycle of life, death and rebirth.

The front of a monastery may also feature enormous *mani dungkhor* – giant prayer wheels stuffed with thousands of copies of the Buddhist mantra *om mani padme hum* ('hail to the jewel in the lotus').

This mantra also appears on the smaller prayer wheels around the outer wall and on the fluttering prayer flags outside. On the monastery roof you may see a statue of two deer on either side of the Wheel of Law, symbolising the Buddha's first sermon at the deer park of Sarnath.

Cultural Considerations

Visitors are welcome in most monasteries, but stick to the following guidelines:

» Remove your shoes and hat before you enter a gompa.

» Ask before taking photos and avoid taking photos during prayers.

» Do not smoke anywhere in the main compounds.

» Do not step over or sit on the monks' cushions, even if no one is sitting on them.

» During ceremonies, enter quietly and stand by the wall near the main entrance; do not walk around while monks are engaged in rituals.

» Always walk around stupas and chörtens (Tibetan-style stupas) in a clockwise direction and, likewise, spin prayer wheels clockwise.

» It is appropriate to make an offering – a khata (Tibetan prayer scarf) is traditional, or cash donations help fund the monastery and its charitable works in the community.

courses, staying with local families. The noticeboard is a good place to find a language tutor or room for rent.

✨ Festivals & Events

Losar RELIGIOUS

Bodhnath goes into spiritual overdrive every year in February or March for the Tibetan New Year. Long copper horns are blown, a portrait of the Dalai Lama is paraded around, thousands of pilgrims throng the stupa, and monks from the surrounding monasteries perform masked *chaam* (religious dances).

Buddha Jayanti RELIGIOUS

April/May is another good time to visit, as Buddhists everywhere celebrate the birth of the Buddha. Thousands of butter lamps are lit by devotees and an image of the Buddha is paraded by elephant around the stupa.

🛏 Sleeping

The guesthouses in the tangle of lanes north and east of the stupa offer an interesting and much more peaceful alternative to basing yourself in Kathmandu.

Lotus Guest House GUESTHOUSE $
(☑4472320; s/d/tr Rs 400/700/750, without bathroom s/d Rs 350/600) This calm, contemplative guesthouse is located close to Pal Dilyak Gompa. Rooms are spread over two floors around a marigold-fringed garden lawn and the bathrooms are so clean they sparkle.

Pema Guest House GUESTHOUSE $
(☑4495662; pemaguesthouse@hotmail.com; r from Rs 850, without bathroom from Rs 500, deluxe r Rs 1050; ☎) This tidy house is set in a neat courtyard garden. The spacious rooms on the upper levels get lots of natural light and there are terraces on each level where you can sit and ponder the nature of existence. Ground-floor rooms are darker.

Tharlam Guest House GUESTHOUSE $
(☑4915878; tharlamgh@yahoo.com; s/d from Rs 400/600, ste Rs 1000; ☎) Part of the Tharlam Gompa, this huge place looks a bit like a Spanish holiday villa. Rooms have rather bright carpets but are large and well appointed, and there are stupa views from the rooftop.

Dragon Guest House HOTEL $
(☑4479562; dragon@ntc.net.np; d Rs 600, s/d without bathroom Rs 385/550) This friendly, family-run place is set in a peaceful location north of Shechen Tennyi Dargyeling Gompa, and staff keep the rooms and pleasant garden looking spick and span. To get here, walk north through the gate beside the Shechen Guest House.

Shechen Guest House GUESTHOUSE $
(☑4479009; www.shechenguesthouse.com.np; s/d/tr Rs 900/1235/1715; ☎) Located at the back of the Shechen Tennyi Dargyeling Gompa, this agreeable guesthouse caters to a mix of long-term dharma students, shaven-scalped Buddhist groups and ordinary travellers. Tibetan fabrics add a dash of colour to the uncluttered bedrooms and the attached **Rabsel Garden Café** cooks up excellent vegetarian food. To get here, enter the monastery compound and turn left, then right beside a line of giant chörten (Tibetan-style stupa).

Valley Guest House HOTEL $
(☑4915241; www.thevalleyguesthouse.com; s/d from Rs 1100/1650, ste Rs 2750; ☎) Owned by a Dutch-Nepali couple, this modern and marbly place is popular with long-term dharma students and there are excellent rooftop views to the Bodhnath Stupa. Rooms are very clean and spacious and some come with a balcony.

Hotel Norbu Sangpo HOTEL $$
(☑4482500; www.hotelnorbusangpo.com; s/d from US$20/30, apt US$35; ☎) Hidden away in the backstreets northeast of the Bodhnath Stupa, this very private place has delightful lawn seating and big rooms with all mod cons. There are common balconies on every level. The apartments offer easily the best value, with sitting room and kitchen and great-value monthly rates (US$315). Rates include tax.

PRK Guest House GUESTHOUSE $
(Pal Rabten Khansar; ☑4465055; www.sakyatharig.org.np; s/d Rs 660/880, deluxe r Rs 1100; @) This surprisingly stylish guesthouse is run by the next-door Sakya Tharig Gompa. The spacious, carpeted deluxe rooms are very comfortable and offer the best value; other rooms are smaller. Out back is an ornamental garden with a large stupa, plus there's a nice rooftop.

🍴 Eating

Buddhist Bodhnath is nirvana for vegetarians. Traveller-oriented rooftop restaurants ring the stupa and offer superlative views, or for cheaper eats, head to the back lanes radiating out from the stupa, where any building with a curtain across an open door is a local cafe serving Tibetan momos (dumplings) and *thukpa* (noodle soup). Unless otherwise stated, the following restaurants open from 8am to 9pm.

Flavor's Café INTERNATIONAL $$
(☑4498748; meals Rs 325-400; ☺7.30am-9.30pm; ☎☑) Formerly New Orleans, this well-run place has changed its name but not its menu, which covers everything from Cajun chicken to *tom yam* soup, plus good coffee and pastries. Choose a table in the calm, covered courtyard or upstairs on the roof, for partial stupa views.

Saturday Café VEGETARIAN $
(mains Rs 60-200; ☎☑) Looking more like something you'd find in Portland, Oregon, this multistorey cafe serves healthy vegetar-

ian meals, organic soups, excellent cakes and organic coffee. The mushroom momos and rhododendron squash are worth trying. Come early for a seat with a view on the rooftop.

Double Dorjee Restaurant   TIBETAN $
(dishes Rs 80-180) On the lane north of the stupa, this cosy Tibetan-run place caters to backpackers and the dharma crowd with rock-bottom prices, tasty Tibetan and Western food, and soft sofas to relax in.

Garden Kitchen   INTERNATIONAL $
(mains Rs 85-280) A partly open-air place near the Valley Guest House, serving the usual globe-trotting menu in quiet and pleasant surroundings. Reasonable prices attract many long-term dharma students.

Café du Temple   INTERNATIONAL $$
(☑2143256; www.cafedutemple.com.np; mains Rs 300-400, set meals Rs 500-600; ⊙from 9am) Run by the same people as the Café du Temple in Patan, this smart and efficient place targets tour groups with a variety of Indian, Chinese and Tibetan dishes, plus unbeatable views.

Stupa View Restaurant   INTERNATIONAL $$
(☑4914962; mains Rs 300-450, set meals Rs 700; ⊙9am-9pm; ☑) The views are as good as they claim at this superior traveller-oriented place to the north of the stupa. The meze platters for two are excellent, as are the vegetarian set meals and clay-oven pizzas.

White Dzambala Tibetan Restaurant   CHINESE $$
(mains Rs 320) It's hard not to feel a twinge of guilt tucking into Chinese food in Tibetan Bodhnath, but this doesn't seem to deter the local Tibetan businessmen and monks who come here to tuck into authentic Sichuanese *gongbao jiding* (chicken with peanuts) or to nurse a *wanzi* fruit tea in the charming garden pavilions. It's just 40m from the stupa but sees almost no tourists.

🛍 Shopping

The stupa is ringed by shops selling Tibetan crafts, thangkas, votive objects and Tibetan cowboy hats, but prices are high compared to other parts of Kathmandu so bargain hard. For tea bowls, butter lamps, prayer flags and juniper incense, try the shops on the alleyway leading north from the stupa.

Several shops sell Tibetan 'singing bowls', beloved by new age Tibetophiles, which have an alloy of seven metals that creates a ring-ing sound when you rotate a dowel around the rim, said to be conducive to meditative thought.

Tsering Art School Shop   HANDICRAFTS
(Shechen Tennyi Dargyeling Gompa; ⊙9am-5pm Mon-Fri, to noon Sat) The shop at Shechen gompa has an on-site tailor and a workshop that produces thangkas, incense and sculptures. The shop also sells Buddhist reference books and CDs.

ℹ Information

Dharma Cyber (per hr Rs 50; ⊙9am-7pm) One of many internet cafes and communications centres, north of the main stupa.
Kunphen Tibetan Medical Centre
(☑4251920; ⊙9am-noon & 2-5pm) If you fancy trying out Tibetan traditional medicine, pay a visit to this clinic near Tsamchen Gompa. Diagnosis is based on the speed and regularity of the pulse and the condition of the tongue, and illnesses are treated with Himalayan herbs.

ℹ Getting There & Away

From Kathmandu, the easiest way to reach Bodhnath is by taxi (Rs 300 one way), but you can also come by bicycle (watch the traffic), by bus from Ratna Park bus station (Rs 15, 30 minutes) or by tempo from Kantipath (Rs 15, routes 2 and 28).

There's also an interesting short walk between Bodhnath and Pashupatinath (see p118), or you could combine Bodhnath with a visit to Gokarna Mahadev Temple and Kopan Monastery (see the boxed text, p160).

Around Bodhnath

KOPAN MONASTERY
On a hilltop north of Bodhnath, **Kopan Monastery** (☑01-4821268; www.kopan-monastery.com) was founded by Lama Thubten Yeshe, who died in 1984, leading to a worldwide search for his reincarnation. A young Spanish boy, Osel Torres, was declared to be the reincarnated lama, providing the inspiration for Bernardo Bertolucci's film *Little Buddha*. Lama Tenzin Osel Rinpoche no longer resides at Kopan, but visitors are welcome to explore the monastery and many people come here to study Buddhist psychology and philosophy.

You can visit Kopan on the pleasant walk between Bodhnath and the Gokarna Mahadev Temple (see boxed text, p160) or even from Nagi Gompa in Shivapuri Nagarjun

National Park. A taxi here from Kathmandu costs Rs 400 to Rs 500.

☙ Courses

Kopan Monastery MEDITATION
(☎01-4821268; www.kopan-monastery.com) Kopan is probably the best place in the Himalaya to learn the basics of meditation and Tibetan Buddhism. The reasonably priced and popular seven-day (US$80) or 10-day (US$110) courses are generally given by foreign teachers. There's also a popular annual one-month course (US$430) held in November, followed by an optional seven-day retreat.

THE NORTHERN & NORTHWESTERN VALLEY

There are several interesting detours to the north and northwest of the capital, which can easily be visited by bus, tempo, taxi, rented bicycle or motorcycle, or even on foot.

Ichangu Narayan

About 3km northwest of Swayambhunath, **Ichangu Narayan** (admission free; ⊘dawn-dusk) is one of several important temples dedicated to Vishnu in his incarnation as Narayan, the 'eternal man'. Built in the two-tiered pagoda style, the temple was founded in around AD 1200 and its courtyard is dotted with ancient Garuda statues and other Vaishnavite symbols.

The walk here starts opposite the Buddha Amideva Park on the Ring Rd and climbs steeply through small villages to reach the temple compound. On the way you'll pass a line of handsome lotus-bud-style Shiva shrines.

Getting here from Kathmandu by bike is a long slog, but it's an easy freewheel on the way back down and you can break the trip at Swayambhunath.

Nagarjun Hill (Shivapuri Nagarjun National Park)

If you continue uphill from Balaju on the road towards Trisuli Bazaar, you'll reach this **protected area** (admission Rs 250; ⊘entry 7am-2pm, visitors must exit by 5pm), also known as the Rani Ban (Queen's Forest), now formally part of Shivapuri Nagarjun National Park. This protected forest is one of the last undamaged areas of woodland in the valley, providing a home for pheasants, deer and monkeys. It's a peaceful spot but safety is a consideration. Female visitors are discouraged from walking here alone after two foreign tourists were murdered in the reserve in 2005.

The 2095m summit of the hill – accessible by the winding unpaved road or a two-hour hike on the footpath leading directly up the hill – is a popular Buddhist pilgrimage site and there's a small shrine to Padmasambhava. The viewing tower offers one of the valley's widest mountain panoramas, stretching all the way from the Annapurnas to Langtang Lirung (a plaque identifies the peaks).

Several Kathmandu-based adventure companies run introductory rock-climbing courses here. **Hardcore Nepal** (Map p80; ☎9813463599; www.hardcorenepal.com; Bhagwati St, Thamel) offers a four-day climbing clinic (US$250), which teaches you the basics about knots, anchors and safety to give you the confidence to climb solo. The course is based in Nagarjun Hill, before moving onto more technical climbs in Hattiban and Bimalnagar. Hardcore also offers guided climbs (half/full day US$45/65) and morning abseils (US$25) here.

❶ Getting There & Away

The main entrance to the reserve is at Phulbari, about 2km north of Balaju. A ride up to the summit makes for a fine motorbike excursion.

Budhanilkantha

The Kathmandu Valley is awash with ancient temples and sacred sites, but Budhanilkantha is a little bit special. For one thing, it lies off the main traveller circuit, so most visitors are local devotees. This gives Budhanilkantha a uniquely mystical air – butter lamps flicker in the breeze, incense curls through the air, and devotees toss around *tika* powder like confetti.

The focal point of the devotions at Budhanilkantha is a large **reclining statue** (admission free; ⊘dawn-dusk) of Vishnu as Narayan, the creator of all life, who floats on the cosmic sea. From his navel grew a lotus and from the lotus came Brahma, who in turn created the world. The 5m-long Licchavi-style image was created in the 7th or 8th century from one monolithic piece of black stone and hauled here from outside the valley by devotees. It's one of the most impressive pieces of sculpture in Nepal, and that's saying something!

Only Hindus can approach the statue to leave offerings of fruit and flower garlands, but visitors can view the statue through the fence that surrounds the sacred tank. Narayan slumbers peacefully on the knotted coils of Ananta (or Shesha), the 11-headed snake god who symbolises eternity. In each hand, Narayan holds one of the four symbols of Vishnu: a chakra disc (representing the mind), a conch shell (the four elements), a mace (primeval knowledge) and a lotus seed (the moving universe).

Vaishnavism (the worship of Vishnu) was the main sect of Hinduism in Nepal until the early Malla period, when Shiva became the most popular deity. The Malla king Jayasthithi is credited with reviving the Vishnu cult by claiming to be the latest incarnation of this oft-incarnated god. Every subsequent king of Nepal has made the same claim, and because of this they are forbidden, on pain of death, from seeing the image at Budhanilkantha.

Vishnu is supposed to sleep through the four monsoon months and a great festival takes place at Budhanilkantha for **Haribodhini Ekadashi** – the 11th day of the Hindu month of Kartik (October–November) – when Vishnu is said to awaken from his annual slumber.

🛏 Sleeping & Eating

There are no budget sleeping options in the area. The road to the sacred pavilion is lined with bhojanalayas (stalls) serving *sel roti* (rice-flour doughnuts), *channa puri* (fried bread with chickpeas), pakora (battered vegetables) and outsized pappadums.

TOP CHOICE **Shivapuri Heights** COTTAGE $$
(☏01-4372518, 9851012245; www.shivapuricottage.com; s/d from US$60/90, without bathroom US$50/60, 2-/3-bedroom cottage US$140/290) Perched on the hillside above Budhanilkantha, Shivapuri Heights offers a peaceful, private bolthole away from the chaos of Kathmandu. There are two cottages for hire, both decked out with tasteful furniture and modern conveniences. You can rent the whole cottage (the larger one houses six) or just a room; either way, breakfast and dinner are included and staff are on hand to lead you on guided forest walks. It's a

15-minute uphill walk from Budhanilkantha; staff can arrange transport on request.

Park Village Resort RESORT $$
(☏01-4375280; www.ktmgh.com; s/d from US$60/70; ☀) Part of the Kathmandu Guest House group, this delightful hotel feels like a country retreat, despite being smack in the middle of Budhanilkantha. The tidy rooms and self-contained, comfortable cottages are surrounded by leafy gardens full of meditation spaces and statuary, and there's a lovely pool and spa. The hotel also offers various spa treatments and activities, including bird-spotting tours to Shivapuri Nagarjun National Park.

❶ Getting There & Away

From Kathmandu, No 5 minibuses run from the northern end of Kantipath to the main junction in Budhanilkantha (Rs 20, 35 minutes). There are also tempos (from Sundhara) and buses (from both Gongabu and Ratna Park bus stations). The shrine is about 100m uphill from the junction. From Thamel, a taxi costs around Rs 500 one way or Rs 1000 return.

By bicycle it's a gradual, uphill haul of 15km.

Shivapuri Nagarjun National Park

The northern part of the Kathmandu Valley rises to the sprawling forests of **Shivapuri Nagarjun National Park** (☏01-4370355; admission Rs 250, mountain bike Rs 500), upgraded to national park status in 2002 to protect the valley's main water source, as well as 177 species of birds and numerous rare orchids. This is one of the last areas of woodland left in the valley, and the forest is alive with monkeys, and maybe even leopards and bears.

In the past the park was mainly visited by trekkers en route to Helambu, but today the reserve is a popular destination for birdwatching tours from Kathmandu. Several trekking and mountain-bike routes crisscross the park, including the challenging Scar Rd cycle path – see p292.

You can combine a nature-spotting tour with a trip to the Tibetan nunnery of **Nagi Gompa**, about 3km uphill from the main gate above Budhanilkantha. Around 100 nuns are resident and there are soaring valley views – you can walk here from Budhanilkantha in 1½ hours or drive in 20 minutes by motorcycle or hired 4WD.

Bodhnath's Ka-Nying Sheldrup Ling Gompa holds **retreats** here for foreign students every November.

From the gompa it's possible to climb steeply for about three hours to reach **Shivapuri Peak** (2725m), via Baghdwar (where the source of the holy Bagmati River pours out of two stone tiger mouths), returning to the park entrance via the Pani Muhan water tank, for a very long day of around seven hours. This is a serious hike that you shouldn't do alone. Take a map, plenty of water and preferably a guide.

There are several easier **walks** from Nagi Gompa. Consider the relaxing downhill stroll to Budhanilkantha, or continue south along the ridgeline for three hours to reach Kopan Monastery and Bodhnath. Another good option on foot or by mountain bike is to follow the dirt track east to Mulkarkha and then descend to Sundarijal – a mostly level 11km trip.

PATAN

📝 01 / POP 190,000

Once a fiercely independent city-state, Patan (pronounced *pah*-tan) is now almost a suburb of Kathmandu, separated only by the murky Bagmati River. Many locals still call the city by its original Sanskrit name of Lalitpur (City of Beauty) or by its Newari name, Yala. Almost everyone who comes to Kathmandu also visits Patan's spectacular Durbar Sq – arguably the finest collection of temples and palaces in the whole of Nepal.

Another good reason to come here is to take advantage of the shops and restaurants set up to cater to the aid workers and diplomats who live in the surrounding suburbs. Then there are Patan's fair-trade shops, selling superior handicrafts at fair prices and channelling tourist dollars to some of the most needy people in Nepal.

Most people visit Patan on day trips from Kathmandu and, as a result, the accommodation offerings are rather limited. On the flip side, Patan becomes a different place once the crowds of day-trippers retreat across the Bagmati. If you stay here, you'll be able to explore the myriad *tole* (squares) and bahal (courtyards) at your leisure.

History

Patan has a long Buddhist history, which has even had an influence on the town's Hindu temples. The four corners of the city are marked by stupas said to have been erected by the great Buddhist emperor Ashoka in around 250 BC.

The town was ruled by local noblemen until King Shiva Malla of Kathmandu conquered the city in 1597, temporarily unifying the valley. Patan's major building boom took place under the Mallas in the 16th, 17th and 18th centuries.

◉ Sights

Most of the famous sights are centred on Durbar Sq. Don't miss the walking tour of the courtyards to the north (p136). We describe the temples in Durbar Sq as you visit them from north to south.

DURBAR SQUARE

As in Kathmandu, the ancient Royal Palace of Patan faces on to a magnificent **Durbar Square** (Royal Square; Map p132; foreigner/SAARC Rs 200/25; ⊙ticket office 7am-7pm). This concentrated mass of temples is perhaps the most visually stunning display of Newari architecture to be seen in Nepal, despite current renovation and scaffolding. Temple construction in the square went into overdrive during the Malla period (from the 14th to 18th centuries), particularly during the reign of King Siddhinarsingh Malla (1619–60).

The entry fee is payable at the southern end of Durbar Sq – for repeated visits ensure that your visa validity date is written on the back of your ticket.

Bhimsen Temple   TEMPLE
(Map p132) At the northern end of Durbar Sq, the Bhimsen Temple is dedicated to the god of trade and business, which may explain its prosperous appearance. One of the five Pandavas from the Mahabharata, Bhimsen is credited with superhuman strength – he is often depicted as a red muscleman, lifting a horse or crushing an elephant under his knee.

The three-storey pagoda has an unusual rectangular plan that sets it apart from other temples in Patan.

The current temple was completely rebuilt in 1682 after a fire and was later restored after the 1934 earthquake, and again in 1967. It's currently under renovation. Non-Hindus can enter and climb to the upper level (the inner sanctum is usually upstairs in Bhimsen temples) to view the wild-eyed statue of Bhimsen.

Manga Hiti
WATER TANK

(Map p132) Immediately across from Bhimsen Temple is the sunken Manga Hiti, one of the water conduits with which Patan is liberally endowed. The tank contains a cruciform-shaped pool and three wonderfully carved *dhara* (water spouts) in the shape of makara (mythical crocodile-elephants). Overlooking the tank are two wooden pavilions known as the **Mani Mandap**, which were built in 1700 for use in the elaborate ceremonies at royal coronations – one of the shelters features a serpent-backed throne.

Vishwanath Temple
HINDU TEMPLE

(Map p132) South of the Bhimsen Temple stands the Vishwanath Temple, sacred to Shiva. This elaborately decorated two-tiered pagoda was built in 1627 and it features some particularly ornate woodcarving, especially on the friezes above the colonnade. Also noteworthy are the fine stone carvings of Ganesh set into the brick walls. On the west side is a statue of Shiva's loyal mount, Nandi the bull, while the east side features two stone elephants with mahouts, one crushing a man beneath its foot. When the doors are open, you can view the enormous lingam inside.

Krishna Mandir
HINDU TEMPLE

(Map p132) Continuing into the square, you can't miss the splendid Krishna Mandir built by King Siddhinarsingh Malla in 1637. Constructed from carved stone – in place of the usual brick and timber – this fabulous architectural confection shows the clear influence of Indian temple design. The temple is one of the most distinctive monuments in the valley and it is often depicted on the ornate brass butter lamps hung in Nepali homes.

The temple consists of three tiers, fronted by columns and supporting a north Indian–style shikhara. Non-Hindus cannot enter to view the statue of Vishnu as Krishna, the goatherd, but you'll often hear temple musicians playing upstairs. Vishnu's mount, the man-bird Garuda, kneels with folded arms on top of a **column** facing the temple. The delicate stone carvings along the beam on the 1st floor recount events from the Mahabharata, while the beam on the 2nd floor features scenes from the Ramayana.

A major festival, **Krishna Jayanta**, also known as Krishnasthami, is held here in the Nepali month of Bhadra (August–September) for Krishna's birthday.

Jagannarayan Temple
HINDU TEMPLE

(Map p132) Fronted by a pair of barrel-chested lions, the two-storey Jagannarayan (or Char Narayan) Temple is dedicated to Vishnu as Narayan, the creator of the universe. Dating from 1565, it is said to be the oldest temple in the square, and its roof struts are alive with carvings of couples engaged in saucy goings-on.

King Yoganarendra Malla's Statue
MONUMENT

(Map p132) South of the Jagannarayan Temple is a tall column topped by a striking brass statue of King Yoganarendra Malla (1684–1705) and his queens, installed in 1700. Above the king's head is a cobra, and above the cobra is a small brass bird – legend has it that as long as the bird remains, the king may still return to his palace. Accordingly, the door and window of the palace are always kept open and a hookah is kept ready should the king ever decide to come back. A rider to the legend adds that when the bird flies off, the elephants in front of the Vishwanath Temple will stroll over to Manga Hiti for a drink!

Behind the statue of the king are three smaller **Vishnu temples**, including a brick-and-plaster shikhara temple, built in 1590 to enshrine an image of Narsingha, Vishnu's man-lion incarnation.

Hari Shankar Temple
HINDU TEMPLE

(Map p132) The three-storey temple to Hari Shankar, a curious hybrid deity that has half the attributes of Vishnu and half the attributes of Shiva, has roof struts carved with scenes of the tortures of the damned, in contrast to the erotic scenes more commonly seen on temple roofs. It was built in 1704–05 by the daughter of King Yoganarendra Malla.

Taleju Bell
MONUMENT

(Map p132) South of the Hari Shankar Temple is a huge, ancient bell, hanging between two stout pillars, erected by King Vishnu Malla in 1736. Petitioners could ring the bell to alert the king to their grievances. The huge brass chains attached to the bell look almost as solid as the stone columns that support them. Behind the bell pavilion is a **fountain** crossed by an ornamental bridge.

Krishna Temple
HINDU TEMPLE

(Chyasim Deval; Map p132) This attractive, octagonal stone temple completes the 'front line' of temples in the square. It has strong

Patan

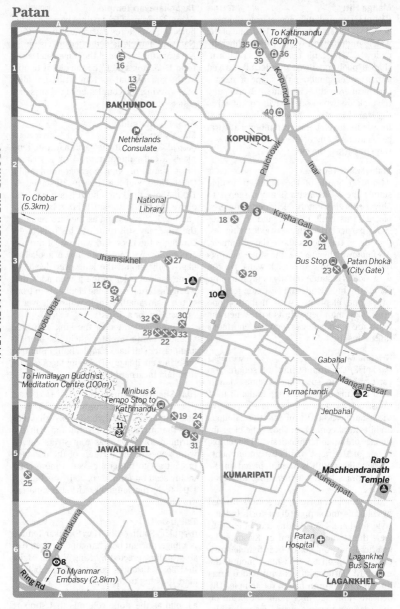

architectural similarities to the Krishna Temple at the north end of the square. The tiered structure was built in 1723 in a style clearly influenced by the stone temples of northern India.

Royal Palace PALACE
(Map p132) Forming the whole eastern side of Durbar Sq, the Royal Palace of Patan was originally built in the 14th century, but was expanded massively during the 17th and 18th centuries by Siddhinarsingh Malla,

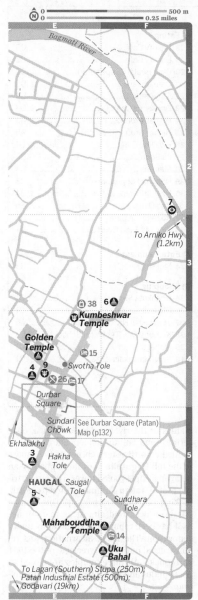

of 1934, but the palace remains one of the architectural highlights of Nepal.

Behind the extravagant facade, with its overhanging eaves, carved windows and delicate wooden screens, are a series of connecting courtyards and three **temples** dedicated to the valley's main deity, the goddess Taleju. The **Bhairab gateway** leading to the central courtyard – known as Mul Chowk – is flanked by two stone lions and colourful murals of Shiva in his wrathful incarnation as Bhairab. Strings of buffalo guts are hung above the door in his honour.

The northern courtyard is reached through the **Golden Gate** (Sun Dhoka). Installed in 1734, this finely engraved and gilded gateway is topped by a golden torana (pediment) showing Shiva, Parvati, Ganesh and Kumar (an incarnation of Skanda, the god of war). Directly above the gateway is a window made from gold foil wrapped around a timber frame, where the king once made public appearances. The gateway now forms the entrance to the Patan Museum.

[TOP CHOICE] **Patan Museum** MUSEUM
(Map p132; ☏5521492; www.patanmuseum.gov.np; foreigner/SAARC Rs 250/75; ⊗10.30am-4.30pm, last admission 4pm) Formerly the residence of the Malla kings, the section of the palace surrounding Keshav Narayan Chowk now houses one of the finest collections of religious art in Asia. Initially funded by the Austrian government, the museum is a national treasure and an invaluable introduction to the art, symbolism and architecture of the valley.

The collection is displayed in a series of brick and timber rooms, linked by steep and narrow stairways. There are informative labels on each of the hundreds of statues, carvings and votive objects, allowing you to put a name to many of the deities depicted at temples around the valley.

There are also some interesting displays on the techniques used to create these wonderful objects, including the art of repoussé and the 'lost-wax' method of casting. Gallery H at the back of the complex, near the cafe, houses some fascinating photos of Patan at the turn of the 19th and 20th centuries.

You need at least an hour, and preferably two, to do this place justice, and it's worth taking a break at the excellent Museum Café before diving in for another round. The museum also has a shop selling reproductions of some of the works displayed inside. For

Srinivasa Malla and Vishnu Malla. The Patan palace predates the palaces in Kathmandu and Bhaktapur and it was severely damaged during the conquest of the valley by Prithvi Narayan Shah in 1768. More restoration was done after the great earthquake

AROUND THE KATHMANDU VALLEY PATAN

Patan

a sneak preview of the museum's highlights and the story of its renovation, go to www.asianart.com/patan-museum. Photography is not allowed.

Mul Chowk
COURTYARD

(Map p132) South of the Patan Museum, a gateway opens onto the stately Mul Chowk, the largest and oldest of the palace's three main chowks (squares). The original buildings were destroyed by fire in 1662 but rebuilt just three years later by Srinivasa Malla. If the doors happen to be open when you visit, you can enter the square to view the exquisitely carved windows and balconies and the three temples dedicated to Taleju, the personal deity of the Malla kings.

As you enter through the Bhairab gateway, the first thing you will notice is the small, gilded **Bidya Temple** in the middle of the square, beside a wooden post used to secure animals for sacrifices. To the south is the **Taleju Bhawani Temple**, flanked by

statues of the river goddesses Ganga, on a tortoise, and Jamuna, on a makara.

At the northeastern corner of the square is the tall **Degutalle Temple**, topped by an octagonal triple-roofed tower. The larger, triple-roofed **Taleju Temple** is directly north, looking out over Durbar Sq. This temple has been destroyed almost as many times as it has been rebuilt and is currently under renovation. The latest incarnation was reconstructed out of the wreckage of the 1934 earthquake. All three temples are closed to non-Hindus and actually rarely open to anyone.

Sundari Chowk
COURTYARD

(Map p132) South of Mul Chowk is the smaller Sundari Chowk, arranged around a superbly carved sunken water tank known as the **Tusha Hiti**. Unfortunately, the courtyard is closed to the public, but swing by the gateway to view the gilded metal window over the entrance, which is flanked by windows of carved ivory. Nearby are three magnificent statues of **Hanuman** (barely recognisable beneath layers of orange paint), **Ganesh** and Vishnu as **Narsingha**, the man-lion, tearing out the entrails of a demon (see the boxed text, p162).

NORTH OF DURBAR SQUARE

The following sights are north of Durbar Sq. They can be visited as part of the walking tour on p136.

Golden Temple (Kwa Bahal)　BUDDHIST TEMPLE

(Hiranya Varna Mahavihara; Map p128; foreigner/SAARC Rs 50/10; ☉dawn-dusk) This unique Buddhist monastery is just north of Durbar Sq. It was allegedly founded in the 12th century, and it has existed in its current location since 1409. Entry is via an ornate narrow stone doorway to the east or a wooden doorway to the west, inside one of the interlinked bahal on the north side of Nakabhil.

Entering from the east, note the gaudy lions and the 1886 signature of Krishnabir, the master stonemason who sculpted the fine doorway with its frieze of Buddhist deities. This second doorway leads to the main courtyard of the Golden Temple, so named because of the gilded metal plates that cover most of its frontage. Shoes and leather articles must be removed if you enter the inner courtyard. Look for the tortoises pottering around the compound – these are the temple guardians. The main priest of the temple is a young boy under the age of 12, who serves for 30 days before handing the job over to another young boy.

The temple itself is a magnificent example of courtyard temple architecture. Two elephant statues guard the doorway and the facade is covered by a host of gleaming Buddhist figures. Inside the main shrine is a beautiful statue of Sakyamuni (no photos allowed). To the left of the courtyard is a statue of Green Tara and in the right corner is a statue of the Bodhisattva Vajrasattva wearing an impressive silver-and-gold cape.

Facing the main temple is a smaller shrine containing a 'self-arisen' *(swayambhu)* chaitya (small stupa). The four corners of the courtyard have statues of four Lokeshvaras (incarnations of Avalokiteshvara) and four monkeys, which hold out jackfruits as an offering. A stairway leads to an upper-floor chapel dedicated to a white eight-armed Avalokiteshvara, lined with Tibetan-style frescoes including a wheel of life. Finally, as you leave the temple, look up to see an embossed Kalachakra mandala mounted on the ceiling.

It's worth ducking south towards Durbar Sq to see the small, two-tiered **Uma Maheshwar Temple** (Map p128) and the handsome stone **Gauri Shankar Temple** (Map p128), in the Indian shikhara style. Across the road, the Buddhist **Maru Mandapa Mahavihar** (Map p128) is set in a small courtyard.

Kumbeshwar Temple　HINDU TEMPLE

(Map p128) Due north of Durbar Sq is the eye-catching Kumbeshwar Temple, one of the valley's three five-storey temples. This tall, thin mandir (temple) features some particularly artistic woodcarving, and it seems to defy gravity as it towers above the surrounding houses. A large Nandi statue and central lingam indicate that the shrine is sacred to Shiva.

The temple platform has two ponds whose water is said to come straight from the holy lake at Gosainkund, a weeklong trek north of the valley (see p287). Bathing in the tank at Kumbeshwar Temple is said to be as meritorious as making the arduous walk to Gosainkund.

ASHOKA STUPAS

Legend claims that the four ancient stupas marking the boundaries of Patan were built when the great Buddhist emperor Ashoka visited the valley 2500 years ago. All are worth a quick visit, especially during the auspicious full moon of August when Buddhist and Tibetan pilgrims walk around all four stupas in a single day.

» **Northern Stupa** (Map p128) Just beyond the Kumbeshwar Temple, on the way to the Sankhamul ghats.

» **Lagan (Southern) Stupa** (off Map p128) Just south of the Lagankhel bus stand, crowning a hilltop and offering good views over southern Patan.

» **Western Stupa** (Map p128) Covered in grass beside the main road at Pulchowk. A set of steps leads uphill to the Aksheshwor Mahavihar, a courtyard-style Buddhist monastery on the hilltop.

» **Eastern Stupa** Well to the east of the centre, across Kathmandu's Ring Rd.

The surrounding square is dotted with temples sacred to Bhairab and Baglamukhi (Parvati). Local women gather at the tank known as **Konti Hiti** to socialise, wash clothes and fill up their water jugs. Down an alley to the north of the temple is the Kumbeshwar Technical School (see p140).

From here you can detour north to see the Northern Stupa, one of four marker shrines showing the old city limits of Patan.

SOUTH OF DURBAR SQUARE

The following sights are south of Durbar Sq in the backstreets south of Mangal Bazar, the main local shopping street. If you continue south, you will reach the busy marketplace surrounding the Lagankhel bus stand.

I Baha Bahi   MONASTERY
(Map p128) Just a one-minute walk south of Durbar Sq, a large new-looking doorway flanked by black lions with Cheshire-cat grins leads to a quiet bahal containing the I

Baha Bahi. This handsome Buddhist monastery was founded in 1427 and the structure was restored in the 1990s by a team of archaeologists from Japan.

Minnath Temple   TEMPLE
(Map p128) Just 200m south of I Baha Bahi, a large water tank marks the entrance to a courtyard strewn with wooden beams. In the centre is the brightly painted, two-tiered Minnath Temple, dedicated to the Bodhisattva Jatadhari Lokesvara, who is considered to be the little brother of Rato Machhendranath.

The temple was founded in the Licchavi period (3rd to 9th centuries) but the multi-armed goddesses on the roof struts were added much later. Note the metal pots and pans nailed to the temple rafters by devotees. The timbers surrounding the temple are assembled into a chariot every year to haul the statue of Minnath around town as part of the Rato Machhendranath Festival.

Durbar Square (Patan)

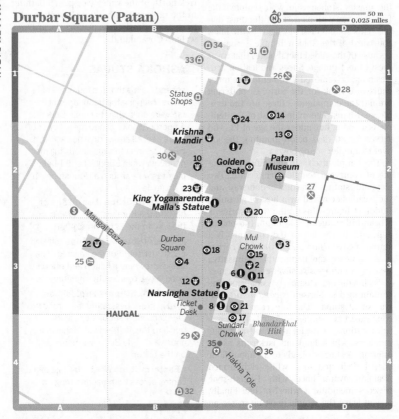

Rato Machhendranath Temple   TEMPLE
(Map p128) Almost directly across the road
from the Minnath Temple, down an alley, a
white-columned gateway leads to the wide,
open square containing the revered Rato
Machhendranath Temple. Dedicated to the
god of rain and plenty, the temple, like so
many in Nepal, blurs the line between Buddhism and Hinduism. Buddhists regard
Rato (Red) Machhendranath as an incarnation of Avalokiteshvara, while Hindus see
him as an incarnation of Shiva.

Set inside a protective metal fence, the
towering three-storey temple dates from
1673, but there has been some kind of temple on this site since at least 1408. The temple's four ornate doorways are guarded by
stone snow lions and at ground level on the
four corners of the temple plinth are curious
yeti-like demons known as *kyah*.

Mounted on freestanding pillars at the
front of the temple is a curious collection of
metal animals, including a peacock, Garuda,
horse, buffalo, lion, elephant, fish and snake.
Look up to see the richly painted roof struts
of the temple, which show Avalokiteshvara
standing above figures being tortured in hell.

The temple comes into its own during
the Rato Machhendranath Festival in April–
May.

Mahabouddha Temple   BUDDHIST TEMPLE
(Map p128; foreigner/SAARC Rs 50/25) To reach
the Mahabouddha Temple, you must walk
southeast from Durbar Sq along Hakha Tole,
passing a series of small Vaishnavite and
Shaivite temples. When you reach Sundhara
Tole, with its temple and sunken hiti (water
tank) with three brass water spouts, turn
right and look for the tiny doorway leading
to the temple.

As you step through, the temple suddenly looms above you, crammed into a tiny
courtyard like a plant straining to get some
sunlight. Built in the Indian shikhara style,
the shrine takes its name from the hundreds
of terracotta tiles that cover it, each bearing an image of the Buddha. The temple is
loosely modelled on the Mahabouddha Temple at Bodhgaya in India, where the Buddha
gained enlightenment.

AROUND THE KATHMANDU VALLEY PATAN

Durbar Square (Patan)

RATO MACHHENDRANATH FESTIVAL

The image in the Rato Machhendranath Temple may look like a crudely carved piece of painted wood, but each year it forms the centrepiece for the **Rato Machhendranath Festival** in the Nepali month of Baisakh (April–May). Immediately prior to the festival, the scattered timbers of Rato Machhendranath's chariot are gathered and assembled and the statue is installed on his awesome coach on the fourth day of the light fortnight of Baisakh. It takes a full month to move the chariot across Patan to Jawalakhel, where the chariot is finally dismantled. Machhendranath is considered to have powers over rain and, since the monsoon is approaching at this time, this festival is essentially a plea for generous rains.

The towering main chariot is accompanied for much of its journey by a smaller chariot, which contains the image of Rato Machhendranath's companion, Jatadhari Lokesvara, which normally resides in the Minnath Temple. The highlight of the festival is the Bhoto Jatra, or showing of the sacred vest. According to the legend, the jewelled vest was given to the god for safe keeping after a dispute between two potential owners. Every year, the vest is displayed three times in order to give the owner the chance to claim it.

From Jawalakhel, Rato Machhendranath is conveyed on a khat (palanquin) to his second home in the village of Bungamati, 6km to the south, where he spends the next six months of the year, before returning to Patan. The main chariot is so large and the route is so long that the Nepali army is often called in to help transport it.

The temple dates from 1585, but it was ruined by the 1934 earthquake and totally rebuilt. Unfortunately, without plans to work from, the builders ended up with a different-looking temple, and had enough bricks and tiles left over to construct a smaller shrine to Maya Devi, the Buddha's mother, in the corner of the courtyard!

The surrounding lanes are full of shops selling high-quality Patan-style metal statues of Hindu and Buddhist deities, and these shops even spill into the square around the temple. The roof terrace of the shop at the back of the courtyard has a good view of the temple and there's no undue pressure to buy.

Uku Bahal   BUDDHIST MONASTERY
(Rudra Varna Mahavihar; Map p128) South of the Mahabouddha Temple, this ancient Buddhist monastery is one of the best known in Patan.

The main courtyard is jam-packed with statuary and metalwork – dorjes (thunderbolt symbols), bells, peacocks, elephants, Garudas, rampant goats, kneeling devotees, a regal-looking statue of a Rana general and, rather incongruously, a pair of Victorian-style British lions that look like they could have been lifted straight from London's Trafalgar Sq.

The monastery has been used for centuries, and the wooden roof struts are some of the oldest in the valley, but much of what you can see today dates back to the 19th century. Behind the monastery is a Swayambhunath-style stupa accessed by a side door.

WEST OF DURBAR SQUARE
Zoo   ZOO
(Map p128; ✆5528323; adult/child Rs 250/150; ☺10am-5pm) Nepal's only zoo is in the southwestern part of Patan by the Jawalakhel roundabout. The animals live in better conditions than you might expect and there are always crowds of local kids being wowed by such exotic creatures as elephants, tigers, leopards, hyenas, gaur, deer, blue bulls, gharials, giant tortoises, langur monkeys and some very noisy hippos. People routinely get freaked out by the giant 60cm-long squirrels. Kids can take an elephant ride at 1pm (Rs 100).

🏃 Activities & Courses

Himalayan Buddhist
Meditation Centre   MEDITATION
(HBMC; off Map p128; ✆9841224368; www.fpmt -hbmc.org; Dobigat; ☺8am-9pm) This friendly dharma centre offers guided meditations and talks on Tibetan Buddhism, with free guided meditation on Saturday mornings and regular Buddhist teachings. The centre also offers t'ai chi and reiki classes, a five-day yoga course and local pilgrimage walks. There's also a vegetarian restaurant and a library.

Pranamaya Yoga
YOGA

(Map p128; ☎9851002920; www.pranamaya-yoga. com; classes Rs 600) Yoga classes opposite Moksh Live; see p77.

✦✦ Festivals & Events

Rato Machhendranath Festival
RELIGIOUS

Patan's most dramatic festival takes place in April–May.

Janai Purnima Festival
RELIGIOUS

Thousands of pilgrims visit the Kumbeshwar Temple in July–August, as members of the Brahmin and Chhetri castes replace the sacred thread they wear looped over their left shoulder. A silver-and-gold lingam is set up in the tank and devotees take a ritual bath while *jhankri* (faith healers) in colourful headdresses dance around the temple beating drums.

🛏 Sleeping

Not many tourists overnight in Patan, which is a shame because there's a small but good spread of accommodation for all budgets.

Traditional Homes Patan Durbar Square
BOUTIQUE HOTEL $$

(Map p128; ☎5551184; www.traditionalhomes. com.np; s/d/ste US$60/70/100; 🛜) Just 50m from Durbar Sq, this 70-year-old traditional house has just been revamped into a stylish, exclusive hotel. Unlike most traditional homes, the six rooms here are actually bright and full of modern design touches such as pressed-concrete floors, reclaimed wood and traditional-style *makal* (braziers) to provide winter heat. Bathrooms are small due to the nature of the house but the rooms are spacious and lower floors enjoy a private terrace. The good restaurant serves up authentic Newari food and even offers cooking classes.

Newa Chén
BOUTIQUE HOTEL $$

(Map p128; ☎5533532; www.newachen.com; s/d US$25/40, without bathroom US$20/30, deluxe US$30/45; 🛜@) Housed inside the Unesco-restored Shestha House mansion, this similarly boutique but less modern hotel offers a window onto what it must have been like to be a well-to-do resident of Patan in centuries past. Rooms are all different but are decked out in traditional style, with divan seating areas and coir matting on the floors, and there's a nice living room. Anyone over 5ft 6in will feel a bit cramped. Rates include breakfast.

Summit Hotel
RESORT $$$

(Map p128; ☎5521810; www.summit-nepal.com; budget s/d €25/30, s/d from €70/80; ❄@🛜) Expats and NGOs like to keep the Summit secret so that there is room when relatives and friends come to visit. The Dutch-founded resort-style hotel is built in mock-Newari style, with lots of red brick and carved timber, and the atmosphere is superbly romantic and relaxed. The swimming pool comes into its own in summer, while multiple fireplaces keep things snug in winter, especially in the cosy bar. The budget rooms with shared bathrooms in Holland House are aimed at students, but the Garden View and larger and pricier Himalayan View rooms are delightful. The hotel is tucked away in the quiet lanes west of Kopundol, offering fine views over Kathmandu. The weekend barbecues are a highlight.

Mahabuddha Guest House
GUESTHOUSE $

(Map p128; ☎5540575; mhg@mos.com.np; s/d Rs 450/600; @) Southeast of Durbar Sq, across the road from the Mahabouddha Temple, this is a simple but decent budget choice, with tidy, cared-for rooms and an internet cafe. Rooms can be dark, so aim for one higher up. The singles are particularly poky. Rates include tax.

Café de Patan
HOTEL $

(Map p132; ☎5537599; www.cafedepatan.com; r with/without bathroom Rs 800/600) This courtyard hotel is almost on Durbar Sq and there's a rooftop garden and a pleasant downstairs cafe. The neat, modern rooms get plenty of light, but only two have bathrooms.

Hotel Greenwich Village
HOTEL $$

(Map p128; ☎5521780; www.greenwichnepal.com; s/d from US$75/85, deluxe r US$95; ❄🛜🛜) In the same area as the Summit Hotel, the oddly named Greenwich Village is peaceful and secluded, though less luxurious than the rates might suggest. Rooms are smart and comfortable but you'll probably spend most of your time at the lovely poolside patio and cafe. Foreign exchange and free airport pick-up are useful perks, as is free breakfast.

✗ Eating

Several restaurants overlook Durbar Sq, offering magical views, and are aimed squarely at day-tripping tour groups. Unless otherwise stated, the following restaurants are open from 8am to 8pm.

AROUND THE KATHMANDU VALLEY PATAN

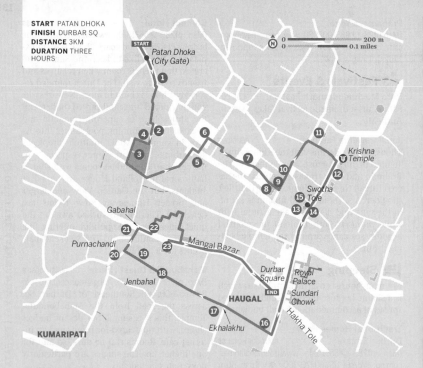

START PATAN DHOKA
FINISH DURBAR SQ
DISTANCE 3KM
DURATION THREE
HOURS

START

Patan Dhoka
(City Gate)

① ② ④ ③ ⑤ ⑥ ⑦ ⑧ ⑨ ⑩ ⑪ ⑫

Krishna Temple

Swotha Tole ⑮ ⑬ ⑭

Gabahal ㉑ ㉒ ㉓

Purnachandi ⑲
⑳ ⑱

Mangal Bazar

Jenbahal

Durbar Square *Royal Palace*

END

Sundari Chowk

HAUGAL

⑰ ⑯

Ekhalakhu

Hakha Tole

KUMARIPATI

N 0 — 200 m
0 — 0.1 miles

Walking Tour
Patan

> This route gives a great insight into the communal lifestyle and traditional layout of Newari villages, with their bahal, hiti and *tun* (wells). The first part of the walk starts at Patan Dhoka, ends at Durbar Sq and takes under two hours. After visiting Durbar Sq and grabbing some lunch it's worth continuing on part two of the walk, which takes you past the interesting temples and bahal of southwest Patan, returning in 45 minutes to Durbar Sq.

From Patan Dhoka, stroll southeast to a handsome two-storey ① **Ganesh shrine**, then turn right into ② **Sulima Square**, a crumbling brick-lined square with a 17th-century Mahadev (Shiva) shrine. On the east side of the square is the derelict house of a famous 16th-century Tantric master. Continue south to the ③ **Pim Bahal Pokhari** pond and go around it anticlockwise, past the three-tiered ④ **Chandeswari Temple** built in 1663. On the west side is a 600-year-old whitewashed stupa that was damaged by Muslim invaders in 1357.

At the road junction, walk northeast past fine wooden windows and copper-chasing workshops to a large square at Nakabhil. On the south side is the courtyard-style ⑤ **Lokakirti Mahavihar**, a former Buddhist monastery that is now used to store parts of the chariot used during the Rato Machhendranath Festival; you can see the runners by the front door. Masked dances are performed on the *dabali* (platform) in front of the monastery during festival time. An alley leads north off the square, sign-posted 'Bhaskar Varna Mahavihar', to the ⑥ **Nyakhuchowk Bahal**. The courtyard is full of ancient chaitya (small stupas) and in the centre is a white stupa and a gaudy 4m statue of Sakyamuni.

Head past a row of stupas to the eastern wall and go through the covered entrance (signed 'please mind your head'), straight across an alley, into another chaitya-filled courtyard, the ⑦ **Naga Bahal**. Walk past the statue of a bull surrounded by prayer wheels to a painting of a naga (snake spirit) on the wall, repainted every five years during the Samyak festival and safe behind bars.

Go through the eastern passageway to a further courtyard with the red-walled Harayana Library in the southwestern corner. Follow a diagonal path past the carved wooden frontage of an ancient monastery to the southeastern corner and walk beneath a wooden torana (pediment) to enter the **8** **Golden Temple** (p131).

After visiting the temple, exit east onto the main street, then turn left. You'll soon see a small blue sign for the courtyard-style **9** **Manjushri Temple**. From here, continue north past a group of ancient **10** **megaliths**, possibly the oldest objects of worship in the Kathmandu Valley, and continue to the **11** **Kumbeshwar Temple** (p131).

From this temple, head east and take a right (south) back to Durbar Sq. This road is lined with shrines to different incarnations of Vishnu, including a north Indian–style Krishna Temple and the two-tiered **12** **Uma Maheshwar Temple**. Peer inside the temple (it's the back of the two temples) to see a very beautiful black-stone relief of Shiva and Parvati in the pose known as Uma Maheshwar – the god sitting cross-legged with his shakti leaning against him rather seductively.

Further south, at Swotha Tole, are the pagoda-style **13** **Rada Krishna Temple**, the Garuda-fronted **14** **Narayan Temple** and another Indian-influenced **15** **Krishna Temple**. A few more steps will take you to Durbar Sq.

After lunch in Durbar Sq, start the second part of the walk by walking south from Durbar Sq, then take the lane leading west to the **16** **Bishwakarma Temple**, whose entire facade is covered in sheets of embossed copper. The temple is dedicated to the patron deity of carpenters and craftspeople, which is appropriate, as you can hear many of them banging hammers in the surrounding workshops.

Continuing northwest, at the first junction, Ekhalakhu, there are several Nepali-style **17** **Vishnu shrines**, one with a kneeling Garuda statue. Continue past a Ganesh shrine and Shiva shrine to Jenbahal and a brightly painted, three-tiered **18** **Ganesh Temple**. Continue west past a stone shikhara-style **19** **Narayan Temple**.

At Purnachandi junction, detour south to see a substantial, three-tiered **20** **Kali Temple** on the south side of a large water tank,

then walk north past another pagoda-shaped **21** **Vaishnavite Temple** to the junction at Gabahal.

Turn right and look for a small gateway on the left leading to **22** **Bubahal**, a courtyard full of Buddhist statues and chaityas in front of the ornate Yasodhara Mahavihar Temple.

Here's where things get fun! It's possible to continue east along the main road to reach the Haka Bahal but it's much more fun to detour there through the maze of interconnecting courtyards. Follow our instructions, leave a popcorn trail and if in doubt turn right. From the Bubahal courtyard take the far right entryway beside a stone chaitya into a hidden brick courtyard with ornate wooden carvings. Continue through the far (northeast, or middle) corner into another small courtyard and straight through that, through a dark alleyway to another courtyard. Jog right into another courtyard that has a small printing press and then continue south through a small courtyard to a larger courtyard (the sixth!) with a Vishnu Temple. From here you can rejoin the main road to the south and take a right to see the Haka Bahal.

Assuming you aren't hopelessly lost (well done!), pop into **23** **Haka Bahal**, the restored courtyard of the Ratnakar Mahavihar, linked to Patan's Kumari (living goddess) cult. The red sign pointing to the 'Living Goddess' is something you don't see every day! Continue east through Mangal Bazar to finish at the south end of Durbar Sq for a well-deserved cup of tea.

EXPAT EATS

The area around Pulchowk and Jawalakhel is a favourite hang-out of diplomats, NGO staff and other expats, and it feels a long way from the tourist crowds of Thamel or Patan's Durbar Sq. There are now so many restaurants here that locals have dubbed the area 'Jhamel'.

Bakery Café (Map p128; mains Rs 60-200; www.nanglo.com.np; ⊙10.30am-9.30pm; ☎) All the branches of this excellent chain provide work for deaf Nepalis. Patan has two branches – one by the main roundabout at Jawalakhel and one opposite UN House at Pulchowk. Both offer good-value coffee, momos, dosas, sizzlers and sandwiches.

Sing Ma Food Court (Map p128; mains Rs 300-360; ⊙8.30am-9pm Sun-Fri) For the authentic tastes of Malaysia, the noodle soups, *nasi lemak* (coconut rice with anchovies) and beef-fillet *rendang* (dry coconut curry with lime leaves) are the real *mamak* (Malay Tamil) deal.

Masala (Map p128; mains Rs 245-365; ⊙10am-10pm) Quality Indian food is surprisingly hard to find in Kathmandu or Patan, but this tasty place plugs the gap, with an excellent menu of Mughlai and tandoori dishes.

Red Dingo (Map p128; ☑6914960; www.thereddingo.com; mains Rs 250-380; ⊙7am-9pm; ☎) No prizes for guessing the origins of the owners of this Aussie bistro near the Jawalakhel roundabout. Come for hearty meat pies, elegant salads and Modern Australian mains.

New Orleans (Map p128; ☑5522708; mains Rs 270-380; ⊙8am-10pm; ☎) Set around a pleasant courtyard that is often full of expats with laptops, this branch of the popular Thamel restaurant serves everything from Goan-style *bekti* fish to Mongolian beef, plus there's on-site shiatsu massage (Rs 800 per hour). There's an organic farmers market here every Sunday morning.

La Soon (Map p128; mains Rs 200-385; ⊙noon-10pm) Recently reinvented in a Malian-style adobe building near Pulchowk, this lively restaurant and bar is run by a Swiss-Ghanaian couple, and the menu is an interesting fusion of Asian, French and African influences.

Roadhouse Cafe (Map p128; ☑5521755; pizzas Rs 420-475; ⊙11am-10pm) A chintzy branch of the ever-popular Thamel pizza parlour, with a relaxed, family vibe.

Cafereena (Map p128; www.cafereena.com.np; mains Rs 150-365) A nice courtyard restaurant firmly aimed at the business lunch crowd, with 35 types of momos (try the paneer peanut variety), plus excellent-value Indian, Thai and Nepali set lunches.

For when you can't face battling Patan traffic, **Foodmandu** (☑4102588; www.foodmandu. com) offers delivery from over 65 local restaurants with no fee for a minimum purchase. **New York Pizza** (☑5520294; Kopundol; pizzas from Rs 350) offers free delivery of its American-style pizzas.

For a classy dinner for two while in Patan, consider the expat-oriented restaurants around Pulchowk.

Museum Café INTERNATIONAL $$
(Map p132; ☑5526271; mains Rs 200-450; ⊙9am-5pm) In the rear courtyard of the Patan Museum, this stylish open-air place is run by the team behind the Summit Hotel. Prices are high but so is the quality of the food, mainly soups, sandwiches and salads, and the garden terrace setting feels elegant and refined. You don't need to buy a museum ticket to eat at the cafe.

Si Taleju Restaurant & Bar INTERNATIONAL $
(Map p132; mains Rs 175-250) A narrow, towering place with four floors, each with a different feel. Best is the top-floor dining room with magical views north across Durbar Sq to the mountains beyond. You'll find all your favourites on the menu and the prices are surprisingly reasonable.

Kwalkhu Café INTERNATIONAL $
(Map p128; mains Rs 115-320) An island of calm in the courtyard of the Unesco-restored Rajbhandari House, this peaceful cafe has a delightful back terrace and a solid menu

of Nepali, Tibetan, Chinese and Continental food.

Dhokaima Café   INTERNATIONAL $$
(Map p128; ✆5522113; mains Rs 200-540; 🖥) A sophisticated cafe set inside a Rana-era storehouse by the Patan Dhoka gateway. Shaded by a sprawling walnut tree, the courtyard garden is a peaceful place to enjoy a great range of light and healthy dishes, such as the rocket salad with apple, pear and cheese, or a sandwich and soup combo, plus good coffee and cakes.

Café Cheeno   INTERNATIONAL $$
(Map p128; www.cafecheeno.com; mains Rs 250-475; ⊙7.30am-9pm) Another great place just outside Patan Dhoka, with a nice garden, good salads and soups, tasty breakfast crêpes and a 'Wellness Sanctuary' for massage and treatments.

Café de Patan   INTERNATIONAL $$
(Map p132; www.cafedepatan.com; dishes Rs 200-300) Southwest of Durbar Sq behind a small Uma Maheshwar Temple, this quiet place is a long-running travellers' favourite, with an open-air courtyard and a rooftop garden (though no real views). The menu runs to momos, pizza and chop suey.

Café du Temple   INTERNATIONAL $$
(Map p132; ✆5527127; www.cafedutemple. np; mains Rs 250-400, set meals Rs 600) A tour-group favourite at the north end of Durbar Sq. The airy rooftop tables are covered by red-and-white sun umbrellas and the menu runs from Chinese fried rice to daal bhaat, via chicken stroganoff. The nearby **Old House Café** is similar.

Third World Restaurant   INTERNATIONAL $$
(Map p132; mains Rs 250) Located on the quiet western side of the square, with good rooftop views of the Krishna Mandir.

Higher Ground   CAFE, BAKERY $
(Map p128; www.higherground.com.np; Jawalakhel junction; coffee Rs 70, mains Rs 100-200; ⊙7am-8pm Sun-Fri; 🖥) Good 'cafe with a conscience' and bakery with good breakfast wraps, waffles and French toast, plus lunches, smoothies and baked goods. The organisation trains marginalised and underprivileged women as bakers. There's a branch opposite DFID in Ekantakuna.

Namaste Supermarket   SUPERMARKET
(Map p128; Pulchowk; ⊙8.30am-8pm) Sharing a building with the Hotel Narayani, this is where expats come to stock up on quality local produce and the tastes of home.

Bhat Bhateni Super Store   SUPERMARKET
(Map p128; www.bhatbhatenionline.com, www. bbsm.com.np; Krishna Gali; ⊙7.30am-8.30pm) The largest supermarket in town.

☆ Entertainment

Moksh Live   LIVE MUSIC
(Map p128; ✆5528362; Gyanmandala, Jhamsikhel; ⊙11am-11pm Tue-Sun) Moksh has some of the best live rock, funk and folk music in town (not just the standard cover bands), most frequently on Friday. Other nights there are pizzas from the outdoor oven and espresso from Himalayan Java.

🔒 Shopping

Patan is a famous centre for bronze casting, repoussé work and other metal arts. Most of the statues that you see on sale in Kathmandu are actually made in Patan, and you can save money by buying them at their source.

There are dozens of metalwork shops north and west of Durbar Sq, and more around the Mahabouddha Temple. The price of a bronze statue of a Buddhist or Hindu deity can range from Rs 3000 to more than Rs 100,000, depending on the size, the complexity of the casting, the level of detail and the amount of gilding and enamelling on the finished statue.

Patan is also the best place in the valley for interior design and fair-trade products, mostly on the Kopundol hill. The Jawalakhel area around the zoo has several carpet shops.

Jawalakhel Handicraft Centre   CARPETS
(Map p128; ✆5521305; ⊙9am-noon & 1-5pm Sun-Fri, 10am-5pm Sat high season) Anyone who appreciates carpets should visit this Tibetan refugee cooperative, where Nepal's enormous carpet industry was essentially born in 1960. You can watch the carpet-makers at work (the centre employs 1000 refugees) before shopping upstairs for the finished article. The quality is high, there is a good selection, the prices are fixed, credit cards are accepted and staff can arrange shipping for you. Carpet quality depends on knots per inch and the price is worked out per sq metre. A 60-/100-knot carpet made with Tibetan wool costs around US$100/220 per sq metre. The size of a traditional Tibetan carpet is 1.8m by 90cm.

AROUND THE KATHMANDU VALLEY PATAN

Mahaguthi   FAIR TRADE
(Map p128; ☑5521607; www.mahaguthi.org;
⊙10am-6.30pm Sun-Fri, to 5pm Sat) Mahaguthi
was founded by a Nepali disciple of Mahat-
ma Gandhi and its Kopundol showroom is a
treasure house of dhaka weavings, handmade
paper, ceramics, block prints, pashminas,
woodcrafts, jewellery, knitwear, statues, singing bowls, embroidery and Mithila paintings
(see the boxed text, p258). There's a smaller
branch in Kathmandu's Lazimpat district.

Dhukuti   FAIR TRADE
(Map p128; ☑5535107; www.acp.org.np; ⊙9am-
7pm) The Kopundol road linking Patan and
Kathmandu is lined with shops that support the work of craft cooperatives around
the country, channelling money directly
from travellers to disadvantaged and neglected communities. Dhukuti packs in
three floors of home furnishings, textiles,
shawls, scarves, bags and rugs from the
Nupri region of Manaslu, and even has
Christmas decorations, created by over
1200 low-income producers.

Sana Hastakala   FAIR TRADE
(Map p128; ☑5522628; www.sanahastakala.org;
⊙9.30am-6pm Sun-Fri, to 5pm Sat) Another
recommended place for paper, batiks, Mithila crafts, felt products and clothing woven
from natural fibres.

Dhankuta Sisters   FAIR TRADE
(Map p128; ☑5203209; ⊙11am-5.30pm Sun-Fri)
Come here for tablecloths, cushion covers
and clothing made from dhaka cloth from
eastern Nepal.

Kumbeshwar Technical School FAIR TRADE
(Map p128; ☑5537484; www.kumbeshwar.
com; ⊙9am-1pm & 2-5pm Sun-Fri) Near the
Kumbeshwar Temple in the backstreets of
Patan, this small workshop provides disadvantaged low-caste families with training,
education and a livelihood, producing carpets, knitwear and woodcarvings. Sales from
the showroom help fund the work of the attached primary school.

Patan Industrial Estate   HANDICRAFTS
(off Map p128; ☑5521367; www.patan.com.np;
⊙10am-5pm Sun-Fri) Despite the unpromising
name, this tourist-oriented crafts complex
boasts a number of workshop showrooms
selling high-quality carpets, woodcarvings
and metalwork. It's around 500m south of
Lagankhel bus stand.

❶ Information

There are banks with ATMs at Mangal Bazar, at
the south end of Durbar Sq, and at Pulchowk and
Jawalakhel.
Patan Hospital (Map p128; ☑5522295;
www.patanhospital.org.np; Lagankhel) The
best in the Kathmandu Valley.

❶ Getting There & Away

You can get to Patan from Kathmandu by bicy-
cle, taxi, bus or tempo. The trip costs around
Rs 250 by taxi. If you come under your own
steam, go south from the Tundikhel to the
National Stadium in Tripureshwar, passing the
striking, lion-topped Tripureshwar Mahadev
Temple, and cross the Bagmati to Kopundol.
At the top of the hill, bear right after the Hotel
Himalaya to reach Patan Dhoka.

Safa (electric) tempos (Rs 12, route 14A) leave
from Kantipath's Sundhara stop, near the Kathmandu main post office. Double-check the destination when getting in, as some run to Mangal
Bazar/Durbar Sq while others to Lagankhel bus
stand, in the south of the city. In the reverse
direction, ask for Kantipath or RNAC. Local
buses and minibuses run frequently between
Kathmandu's Ratna Park bus station and Patan
Dhoka or the chaotic Lagankhel bus stand
(Rs 15, 20 minutes).

Buses and faster minibuses to the southern
valley towns leave when full from Lagankhel.
There are regular services till nightfall to Godavari (Rs 21, 45 minutes), Bungamati (Rs 14, 40
minutes) and Chapagaon (Rs 15, 45 minutes).
There are also frequent buses to Bhaktapur
(Rs 20, 30 minutes).

An interesting route back to Kathmandu is to
continue northeast from the Northern Stupa
down to the riverside ghats at Sankhamul,
across the footbridge over the Bagmati River
and then up to the Arniko Hwy near the big con-
vention centre, from where you can take a taxi or
minibus back to Thamel.

BHAKTAPUR

☑01 / POP 65,000
The third of the medieval city-states in the
Kathmandu Valley, Bhaktapur is also the
best preserved. Many Nepalis still use the old
name of Bhadgaon (pronounced *bud*-gown)
or the Newari name Khwopa, which means
City of Devotees. The name fits – Bhaktapur
has not one but three major squares full of
towering temples that comprise some of the
finest religious architecture in the entire
country.

From a visitor's perspective, this is a place to wander around aimlessly, soaking up the atmosphere. Narrow cobblestone streets wind between the red-brick houses, joining a series of squares and courtyards that are peppered with temples, statues, cisterns and wells. The contents of any one of these historic squares could fit out a decent-sized museum.

The town's cultural life is also proudly on display. Artisans weave cloth and chisel timber by the roadside, squares are filled with drying pots and open kilns, and locals gather in communal courtyards to bathe, collect water and socialise – often over intense card games. Visitors must pay a steep entry fee of US$15 to view this tapestry of Nepali life, which goes into protecting and maintaining the temples.

History

As with many other towns in the valley, Bhaktapur grew up to service the old trade route from India to Tibet, but the city became a formal entity under King Ananda Malla in the 12th century. The oldest part of town, around Tachupal Tole, was laid out at this time.

From the 14th to the 16th century, Bhaktapur became the most powerful of the valley's three Malla kingdoms, and a new civic square was constructed at Durbar Sq in the west of the city.

Many of the city's most iconic buildings date from the rule of King Yaksha Malla (1428–82), but there was another explosion of temple-building during the reign of King Bhupatindra Malla in the 18th century. At its peak the city boasted 172 temples and monasteries, 77 water tanks, 172 pilgrim shelters and 152 wells.

The 15th-century Royal Palace in Durbar Sq was the principal seat of power in the valley until the city was conquered by Prithvi Narayan Shah in 1768 and relegated to the status of a secondary market town. An earthquake that hit in 1934 caused major damage to the city but locals were able to restore most of the buildings, though you can still see the occasional unoccupied temple plinth.

Bhaktapur's streets were paved and extensively restored in the 1970s by the German-funded Bhaktapur Development Project, which also established proper sewerage and waste-water management facilities.

◉ Sights

To dive into the backstreets of Bhaktapur, follow the walking tour on p150.

TAUMADHI TOLE
Nyatapola Temple   HINDU TEMPLE
(Map p146) You will be able to see the sky-high rooftop of the Nyatapola Temple long before you reach the square. With five storeys towering 30m above Taumadhi Tole, this is the tallest temple in all of Nepal and one of the tallest buildings in the Kathmandu Valley.

This perfectly proportioned temple was built in 1702 during the reign of King Bhupatindra Malla, and the construction was so sturdy that the 1934 earthquake caused only minor damage (the upper storey was rebuilt).

The temple is reached by a stairway flanked by stone figures of the temple guardians. At the bottom are the legendary Rajput wrestlers Jayamel and Phattu, depicted kneeling with hefty maces. Subsequent levels are guarded by elephants with floral saddles, lions adorned with bells, beaked griffons with rams' horns and finally two goddesses – Baghini and Singhini. Each figure is said to be 10 times as strong as the figure on the level below.

The temple is dedicated to Siddhi Lakshmi, a bloodthirsty incarnation of the goddess Durga (Parvati). The idol of the goddess is so fearsome that only the temple's priests are allowed to enter the inner sanctum, but less brutal incarnations of the goddess appear on the torana above the door, beneath a canopy of braided snakes, and also on the temple's 180 carved roof struts. In a classic piece of religious crossover, the Buddhist eight lucky signs are carved beside the temple doorways.

Bhairabnath Temple   HINDU TEMPLE
(Kasi Vishwanath, Akash Bhairab; Map p146) The broad-fronted, triple-roofed Bhairabnath Temple is dedicated to Bhairab, the fearsome incarnation of Shiva, whose consort occupies the Nyatapola Temple across the square. The first temple on this site was a modest structure built in the early 17th century, but King Bhupatindra Malla added an extra storey in 1717 and a third level was added when the temple was rebuilt after the 1934 earthquake. The final version of the temple has a similar rectangular plan to the Bhimsen Temple in Patan's Durbar Sq.

Casually stacked against the north wall of the temple are the enormous wheels and

Bhaktapur

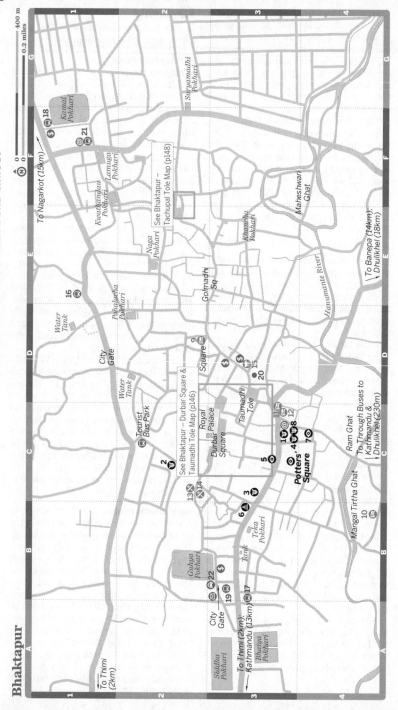

Bhaktapur

AROUND THE KATHMANDU VALLEY BHAKTAPUR

runners from the chariot used to haul the image of Bhairab around town during the Bisket Jatra Festival in mid-April. More chariot runners are piled up on the north side of the Nyatapola Temple.

Despite Bhairab's fearsome powers and his massive temple, the deity is depicted here as a disembodied head just 15cm high! A small hole in the central door (below a row of carved boar snouts) is used to push offerings into the temple's interior, but priests gain entry through the small Betal Temple, on the south side of the main pagoda.

The temple's facade is guarded by two brass lions holding the Nepali flag, the only national flag that is not rectangular or square. To the right of the door is an image of Bhairab painted on rattan, decorated with a gruesome garland of buffalo guts. Head here at dusk to hear traditional devotional music.

Next to the temple is a sunken hiti with a particularly fine spout in the form of a makara.

Til Mahadev Narayan Temple   HINDU TEMPLE
(Map p146) The third interesting temple at Taumadhi Tole is hidden away behind the buildings at the south end of the square. The Til Mahadev Narayan Temple is set in an untidy courtyard, but this is actually an important place of pilgrimage and one of the oldest temples in the city. An inscription states that the site has been in use since 1080 and that the image of Til Mahadev was installed here in 1170.

The double-tiered temple is fronted by an elegant kneeling Garuda statue on a pillar and two columns bearing the sacred sankha and chakra symbols of Vishnu. In case Shiva was feeling left out, a lingam symbol on a yoni base (the Shaivite symbol for the male and female genitals) stands behind a grill in front and to one side of the temple. A plaque to the right of the door depicts the Buddhist deity Vajrayogini in a characteristic pose with her left leg high in the air.

DURBAR SQUARE
Bhaktapur's Durbar Sq was once much more crowded than it is today. Victorian-era illustrations show the square packed with temples and buildings, but the disastrous earthquake of 1934 reduced many of the temples to empty brick plinths, with lion-guarded stairways leading to nowhere.

Expect to be approached by a string of would-be guides and thangka-painting-school touts as you walk around.

Erotic Elephants Temple   HINDU TEMPLE
(Map p146) Outside the main Durbar Sq entrance gate is this little piece of architectural whimsy on the roof of the small Shiva Parvati Temple. Giving graphic representation to the lyric 'birds do it, bees do it...', the temple roof struts feature camels, cows and even elephants engaged in the act of making sweet love, usually in the missionary position!

Shiva Parvati Temple
HINDU TEMPLE

(Map p146) Similar to Nyatapola Temple, this much smaller version also features pairs of statues of elephants, lions, bulls and the wrestlers Jayamel and Phattu leading up the stairs.

Indrayani Temple
HINDU TEMPLE

(Map p142) Just outside the square, head down the path near the hiti that leads down the stairs to this atmospheric Kali temple that was built around a gnarled pipal tree. Blood flows on Saturdays with animal sacrifices.

Ugrachandi & Bhairab Statues
MONUMENT

(Map p146) As you enter Durbar Sq through the western gate, look left to a gateway flanked by two stocky stone lions, erected by King Bhupatindra Malla in 1701. On either side are statues of the terrible Bhairab, the rending, sundering incarnation of Shiva, and his consort on the left side, the equally terrible Ugrachandi (Durga). It is said that the unfortunate sculptor had his hands cut off afterwards, to prevent him from duplicating his masterpieces.

Ugrachandi has 18 arms holding various Tantric weapons symbolising the multiple aspects of her character. She is depicted casually killing a demon with a trident to symbolise the victory of wisdom over ignorance. Bhairab gets by with just 12 arms, one holding two heads impaled on a spear and another holding a cup made from a human skull. The statues originally guarded a courtyard that was destroyed in the 1934 quake.

Char Dham Temples
HINDU TEMPLES

(Map p146) Standing at the western end of Durbar Sq, the four Char Dham temples were constructed to provide spiritual merit for pilgrims who were unable to make the journey to the Indian state of Uttaranchal to visit its famed Char Dham temples.

Temples here include the terracotta shikhara-style **Kedarnath Temple**, dedicated to Shiva, which was destroyed by the 1934 earthquake and renovated by a German team in 1990 using original materials. The two-roofed **Gopi Nath Temple** (also called Jagharnath) features different incarnations of Vishnu on the ceiling struts and a statue of Garuda on the pillar at the entrance.

The small, four-pillared **Rameshwar Temple**, topped by an ornate white dome, is still standing despite its distinct lean courtesy of the 1934 earthquake. The **Badrinath Temple** is sacred to Vishnu in his incarnation as Narayan.

Royal Palace
PALACE

(Map p146) The northern half of the square is taken up by Bhaktapur's Royal Palace. This vast compound was founded by Yaksha Malla and added to by successive kings, but only half a dozen of the 99 courtyards survived the 1934 earthquake. The only parts of the palace open to visitors are the western wing, which houses the National Art Gallery, and a section of the eastern wing, reached through the Golden Gate.

National Art Gallery

(foreigner/SAARC Rs 100/40, camera/video Rs 50/200; ☉10.15am–3.45pm Tue-Sun, to 3pm Mon, to 5pm mid-Jan–mid-Oct) The western end of the palace contains the best of the three museums in Bhaktapur. The entrance to the gallery is flanked by two huge guardian lions, one male and one female. Beside the lions are some imposing 17th-century statues of Hanuman the monkey god, in his four-armed Tantric form, and Vishnu, as the gut-ripping Narsingha.

Inside the gallery you can view an extensive collection of Tantric cloth paintings – the Hindu version of Buddhist thangkas – as well as palm-leaf manuscripts and metal, stone and wooden votive objects, some of which date to the 12th century. Look out for depictions of the nightmarish Maha Sambhara, with 21 faces and an unbelievable number of arms, as well as scenes from the Karma Sutra. Also here are portraits of all the Shah kings, except Gyanendra (the last of the Nepali kings), who has been neatly excised from the gallery. Keep hold of your ticket as this also covers the Woodcarving Museum and Brass & Bronze Museum in Tachupal Tole.

Golden Gate

You can't miss the magnificent Golden Gate, or Sun Dhoka, with its fabulous portal, topped by a frieze of Hindu deities, set into a bright red gatehouse surrounded by the white palace walls. Construction of the gate and palace began during the reign of King Bhupatindra Malla (r 1696–1722), and the project was completed by his successor, Jaya Ranjit Malla, in 1754. The death of Jaya Ranjit Malla marked the end of the Malla dynasty and the end of the golden age of Newari architecture in Nepal.

The level of detail on the repoussé work on the Golden Gate is extraordinary. The gilded torana features a fabulous Garuda wrestling with a number of supernatural serpents, his sworn enemies. Below is a four-headed and 10-armed figure of the goddess Taleju Bhawani, the family deity of the Malla kings. There are temples to Taleju in the royal palaces in Kathmandu and Patan as well as Bhaktapur.

The Golden Gate opens to the inner courtyards of the **55 window palace**, which, you guessed it, has 55 intricate wooden windows stretching along its upper level. Immediately within the gate is a pair of enormous **war drums**, which were used to rouse the city in the event of attack. From here you'll pass the two statues of traditionally dressed guards standing either side of an ornate door, brought here from Rajhastan.

Taleju Temple

Continuing on you'll reach the main entrance to **Mul Chowk**, the oldest part of the palace and the site of Taleju Temple, built in 1553. One of the most sacred temples in Bhaktapur, only Hindus can enter, but you can admire its entrance, which is fronted by magnificent woodcarvings. Photography is prohibited.

Naga Pokhari

Continuing on around the corner from Mul Chowk is this 17th-century **water tank** used for the ritual immersion of the idol of Taleju. The pool is encircled by a writhing stone cobra and more serpents rise up in the middle and at the end of the tank, where water pours from a magnificent dhara in the form of a goat being eaten by a makara.

King Bhupatindra Malla's Column   MONUMENT

(Map p146) With hands folded in a prayer position, the bronze statue of King Bhupatindra Malla sits atop a column in front of the Vatsala Durga Temple. The statue was created in 1699 and it mirrors the similar statues in the Durbar Sqs of Kathmandu and Patan. He was the best known of the Malla kings of Bhaktapur, and contributed to much of the architecture in town.

Vatsala Durga Temple   HINDU TEMPLE

(Map p146) Beside the king's statue and directly in front of the Royal Palace is this stone temple, which was built by King Jagat Prakash Malla in either 1672 or 1727 (depending on which inscriptions you trust). This is Bhaktapur's answer to the Krishna Mandir in Patan, and it follows similar Indian architectural rules. Note the mythical beasts bursting out from the sides of the shikhara and the detailed carvings of multi-armed deities in the false windows on the second level. Beside the temple is an ornate sunken **hiti** containing a fine stone dhara in the form of a makara, topped by a crocodile and a frog.

Taleju Bell   MONUMENT

(Map p146) In front of the Vatsala Durga Temple is a large bell, which was erected by King Jaya Ranjit Malla in 1737 to mark morning and evening prayers at the Taleju Temple. A smaller bell on the plinth of the Taleju Temple is known as the 'barking bell'. According to legend, it was erected by King Bhupatindra Malla in 1721 to counteract a vision he

---

BISKET JATRA AT KHALNA TOLE

Held annually in the Nepali month of Baisakh (typically in the middle of April), the dramatic Bisket Jatra Festival heralds the start of the Nepali New Year. The focal point of the celebrations is the mighty chariot of Bhairab, which is assembled from the timbers scattered beside the Bhairabnath Temple and Nyatapola Temple in Taumadhi Tole. As the festival gets under way, the ponderous chariot is hauled through the streets by dozens of devotees to Khalna Tole, with Betal, Bhairab's sidekick from the tiny temple behind the Bhairabnath Temple, riding out front like a ship's figurehead. Bhadrakali, the consort of Bhairab, follows behind in her own chariot.

The creaking and swaying chariots lumber around the town, pausing for a huge tug of war between the eastern and western sides of town. The winning side is charged with looking after the images of the gods during their week-long sojourn in Khalna Tole's octagonal *path* (pilgrim shelter). The chariots then skid down the steep road leading to Khalna Tole, where a huge 25m-high lingam is erected in a stone base shaped like a yoni.

As night falls the following day (New Year's Day), the pole is pulled down in another violent tug of war, and as the pole crashes to the ground, the new year officially commences. Bhairab and Betal return to Taumadhi Tole, while Bhadrakali goes back to her shrine by the river. It certainly beats 'Auld Lang Syne'...

Bhaktapur – Durbar Square & Taumadhi Tole

had in a dream, and to this day dogs are said to bark and whine if the bell is rung – which could have a physical explanation in terms of resonance frequencies. With the amount of dogs in town, it's probably a good thing the bell is chained so it can't be rung.

Chyasilin Mandap   MONUMENT
(Map p146) The octagonal pavilion known as Chyasilin Mandap was in fact created in 1990 using components from a temple that was destroyed in the 1934 earthquake and reassembled around a metal frame.

Pashupatinath Temple   HINDU TEMPLE
(Map p146) Behind the Vatsala Durga Temple, the Pashupatinath Temple is dedicated to Shiva as Pashupati and is a replica of the main shrine at Pashupatinath. Originally built by King Yaksha Malla in 1475 (or 1482), it is the oldest temple in the square. Like many temples, the roof struts feature erotic images, but what exactly the dwarf is doing with that bowl takes things to a new level.

Siddhi Lakshmi Temple   HINDU TEMPLE
(Lohan Dega, Stone Temple; Map p146) By the southeastern corner of the palace stands the attractive 17th-century Siddhi Lakshmi Temple. The steps up to the temple are flanked by male and female attendants, each leading a child and a rather eager-looking dog. On successive levels the stairs are flanked by horses, garlanded rhinos, human-faced lions and camels. The temple itself is built in the classic shikhara style, commonly seen in the north of India.

Behind the temple is a neglected corner of the square that contains a small, red-brick **Vatsala Temple** and a pair of lost-looking curly-haired **stone lions** who, depending on what theory you subscribe to, are either guarding the palace or the site of a lost temple that crumbled to dust in the 1934 earthquake.

Bhaktapur – Durbar Square & Taumadhi Tole

Fasidega Temple HINDU TEMPLE
(Map p146) The large and plain Fasidega Temple is notable more as a landmark than for any great architectural merit. If you look towards Bhaktapur from vantage points such as Changu Narayan (p156), the white bulk of the Fasidega is always an easy landmark to pick out. The shrine is dedicated to Shiva and it sits atop a six-level plinth with guardian elephants, lions and cows. Inside is a substantial lingam.

Tadhunchen Bahal BUDDHIST TEMPLE
(Chatur Varna Mahavihara; Map p146) Walking east from Durbar Sq, you'll pass the gateway to the restored Tadhunchen Bahal monastery, tucked between souvenir shops. This Buddhist temple is linked to the cult of the Kumari, Bhaktapur's living goddess. Bhaktapur actually has three Kumaris, but they lack the political importance of Kathmandu's (see the boxed text, p66).

In the inner courtyard the roof struts on the eastern side have unusual carvings that show the tortures of the damned. In one, a snake is wrapped around a man, another shows two rams butting an unfortunate's head, while a third strut shows a nasty tooth extraction being performed with a large pair of pliers!

TACHUPAL TOLE
Tachupal Tole was the original central square of Bhaktapur and it formed the official seat of Bhaktapur royalty until the late 16th century.

Dattatreya Temple HINDU TEMPLE
(Map p148) At the east end of the square, the eye-catching Dattatreya Temple was originally built in 1427, supposedly using the timber from a single tree. The slightly mismatched front porch was added later. The temple is dedicated to Dattatreya, a curious hybrid deity, blending elements of Brahma, Vishnu and Shiva. Judging from the Garuda statue and the conch and chakra disc mounted on pillars supported by stone

turtles in front of the temple, Vishnu seems to have come out on top.

The three-storey temple is raised above the ground on a brick and terracotta base, which is carved with erotic scenes, including unexpected humour where one bored-looking woman multitasks by washing her hair while being pleasured by her husband. The main steps to the temple are guarded by statues of the same two Malla wrestlers who watch over the first plinth of the Nyatapola Temple.

Bhimsen Temple HINDU TEMPLE

(Map p148) At the other end of the square, this two-storey, 17th-century temple is sacred to Bhimsen, the god of commerce. The squat rectangular structure has an open ground floor and an inner sanctum on the second level. In front is a platform with a small double-roofed Vishnu/Narayan Temple and a pillar topped by a brass lion with his right paw raised. Steps lead down behind it to the deeply sunken Bhimsen Pokhari tank.

Pujari Math HISTORIC BUILDING

(Map p148) The square is flanked by a series of ornate brick-and-timber buildings that were originally used as maths (Hindu priests' houses). The best known is the Pujari Math, which was constructed in the 15th century during the reign of King Yaksha Malla, but rebuilt in 1763. It now serves as the Wood-

carving Museum. German experts renovated the building in 1979 as a wedding gift for the then King Birendra.

The most famous feature of this handsome mansion is the superb 15th-century **Peacock Window**, visible from the narrow alley on the right-hand side. This is widely regarded as the finest carved window in the valley and it appears on countless postcards. Many surrounding shops sell miniature wooden copies of the window as souvenirs.

Woodcarving Museum MUSEUM

(Map p148; foreigner/SAARC Rs 100/40, camera/video Rs 50/200; ⊘10am-4pm Wed-Sun, to 3pm Mon, to 5pm winter) This museum has some fine examples of Bhaktapur woodcarving displayed in dark, creaky rooms. There isn't enough light to justify paying the camera fee, but it's worth a visit, not least for the extravagantly carved windows in the inner courtyard. The same ticket covers entry to the nearby Brass & Bronze Museum and the National Art Gallery.

Brass & Bronze Museum MUSEUM

(Map p148; foreigner/SAARC Rs 100/40, camera/video Rs 50/200; ⊘10am-5pm Wed-Sun, to 3pm Mon, to 5pm winter) Directly across from the Woodcarving Museum, in another old math with similar lighting problems, this museum has some excellent examples of traditional

Bhaktapur – Tachupal Tole

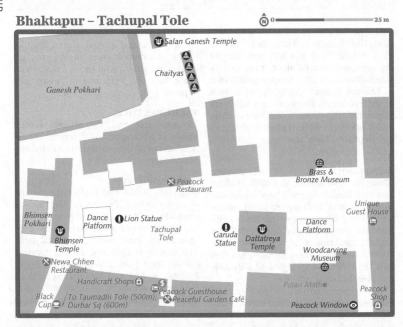

BHAKTAPUR'S PONDS

Around the outskirts of Bhaktapur are a series of enormous tanks, constructed in the medieval period to store water for drinking, bathing and religious rituals. The tanks still play an important role in the social life of Bhaktapur – in the mornings and afternoons, locals gather by the ponds to bathe, socialise, take romantic walks and feed the giant carp and turtles that keep the water free from detritus.

The most impressive tank is the ghat-lined **Siddha Pokhari** (Map p142) near the main bus park. This rectangular reservoir is set inside an enormous wall that is broken by rest houses and towers that have been consumed by the roots of giant fig trees. You can buy bags of corn and rice to feed the fish for a few rupees.

During the annual festival of **Naga Panchami** in the Nepali month of Saaun (July–August), residents of Bhaktapur offer a bowl of rice to the nagas (serpent spirits who control the rain) who live in the Siddha Pokhari. According to legend, a holy man once attempted to kill an evil naga who lived in the lake by transforming himself into a snake. An attendant waited by with a bowl of magical rice to transform the yogi back into human form, but when the victorious holy man slithered from the water, his terrified assistant fled, taking the holy rice with him and leaving the yogi trapped for eternity in his scaly form. To this day, locals leave a bowl of rice out at Naga Panchami in case the snake-yogi decides to return.

Other significant tanks include the nearby Bhaiya Pokhari (across the road to the south), the Guhya Pokhari (across the road to the east) and the Kamal Pokhari (at the northeast end of Bhaktapur on the road to Nagarkot).

metalwork, including ceremonial lamps and ritual vessels from around the valley. Hold on to your ticket to avoid paying entry at the other museums.

Salan Ganesh Temple HINDU TEMPLE
(Map p148) On the north side of Tachupal Tole is an open area with a small temple dating from 1654. Backed by a large tank, the open temple is ornately decorated, but the image is a natural rock with only the vaguest elephant-head shape.

THE WESTERN GATE TO TAUMADHI TOLE
Ni Bahal BUDDHIST TEMPLE
(Jetbarna Maha Bihar; Map p142) Located before the major junction, look for the tiny, tunnel-like entrance to this small Buddhist temple dedicated to Maitreya Buddha, the future Buddha. The courtyard contains a very old whitewashed chaitya and several Buddhist shrines. Next to the gatehouse to the courtyard is an enormous pilgrims' rest house with finely carved timbers.

Jaya Varahi Temple HINDU TEMPLE
(Map p142) Situated on the road to the Mangal Tirtha Ghat, the red-brick Jaya Varahi is dedicated to Parvati as the boar-headed Varahi. Look for two very different depictions of the goddess on the torana above the central doorway and the torana over the window above. At the eastern end of the temple is the entrance to the upper floor, flanked by stone lions and banners.

Nasamana Square SQUARE
(Map p142) This square lost its temples in the 1934 quake, but it still has a large Garuda statue praying to a vanished Vishnu shrine. Also here is a stone hiti with a spout in the shape of a goat being eaten by a makara.

Jyotirlingeshwar Temple HINDU TEMPLE
(Map p142) Nearby to Nasamana Sq is the tall shikhara housing an important lingam, and two small Shiva shrines by a tank filled with alarmingly green algae. Continue straight and you will pass a turning on the right to Potters' Sq.

TOP CHOICE **Potters' Square** SQUARE
(Map p142) Hidden by the alleyways leading south from the curving road to Taumadhi Tole, Potters' Sq is exactly what you would expect – a huge public square, full of treadle-power potters' wheels and rows of clay pots drying in the sun. This is the centre of Bhaktapur's ceramic industry, and it's a fascinating place to wander around. Several shops sell the finished article, and you can see the firing process at the back of the square, which is lined with mud-covered straw kilns. During the harvest in October, everywhere

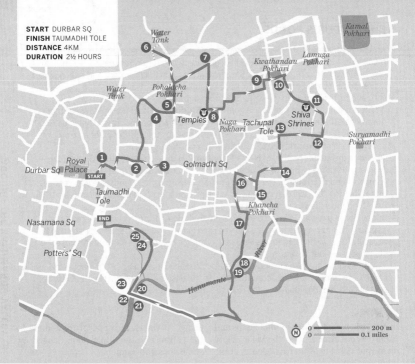

START DURBAR SQ
FINISH TAUMADHI TOLE
DISTANCE 4KM
DURATION 2½ HOURS

Kamal Pokhari

Water Tank

Lamuga Pokhari

Kwathandau Pokhari

Water Tank

Pohalacha Pokhari

Shiva Shrines

Temples

Naga Pokhari

Tachupal Tole

Suryamadhi Pokhari

Royal Palace

Durbar Sq

START

Golmadhi Sq

Taumadhi Tole

Nasamana Sq

END

Khancha Pokhari

Potters' Sq

Hanumante

N

0 — 200 m
0 — 0.1 miles

Walking Tour
Bhaktapur

❯ The following walking tour takes you through the backstreets that reveal a more complete picture to the living museum that is Bhaktapur.

Starting from the northeastern corner of Durbar Sq, walk to the east of the Fasidega Temple, passing a multicoloured **① Ganesh shrine**, where the god is worshipped in the form of a rock that naturally resembles an elephant's head. Turn to the right to reach a square with disused palace buildings and a ruined temple plinth. Walk around the north side of the square and exit at the northeast corner past the hiti, by the strut-roofed **② Tripurasundari Temple**, sacred to one of the Navadurgas (see the boxed text, p155). Continue east passing several local confectionery shops selling milk-based Indian sweets, where the road bends right at a brick Narayan shrine. Past the next alley, a doorway leads into a cramped bahal containing a small **③ Bhimsen Temple**, which was created from remains of the Lun Bahal, a 16th-cen-

tury Buddhist monastery. Note the pots and pans nailed to the roof struts by devotees.

Head back to the Narayan shrine, take a right and head 200m to the unassuming brick facade of the **④ Ganesh Temple**, with fine figures of the elephant-headed deity on its torana and an unusual terracotta Ganesh window above the door.

At the next junction take a right, past some lovely carved windows, and then swing left past a small **⑤ Mahakali shrine** with caged windows and buffalo horns, and the Pohalacha Pokhari tank, to a city ticket office. Continue by the ticket office to the Bhaktapur-Nagarkot road, where you take a left and cross the road to climb the small hillock to a large **⑥ Mahakali Temple**, which has an eccentric collection of statues inside a gated pavilion. Note the buffalo entrails draped over the guardian statues inside the temple.

Return to the ticket office and take a left until you reach a brick square containing a tiny, yellow-roofed **⑦ Mahalakshmi Temple**, sacred to the goddess of wealth. Turn right (south) and continue straight to a large tank, the ⑧ **Naga Pokhari**, where saffron colour threads are dried on large racks beside the lurid green waters. On the western side of the tank is a cluster of small temples to various Hindu deities, and in the middle is a statue of a rearing cobra.

Pass along the north side of the tank, turn left and cross a tiny courtyard with lovely woodcarvings and a central chaitya. Continue out the far end past another courtyard. On the left you'll see the white stucco pillars that mark the entrance to the ⑨ **Mul Dipankar Bihar**, enshrining an image of Dipankar, the Buddha of Light.

Continue east to the road junction, and turn left by a lotus-roofed Vishnu shrine, to reach the large Kwathandau Pokhari. Head right at the tank and you'll pass the ⑩ **Nava Durga Temple**, a Tantric Shaivite temple with a fine gilded torana. Only Hindus are allowed to enter.

Continue southeast through a wide square full of drying ceramic pots, brick Shiva shrines and houses with carved balconies. Follow the lanes south past the ⑪ **Toni Hagen house**, restored in honour of the famous Swiss geologist. Continue to the junction by a stupa and a dance platform, on the main east–west road. Turn right and immediately on your left you'll see the elaborate entrance to the ⑫ **Wakupati Narayan Temple**, built in 1667. The courtyard is full of spinners and wood-whittlers, and women winnow rice here in the harvest season using flat baskets as fans. The ornate, golden temple is fronted by an entourage of five Garudas supported on pillars on the backs of turtles.

Continue from here past the centuries-old wooden frontage of the ⑬ **Brahmayani Temple**, fronted by two lions and sacred to the patron goddess of Panauti, and then on to Tachupal Tole.

From here turn left down the side of the Pujari Math, passing the famous Peacock Window. Follow the road around south and turn right at the small square with a ⑭ **Vishnu Temple** on an octagonal plinth.

Go straight down an atmospheric alley lined with brick houses and follow it around to the left, then to the right into a large square. Detour south from this square down a wide cobbled road to reach a large statue of ⑮ **Sakyamuni**, the historical Buddha, overlooking the river from the east end of the Khancha Pokhari tank.

Return to the square and take a left and walk west towards the main road linking Taumadhi Tole and Tachupal Tole. Just before the junction is the unassuming gateway to the ornate Inacho Bahal, containing the narrow ⑯ **Sri Indravarta Mahavihar**, a 17th-century Buddhist temple topped by a lopsided miniature pagoda roof. From here, the walk gets really interesting. Rather than following the road to Taumadhi Tole, walk south towards the Hanumante River, passing the other end of the Khancha Pokhari and the ⑰ **Munivihar**, a rapidly expanding modern Buddhist temple. At the bottom of the hill is an impressive collection of ⑱ **chaityas**, **Shiva statues**, **Shaivite shrines** and **lingams**, including a bas-relief of a nude Shiva (obviously pleased to see you!) beside what could well be the two largest Shiva lingams in Nepal.

Duck left beside the Ram Janaki Mandir to another splendid collection of statues at ⑲ **Hanuman Ghat**. Note the exquisitely carved images of Ganesh, Sakyamuni, Ram and Sita, Hanuman and Vishnu/Narayan, reclining on a bed of snakes. Hindu yogis often come here to meditate.

Cross the bridge and follow the road uphill, then turn sharply right after the Happy Home School onto a brick-lined path that runs west along the riverbank. Look north to see the tower of the Nyatapola Temple rising above the rooftops across the river as you pass another ticket booth and the garish ⑳ **Bhimsen Temple** fronted by a carved tiger on a column.

Follow this wide road to the river past some modern cremation plinths at ㉑ **Chuping Ghat**. Just across the river, turn left past a Hanuman statue on the riverbank and nip into the campus of the ㉒ **Kathmandu University Department of Music**, where the sound of traditional music wafts over the peaceful ornamental gardens. It's closed on Saturday.

Above the river is the wide open square of ㉓ **Khalna Tole**, the setting for the spectacular Bisket Jatra Festival (see the boxed text, p145). In the middle of the square, note the huge stone yoni where the giant lingam is erected (you may have to pick your way through mountains of drying rice and grain to get here).

To finish, walk north along the river at the bottom of the square and follow the curving path uphill past the modern ㉔ **Kumari Temple** and the ㉕ **Bhagwati Temple**, emerging on the southern side of Taumadhi Tole.

that is not covered by pots is covered by drying rice.

On the northern side of the square a small hillock is topped by a shady pipal tree and a **Ganesh shrine**, surrounded by piles of straw for the pottery kilns. In the square itself is a solid-brick **Vishnu Temple**, which was constructed from remnants of temples destroyed in the 1934 quake, and the double-roofed **Jeth Ganesh Temple**, whose priest is chosen from the Kumal (potters') caste.

Those interested in henna body art can learn the art of *mehndi* at **Surekha Mahenadi Classes** (☑9849171280) in a small house south of Potters' Sq.

★☆ Festivals & Events

Bisket Jatra   HINDU
Bhaktapur celebrates Bisket Jatra (Nepal's New Year's Day) in mid-April with a stupendous chariot festival (see the boxed text on p145).

Gai Jatra   HINDU
Bhaktapur is the best place to witness the antics of Gai Jatra (see p20), where cows and boys dressed as cows are paraded through the streets. It's not quite the running of the bulls at Pamplona, but it's all good fun.

🛏 Sleeping

⦿ CHOICE Sunny Guest House   GUESTHOUSE $$
(Map p146; ☑6616094; www.sunnyguesthouse nepal.com; s/d/tr incl breakfast US$25/35/45; 🛜) This long-established place scores extra points for the sunny disposition of its staff and an excellent location at the north end of Taumadhi Tole. The building is a wonderful Newari design, there's a superior rooftop restaurant and rooms have screen-printed bedspreads and carved wooden lattice windows.

Ganesh Guest House   GUESTHOUSE $
(Map p142; ☑6611550; www.ganeshguesthouse. com; r with/without bathroom Rs 500/300; @🛜) A favourite for budget travellers, this laid-back guesthouse gets rave reviews for its cheap rates, friendly staff and piping-hot showers. Its restaurant is a good hang-out spot.

Siddhi Laxmi Guest House   GUESTHOUSE $
(Map p146; ☑6612500; siddhilaxmi.guesthouse@ gmail.com; s/d from Rs 700/1200; 🛜) Sharing a courtyard with the Til Mahadev Narayan Temple, this Newari-inspired guesthouse

has comfortable rooms to suit all budgets. Most have TVs, balconies and decent views, and there's a rooftop garden and a homely restaurant downstairs. Staff are friendly and the owner is a genuine character. A pair of earplugs will come in handy, as there are barking dogs and ringing bells to contend with. Healthy discounts are available.

Khwopa Guest House   GUESTHOUSE $
(Map p142; ☑6614661; www.khwopa-guesthouse. com.np; s/d from Rs 800/1200; 🛜) Just south of Taumadhi Tole, this pocket-sized family-run guesthouse is a rare budget choice in expensive Bhaktapur. The vibe is easygoing and friendly.

Shiva Guest House   GUESTHOUSE $
(Map p146; ☑6613912; www.shivaguesthouse.com; s/d US$15/20, without bathroom US$6/10; 🛜) A well-maintained place on Durbar Sq with comfy rooms and a heartfelt welcome. Ask for a corner room if you want a view. Discounts of 20% are available from December to August.

Peacock Guesthouse   GUESTHOUSE $
(Map p148; ☑6611829; www.peacockguesthouse nepal.com; r from Rs 600; 🛜) Right on Tachupal Tole, this wonderful 15th-century building ticks many boxes. It has comfortable, cheap rooms and historic character – though anyone over 6ft might struggle with its low ceilings. Also has an attractive front courtyard, from which woodworkers chip away.

Cosy Hotel   HOTEL $$
(Map p146; ☑6616333; www.cosyhotel.com.np; r incl breakfast US$25-55; ❀@🛜) Tucked away on a narrow road to Potters' Sq, you might not get views here, but this business-chic hotel definitely lives up to its name, with sparkling rooms, lovely big beds, bathtubs and double-glazed windows. Toothbrushes, mineral water and sweets are thoughtful gestures. Rooms can sleep up to three, and the cheapest has a common bathroom.

Nyatapola Guest House   GUESTHOUSE $
(Map p142; ☑6614599; www.nyatapolacrafts.com; s/d without bathroom Rs 500/700; 🛜) Located above a craft shop in a street with plenty of Newari flavour, Nyatapola's rooms are spacious and its beds have traditional cotton mattresses. Shared bathrooms are modern and shiny clean. It's owned by a family of woodcarvers, and they can arrange lessons on the craft.

Golden Gate Guest House GUESTHOUSE $
(Map p146; 6610534; www.goldengateguest
house.com; s/d Rs 700/1000, without bathroom
Rs 400/600;) A quiet courtyard and attentive staff are the drawcards at this brick-
built guesthouse between Durbar Sq and
Taumadhi Tole. Rooms won't win any design
awards, but they're clean and some have balconies. The rooftop offers views towards the
Fasidega Temple in one direction and the
Nyatapola Temple in the other.

Pagoda Guest House GUESTHOUSE $$
(Map p146; 6613248; www.pagodaguest
house.com.np; s/d US$15/35, without bathroom
US$10/12;) A cute family-run place in the
northwest corner of Taumadhi Tole, set back
from the hubbub and piled high with pot
plants. Its six rooms are all different, but
well appointed. There's also a decent rooftop
restaurant. It also manages the next-door
Newa Guest House (6916335), a more up-
market choice with tasteful rooms that have
splendid temple views.

Unique Guest House GUESTHOUSE $
(Map p148; 6611575; www.uniqueguesthouse.
com; s/d from US$10/15) Above a souvenir
shop, this creaky and slightly claustrophobic
old building opens right up to Tachupal Tole
with unbeatable views of Dattatreya Tem-
ple. There is one room per floor, and barely
space to swing a shopping bag on the stairs.

Greenland Guest House GUESTHOUSE $
(6618115; www.greenlandbhaktapur.com; r with/
without bathroom Rs 1200/800;) Set on the
edge of the forest on the western side of
Bhaktapur, this midrange resort is surround-
ed by lovely quiet lawns and trees full of fly-
ing foxes (fruit bats). Rooms are smart, clean
and comfortable, and the showers are set in
giant beaten-copper dishes.

Bhadgaon Guest House GUESTHOUSE $$
(Map p146; 6610488; www.bhadgaon.com.np;
Taumadhi Tole; s/d from US$30/35;) An up-
date of a traditional Newari building, this
place has it all – a courtyard restaurant, a
rooftop balcony with perfect views and a
coveted deluxe room with a private balcony
overlooking Taumadhi Tole. Rooms are
modern-looking rather than traditional, but
they are excellent value. Its annexe across
the square is less appealing.

Hotel Heritage BOUTIQUE HOTEL $$$
(Map p142; 6611628; www.hotelheritage.com.
np; s/d from US$100/110;) Outside the

boundaries of the old town, this multistorey
red-brick Newari building is an interesting
blend of old and new – incorporating original
parts such as windows and bricks into its
design. While it's well overpriced, it remains
the plushest option in Bhaktapur with all of
the mod cons and thoughtful touches.

✕ Eating & Drinking

Cafe Beyond KOREAN $
(Map p142; mains Rs 130-250; 7am-8pm) In a
town with little variation between menus,
this Korean restaurant makes for a great
point of difference. Run by an NGO that pro-
motes local organic farming, Cafe Beyond
serves a good range of fresh-tasting food,
most of which is grown in the cafe's own ve-
gie garden. It's an alluring little restaurant,
decked out with funky decor, while outside
is a peaceful garden. It also serves *soju* (rice
liquor from Korea) and has a coffee machine.

Newa Chhen Restaurant NEPALI $
(Map p148; mains from Rs 70) Slightly rundown
and dingy, the food however is cheap and
tasty. It gets points for excellent Newari
dishes and a corner table with killer views
over the square.

Shiva's Café Corner CAFE $
(Map p146; espresso Rs 110, mains Rs 150-375;)
With an espresso machine and free wi-fi,
this inviting cafe is a good spot for breakfast.

Café Nyatapola NEPALI, INTERNATIONAL $$
(Map p146; mains Rs 135-325, set meals from
Rs 625; 8am-7pm) Out in the square at Taumadhi Tole, this place is touristy and pricey,
but what a setting! Tables are set on the balconies of a historic pagoda temple – there
are even erotic carvings on the roof struts.
The menu covers the usual Nepali, Chinese
and Continental standards, and a portion of
the profits supports a local hospital.

**Watshala Garden
Restaurant** NEPALI, INTERNATIONAL $$
(Map p146; mains Rs 150-300;) Set in a pot-
plant-filled courtyard behind the Shiva
Guest House, this place is a genuine retreat
from the Durbar Sq crowds. Sit back with a
cold beer and gently exhale...

Palace Restaurant NEPALI, INTERNATIONAL $$
(Map p146; mains Rs 150-350) Opposite the
Royal Palace in a long, historic building, this
regal place offers the chance to dine with a
view that used to be reserved for the Malla
kings.

KING OF CURDS

While in Bhaktapur, be sure to try the town's great contribution to the world of desserts – *juju dhau*, 'the king of curds'. Just how special can yoghurt be, you might ask? Well, this could just be the richest, creamiest yoghurt in the world! You'll find this delicacy in many tourist restaurants, but the best places to try it are the hole-in-the-wall restaurants between Durbar Sq and the public bus stand (look for the pictures of bowls of curd outside). King curd comes set in an earthenware bowl for Rs 25.

Namaste Cafe   CAFE **$$**
(Map p146; mains Rs 120-300) Cosy upstairs cafe decked out in attractive decor, with great views of Taumadhi Tole.

Peaceful Garden Café   NEPALI, INTERNATIONAL **$**
(Map p148; dishes from Rs 140) This sleepy outdoor eatery, in a courtyard behind the souvenir shops on the south side of the square, does the usual menu, but at good prices.

Peacock Restaurant   NEPALI, INTERNATIONAL **$$**
(Map p148; mains Rs 200-345) Tachupal Tole's answer to Café Nyatapola in a wood-fronted math on the north side of the square is atmospheric, and the food is decent enough.

Black Cup   CAFE
(Map p148; espresso Rs 75) Staffed by enthusiastic local students, this small coffeehouse serves decent espressos, lattes etc. It's a handy retreat from Tachupal Tole. It has another branch, **Himalayan Java** (Map p142) near Taumadhi Tole.

Black Olive   BAR
(Map p146) With live music on weekends and a decent cocktail list, this is a good place to head for a drink. Choose between a rooftop beer garden or swanky downstairs bar. Also does decent food.

🛍 Shopping

Bhaktapur is famed for its **pottery**, which is sold in a staggering number of souvenir shops around the main squares, particularly at Tachupal Tole and Taumadhi Tole. There's also some good metalwork on sale – look out for beaten metal dishes embossed with Buddhist symbols and ornate brass butter lamps in the shape of the Krishna Temple in Patan's Durbar Sq.

Many small factories in Bhaktapur produce **handmade paper** from the pulp of the *lokta* (daphne) bush, which is sold all over town as cards, notepads, photo albums, envelopes and other stationery items.

Bhaktapur has long been renowned for its **woodcarving**, and this craft is now used to make objects that fit well into Western homes. Some of the best work is sold from the stalls around Durbar Sq and the alley beside the Pujari Math. Miniature models of the famous Peacock Window are always popular souvenirs.

Peacock Shop   HANDICRAFTS
(Map p148; ◷9am-6.30pm, workshop closed Sat) This good paper emporium is near the Peacock Window, down the side of Pujari Math. Prices are higher than some other stores, but so is the quality, and you can visit the workshop to observe the pressing, drying, smoothing, cutting and printing of the paper.

ℹ Information

To enter Bhaktapur you must pay a hefty fee of US$15. SAARC nationalities pay Rs 100 and children under 10 are free. This fee is collected at over a dozen entrances to the city and your ticket will be checked whenever you pass one of the checkpoints. If you are staying here for up to a week, you need only pay the entrance fee once, but you must ask the ticket desk to write your passport number on the back of the ticket.

For longer stays (up to one year), a Bhaktapur Visitor Pass is available within a week of purchasing your entry ticket. You need two passport photos and a photocopy of your visa and passport details.

The **tourist information centre** (Map p146; Durbar Sq; ◷6am-7.30pm) has maps and free internet for 30 minutes. Around Taumadhi and Tachupal Toles, there are moneychangers and several internet cafes.

Guides touting their services around Durbar Sq charge Rs 200 per hour. Look out for the booklet *Bhaktapur: A Guide Book,* published by the **Bhaktapur Tourism Development Committee** (www.btdc.org.np) and sold in local shops.

ℹ Getting There & Away

Bicycle

The Arniko Hwy to Bhaktapur carries a lot of bellowing, belching buses and trucks, so it's better to follow the parallel road to Bhaktapur past the northern end of Thimi. **Green Valley Mountain Bike** (Map p142; ☏9841495695) have mountain bikes for hire (per day Rs 500), and information on trails in the area.

Bus, Minibus & Taxi

Taxis from Kathmandu cost between Rs 700 to Rs 800 one way. Express minibuses run very frequently from Kathmandu's Bagh Bazar bus stand (Rs 50, one hour) until nightfall, dropping off next to the Guhya Pokhari, a short walk west of Durbar Sq. For Thimi (Rs 13, 20 minutes), take a local bus rather than an express bus. Buses also run along the highway south of Bhaktapur from the Lagankhel bus stand in Patan (Rs 20, 30 minutes).

Kathmandu buses also leave from a stand at the northeastern edge of Bhaktapur by the Lamuga Pokhari. The stand for buses to Nagarkot (Rs 35, 1½ hours, from 7am to 5.30pm) is nearby, beside the Kamal Pokhari tank. A taxi from here takes 45 minutes and costs around Rs 800. Buses to Changu Narayan (Rs 15, 30 minutes) leave every 30 minutes or so from the junction with the Changu Narayan road.

For Dhulikhel (Rs 35, one hour) or anywhere further east, you'll have to walk 20 minutes south across the river to the Arniko Hwy to catch a (probably packed) through bus from Kathmandu. Count on around Rs 900 for a taxi to Dhulikhel.

AROUND BHAKTAPUR

Suriya Binayak Temple

South of Bhaktapur, on the south side of the Arniko Hwy, Suriya Binayak is an important Ganesh temple dating back to the 17th century. The white shikhara-style temple contains some interesting statuary, but the main attraction is the peaceful setting and the walk uphill above the temple to a hillside with sweeping views over Bhaktapur. The temple is flanked by statues of Malla kings and a large statue of Ganesh's vehicle, the rat.

To get here, take the road south from Potters' Sq to Ram Ghat (where there are areas for ritual bathing and cremations) and cross the river to the Arniko Hwy. On the other side, it's a 1km walk along the road to the start of the steps to the temple. Bank on around 30 minutes from Taumadhi Tole.

Thimi

Thimi, known historically as Madhyapur, was once the fourth-largest town in the valley. Today, it's a sleepy backwater but its winding, brick-paved streets are lined with medieval temples. The town takes its modern name from the Newari phrase for 'capable people', which is fitting as the town is a major centre for the production of pottery and papier-mâché masks. You'll pass a string of mask shops on the road that cuts across the north end of town towards Bhaktapur.

Its most well-known temple is 16th-century **Balkumari Temple**, dedicated to one of Bhairab's shaktis. The goddess' peacock vehicle is depicted on a column in front of the temple, as well as each corner of the temple. It's the focus for the **Balkumari Jatra**, a festival where Thimi welcomes the new year (around mid-April) with riotous scenes as the 32 khats (palanquins) whirl around the temple while red powder is hurled at them.

A passage on the south side of the square leads to Thimi's **potters' square**, which is full of kilns made from straw covered with ash.

One kilometre north of Thimi is the village of **Bode**, famous for its 17th-century **Mahalakshmi Temple**, with a small image of Narayan reclining on his snake bed just behind.

❶ Getting There & Away

Any of the Bhaktapur-bound minibuses from Kathmandu will be able to drop you at Thimi (Rs 20, 40 minutes), either at the southern gateway on the Arniko Hwy, or on the back road at the north end of Thimi.

If you are bicycling to Bhaktapur, the northern (old) road offers a far more pleasant ride. The road branches off the Arniko Hwy to the east of the runway at Tribhuvan Airport.

NAVADURGA DANCERS

The colourful masks sold around Bhaktapur and Thimi are not just souvenirs. Every year, as part of the Dasain celebrations in September or October, local residents perform frenetic dances in Bhaktapur's public squares, during which they are said to be possessed by the spirits of the Navadurga, the nine incarnations of the fearsome consort of Shiva. The masks worn by dancers are cremated ever year and new masks are made from the ashes, mixed with black clay from the fields around Bhaktapur. Although most of the masks for sale in Bhaktapur are made for the tourist market, they are full of Tantric symbolism. Popular figures include Ganesh, Kali, Bhairab, boar-headed Varahi, red-faced Kumari and roaring Sima and Duma, the eerie harbingers of death.

Changu Narayan Temple

Perched atop a narrow ridge due north of Bhaktapur, the beautiful and historic temple of Changu Narayan is a living museum of carvings from the Licchavi period. The temple is a Unesco World Heritage Site and rightly so, because the statues, and the temple itself, are genuine works of art. Despite being only 6km from Bhaktapur and 22km from Kathmandu, the temple attracts relatively few visitors, which is part of its appeal.

◉ Sights

Changu Narayan Temple HINDU TEMPLE
(foreigner/SAARC Rs 100/25; ⊘dawn-dusk) Built in the two-tiered pagoda style, the shrine is guarded on all sides by pairs of mythical beasts – lions, elephants and ram-horned griffons – and its roof struts feature some amazingly intricate carvings of Tantric deities. The statue inside shows Vishnu as Narayan, the creator of all life, but the beautifully decorated metal-plate doors are only opened for rituals and only Hindus may enter.

Facing the west door is a kneeling figure of Garuda said to date from the 5th century. In front of this statue is the oldest stone inscription in the valley, dating from AD 464, which recalls how the king persuaded his mother not to commit *sati* (ritual suicide) after his father's death. Two large pillars carry a conch and chakra disc, the traditional symbols of Vishnu.

Dotted around the courtyard are a series of extraordinary carvings dating from the Licchavi era, showing Vishnu in his various avatars (incarnations). In the southwest corner of the compound, Vishnu appears as Narsingha (his man-lion incarnation), disembowelling a demon with his fingers, and as Vikrantha (Vamana), the six-armed dwarf who transformed himself into a giant capable of crossing the universe in three steps to defeat King Bali (look for his outstretched leg).

To the side of these images is a broken slab showing a 10-headed and 10-armed Vishnu, with Ananta reclining on a serpent below. The scenes are divided into three sections – the underworld, the world of man and the heavens. In the northwest corner of the compound is an exquisite 7th-century image of Vishnu astride Garuda, which is illustrated on the Rs 10 banknote.

The squat temple in the southeast corner of the complex is dedicated to the Tantric goddess Chhinnamasta, who beheaded herself to feed the bloodthirsty deities Dakini and Varnini.

Down the steps leading east from the temple complex are the one-storey Bhim-

Changu Narayan Temple

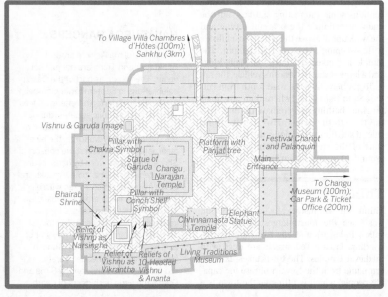

sen Pati, with its stone guardians, and the remains of a Malla-era royal palace.

Living Traditions Museum
MUSEUM
(www.livingtraditionsmuseum.org; foreigner/Nepali Rs 250/60; ⊙10am-4pm Tue-Sun) Just opening its doors at the time of research, this well-curated museum, housed in a restored building surrounding Changu Narayan Temple, features over 400 exhibits covering artefacts and displays on ethnic groups from the Kathmandu Valley, the Terai, Middle Hills and Himalayan Highlands.

Changu Museum
MUSEUM
(admission Rs 200; ⊙8am-5pm) The single brick-paved street in Changu village climbs from the car park and bus stand past the privately owned Changu Museum, which offers a quirky introduction to traditional village life. The owner will give you a whistlestop tour of such oddities as a rhino-skin shield, a raincoat made of leaves, a 500-year-old dishwashing rack and some 225-year-old rice. There's also a fascinating coin collection, including leather coins from the 2nd century and one that equates to one-eighth of a paise – meaning 800 pieces are needed to make one rupee!

🛏 Sleeping & Eating

There are several tourist-oriented restaurants at the start of the village, or you can grab a meal at one of the guesthouses. Viewpoint Rooftop Restaurant near the temple is probably the best.

Changu Guest House
GUESTHOUSE $
(☑01-5090852; saritabhatta@hotmail.com; r US$10-15) Just outside the temple entrance, this family-owned brick guesthouse has sunny rooms with tasteful decor, some with balconies that look out to Bhaktapur. It's run by two young brothers who are passionate about promoting their hometown and are very knowledgeable on the region. They can also arrange visits to local Tamang villages.

Village Villa Chambres d'Hôtes
GUESTHOUSE $
(☑9841480637; r Rs 450-600) A short walk downhill from the temple in the pastoral village of Kapahity, this bright green family house has rooms ranging from spacious to boxy. It also has less appealing tin-roofed A-frame huts (rooms with/without bathroom Rs 300/250) near the temple.

ⓘ Getting There & Away

Regular public buses run the 6km between Changu Narayan and Bhaktapur (Rs 15, 30 minutes), with the last bus around sunset. A taxi from Kathmandu costs around Rs 1500 return, or Rs 500 from Bhaktapur.

By bike or on foot, it's a steep climb uphill from Bhaktapur (one hour), but an easy downhill trip on the way back. If you're headed to Nagarkot you can take the footpath east to Tharkot and catch a bus for the final uphill stretch.

THE NORTHEASTERN VALLEY

Most travellers miss this corner of the valley, which means things are blissfully peaceful and quiet. It's a great destination for mountain biking, motorbiking as well as hiking excursions.

Gokarna Mahadev Temple

Set beside the Bagmati River, which at this stage is a comparatively clear mountain stream, the Gokarna Mahadev (Gokarneshwar, or Lord of Gokarna) Temple is an easy 4km trip from Bodhnath on the road to Sundarijal. Dedicated to Shiva as Mahadeva (Great God), this handsome three-tiered temple is a fine example of Newari pagoda style, but the main reason to come is to see the exquisite stone carvings dotted around the compound, some dating back more than a thousand years.

The sculptures provide an A to Z of Hindu deities, from Aditya (the sun god), Brahma and Chandra (the moon god) to Indra (the elephant-borne god of war and weather) and Ganga (with four arms and a pot on her head from which pours the Ganges). Vishnu is depicted as Narsingha, making a particularly thorough job of disembowelling the demon Hiranyakashipu, while Shiva makes several appearances, including as Kamadeva, the god of love, complete with one suitably erect celestial body part.

The god Gauri Shankar is interesting since it contains elements of both Shiva and Parvati. The goddess appears on her own in a particularly elegant statue in the northwest corner of the compound. The Brahma figure in the southwest corner appears to have only three heads (he should have four) until you peer around the back and discover the hidden head. Many of the deities have

Gokarna Mahadev Temple

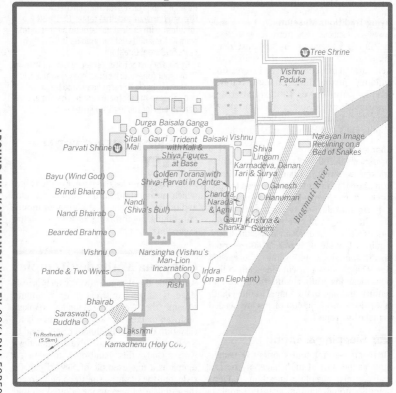

Tree Shrine

Vishnu
Paduka

Durga Baisala Ganga

Sitali Gauri Trident Baisaki Vishnu

Parvati Shrine Mai

Shiva Figures
with Kali &
at Base

Shiva
Lingam

Narayan Image
Reclining on a
Bed of Snakes

Bayu (Wind God)

Golden Torana with
Shiva-Parvati in Centre

Karmadeva, Danan
Tari & Surya

Brindi Bhairab

Chandra,

Ganesh

Nandi
(Shiva's Bull)

Narada
& Agni

Hanuman

Nandi Bhairab

Gauri Krishna &
Shankar Gopini

Bearded Brahma

Vishnu

Narsingha (Vishnu's
Man-Lion
Incarnation)

Indra
(on an Elephant)

Pande & Two Wives

Rishi

Bhairab

Saraswati
Buddha

To Bodhnath
(5.5km)

Lakshmi

Kamadhenu (Holy Cow)

Bagmati River

one foot on their *vahana* (spiritual vehicle). Shiva's vehicle **Nandi** appears as a large statue made of brass laid over a stone base, in front of the main temple, and Shiva is venerated in the form of an enormous lingam inside the main chamber. There's some fine woodcarving on the temple struts.

Behind the temple, just above the river, is the **Vishnu Paduka**, a low pavilion enshrining a metal plate with a footprint of Vishnu. Just in front is an image of **Narayan** reclining on a bed of snakes, just like the images at Budhanilkantha and Balaju. To the north of the pavilion is a remarkable **shrine** that has almost been consumed by a fig tree that must have started as a seed on its roof.

Nepalis who have recently lost a father often visit the temple, particularly during Gokarna Aunsi, the Nepali equivalent of Father's Day, which falls in September.

ⓘ Getting There & Away

You can walk, cycle, take a minibus from Kathmandu's Ratna Park station (Rs 25, 45 minutes) or Bodhnath (or Jorpati), or hire a taxi (Rs 700 one way from Kathmandu or Rs 400 from Bodhnath). For a great day of biking you can combine a visit to the temple with a trip to Sankhu.

Gokarna Forest

The 188-hectare forest at Gokarna was formerly set aside as a hunting reserve for the Nepali royal family, which saved it from the woodcutters. Today, the sound of gunshots has been replaced by the thwack of flying golf balls.

The forest forms part of the **Gokarna Forest Resort** (☏ 01-4450444; www.gokarna.com; ⊙ 7.30am-sunset), which was designed by the team behind the famous Gleneagles course in Scotland. A change of ownership from Le Meridien to a local group has not affected the high standards at the resort. Green fees for 18 holes are Rs 4000 on weekdays and Rs 5000 at weekends, and you can rent clubs, shoes and caddies for an extra Rs 2200.

If you stay here, you can pamper yourself with all sorts of luxury spa treatments, and the resort can arrange guided forest walks to the Bandevi (Forest Goddess) Temple and the Gokarna Mahadev Temple (one hour).

At the entrance to the resort spa is a 200-year-old pipal tree, where the Buddha (played by Keanu Reeves, of all people) in Bertolucci's film *Little Buddha* was tempted by the demon Mara and called the earth to witness his victory. Not a lot of people know that...

🛏 Sleeping

Gokarna Forest Resort RESORT **$$$**
(☏01-4451212; www.gokarna.com; s/d from US$160/180, incl breakfast) Top-of-the-line accommodation is provided in this sublimely peaceful former–Le Meridien property. Wicker furniture and dark timber lend a colonial feel, and the surrounding forest is alive with deer and monkeys. The new block is luxurious, but for real character, book a room in the Rana-era Hunter's Lodge. A taxi from Kathmandu will cost around Rs 700 one way.

Sankhu

The red-brick town of Sankhu was once an important stop on the old trade route from Kathmandu to Lhasa (Tibet), and you can still see signs of its former prosperity. The main attraction is the imposing Vajrayogini Temple on the hillside north of the village, but it's worth taking time to explore the winding brick backstreets and squares of the sleepy old town (there's a faded map by the bus stand).

◎ Sights

Vajrayogini Temple TEMPLE
To reach Sankhu's most famous temple, you should walk north from the bus stand under a colourful deity-covered archway, jogging around Dhunla Tole. As you leave the village, an interesting collection of lingam shrines (one-half destroyed by a tree) and finely crafted statues of Ganesh, Vishnu and Hanuman will show you are on the right path. Shortly afterwards the road forks at a bend; turn left and head downhill to reach the pedestrian steps to the temple or right by bike or car to reach the parking area about halfway up.

Having found the steps, join the pilgrims climbing the hill to reach a gorgeous complex of temples, surrounded by Newari-style mansions and set in a grove of gnarled trees. The stately, three-tiered Vajrayogini Temple has an amazing gilded doorway flanked by images of Bhairab, Garuda and other celestial beings, but the image of the revered female yogi is only visible when the priest opens the doors for devotees (no photos). Although the goddess Vajrayogini is nominally a Buddhist deity, the complex also features plenty of Hindu iconography. The other temple in the main courtyard enshrines a huge chaitya and its roof struts are decorated with images of Buddhist protector deities. Immediately behind this temple is a chaitya with four Buddha images mounted on a yoni base – a striking fusion of Hindu and Buddhist iconography.

The 40-minute climb from the bus station up the stone steps to the temples is steep and hot for the second half but water spouts along the route offer a chance to cool off. About halfway up is a shelter with carvings of an anorexic-looking Kali and an overweight orange Ganesh. A natural **stone lingam** represents Bhairab, and sacrifices are made at its foot. If you climb the stairway above the Vajrayogini temple, you will

HIKING THE SHORTCUT BETWEEN CHANGU NARAYAN & SANKHU

From Changu Narayan there's an interesting shortcut north to the Bodhnath–Sankhu road, allowing a detour to Sankhu and Bodhnath on your way to Kathmandu. From the northern entrance of the Changu Narayan Temple, follow the obvious path that drops to Manohara River, where you cross over the bridge. This brings you out to the Sankhu road at Bramhakhel, about 4km southeast of Gokarna. Frequent minibuses head east and west from here.

Coming from the other direction, you'll see a small sign for Changu Narayan on a building wall on the south side of the road as you enter Bramhakhel. It's a five-minute walk across fields to the river and temporary bridge, then a steep and tiring 45-minute scramble up the hill to the temple – look for the golden rooftop on the final bump of the spur running down from the eastern edge of the valley.

GOKARNA–KOPAN–BODHNATH WALK

There's a pleasant walking or biking route between Gokarna and Bodhnath via the monastery at Kopan. The obvious trail starts just opposite the Gokarna Mahadev Temple, to the right of a series of four roadside statues (signposted 'Sahayogi Multiple College'), and branches left at the college. After five minutes, join the tarmac road as it follows the side of a pine-clad hill. Stay on the paved road as it climbs, offering views of the valley below and the yellow walls of Kopan Monastery ahead atop a hill.

After another 10 minutes, branch left onto a dirt road, which soon becomes a footpath. After another couple of minutes, branch left, passing below Rato Gompa, and follow the hillside to a saddle on the ridge. Where the path forks, take the trail heading uphill to the right, passing another small monastery before reaching the entrance to Kopan (45 minutes).

From Kopan, follow the main road south for 40 minutes to Bodhnath, or jump on one of the frequent minibuses. Travelling on foot, branch off to the left before you hit the built-up area of Bodhnath to reach the stupa.

reach a rest house for pilgrims and several small tea stands.

🛏 Sleeping

Backspace COTTAGE **$$**
(☑9751003265; www.backspacenepal.com; s/d Rs 1750/2500, incl breakfast) With just one room available in the only accommodation in town, you are guaranteed solitude at this rural retreat by the entrance to town. The simple but cosy suite comes with a mini-kitchen and a bathroom with hot water, as well as a fire pit and bicycles for rent, and the owners can arrange a cooking class. Breakfast comes delivered in an outdoor iron box, maximising privacy. Reservations are essential.

❶ Getting There & Away

Buses and minibuses on route 30 run to Sankhu from Kathmandu's Ratna Park bus station (Rs 30, one hour). The last bus back to Kathmandu leaves Sankhu around 6pm. Minibuses on route 4 pass by Patan.

It's an easy 20km cycle to Sankhu from Kathmandu, or an even easier motorcycle ride. Head to Bodhnath and turn right at Jorpati, then skirt around the Gokarna Forest. If you are walking, you can continue from Sankhu to Changu Narayan by crossing the Manohara River near Bramhakhel – see the boxed text on p159.

THE SOUTHERN VALLEY

There are some fascinating temples and Buddhist monasteries in the southern part of the Kathmandu Valley, but it's hard to see too many together in a single day trip, as the villages are strung out on four different roads branching south from the Kathmandu Ring Rd. There's a useful dirt-road shortcut that links the roads to Godavari and Chapagaon, and a walking-only route linking the road to Bungamati and Chobar on the way to Dakshinkali.

Kirtipur
☑01

Just 5km southwest of Kathmandu, the sleepy town of Kirtipur has a wonderful sense of faded grandeur thanks to the impressive medieval temples dotted around its backstreets. When Prithvi Narayan Shah stormed into the valley in 1768, he made a priority of capturing Kirtipur to provide a base for his crushing attacks on the Malla kingdoms. Kirtipur's resistance was strong, but eventually, after a bitter siege, the town was taken. The inhabitants paid a terrible price for their brave resistance – the king ordered that the nose and lips be cut off every male inhabitant in the town, sparing only those who could play wind instruments for his entertainment.

As you approach Kirtipur from the Ring Rd, the old town is up the hill straight ahead, best approached by following the main road to the right and climbing the hillside on a wide flight of steps.

◎ Sights

Everything of interest in Kirtipur is at the top of the hill above the road into town.

Bagh Bhairab Temple HINDU TEMPLE
In a courtyard off the north side of the main square is an imposing Bhairab Temple with an incredible armoury of *tulwars* (swords)

and shields belonging to the soldiers defeated by Prithvi Narayan Shah. Befitting the militaristic mood, animal sacrifices are made here early on Tuesday and Saturday mornings.

Main Square
SQUARE

Ringed by the former residences of the royal family of Kirtipur, this square is now a popular hang-out for locals. In the middle is a large tank and a whitewashed Narayan Temple guarded by lions and griffons.

Uma Maheshwar Temple
HINDU TEMPLE

From the main square, go right heading west through the village to a Ganesh shrine and a stone stairway that climbs to the triple-roofed Uma Maheshwar Temple. It's flanked by two stone elephants, decked out in spiked saddles to discourage children from sitting on them! The temple was originally built in 1673 with four roofs, but one was lost in the earthquake of 1934. This was the spot where Kirtipur's residents made their last stand during the 1768 siege.

Nagar Mandap Sri Kirti Vihar
BUDDHIST TEMPLE

At the bottom of the hill, follow the left fork of the main road around the base of the hill to this classic Thai-style *wat* (Buddhist monastery) inaugurated by the Supreme Patriarch of Thailand in 1995.

Lohan Dehar
HINDU TEMPLE

From the main square, take a turn right, exiting at the southeast corner of the square to reach the 16th-century stone shikhara-style Lohan Dehar.

Chilanchu Vihara
BUDDHIST TEMPLE

Built in 1515, this stately stupa crowns the hilltop and the harmika above the dome is painted a rich blue. The main stupa is surrounded by a garden of chaitya and fronted by a giant dorje symbol. To get here, turn left from Lohan Dehar, then right through a brick gate and cross a large square. The next right will take you to a shrine gripped by the roots of an enormous fig tree, and opposite the gateway is the *vihara*.

⇌ Courses

Kagyu Institute of Buddhist Studies
MEDITATION, BUDDHISM

(KIBS; ✆4331679; www.kirtipur.org) Aspiring scholars of Buddhism can arrange various courses, from four-day dharma studies to three-year certificates, at this peaceful hilltop gompa. Personal retreats and thangka painting courses are also offered. Application forms are available online.

🛏 Sleeping & Eating

Kirtipur Hillside Hotel
HOTEL $

(✆4334010; www.kirtipurhillside.com.np; s/d US$15/25, without bathroom US$12/20) A great option for those wanting to escape Kathmandu's fumes, with large and clean rooms – the best of which look out to the valley, with the Himalaya looming in the distance. Some rooms have balconies. There's some great artwork (painted by the manager) and a pleasant rooftop restaurant.

TOP CHOICE Kirtipur View Point Restaurant
NEPALI, INTERNATIONAL $

(mains Rs 50-150) Tasty Newari food, cheap beer and fantastic views make this a great stopover for lunch or an afternoon snack. Its rooftop is the prime viewing area, looking out to mountains ahead, or Uma Maheshwar Temple to the side.

❶ Getting There & Away

Minibuses leave regularly for Kirtipur from Kathmandu's Ratna Park bus station (Rs 15, 30 minutes); the last is at 7pm. Taxis charge around Rs 500.

It takes around one hour to Kirtipur by mountain bike from Kathmandu; turn south off the Ring Rd at Balkhu and follow the tarmacked Chobar road to the turn-off to Kirtipur.

Chobar

The tiny village of Chobar, 6km from Kathmandu, tops a hill overlooking the Bagmati River where it flows through the Chobar Gorge, allegedly chopped out by the sacred sword of Manjushri. The village itself is lovely, with a tangle of old streets surrounding a famous temple, but the gorge has been ravaged by mining to supply cement for construction in Kathmandu.

⊙ Sights & Activities

Adinath Lokeshwar Temple
HINDU TEMPLE

In the village of Chobar is the curious Adinath Lokeshwar Temple, originally built in the 15th century. It's a handsome three-tiered Newari temple and its roof struts, walls and courtyard are adorned with hundreds of metal plates, cups, dishes, knives, ladles and ceremonial vessels, nailed there by newlyweds to ensure a happy married

NARSINGHA

The image of Vishnu in his man-lion incarnation as Narsingha (or Narsimha) can be seen all over the Kathmandu Valley. The deity is normally depicted gleefully disembowelling the demon Hiranyakashipu with his bare hands, recalling a famous legend from the Bhagavata Purana. Because of a deal made with Brahma, the demon was granted special powers – he could not be killed by man or beast, either inside or outside, on the ground or in the air, by day or by night, nor by any weapon. Vishnu neatly got around these protections by adopting the form of a man-lion and killing the demon with his fingernails, at dusk, on his lap, on the threshold of the house. You can see statues of Narsingha at his grisly work at the Gokarna Mahadev Temple, in front of the palace in Patan (p130) and just inside the Hanuman Dhoka entrance in Kathmandu (p68).

life. The temple is sacred to both Hindus and Buddhists, and in front is an octagonal stone shikhara temple fronted by a gilded dorje symbol.

A tangle of lanes leads off the square in front of the temple to the main part of the village and a small Tibetan Buddhist monastery.

Jal Binayak Temple HINDU TEMPLE
Built in 1602, Jal Binayak Temple is one of the valley's most important Ganesh shrines. The temple's three-tiered roof struts depict eight Bhairabs and the eight Ashta Matrikas (Mother Goddesses) with whom Ganesh often appears. It has scenic views from the base of the gorge, with plenty of birdlife about. It's accessed from a car park off the main road.

Manjushree Park & Cave CAVING
(park entry Rs 50, short/medium/long caving US$3/5/10) Looking over Chobar Gorge, Manjushree Park is popular with romancing teenagers, but is of more interest to foreigners for its caves. At 3250m, it's said to be the longest in South Asia. Only 350m of the cave is open to visitors, and accessed from five different entry points – the largest of which is Bagh Gohpha, which involves clambering through a series of warren-like tunnels.

Headlamps and guides are included in the price.

✖ Eating

While there's no accommodation in Chobar, there are a couple of good spots for a feed.

Hira's Coffee Shop CAFE **$**
(snacks from Rs 65; ⊘7am-5pm) On the wide lane south of Jal Binayak Temple in Chobar Village is this intimate and quaint cafe in a village house.

Kathmandu View Cottage NEPALI **$**
(mains Rs 70-300) Reached by turning north off the road into Chobar, this tasteful garden restaurant with tables in bamboo huts looks out over the rooftops of Kathmandu.

ℹ Getting There & Away

To reach Chobar, follow the road that turns south off the Kathmandu Ring Rd at Balkhu and follow the Bagmati River. There are no direct buses here, but any bus to Pharping or Dakshinkali can drop you at the turn-off, a 10-minute walk below the village, for around Rs 20. A taxi from Kathmandu will cost Rs 500 one way. You can also walk here from Kirtipur in around an hour, via the village of Panga, which has several old temples, including the revered Vishnu Devi Mandir.

Pharping

01

About 19km south of Kathmandu, Pharping is a thriving Newari town whose ancient Buddhist pilgrimage sites have been taken over by large numbers of Tibetans. Pharping lies on the road to Dakshinkali and it's easy to visit both villages in a day by bus or bicycle. En route you'll pass the pond at Taudaha, allegedly home to the nagas released from the Kathmandu lake. More Buddhist monasteries are opening up around here every year, some of which accept foreign dharma students.

⊙ Sights

Shesh Narayan Temple HINDU TEMPLE
About 600m downhill from the main junction at Pharping, in the direction of Kathmandu, the Shesh (or Sekh) Narayan Temple is a highly revered Vishnu shrine surrounded by ponds and statues, tucked beneath a rocky cliff wall and a **Tibetan monastery**. The main temple was built in the 17th century, but it's believed that the cave to the right (now dedicated to Padmasambhava, or

Guru Rinpoche) has been a place of pilgrimage for far longer.

There are some artfully carved Licchaviera statues in the courtyard, including lively depictions of Ganesh and Hanuman. The surrounding ponds are full of koi carp and semisubmerged carvings, including an image of Aditya, framed by a stone arch. If you are lucky you might catch devotional religious music being played in the pavilion by the pools.

THE PILGRIMAGE ROUTE

The best way to visit the sights of Pharping is to join the other pilgrims on an easy, clockwise pilgrimage circuit (a *parikrama* in Nepali, or kora in Tibetan) taking one to two hours.

Auspicious Pinnacle Dharma
Centre of Dzongsar   BUDDHIST TEMPLE
As you enter the town from the main road, take the first right and head uphill, passing a **Guru Rinpoche statue** in a glass case. Next to the statue is a giant chörten that contains 16 enormous prayer wheels.

Ralo Gompa   BUDDHIST TEMPLE
A large white Ralo Gompa with a brightly painted chörten. It's located up the hill past the line of Tibetan restaurants.

Sakya Tharig Gompa   BUDDHIST TEMPLE
Next door to Ralo Gompa, this is another enormous and brightly painted chörten – step inside to see hundreds of miniature chörten and statues of Guru Rinpoche set into alcoves in the walls.

Drölma Lhakhang   BUDDHIST TEMPLE
The shrine is sacred to both Hindus and Buddhists, who identify Saraswati as Tara. It's accessed via a set of steps to the right of Sakya Tharig Gompa. To the right of this chapel is the **Rigzu Phodrang Gompa**, which contains an impressive frieze of statues, with Guru Rinpoche surrounded by his fearsome incarnations as Dorje Drolo (riding a tiger) and Dorje Porba (with three faces, Garuda-like wings and a coupling consort).

Guru Rinpoche Cave   BUDDHIST SHRINE
Climb the steps from Drölma Lhakhang, passing a rocky fissure jammed full of *tsha tsha* (stupa-shaped clay offerings) and cracks stuffed with little bags of wishes and human hair. Eventually you'll come to the walls of a large white monastery, inside which is a small cave (also known as the Gorakhnath Cave). Take off your shoes and duck between

the monastery buildings to reach the soot-darkened cavern, which is illuminated by butter lamps and a Liza Minnelli–style row of coloured light bulbs.

Vajra Yogini Temple   BUDDHIST TEMPLE
This sacred 17th-century Newari-style temple is devoted to the Tantric goddess Vajrayogini. One of the few female deities in Buddhist mythology, Vajrayogini was a wandering ascetic who achieved a level of enlightenment almost equivalent to the male Buddhas. Note the lovely Rana-style buildings around the courtyard. The temple is accessed down a flight of stairs leading from the Guru Rinpoche Cave.

🛏 Sleeping & Eating

Along the main road uphill from Pharping bazaar are numerous Tibetan restaurants serving momos, *thukpa* and butter tea to hungry pilgrims.

Family Guest House   GUESTHOUSE $
(☑4710412; r with/without bathroom Rs 700/500) The only choice in the middle of Pharping, opposite the Guru Rinpoche Statue, this well-run guesthouse is right on the pilgrim circuit and has a good rooftop restaurant.

Hotel Ashoka   GUESTHOUSE $
(☑4710057; bungalow r Rs 500, r Rs 600-700) On the road that passes around Pharping to Dakshinkali, Ashoka has a peaceful location, with sublime views from the rooms in the main building.

Dakchhinkali Village Inn   HOTEL $$
(☑4710053; www.dakchhinkali.com; s/d/tr from US$30/40/45) At the far end of Pharping by the gate marking the route to Dakshinkali, this midrange resort has an inviting garden setting, and rooms in its farmhouse-like building have great mountain views. Discounts of 30% or more are usually available.

Hattiban Resort   RESORT $$$
(☑4710122; nepal@intrek.wlink.com.np; s/d US$80/90; @☎) Perched on a ridge high above the valley in a pine forest, this small resort has 30 good-quality rooms, most with balconies that make the most of the stunning Himalayan views. Popular with German tourists, the rooms are huge, with big comfy beds, heaters and modern bathrooms. From the resort you can make an excellent three-hour (return) hike up to the peak of Champa Devi (2249m). Its main drawback is that it's very inaccessible; to get here you'll

need a car to travel 2km on a steep, rutted dirt road that branches off about 3km north of Pharping. The condition of the road varies so ask the hotel about arranging transfers. A taxi from town is around Rs 1000.

❶ Getting There & Away

Buses on route 22 leave throughout the day for Pharping from Kathmandu's Ratna Park bus station (Rs 27, 1½ hours), continuing to Dakshinkali; buses also leave from Shahid Gate (Martyrs' Memorial; Rs 21, two hours). The last bus back to Kathmandu leaves around 5.30pm.

Around Pharping

DAKSHINKALI

The road from Pharping continues a few kilometres south to the blood-soaked temple of Dakshinkali, a favourite Hindu pilgrimage destination. Set at the confluence of two sacred streams in a rocky cleft in the forest, the temple is dedicated to the goddess Kali, the most bloodthirsty incarnation of Parvati. To satisfy the blood-lust of the goddess, pilgrims drag a menagerie of chickens, ducks, goats, sheep, pigs and even the occasional buffalo up the path to the temple to be beheaded and transformed into cuts of meat by the temple priests, who are also skilled butchers.

Once the sacrifice is made, the meat goes in the pot – pilgrims bring all the ingredients for a forest barbecue and spend the rest of the day feasting in the shade of the trees. Saturday is the big sacrificial day, and the blood also flows freely on Tuesday. For the rest of the week Dakshinkali is very quiet. During the annual celebrations of Dasain in October the temple is washed by a crimson tide and the image of Kali is bathed in the gore.

The approach to the temple from the bus stand winds through a religious bazaar, which is often hazy with smoke from barbecue fires. Local farmers sell their produce here to go into the post-sacrifice feasts, along with piles of marigolds, coconuts and other offerings for the goddess. Only Hindus can enter the temple courtyard where the image of Kali resides, but visitors can watch from the surrounding terraces. However, remember that the sacrifices are a religious event, with profound spiritual significance for local people, and not just an excuse to snap gruesome photos.

A pathway leads off from behind the main temple uphill to the small **Mata Temple** on the hilltop, which offers good views over the forest. Several snack stalls at the Dakshinkali bus park serve reviving tea and pappadums.

❶ Getting There & Away

Buses on route 22 run to Dakshinkali regularly from Kathmandu's Shahid Gate (Martyrs' Memorial) and Ratna Park bus station (Rs 37, 2½ hours). There are extra buses on Tuesday and Saturday to accommodate the pilgrimage crowds. From Pharping it's an easy 1km downhill walk or ride, but a steep uphill slog in the other direction.

DOLLU

Located 3km before Pharping on the road from Kathmandu, a side road turns north along a small valley to the village of Dollu, passing several huge Tibetan Buddhist monasteries, including the **Rigon Tashi Choling**, which contains some fine murals and statuary, including a fearsome image of Guru Dorje Drolo and his tiger.

If you walk a few hundred metres towards Kathmandu from the Dollu junction, you will reach a cluster of houses tucked into a hairpin bend, where a track leads uphill to the enormous **Neyndo Tashi Choling** monastery. This newly constructed gompa looms over the surrounding landscape like a scene from *Howl's Moving Castle* and the main prayer hall contains some stunning mural work and a 15m-high statue of Sakyamuni. There are nearly 200 monks here, so the morning and evening prayer ceremonies are quite an experience.

Bungamati

Across the Bagmati River from Chobar, Bungamati is a classic medieval village, dominated by the shikhara of its main temple. Exploring the atmospheric pedestrian-only streets is a great way to pass a few hours. Many locals make a living as woodcarvers and there are several workshops and showrooms around the main square. To get here from the bus stand, follow the wide road south, then turn right, and then right again at an obvious junction by a Ganesh shrine.

◉ Sights

Rato Machhendranath Temple HINDU TEMPLE
Bungamati is the birthplace of Rato Machhendranath, the patron god of Patan, and for six months of the year the deity resides in the enormous shikhara in the main vil-

lage square (he spends the rest of his time at the Rato Machhendranath Temple in Patan). The process of moving him backwards and forwards between Patan and Bungamati is central to one of the most important festivals in the valley – see the boxed text, p135.

The chowk around the temple is one of the most beautiful in the Kathmandu Valley – here you can see the beating heart of a functioning Newari town. During harvesting season (October to November) you'll see villagers winnowing rice here.

Bhairab Temple   HINDU TEMPLE

On one side of the main square is a double-tiered temple that enshrines a ferocious-looking brass mask of Bhairab in front of a brass vessel in the shape of a *kapala* (human-skull bowl). Around the square you'll hear the tap-tap of woodcarvers' chisels.

Bungamati Culture Museum   MUSEUM

(admission Rs 25; ☺10am-4pm Sat-Thu) On the narrow lane towards the main square is this low-key, dusty museum displaying cultural objects from the area.

Dey Pukha   POND

(Central Pond) If you leave the main square by the northern gate (opposite the Bhairab Temple), you'll pass a crumbling Buddhist courtyard monastery and an assortment of chaityas and shrines, then the brick-lined water tank of the Dey Pukha.

Karya Binayak Temple   HINDU TEMPLE

Halfway between Bungamati and Khokana, this temple is dedicated to Ganesh. Local pilgrims flock here on Saturdays for a *bhoj* (feast) and some *bhajan* (devotional music) – the Newari version of a barbecue and sing along. To reach the temple, turn left when the path from Bungamati meets a larger track by a school.

❶ Getting There & Away

Buses to Bungamati leave frequently from Patan's Lagankhel station (Rs 14, 40 minutes), or you can get here easily by bike or motorcycle, turning off the Kathmandu Ring Rd at Nakhu.

Khokana

Another delightful Newari town, Khokana is smaller and sleepier than Bungamati, but it's still worth a quick look around this living museum. The main road leads through the village, which is like a window back in time,

with mattress-makers stuffing cases with cotton, farmers baling straw, tailors stitching and women spinning wool and winnowing rice. It was seriously damaged in the 1934 earthquake. In the main village square is the triple-tiered **Shekala Mai Temple** (also known as Rudrayani), with carved balconies covered by fretwork screens. The five-day Khokana Jatra festival, with its masked dancers, is usually held in October and is a good time to visit.

You'll need to pay Rs 20 to visit the town, collected at the tourist information centre. The fee goes to general upkeep of the village's streets.

Chapagaon

Chapagaon is an attractive Newari village of tall brick houses, but its central square is cut in two by the road to Tika Bhairab and the rumbling gravel lorries rather destroy the atmosphere. Beside the road are a number of shrines, including temples to Bhairab, Krishna and Narayan, but the main attraction here is the **Vajra Varahi Temple** (parking Rs 5), about 500m east of the main road on the back route to Godavari (turn left by the Narayan Temple).

Set in a peaceful wood, this important Tantric temple was built in 1665 and it attracts lots of wedding parties, pilgrims and picnickers who descend en masse on Saturdays. Visitors pour milk and offerings over the statue of a bull in front of the temple and make similar offerings to the image of Vajra Varahi, an incarnation of the 'female Buddha' Vajrayogini. There are lots of birds in the forest – check the sign by the car park for a list of species.

For a bit of exploring further afield, you can head towards the **Lele Valley**, which runs east off the valley of the Nakhu Khola, about 5km south of Chapagaon. Few tourists make it out here and the valley offers a window into a way of life that is fast vanishing in other parts of the Kathmandu Valley.

To get to Lele, follow the trucking road south from Chapagaon to the **Tika Bhairab**, a large rock shrine with a multicoloured painting of Bhairab, set at the confluence of two rivers. Buses run here from Chapagaon.

❶ Getting There & Away

Local minibuses leave from Lagankhel in Patan to Chapagaon (Rs 15, 45 minutes) or direct to the Vajra Varahi Temple (Rs 17). You can cycle from the Kathmandu Ring Rd in around the same time (the turn-off is south of Patan near Satdobato).

The road to the Vajra Varahi Temple continues through peaceful countryside to meet the Godavari road just south of Bandegaon. You can walk it in about an hour or cycle it in 20 minutes.

Godavari

🗾 01

Godavari is best known for the green fingers of its inhabitants. The village is home to Nepal's Royal Botanical Gardens and the approach road is lined with the nurseries that supply Kathmandu with flowers and potted plants. The 10km road from the Kathmandu Ring Rd forks in the middle of Godavari – the left fork goes to the botanical gardens while the right fork climbs past the Naudhara Kunda temple and turns into a dirt track running up to Pulchowki Mountain.

⊙ Sights

If you plan on walking the remote trails in the forests surrounding Godavari, it's a good idea to get a guide, with locals warning of robberies. Hotels or restaurants should be able to help with a guide.

Royal Botanical Gardens   GARDENS
(foreigner/SAARC Rs 100/25, camera/video Rs 10/100, child under 10yr 50% discount; ⊙10am-5pm, to 4pm mid-Nov–mid-Feb) The verdant botanical gardens are a quiet and peaceful spot for a walk or picnic, except on Friday and Saturday when the place is overrun with schoolkids. The visitor centre has some good exhibits on Nepal's flora and in the middle is the decorative Coronation Pond with its 7m commemorative pillar.

Godavari Kunda   HINDU SITE
If you turn to the right at the junction before the Royal Botanical Gardens, you'll reach a cluster of local restaurants and the Godavari Kunda – a sacred spring marked by a neat line of Shaivite shrines. Every 12 years (the next is 2015) thousands of pilgrims come here to bathe and gain spiritual merit. Next door is the large O Sal Choling Godavari Tibetan monastery.

Godavari Kunda Community Forest FOREST
Across the road from Godavari Kunda is a tiny scenic lake that leads to the entrance of a 147-hectare woodland, which is managed by local people and provides a haven for 300 species of birds.

Naudhara Kunda   HINDU TEMPLE
(Pulchowki Mai Temple) The three-tiered pagoda is dedicated to one of the Tantric mother goddesses and the two large pools before the temple compound are fed by nine spouts (known as the Naudhara Kunda) that represent the nine streams that flow from Pulchowki Mountain. It's located along the road at the junction by St Xavier's School, which veers off to the right. The temple sits at the mouth of the **Naudhara Community Forest** (admission Rs 20), 147 hectares of locally managed woodland, established with support from **Bird Conservation Nepal** (www.birdlifenepal.org).

Shanti Ban Buddha   BUDDHIST SHRINE
(www.shantiban.com) On the hillside above Godavari is an enormous golden Buddha image, created by local Buddhists who were inspired by the Japanese Peace Pagoda movement. To reach the statue, take the signposted road to the right at the end of the village, and then a steep stair climb to get here.

Himalayan Brewery   BREWERY
(🗾9851075922; www.himalayanbreweries.com; ⊙9am-5pm Sun-Fri) While no official tours are run here, with prior arrangements you should be able to organise someone to show you around the second oldest brewery in Nepal – established in 1983. It's a fascinating look behind the scenes, taking you through the production process that sees 30,000 bottles of beer filled a day, as well as its interesting recycling plant.

🛏 Sleeping & Eating

There's nothing in the way of budget hotels here, but there are a few cheap restaurants in front of the Godavari Kunda where daytrippers can grab a bite of lunch for not too many rupees. Godawari Restaurant and Evergreen Restaurant are both good choices.

Hotel View Bhrikuti   HOTEL $$
(🗾5560471; www.hotelviewbhrikuti.com.np; s/d incl breakfast US$60/70; @🤚) An attractive businesslike hotel, rooms here are large and surprisingly plush, with mod cons such as minibars, modern bathrooms and cable TV. It has an appealing rooftop garden too, with postcard mountain views on a clear day.

Godavari Village Resort   RESORT $$$
(🗾5560675; www.godavariresort.com.np; s/d incl breakfast US$150/165; @🤚🏊) A comfortable modern escape for city dwellers, Godavari Village Resort sprawls down a hillside with

views across paddy fields to the mountains. It's also a conference centre, with plenty of lawn, a big pool, a sauna, a spa and tennis courts. Its swish restaurant is a good spot for lunch, with an outdoor balcony to enjoy the views. To get here look for the signposted road, about 3km south of Godavari, off the main road.

❶ Getting There & Away

Local minibuses (No 5) and buses (No 14) run between Lagankhel in Patan and Godavari (Rs 21, 45 minutes). The road is in good condition for cycling or motorcycling, but watch for trucks headed for the mines near Tika Bhairab.

Around Godavari

HARISIDDHI

About 7km northwest of Godavari, on the main road, Harisiddhi is notable for the towering, four-tiered **Harisiddhi Bhagwan Temple** on its brick-paved market square. Dedicated to one of the fearsome incarnations of Durga, the temple has been painted in bright colours by local devotees. Any bus bound for Godavari can drop you here.

BISHANKHU NARAYAN

If you're looking for an excuse to get off the beaten track, the shrine of Bishankhu Narayan may do nicely. Dedicated to Vishnu, this chain-mail-covered shrine is reached by a steep stairway that climbs to the temple and then drops into a narrow fissure in the rock, where pilgrims test their sin levels by trying to squeeze through the tiny gap. If you get stuck, the sin in question is either gluttony or pride...

The unsealed 3km road to Bishankhu Narayan starts at Bandegaon on the Godavari road, and runs southeast over a small stream. At Godamchowr village, take the left fork at the football ground and climb for about 2km to reach the shrine.

PULCHOWKI MOUNTAIN

This 2760m-high mountain is the highest point around the valley and there are magnificent views from the summit, also home to the sacred **Pulchowki Mai Temple**. Here you'll find over 570 species of flowering plants and it's a popular spot for **birdwatching**, home to one-third of all the bird species in Nepal. There have been rumours for years that the government will turn this into a national park. The mountain is famous for its springtime (March–April)

flowers, in particular its magnificent red and white rhododendrons.

To get here, the only options are a full-day hike along dirt tracks from Naudhara Kunda, or a very rough unsealed road that is only suitable for 4WDs, mountain bikes or trail motorcycles. There are no facilities so bring water, food, a compass and fellow travellers for company (trekkers have been robbed here in the past). It's about a six-hour return hike.

THE VALLEY FRINGE

Beyond Bhaktapur the landscape starts to rise, revealing views north to the rugged mountain wall of the Himalaya, which is rarely visible from the bottom of the valley. Technically, most of the following towns are outside the valley, on the roads to Langtang or the Tibetan border, but it is easy to visit these places on day trips or overnight stays from Kathmandu. See p292 for possible cycling routes through the eastern valley.

Nagarkot

📱 01 / ELEV 2175M

Competing with Dhulikhel and Kakani, Nagarkot is perhaps the best place to view the Himalaya from the comfort of your hotel balcony. Just 32km from Kathmandu, the village is packed with hotels, stacked up on a ridge facing one of the broadest possible views of the Himalaya. Between October and March a trip to Nagarkot will nearly always be rewarded with a view, but be warned the mountains are notorious for disappearing behind cloudy skies on any given day (or hour). It can get very cold at Nagarkot, so bring warm clothing.

◉ Sights & Activities

Other than taking it easy and admiring mountain views, day hikes in the area are the main activities to keep you busy.

Views   LOOKOUT

Nagarkot only exists because of the views, as there is not much else to the village. But what views! From any clear point on the ridge, you can take in a panorama, from Dhaulagiri in the west to Mt Everest (little more than a dot on the horizon) and Kanchenjunga in the east, via Ganesh Himal (7406m), Langtang Lirung (7246m), Shisha

Nagarkot

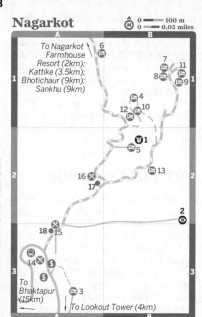

N 0 ——— 100 m
    0 ——— 0.05 miles

To Nagarkot
Farmhouse
Resort (2km);
Kattike (3.5km);
Bhotichaur (9km);
Sankhu (9km)

To Bhaktapur (15km)

To Lookout Tower (4km)

Nagarkot

Pangma (8012m), Dorje Lakpa (6975m) and Gauri Shankar (7146m).

The most popular place is the **Lookout Tower**, perched 2164m on a ridge, with killer 360-degree views at sunrise. It's around an hour's walk (4km) south from the village, or otherwise Nagarkot Guide.com runs sunrise bus tours (Rs 250) here at approximately 5.30am if you're not up for the dark, chilly morning walk. Another good vantage point is from the **Mahakali Temple** on the small hilltop near several of the hotels.

Paneer Cheese Factory   CHEESE FACTORY
(☏9841761643; ⊙10-11am) If you've got time on your side, you might want to pop in to this small but interesting factory for a quick look at how the cheese is produced. To get here take the downhill path from Hotel Shivapuri on the main road.

Day Hikes   WALKING
A popular trail is the four- to five-hour trek loop around Nagarkot, which passes through Rohini Bhanjyang and scenery of terraced hills, fields of mustard flowers and rustic mudbrick farmhouses belonging to Tamang and Gurung people. Get in touch with the tour company NagarkotGuide (www.nagarkotguide.com) for detailed information on local trekking routes.

Rock Climbing   ROCK CLIMBING
(☏9851115014; www.himalayantrailfinder.com) It's an activity that's very much in its infancy, but climbers keen for some action can tackle a 25m rock here (US$65). It's arranged through Himalayan Trailfinder, and the price also includes homestay, basic meals and transport from Kathmandu.

🛏 Sleeping

Nagarkot has numerous guesthouses and hotels that take advantage of the views on the north side of the ridge, and charge a premium for the privilege. However, most of the hotels offer significant discounts so always ask when you book or check in.

TOP CHOICE Fort Resort   RESORT $$$
(☏6680149; www.mountain-retreats.com; s/d/ste US$90/110/160; @☎) At the end of the track branching off near the Hotel New Dragon, this is by far Nagarkot's most stylish resort. It's a towering place, built in the Newari red-brick style, and the immaculately trimmed garden terrace looks out over a natural amphitheatre of peaks. It's set on a property

of 5 hectares, and was the location of the fort (kot) that gave Nagarkot its name. The dignified rooms and suites are set in stylish cottages or in the main building, some with rustic woodfire furnaces. Its restaurant does great food, and grows many of the vegetables from its own garden. There's also a library with some excellent books on Nepal.

Hotel at the End of the Universe
GUESTHOUSE $
(☑ 6680011; www.endoftheuniverse.com.np; r without bathroom Rs 500-900, cottages Rs 1500, ste Rs 3500-4500; ☎) As well as a great name, this eclectic resort offers an intriguing selection of cottages, bamboo cabins and gingerbread-style cottages, set in a verdant garden. The gigantic suites have multiple bedrooms and huge lounges – perfect for families. There's an atmospheric hippie-style restaurant with big windows looking out to mountains. Also has free water to refill your bottle.

Hotel Green Valley
HOTEL $
(☑ 6680078; loveghishing_355@yahoo.com; r from Rs 700, deluxe Rs 2500; ☎) A top location that looks out to memorable Himalayan vistas, the cheaper rooms here are probably the best deal in town – especially if you snare a discount.

Hotel Sunshine
HOTEL $$
(☑ 6680105; www.sunshinehotel.com.np; s/d US$40/50) An attractive red-brick hotel with room rates that correspond to the quality of the view. The best rooms (numbers 206 and 306) on the upper levels have windows on three sides, facing directly onto the panorama.

Nagarkot Farmhouse Resort
RESORT $$
(☑ 6202022; www.nagarkotfarmhouse.com; s/d incl half-board US$32/50) Well away from the main hotel sprawl, this highly recommended place feels like an exclusive country retreat. It has an attractive Tibetan Buddhist motif throughout and even its own stupa and meditation room. The best rooms are in the Newari-inspired brick complex on the edge of the garden, with tiled floors, spotless bathrooms and deck chairs on the balconies, which face a sensational sweep of peaks. Room 15 has windows on two sides. The resort is about 2km past the Hotel Country Villa down the dirt track to Sankhu.

Hotel Country Villa
RESORT $$
(☑ 6680128; www.hotelcountryvilla.com; s/d/ste US$70/80/100; ✴☎) Down the dirt road to Sankhu, this classy place feels like a modern resort, with a stylish dining room and bedrooms livened up by prints of Robert Powell's paintings of Nepal. The bright rooms have blond-wood details and modernist carpets that were handwoven in the Kathmandu Valley. The suites here are fantastic value.

Club Himalaya Resort
RESORT $$
(☑ 6680080; www.nepalshotel.com; s/d incl breakfast from US$65/80; @☎✴) The swankiest place in town, this resort has large, modern rooms with all the mod cons that make it terrific value. The views from the terraces and rooms are probably the best in town. It has the bonus of a heated pool, Jacuzzi and massage services, and a private helipad if you want to arrive in style. It's just uphill from the bus stand on the main road.

Nirvana Village Resort
GUESTHOUSE $
(☑ 9841072508; r Rs 300-500) The only genuine budget option in town, Nirvana Village has a mellow old-school traveller vibe with a psychedelic restaurant and appealing location overlooking a valley. However, it falls short of its potential with poorly maintained rooms.

Peaceful Cottage
HOTEL $
(☑ 6680077; www.nagarkothotels.blogspot.com, peacefulcottage@hotmail.com; r US$33, without bathroom US$12; ☎) The best of a group of cheapies on a side track leading north off the dirt road to Kattike. It's an architectural hodgepodge but there are good views from the top of the octagonal tower. The plywood box rooms are fairly gloomy, but the deluxe rooms with bathrooms and carved bedsteads are more inviting.

Hotel Nagarkot Besso
HOTEL $
(☑ 6680119; www.hotelbesso.com; r Rs 1200-2000) Next door to Hotel Green Valley, Besso has giddying panoramic mountain views and comfortable, modern rooms with appealing interior decor.

New Elephant Head
HOTEL $
(☑ 6680031; www.hotelelephanthead.com; r Rs 800-1500; ☎) Being your typical modern Nepali hotel, this place may not be bursting with character, but it gets the job done with affordable, large, carpeted rooms, good hot-water bathrooms, views and a homely upstairs restaurant.

Sherpa Alpine Cottage
GUESTHOUSE $
(☑ 6680015; www.sherpacottage.com; r from Rs 600) Basic cottages that are right for the price, most with memorable views. There's

HIKING & CYCLING TO/FROM NAGARKOT

There are a number of hiking and cycling routes in this area, best walked downhill from Nagarkot. Nepa Maps' 1:25,000 *Nagarkot – Short Trekking on the Kathmandu Valley Rim* is useful, though its 1:50,000 *Around the Kathmandu Valley* is probably good enough.

Bottled water is mostly unavailable on these routes, so be sure to pack plenty of water.

To Dhulikhel (Four to Seven Hours from Nagarkot)

With the Kathmandu Valley Cultural Trekking Trail being established by NETIF (www.netif-nepal.org), there's now a direct 20km trail to Dhulikhel. While for the most part it's well signed, there remains some confusing sections, so you'll probably need to ask passing villagers for directions along the way. The trail starts past Club Himalaya Resort, following the road past the army barracks. Keep an eye out for the sign to Dhulikhel, which leads you to the village of Rohini Bhanjyang. From here follow the road straight (don't take the left or right paths) and take the hill up, where you'll need to turn left at the intersection. After 1km take the small trail on the right that's a steep downhill into the valley, leading you to the villages of Kankre and Tanchok. At Tanchok take the main jeep track and follow it uphill to Tusal. Head right to Opi where you cross the main jeep track and on to the final 5km stretch to Dhulikhel, crossing over the Arniko Hwy to Himalayan Horizon Hotel – 500m from the bus park.

To Changu Narayan (4½ Hours from Nagarkot, 1½ Hours from Tharkot)

From Nagarkot, it's an easy stroll along the spur to Changu Narayan. The trail runs parallel to the road to Bhaktapur along the ridge, branching off at the sharp hairpin bend at Tharkot (marked on some maps as Deurali Bhanjhang). Catching a bus to here from Nagarkot will save you the tedious first half of the walk.

From the bend, follow the middle dirt road up into the Tilkot Forest and keep to the left. The track climbs uphill through a pine forest for about 20 minutes to the top of the ridge and then follows the ridgeline, dropping gently down to Changu Narayan. On clear days there are good views of the Himalaya. You can follow this track on foot or on a mountain bike or motorcycle.

In the reverse direction, pick up the track near the Changu Narayan Hill Resort, and take the middle road where the track splits. See the boxed text on p159 for details of the temple and onward hikes to Bodhnath and Sankhu.

---

also a pleasant alfresco restaurant, with tables in huts around a terraced garden overlooking the valley.

✖ Eating

Most people eat at the lodges, but there are a few independent restaurants.

TOP CHOICE **Berg House Café**   INTERNATIONAL $
(dishes Rs 80-350) By the main junction on the highway, this colourful cafe is packed with fossils, gnarled tree roots and other found bits of bric-a-brac, and the traveller-oriented menu runs to pizzas, sandwiches and steaks.

Food Republic   INDIAN, INTERNATIONAL $
(dishes Rs 160-320; @🛜) Great for tandoori Indian and also a few unexpected international dishes such as shwarma wraps. There are computers too if you want to get online.

Kumari Bakery Cafe   NEPALI $
(dishes Rs 80-200; @🛜) A warm and cosy wooden teahouse that does the usual dishes at good prices; there are newspapers and magazines to read if you want to hang out.

ℹ Information

The **Nagarkot Naldum Tourism Development Committee** (NNTDC; ☏9851043518; www.netif-nepal.org; ☺10am-5pm Sun-Fri) and the private tour company **Nagarkot Guide.com** (☏6680150; www.nagarkotguide.com) both have good information on walks in the area and can arrange guides starting from Rs 1000.

There are several ATMs near the bus park, while internet is available at Nagarkot.com and Food Republic.

ℹ Getting There & Away

There's a direct tourist minibus that runs daily to Kathmandu (Rs 250, two hours), departing Na-

To Sankhu (2½ Hours from Nagarkot)

The quickest route from Nagarkot is via a dirt road that leads all the way to Sankhu. Take the northwest road down to the Nagarkot Farmhouse Resort and follow switchbacks down to the village of **Kattike**, which has a teahouse for refreshments. Go left at the junction at the edge of town. You can continue all the way down this track, or take a minor road that turns off sharply to the right after 15 minutes. Follow this track for 20 minutes as it shrinks to a trail and then take a sharp left downhill past several houses to rejoin the main track. From here it's an hour's slog to Sankhu village.

A more scenic route along village trails starts from just past the Nagarkot bus park, where you take a right downhill and continue on to the village of Bakhrigaun. From here you keep following trails that take you through to the main track joining at Bisambhar.

To Sundarijal (One to Two Days from Nagarkot)

It takes two easy days – or one very long day – to skirt around the valley rim to Sundarijal, from where you can travel by road to Gokarna, Bodhnath and Kathmandu, trek for another day along the valley rim to Budhanilkantha, or start the treks to Helambu or Gosainkund. Accommodation is available at Bhotichaur and Sundarijal in local guesthouses, but the trails can be confusing so ask for directions frequently.

Start by following the Sankhu trail as far as Kattike (about one hour), then turn right (north) to Jorsim Pauwa. Walk further down through Bagdhara to Chowki Bhanjyang (about one hour) and on for one more hour through Nagle to **Bhotichaur**, a good place to stop overnight in a village inn.

On day two, walk back up the trail towards Chowki Bhanjyang and take the fork leading uphill by a chautara (porters' resting place). This path climbs uphill to cross a ridge line before dropping down on the middle of three trails to Chule (or Jhule). Here the path enters the Shivapuri Nagarjun National Park and contours around the edge of the valley for several hours, before dropping down to Mulkarkha, on the first stage of the Helambu trek. From Mulkarkha, it's an easy descent beside the water pipeline to Sundarijal.

An alternative route runs northwest from Bhotichaur to **Chisopani**, the first overnight stop on the Helambu trek, which has several trekking lodges. The next day, you can hike southwest over the ridge through Shivapuri Nagarjun National Park to Sundarijal.

garkot at 10.15am from outside Nagarkot.com. From Kathmandu, buses depart at 1.30pm out front of Hotel Malla in Lainchhaur. To get here by public bus you'll need to transfer at Bhaktapur (Rs 35, one hour) and jump on another bus to Nagarkot, which leave every 30 minutes. There are also buses from here to Sankhu and Bodhnath.

A one-way taxi to Nagarkot costs around Rs 1500 from Kathmandu, or Rs 2500 for a return trip with an hour or so to view the peaks. Walking to, or preferably from, Nagarkot is an interesting alternative.

Banepa

POP 16,000

The first major town you reach heading east out of the valley, Banepa is a lot more attractive once you get off its hellish highway and into the brick-paved backstreets snaking north from the highway. It's worth spending an hour or so exploring, with a number of Hindu and Buddhist temples. Most were built in the 14th and 16th centuries, when Banepa was an important stop on the trade route to Tibet, boasting trade links as far afield as the Ming dynasty on the east coast of China.

Legend has it that the people of this valley were once terrorised by a demon known as Chand, who was defeated by one of the fearsome incarnations of Parvati, earning the goddess a new title – Chandeshwari, 'Slayer of Chand'. The **Chandeshwari Temple** has an enormous mural of Bhairab on its wall, and is a popular pilgrimage spot where animals are sacrificed here on feast days.

Located in front of the temple is a row of columns supporting statues of a menagerie of animals, and the struts supporting the triple-tiered roof show the eight Ashta Matrikas and eight Bhairabs.

On the north side of the approach road is a smaller temple dedicated to the 'Mother of Chandeshwari'.

ⓘ Getting There & Away

Regular buses leave from Kathmandu's Ratna Park bus station (Rs 35, two hours) and continue on to Dhulikhel and beyond.

Buses going to Panauti (Rs 13, 20 minutes) turn off the Arniko Hwy at the main Banepa junction.

Dhulikhel

☎ 011 / POP 9800 / ELEV 1550M

Dhulikhel is a popular place to observe the high Himalaya, and the views easily compete with Nagarkot. From the edge of the ridge, a stunning panorama of peaks unfolds, from Langtang Lirung in the east, through Dorje Lakpa to the huge bulk of Gauri Shankar and nearby Melungtse (7181m) and as far as Numbur (5945m) in the east.

Dhulikhel has one big advantage over Nagarkot – it's a real Newari town, with a temple-lined village square and a life outside of exposing tourists to the views.

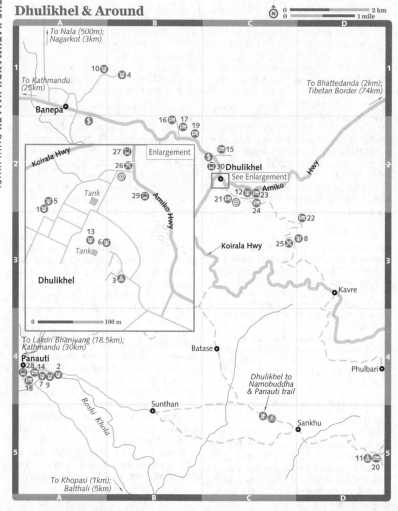

Dhulikhel & Around

◎ Sights

Shiva Temple
HINDU TEMPLE

If you take the road leading southeast from the bottom of the square for 2km, you'll pass a playing field and the turn-off of the road to the Kali Temple. Just beyond this junction, a Ganesh shrine marks the path down to a picturesque little temple at the bottom of a gorge. The temple enshrines a four-faced lingam topped by a metal dome with four nagas arching down from the pinnacle. Note the statues of a Malla royal family in the courtyard. The trickling stream flowing through the site gives it added atmosphere.

Old Town
NEIGHBOURHOOD

The old part of the town is an interesting area to wander around. The main square contains a triple-roofed **Hari Siddhi Temple** and a three-tiered **Vishnu Temple** fronted by two worshipful Garudas in quite different styles and heights. Northwest of the square are the modern **Gita Temple** and the three-tiered, Newari-style **Bhagwati Shiva Temple**.

Kali Temple
VIEWPOINT, HINDU TEMPLE

If you don't mind a steep 30-minute uphill climb, you can head up a series of shortcuts on concrete steps to reach this modern hilltop temple for excellent mountain views. The site is occupied by the army, but there's a viewing tower that attracts hordes of local sightseers at weekends and villagers sell *suntala* (small oranges) beside the path in autumn. On the way you'll pass **Shanti Ban**, a massive golden statue of Buddha.

It's also the way to Namobuddha, so if you plan on heading there, it makes sense to save the walk up here till then.

🏃 Activities

Day hike to Namobuddha
WALKING

The hike or mountain-bike trip from Dhulikhel to Namobuddha is a fine leg-stretcher, and one of the most popular activities for visitors here. It takes about three hours each way, or you can continue to Panauti in around two more hours. From Dhulikhel the trail first climbs up to the Kali Temple lookout then drops down to the left after the Deurali Restaurant for half an hour to the village of **Kavre**, by the new road to Sindhuli. Cross the road and walk down beside prayer flags for around an hour to the village of **Phulbari**. As you crest the ridge, you'll see a Tibetan monastery on a hilltop, with Namobuddha just below it. To reach the stupa, take the right branch where the path forks. The trail is well signed, so you shouldn't need a guide to get here.

🛏 Sleeping

Most of the expensive places with good views are strung out on dirt roads leading off the highway. The cheapies are down the winding back road that leads southeast from the main square.

Shiva Guest House
GUESTHOUSE $

(☎9841254988; d Rs 700, without bathroom Rs 300-500) A delightful family-run farmhouse with five clean rooms, and great views from the upper floors and rooftop. Food comes fresh from the organic garden and you can pick mandarins and other fruit right off the trees. It's reached by stairs leading up from the Shiva Temple. It's a 15-minute walk from the bus station.

Tashidhalek Guest House
GUESTHOUSE $

(☎9841310604; www.bhattidadavillage.com; r Rs 400, without bathroom Rs 200) On the edge of the Tamang village of Bhattedanda, Tashidhalek has a fantastic pastoral setting that gives it that end-of-the-road feel. Most of the rooms enjoy mountain views (some from the bathroom), and one has a private balcony. Its lovely rooftop has even better views. There's a pleasant little restaurant, and they grow most of their own vegetables. The owner can pick you up on his motorbike from the bus park, otherwise it's a 30-minute walk here.

Mirabel Resort
HOTEL $$

(☎490972; www.mirabelresorthotel.com; s/d Rs 2600/3200; 🛜) This large, comfortable resort would look more at home on a Balearic island, with its tiled white villas and hacienda vibe. Terrific value, its rooms have balconies facing the Himalayan vista, and you can also admire the peaks from the rooftop and gardens. There are also cheaper rooms (Rs 1500) in another building, but no views.

Nawaranga Guest House
GUESTHOUSE $

(☎490226; r Rs 500, without bathroom Rs 300) A real blast from the past, this arty guesthouse has been around for nearly 40 years. Rooms are basic but the price is right and the restaurant and communal areas are full of paintings for sale. It's southeast of the main chowk, on the back road towards the Shiva Temple.

Tamang Family Homestay
GUESTHOUSE $

(☎9841427881; www.bhattedandahomestay.com; s/d without bathroom Rs 400/700) A half-hour's walk from Dhulikhel in the village of Bhattedanda, this chilled-out Tamang family-run guesthouse is in a brightly painted building that's draped in prayer flags. Rates here include meals, which you eat with the family in their atmospheric kitchen. There's also free yoga each morning during the warmer months. If you call ahead they can pick you up for free from the bus station.

Himalayan Horizon Hotel
HOTEL $$

(☎490296; www.himalayanhorizon.com; s/d from US$65/75; 🛜) Also known as the Hotel Sun-n-Snow, this huge place uses traditional brickwork and woodcarving to create a Newari ambience. It's not quite 'old Dhulikhel' but the restaurant and garden terrace are great and the rooms have sublime views of the snow peaks.

High View Resort
HOTEL $$

(☎490048; www.highviewresort.com; deluxe s/d US$60/65; 🛜) A 1980s atmosphere pervades this secluded place, about 700m past the Himalayan Horizon and then a stiff five-minute climb up some steps. The styling is a little dated but the huge deluxe rooms come with a private balcony and the views are superb. Discounts can bring rates down by as much as 50%.

Panorama View Lodge
HOTEL $

(☎680786; www.panoramaviewlodge.com.np; s/d/tr Rs 800/1200/1500; 🛜) An option for those who really want to get away from it all, this place offers the full 'panorama view' plus good food and inviting rooms. Just don't expect crowds of people for company. The hotel is 2km above town on the dirt track to the Kali Temple.

Snow View Guest House
GUESTHOUSE $

(☎9841482487; r Rs 600) Probably the cheapest place with a proper mountain view, the Snow View is an annexe to a family home, set beside a pleasant garden restaurant. Only two rooms look directly onto the mountains but the rooftop has enough views for everybody.

Dhulikhel Lodge Resort
HOTEL $$

(☎490114; www.dhulikhellodgeresort.com; s/d from US$70/80; 🛜) Modern but built in a vaguely traditional style, this place has cracking views (particularly from the top-floor rooms) and the great circular fireplace in the bar provides an après-ski atmosphere, while the coffee bar is equally inviting.

Eating

There's very limited choice of places to eat, and most travellers opt to dine at their hotels. If you're headed to the Kali Temple you could grab breakfast or a snack at the nearby Deurali Restaurant.

Newa Kitchen
INTERNATIONAL, NEPALI $

(dishes Rs 60-250) Upstairs eatery by the bus stand with a full menu of Nepali, Indian, Chinese and European standards.

ℹ Information

There's a Nabil ATM at the junction of the main and BP roads, while there's internet across the road from Newa Kitchen.

ℹ Getting There & Away

Frequent buses to Dhulikhel leave from Kathmandu's Ratna Park bus station (Rs 46, two hours), passing Bhaktapur (Rs 28, 45 minutes) en route. The last bus goes back to Kathmandu at around 6.30pm. A taxi from Kathmandu costs about Rs 1700, or about Rs 900 from Bhaktapur. Buses to Namobuddha pass through around every two hours from the corner of the Arniko and BP highways.

The walk to Dhulikhel from Nagarkot is an interesting alternative; see the boxed text on p170 for details.

Panauti

☑ 011

Tucked away in a side valley off the Arniko Hwy, about 7km south of Banepa, Panauti sits at the sacred confluence of the Roshi Khola and Pungamati Khola. A third 'invisible river' called the Padmabati is said to join the other two rivers at Panauti, making this a particularly sacred spot. Accordingly, there are some fabulously ancient temples that have stood the test of time partly because of Panauti's legendary resistance to earthquakes. Sadly, this didn't help in 1988 when a tremor damaged several buildings in the village. The places covered in the Panauti section can be found on Map p172.

Panauti was once a major trading centre with its own royal palace but today the

---

WORTH A TRIP

NAMOBUDDHA

Along with Bodhnath and Swayambhunath, the stupa at **Namobuddha** is one of the three most important Buddhist pilgrimage sites in Nepal, attracting large numbers of Tibetans from Nepal, India and Tibet itself.

The site is sacred due to the inspiring legend about the Buddha, who, when in a previous life as a prince, encountered a tigress that was close to death from starvation and unable to feed her cubs. In an act of compassion he allowed the hungry tigress to consume him, a deed that transported him to the higher realms of existence. A marble tablet depicts the event in a small cave up the forested path to the left of the stupa. At the top of the hill is also the magnificent **Thrangu Tashi Yangtse Monastery**, a sprawling monastic complex of Tibetan Buddhist temples and monasteries with gleaming golden arched roofs. It was officially opened in December 2008.

While most foreigners visit as a day trip, it's possible to stay overnight at the **monastery** (☑ 9841112171; www.namo-buddha.org/namobuddha.html; r incl meals per person Rs 400-800), and you'll eat at the same time as the monks. You'll need to arrange it in advance. There are also several teahouses by the stupa where you can get a basic lunch.

Namobuddha Resort (☑ 9851106802; www.namobuddharesort.com; s €30-40, d €35-50; @ 🔊) is the other sleeping option, a delightful eco-retreat that's a 20-minute walk from Namobuddha stupa. Its tasteful cottages are spread throughout its garden and feature charming Nepali-inspired decor and Himalayan views. It's all organic here, and they bake their own sourdough bread, grow their own vegetables and even make their own paneer cheese for the entirely vegetarian menu. If its peaceful setting and mountain views don't relax you, there's also a sauna, flotation tank and yoga-meditation hall. Reservations are highly recommended.

Most people arrive at Namobuddha via the walking trail from Dhulikhel. However, there's a road here, too, and buses (Rs 45, 20 minutes) heading to/from Banepa and Dhulikhel leave at the bottom of the hill near the stupa. A taxi from Dhulikhel is around Rs 400.

From Namobuddha, a trail also descends from the right side of the stupa through forest to the small village of **Sankhu** (distinct from the other village called Sankhu that is mentioned in this chapter), with temples and riverside ghats. Shortly after, the track splits – the right fork leads to Batase and Dhulikhel, while the left fork winds past terraced fields to **Sunthan** and **Panauti**, about 2½ hours from Namobuddha. As you approach Panauti, cross the stream over a suspension bridge to the ghats and then follow the road as it curves round to the Indreshwar Mahadev Temple.

TRICKERY & REPENTANCE AT PANAUTI

Legend has it that Ahilya, the beautiful wife of a Vedic sage, was seduced by the god Indra, who tricked her by assuming the shape of her husband. When the sage returned and discovered what had happened he took his revenge by causing Indra's body to become covered in yonis – female sexual organs! Naturally, Indra was somewhat put out by this and for many years he and his wife Indrayani repented at the auspicious *sangam* (river confluence) at Panauti.

Parvati, Shiva's consort, took pity upon Indrayani and turned her into the invisible river, Padmabati, but it was some years before Shiva decided to release Indra from his strange affliction. The god appeared in Panauti in the form of a giant lingam and when Indra bathed in the river, his extranumerary yonis disappeared. Locals maintain that this miraculous Shiva lingam is the one enshrined in the Indreshwar Mahadev Temple.

village is a serene backwater, and all the more appealing for that. Most people visit on day trips, but we recommend staying over and exploring the streets at dawn and dusk, when they are at their most magical. As well as its ornate temples, the village has some striking Rana-era mansions, which have been restored with assistance from the French government.

◉ Sights

All of the following are located in Panauti's old town.

Indreshwar Mahadev Temple   HINDU TEMPLE
(foreigner/SAARC incl guide & entry to museum Rs 300/100; ⊙7am-5.30pm) Panauti's most famous temple is set in a vast courtyard full of statuary in the middle of the isthmus between the two rivers. Topped by a three-storey pagoda roof, the temple is a magnificent piece of Newari architecture. The first temple here was founded in 1294 but the shrine was rebuilt in its present form in the 15th century. The lingam enshrined here is said to have been created personally

by Shiva. The woodcarvings on the temple's windows, doorways and roof struts are particularly fine, and the erotic carvings here are subtle and romantic rather than pornographic.

To the south of the main temple is the rectangular **Unamanta Bhairab Temple**, with three faces peering out of the upstairs windows. Located within is a statue of Bhairab, accompanied by goddesses. A small, double-roofed Shiva temple stands in one corner of the courtyard, and a second shrine containing a huge black image of Vishnu as Narayan faces the temple from the west.

Inside the temple compound is also the **Panauti Museum**, an interesting collection of artefacts from the region, and original sections from the Indreshwar Mahadev Temple.

Brahmayani Temple   HINDU TEMPLE
Dating from the 17th century, the three-tiered Brahmayani Temple was built to honour Brahmayani, the chief goddess of the village. The image from the temple is hauled around town during the lively annual chariot festival, marking the end of the monsoon. To get here, cross a small suspension bridge to the north bank of the Pungamati Khola.

Krishna Narayan Temple   HINDU TEMPLE
Cross back to the south bank over the weir, then take another bridge back to the end of the spur, which is covered by the shrines and statues of the Krishna Narayan Temple.

There are also temples to various incarnations of Vishnu here – the largest temple has roof struts depicting Vishnu as the carefree, flute-playing Krishna. Many of the shrines are embellished with Rana-era stucco-work.

Civic Square   SQUARE
There are some interesting buildings in the middle of the village. Walk west along the northern brick lane and turn right just before you reach the main road. You'll soon come to a large square with a music platform, a large white stupa, a Brahmayani Temple and classic Newari-style architecture.

Panauti Peace Gallery   MUSEUM
(admission Rs 100; ⊙8am-5pm) Next to the tourism office in a rickety building, this museum has a rambling collection, including an antique walking-stick sword, straw-brush comb and the gall bladder of an elephant!

✨ Festivals & Events

Chariot Festival   RELIGIOUS

Held at the end of the monsoon each year (usually in September), when images of the gods from the town's various temples are drawn around the streets in wooden chariots, starting from the town's main square.

Magh Sankranti   RELIGIOUS

Every year during the Nepali month of Magh (usually January), pilgrims come to Panauti to bathe at the confluence of the two rivers to celebrate the end of the month of Poush, a dark time when religious ceremonies are forbidden. Every 12 years – next in 2022 – this is accompanied by a huge *mela* (fair) attracting devotees and sadhus from all over Nepal.

🛏 Sleeping & Eating

There are options for homestays in the area, arranged through the tourism centre or Ananda Café.

There were plans for Yomari Café to reopen in a new location in the courtyard of Panauti Peace Gallery.

Ananda Café & Guest House   GUESTHOUSE $

(☏6211924; s/d Rs 300/500) Set in an authentic village house, with drying corn cobs in the windows, rooms here are creaky and full of character. There's a fantastic outdoor garden with a table and chairs, surrounded by sprouting vegetables used for meals. It's opposite the Indreshwar Mahadev Temple.

Hotel Panauti   HOTEL $

(☏440055; www.hotelpanauti.com; r Rs 1000, without bathroom Rs 500; @) An above-average hotel with a superior rooftop restaurant, set under a thatched canopy. The giant rooms without bathrooms are better value than the rooms with bathrooms and TVs.

ℹ Information

The **Panauti Tourism Centre** (☏440093; www. panauti.com.np) at the start of the old town has good brochures, and can arrange guides and homestays. It also offers free internet, but there's only one computer.

ℹ Getting There & Away

Buses run frequently between Panauti and Kathmandu's Ratna Park bus station (Rs 53, 1½ to two hours); the last bus leaves Panauti at 5.30pm. For Dhulikhel you'll have to change in Banepa (Rs 12, 20 minutes). See the boxed text on p175 for information on walking to Panauti from Dhulikhel.

Around Panauti

Many of the small villages dotted around the valley have Newari-style temples and traditional brick architecture. Get hold of Nepa Maps' 1:50,000 *Around Kathmandu Valley* map and explore. One place to check out is the village of **Shrikandapur**, just off the Banepa–Panauti road. On the hilltop is a three-tiered Bhairab Temple with good views over the valley.

At Balthali, 7km southeast of Panauti, the **Balthali Resort** (☏01-4108210; www.balthalivil lageresort.com; s/d incl breakfast US$40/50) can arrange all sorts of volunteering and cultural immersion activities and treks to the surrounding villages. The resort is perched on the hilltop above Balthali village, with sweeping Himalayan views. To get here from Panauti, take a bus (Rs 15, 15 minutes) or walk along the road for an hour, crossing the river after Khopasi.

BEYOND THE VALLEY

The following destinations lie outside the Kathmandu Valley on the roads north to Syabrubesi and Kodari, on the Tibetan border. You can only cross into Tibet on an organised tour, but a trickle of independent travellers come up this way on overnight trips to peer wistfully at the Tibetan border. This is also the birthplace of Nepal's adventure-sports industry.

Arniko Highway to Tibet

The Arniko Hwy provides Nepal's overland link with Tibet and China. Beyond Barabise, the road is particularly vulnerable to landslides and sections are likely to be closed temporarily during the monsoon months (May to August). Even when the highway is open it's of limited use in breaking India's commercial stranglehold on Nepal, as it's still cheaper to ship Chinese goods via Kolkata (Calcutta) than to truck them through Tibet. The road attracts some mountain bikers, though bus and truck traffic can be heavy. The main towns covered in this section can be found on Map p270. To Borderlands or the Last Resort is a drive of around 3½ hours.

BARABISE

Strung out along the Arniko Hwy, Barabise is the region's main bazaar town but there's little reason to visit except to change buses. If you get stuck overnight, the central **Him Shrinkhala Guest House** (r Rs 500-600) and **Bhotekoshi Guest House** (r Rs 350-850) both have some good rooms. **Mata Chandeshwori Hotel** (r Rs 250-800) has grubby rooms but a pleasant restaurant.

Buses run frequently from the north end of town to Kodari (Rs 60 to Rs 75, three hours, last bus 5pm) and from the south end of town to Kathmandu (Rs 200, four hours, last bus 4pm).

BORDERLANDS RESORT

Tucked away in a bend of the Bhote Kosi River, 97km from Kathmandu and 15km from Tibet, the superb **Borderlands Resort** (Map p270; ☎01-4701295; www.borderlandresorts. com; accommodation with meals per person US$32-50, adventure packages per night from US$60)

is one of Nepal's top adventure resorts. Adrenaline-charged activities include rafting, trekking and canyoning but you can also just kick back and enjoy the peace and quiet. The riverside resort is centred on an attractive bar and dining area, surrounded by thatch-roofed safari tents dotted around a lush tropical garden. Massage is planned.

Most people visit on a package that includes activities, accommodation, meals and transport from Kathmandu – drop in to the resort's Kathmandu office (Map p80) next to the Northfield Cafe in Thamel to discuss the options. Two days of canyoning/rafting/cycling cost US$135/120/155, including transportation, food and accommodation, and there are plenty of combo options. The resort supports several local schools.

LAST RESORT

Thrill-seekers also drop off the Kodari road – quite literally – at the **Last Resort** (Map p270; ☎01-4700525; www.thelastresort.com.np; accom-

---

ADVENTURE SPORTS ON THE ROAD TO TIBET

The Ultimate Bungee

The bungee at the Last Resort straddles a mighty 160m drop into the gorge of the Bhote Kosi and ranks as one of the world's longest bungee jumps (higher than the highest bungee in New Zealand). The roars and squeals of free-falling tourists echo up and down the valley for miles.

As if the tallest bungee in Asia wasn't enough, the fiendish minds at the resort have devised the 'swing', a stomach-loosening eight-second free fall, followed by a Tarzan-like swing and then three or four pendulum swings back up and then down the length of the gorge. We feel ill just writing about it.

A swing or bungee costs €65 from Kathmandu (including return transport) or €58 if you are already up at the Last Resort. Extra jumps or swings cost an €20. For €15 you can reveal your inner wisdom and travel up to watch someone else jump and enjoy the looks on everyone else's faces when they catch their first glimpse of how deep a 160m gorge really is. The price includes whatever lunch you can muster, wisely served up *after* the jump.

Canyoning

This exciting sport is a wild combination of rappelling/abseiling, climbing, sliding and swimming that has been pioneered in the canyons and waterfalls near the Last Resort and Borderlands.

Both companies run two-day canyoning trips for about US$100, or you can combine two days of canyoning with a two-day Bhote Kosi rafting trip for US$200 (half this for one day's canyoning and one day's rafting). On day one you drive up from Kathmandu, have lunch, get some basic abseiling training and then practise on nearby cascades. Day two involves a trip out to more exciting falls, with a maximum abseil of up to 45m. Most canyons involve a short hike to get there.

Canyoning is not possible during the monsoon. It's best to bring a pair of closed-toe shoes that can get wet as these are better than sandals. Hiking shoes, a water bottle and bathing suits are also required and a waterproof camera is a real bonus. After November wetsuits are a must and are provided.

modation with transport & meals €40, overnight stay with activities €65-115). Set in a gorgeous spot on a ridge above the raging Bhote Kosi River, 12km from the Tibetan border, the resort is reached by a vertiginous suspension bridge that acts as a launch pad for Nepal's only bungee jump.

Accommodation at the resort is in comfortable and private two- or four-person safari tents, set around a soaring stone-and-slate dining hall and bar. Most people visit on all-inclusive adventure packages – as well as swinging from a giant elastic band, you can combine rafting, trekking, mountain biking and canyoning. An overnight bungee and rafting package costs around €115.

For less endorphin-motivated travellers, there are gas-heated showers, a plunge pool and a sauna and spa, making it slightly more luxurious than Borderlands and a great place to escape the city or relax en route to or from Tibet. Package rates include accommodation, meals and transport to and from Kathmandu – drop into the Kathmandu office (Map p80) near the Kathmandu Guest House for more information and to book.

KODARI

The road linking Kathmandu and Lhasa was constructed in the 1960s, but political wrangles and the ever-present risk of landslides prevented the Arniko Hwy from ever becoming a mainstream route between the two countries. Even today, traffic on the road from Barabise to Kodari is mainly limited to freight trucks and the occasional overland jeep tour.

It is not possible for foreigners to enter Tibet here except as part of an organised tour with a group Chinese visa and Tibetan travel permit. However, quite a few people traipse up to the border to pose for photos on the **Friendship Bridge** that separates the two countries. From here, everything to the north is Tibet, though at this elevation there is no real difference in the landscape. The nearest Tibetan town is Khasa (Zhangmu), about 8km uphill from the border.

It's worth taking a 15-minute walk up the steps opposite the Friendship Restaurant to the hilltop **Liping Gompa** for views over the Chinese side of the border, with its long lines of trucks snaking up the hill towards Khasa. The small main gompa is left at the trail junction; a charming meditation retreat and stupa is a 10-minute walk uphill to the right. Liping is the local name for Kodari.

🍽 Sleeping & Eating

Unless you are stuck for transport, you are better off heading to either the Last Resort or Borderlands.

Kailash Manasarovar Hotel & Guest House HOTEL $
(☎011-480022; kmansarobar@gmail.com; r Rs 600) The best option, a 10-minute walk downhill from the Kodari bazaar, with private bathrooms (but no hot water), a good restaurant and balcony seating.

Mt Kailash Guest Home GUESTHOUSE $
(☎011-480116; d Rs 700) Another decent place with a restaurant, located in the central Kodari bazaar.

ℹ Information

Bank of Kathmandu (⊙10am-3pm Sun-Thu, to 1pm Fri) About 20m below the immigration office, changes cash US dollars only.

Immigration office (⊙8am-5pm) Just before the Friendship Bridge, offers tourist visas on arrival at standard rates, but you must pay in cash US dollars and you'll need one photo.

Nepal Bangladesh (NB) Bank (⊙10am-5pm Sun-Fri) Two doors down, also changes cash US dollars.

ℹ Getting There & Away

There are four daily buses to Kathmandu (Rs 230 to Rs 350, 4½ hours) – the last bus at 1.30pm runs express. Otherwise take a local bus to Barabise (Rs 75 to Rs 125, three hours, last bus 5pm) and change there.

After 2pm your only option to get to Kathmandu the same day is to take a taxi for around Rs 3000 (Rs 800 per seat), but you'll struggle to find a willing driver after 5pm. Hitching is possible on this route, though you'll likely have to pay for your ride.

The Road to Langtang

A tarmac road heads northwest out of Kathmandu towards Dhunche, offering fantastic views of the Ganesh Himalaya as it gains the ridge at Kakani. Beyond Trisuli Bazaar, the road deteriorates and is travelled mainly by mountain bikers and trekkers headed for the Langtang region (see p283).

At Trisuli Bazaar an upgraded road branches southwest to Dhading and Malekhu, on the Kathmandu–Pokhara (Prithvi) Hwy, offering a shortcut route to Bandipur and Pokhara and a possible bicycle ride taking in Kakani, Trisuli Bazaar, Dhading and Malekhu. See Map p183 for this route.

WORTH A TRIP

NUWAKOT

The small village of Nuwakot (Nine Forts), just southeast of Trisuli Bazaar, is one of those untouched Newari townships that seems to float somewhere between the 17th and 21st centuries. It's one of Nepal's undiscovered gems.

The village is centred on its Durbar Sq, currently occupied by the army. The centrepiece is the **Saat Tale Durbar** (admission Rs 150; ☉10am-4pm Tue-Sun), a seven-storey fortress built in 1762 by Prithvi Narayan Shah as his family palace after taking the town. The town served as Nepal's capital until Shah conquered the Kathmandu Valley six years later. This was also where the great king died in 1775. You can climb to the 3rd-floor residency, the 6th-floor 'room of death' (a jail) and a cramped top-floor lookout.

Two other buildings, the Ranga Mahal (a Malla entertainment hall) and Garad Ghar (Tilganga Ghar), frame the courtyard but both are currently occupied by the police and army. Just above Durbar Sq is the large **Taleju Temple**, said to date from the 15th century, when Nuwakot was ruled by its own royal family.

Nearby is the golden-roofed **Bhairab Temple**, said to be one of Nepal's oldest, and used for animal sacrifices during the annual Sinduri Jatra festival. The temple is flanked by two pilgrim rest houses.

There are several possible walks around Nuwakot, including to the new **viewpoint** tower at the Kalika Temple and to the nearby hilltop **Malika Temple**.

The enterprising chaps at Himalayan Encounters (p42) run **Famous Farm** (☎01-4700426; www.himalayanencounters.com; s/d B&B US$45/55, full board US$60/80), a charming lodge in a pair of artfully converted old village houses. The 11 comfortable rooms are surrounded by a serene and peaceful garden, with views over the Trisuli Valley, and the open kitchen serves up superb organic food (cookery lessons are possible). It's one of Nepal's most serene getaways and it's worth staying at least two nights.

Getting to Nuwakot can be a little awkward. There are three direct buses a day from Kathmandu (Rs 160, four hours), or you can get here via a steep 7km (1½-hour) uphill hike from Bidur, on the bus route to Trisuli Bazaar. A taxi from Kathmandu costs a steep Rs 6000, plus Rs 1500 for an overnight wait.

KAKANI

Most of the towns around Kathmandu sit at the bottom of the valley – you have to travel to the valley rim to get decent views of the Himalaya. Set atop a ridge at 2073m, just off the road to Trisuli Bazaar, Kakani is the quieter, more peaceful cousin of Dhulikhel and Nagarkot. From a series of high points along the ridge, there are magnificent views of the Himalayan skyline stretching all the way from Annapurna to Everest, via Manaslu, Ganesh Himal, Gauri Shankar, Dorje Lekpa and Shishapangma. Part of the fun is getting here – the 24km road that winds uphill from Balaju makes for a challenging cycle ride and an even better motorcycle trip.

◉ Sights

Apart from staring open-mouthed at the view, there's not much to do. In the middle of the village, the meticulously tended **Thai Memorial Park** commemorates the final resting place for 113 passengers of a Thai Airlines plane that crashed near Gosainkund in 1992. On the other side of the hill is the **International Mountaineer Memorial Park**, with an artificial climbing wall.

The handsome colonial mansion at the start of the village was built as a summer villa for the British embassy, but it's closed to visitors.

🛏 Sleeping & Eating

Kakani Mountain View Hotel   HOTEL **$$**
(☎9802010210; www.kakanimountainview.com; r Rs 1500-2000, r without bathroom Rs 1200; @🛜) This is the best-run place on the ridge, offering seven clean rooms, a good restaurant and eager-to-please staff, though the location means you don't get any direct mountain views.

Tara Gaon Resort Hotel   CHALET **$**
(☎01-4672792; taragaon@enet.com.np; s/d US$12/16) This old-school government hotel offers good food and sublime views from its lawns but, though clean, the four old-

fashioned rooms are quite tired. Come for lunch or a sunset beer. Rates include tax.

View Himalaya Resort   HOTEL $
(☎01-6915706; r Rs 1200-1500) Newly rebuilt on the ridgeline above the road, this place does what is says on the label. The restaurant and most of the rooms offer great mountain views.

ⓘ Getting There & Away

Kakani is 1½ hours from Kathmandu by bus or motorcycle but you'll burn plenty of calories powering up here by bicycle. It's uphill all the way, but there are numerous trout restaurants where you can stop for a break. It's a thrilling freewheel back to Kathmandu but watch for trucks or buses on the corners. See p292 for details of the route to Kakani and on through Shivapuri Nagarjun National Park.

The road to Kakani turns off the Kathmandu–Trisuli Bazaar road just before the Kaulithana police checkpoint, at the crest of the hill. Frequent buses bound for Trisuli Bazaar can drop you at the junction (Rs 50, 1½ hours) and you can walk the 4km to Kakani in 45 minutes. A taxi from Kathmandu costs Rs 3000 return.

Kathmandu to Pokhara

Best in Culture

» Gorkha Durbar (p187)

» Bandipur's Newari architecture (p186)

» Manakamana Temple (p184)

» Gorkha Museum (p186)

Best in Adventure

» Rafting on the Trisuli (p184)

» Paragliding in Bandipur (p189)

» Rock climbing at Bimalnagar (p189)

» Caving in Siddha Gufa (p189)

» Canyoning near Mugling (p184)

Why Go?

Before you sprint from Kathmandu to Pokhara, consider the 206km of classic Middle Hills countryside that you will pass through en route. The hills that flank the Prithvi Hwy are dotted with historic villages and ancient temples, but visitors often see nothing of this area apart from the views flashing by outside the bus windows.

Better yet, forget the bus altogether and grab a paddle to join a white-water rafting trip that tumbles along the Trisuli River. With white, sandy beaches along the way, it's also a good opportunity to slow down and laze in a hammock.

The river runs parallel with the highway, so there's no excuse not to visit atmospheric towns like Gorkha or Bandipur. The latter is a slice of Europe in the middle of gorgeous countryside – with no traffic, restaurants with tables set up on the street and quaint Newari architecture.

When to Go

The best time to travel between Kathmandu and Pokhara is during the winter months of November to January, which will maximise your chances of catching sweeping Himalayan views during glorious mild sunny days. For those planning to tackle the Trisuli River on a rafting expedition, you should aim to visit from October to December or March to May for rollicking rapids and camping on sandy river beaches. Even more adventurous souls wanting to head up into the skies can arrange tandem paraglide flights in Bandipur between September and June.

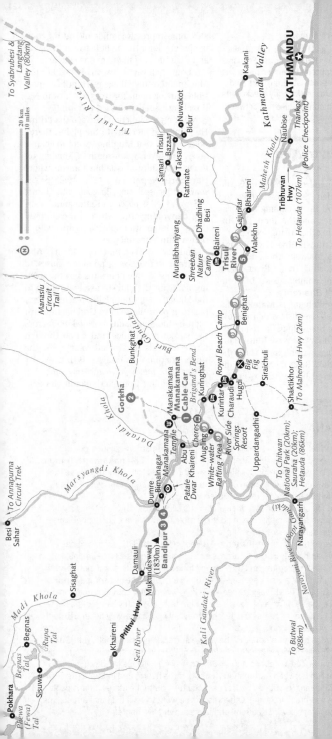

Kathmandu to Pokhara Highlights

1 Fly like a yogi on the exhilarating **Manakamana cable car** (p184)

2 Walk in the footsteps of royalty at Gorkha's magnificent hilltop **Gorkha Durbar** (p187)

3 Step back in time among the Newari houses of **Bandipur** (p186), on the ancient trade route to India

4 Walk to caves, viewpoints, villages and mountain shrines in the **Bandipur hills** (p189)

5 Fly down the Trisuli River on Nepal's most accessible **white-water rafting trip** (p297), before chilling out at one of its beach camps

ⓘ Getting There & Away

Several dozen public and tourist buses and mini-vans run daily between Kathmandu and Pokhara, linking most of the important towns en route. The winding journey takes at least seven hours, and longer if the bus has to stop for army checkpoints.

For details of the mountain-bike ride between Kathmandu and Pokhara, see p293.

Kathmandu to Abu Khaireni

The main thoroughfare to Pokhara is the Prithvi Hwy, which runs west along the gorge of the Trisuli River, passing the turn-off for Narayangarh and the Terai. (For information on rafting the Trisuli, see p297.)

From Naubise, the Prithvi Hwy follows the valley of the Mahesh Khola to meet the twisting, contorting Trisuli River. Many white-water rafting companies set off from the small village of **Bhaireni**.

The next big settlement is **Malekhu**, famous for its smoked river fish, which are sold from long wooden rakes along the roadside.

Following the highway west from Malekhu, the next village is **Benighat**, where the roaring Buri Gandaki River merges with the Trisuli. The increased bore of the river creates some impressive rapids and rafting companies break for the night between Benighat and Charaudi, about 20km downstream.

About halfway between Benighat and Mugling, the tiny village of **Hugdi** is a possible starting point for treks to Chitwan National Park – see the boxed text, p190.

Marking the junction between the Prithvi Hwy and the highway to the plains, there's no reason to visit **Mugling** except to change buses. However, 10km south of Mugling on the road to Chitwan is Jalbire Canyon, where **Hardcore Nepal** (Map p80; ☎9813463599; www.hardcorenepal.com; Bhagwati St, Thamel; US$75), which is based in Kathmandu, operates **canyoning** trips where you can abseil down a 100m waterfall, climaxing with a plunge into a natural pool.

Another dusty junction town, **Abu Khaireni** is the access point for buses to Gorkha (Rs 55, one hour). It's also the starting point for the four- to five-hour climb to the Manakamana Temple. To reach the temple, turn onto the road to Gorkha and turn right by the Manakamana Hotel, then cross the suspension bridge and climb through terraced fields and small villages to the ridge. There are several ATMs, but regular power cuts mean you can't rely on them. Any bus going from Kathmandu (Rs 250,

---

WORTH A TRIP

MANAKAMANA

From the tiny hamlet of Cheres (6km before Mugling), an Austrian-engineered cable car soars up an almost impossibly steep hillside to the ancient **Manakamana Temple** (☉daylight), one of the most important temples in the Middle Hills. Hindus believe that the goddess Bhagwati, an incarnation of Parvati, has the power to grant wishes, and newlyweds flock here to pray for male children.

But this good fortune comes at a price – pilgrims seal the deal by sacrificing a goat, chicken or pigeon in a gory pavilion behind the temple. There's even a dedicated carriage on the cable car for sacrificial goats.

Built in the tiered pagoda style, the temple dates back to the 17th century. It has a stunning Himalayan backdrop. On Saturdays and other feast days, Manakamana almost vanishes under a sea of pilgrims and the paving stones run red with sacrificial blood.

Part of the highlight of a visit here is getting to the temple in the awesome **Manakamana cable car** (adult US$12, luggage per 1kg Rs 8; ☉9am-noon & 1.30-5pm, from 8am Sat), which rises more than 1000m as it covers the 2.8km from the Prithvi Hwy to the Manakamana ridge. The price for goats is Rs 130 but they only get a one-way ticket... Expect long queues on weekends and holidays.

There are dozens of pilgrim hotels in the village surrounding the temple, with **Sunrise Home** (☎064-460055; r with bathroom from Rs 500) having spotless, spacious rooms with fans and TVs. Prices almost double on Saturdays and religious holidays.

All buses that run between Kathmandu (Rs 200, three hours) and Pokhara (Rs 250, four hours) or Chitwan (Rs 150, 1½ hours) pass the turn-off to the Manakamana cable car (look for the red-brick archway). Otherwise if you want to walk to Manakamana, the trail starts at the village of Abu Khaireni, and takes around five hours.

three hours) to Pokhara (Rs 180, two hours) can drop you at Abu Khaireni. For Bandipur, you'll need to head via Dumre.

🛏 Sleeping & Eating

Royal Beach Camp   HOTEL, CAMPGROUND **$$**
(☎9741010866, 01-4700531; www.royalbeachnepal. com; tent incl full board US$25, bungalow US$35, r with/without bathroom US$60/75; ☀) While it caters primarily to those on rafting or kayaking packages, Royal Beach Camp's soft sandy beach, hammocks and outdoor restaurant/bar also make it a great spot to chill out along the river for a day or two. There are pricey rooms in the new building, or permanent tents and bungalows near the water. It's near Charaudi, and three hours by bus from Kathmandu or Pokhara (Rs 300).

River Side Springs Resort   LODGE **$**
(☎056-540129; www.rsr.com.np; permanent tents s/d US$25/30, cabins s/d US$50/60; ❋☀) Around 10km before Manakamana, this sophisticated, colonial-style resort occupies a prime piece of real estate on the banks of the Trisuli. Popular with tour groups, accommodation is in Japanese-inspired cabins or permanent tents. With a good restaurant, an extravagant ring-shaped swimming pool (nonguests Rs 275) and a sandy beach, it's a popular stopover for daytrippers.

Big Fig   CAFE **$**
(www.himalayanencounters.com; mains from Rs 100) Part of an attractive little roadside village, Big Fig is a good stopover for a bite and to stretch your legs. Its outside tables look over the Trisuli River, and a magnificent suspension bridge leads to a sandy beach at Himalayan Encounter's rafting camp, the Trisuli Centre.

Shreeban Nature Camp   LODGE **$$**
(☎01-4258427; www.shreeban.com.np; outside Dhading; 1 night, 2-day package per person €35) It's a low-key operation, but with a program of trekking, birdwatching, and cultural activities, lovers of the outdoors should consider stopping by. You'll need to make prior arrangements before visiting.

Gorkha

☎ 064 / ELEV 1135M
About 24km north of Abu Khaireni, Gorkha is famous as the birthplace of Prithvi Narayan Shah, who unified the rival kingdoms of Nepal into a single cohesive nation in 1769, but the Shah dynasty ended with the igno-

Gorkha

minious 'retirement' of Gyanendra Shah in 2008.

Nevertheless, Gorkha is still an important pilgrimage destination for Newars, who regard the Shahs as living incarnations of Vishnu.

The main attraction is the Gorkha Durbar (see boxed text, p187), the former palace of the Shahs, which looks over Gorkha from a precarious ridge. There are also historic temples dotted around the old part of Gorkha.

◎ Sights

Old Town   NEIGHBOURHOOD
Immediately above the bus stand is the fortified **Ratna Temple**, the former Gorkha

Gorkha Durbar

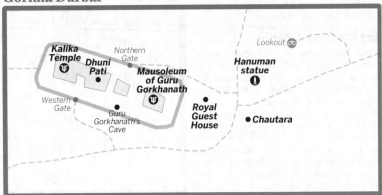

KATHMANDU TO POKHARA BANDIPUR

residence of King Gyanendra, which is now unoccupied. If you follow the road uphill, you'll reach the two-tiered temple dedicated to **Vishnu**; a squat white temple with the Nandi statue that's dedicated to **Mahadev** (Shiva); and a small, white shikhara (temple tower) by the tank, which is sacred to **Ganesh**.

Gorkha Museum   MUSEUM
(admission foreigner/SAARC Rs 50/20, camera fee Rs 200/100; ⊙10.30am-4.30pm, to 3.30pm winter Wed-Mon) Housed inside the grand Tallo Durbar, a Newari-style palace built in 1835, the museum's exhibits are limited, but it's interesting to see the finely carved timbers up close. It's set in 3.5 hectares of garden, which are nice for a stroll.

🛏 Sleeping & Eating

Most of the hotels in Gorkha are strung out along the road that runs up to the bus stand.

The best restaurants are at the Hotel Gorkha Bisauni and Gurkha Inn, but there are numerous cheap *bhojanalayas* (snack restaurants) near the bus stand.

Hotel Gorkha Bisauni   HOTEL $
(☑420107; gh_bisauni@hotmail.com; r with bathroom Rs 800-1200, r without bathroom from Rs 400; 🛜) Set in landscaped grounds located about 500m downhill from the bus stand, this agreeable midrange place has carpets, TV and private or shared bathrooms with hot showers, and the restaurant serves a little bit of everything. Rooms vary from dingy to plush. The outdoor terrace is a wonderful spot at sunset.

New Hotel Gorkha Prince   GUESTHOUSE $
(Prince Hotel; ☑420030; r without bathroom Rs 300) It's bare bones, but with rooms that look out to the hills at this price, who cares? New Hotel Gorkha Prince is also handy for the bus stand.

Gurkha Inn   HOTEL $
(☑420206; s/d US$30/40; @) It's overpriced and could do with a fresh lick of paint, but we like the Gurkha Inn. This probably has something to do with the lovely, stepped garden facing the valley, the cosy patio restaurant and the bright, airy rooms.

Gurung Hotel & Lodge   GUESTHOUSE $
(☑9803690184; r with/without bathroom Rs 250/200) Rooms are quite rundown, but its location right in the heart of the old town is the best of all hotels in Gorkha.

ⓘ Getting There & Away

The bus stand is right in the middle of town and there are ticket offices at either end of the stand.

There are three daily buses to Pokhara (Rs 180, five hours) and numerous buses (Rs 250, five hours) and microbuses (Rs 320, four hours) to Kathmandu from 6.15am until 2.20pm. A single microbus leaves Gorkha at 7am for Bhairawa (Rs 300, six hours) or there are regular buses to Narayangarh (Rs 175, two hours) until midday.

Bandipur

☑065 / ELEV 1030M
Draped like a scarf along a high ridge above Dumre, Bandipur is a living museum of Newari culture. Its winding lanes are lined with tall Newari houses and people here

DON'T MISS

GORKHA DURBAR

Regarded by many as the crowning glory of Newari architecture, **Gorkha Durbar** (admission Rs 50, camera Rs 200; ⊙6am-6pm) is a fort, a palace and a temple all-in-one. This magnificent architectural construction is perched high above Gorkha on a knife-edge ridge, with superb views over the Trisuli Valley and glimpses north to the soaring peaks of the Annapurna and Ganesh Himalaya.

As the birthplace of Prithvi Narayan Shah, the Durbar has huge significance for Nepalis. The great Shah was born here around 1723, when Gorkha was a minor feudal kingdom. Upon gaining the throne, Prithvi Narayan worked his way around the Kathmandu Valley, subduing rival kingdoms and creating an empire that extended far into India and Tibet.

The Durbar is an important religious site, so leather shoes and belts etc should be removed. Most pilgrims enter through the western gate, emerging on an open terrace in front of the exquisite **Kalika Temple**, a psychedelic 17th-century fantasy of peacocks, demons and serpents, carved into every available inch of timber. Only Brahmin priests and the king can enter the temple, but non-Hindus are permitted to observe from the terrace.

The east wing of the palace complex contains the former palace of Prithvi Narayan Shah. Like the temple, the **Dhuni Pati** palace is covered in elaborate woodcarvings, including a magnificent window in the shape of Garuda. At the east end of the palace is the mausoleum of **Guru Gorakhnath**, the reclusive saint who acted as a spiritual guide for the young Prithvi Narayan.

If you leave via the northern gate, you'll pass the former **Royal Guest House** – note the erotic roof struts and the crocodile carvings on the window frames.

Down from here is a vividly painted **Hanuman statue**, and a path leading to a large **chautara** (stone resting platform) on an exposed rocky bluff with awesome views and a set of carved stone footprints, attributed variously to Sita, Rama, Gorakhnath and Guru Padmasambhava.

To reach the Durbar, you must climb an exhausting stairway of 1500 stone steps, snaking up the hillside.

seem to live centuries before the rest of the country. It's hard to believe that somewhere so delightful has managed to escape the ravages of unchecked tourist development.

The Bandipur Social Development Committee has opened Bandipur up to tourism. With help from the owners of the adventure company Himalayan Encounters (see p77), derelict buildings have been reborn as cafes and lodges, and temples and civic buildings have been pulled back from the edge of ruin. With its glorious 18th-century architecture, absence of motorised vehicles and restaurant tables set out on the bazaar, it has a distinct European feel. Yet Bandipur remains very much a living community, full of farmers and traders going about their business.

Bandipur was originally part of the Magar kingdom of Tanahun, ruled from nearby Palpa (Tansen), but Newari traders flooded in after the conquest of the valley by Prithvi Narayan Shah.

The town became an important stop on the India-Tibet trade route until it was bypassed by the Prithvi Hwy in the 1960s.

 Sights

Thani Mai Temple   VIEWPOINT
Perched atop Gurungche Hill, the main reason to climb up to Thani Mai is for its spectacular sunrise views. On a clear morning it has some of the most memorable 360-degree vistas in the country, with the Himalaya stretching out along the horizon, while the valley beneath is cloaked in a thick fog that resembles a white lake. The trail starts near the school at the southwest end of the bazaar, and is a steep 30-minute walk.

Siddha Gufa   CAVE
Making for a popular half-day trip, at 437m deep and 50m high, Siddha Gufa is said to be the largest cave in Nepal. Its cathedral-like chasm is full of twisted stalactites and stalagmites and hundreds of bats chirp and whistle overhead. Guides (Rs 300) are compulsory and await you at the cave's entrance. Flashlights (Rs 100) are also available for hire. Getting here is definitely a trek, taking 1½ hours one way. Follow the signs starting from the north end of the village, taking you

Bandipur

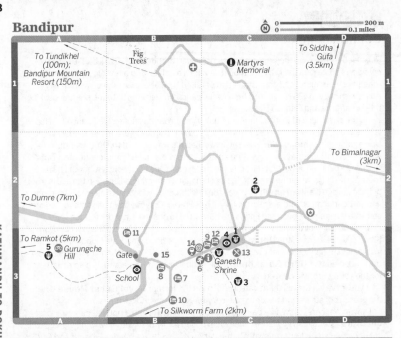

Bandipur

◎ Sights

1 Bindebasini Temple...............................C3
2 Khadga Devi Temple C2
3 Mahalaxmi Temple C3
4 Padma Library..C3
5 Thani Mai Temple A3

⊙ Activities, Courses & Tours

6 Blue Sky Paragliding............................B3

▣ Sleeping

7 Bandipur Guest House..........................B3
8 Bandipur Village Resort.......................B3
9 Gaun Ghar...C3

10 Green Hills View Lodge.........................B3
11 Hotel Depche B3
12 Old Inn Bandipur...................................C3

✕ Eating

Gaun Ghar ....(see 9)
13 Ke Garne Café..C3

◎ Drinking

14 Hill's Heaven..B3
Monkey's Flunky............................(see 13)

ℹ Transport

15 Jeeps to Dumre B3

along a dirt path running north over the edge of the ridge, turning right at the obvious junction. The stone path is slippery so mind your step. From here it's a 25-minute walk downhill to Bimalnagar for buses to Pokhara or Kathmandu.

Tundikhel
VIEWPOINT

In centuries past, traders would gather on this flat-topped ridge to haggle for goods from India and Tibet before starting the long trek to Lhasa or the Indian plains. It was also a former parade ground for Gur-

khas serving with the British Army. These days it's all about the views. At dawn and sunset, the clouds peel back to reveal a stunning panorama of Himalayan peaks that include Dhaulagiri (8167m), Machhapuchhare (6997m), Langtang Lirung (7246m), Manaslu (8162m) and Ganesh Himal (7406m). Things get rather rowdy here on weekends during the picnic season from October to November.

At the start of the Tundikhel are five enormous fig trees. In Nepali mythology, the different types of fig are symbols for different Hindu gods, and Vishnu, Brahma and Hanuman are all represented here.

Silkworm Farm
FARM

(☑520104; admission by donation; ⊘10am-4pm Sun-Fri) A more offbeat choice, a visit to Silkworm Farm takes you through the fascinating process of how silk is produced. The farm comprises orchards of mulberry plants, which are grown for worm food – the worms themselves are reared indoors, usually from August to December and March to May. But you can visit anytime, with someone on hand to explain the process using jars of preserved displays. To get here follow the road past Green Hills View Lodge downhill for around 2km.

Bindebasini Temple
HINDU TEMPLE

At the northeast end of the bazaar (which is the main shopping strip) this ornate, two-tiered temple is dedicated to Durga. Its ancient walls are covered in carvings and an elderly priest opens the doors each evening. Facing the temple across the square is the **Padma library**, a striking 18th-century building with carved windows and beams. Nearby, a set of stone steps runs off east to the small **Mahalaxmi Temple**, another centuries-old Newari-style temple.

Khadga Devi Temple
HINDU TEMPLE

A wide flight of stone steps leads up the hillside to this barn-like temple, which enshrines the sword of Mukunda Sen, the 16th-century king of Palpa (Tansen). Allegedly a gift from Shiva, the blade is revered as a symbol of shakti (consort or female energy) and once a year during Dasain it gets a taste of sacrificial blood.

🏃 Activities

Day Hikes
WALKING

It's easy to pass several peaceful days exploring the hills around Bandipur. There are dramatic Himalayan views and the countryside is a gorgeous patchwork of terraced rice and mustard fields and small orchards. Most guesthouses can arrange walking guides for around Rs 500.

Along with Siddha Gufa (see p187), one of the most popular walks is to the Magar village of **Ramkot**. The scenic four-hour (return) walk takes you to this charming and friendly little village where there are some traditional round houses. There's nowhere to buy food or water here, so pack a lunch,

which you can enjoy under the two banyan trees atop the hill, with a great Himalayan backdrop. Enquire with the Old Inn Bandipur about homestays in the village.

Blue Sky Paragliding
GLIDING

(☑520091; www.paragliding-nepal.com; ½/1hr €70/100) Blue Sky Paragliding is the first company to bring paragliding to Bandipur, with tandem or solo flights taking you over some stunning views. There are four flights per day, with sunset being the most popular.

Hardcore Nepal
ROCK CLIMBING, CAVING

(☑9813463599; www.hardcorenepal.com; Kathmandu; rock climbing US$65, caving US$65) Keen climbers can tackle the 40m limestone wall along the highway in Bimalnagar, a couple of kilometres east of Dumre. Hardcore Nepal can also arrange caving in Siddha Gufa, involving abseiling 70m through the ceiling entrance.

🛏 Sleeping & Eating

There's no shortage of accommodation in Bandipur to suit all budgets. The main bazaar has probably the cheapest rooms, but most with rock-hard beds.

🄼 Old Inn Bandipur
INN $$

(☑520110; info@himalayanencounters.com; s/d/tr incl breakfast without bathroom US$45/55/65, with bathroom US$60/75/90) Run by the highly professional team behind Himalayan Encounters, this beautifully restored mansion offers atmospheric rooms full of Buddhist and Newari art, set around a terracotta terrace facing the mountains. Take your pick from rooms with views of mountains or those looking out to charming streetscape. Some rooms are on the cosy side (and watch your head!), but newer rooms are spacious with private bathrooms, and some with balconies.

Hotel Depche
LODGE $

(☑9841226971; hoteldepche@hotmail.com; r with/without bathroom Rs 1200/800) A hidden gem on the outskirts of Bandipur, this attractive mudbrick cottage is tucked away among the fields. While the rooms themselves lack character (they're more your typical modern rooms), the courtyard and rooftop are the real appeal of this place.

Bandipur Guest House
GUESTHOUSE $

(☑520041; r with/without bathroom Rs 500/400; 🔊) Housed in a majestic, crumbling old shop-house at the start of the bazaar, the welcoming Bandipur Guest House offers

TREKKING TO CHITWAN

From tiny Hugdi, you can trek south into the homeland of the Chepang tribe, reaching Sauraha (p230) on the edge of Chitwan National Park in five days. Trekkers stay in rustic teahouses and homestays in the villages of Hattibang, Jyandala, Gadi and Shaktikhor.

On the way, you can visit forts and mountain viewpoints, go birdwatching and get involved in a variety of cultural activities. Contact trekking operators in Kathmandu or Pokhara for further details.

simple wooden rooms with tiny balconies overlooking the Newari-style village. The attached restaurant serves some good meals, including Newari specialities, such as *jhwai khattee* (warm local wine with millet, ghee, rice and honey).

Green Hills View Lodge GUESTHOUSE $
(☑520064; greenhills@yahoo.com; r Rs 250-300) Another converted house, with simple rustic rooms and great valley views. Also has an attractive rooftop area and homely restaurant.

Bandipur Mountain Resort HOTEL $$
(☑520125; www.islandjungleresort.com.np; s/d with full board US$35/40; ☎) A calm midrange resort that benefits from a lovely setting, surrounded by swishing pines at the west end of Tundikhel. Rooms are a little dated but they're not bad for the price and all have great mountain views. Popular with tour groups; reservations are essential.

Bandipur Village Resort HOTEL $
(☑520143; bandipurvillageresort@gmail.com; s/d from 700/1200; ✳☎) The first hotel you'll pass arriving from the jeep stand, the Village Resort has an attractive historic facade, but rooms themselves are in the modern, concrete building out the back. It's a good option if you're looking for comfort. Some rooms have amazing mountain views – also appreciated from the rooftop. Food here is pretty good, and the crispy mushrooms make a great snack with a cold beer. Staff are friendly and helpful.

Gaun Ghar NEPALI $$
(☑520129; www.gaunghar.com; s/d incl breakfast US$65/130; mains nonveg/veg platter Rs 715/500)

Another renovated historic home, Gaun Ghar is almost a carbon copy of Old Inn Bandipur (its next-door neighbour). Beds are fitted with electric blankets for chilly winter nights. It's also the best place to try Newari food, with many of its ingredients organic and specialities like *neurow* (local fern).

Ke Garne Café NEPALI, INTERNATIONAL $
(snacks from Rs 50) The name of this cosy cafe means 'What to do?' so here are some suggestions for you: sip tea, munch on Nepali snacks, play giant chess on the cafe's terrace, or head upstairs to the cosy **Monkey's Flunky** bar.

Hill's Heaven NEPALI $
(meals from Rs 70-180; ☎) On the main strip, Hill's Heaven is popular for its cheap beer and free wi-fi.

❶ Information

The **Bandipur Tourist Information Counter** (www.bandipurtourism.com; ☉10am-5pm Sun-Fri) has brochures and basic information on the area. Guides can be arranged for around Rs 500 for a half-day.

There's no ATM in Bandipur, with the closest being at Dumre – a 30-minute drive. You can get online at **Cyber Café** (per hr Rs 40) in the bazaar.

❶ Getting There & Away

The road to Bandipur branches off the Prithvi Hwy about 2km west of Dumre; jeeps hang around by the junction charging Rs 50 per person. The first jeep is at 7am and the last at 4pm, departing every 45 minutes or when full.

Dumre

About 17km west of Abu Khaireni, Dumre is yet another dusty highway town, and is visited solely as a connecting point for jeeps to Bandipur (Rs 50 per person, Rs 300 for the whole jeep, one hour) that loiter around on the highway about 200m west of the Besi Sahar junction. It's also a handy point to head to Besi Sahar, the starting point for the Annapurna Circuit Trek. There are several ATMs here.

There are regular buses and microbuses to Kathmandu (Rs 300) and Pokhara (Rs 200). From the main junction, local buses and minivans also run regularly to Besi Sahar (Rs 100 by bus, Rs 150 by minivan, three hours).

Pokhara

061 / POP 250,000 / ELEV 884M

Best Places to Eat

» Krishna's Kitchen (p207)
» Moondance Restaurant (p205)
» Caffe Concerto (p206)
» Koto (p206)
» China Town (p205)

Best Places to Stay

» Temple Tree Resort & Spa (p200)
» Hotel Travel Inn (p199)
» Fish Tail Lodge (p202)
» Chhetri Sisters Guest House (p203)
» Maya Devi Village (p204)

Why Go?

Peaceful Pokhara has a prime position beside a deep green lake, nestling among forested hills with a picture-postcard backdrop of gleaming Himalayan peaks. But Pokhara has two personalities. Behind Lakeside Pokhara, the one most tourists see, is a sprawling trade centre bustling with all the trappings of modern commerce but with pockets of old Newari architecture. Meanwhile, back at Lakeside Pokhara, the scene is a chilled-out version of Thamel where traffic fumes have been swapped for fresh mountain air and the racing motorbikes for paddle boats.

Lakeside Pokhara provides rest and recreation for many a weary traveller. Whether you've just returned from a three-week trek or endured a bus trip from hell, Lakeside is the perfect place to recharge the batteries. Yet there's much more to it than a laid-back charm. It also has a booming adventure sports industry, and is arguably the best paragliding venue on the globe. And, of course, it's the gateway to the world-famous Annapurna treks.

When to Go
Pokhara

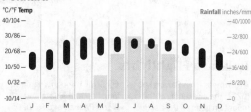

Oct–Mar Ideal time to visit, when the mountains (mostly) reveal their grandeur.

28 Dec–1 Jan Enjoy food and cultural shows at the Pokhara Street festival.

Apr Tourists and locals alike celebrate the Nepali New Year in Pokhara.

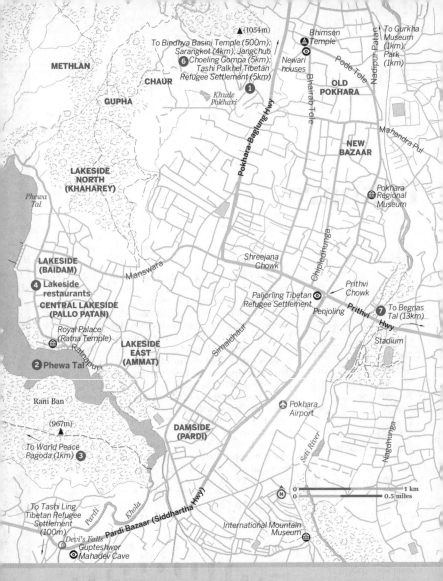

Pokhara Highlights

1 Witness from **Sarangkot** (p212) the awakening of the mountain gods as the rising sun illuminates the Himalayan peaks

2 Paddle a colourful boat out to the middle of **Phewa Tal** to capture an unbelievable reflection of the Annapurna Range

3 Stroll through a verdant forest up to the dazzling white **World Peace Pagoda** (p205) to capture a bird's-eye view of Pokhara with its magnificent mountain backdrop

4 Celebrate your trekking triumph with a delicious meal and a cold beer at one of Lakeside's **restaurants** (p205)

5 Soar like an eagle as you follow the thermals while tandem **paragliding** (p198)

6 Learn the survival story of Tibetan refugees and listen to chanting monks at **Jangchub Choeling Gompa** (p195)

7 Escape the Lakeside crowds and explore the quiet shores of **Begnas Tal** (p213)

Climate
Pokhara sits about 400m lower than Kathmandu so the autumn and winter temperatures are generally much more comfortable. Even in winter you can get away with a T-shirt during the daytime and you'll only need a sweater or jacket for evenings and early morning starts. From June to September the skies open and the mountains spend a lot of time behind blankets of cloud.

Dangers & Annoyances
There's been the occasional serious mugging on solo walkers trekking up to the World Peace Pagoda and around Sarangkot, and attacks on solo women near trance parties. Clearly there's a safety in numbers message for both activities.

◉ Sights

Phewa Tal   LAKE
(Map p201) Phewa Tal is the travellers' focal point in Pokhara, and is the second largest lake in Nepal. In contrast to the gaudy tourist development of Lakeside, the steep southwestern shore is densely forested. The lush Rani Ban, or Queen's Forest, gives the still waters a deep emerald hue. On clear, calm days, the Annapurna mountains are perfectly reflected in its mirror surface.

You can take to the lake in one of the brightly painted *doongas* (boats) available for rent at Lakeside (see p197). Many people walk or cycle around the lakeshore – the trek up to the World Peace Pagoda (see the boxed text, p205, for details) affords breathtaking views over the tal and the mountains beyond.

Mountains   MOUNTAINS
Forming a spectacular backdrop to Pokhara is the dramatic Annapurna Massif. Most prominent is the emblematic Mt Machhapuchhare ('Fish Tail' in Nepali), whose triangular mass looms large over the town, and remains the only virgin mountain in Nepal set aside as forbidden to be climbed.

From west to east, the peaks are Hiunchuli (6441m), Annapurna I (8091m), Machhapuchhare (6997m), Annapurna III (7555m), Annapurna IV (7525m) and Annapurna II (7937m).

A word of warning: the mountains can occasionally disappear behind cloud for several days, particularly during the monsoon season.

Varahi Mandir   HINDU TEMPLE
(Map p201) Pokhara's most famous Hindu temple, the two-tiered pagoda-style Varahi Mandir, stands on a small island near the Ratna Mandir (Royal Palace). Founded in the 18th century, the temple is dedicated to Vishnu in his boar incarnation, but it's been extensively renovated over the years and is inhabited by a loft of cooing pigeons. Rowboats to the temple (Rs 50 return) leave from near the city bus stand in Lakeside.

Old Pokhara   HISTORIC BUILDINGS
(Map p196) For a taste of what Pokhara was like before the trekking agencies and tourist restaurants set up shop, head out to the old town, north of the bustling Mahendra Pul. The best way to explore is on foot or by bike.

From the Nepal Telecoms building at Mahendra Pul, head north along Tersapati, passing a number of **religious shops** selling Hindu and Buddhist paraphernalia. At the intersection with Nala Mukh, check out the **Newari houses** with decorative brickwork and ornately carved wooden windows.

Continue north on Bhairab Tole to reach the small two-tiered **Bhimsen Temple**, a 200-year-old shrine to the Newari god of trade and commerce, decorated with erotic carvings. The surrounding square is full of shops selling baskets and ceramics.

About 200m further north is a small hill, topped by the ancient **Bindhya Basini**

POKHARA SIGHTS

WORTH A TRIP

PHEWA TAL CIRCUIT

If you get an early start, it's possible to walk right around the shore of Phewa Tal, beginning on the path to the World Peace Pagoda. Starting from the pagoda, continue along the ridge to the village of Lukunswara and take the right fork where the path divides. Once you reach Pumdi, ask around for the path down to Margi on the edge of the lake. From Margi, you can either cut across the marshes over a series of log bridges or continue around the edge of the valley to the suspension bridge at Pame Bazaar, where a dirt road continues along the northern shore to Pokhara. If you run out of energy, local buses pass by every hour or so. See Map p214.

Temple. Founded in the 17th century, the temple is sacred to Durga, the warlike incarnation of Parvati, worshipped here in the form of a saligram.

International Mountain Museum MUSEUM
(Map p196; ☑460742; www.mountainmuseum.org; foreigner/SAARC Rs 300/100; ☺9am-5pm) This immense barn of a museum is devoted to the mountains of Nepal and the mountaineers who climbed them. Inside, you can see original gear from many of the first Himalayan ascents, as well as displays on the history, culture, geology, and flora and fauna of the Himalaya.

Now that you've been inspired, outside there's a 21m climbing wall and a 9.5m-high climbable model of Mt Manaslu. A taxi here from Lakeside will cost you around Rs 500 return.

Gurkha Museum MUSEUM
(Map 196; ☑541966; foreigner/SAARC Rs 150/80, camera Rs 10; ☺8am-4.30pm) Located just north of Mahendra Pul, near the KI Singh Bridge, the Gurkha Museum celebrates the achievements of the renowned Gurkha regiment. Accompanied by sound effects of machine-gun fire, it covers Gurkha history from the 19th-century Indian Uprising, through two World Wars to current-day Afghanistan, with a fascinating display on Gurkhas who have been awarded the Victoria Cross medal.

Pokhara Regional Museum MUSEUM
(Map p196; ☑520413; foreigner/SAARC Rs 30/10; ☺10am-5pm, to 3pm Mon, to 4pm in winter, closed Tue) North of the bus station on the road to Mahendra Pul, this little museum is devoted to the history and culture of the Pokhara Valley, including the mystical shamanic beliefs followed by the original inhabitants of the valley.

Seti River Gorge PARK
The roaring Seti River passes right through Pokhara, but you won't see it unless you go looking. The river has carved a deep, narrow chasm through the middle of town, turning the water milky white in the process. The best place to catch a glimpse of the Seti River is the **park** (Map p196; adult Rs 25; ☺7am-6pm) just north of Old Pokhara near the Gurkha Museum.

Devi's Falls WATERFALL
(off Map p196; adult Rs 20; ☺6am-6pm) Also known as Patale Chhango, this waterfall marks the point where the Pardi Khola stream vanishes underground. When the stream is at full bore after monsoon rains, the sound of the water plunging over the falls is deafening.

According to locals, the name is a corruption of David's Falls, a reference to a Swiss visitor who tumbled into the sinkhole and drowned, taking his girlfriend with him. The falls are about 2km southwest of the airport on the road to Butwal, just before the Tashi Ling Tibetan camp.

Gupteshwor Mahadev Cave CAVE
(Map p196; first cave adult Rs 30, second cave Rs 100; ☺6am-6pm) Across the road from Devi's Falls, this venerated cave contains a huge

BRAVEST OF THE BRAVE

It might seem like an odd leftover from the days of empire, but the British army maintains a recruiting centre on the outskirts of Pokhara. Every year hundreds of young men from across Nepal come to Pokhara to put themselves through the rigorous selection process to become a Gurkha soldier.

Prospective recruits must perform a series of backbreaking physical tasks, including a 5km uphill run carrying 25kg of rocks in a traditional doko basket. Only the most physically fit and mentally dedicated individuals make it through – it is not unheard of for recruits to keep on running with broken bones in their determination to get selected.

Identified by their curved khukuri knives, Gurkhas are still considered one of the toughest fighting forces in the world. British Gurkhas have carried out peacekeeping missions in Afghanistan, Bosnia and Sierra Leone, and Gurkha soldiers also form elite units of the Indian Army, the Singapore Police Force and the personal bodyguard of the sultan of Brunei.

The primary motivation for most recruits is money. The average daily wage in Nepal is less than one British pound, but Gurkha soldiers earn upwards of UK£1000 per month, with a commission lasting up to 16 years and a British Army pension for life, plus the option of settling in Britain on retirement.

POKHARA IN...

Two Days

Start your day browsing through the **souvenir shops** and **cafes** of Lakeside before renting a colourful boat for a leisurely paddle on **Phewa Tal**. After lunch on the strip climb up to the sublime **World Peace Pagoda** for more incredible views. On day two get up early to watch the sunrise light up the Himalaya at **Sarangkot**. On the return to Lakeside stop off in **Old Pokhara** and visit the **Gurkha Museum**.

Four Days

Consider hiring a bike and riding north around the lake, before visiting one of the **Tibetan refugee settlements** around Pokhara. Drop in on **Devi's Falls**, and muster the courage to have a go at **tandem paragliding** with a Himalayan backdrop. Get some background research on your trek at the **International Mountain Museum** and vary it up by wriggling through the **Bat Cave**.

One Week

Consider the short trek to **Poon Hill** or the four-day **Annapurna Skyline Trek**. Head out to **Begnas Tal** to spend a peaceful night and explore the villages on the northern shore of **Phewa Tal**.

---

stalagmite worshiped as a Shiva lingam. The Rs 30 ticket only covers the temple cave, the Rs 100 ticket allows you to clamber through a tunnel behind the shrine, emerging in a damp cavern adjacent to the thundering waters of Devi's Falls.

Tibetan Settlements REFUGEE CAMP
Many of the Tibetan refugees who hawk souvenirs in Lakeside live in the Tibetan refugee settlements within and around Pokhara.

The largest settlement close to Pokhara is **Tashi Palkhel** (Map p214), about 5km northwest of Pokhara at Hyangia, on the road to Baglung. With prayer flags flapping in the breeze in the rocky valley, it genuinely feels like you're in Tibet. The colourful **Jangchub Choeling Gompa** in the middle of the village is home to around 200 monks. Try to time your visit in the afternoon to experience the rumbling of monks chanting and horns blowing during the prayer session (held 3.30pm to 5pm).

Masked dances are held here in January/February as part of the annual Losar (Tibetan New Year) celebrations.

To reach the gompa you have to run the gauntlet past an arcade of very persistent handicraft vendors. A '*tashi delek*' (a greeting in Tibetan) will win many smiles here. Nearby is a chörten piled with carved mani stones bearing Buddhist mantras and a carpet-weaving centre, where you can see all stages of the process and buy the finished article. If you'd like to spend the night, **Friend's Garden** ([icon]9806535582; r without bathroom Rs 250) has spartan rooms and a restaurant serving Tibetan food. A few other hole-in-the-wall restaurants, such as Rita's (no English sign), serve excellent *thukpa* (Tibetan noodle soup) and momos (dumplings). You can reach Tashi Palkhel by bike, bus, taxi or foot.

About 3km south of Lakeside, on the road to Butwal and near Devi's Falls, is the smaller settlement of **Tashi Ling** (Map p196). Near the entrance of the camp is a small open space where handicraft purveyors set up stalls and entice visitors to part with cash. There's also a small carpet factory and showroom (see Shopping p208). A smaller settlement, **Paljorling** (Map p196), resides in the city centre near Prithvi Chowk.

[icon] Activities

There are some fascinating short treks in the lower foothills around Pokhara with epic views of the Annapurna Himalaya, see p266 for details. See p364 for information on courses, and p352 for volunteering opportunities in Pokhara.

Avia Club Nepal SCENIC FLIGHTS
(Map p201; [icon]465944; www.aviaclubnepal.com) Avia offers exhilarating microlight flights around the Pokhara Valley. In 15 minutes (€65) you can buzz around the World Peace Pagoda and lakeshore, but you'll need 30 minutes (€110) or one hour (€185) to get up above Sarangkot for the full Himalayan panorama.

Ganden Yiga Chopen Meditation Centre
MEDITATION

(Pokhara Buddhist Meditation Centre; Map p201; www.pokharabuddhistcentre.com; 3-day course incl room & meals Rs 4000) This calm place holds three-day meditation and yoga courses that start every Friday at 2.45pm. There are also daily sessions – enquire at the centre.

Nepali Yoga Centre
YOGA

(Map p201; www.nepaliyoga.com; 1½hr Rs 400; 7.30-9.30am, 4.30-6pm) Program includes

Greater Pokhara

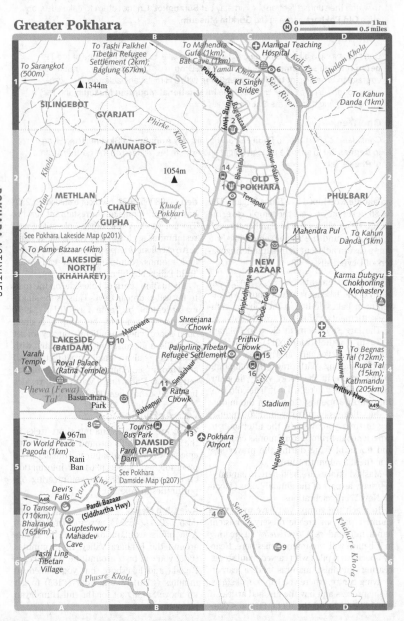

daily meditation and Hatha yoga classes. One-day to five-day courses also available.

Skyzip Highground Nepal   ADVENTURE SPORTS
(Map p214; ☑521882; www.highgroundnepal.com; admission US$100) Although still under construction when we visited, this awesome zipline starting at Sarangkot was boasting it would be the highest, longest and fastest zipline in the world.

Sadhana Yoga   YOGA
(Map p214; ☑464601, 9846078117; www.sadhana -asanga-yoga.com; 1 day from Rs 3000) This retreat is secluded in the village of Sedi Bagar, 2.5km northwest of Lakeside. One- to 21-day courses in Hatha yoga include tuition, steam and mud baths, accommodation and meals. Enquire about yoga treks.

Boating

Heading out onto the calm waters of Phewa Tal is the perfect way to unwind and gain a spectacular reflective mountain view. Colourful wooden *doongas* are available for rent at several boat stations, including near the city bus stand and next to the Fewa Hotel. Rates start at Rs 350 per hour with a boatman, or Rs 300/700 per hour/day if you paddle yourself. You can also rent aluminium pedalos (Rs 300 per hour) and sailboats (Rs 400 per hour, or Rs 450 per hour for lessons). Weak swimmers should rent a lifejacket at Rs 20. Another popular way to explore Phewa Tal is by kayak; see Ganesh Kayak Shop, p198.

Cycling & Mountain Biking

Cycling is a great way to get around Pokhara, whether you are visiting the mu-seums, braving the bazaar or just cruising Lakeside. Indian mountain bikes are available from dozens of places on the strip in Lakeside and cost around Rs 50/200 per hour/day.

For a description of the bike trip out to Sarangkot and Naudanda see p297. Contact any of the Lakeside travel agents for details of mountain-biking trips in the hills around Pokhara.

Horse Riding

Travel agents in Pokhara offer pony treks to various viewpoints around town, including Sarangkot, Kahun Danda and the World Peace Pagoda. Half-day trips (US$15) stick to the lakeshore; you'll need a full day (US$23) to reach the viewpoints.

Kayaking & Rafting

Pokhara is a good place to organise rafting trips, particularly trips down the Kali Gandaki and Seti Rivers. Half-day rafting/ kayak trips start at US$45/65 per person. All-inclusive overnight rafting trips start at US$80 per person and trips can be as long as 10 days.

Kayak clinics (US$55 per day) are held on the Seti River and scenic drifts down the Narayani River to Chitwan National Park can be arranged. See p292 for more information. Pokhara-based operators include the following:

Paddle Nepal   RAFTING
(Map p201; ☑207077; www.paddlenepal.com) As well as rafting, there are four-day beginner kayak clinics and canyoning expeditions.

POKHARA ACTIVITIES

Greater Pokhara

PARAHAWKING

Created by British falconer Scott Mason, **parahawking** (www.parahawking.com; tandem flights €130) is unique to Pokhara and is a must for thrill seekers and bird-of-prey lovers. Parahawking involves a combination of falconry and paragliding where raptors are trained to lead gliders to the best thermal currents. As a reward for their guidance, a whistle is blown to call in the bird to land on your outstretched gloved arm for you to feed it in mid air! All the parahawking birds (Egyptian vultures and black kites) are taken in as injured or orphaned birds unable to survive in the wild, and you can see them at their roost at the **Himalayan Raptor Centre** at Maya Devi Village (see p204) where falconry lessons are available. **Tandem parahawking** trips are organised through Blue Sky Paragliding (see p198) and a portion of the cost helps fund vulture conservation projects in Nepal.

Rapid Runner RAFTING
(Map p201; ☎462024; www.rapidrunnerexpeditions.com; 2-day family rafting from adult/child US$90/70) Offers kayak clinics and 'ducky trips' (which are gentle paddles in small rafts), in addition to serious white-water rafting trips.

Adrenaline Rush Nepal RAFTING
(Map p201; ☎229952; www.adrenalinenepal.com) Big white-water rafting trips are supplemented by river 'tubing' and canyoning; add-on treks can also be organised.

Ganesh Kayak Shop KAYAKING
(Map p201; ☎462657; www.ganeshkayak.com; 4-day kayaking & camping safaris US$225) Ganesh Kayak Shop, beside the Moondance Restaurant, also rents out kayaks for Rs 200/500/650 per hour/half-day/day for paddling in Phewa Tal.

Paragliding

Soaring through the air at nearly 800m among gliding Himalayan raptors against a backdrop of the snow-capped Annapurna is a once-in-a-lifetime experience. Operators usually offer both 20-minute (€80) and 45-minute (€120) flights.

Paragliding only operates during fine weather between October and April, as the season closes for the monsoon. Numerous operators have started up in recent years; listed below are experienced and recommended companies.

Blue Sky Paragliding ADVENTURE SPORTS
(Map p201; ☎464737; www.paragliding-nepal.com) With more than a decade of paragliding experience in Nepal, Blue Sky offers pilot courses and multiday paratrekking as well as parahawking.

Frontiers Paragliding ADVENTURE SPORTS
(Map p201; ☎466044; www.himalayan-paragliding.com) Another of the pioneering companies, Frontiers also offers pilot courses and multi-day tours in addition to the popular tandem flights.

Sunrise Paragliding ADVENTURE SPORTS
(Map p201; ☎463174; www.sunrise-paragliding.com) Sunrise similarly offers courses and tours, and as a paragliding company it has stood the test of time.

Swimming

The cool waters of Phewa Tal may beckon on a hot day, but there's a fair bit of pollution, so if you do swim it's advisable that you hire a boatman to take you out to the centre of the lake. Keep a watch for currents and don't get too close to the dam in Damside.

Several upmarket hotels let nonguests swim in their pool for a fee, including Hotel Barahi (Rs 340; see p200), Fish Tail Lodge (Rs 300; see p202) and Temple Tree Resort & Spa (Rs 600; see p200).

Walking

Even if you don't have the energy or perhaps the inclination to attempt the Annapurna Circuit, there are plenty of short treks in the hills around Pokhara. If you just want to stretch your legs and escape the crowds, stroll along the north shore of Phewa Tal. A paved walkway runs west along the shoreline to the village of Pame Bazaar, where you can pick up a bus back to Pokhara or continue on a circuit of Phewa Tal (see the boxed text on p193).

Another hike is the three-hour trip to the viewpoint at **Kahun Danda** (1560m) on the east side of the Seti River. There's a viewing tower on the crest of the hill, built over the ruins of an 18th-century fort. The easiest trail to follow begins near the Manipal Teaching Hospital in Phulbari – ask for directions at the base of the hill.

One of the most popular walks around Pokhara is the trip to the World Peace Pagoda (see the boxed text on p205). For longer walks in the Pokhara area, see p266.

☞ Tours

Travel agents in Pokhara can arrange local tours and activities, and it's easy to rent a bike and do things under your own steam.

Tibetan Encounter GUIDED TOUR
(Map p201; ☎464586; www.tibetan-encounter. com; half-/full-day tour US$45/60) This is a great way to experience Pokhara's refugee settlements and learn about Tibetan culture, traditional foods and medicine, and the contemporary life of Tibetan refugees in Nepal. Tibetan Encounter can also arrange long-term homestays and overnight tours to Jampaling Tibetan Settlement.

✵ Festivals & Events

Country-wide festivals are listed in the Month by Month feature (p19). The following festivals are specific or significant to Pokhara:

Pokhara Street Festival STREET FESTIVAL
Lakeside comes alive with a festive spirit during this annual festival (28 December to 1 January), when the main strip closes to traffic as restaurants set up tables on the road. Visitors cram the street to enjoy food, parades, performances and carnival rides.

Phewa Festival NEW YEAR
Celebrations for the Nepali New Year, in April, organised by the Pokhara hotel association to promote tourism.

Bagh Jatra NEWARI
Every August, Pokhara's Newari community celebrates this three-day festival that recalls the slaying of a deadly marauding tiger.

Losar BUDDHIST
(Tibetan New Year) Tibetan Buddhists hold celebrations and masked dances at gompas around Pokhara in January/February.

🛏 Sleeping

Most people stay in Lakeside, a strip of hotels, travel and trekking agents, restaurants

and souvenir shops. People looking for more peace and quiet tend to head to the north end of the strip or go south to Damside. All hotels will hold your luggage if you plan on trekking.

Most will add a 10% service charge, while midrange and top-end hotels load the bill with 13% VAT on top of the combined tariff and service charge. It's always worth asking for a discount, particularly during low season when most places offer discounts of between 20% and 30%.

LAKESIDE

As the main traveller centre in Pokhara, Lakeside is packed with hotels. You can set up your tent for free in the scrappy **camping ground** (Map p201), next to the lake at Camping (Hallan) Chowk. However, there are no facilities, and the nearest toilets are at neighbouring restaurants.

CENTRAL LAKESIDE

This is the heart of the action at Lakeside, where you are never more than 20m away from a budget hotel and traveller restaurant.

Butterfly Lodge HOTEL $
(Map p201; ☎461892; www.butterfly-lodge.org; s/d from Rs 750/1200, without bathroom Rs 450/600, r with aircon Rs 4000-5000; ❄) Spread over four villas, Butterfly Lodge has clean, big rooms (some are designated non-smoking), and there's a lovely lawn with banana lounges. Staff are very helpful and some of the money goes to the Butterfly Foundation supporting local children.

Hotel Travel Inn HOTEL $
(Map p201; ☎462631; www.hoteltravelin.com; s/d inc breakfast US$7/15, s/d with aircon from US$30/40; ❄🛜) Although catering for all budgets, even the cheapest rooms are spotless. It's worth the step up to deluxe for the comfy beds and bathtubs. The owner here claims tourists want three things: cleanliness, friendliness and quietness, and this modern hotel delivers on all fronts. It's the UN's choice of hotel when it's in town.

Lake City Hotel HOTEL $
(Map p201; ☎464240; www.lakecityhotel.com; dm Rs 220, s/d Rs 600/800, without bathroom Rs 330/440, ste Rs 2000; ❄🛜) Formerly Amrit Guesthouse, Lake City's motel-like facade – which is arranged around a courtyard – may lack character but its rooms are surprisingly comfortable. Newer rooms sport wonderful stone-lined bathrooms. There's also a

rooftop restaurant with a fireplace and lake views. Its recycling bins and refillable water supply (Rs 10 per bottle) set an excellent example.

Hotel Peace Plaza   HOTEL $

(Map p201; ✆461505; www.hotelpeaceplaza.com; r US$15-40; ❈❂) This centrally located, modern four-storey building comprises spotless rooms (many with lake views) with soft beds, a desk, a bar fridge and satellite TV. Some also have a bathtub. And there's a bright restaurant/cafe downstairs.

Tranquility Lodge   GUESTHOUSE $

(Map p201; ✆463030; www.baidam.com; s/d US$10/15; ❂) Set back from the road in a well-tended shady garden and a swath of lawn, Tranquility Lodge has an air of peace and privacy. There are just seven double rooms that are homely, tidy and clean.

Little Tibetan Guest House   GUESTHOUSE $

(Map p201; ✆531898; littletibgh@yahoo.com; s/d from Rs 700/1000) This Tibetan-run lodge east of Camping Chowk is rightly popular for its calm and relaxed atmosphere. Rooms are elegantly decorated with Tibetan wall hangings and bedspreads. Balconies overlook a serene garden and while there's no restaurant, bed and breakfast packages are available.

Hotel Fewa   HOTEL $$

(Map p201; ✆463151; www.hotelfewa.com; s/d US$20/25, s/d cottage US$40/45; ❂) In a town with little variation between lodgings, Hotel Fewa gets marks for its rustic stone cottages set right on the lake. A long-time favourite, the cottages with a loft make for a memorable stay, and include a fireplace and Buddhist motifs. The rooms in the back building are overpriced and lack the same charm.

Hotel Barahi   HOTEL $$$

(Map p201; ✆460617; www.barahi.com; s/d US$57/79, deluxe US$115/145; ❈❂❀) The stone-clad Hotel Barahi has a sparkling pool and very smart deluxe rooms with small balconies. Though these rates include all taxes, the standard rooms are still disappointing. It has 24-hour room service and a nightly cultural show. Many rooms boast incredible mountain vistas.

LAKESIDE EAST

Lakeside East is separated from Central Lakeside by the Royal Palace, but it doesn't take long to walk between the two.

Temple Tree Resort & Spa   LUXURY HOTEL $$$

(Map p201; ✆465819; www.templetreenepal.com; s/d from US$160/180; ❈❂❀) Tricked-out Temple Tree looks a little incongruous in Budgetsville Lakeside. Is this a sign of things to come? Plenty of timber and slate and straw-coloured render add delightful earthy tones. The standard rooms aren't huge but are exceptionally comfortable and most sport a bathtub and private balcony. There are two restaurants, a health spa, and a bar beside the pool.

Peace Eye Guest House   HOTEL $

(Map p201; ✆461699; www.peaceeye.co.uk; s/d Rs 500/700, without bathroom Rs 300/500; ❂) Established in 1977, the chilled-out Peace Eye retains all the qualities that attracted the original visitors to Pokhara 30 years ago. Cheap, laid-back and friendly, its brightly decorated rooms are smallish, but well-kept and clean. It also has a vegetarian restaurant and small German bakery.

Gauri Shankar Guest House   HOTEL $

(Map p201; ✆462422; www.gaurishankar.com; dm Rs 150, s Rs 450-1000, d Rs 500-1300; ❂) Calm, quiet and reasonably priced, Gauri Shankar has cosy, bright rooms set in a secluded garden of pebbles and bushes. The better and pricier rooms are upstairs. It has a garden cafe for breakfasts and a TV common room; its atmosphere is social and friendly.

Sacred Valley Inn   HOTEL $

(Map p201; ✆461792; www.sacredvalleyinn.com; r with/without bathroom US$12/10, upstairs US$18-25; ❂) Set in a shady garden across from the Royal Palace, Sacred Valley is a long-established traveller favourite. All the rooms are well maintained and those upstairs have gleaming marble floors and windows on two sides, allowing in plenty of light. Attached is the pleasant Monsoon Café.

Hotel Yeti   HOTEL $

(Map p201; ✆462768; www.hotelyeti.com.np; s/d from Rs 600/700) Draped in vines that flower bright red or yellow (depending on the time of year), Hotel Yeti's striking facade makes an excellent first impression. Rooms vary but all are good value and the manager here is very helpful. The neat garden is shared with neighbouring, and similar, Hotel Bedrock.

Blue Planet Lodge   HOTEL $$

(Map p201; ✆465706; www.blueplanetlodge.com; r inc breakfast €25-50) Having moved to new

Pokhara Lakeside

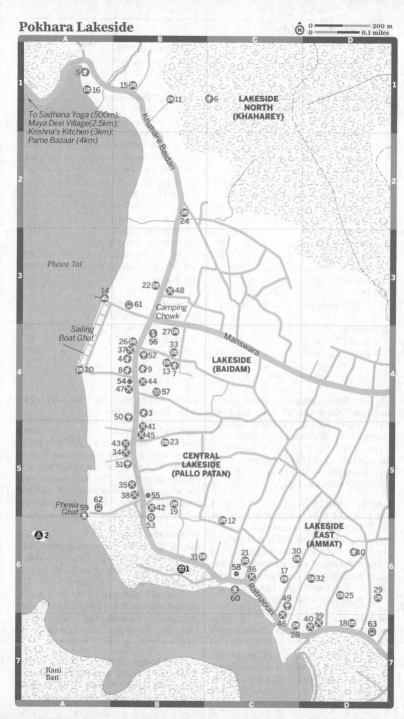

To Sadhana Yoga (500m);
Maya Devi Village(2.5km);
Krishna's Kitchen (3km);
Pame Bazaar (4km)

Phewa Tal

Camping Chowk

Sailing Boat Ghat

LAKESIDE NORTH (KHAHAREY)

LAKESIDE (BAIDAM)

Manswara

Khahare Baidan

CENTRAL LAKESIDE (PALLO PATAN)

Phewa Ghat

LAKESIDE EAST (AMMAT)

Ratnapuri

Rani Ban

Pokhara Lakeside

Sights

1	Ratna Mandir (Royal Palace)	B6
2	Varahi Mandir	A6

Activities, Courses & Tours

	3 Sisters Adventure Trekking	(see 15)
	Adrenaline Rush	(see 45)
3	Avia Club Nepal	B4
4	Blue Sky Paragliding	B4
5	Cosmic Brontosaurus Language School	A1
	Frontiers Paragliding	(see 3)
6	Ganden Yiga Chopen Meditation Centre	C1
	Ganesh Kayak Shop	(see 42)
	Heart & Tears	(see 50)
7	Nepali Yoga Centre	B4
8	Paddle Nepal	B4
	Rapid Runner	(see 37)
9	Sunrise Paragliding	B4
10	TAAN	D6
	Tibetan Encounter	(see 3)

Sleeping

11	Banana Garden Lodge	B1
12	Blue Planet Lodge	C6
13	Butterfly Lodge	B4
14	Camping Ground	A3
15	Chhetri Sisters Guest House	B1
16	Freedom Café & Bar	A1
17	Gauri Shankar Guest House	C6
18	Highland Rest House	D7
19	Hotel Barahi	B5
20	Hotel Fewa	A4
21	Hotel Nirvana	C6
22	Hotel Peace Plaza	B3
23	Hotel Travel Inn	B5
24	Hotel Tropicana	B2
25	Hotel Yeti	D6
26	Lake City Hotel	B4
27	Little Tibetan Guest House	B4
28	Mt Kailash Resort	C7
29	Nanohana Lodge	D6
30	Peace Eye Guest House	C6
31	Sacred Valley Inn	B6
32	Temple Tree Resort & Spa	D6
33	Tranquility Lodge	B4

Eating

34	Boomerang Restaurant & German Bakery	B5
35	Byanjan	B5
36	Caffe Concerto	C6
37	China Town	B4

digs, Blue Planet Lodge has become a midrange hotel with a range of rooms including seven 'chakra' rooms: energised with the colours of the rainbow, special stones and singing bowls. There is also a meditation and yoga hall with a Nepali yoga master. The rates shown here include all taxes and there is a 20% discount for singles.

Nanohana Lodge HOTEL $

(Map p201; ☎464478; www.nanohanalodge.com; r US$10-18;) This banana-yellow hotel is spotless and well managed and represents good value. Each level has a balcony with table and chairs and some rooms have cracking Annapurna views. It's close to the Lakeside restaurants and is associated with the nearby Fewa Lake Restaurant.

Hotel Nirvana HOTEL $

(Map p201; ☎463332; hotelnirvana@hotmail.com; r US$10-20, s/d without bathroom Rs 500/600;) Almost invisible behind a giant bougainvillea hedge, Hotel Nirvana is a much-loved, fastidiously clean place with a prim garden and spacious rooms with colourful bedspreads and curtains. The rooms get pricier as you climb the stairs.

Highland Rest House HOTEL $

(Map p201; ☎462173; r US$10-20) This bright yellow hotel, formerly the popular Pension Tushita, was still under renovation when we visited. Nevertheless, the airy rooms were spotlessly clean and represented excellent value. The attached open-sided, lake-view restaurant also makes a good impression.

Mt Kailash Resort HOTEL $$

(Map p201; ☎465703; www.mtkailashresort.com; s/d from US$55/65;) This is a comfortable and professionally managed choice with discounts available for longer stays. The modern well-appointed rooms have a double and a single bed with possibly the best mattresses in Lakeside. The bright and airy upper-floor rooms have mountain views, and there is a health spa and a restaurant.

Fish Tail Lodge LUXURY HOTEL $$$

(Map p196; ☎465201; www.fishtail-lodge.com.np; s/d from US$170/180, Heritage r US$200;) Reached by a rope-drawn pontoon from

Basundhara Park, Fish Tail is charmingly understated and Heritage rooms are housed in low slate-roofed bungalows in a lush tropical garden. Rooms 16, 17 and 18 have excellent lake and mountain views but you'll need to book well in advance. Profits here are donated to a trust that helps cardiac patients in Nepal.

LAKESIDE NORTH

Things become simpler, quieter, and cheaper as you head north from Camping Chowk towards Khaharey. It's a perfect location for anyone seeking an added calmness, while being close enough to walk to the action of Central Lakeside.

Chhetri Sisters Guest House　　HOTEL **$$**
(Map p201; ☎462066, 462912; www.3sisters adventure.com/Accomodation; s/d inc breakfast US$20/30, without bathroom US$15/25; ☎) Much smarter than the surrounding hotels, this tidy pink-brick lodge is owned by the same folk as 3 Sisters Adventure Trekking (see p30). Rooms are tastefully decorated and the location is peaceful, but the hotel is very popular so booking ahead is advised.

Banana Garden Lodge　　GUESTHOUSE **$**
(Map p201; ☎464901; s/d without bathroom Rs 200/300) The best and brightest of a cluster of budget guesthouses among the terraced fields, Banana Garden Lodge benefits from genial owners and a lovingly maintained garden. There are two shared solar-heated showers and the owners provide home-style Nepali meals.

Hotel Tropicana　　HOTEL **$**
(Map p201; ☎462118; www.hoteltropicana.com.np; r US$10-30; ☎) This time-honoured hotel of more than 20 years has large, spotless rooms with great lake and mountain views from the upper floors. Rooms on the 3rd floor (US$20) are the best value. The swing chair upstairs is a lovely spot to read a book, looking out to the lake.

Freedom Café & Bar　　HUT **$**
(Map p201; ☎9808686790; freedomcafe@hot mail.com; r without bathroom Rs 600; ☎) Will this picturesque pseudo village of bamboo huts right on the lakeshore stand the test of time? The huts are very basic – one bed, one window, one desk – with no attached bathrooms. Outside each hut is a cute dining

LOCAL KNOWLEDGE

PHUNTSOK YOUGYEL

Phuntsok Yougyel is a schoolteacher, musician and Tibetan refugee. His father and mother fled Tibet in 1961. Phuntsok grew up in Jampaling refugee camp east of Pokhara before moving with his family to Tashi Gang Settlement, a tiny settlement adjacent to the larger Tashi Palkhel, in Hyangia, about 5km northwest of Pokhara.

What can travellers see when visiting the Tibetan settlements around Pokhara?
They can spend time with the Tibetan community. Have their questions about Tibet and the refugee situation answered, learn a little about Tibetan Buddhism, and even visit a monastery.

And what can they take home? The handicraft stalls and carpet workshops are two of the few ways to make a living within the settlements. Apart from small business, there are not many opportunities for work for refugees.

Tell us about the Tibetan Brothers' Band. We are eight members, all Tibetan guys, all passionate about playing music, and we have been playing for about five years. Our aim is to play traditional Tibetan music as well as occasionally combining them in a folk-rock fusion. We play at three special concerts each year at Tashi Palkhel: The Dalai Lama's birthday (6 July), International Human Rights Day (10 Dec), and Losar (Tibetan New Year).

area on bamboo stilts that is shared with the attached chilled-out restaurant where occasional amplified music events occur.

DAMSIDE

The area around Phewa Dam is officially known as Pardi, but most people call it Damside. It was one of the first areas to be developed for tourists but it feels very quiet these days. The advantages here over Lakeside are its quietness, local flavour and incredible mountain views. It's worth investing in a rental bike to get between here and Lakeside.

Dragon Hotel   HOTEL **$$**
(Map p207; ☑460391; www.dragonhotelpokhara. com; s/d US$15/20; ☀) A huge building that is reached through a private courtyard, Dragon Hotel is a Pokhara survivor of almost 40 years. Although conferences are gradually overtaking tourism as the main business here, the rooms are spacious and charming with parquetry floors and Tibetan carpets. The foyer is full of Tibetan knick-knacks.

Hotel Mona Lisa   HOTEL **$$**
(Map p207; ☑463863; s/d US$20/30, with air-con US$40/50; ☀) The best and brightest of several similar places in this area, Hotel Mona Lisa tempts Japanese visitors with brightly coloured rooms and lounges with low *kotatsu* tables and cushions. Rooms are spotless and the best have balconies with mountain and lake views.

ELSEWHERE

You don't have to stay in Lakeside. There are budget hotels and luxury lodges outside the centre, across the lake, by the Seti River and high in the hills east of town.

Maya Devi Village   HUT **$$**
(Map p214; ☑463650; www.mayadevivillage.com; Khapaudi; r €36) Run by the friendly folks from Blue Sky and Frontiers Paragliding, this ultra-relaxed spot at the north end of the lake is on the road to Pame village. Accommodation is in tricked-out, thatched, round huts with a balcony, bathroom and second storey. Also here is a recommended restaurant-bar (p207) and several well-trained raptors (see p198).

Park Anadu Restaurant & Lodge   HOTEL **$**
(Map p214; ☑9846025557; r without bathroom from Rs 400) Perched high on Phewa Tal's western shore, the secluded Park Anadu has unbeatable views with rooms opening up to a perfect lake vista framed by a Himalayan backdrop. Situated a 20-minute boat trip from Lakeside (free transit back and forth), the simple rooms share a common bathroom with bucket hot water. There is an inexpensive restaurant here.

 Tiger Mountain Pokhara Lodge   HOTEL **$$$**
(Map p214; ☑691887, in Kathmandu 01-4361500; www.tigermountainpokhara.com; cottages per person US$250; ☀@☎☀) This lodge is set on a

lofty ridge about 10km east of Pokhara, and the owners have made a real effort to make it blend into the surroundings. Rooms are contained in stylish stone bungalows and there's an amazing mountain-view swimming pool. Rates include meals and transfers to/from Pokhara. Tiger Mountain prides itself on its sustainable tourism, such as growing its own produce and minimising imported goods.

Fulbari Resort LUXURY HOTEL **$$$**
(Map p214; ☏523451; www.fulbari.com; r from US$175, ste from US$400; ❄@☎☀) Dramatically sited on the bank of the Seti River Gorge south of Pokhara, the Fulbari is a vast, five-star resort hotel. It's far enough from town for uninterrupted mountain views, and beyond the stunning lobby you'll find every conceivable luxury, including a huge pool, health spa, tennis courts and golf club.

 Eating

Lakeside has numerous restaurants, bars and cafes serving up Western, Nepali, Indian and Chinese food to hungry travellers and trekkers. Restaurants are open from 6am to 10pm.

LAKESIDE

CENTRAL LAKESIDE

Moondance Restaurant INTERNATIONAL **$$**
(Map p201; mains Rs 150-590; ☎) The much-loved Moondance is a Lakeside institution and deservedly so. Quality food, good service and a roaring open fire all contribute to the popularity of this tastefully decorated restaurant. Its menu features salads, pizzas, imported steaks and excellent Indian and Thai curries. For dessert, the lemon meringue pie is legendary.

Punjabi Restaurant VEGETARIAN, INDIAN **$**
(Map p201; mains Rs 155-265) An authentic, Punjabi-run place churning out tasty vegetarian curries and tandoori breads. The front section has an inviting atmosphere with wicker lanterns and candles. The paneer curries are excellent and a *masala dosa* makes for a wonderful light lunch.

China Town CHINESE **$$**
(Map p201; mains Rs 110-350) With red-tassled lanterns and paintings of rotund children riding goldfish, this is a bona fide Chinatown experience. The Chinese chef creates

WALKING TO THE WORLD PEACE PAGODA

Balanced on a narrow ridge high above Phewa Tal, the brilliant-white World Peace Pagoda (Map p214) was constructed by Buddhist monks from the Japanese Nipponzan Myohoji organisation to promote world peace. In addition to the access road, there are three walking paths up to the pagoda and several small cafes for snacks and drinks once you arrive.

The Direct Route (One Hour)

The most obvious route up to the pagoda begins on the south bank of Phewa Tal, behind the Fewa Resort. Boatmen charge around Rs 350 to the trailhead from Lakeside and the path leads straight up the hillside on cut stone steps. Ignore the right-hand fork by the small temple and continue uphill through woodland to reach the ridge just west of the pagoda. You can either continue on to Pokhara via the scenic route (described below) or go back the way you came.

The Scenic Route (Two Hours)

A more interesting route to the pagoda begins near the footbridge over the Pardi Khola, just south of the Phewa dam. After crossing the bridge, the trail skirts the edge of paddy fields before turning uphill into the forest near a small brick temple. From here the trail climbs for about 2km through gorgeous open sal forest and follows the ridge west. When you reach a clearing with several ruined stone houses, turn left and climb straight uphill to reach the flat, open area in front of the pagoda. An alternative starting point for this route is Devi's Falls – a small but obvious trail crosses the paddy fields behind the falls and runs up to meet the main path at the bottom of the forest.

The Easy Route (20 Minutes)

For views without the fuss, take a local bus from the public bus stand to Kalimati on the road to Butwal for Rs 10. Several small trails lead up from the road to the school in Kalimati village and on to the entrance to the pagoda.

authentic Cantonese and Sichuan dishes with a delicious selection of duck and pork dishes. We recommend the spicy mapo dofu and gong bao chicken.

Olive Café
INTERNATIONAL $$$

(Map p201; mains Rs 320-500) At night this cosy cafe morphs into a romantic restaurant with a snug garden for private dining or street-side seating for people-watching. The exceptional menu includes a selection of excellent Indian curries, while well-executed dishes of Australian steak and Norwegian salmon top out the menu.

Once Upon a Time
INTERNATIONAL $$

(Map p201; mains Rs 130-595) Another laid-back tourist restaurant, this place has a good combo of suave European cafe vibe up front, and traditional Nepali out back. The multi-cuisine menu is much the same as others, though the Nepali and Indian dishes here are above average and they try to cater to special dietary requirements.

Mike's Restaurant
INTERNATIONAL $$

(Map p201; breakfast Rs 245, sandwiches from Rs 180; ☎) An enterprise from the late Mike, of Mike's Breakfast fame in Kathmandu, the Lakeside setting makes it a delightful spot for a hearty breakfast. Among the wide range of dishes are several Mexican options. The lakeside tables are a great place to camp with an evening drink.

New Everest Steak House
STEAKHOUSE $$$

(Map p201; mains Rs 650-2000) Carnivores flock to this old-fashioned steakhouse for 5cm-thick hunks of freshly grilled beef flown in from West Bengal. Take your pick from an impressive selection of 34 versions of steak sauces, including the 'Swiss style pizza' and the 'Really red wine sauce'.

Boomerang Restaurant & German Bakery
INTERNATIONAL $$

(Map p201; mains Rs 170-400; ☎) The best of the 'garden and dinner show' places, Boomerang has a large, shady garden with fresh flowers on each table. The food is very good, as is its Lakeside setting. There's a cultural show nightly from 7pm. The roadside German bakery is also recommended.

Maya Pub & Restaurant
INTERNATIONAL $$

(Map p201; mains Rs 175-375) Serving up travellers' fare since 1989, the atmospheric Maya is still going strong. The walls are decorated with colourful images of Hindu deities, and its comfortable wicker furniture makes a great spot to people-watch with a pizza, pasta, momos, or Nepali thali and a cold beer.

Byanjan
INTERNATIONAL $$

(Map p201; mains Rs 140-390) This eatery associated with Hotel Barahi (p200) uses chilled white-and-blue décor, raw rocks and subtle lighting to achieve a modern-global air of sophistication. The menu is wide-ranging with Chinese, Thai, Indian and Nepalese dishes. If the low tables look uncomfortable, head upstairs or out the back into the garden.

Koto
JAPANESE $$

(Map p201; set meals Rs 320-730; ☺11.30am-3pm & 6-9pm) Though it never seems busy, Koto is the real deal, and its authentic Japanese food is prepared and presented with great care. The set meals that include miso soup and rice are the way to go. The barbecued teriyaki beef is highly recommended.

Pokhara Thakali Kitchen
NEPALI $$

(Map p201; thali Rs 190-380; ☺11am-9pm) Attached to the Hotel Trek-o-Tel this small atmospheric restaurant specialises in regional Thakali cuisine presented as thalis, each with three curries – choose veg or non-veg, standard or special. There is an entrance off the side street to the north of the hotel.

LAKESIDE EAST

TOP CHOICE Caffe Concerto
ITALIAN $$$

(Map p201; mains Rs 350-700; ☎) Potted marigolds, an open fireplace and jazz on the stereo add to the bistro atmosphere at this cosy Italian place. The thin-crust pizzas come in two sizes and are the best in town. The pasta dishes are authentic, wine is available by the glass, and the espresso and gelato are superb. *Bellissimo*!

Lhasa Tibetan Restaurant
TIBETAN, INTERNATIONAL $$

(Map p201; meals Rs 175-360) Soothing temple music and Tibetan flags on the ceiling add a relaxed atmosphere to this big Tibetan eatery. Going strong since 1982, the menu has an excellent range of Tibetan dishes, including momos and *thukpa,* and you can warm up after dinner with a tankard of *tongba* (warm millet beer).

La Bella Napoli
ITALIAN, INTERNATIONAL $$

(Map p201; mains Rs 195-420; ☎) Another stalwart on the strip, this traveller restaurant specialises in tasty homemade pasta and decent pizzas, though it tries its hand at just about everything.

LAKESIDE NORTH

Things get decidedly quieter as you go north of Camping Chowk (aka Hallan Chowk), but there are plenty of rustic restaurants with a sleepy charm, and an unexpected gem of a Thai restaurant.

TOP CHOICE **Krishna's Kitchen**   THAI $$$

(off Map p214; ☑9846232501; www.krishnaskitchen. com; Khapaundi Cove; mains Rs 305-555; ☺10am-11pm; ☎) Krishna's is a superb Thai garden restaurant nestling at the north end of Phewa Tal. Homemade tofu, organic herbs and vegetables, and professional presentation mean this would be a great Thai restaurant anywhere. All your favourites plus many unexpected dishes grace the menu. And to match the excellence of the food there are gourmet teas and a quality wine list. Walk, cycle or taxi the 3km from Lakeside. The restaurant can organise a taxi back to your hotel.

Maya Devi Village   CAFE $$

(Map p214; ☑463650; ☺7am-6pm) Right beside the paragliding landing zone, this relaxed spot north of the lake is on the road to Pame Bazaar. It is best known for its BLT sandwiches (Rs 250) and social Sunday afternoon barbecues (Rs 750 for all you can eat). It's an excellent 3km bike ride or walk from central Lakeside.

Sweet Memories Restaurant INTERNATIONAL $$

(Map p201; mains Rs 145-360) This exceptionally friendly, laid-back, family-run restaurant serves all the usual traveller fare, with standouts including sizzlers and eggplant lasagne.

DAMSIDE

In Damside there are several *sekuwa* restaurants, where succulent morsels of spicy chicken are barbecued before your eyes. The dish goes down a treat with a cold beer on a warm afternoon. Look for the smoky barbecues and the throng of locals' motorbikes parked out front (afternoons only).

German Bakery   BAKERY $

(Map p207; cakes Rs 40-180) This is one of the original 'German bakeries' and supplies cafes from Pokhara to Jomsom. Come here for breakfasts, decent coffee plus sweet cheesecake (Rs 105), Danish pastries (Rs 40) and apple crumble (Rs 95).

Don't Pass Me By   INTERNATIONAL $$

(Map p207; mains Rs 100-280) The pick of the Damside eateries is this cosy restaurant that sits smack on the edge of the lake. It has

Pokhara Damside

Pokhara Damside

good travellers' fare, and the outdoor seating among colourful flowers is peaceful and delightful.

Drinking

TOP CHOICE **Olive Café**   CAFE

(Map p201; espresso from Rs 170, mains Rs 320-500) This sophisticated yet relaxing cafe is brought to you by the folks from Moondance Restaurant (see p205). With Italian espresso, Baskin Robbins ice cream and their very own mischievously sweet Machhapuchhare cake, it makes a great place to break a shopping spree. At night it becomes a romantic restaurant (see p206).

Busy Bee Café BAR

(Map p201) The Busy Bee has live bands rocking to headbanging locals every night and there's a courtyard with a fire pit, which is a great spot to meet other travellers. There's also a smoky pool room down in the den. Look out for Busy Bee's furry resident mascot on the bar.

Club Amsterdam BAR

(Map p201) The boisterous and loud Club Amsterdam is an old favourite on the Lakeside strip. With live music, pool tables, cocktails and mocktails, and football on the TV, it's got it all covered. Head for the fire pit out back if you want a conversation.

All That Jazz BAR

(Map p201; live music 7-10.30pm) Dark, smoky and intimate, it's everything a jazz bar should be. Live jazz musicians swing to an appreciative audience who sit at small tables below the stage. It's located above Punjabi Restaurant.

Bullet Basecamp BAR

(Map p196; Jarebar; ☉4-11.30pm; ☎) Away from the Lakeside glitz and adjacent to a motorcycle repair workshop, Bullet Basecamp has an unmistakable storyline. Sprockets, driveshafts and Tata truck grills have been turned into light fittings and bar furniture. Each night has a different theme and different drink specials. If you are travelling on an Enfield, this place is a must-do pitstop. It's located about a kilometre east of Camping Chowk on Phewa Marg.

Am/Pm Organic Café CAFE

(Map p201; espresso from Rs 90) This shack run by a Nepali trained as a barista in London has organic Himalayan coffee from Palpa and tasty pastries from its German Bakery.

Old Blues Bar BAR

(Map p201; ☉4-11.30pm) A super-relaxed option, the Blues Bar is popular with stoners, and large banners of Jimi Hendrix and John Lennon add to its appeal.

Club Paradiso BAR

(Map p201; ☉noon-11.30pm, shows from 7.30pm) If you are after noise, momos, alcohol and alcoves, try Paradiso. After weeks in the hills this loud and brash teenager hangout may be just what you need.

☆ Entertainment

Several restaurants located along the strip have nightly Nepali cultural song-and-dance shows that are enthusiastic, if not entirely authentic, and there is no additional charge.

Pokhara nightlife generally winds down around 11pm, but a handful of bars flaunt the rules and rock till around midnight. Local bands move from bar to bar (see Drinking, p207) on a nightly rotation, playing covers of Western rock hits.

Every month full-moon raves are held at Pame Bazaar, which – while far from the scale of the raves at Goa or Ko Pha Ngan – are worth checking out if trance music is your thing.

Hotel Barahi TRADITIONAL DANCE

(Map p201; ☉6.30pm) Bookings are required for the buffet dinner and cultural show from 6.30pm (Rs 1150). If you reserve a table early, you can use the pool for free during the day.

Boomerang Restaurant & German Bakery TRADITIONAL DANCE

(Map p201; ☉7pm) A long-standing popular restaurant (see p206) with an evening cultural show.

Fewa Paradise Restaurant TRADITIONAL DANCE

(Map p201; ☉6.30pm) An all-day restaurant with a traveller menu and an evening song-and-dance show.

Hungry Eye Restaurant TRADITIONAL DANCE

(Map p201; ☉6.30pm) Another long-standing dinner and show venue. This one is indoors.

🔒 Shopping

If you've been to Thamel in Kathmandu, you know what to expect. Dozens of traveller boutiques in Lakeside sell pirate CDs, Buddhist masks, prayer flags, counterfeit trekking gear, wall hangings, khukuri knives and antiques of dubious antiquity. Pokhara is also a good place to pick up saligram fossils.

As well as the shops in Lakeside, legions of Tibetan refugee women wander from restaurant to restaurant offering Tibetan knick-knacks for sale. For an even greater selection of Tibetan arts and crafts, including handmade carpets, head to the Tashi Palkhel and Tashi Ling Tibetan communities, respectively north and south of Pokhara – see p195.

JOMSOM

With the upgrading of the path to Jomsom (Dzongsam) into a road, growing numbers of travellers are heading north to this mountain village and making short treks from there. Taking the bus or flying here brings you closer to the peaks. With a few days to spare, you could walk south to Marpha or go east to Kagbeni and Muktinath (see p274). Hotels can arrange porters for around Rs 800 per day.

To visit, you must pay the Rs 2000 fee for the Annapurna Conservation Area Project (ACAP) and present your receipt and Trekking Information Management System (TIMS) permit (see p210) at the police checkpoint by the ACAP visitor centre. The nearby **Machhapuchhare Bank** (9am-2.30pm Sun-Thu, 9am-12.30pm Fri) changes cash and travellers cheques and has an ATM. Internet access is available at the **Rural Information Center** (Rs 5-8 per min; 8am-6.30pm) and Alka Marco Polo hotel.

At the west end of town a concrete stairway leads to the **Mustang Eco Museum** (admission Rs 50; 10am-5pm Tue-Sun, to 3pm Fri, to 4pm in winter), which is worth a visit for its displays on herbal medicine and its recreated Buddhist chapel. Just north of here is the airport, where you'll find the main hotels, restaurants, shops and airline offices.

Xanadu Guesthouse (069-440060; chandramohangauchan@yahoo.com; r from Rs 500, r without bathroom Rs 150) is popular for its clean rooms, excellent restaurant and laundry service. Other good places on the main drag include Snowland, Trekkers Inn, Majesty, Moonlight and Tilicho hotels, all with rooms between Rs 350 and 800, as well as Rs 150 to 250 for boxy rooms without a bathroom.

More upmarket options include rambling **Om's Home** (069-440042; omshome@wlink.com.np; s/d Rs 400/500, deluxe Rs 700/800), with private, tiled hot-water bathrooms, a sunny courtyard and a table-tennis table, and the **Alka Marco Polo Hotel** (069-440007; r Rs 800-1000; @), which accepts credit cards and boasts a sauna (Rs 500) and internet access.

Tara Air (www.taraair.com), **Sita Air** (www.sitaair.com.np), **Agni Air** (www.agniair.com) and **Nepal Airlines** (www.nepalairlines.com.np) operate flights between Pokhara and Jomsom (US$76 to US$82, 20 minutes) and have offices where you can book and reconfirm tickets. All flights depart between 7am and 9am. Buses and share-4WDs operate on the road to/from Beni (Rs 900, seven to nine hours), which is 45km west of Pokhara, and where you can board a bus to Pokhara (Rs 220, four hours). Road blockages (where you may need to carry your gear over a landslide to find waiting vehicles) are fairly common, especially after heavy rain. Ask your hotel about 4WDs east to Muktinath (Rs 800, three hours).

There are numerous supermarkets in Lakeside where you can stock up on chocolate, biscuits, toiletries and other goods before heading out on your trek.

Nepal Mandala Bookshop   BOOKS
(Map p201) There is no dearth of bookshops in Lakeside but Nepal Mandala probably has the best selection of books and maps in town.

Sherpa Adventure   OUTDOOR EQUIPMENT
(Map p201) Upstairs and above Ganesh Kayak Shop, Sherpa Adventure is the place to find outdoor gear that is of a better quality than most of the counterfeit stuff that dominates the bazaar.

❶ Information

Emergency

The direct phone number for the police is 100. For medical emergencies, see Medical Services, p210. The **tourist police** (Map p207; 462761) are located in Damside at the same site as the tourist office and they operate a small booth opposite Moondance Restaurant.

Immigration Office

The **immigration office** (Map p196; 465167; Ratna Chowk; visa extensions 10.30am-1pm Sun-Thu, 10am-noon Fri, office hours 10am-5pm Sun-Thu, to 3pm Fri) is 1km northeast of Damside. Visa extensions cost US$30 for 15 days, and US$2 per extra day (up to 15 extra days), while a 60-day extension is US$120 – bring your passport and a passport photo, plus the visa

TREKKING PERMITS

If you plan to trek anywhere inside the Annapurna Conservation Area, you'll need a permit from the **Annapurna Conservation Area Project** (ACAP; Map p207; ☏061-463376; ☺10am-5pm Sun-Fri, to 4pm Sat, to 4pm winter) in Damside.

The admission fee to the conservation area is Rs 2000/200 (foreigner/SAARC) and permits are issued on the spot (bring two passport-sized photos). There are ACAP checkpoints throughout the reserve and if you get caught without a permit, the fee rises to Rs 4000/400 (foreigner/SAARC). Independent trekkers without a guide will need to register with the **Trekkers Information Management System** (TIMS; www.timsnepal.com), which can be purchased from the **Nepal Tourism Board** (☺10am-5pm Sun-Fri) or the office of the **Trekking Agencies Association of Nepal** (TAAN; Map p201; ☺10am-5pm). Another two passport-sized photos are necessary for TIMS, which costs the equivalent of US$10 in Nepali currency if booking through a local registered travel agent or US$20 for totally independent trekkers.

fee in Nepali rupees. There are photo booths outside the office. For more on visa extensions see p371.

Internet Access

Internet cafes charge Rs 50 to 80 per hour, usually with a minimum 15-minute charge. Those in the centre of Lakeside, such as **MS Communications** (Map p201; per hour Rs 80, min Rs 25 for 15 min), charge the most. However, free wi-fi is available at most Lakeside hotels and many restaurants.

Laundry

Hotels can arrange same-day laundry services if you drop your clothes off first thing in the morning, or there are plenty of small laundry shops along the strip in Lakeside. They charge Rs 50 to 100 per kilogram.

Medical Services

There are several pharmacies in Lakeside selling everyday medicines, antibiotics and first-aid supplies.

For anything serious, head to **Western Regional Hospital** (Map p196; ☏520066), also known as the Gandaki Hospital, on the east bank of the Seti River.

Money

There are plenty of foreign-exchange offices in Lakeside that change cash and travellers cheques in major currencies. All are open daily but rates are better at the **Standard Chartered Bank** (Map p201; ☏462102; ☺9.45am-4.15pm Sun-Thu, to 1.15pm Fri), near Camping (Hallan) Chowk. There are several ATMs along the main strip in Lakeside, including Standard Chartered Bank, that accept foreign cards.

Post

The main **post office** (Map p196; ☺10am-5pm Sun-Thu, to 3pm Fri) is a hike from Lakeside at Mahendra Pul. There's a much smaller branch in Lakeside East (Map 201), though alternatively most bookstores in Lakeside sell stamps and have a post box for letters and postcards.

If you want to send anything valuable, **UPS** (Map p201; ☏463209) in Lakeside is reliable.

Telephone

Mobile phone reception is good and there are numerous outlets selling recharge vouchers for the major companies. Internet cafes in Lakeside offer phone calls to Europe and most other places for around Rs 50 per minute.

Tourist Information

Nepal Tourism runs a helpful **tourist office** (Map p207; ☏465292; ☺10am-1pm & 2-5pm Sun-Fri) in Damside, sharing a building with the Annapurna Conservation Area Project.

Travel Agencies

Most of the travel agents in Lakeside can book tours, flights and bus tickets. The following travel agents are reputable.

Adam Tours & Travels (Map p201; ☏461806; www.adamnepal.com) IATA-accredited agency for international flights.

Blue Sky Travel & Tours (Map p201; www.blue-sky-tours.com)

Wayfarers (Map p201; ☏463774; www.wayfarers.com.np) See p104 for details.

Getting There & Away

Air

There are numerous flights to Kathmandu (US$86 to US$98, 25 minutes) all day, weather permitting, with **Buddha Air** (Map p207; ☏465998; www.buddhaair.com), **Yeti Airlines** (Map p207; ☏464888, airport 465888; www.yetiairlines.com), **Guna Air** (Map p207; ☏465887; www.gunaairlines.com), **Nepal Airlines** (Map p207; ☏465021, airport 465040;

www.nepalairlines.com.np), **Sita Air** (Map p207; ☑465364; www.sitaair.com.np) and **Agni Air** (Map p196; ☑462968; www.agniair.com) sharing the load. There are great Himalayan views if you sit on the right-hand side of the plane heading into Pokhara (or the left on the way to Kathmandu).

Nepal Airlines, Sita Air, Agni Air and a division of Yeti Airlines called **Tara Air** (Map p207; ☑464888, airport 465888; www.taraair. com) have daily flights to Jomsom (US$80, 20 minutes). Nepal Airlines also flies to Manang (US$95, 25 minutes) on Monday, Wednesday and Friday.

All the airlines have offices opposite the airport near Mustang Chowk but it's often easier to use the services of one of the travel agents in Lakeside.

Don't forget the domestic departure tax from Pokhara Airport (and all other domestic airports) is Rs 200.

Bus

There are three bus stations in Pokhara. Tourist buses that go to Kathmandu and Royal Chitwan National Park leave from the **tourist bus park** (Map p207) at Mustang Chowk. The dusty and chaotic **Main Pokhara bus park** (Map p196) at the northeast end of the Pokhara airstrip has buses to Kathmandu and towns in the Terai. You will find the main ticket office at the back and the night buses office at the top of the steps near the main highway. Buses going to the trailheads for the Annapurna Conservation Area leave from the **Baglung bus park** (Map p196), about 2km north of the centre on the main highway.

TO/FROM KATHMANDU

The bus trip between Kathmandu and Pokhara takes six to eight hours, depending on the condition of the road. Tourist buses (Rs 450 to 500) are the most hassle-free option and leave from the tourist bus park at 7.30am. Taxis meet the

tourist buses on arrival but brace yourself for Pokhara's notorious hotel touts.

Greenline (Map p201; ☑464472; www.green line.com.np) has a daily air-con bus to Thamel (US$18 with lunch, six to seven hours) at 8am from its Lakeside East office. **Golden Travels** (Map p201; ☑460120) has a similar service to Durbar Marg (US$15 with lunch) in central Kathmandu, leaving from the tourist bus park.

Public buses to Kathmandu (day/night Rs 390/450) leave from the main public bus station. Faster microbuses run to Kathmandu (Kalanki) for Rs 400, leaving from the highway in front of the public bus stand.

Stops along the road to Kathmandu include Dumre (Rs 90, two hours), Abu Khaireni (Rs 120, three hours) and Mugling/Manakamana (Rs 130, four hours).

There are also four daily direct buses going to Gorkha (Rs 280, five hours). See the Kathmandu to Pokhara chapter, p182, for more information on sights and stopovers along the way.

TO/FROM CHITWAN NATIONAL PARK

The best way to get to Chitwan is by tourist bus. Buses leave the tourist bus park daily at 7.30am for Sauraha (Rs 400 to 450, seven hours), arriving at Bachhauli, a 15-minute walk from town, or there are jeeps waiting to transfer travellers to their hotel – see p221 for details.

Greenline has a daily air-con bus to Sauraha (US$15 including lunch, 5½ hours) at 8am from its Lakeside East office (the return journey drops off at the tourist bus park).

TO/FROM THE INDIAN BORDER

The closest border crossing to Pokhara is Sunauli, which is just south of the town of Bhairawa. See the individual towns in the Terai & Mahabharat Range chapter for more details on transport to India.

Travel agents might try to tempt you with the offer of tourist buses to the border and direct

POKHARA TO BENI BUS STOPS

STOP	FARE (RS)	DURATION (HR)	TREK
Hyangja	30	1	Ghachok trek
Phedi	45	1½	Annapurna Sanctuary Trek
Naya Pul	90	2	Ghorepani (Poon Hill) to Ghandruk trek, Annapurna Sanctuary Trek, Annapurna Circuit Trek
Baglung	140	3	Annapurna Circuit Trek
Beni	220	4	Annapurna Circuit Trek

buses to towns in India. Don't be fooled – there are no tourist buses to Sunauli and no through-buses to India; without exception, you must change at the border.

There are two (sometimes three) buses to Bhaiwara (Rs 500, seven to nine hours), via Narayangarh (departing 7.15am) or the Siddhartha Hwy (the speedier option, departing at 6.30am), from the tourist bus park. From the main Pokhara bus park there are nearly 20 day and night buses daily for Bhairawa (Rs 380/450 day/night, eight hours), where you can pick up a local bus to the border post at Sunauli.

There are day/night buses heading to Birganj (Rs 380/450, nine hours), Nepalganj (Rs 740/850, 12 hours), Mahendranagar (Rs 1050, 16 hours) and Kakarbhitta (Rs 1500, 17 hours).

TO/FROM THE TERAI

As well as the buses to the Indian border, there are regular day/night services to Narayangarh (Rs 250, five hours), where you can change to buses heading east and west along the Mahendra Hwy. A few buses go to Janakpur (Rs 550, 10 hours). All buses leave from the main Pokhara bus park.

Most buses go via Mugling, but there are also buses along the dramatic Siddhartha Hwy to Butwal (Rs 360, six hours) via Tansen (Rs 300, five hours).

TO/FROM TREKKING ROUTES

Buses to the trailheads for most treks in the Annapurna Conservation Area leave from the Baglung bus park. One important exception is the Annapurna Circuit Trek, which normally starts at Besi Sahar. See p274.

Buses leave about every half-hour from 5.30am to 3.30pm. Cranky old Toyota taxis leave from the same bus stand – the fare is Rs 900 to Phedi and Rs 1500 to Naya Pul, Rs 2000 to Baglung and Rs 4000 to Beni (from where you can now get a jeep to Jomsom for Rs 500).

For Besi Sahar (Rs 250, five hours), there are two early morning and two lunchtime buses from the main Pokhara bus park and tourist bus park, or you can take any bus bound for Kathmandu and change at Dumre.

ⓘ Getting Around

Bicycle

There are lots of bicycle rental places at Lakeside charging Rs 50/200 per hour/day.

Bus

Small local buses shuttle between Lakeside, the airport, the public bus stand and Mahendra Pul but routes are erratic and there isn't much space for baggage. Fares start at Rs 20.

Local buses to Pame Bazaar (Rs 20) and other places on the north shore of Phewa Tal leave

Camping (Hallan) Chowk every hour or so until mid-afternoon. Buses to Begnas Tal (Rs 50) leave from the main bus stand.

Motorcycle

Several places in Lakeside rent out motorcycles and scooters for around Rs 300 per day not including fuel. A helmet will be provided, and if you don't wear it the police are likely to fine you and impound the bike. Check the bikes out first to make sure they start easily, brake smoothly and the lights work.

Hearts & Tears (Map p201; ☑9846020293; www.heartsandtears.com) is tucked away in the entrance to Busy Bee Café. It's a great place to learn to ride (it rents bikes from €45 per day) or join a motorcycle tour around Nepal. **Raju Bullet Surgery** (Map p196; ☑9806511845; Jarebar) is, as the name implies, a motorcycle workshop specialising in Royal Enfield Bullets. It's adjacent to the Bullet Basecamp bar (see p208).

Taxi

Taxis meet tourist buses at the tourist bus park (Mustang Chowk), but you can expect a hotel tout to come along for the ride. The fare to Lakeside is Rs 150 whether you take the tout's advice or not, so insist on being taken where you want to go. Heading out from Lakeside, you'll pay Rs 150 to the main Pokhara bus park and the airport, and Rs 200 to the Baglung bus park. Taxis from the airport charge at least Rs 200 to Lakeside.

AROUND POKHARA

Trekking in the Annapurna Conservation Area Project is easily the biggest attraction around Pokhara (see p274 for details) but you don't have to be a seasoned trekker to appreciate the glory of the peaks. There are several dramatic viewpoints on the rim of the Pokhara Valley that can be reached by foot, taxi, mountain bike or rented motorcycle from Pokhara. For short treks around Pokhara see p266.

Sarangkot

The view of the Annapurna Himalaya from Sarangkot (adult Rs 25) is almost a religious experience. From here, you can see a panoramic sweep of Himalayan peaks, from Dhaulagiri (8167m) in the west to the perfect pyramid that is Machhapuchhare (6997m) and the rounded peak of Annapurna II (7937m) in the east. Most people come here at dawn or dusk, when the sun picks out the peaks, transforming them from a purple-pink to a celestial gold. If you feel noisy teenagers are ruining the peace at the viewing tower, try walking further along to the secluded grassy helicopter pad (though there are no seats here).

The main village is just below the ridge, but a set of steps leads uphill to a dramatic viewpoint in the ruins of an ancient kot (fort). The army currently occupies it, but photography is fine, as long as you don't take pictures of the soldiers.

There's a ruined fort at **Kaskikot** (1788m), a one-hour walk west of Sarangkot along the ridge road, with similarly jaw-dropping views.

Sleeping & Eating

There are several places to stay and eat in Sarangkot. The cheapest options are along the concrete steps to the fort.

Mountain View Lodge LODGE $
(☎9804180714; s/d Rs 450/550, without bathroom Rs 300/400) The Mountain View doesn't actually have mountain views, but rather it looks out to the soaring Pokhara Valley. Most importantly, it's comfortable, quiet and welcoming.

Sherpa Resort RESORT $
(☎9841456639, in Kathmandu 01-4820201; www.sherparesort.com; r with/without bathroom Rs 700/600) If you've come to Nepal for views of the Himalaya, this is your place. Basic rooms and hard beds are a small sacrifice to wake up with the Himalaya spread out right outside your window. Rooms 201 and 202 are the best picks.

Getting There & Away

Taxi drivers in Lakeside offer dawn rides up to the ridge to catch the sunrise for around Rs 1200. The taxi fare is the same whether the driver waits to drive you back or you walk down. Be prepared for a guide to jump in your taxi who'll do his best to convince of his services, though a guide is unnecessary as it is easy to get to the top via the path.

By motorcycle or mountain bike, follow the road that branches off the Baglung Hwy near the Bindhya Basini Temple. When the road levels out below the ridge, look for the Sarangkot turn-off on the right, opposite a large group of tin-roofed school buildings. For details of the ride out to Sarangkot and on to Naudanda see p297.

A more challenging option is the three- to four-hour walk from Pokhara. The most popular path begins on the highway opposite the Baglung bus park.

The obvious trail runs west across the fields and up the side of Gyarjati Hill, meeting the dirt road at Silangabot, about 1km east of the Sarangkot turn-off.

There's also a scenic route from Phewa Tal but the trail is hard to follow and there have been muggings along this path. The trail begins near the village of Khapeudi on the road to Pame Bazaar (look for the signpost about 50m after the Green Peace Lodge), meeting the road just west of the turn-off to Sarangkot. It's easier to follow this trail on the way down.

Bat Cave & Mahendra Gufa

You won't find Adam West or Christian Bale lurking in the dark and spooky **Bat Cave** (Map p214; Chameri Gufa; adult Rs 20; ⊙7am-5.30pm), but rather thousands of horseshoe bats clinging to the ceiling of a damp and slippery chamber and occasionally chirruping into the darkness – claustrophobics beware. Daredevils can continue to the back of the vault and wriggle out through a tiny chute to the surface.

Torches can be hired for Rs 20, and guides (no fixed rate) can show you the narrow exit tunnel. Ask about tours to other caves in the vicinity. It's easily visited from Pokhara on foot, by bike or by taxi (Rs 600).

Nearby is the underwhelming **Mahendra Gufa** (Map p214; Chameri Gufa; adult Rs 20; ⊙7am-5.30pm), the first large cave to be discovered in Pokhara. The first 125m of the cave is lit only to reveal dusty vandalised limestone formations, some revered as Shiva lingams. Beyond the electric lights there are bats (bring a torch).

Begnas Tal & Rupa Tal

About 10km southeast of Pokhara, a road leaves the Prithvi Hwy for Begnas Tal and Rupa Tal, two gloriously serene lakes that receive few foreign visitors, despite their proximity to Pokhara.

It's a peaceful spot and the mountains of the Annapurna Range are brilliantly reflected in the still waters. Boats can be rented for a leisurely paddle on the lake for Rs 200 per hour.

Rupa Tal is reached via a 3km hike along a trail that winds uphill from the bus stand in Begnas Bazaar. It's much more isolated than Begnas Tal but the surrounding countryside

Around Pokhara

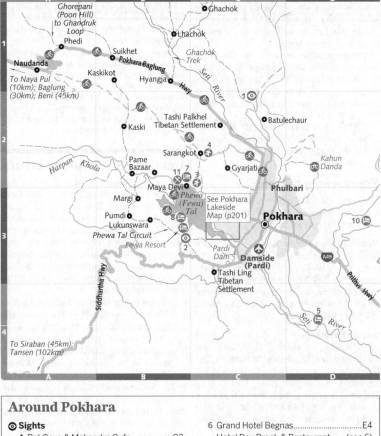

Around Pokhara

is delightful and you can stay at several laid-back teahouses on the ridge overlooking the lake.

🛏 Sleeping & Eating

Grand Hotel Begnas   HOTEL **$**
(Map p214; ☏561129; r Rs 800-1000) Located at the start of the walking trail in Begnas Bazaar, overlooking the dam wall and fish farms, is this edifice of echoing corridors and spacious rooms. It's all pretty soulless but probably the most comfortable option; each room has a double and single bed and a tiled bathroom. There is rooftop dining and a brother of the owner runs the garden restaurant next door.

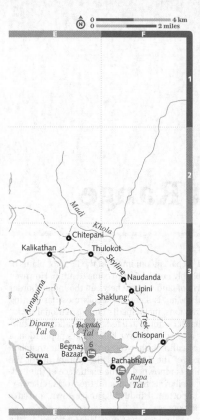

Hotel Day Break & Restaurant   HOTEL **$**
(Map p214; ☏560011; r Rs 500-700) This friendly place has three simple rooms that could do with a clean, but will suffice at a pinch. Access is by a steep ladder of stairs located near the Begnas Bazaar and the reward for the climb is mountain views from the garden and roof.

Rupa View Point   GUESTHOUSE **$**
(Map p214; ☏622098; d old/new bldg Rs 300/750) This family-run place situated above the village of Pachabhaiya, overlooking Rupa Tal, has two basic rooms, plus a building with better rooms and solar hot water. In the evening home-cooked meals are prepared using vegetables from the garden. To get here, follow the signposted path off the main trail, then take the steps on the left, then the path on the right.

❶ Getting There & Away

Buses to Begnas Tal (Rs 50, one hour) stop on the highway opposite the main public bus stand in Pokhara.

By bike or motorcycle, take the Prithvi Hwy towards Mugling and turn left at the obvious junction in Tal Chowk. A taxi will cost Rs 1000 one way.

The Terai & Mahabharat Range

Includes »

Why Go?

Hear the word 'Nepal' and an image of the flat, hot plains of the Terai is probably not the first to come to mind. However, this narrow strip of land wedged between the Indian border and the Himalaya holds some of Nepal's most fascinating and varied attractions, including its famous national parks, Chitwan and Bardia – home to tigers, rhinos and elephants.

The Terai is also home to over half Nepal's population, a colourful mix of cultures showcased through the thatched mud-hut villages of the Tharu and the vibrant art of the Mithila. Lumbini is renowned as the birthplace of the Buddha and attracts pilgrims from around the world. Likewise, Janakpur, an important Hindu pilgrimage town, pulsates with religious fervour.

Rising from the Terai are the Chure Hills, followed by the Mahabharat Range, a region of dramatic gorges, awe-inspiring terracing and enduring mountain towns.

Best Places to Eat

» KC's Restaurant (p232)
» Nanglo West (p244)
» Candy's Place (p248)
» River Sunset Restaurant (p232)

Best Places to Stay

» Travellers Jungle Camp (p230)
» Forest Hideaway (p250)
» Island Jungle Resort (p230)
» Lumbini Village Lodge (p240)

When to Go

Bhairawa

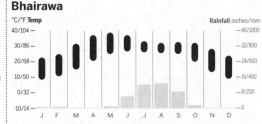

Oct–March	Nov–Dec	Late Dec
Ideal climate to visit the Terai; best wildlife viewing from January.	See Sita Bibaha Panchami, celebrating Sita's marriage to Rama.	Chitwan Festival is known for its elephant race; it also has food stalls.

History

In 563 BC, the queen of the tiny kingdom of Kapilavastu gave birth to a son named Siddhartha Gautama. Thirty-five years later, under a Bodhi (pipal) tree at Bodhgaya in India, Buddhism was born. The Indian Buddhist emperor Ashoka made a famous pilgrimage here in 249 BC, leaving a commemorative pillar at the site of the Buddha's birth in Lumbini.

Nepal also played a pivotal role in the development of Hinduism. Sita, the wife of Rama and heroine of the Ramayana, was the daughter of the historical king Janak, who ruled large parts of the plains from his capital at Janakpur. Janak founded the Mithila kingdom, which flourished until the 3rd century AD when the Guptas from Patna seized its lands.

The depopulation of the Terai began in earnest in the 14th century, when the Mughals swept across the plains of northern India. Hundreds of thousands of Hindu and Buddhist refugees fled into the hills, many settling in the Kathmandu Valley, which later rose to prominence as the capital of the Shah dynasty. Aided by legions of fearsome Gurkha warriors, the Shahs reclaimed the plains, expanding the borders of Nepal to twice their modern size.

Although the British never conquered Nepal, they had regular skirmishes with the Shahs. A treaty was signed in 1816 that trimmed the kingdom to roughly its current borders. Nepal later regained some additional land (including the city of Nepalganj) as a reward for assisting the British in the 1857 Indian Uprising.

Most of the Terai was heavily forested until the late 1950s. There were scattered settlements and the indigenous Tharu people were widely dispersed through the region. In 1954, drainage programs and DDT spraying markedly reduced the incidence of malaria, enabling mass migration from India and the hills. Fertile soils and easy accessibility led to rapid development.

Today, the Tharu are one of the most disadvantaged groups in Nepal, and huge areas of the forest have been cleared for farmland. Nevertheless, patches of wilderness remain, conserved in a series of national parks and community forests.

Despite the end of the Maoist insurgency, the Terai is still not entirely free of political instability. The region has seen the emergence of Madhesi insurgent groups that have launched an often-violent campaign for greater equality. It's advisable to stay informed of the situation if travelling in the region.

Climate

The Terai has a similar climate to the northern plains of India: hot as a furnace from May to October and drenched by monsoon rains from June to September. Try to visit in winter (November to February) when skies are clear and temperatures are moderate.

ⓘ Getting There & Away

The Terai is easily accessible from Kathmandu and Pokhara in Nepal and from West Bengal, Bihar and Uttar Pradesh in India. The Indian rail network passes close to several of the most important border crossings and there are frequent bus and air connections from the Terai to towns and villages across Nepal.

ⓘ Getting Around

The annual monsoon rains can severely affect transport in the region – dirt roads turn to mud, dry streambeds become raging torrents, and roads and bridges are routinely washed away.

BICYCLE

On the face of it, the Terai is well suited to cycling: much of the terrain is pool-table flat and there are villages every few kilometres. However, the condition of the roads, the traffic density and unpredictable driver behaviour require riders to be super-alert and highly cautious. If you run out of steam or courage along the way, you can usually put your bike on the roof of a bus. See p296 for details of biking routes from Kathmandu to Hetauda and Hetauda to Mugling, as well as general biking information.

BUS

Buses and microbuses are the main form of transport around the Terai. However, road safety can be an issue, particularly for night travel. To maximise safety, travel in daylight hours and avoid the front seats.

Roof riding is prohibited in the Kathmandu Valley, but there is no such restriction in the Terai. Riding on the luggage rack with the wind in your hair can be an exhilarating experience, but you will need to protect yourself from the elements. See p379 for more details on bus travel.

CENTRAL TERAI

The Central Terai is the most visited part of the plains. The highway from Mugling to Narayangarh is the principal route south from Kathmandu and Pokhara, and the border crossing at Sunauli is the most popular

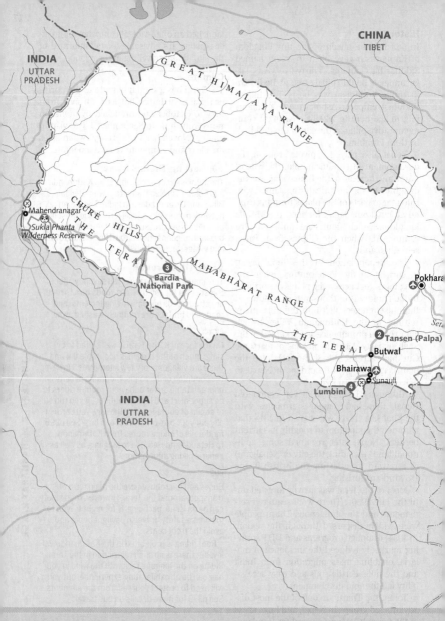

The Terai & Mahabharat Range Highlights

1 Take a rolling ride on an elephant's back to spot tigers and one-horned rhinos in **Chitwan National Park** (p221)

2 Explore the cobblestone streets of medieval **Tansen**

(Palpa) (p243) before hiking down to the abandoned palace of Ranighat.

3 Raft the mighty Geruwa River and follow it with a

jungle walk in pristine **Bardia National Park** (p249)

4 Cycle among Buddhist temples through the peaceful landscaped grounds of **Lumbini** (p236)

5 Visit Mithila women while they make their signature art in **Janakpur** (p256)

6 Stroll through **Ilam's** (p263) peaceful manicured tea gardens

7 Visit a traditional **Tharu village** (of which there are many throughout the Terai; see p226 for some examples), or mingle with a sea of pilgrims at one of the Terai's colourful festivals

8 Spot a rare Bengal florican and other marvellous wildlife in **Koshi Tappu Wildlife Reserve** (p259)

border crossing between Nepal and India. Its chief attractions include Chitwan National Park, which rightfully remains high on most visitors' to-do lists, and Lumbini, the revered birthplace of the Buddha.

Narayangarh & Bharatpur

📞056

Narayangarh (also Narayangadh and Narayangat) sits on the banks of the Narayani River, where the Mugling Hwy, the major road into the hills to Kathmandu and Pokhara, meets the Mahendra Hwy, which runs the length of Nepal from Mahendranagar to Kakarbhitta. Along with its twin city Bharatpur, which has an airport, it's an important hub, with visitors on their way to or from Chitwan National Park, India and Kathmandu.

Nabil Bank (◷10am-5pm Sun-Thu, 10am-3pm Fri) has both foreign exchange and an ATM accepting foreign cards. Check your email at **Pulchowk Cyber Cafe** (Pulchowk; per hr Rs 25; ◷7.30am-8.30pm).

🛏 Sleeping & Eating

Hotel Gangotri   HOTEL **$$**
(📞525746; www.hotelgangotri.com; Pulchowk, Narayangarh; r from Rs 750, with air-con Rs 1100-1450; ❄🛜) About 100m along the Mugling Hwy, towards Mugling from the Pulchowk intersection, the Gangotri has boxy standard rooms, slightly better air-cooled rooms with TVs, and comfortable air-con rooms in the new wing. The attached Chitwan Café & Restaurant (mains Rs 150 to 220) is best for its Indian dishes.

Hotel Satanchuli   HOTEL **$**
(📞521151; Narayangarh; s/d Rs 500/800, without bathroom Rs 400/600) This hotel, undergoing renovations at the time of writing, is the best option near the Pokhara bus stand. It's clean, has river views, and you can jump straight out of bed and onto the bus.

Hotel Global   HOTEL **$$**
(📞525513; www.hotel-global.com.np; Chaubiskoti Chowk, Bharatpur; s US$20-40, d US$25-50; ❄@🛜) This business hotel boasts manicured gardens and a palm-fringed swimming pool, only a short walk from the airport. The standard rooms are a little undersized, while the 'deluxe' options offer more comfort and all amenities.

New Kitchen Cafe   INTERNATIONAL **$**
(📞520453; mains Rs 170-200; ◷9am-10pm; ❄) Just south of the bridge over the Narayani, this busy restaurant serves the best food in town in either the air-con dining room or small garden. The menu is extensive, though the set meals (Indian and Nepali *thalis*) are probably the best choice.

ⓘ Getting There & Away

Bharatpur Airport (2km south of Narayangarh) is the closest airport to Chitwan National Park. There are several daily flights to/from Kathmandu (US$88, 30 minutes) with **Buddha Air** (📞528790) and **Yeti Airlines** (📞523136).

The main bus stand in Narayangarh is called the Pokhara bus stand, and it is found at the east end of Narayangarh on the highway to Mugling. Buses/microbuses run regularly to Pokhara (Rs 210/250, five hours) and Kathmandu (Rs 300/380, five hours). A few buses also run to Gorkha (Rs 120, three hours) and local

---

NEPAL–INDIA BORDER CROSSINGS

Heading from east to west, you can cross between India and Nepal at the points listed below. The Sunauli crossing is by far the most popular route between the two countries, but immigration staff are used to seeing foreign tourists at all the crossings. Nepali visas are available on arrival: you'll need one passport photo and US dollars cash for the visa fee. For more on crossing between Nepal and India, see the boxes throughout this chapter and p375.

BORDER CROSSING (NEPAL TO INDIA)	ONWARDS TO:
Mahendranagar to Banbassa (p252)	Delhi & hill towns in Uttaranchal
Belahiya to Sunauli (p235)	Varanasi, Agra & Delhi
Nepalganj to Jamunaha/Rupaidha Bazaar (p247)	Lucknow
Birganj to Raxaul Bazaar (p255)	Patna & Kolkata
Kakarbhitta to Panitanki (p264)	Darjeeling, Sikkim & Kolkata

Central Terai

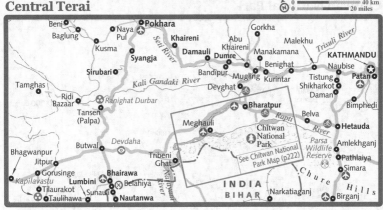

0 — 40 km
0 — 20 miles

buses head to Devghat (Rs 15, 20 minutes). Buses to Kathmandu can also be caught at the busy Pulchowk intersection.

The Bharatpur bus park is about 1km south of the airport. From here there are buses to Butwal (Rs 180, three hours), Sunauli/Bhairawa (Rs 200, three hours), Birganj (Rs 180, three hours), Janakpur (Rs 350, six hours), Biratnagar (Rs 575, nine hours), Kathmandu (Rs 300, five hours), Nepalganj (Rs 630, 10 hours), Kakarbhitta (Rs 715, 12 hours) and Mahendranagar (Rs 850, 12 hours).

For Sauraha, you can take a local bus from the side of the Mahendra Hwy south of Pulchowk (just before you reach the next intersection) to Tandi Bazaar/Sauraha Chowk (Rs 30, 20 minutes). From there you can take a share/reserve jeep (Rs 50/600) to Bachauli bus park, but it's much quicker to take a taxi all the way from Pulchowk (Rs 1500).

Around Narayangarh

DEVGHAT

Hidden away in the forest 6km northeast of Narayangarh, Devghat marks the sacred confluence of the Kali Gandaki and Trisuli Rivers, two important tributaries of the River Ganges. Hindus regard the point where the rivers meet as especially sacred and many elderly high-caste Nepalis come here to live out their final years and eventually die on the banks of the holy river. Far from being gloomy, the calm, contemplative atmosphere is wonderfully soothing after the hectic pace of the plains.

The village is reached via a suspension footbridge high over the rushing waters of the Trisuli. The best way to experience Devghat is to wander the streets, which are lined with ashrams and temples that hum and ring with chants and clashing cymbals. On the first day of the Nepali month of Magh (mid-January), thousands of pilgrims flock to Devghat to immerse themselves in the river to celebrate the Hindu festival of Magh Sankranti.

Local buses to Devghat (Rs 15, 20 minutes) leave from the Pokhara bus stand in Narayangarh.

Chitwan National Park

♫056

Chitwan National Park is one of the premier drawcards in Nepal. The World Heritage–listed reserve protects over 932 sq km of forests, marshland and rippling grassland, and is home to sizeable populations of wildlife. It's little wonder this place is so popular.

Meaning 'Heart of the Jungle', Chitwan is famous as one of the best wildlife-viewing national parks in Asia, and you'll have an excellent chance of spotting one-horned rhinos, deer, monkeys and 450 species of birds. If you're extremely lucky, you'll see leopards, wild elephants and sloth bears – though it's the once-in-a-lifetime chance to spot a majestic royal Bengal tiger that attracts people in their droves.

Sadly, Chitwan lost many animals during the decade-long Maoist insurgency, when the army were preoccupied with the conflict and unable to provide adequate protection from poachers. However, the good news is that recent census figures show rhino numbers are substantially increasing (503 individuals

Chitwan National Park

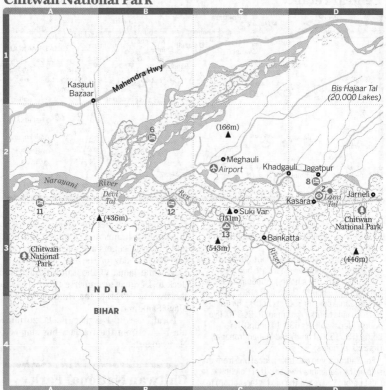

Chitwan National Park

◎ Sights

in 2011) and tiger numbers are steadily increasing (around 125 adults in 2010).

The best option for experiencing Chitwan National Park is to stay in one of the luxury lodges located deep inside the park. Clearly this experience doesn't come cheaply, and with calls for the removal of all lodges from the park getting louder, the future of this option looks uncertain. At the time of writing,

the government had set a date for closure of these lodges at 15 July 2012. In response, the lodges have bought land just outside the national park to develop new accommodation.

Most budget travellers opt for the more affordable lodging in Sauraha, a tourist village on the northern bank of the Rapti River on the edge of the park. It has a lively backpacker scene, and while many enjoy its so-

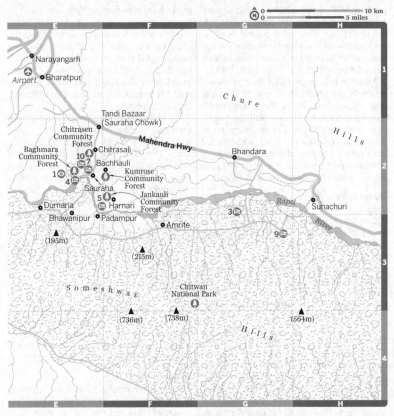

cial nature, and it is a great place to have a beer watching the sunset over the river, others are let down by its insensitive and overly commercial development.

Two whole days in the park is really the minimum for wildlife spotting. The nature of dense jungle, tall grass and the nocturnal hours kept by many animals are all factors that make spotting animals far from guaranteed. A good approach is to treat wildlife viewing as one would the pastime of fishing: some days you'll get plenty of bites, others not a nibble. Irrespective, it's all about the thrill of the chase and being out and about in tiger and rhino country. Be aware that the popular four-day, three-night packages include a day of travel at either end.

History

Chitwan National Park was created in 1973, but the area has been protected since at least the 19th century as a hunting reserve. Brit-

ain's King George V and his son, the young future Edward VIII, managed to slaughter a staggering 39 tigers and 18 rhinos during just one blood-soaked safari to Chitwan in 1911. Despite the occasional slaughter, Chitwan's status as a hunting reserve probably protected more animals than were killed.

Until the late 1950s, the only inhabitants of the Chitwan Valley were small communities of Tharu villagers, who were blessed with a degree of resistance to malaria. After a massive malaria eradication program in 1954, land-hungry peasants from the hills swarmed into the region and huge tracts of the forest were cleared to make space for farmland.

As their habitat disappeared, so did the tigers and rhinos. By the mid-1960s there were fewer than 100 rhinos and 20 tigers. News of the dramatic decline reached the ears of King Mahendra and the area was declared a royal reserve, becoming a national park in 1973. Some 22,000 peasants were removed from within the park boundaries, but it was only when army patrols were introduced to stop poaching that animal numbers started to rebound. Chitwan was added to the Unesco World Heritage list in 1984.

While animal populations have increased markedly since then, there was an alarming drop in numbers during the Maoist rebellion. Poachers reduced rhino and tiger numbers by a quarter, selling animal parts on to middlemen in China and Tibet. With regular army patrols and several significant arrests of poachers, protection has been restored and wildlife numbers are once again on the rise.

Geography

Chitwan National Park covers an impressive 932 sq km. A further 499 sq km is set aside as the Parsa Wildlife Reserve and multiuse conservation areas have been created in the community forests of Baghmara, Chitrasen, Jankauli and Kumrose, which have been replanted with trees to provide villages with a source of firewood and fodder. Because of the topography, most tourist activities are restricted to the flood plain of the Rapti River.

As well as the river, there are numerous tal (small lakes) dotted around the forest. The most interesting of these, particularly for viewing birds, are **Devi Tal** near Tiger Tops Jungle Lodge and **Lami Tal** near Kasara. There's another group of lakes and pools just outside the park boundary, known collectively as **Bis Hajaar Tal** (literally '20,000 lakes').

Plants

Around 70% of the national park is covered in sal forest; sal is a large-leaved hardwood tree, whose heavy timber is favoured for furniture and boat building. There are also large swathes of *phanta* (grassland), particularly along the banks of the Rapti and Narayani Rivers. Growing up to 8m in height, the local elephant grass provides excellent cover for rhinos and tigers, and food for elephants. In the forest, you'll find shisham, kapok, palash, pipal and strangler fig, and scarlet-flowered kusum trees, as well as the ubiquitous sal.

Animals

Chitwan boasts more than 50 different species of mammals, including rhinos, tigers, deer, monkeys, elephants, leopards, sloth bears, wild boar and hyenas. Birdwatchers can tick off 450 different species of birds,

while butterfly-spotters have identified at least 67 species, some as large as your hand.

The one-horned Indian rhinoceros is the most famous animal at Chitwan and you stand a good chance of seeing one on an elephant safari. Chitwan also has significant populations of gharial crocodiles. See the boxed text, opposite, for more on Chitwan's signature species.

As well as these high-profile animals, you may spot barking deer, spotted deer, hog deer, sambar and massive gaurs (Indian wild oxen). The most commonly seen monkey at Chitwan is the stocky rhesus macaque, but you also have a very good chance of spotting the larger and more elegant grey langur. Spotted deer are often seen following the langurs around, taking advantage of their profligate feeding habits. They also cooperate to alert each other when predators are in the area: the hoots of monkey or deer serve as a good indicator to keep your eyes peeled for a lurking tiger.

Birds seen in Chitwan include bulbuls, mynahs, egrets, parakeets, jungle fowl, peacocks, kingfishers, orioles and various species of drongos. Keen birders should keep an eye out for rare species, such as ruby-cheeked sunbirds, emerald doves, jungle owlets and crested hornbills.

When to Visit

The most comfortable time to visit Chitwan is from October to March, when skies are relatively clear and the average daily temperature is a balmy 25°C. However, the best time to see animals is late January to March when the towering *phanta* grass is slashed by villagers, improving visibility considerably. At other times the grass can grow as tall as 8m, making it difficult to spot animals that may be as close as a few feet away. Jeep safaris are difficult during the monsoon (June to September) when tracks through the park become impassable.

Dangers & Annoyances

Tigers, leopards and rhinos are all quite capable of killing humans, and there have been some serious attacks on tourists. Most people have a good experience on jungle walks, but you should be aware that there's a small but significant risk – being chased by a rhino seems a lot less funny when you consider the phrase 'trampled to death' (see the boxed text, p228).

Insects are another unwelcome aspect of life in the jungle. Mosquitoes in large num-

CHITWAN'S BIG FIVE

Chitwan has some high-profile species that everyone wants to see, including the following.

One-Horned Indian Rhino

Chitwan is one of the last refuges of the rare one-horned Indian rhinoceros (*gaida* in Nepali), and they are one of the most commonly seen animals on elephant safaris in the park. Only about 3000 survive worldwide, most of them in Chitwan and Kaziranga National Park in Assam, India. Sadly, poaching significantly reduced Chitwan's rhino population during the Maoist insurgency, though the good news is the 2011 counts confirmed the population is rebounding with a total of 503 rhinos.

Asian Elephant

The Asian elephant (*hathi*) is the world's second-largest land mammal behind its African counterpart. The elephants you're most likely to see in Chitwan are domestic elephants that ferry visitors around the park on wildlife-spotting safaris, though there's a small population of approximately 25 to 30 wild elephants in the adjoining Parsa Wildlife Reserve plus wandering migrants from Bihar's Valmiki National Park.

Royal Bengal Tiger

This lean, mean killing machine is the top predator in the jungles of Nepal. The intelligence and power of the royal Bengal tiger (*bagh*) make it one of the most feared animals in the subcontinent. Both locals and foreigners have been attacked by tigers at Chitwan – something to think about before joining a guided walk. There are currently around 125 tigers in Chitwan; sightings are rare as tigers lie low during daylight hours. It's said that tigers are a hundred times more likely to spot you, rather than vice versa.

Gharial

The gharial is a bizarre-looking crocodile, with a slender, elongated snout crammed with ill-fitting teeth and a bulbous protuberance at the end of its snout, resembling a *ghara* (local pot) from which it gets its name. Gharials are adept at catching fish, and 110-million-year-old fossils have been found with the same basic body plan, attesting to the effectiveness of the gharial design. Gharials are endangered but there are breeding programs, and young gharials have been released into many rivers in the Terai.

Sloth Bear

These shaggy black bears (*bhalu*), the size of a large dog, have a reputation as the most-feared animal (tiger included) among locals. They get their name from being confused with sloths in the 19th century, owing to their long claws and excellent tree-climbing abilities. The bears' diet is mainly termites and ants – they use their protruding muzzles to vacuum them up through a gap between their teeth, a sound that can be heard up to 100m away.

bers are inescapable year-round. Malaria may be present in some areas of the park, so remember to bring insect repellent. During the monsoon the forest comes alive with *jukha* (leeches).

⊙ Sights

National Park Headquarters　　PARK
(Map p222; ☑521932; ☺6am-6pm) The National Park Headquarters are inside the park at Kasara, about 13km west of Sauraha on the south bank of the Rapti River. Most people visit as part of an organised jungle safari

and there's a small visitor centre with displays on wildlife, including orphaned and injured animals. At the **gharial breeding project** (admission Rs 100) you can see both gharial and marsh mugger crocodiles up close; the program has been a great success in releasing both endangered species back into the wild.

Elephant Breeding Centre　　ZOO
(Map p222; ☑580154; foreigner/SAARC Rs 50/25; ☺6am-6pm) This centre, about 3km west of Sauraha on the far side of the small Bhude

Rapti River, is a must-see sight in Chitwan. Providing many of the elephants for elephant safaris at Chitwan, it's fascinating watching the interaction between mother and baby elephants, as well as the multitask use of their trunk (which has a staggering 40,000 muscles), such as covering themselves in dust to ward off mosquitoes or scratching their backside with a bamboo stick.

The elephants spend much of the day grazing in the jungle, so come before 10.30am or after 3.30pm if you want to see the cute baby elephants. As adorable and harmless as they may seem, treat baby elephants with caution as most have a naughty streak and are surprisingly powerful units.

Morning is a good time to visit. Not only are there fewer tourists, but you also get to watch on as the mahouts (elephant riders) prepare *kuchiis* – elephant sweets made from molasses, salt and rice wrapped in grass. The breeding centre is an easy walk or cycle along the road past Jungle Lagoon Safari Lodge.

Elephant Polo   EXTREME SPORT

About 25km southwest of Narayangarh, the Tharu village of **Meghauli** is a sleepy place full of thatched huts and wandering chickens. However, the town wakes up every December for the annual **Elephant Polo Championships** (www.elephantpolo.com), a jumbo-sized spectacle held on the Meghauli airstrip.

Tharu Cultural Show   TRADITIONAL DANCE

Most of the larger lodges put on shows of traditional Tharu songs and dances for guests, including the popular stick dance, where a great circle of men whack their sticks together in time. It's very much a tourist experience, but the shows are fun and they provide employment for local people. In Sauraha there's a nightly 35-minute performance at the **Tharu Culture Program** (Map p231; tickets Rs 60; ⊘7pm).

Tharu Villages   VILLAGES

Sauraha is surrounded by small Tharu villages, which you can explore by bike or on foot. Resist the urge to hand out sweets, pens and money; instead, if you want to help local people, shop in the village shops or eat in village *bhojanalayas* (basic restaurants). Farming is the main industry and many people still decorate their houses with Mithila paintings and adobe bas-reliefs of animals. The nearest Tharu village is **Bachhauli**, a pleasant cycle or 20-minute walk out through the mustard fields of bright yellow flowers. Here you will find the informative **Tharu Cultural Mu-**

seum & Research Centre (admission Rs 25; ⊘6am-5pm) with colourful murals and exhibits on artefacts and local dress.

Harnari is one of the best villages to get a taste of Tharu culture. Bordering the Kumrose Community Forest, it's less visited than Bachhauli and has a more authentic feel. There's a tiny **Tharu Cultural Museum** (admission by donation) here with displays of ornaments and a *rakshi* distillery pot. If it's closed, ask around and someone will open it up. It's a 20-minute bike ride from Sauraha to get here.

Sapana Village Lodge (see p230) runs excellent tours of Tharu villages and organises activities from walking tours and planting rice in the fields with villagers, to fishing trips and cooking and art classes.

Wildlife Display & Information Centre   MUSEUM

(Map p231; admission Rs 30; ⊘7pm-5pm) Aimed more at school groups than tourists, this educational centre has displays on wildlife, including a rather macabre collection of animal foetuses and reproductive organs in jars, plus skulls, plaster-cast footprints and a collection of animal poo.

 Activities

You'll need to add another Rs 500 to all prices quoted below. This is the cost of a daily park permit. Also, for some activities there is a minimum group size to achieve these per-person costs.

Elephant Safari

For many visitors, lumbering through the jungle on the back of a five-tonne jumbo spotting wildlife is the defining Chitwan experience. It's the best way to see wildlife in the park, offering a fantastic vantage point high above the tall grasses of the *phanta*. The wildlife is much more tolerant of elephants than of noisy jeeps or walkers, and they also effectively mask the scent of humans. Elephants also play an important role in the park on patrols, looking for poachers.

Riding an elephant is thrilling rather than comfortable. Elephants move with a heavy, rolling gait, and three or four passengers are crammed into each wooden howdah (riding platform). Each elephant is controlled by a mahout, who works with the same elephant throughout its life.

Many visitors are upset by the sight of shackled elephants at the breeding centre, as well as their treatment by mahouts, who whack their skulls with sticks and metal hooks to prevent them straying off course. It's one of the unfortunate drawbacks to transforming elephants into domestic animals. The elephants are otherwise treated well and spend a good five hours each day grazing in the park. The WWF has launched an initiative to introduce less severe training methods that involve psychological techniques, compared to the more distressing traditional methods employed by mahouts.

GOVERNMENT-OWNED ELEPHANTS

The national park has its own herd of domesticated elephants; **jungle safaris** (foreigner/SAARC per person Rs 1000/400) leave the **National Park Visitor Centre** (Map p222; ⏱6-9am & noon-4pm) at Sauraha at 8am and 4pm daily, and 7am and 5pm during summer. Children are half-price. There are no advance bookings so you will need to line up early in the morning to purchase a ticket from the Visitor Centre, or better yet organise it through your hotel (a service that helps with the employment of locals). Safaris last one to two hours and run through the dense *phanta* along the Rapti River, a favourite feeding ground for deer and rhinos.

PRIVATELY OWNED ELEPHANTS

Most of the lodges inside the park have their own elephants, and elephant safaris are included in most package tours. In Sauraha, elephants are owned by various resorts and hotels and there is a cooperative, **United Jungle Guide Service** (Map p231; ☎580219), which coordinates the riding business as well as looking after the wear and tear on the elephants and the environment. The best way to arrange these elephant safaris is through your accommodation, as there is no saving in going to the cooperative directly.

Morning and afternoon **safaris** (per person Rs 1050) last 1½ hours and are run in either the Baghmara or Kumrose community forests, which are buffer zones on the northern edge of the park with decent wildlife populations. Although not strictly 'inside' the park, you still need to purchase the park permit. From September to January, spotting wildlife in the community forests is often better than inside the park, where long grass makes visibility difficult.

Jungle Walks

Exploring the park on foot when accompanied by a guide is a fantastic way to get close to the wildlife. Be aware, though, that you enter the park with the real risk of encountering bad-tempered mother rhinos, tigers

ELEPHANT BATH TIME

There are few experiences that create such a feeling of childlike wonder as helping to bathe an elephant. Every day from 11am to noon, the elephants in Sauraha march down to the river near the Hotel River Side (Map p231) for their morning soak and scrub, and everyone turns out to watch the spectacle. If you bring your swimming costume, you can join in the fun. There's no better way of cooling off on a hot day than sitting on the back of a submerged elephant and shouting *chhop!* – if you get the accent right you'll be rewarded with a refreshing trunkful of cold water! Lodges with their own elephants offer similar elephant bathing experiences.

or sloth bears protecting their young. Generally, the bigger the group, the safer the walk, but the experience of your guide counts for a lot. Levels of experience vary and some of the guides have a worryingly devil-may-care attitude to creeping up on rhinos. Therefore, jungle walks are not recommended for the faint-hearted; see the boxed text, p228.

Jungle walks (cost based on 3 walkers half-/full day Rs 800/1000) can be arranged through any of the lodges or travel agents in Sauraha. Rules stipulate two guides are required even if there is only one customer. **United Jungle Guide Service** (Map p231) is a cooperative of around 15 local guides, who provide good options for jungle walks. Before you opt for a whole-day jungle walk, consider the very real risks associated with venturing deep into the park and being far from rescue and medical facilities, possibly without communication.

An alternative is to trek through the Chepang hills to the Kathmandu–Pokhara (Prithvi) Hwy; see p190.

Canoeing

An altogether more relaxing way to explore the park is on a **canoeing trip** (per person from Rs 1150) on the Rapti or Narayani Rivers. You have a good chance of spotting water birds and crocodiles. Typical canoe trips from Sauraha include a one-hour trip downriver followed by a two-hour guided walk back to Sauraha, with a stop at the elephant breeding centre. Canoe trips can be arranged either through your hotel or a booking agency in Sauraha.

JUNGLE SURVIVAL

Chitwan and Bardia national parks are among the few wildlife parks in the world that you can explore on foot when accompanied by a guide. It's both an exhilarating and humbling experience being brought back to a level playing field within the animal hierarchy, where your only protection is the bamboo stick carried by your guide (which can be surprisingly effective in beating off advancing animals). The sound of a twig snapping in the forest or the warning cry of deer and monkey alerting each other of nearby predators will make your heart race.

Jungle walks are a real risk. While dangerous run-ins are not overly common, you'll hear enough stories of tourists experiencing terrifying encounters with animals to make you want to devise a plan of attack if an angry rhino charges at 40km/h in your direction. Nearly all incidents involve protective mothers in the company of their young. The most crucial piece of advice is to never venture into the park without a guide, nor outside the park visiting hours.

Rhinos

Being charged by rhinos is the most common dangerous encounter tourists have in the park. With poor eyesight, rhinos rely on a keen sense of smell that enables them to sniff out threats, which includes humans. If you are charged, the best evasive action according to Eak Krishna Shrestha, naturalist of 25 years, is 'to climb the nearest big tree', which are usually easy enough to climb. Alternatively, hiding behind a tree can be effective, though be prepared for several repeated charges from the rhino. Failing trees, Eak suggests 'running zigzag before dropping an item of clothing or your camera as a decoy'.

Sloth Bears

Due to their unpredictable temperament, sloth bears have the reputation as one of the most-feared animals in Chitwan. Their nocturnal hours make sightings rare, though mothers and cubs sometimes move during the day. Eak, who bears the scars of a sloth bear attack, warns that 'males go for the face; however, females go for down there!' [pointing to his nether region]. 'If in danger, it's best not to run; rather, stay perfectly still and huddle in a group to make you look more threatening, while your guide bangs a stick on the ground to scare it away.'

Tigers

In the unlikely event you cross paths with a tiger, which are known to be extremely shy, the best advice according to Santa Chaudhari, a naturalist from Bardia National Park, is 'not to run; maintain eye contact and back away slowly' – certainly easier said than done. In 2009 Santa had the opportunity to test this theory (see the boxed text, p251).

Elephants

Due to numerous deaths of villagers each year, locals rightfully fear wild elephants. If you are in a threatening situation, the most effective means of escape is to simply run for dear life!

4WD Safari

It may not have quite the same romance as riding through the jungle on the back of an elephant, but **4WD safaris** (cost based on 4 passengers, half-day per person from Rs 1000) are another popular way to explore the park. Animals are less concerned by the rumble of engines than you might suspect and you'll have the opportunity to go further into the jungle. Safaris can be booked either through your hotel or an agency in Sauraha.

Cycling

You can't cycle inside the park, but the surrounding countryside is ideal for bicycle touring, with dozens of small Tharu farming communities to visit. Another possible destination is **Bis Hajaar Tal**, a collection of bird-filled lakes and ponds about 1½ hours northwest of Sauraha, accessible via the Mahendra Hwy. Bicycles can be rented in Sauraha. For details see p234.

For information on a mountain-bike trip that passes Chitwan, see p296.

🛏 Sleeping

You can stay inside or adjacent to the park in a luxury lodge, or at the budget traveller centre of Sauraha on the north bank of the Rapti River.

Many people visit Chitwan on package tours arranged through travel agents in Kathmandu, Pokhara or overseas. This is by far the easiest approach if you plan to stay at one of the upmarket lodges in the park. If you're planning to stay in Sauraha, packages are unnecessary and expensive, and it's easy enough to arrange accommodation and activities independently. Discounts of 20% to 50% are available in the low season, particularly from May to September.

CHITWAN LUXURY LODGES
By far the most atmospheric way to visit Chitwan is to stay at one of the upmarket lodges inside (or adjacent to) the park. The resorts are expensive, but it's hard to put a price on the experience of staying deep in the jungle, surrounded by the sounds of wildlife. Most of the lodges offer a choice of Tharu-style jungle cottages or comfortable safari tents, all with private bathrooms and hot solar showers. The lodges all have bars and restaurants, but there are few other mod cons, reflecting the 'getting back to nature' ethos. Listed prices usually include lodging, meals, jungle activities and a park permit. Transport to the lodges costs extra.

At the time of research there was heightened talk of all the lodges within the national park being forced to relocate outside the park's perimeter before July 2012. While this is not the first call for such relocation, the lodges are preparing for the inevitable move by purchasing land and developing resorts on the park periphery. Such plans and developments are mentioned here, but it will be worth checking the situation before booking.

Tiger Tops Jungle Lodge   LODGE $$$
(Map p222; ☑in Kathmandu 01-4361500; www. tigertops.com; packages per person per night US$350) The original tree-top guesthouse that forged the Tiger Tops brand, its accommodation options in locally built stilt houses remain some of the most characterful anywhere in Nepal. The lodge sits beside the small Reu Khola at the western end of the park and the spacious rooms have solar-powered lights and fans.

Tiger Tops Tented Camp   LODGE $$$
(Map p222; ☑in Kathmandu 01-4361500; www. tigertops.com; packages per person per night US$250) Three kilometres southeast of the Tiger Tops Jungle Lodge in the Surung Valley, this feels much more like a traditional jungle safari. The luxury safari tents have twin beds, modern bathrooms and small balconies, and there's a delightful elevated bar and restaurant.

Tiger Tops Tharu Lodge   LODGE $$$
(☑in Kathmandu 01-4361500; www.tigertops.com; packages per person per night US$250; ☒) This lodge is situated outside and west of the Chitwan National Park, in Nawalparashi, 7km off the Mahendra Hwy at Danda. Built with local material in the traditional architectural style of the Tharu people, it consists of two long houses. Wildlife activities are conducted in the buffer zone and there are tennis and badminton courts, cycling, and cultural shows.

Machan Wildlife Resort   LODGE $$$
(Map p222; ☑in Kathmandu 01-4225001; www. nepalinformation.com/machan; 1-/2-night package US$150/285, additional nights US$135; ☒) At the eastern end of the park, this appealing place has been developed sensitively with well-designed bungalows decorated with Mithila paintings and set among old-growth trees. There's a delightful natural-formed swimming pool. It's the closest resort to the Parsa Wildlife Reserve and wildlife is abundant.

Machan Paradise View   LODGE $$$
(Map p222; ☑in Kathmandu 01-4225001; www. nepalinformation.com/machan; 1-/2-night package US$150/285, additional nights US$135; ☀☎☒) Machan Paradise View is west of Sauraha near the village of Jagatpur and the park headquarters at Kasara. Accommodation includes safari tents and air-con rooms, and activities include excursions to nearby lakes.

Chitwan Jungle Lodge   LODGE $$$
(Map p222; ☑in Kathmandu 01-4442240; www.chit wanjunglelodge.com; 3-day/2-night package from US$275, additional nights US$148) On the south bank of the Rapti River amid sal forest in the eastern part of Chitwan, this ecosensitive resort makes extensive use of thatch and natural materials. There's an inviting open-air bar and restaurant.

Island Jungle Resort
LODGE $$$

(Map p222; ✎in Kathmandu 01-4220162; www.islandjungleresort.com; 3-day/2-night package US$200, additional nights US$80) This resort has a superb location on a large island in the middle of the Narayani River at the western end of the park. The cottages at the main resort are simple but tasteful and decorated with animal paintings. There's a lovely riverside breakfast terrace, plus the obligatory Tharu-style restaurant and bar.

Temple Tiger
LODGE $$$

(Map p222; ✎in Kathmandu 01-4263480; packages per person per night US$250) Surrounded by dense jungle on the south bank of the Narayani River, Temple Tiger offers raised cabins with thatched roofs, each with a private viewing platform overlooking the *phanta*. At the time of writing, Temple Tiger had started construction of a resort just outside the park.

Gaida Wildlife Camp
LODGE $$$

(Map p222; ✎in Kathmandu 01-4215409; www.gaidawildlife.com; s/d US$88/176) The bungalow rooms at Gaida are arranged around the communal dining hut and provide a very basic level of accommodation. It's the closest lodge to Sauraha, so by far the easiest to access, and the only park accommodation on the north bank of the Rapti River.

SAURAHA

Most independent travellers to Chitwan stay in the village of Sauraha on the northern fringes of the park. There are dozens of lodges and hotels here, from upmarket package accommodation to simple guesthouses run by local villagers. Almost all have mosquito nets or insect screening on the windows.

⟨TOP CHOICE⟩ Travellers Jungle Camp
HOTEL $

(Map p231; ✎9855055845; www.nepaljunglecamp.com; budget r Rs 800, deluxe Rs 1200-1500; ✵🖧) This is a long-standing family-owned hotel, where you'll receive a warm welcome, enjoy a relaxing garden, and even meet the resident pachyderm, Chanchal Kali. All rooms are spick and span, while the spacious deluxe rooms have excellent mattresses – a noteworthy item when comparing Sauraha lodges. The owner is well attuned to travellers' needs and, as well as the elephant, you'll find an organic vegie patch out the back.

Royal Park Hotel
HOTEL $$

(Map p231; ✎580061, in Kathmandu 01-4412987; www.royalparkhotel.com.np; r incl breakfast US$30; ✵🖧🗙) Set in extensive parklike gardens, the attractive adobe-and-thatch bungalows boast huge rooms and gorgeous stone- or marble-tiled bathrooms. Upstairs rooms are best with soaring ceilings and inviting balconies. There is a restaurant and regular cultural shows when a group is being hosted.

Sapana Village Lodge
LODGE $$

(off Map p222; ✎580308; www.sapanalodge.com; s/d incl breakfast Rs 2300/3100; ✵🖧) Situated 1.5km north of Sauraha, this relaxing lodge is an excellent option for those with an interest in Tharu culture. Set up with the aim of supporting the local Tharu community, rooms are decked out in charming village-style designs with vibrant paintings, rugs and wicker stools. Its smart restaurant looks out over a flood plain of rice paddies and serves Tharu dishes in addition to other tasty cuisine.

Sauraha Resort
HOTEL $$

(Map p231; ✎580114; www.sauraharesort.com; r Rs 700-2000; ✵) This relaxed, family-run hotel is close to town but tucked back from the street, so quiet all the same. Rooms range from simple twins and larger doubles (with an extra single bed and TV) to air-con doubles. All feature mosquito nets and fans. Although low-key, all the jungle activities can be arranged here and there is a simple restaurant.

Rhino Residency Resort
LODGE $$$

(Map p231; ✎580095, in Kathmandu 01-4420431; www.rhino-residency.com; r incl breakfast US$60; ✵🗙) Right by the entrance to the national park, this resort's elegant colonial styling features comfortable slate-roofed bungalows, Sauraha's best swimming pool, and a bar and restaurant. Contact the company in Kathmandu for discounts on packages and longer stays.

Hotel Shiva's Dream
HOTEL $

(Map p231; ✎580369, in Kathmandu 01-42205973; www.hotelshivasdream.com.np; s/d Rs 700/1000, with air-con Rs 1500/2000; ✵) This comfortable option is run by the same family as Bardia's Forest Hideaway. They are familiar with package and independent tourists alike. The spacious rooms in a three-storey building are tidy enough and there's a garden and separate dining room.

Hotel Hermitage
HOTEL $$

(off Map p231; ✎580090, in Kathmandu 01-4424390; www.nepalhotelhermitage.com; r from

Sauraha

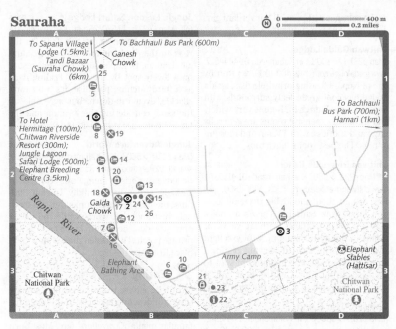

Sauraha

Rs 2000; ❄@☎) Apparently geared to travellers on a package, this lodge nonetheless commands one of the better elevated riverside positions while still an easy stroll from town. All rooms in the moat-surrounded 'boathouse' are large, comfy and cool.

Chitwan Rest House HOTEL $
(Map p231; ☏9845140675, in Kathmandu 01-4266064; kisna107@yahoo.com; r Rs 300-500) Located 500m north of Gaida Chowk, this is a friendly, uberbudget option with basic rooms (no piped hot water) set in neat

adobe cottages with a small but verdant garden and a cheap restaurant.

Chitwan Gaida Lodge
HOTEL $

(Map p231; ☑580083, in Kathmandu 01-4444527; www.gaidalodge.com; r Rs 400-1000; ☎) Run by one of Nepal's leading ornithologists, Gaida Lodge has cool green leafy surrounds with hammocks to lounge in. Rooms vary widely and the more expensive rooms are generally large and spotless, with TV, fan and mosquito nets. The best rooms have tubs.

Chitwan Riverside Resort
HOTEL $$

(off Map p222; ☑580297, in Kathmandu 01-4155372; www.chitwanriverside.com; r Rs 1200-1800; ✳) Here it's all about the idyllic riverside location away from Sauraha. There's a choice between lovely cottages without views or rooms in the newer building with excellent river views. The shaded viewing platform atop the riverbank is a magnificent spot to sit back during sunset with a beer and, if you're lucky, you'll spot some thirsty wildlife.

Chitwan Tiger Camp
HOTEL $$

(Map p231; ☑580060, in Kathmandu 01-4441572; www.chitwantigercamp.com; r Rs 1200-2500) A popular choice, Tiger Camp has welcoming staff, experienced jungle guides and an excellent location on sunset point. The budget rooms are downstairs and fairly standard, while the upstairs rooms with tubs and bamboo decor are worth the extra rupees. Reservations are recommended.

Hotel River Side
HOTEL $

(Map p231; ☑580009; in Kathmandu 01-4425073; www.wildlifechitwan.com; r Rs 800-1500) Take your choice between delightful terracotta-tiled huts or the less atmospheric modern rooms with a balcony delivering unbeatable river views. The cheapest rooms on the bottom floor are unremarkable but decent. There's a riverside restaurant, helpful staff and a garden full of hammocks.

River View Jungle Camp
HOTEL $

(Map p231; ☑580096; rvjcsauraha@hotmail.com; cottages US$10-15) Its pink brick cottages are set along a long garden leading all the way to the river and elephant bathing area. The rooms are tidy with fans, mosquito nets and reliable hot water. It's a good central choice with expert staff and guides. All rooms are similar, so the tariff is at the lower end of the range when occupancy is low and vice versa.

Jungle Lagoon Safari Lodge
LODGE $

(off Map p222; ☑580126, in Kathmandu 01-4258427; www.lagoon.com.np; r Rs 1000) On the road to the elephant breeding centre, Jungle Lagoon is a pleasant low-key 'resort' on a lovely spot by the river. Priding itself as a 'birdwatching paradise', it's a bit ramshackle, even run-down, but agreeable all the same considering the location and the tariff. Rooms are very basic and well worn.

Jungle Adventure World
HOTEL $

(Map p231; ☑580301, in Kathmandu 9841454599; sharad2029@yahoo.com; r Rs 500-700) This rustic lodge comprising bungalows scattered in a shady garden has a mildly Tibetan Buddhist theme. The older bungalows are semi-detached and well worn, while the newer ones are detached with lanterns on each private porch. The garden makes for a great place to escape the heat.

✗ Eating

Most lodges have restaurants and there are several independent places in the main bazaar at Sauraha. All serve cocktails and a familiar menu of travellers' fare. Most open from 6am and close at around 10pm to 11pm. For real bargain-basement meals, there are a few rustic bhojanalayas in the bazaar.

KC's Restaurant
INTERNATIONAL $$

(Map p231; mains Rs 295-475) Rightfully the most popular choice in Sauraha, KC's is set in a cool, thatch-roofed bungalow with an open terrace overlooking the manicured garden and a fire pit at the back for winter dinners. The chefs here look the part and the well-executed menu runs from Nepali and Indian curries to pizzas and pasta. We recommend the top-up-able *thalis* and authentic tandoori dishes.

Sweet Memory Restaurant
NEPALI $

(Map p231; mains Rs 90-200) An attractive family-run shack restaurant with plenty of flowers and pot plants, Sweet Memory prides itself on its home-style cooking. The roast chicken is recommended, and it also serves up good filtered coffee and sweet lime *(mausambi)* juice. By the time you read this it may have moved to Hamro Chowk, the turn-off to Bachauli bus park.

River Sunset Restaurant
INTERNATIONAL $$

(Map p231; mains Rs 95-1250) Attached to the Chitwan Tiger Camp on Sunset Point, this restaurant is one of a cluster of laid-back restaurant-bars that stretch along the sandy banks of the Rapti River. They are most popular during elephant bath time and Sauraha's famous sunset. Here you can sample a mouth-watering barbecue of duck, pork, chicken or buffalo as well as the full range of traveller favourites and, of course, cold beer.

Chitwan Restaurant   INTERNATIONAL $
(Map p231; mains Rs 110-350) This simple gathering of chairs and tables on the sandy riverbank prides itself on its fish dishes and it does seem to manage the coldest beer in these parts. It also makes for a delightful spot to breakfast.

Jungle View Restaurant   INTERNATIONAL $
(Map p231; mains Rs 120-450; ☎) One of a pigeon pair of terrace restaurants overlooking Gaida Chowk, Jungle View has all your traveller favourites, as well as a beer garden and views looking over the main strip. Happy hour brings popcorn with your beer and stretches to several hours.

🛍 Shopping

Souvenir shops in Sauraha sell the usual range of Tibetan and Nepali arts and crafts. Local specialities include tiger pugmark ashtrays, elephant poo paper products, and woodcarvings of elephants and rhinos, including dubious mating scenes.

Happy House   HANDICRAFTS
(Map p231; ✆580026; Gaida Chowk; ⊘7am-9pm) With a good selection of souvenirs, this small, family-run business produces its own honey in various delectable flavours and sells colourful Mithila paintings on handmade paper produced by women's craft cooperatives near Janakpur.

Women's Community Shop HANDICRAFTS
(Map p231; ⊘7pm-5pm) This cooperative outlet, near the visitors centre, sells a small selection of dusty souvenirs including the aforementioned poo paper, with all proceeds going to developing local women's community groups.

❶ Information

Sauraha's **park office** (Map p231; ✆521932; foreigner/SAARC/child under 10yr per day Rs 500/200/free; ⊘ticket office 6-9am & noon-4.30pm) handles admission fees to the park, although this is usually bundled into the overall charge when booking a tour either independently or as a package. You can also book a government elephant safari here; see p227.

The small **National Park Visitors Centre** (Map p231; ⊘6am-4pm) has displays on Tharu culture and wildlife, including dioramas on the Chitwan food chain.

There are several ATMs, though not all accept foreign cards. The Gaurishankar Development Bank and the Himalayan Bank were two that did at the time of research. There are also several private moneychangers accepting foreign currency and travellers cheques. **Chitwan Money Changer** (⊘7am-8pm) does credit card cash advances.

Nearly all hotels and restaurants offer free wireless internet, so the cyber cafes, such as **Sauraha Cyber Cafe** (per hr Rs 100; ⊘7am-10pm), must be feeling the pinch.

❶ Getting There & Away

Air
When there is sufficient demand, Yeti/Tara Airlines has flights from Kathmandu to the tiny airfield at Meghauli for US$108 (30 minutes), and you'll need to make advance arrangements with your lodge for a pick-up. If you're bound for Sauraha, it's better to fly into Bharatpur and take a taxi (Rs 1500). Both Buddha and Yeti offer daily flights to Bharatpur from Kathmandu (US$88, 30 minutes). Travel agents and hotels can make bookings.

Bus
By far the easiest way to reach Chitwan is by tourist bus from Kathmandu. The cost is Rs 400 (eg Baba Travels) to 500 (eg Rainbow Travels) and takes five to seven hours. From Pokhara it costs Rs 400 to 450, and takes about the same time. Buses leave the Thamel end of Kantipath in Kathmandu at around 7am, and from the tourist bus stand in Pokhara at 7.30am. The final stop is Bachhauli tourist bus park, a 15-minute walk from Sauraha. Jeeps, and the dreaded hotel touts, wait to transfer new arrivals to hotels for Rs 50. There's no obligation to commit to staying at any particular resort, regardless of what the touts say. In the opposite direction, buses leave Bachhauli at 9.30am. Any hotel or travel agent can make bookings.

A more comfortable option is the daily aircon bus operated by **Greenline** (Map p231; ✆560126; www.greenline.com.np), which runs to/from Kathmandu or Pokhara for US$15 including brunch. From Kathmandu or Pokhara it leaves at 7.30am; from Bachhauli, it leaves at 9.30am. **Rose Cosmetics** (Map p231; ✆580203) in Sauraha runs a daily microbus to Kathmandu departing at 5am and arriving before noon.

You can also pick up public buses at Tandi Bazaar (also known as Sauraha Chowk) on the Mahendra Hwy, about 6km north of Sauraha. Destinations include Kathmandu, Pokhara and

Bhairawa/Sunauli (Rs 300, five to six hours). For the airport in Bharatpur you can get a local bus from Tandi Bazaar to Narayangarh (Rs 30).

Car

Travel agents and hotels can arrange transfers to Chitwan by private car. The going rate is around US$90 per person, with a minimum of two passengers, and the journey from Pokhara or Kathmandu takes about five hours. Cars usually drop guests off at the turn-offs to the resorts; you must complete the journey by lodge 4WD or elephant!

Raft

A more interesting way to arrive at Chitwan is by river raft. Most of the big Kathmandu rafting operators offer trips down the Trisuli and Narayani Rivers, culminating at the national park, usually as part of a package tour. The rafting experience is more of a leisurely drift – but there are some fine views and the sandy beaches along the riverside offer great camping spots.

Mugling is the main embarkation point on the Prithvi Hwy, about halfway between Kathmandu and Pokhara. It takes two or three days to raft down to Chitwan. Most people combine rafting with a safari package in the national park – expect to pay around US$90 per person for the rafting section of the trip. Rafting companies (see p42) can usually make arrangements.

ⓘ Getting Around

Bicycle & Motorcycle

Several shops in Sauraha rent out bicycles for exploring the surrounding villages; the going rate is Rs 50/180 per hour/day. **Rainforest Guide Office** (Map p231) offers better-than-average bikes for Rs 50/250 per hour/day and motorbikes for Rs 300 per hour.

Jeep & Pony Cart

From Sauraha, a reserved jeep (ie a nonshared vehicle) to the Bachauli bus stand costs Rs 300. By shared *tonga* (pony cart) it will cost Rs 100. A reserved jeep to Tandi Bazaar is Rs 600, while to Bharatpur Airport it costs Rs 1500.

Sunauli & Bhairawa

☎ 071

Sunauli is the most popular tourist border crossing between Nepal and India, seeing scores of people on the way south to Varanasi or Delhi, or northwards to Lumbini, Pokhara and Kathmandu. Most people refer to both sides of the border as Sunauli, though officially the Nepali border town is called Belahiya.

Typical of many border towns, it is dusty and chaotic and you won't want to hang around for any length of time. Most people just get their passports stamped and continue on their way. If you do need to spend a night here there are hotels along the unattractive strip, but it makes more sense to stay in the more relaxed town of Bhairawa 4km north. To further confuse things, Bhairawa is also known as Siddharthanagar, but you can get away with Bhairawa for the town and Sunauli for the border.

Buses run directly from the border to most major towns in Nepal, so unless you plan to stay overnight or are heading to Lumbini, there's no real need to go into Bhairawa.

🛏 Sleeping

SUNAULI

New Cottage Lodge   HOTEL $

(☎521968; s/d Rs 400/600) Travellers on a tight budget need look no further. Rooms here are very basic but those on the 2nd floor offer Western toilets, hot showers and insect screens on the windows. Check a few rooms before deciding on one and settling in.

Hotel Aakash   HOTEL $

(☎524371; aakashshahi@hotmail.com; s/d Rs 800/1000, with air-con Rs 1200/1500; ❄) Although the lobby, air-con and room tariff promise a quantum leap above Sunauli's typical dives, this hotel's rather gloomy and grubby rooms are really only a marginal step up.

BHAIRAWA

Hotel Nirvana   HOTEL $$

(☎4225370; www.nirvanathehotel.com; Paklihawa Rd; s/d incl breakfast US$50/55; ❄@🌐) This is easily the best hotel in town boasting three-star amenities, deep mattresses, a multicuisine restaurant and professional staff. There's also free airport pick-up, a bar and (best of all) a quiet location, so sleep on those wonderful beds is guaranteed. Car travel to/from Lumbini can be arranged. Ask for a discount.

Hotel Glasgow   HOTEL $$

(☎523737; hotelglasgow@gmail.com; Bank Rd; s/d Rs 1000/1100, with air-con Rs 1400/1600; ❄) The best-value place in the centre of town, Hotel Glasgow has comfortable if variable-sized rooms, piping-hot showers, attentive staff and a decent restaurant. It suffers less from road noise than the similar Hotel Yeti.

THE TERAI & MAHABHARAT RANGE SUNAULI & BHAIRAWA

Hotel Yeti
HOTEL $$

(☎520551; hotelyeti@ntc.com; cnr Bank Rd & Siddhartha Hwy; r US$35, with air-con US$40-60; ❄) Yeti has a range of rooms, though the best are usually reserved for the tour groups. Independent travellers may get stuck in rooms with a broken air-conditioner, dodgy plumbing or no hot water. Check all these before deciding on a room and do ask for a discount. Unfortunately, all rooms face the noisy road.

✗ Eating

All the hotels have restaurants serving Nepali, Indian, Chinese and continental dishes. In Sunauli there are small restaurants near the bus station.

Pizza King
INTERNATIONAL $

(mains Rs 95-170) One of the better options in Bhairawa – with a garden of low tables, cushions and atmospheric lighting – it looks better at night than in the glare of daylight. The food is inexpensive and, along with the pizzas, the momos, spring rolls and garlic chicken are recommended.

❶ Information

The government of Nepal runs a small **tourist information office** (☎520304; ⊙10am-5pm Sun-Fri) on the Nepal side of the border. Bhairawa has several banks but it's usually easier to change money at the border. The ATM in Sunauli, beside the Hotel Aakash, accepts only Visa credit cards, while Nabil Bank and Standard Chartered Bank in Bhairawa have ATMs that accept foreign cards. There are net cafes along the strip in Sunauli and around the junction of Bank Rd and New Rd in Bhairawa, charging Rs 25 per hour.

❶ Getting There & Away

Air

Buddha Air (☎526893), **Yeti Airlines** (☎527527) and **Guna Airlines** (☎524260) offer daily flights between Kathmandu and Bhairawa (US$116, 35 minutes). Bhairawa airport is about 1km west of town. A taxi to/from Bhairawa/Sunauli costs Rs 400/500. Airline offices and agents are found around the junction of Bank Rd and Siddhartha Hwy, Bhairawa, near Hotel Yeti.

Bus

Buses for Kathmandu and Pokhara leave from both Sunauli and Bhairawa. From Sunauli, Kathmandu buses (Rs 550, eight hours) leave around 7am. Buses to Pokhara (Rs 550, eight hours) leave at 7am and 8am. After these times and for all other destinations, you will need to head to Bhairawa. Be suspicious of travel agents in India or Nepal who claim to offer 'through tickets' between the two countries: everyone has to change buses at the border.

The most comfortable option is the **Golden Travels** (☎520194) air-con bus to Kathmandu (Rs 1000, six to seven hours); it leaves Kathmandu's Kalanki junction by the southeastern ring road at 7.30am and Sunauli at 7am. Services run daily in conjunction with the Baba Bhairav Travels and Buddha Darshan travel companies.

CROSSING THE BORDER: BELAHIYA TO SUNAULI

Border Hours

The immigration offices on both sides of the border are open 24 hours, but the Indian border post is closed to vehicles from 10pm to 6am. After 7pm and before 7am, you may need to go searching for the immigration officials on either side.

Foreign Exchange

There are no moneychangers on the Indian side of Sunauli. Several moneychangers on the Nepali side of the border exchange Nepali and Indian rupees, as well as cash and travellers cheques in US dollars, UK pounds and euros. Shops and hotels on both sides of the border accept Indian and Nepali rupees at a fixed rate of 1.6 Nepali rupees to one Indian rupee.

Onward to India

All travellers bound for India must change buses at the border. From the bus station on the Indian side of the border, there are direct buses to Varanasi (₹208, 10 hours) leaving in the morning (4.30am to 10.30am) and evening (4.30pm to 7pm). There are also buses to Gorakhpur (₹67, three hours, until 7pm), where you can connect with the Indian broad-gauge railway.

From the bus stand in Bhairawa, there are regular buses to Kathmandu (Rs 467, eight hours) via Narayangarh (Rs 230, three hours). For Pokhara, there are buses (Rs 367, nine hours) via Tansen (Rs 120, five hours) along the Siddhartha Hwy, as well as via the Mugling Hwy (Rs 450, eight hours). Microbuses to Pokhara/Kathmandu cost roughly the same and are marginally faster.

Also from Bhaiwara there are services to Nepalganj (Rs 450, seven hours), and buses leaving every 15 minutes to Butwal (Rs 40, 45 minutes), from where you can connect with many more services heading west. Heading east from Bhairawa, there are buses to Janakpur (Rs 570, eight hours) leaving at 6.10am and 4.30pm, and to Kakarbhitta (Rs 990, 12 hours). Buses heading for Gorkha (Rs 350, six hours) leave early in the morning: it's best to ask locally for the current departure times.

Local buses for Lumbini (Rs 45, one hour) and Taulihawa (Rs 65, three hours) leave from the junction of the Siddhartha Hwy and the road to Lumbini, about 1km north of Bank Rd.

ℹ️ Getting Around

Crowded share jeeps and local buses shuttle between the border and Bhairawa for Rs 10. A rickshaw will cost at least Rs 100.

Lumbini

♪ 071

It was in Lumbini, around the year 563 BC, that one of history's greatest and most revered figures, Siddhartha Gautama – better known as the Buddha – was born. It's no great surprise to learn that the World Heritage–listed Lumbini is of huge religious significance and attracts Buddhist pilgrims from around the world.

Located 22km west of Bhairawa, the spiritual heart of Lumbini is Maya Devi Temple, which marks the spot where Queen Maya Devi gave birth to Siddhartha Gautama. In the adjoining sacred garden you'll find the pillar of Ashoka, ancient ruins of stupas, and maroon- and saffron-robed monks congre-

THE TERAI & MAHABHARAT RANGE LUMBINI

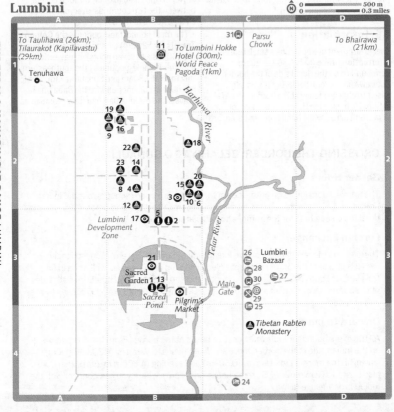

Lumbini

gating under a sprawling Bodhi (pipal) fig decorated with prayer flags.

Maya Devi Temple is set in the middle of the large 4km by 2.5km park grounds known as the Lumbini Development Zone. Designed by Japanese architect Kenzo Tange in 1978, it's a work in progress that comprises landscaped lakes and numerous monasteries that have been constructed by Buddhist communities from around the world.

Most people rush through Lumbini, allowing only a few hours to look around. However, you could easily spend one or two days exploring the zone and its monasteries, and soaking up the peaceful atmosphere.

History

After many years of work at Lumbini, archaeologists are now fairly certain that Siddhartha Gautama, the historical Buddha, was indeed born here. A huge complex of monasteries and stupas was erected on the site by his followers, and the Indian emperor Ashoka made a pilgrimage here in 249 BC, erecting one of his famous pillars.

Shortly after this, an unknown cataclysm affected Lumbini. When the Chinese pilgrim Fa Hsien (Fa Xian) visited in AD 403, he found the monasteries abandoned and the city of Kapilavastu in ruins. Two hundred years later, Hsuan Tang (Xuan Zang), another Chinese pilgrim, described 1000 derelict monasteries and Ashoka's pillar shattered by lightning and lying on the ground.

However, the site was not entirely forgotten. The Nepali king Ripu Malla made a pilgrimage here in 1312, possibly leaving the nativity statue that is still worshipped in the Maya Devi Temple.

Mughal invaders arrived in the region at the end of the 14th century and destroyed the remaining 'pagan' monuments at both Kapilavastu and Lumbini. The whole region then returned to wilderness and the sites were lost to humanity, until the governor of Palpa, Khadga Shumsher Rana, began the excavation of Ashoka's pillar in late 1896.

◉ Sights

Maya Devi Temple   BUDDHIST TEMPLE
(foreigner/SAARC Rs 200/100; ⊙6am-6pm) This temple sits on the site of the birth of the Buddha, according to Buddhist scholars. You will need to buy your entrance ticket 50m north of the gate to the Sacred Garden.

THE TERAI & MAHABHARAT RANGE LUMBINI

At the gate you need to remove your shoes. (A spare pair of socks may be a useful item as there is a fair bit of walking round the garden to see everything and the paving is incomplete.)

Excavations carried out in 1992 revealed a succession of ruins dating back at least 2200 years, including a commemorative stone on a brick plinth, matching the description of a stone laid down by Emperor Ashoka in the 3rd century BC. There are plans to raise a grand monument on the site, but for now a sturdy brick pavilion protects the temple ruins.

You can walk around the ruins on a raised boardwalk. The focal point for pilgrims is a sandstone carving of the birth of the Buddha, reputedly left here by the Malla king, Ripu Malla, in the 14th century, when Maya Devi was worshipped as an incarnation of the Hindu mother goddess. The carving has been worn almost flat by centuries of veneration, but you can just discern the shape of Maya Devi grasping a tree branch and giving birth to the Buddha, with Indra and Brahma looking on. Directly beneath this is a marker stone encased within bulletproof glass, which pinpoints the spot where the Buddha was born.

The **sacred pond** beside the temple is believed to be where Maya Devi bathed before giving birth to the Buddha. Dotted around the grounds are the ruined foundations of a number of brick stupas and monasteries dating from the 2nd century BC to the 9th century AD.

Ashokan Pillar
MONUMENT

The Indian emperor Ashoka visited Lumbini in 249 BC, leaving behind an inscribed sandstone pillar to commemorate the occasion. After being lost for centuries, Ashoka's pillar was rediscovered by the governor of Palpa, Khadga Shumsher Rana, in 1896. The 6m-high pink sandstone pillar has now been returned to its original site in front of the Maya Devi Temple.

Lumbini Museum
MUSEUM

(☑580318; foreigner/SAARC Rs 70/20; ⊙10am-4pm Wed-Mon) Tucked away at the northern end of the compound, this museum is devoted to the life of the Buddha, with artefacts and photos from Buddhist sites around the world.

World Peace Pagoda
BUDDHIST TEMPLE

(☉daylight) Located outside the main compound, but easily accessible by bike, the impressive gleaming white World Peace Pagoda was constructed by Japanese Buddhists at a cost of US$1 million. The shining golden statue depicts the Buddha in the posture he assumed when he was born. Near the base of the stupa is the grave of a Japanese monk murdered by anti-Buddhist extremists during the construction of the monument.

Lumbini Crane Sanctuary
WILDLIFE RESERVE

The wetlands surrounding the World Peace Pagoda are protected as a crane sanctuary and you stand a good chance of seeing rare sarus cranes stalking through the fields. There's no formal entrance to the sanctuary and no admission fee – just stroll into the damp meadows behind the pagoda.

BUDDHIST MONASTERIES

Since the Lumbini Development Zone was founded in 1978, Buddhist nations from around the world have been constructing extravagant monasteries in a dedicated monastic zone. Separated by a long canal, the monastic zone is divided into Mahayana and Theravada sects. Each reflects the unique interpretation of Buddhism of its home nation and together the monasteries create a fascinating map of world Buddhist philosophy.

The site is spread out, so hire a bicycle in Lumbini Bazaar or rent a rickshaw. Unless otherwise stated, all the monasteries are open daily during daylight hours.

West Monastic Zone

The West Monastic Zone is set aside for monasteries from the Mahayana school, which is distinguished by monks in maroon robes and a more clamorous style of prayer involving blowing horns and clashing cymbals.

Panditarama International Vipassana Meditation Centre
MEDITATION

(☑580118; www.panditarama-lumbini.info) Starting at the **Eternal Flame** (just north of the Maya Devi Temple), follow the dirt road along the west bank of the pond to this meditation centre where practitioners can study for a nominal donation.

Drubgyud Chöling Gompa
MONASTERY

Heading north, a track turns west to this classic Tibetan-style gompa built in 2001 by Buddhists from Singapore and Nepal. The mural work inside is quite refined and a gigantic stupa is under construction next door.

Manang Samaj Stupa   BUDDHIST TEMPLE
A small track veers south to this grand yet tasteful chörten (Tibetan reliquary stupa) constructed by Buddhists from Manang in northern Nepal.

**Zhong Hua Chinese
Buddhist Monastery**   MONASTERY
Further west is this elegant monastery, one of the most impressive structures at Lumbini. Reached through a gateway flanked by Confucian deities, this elegant pagoda-style monastery looks like something from the Forbidden City.

Korean Buddhist Temple   BUDDHIST TEMPLE
Not to be outdone, the government of South Korea is (slowly) building a massive temple on the other side of the road.

**Vietnam Phat Quoc
Tu Temple**   BUDDHIST TEMPLE
Just north of the Chinese temple is this charming pagoda-style temple featuring beautiful landscaping and a dragon-decorated roof.

**Mother Temple of the Graduated
Path to Enlightenment**   BUDDHIST TEMPLE
The Austrian Geden International Foundation constructed this complex of stupas and monastery buildings, the latter in classical Greek style. Nearby new monasteries are also planned by the governments of Mongolia and Bhutan.

**Great Drigung Kagyud
Lotus Stupa**   BUDDHIST TEMPLE
(☺8am-noon & 1-5pm) Further north is a second group of Mahayana monasteries, set around an L-shaped pond. This truly extravagant stupa is one of the most beautiful buildings here and was constructed by the German Tara Foundation. The domed ceiling of the main prayer room is covered in Buddhist murals.

Nepal Temple   BUDDHIST TEMPLE
Across from the German monastery is this domed-roof temple that was still being constructed at the time of research.

Sokyo Gompa   MONASTERY
West of the Great Drigung Kagyud Lotus Stupa is this traditional Tibetan-style gompa built by the Japanese Sokyo Foundation.

Linh Son Monastery   MONASTERY
This new monastery constructed by French World Linh Son Buddhists is south of the Great Drigung Kagyud Lotus Stupa and is nearing completion.

East Monastic Zone
The East Monastic Zone is set aside for monasteries from the Theravada school, which is common throughout southeast Asia and Sri Lanka, and recognisable by the monks' saffron-coloured robes.

Royal Thai Buddhist Monastery   MONASTERY
(☺8am-noon & 1-5pm) Close to the north end of the pond, this stunning and imposing *wat* (Thai-style monastery) is built from gleaming white marble.

Myanmar Golden Temple   BUDDHIST TEMPLE
A short cycle ride south reveals one of the oldest structures in the compound. There are three prayer halls in the Myanmar Golden Temple – the most impressive is topped by a corncob-shaped shikhara (tower), styled after the temples of Bagan. Nearby is the **Lokamani Pula Pagoda**, a huge gilded stupa in the southern Burmese style, inspired by the Shwedagon Paya in Yangon.

Gautami Nun's Temple   BUDDHIST TEMPLE
South of Lokamani Pula Pagoda is this modest monastery, the only monastery in the compound built for female devotees.

Sri Lankan Monastery   MONASTERY
Further east, a track leads to the impressive Sri Lankan monastery that's very slowly being built.

Dhama Janami Vipassana Centre   MEDITATION
Towards the canal is this small meditation centre, where followers of the Theravada school can practise. A short walk south from here takes you back to the Eternal Flame, passing a huge **ceremonial bell** inscribed with Tibetan characters.

☞ Tours
Hiring a guide to explain the various sights within the Development Zone is a good way to learn about the Buddhist sites in Lumbini. Otherwise, many hotels and travel agents rent out bicycles for Rs 120 per day.

**Holiday Pilgrims Care
Tour & Travels**   GUIDED TOUR
(☑580432) Attached to Lumbini Village Lodge, this company arranges tours that really get under the surface of life in the Terai. Guides are available for Rs 500 per day, and they provide a free map so you can make your own way around by bike.

✪ Festivals & Events

Buddha Jayanti
BUDDHIST

The most important Buddhist celebration in Lumbini is this annual festival held in April or May, when busloads of Buddhists from India and Nepal come here to celebrate the birth of the Buddha. Pilgrims also come here to worship each **purnima** (the night of the full moon) and **astami** (the eighth night after the full moon).

Rupa Devi
HINDU

Many Hindus regard the Buddha as an incarnation of Vishnu and thousands of Hindu pilgrims come here on the full moon of the Nepali month of Baisakh (April–May) to worship Maya Devi as Rupa Devi, the mother goddess of Lumbini.

🛏 Sleeping & Eating

Most of the budget options are in Lumbini Bazaar (also known as Buddhanagar), the small village opposite the eastern entrance to the Lumbini Development Zone. The upmarket hotels are either in the Development Zone north of the Bhairawa–Taulihawa Rd or on the periphery road around the eastern side of the Development Zone. Most people eat in their hotels.

⭐ TOP CHOICE Lumbini Village Lodge
HOTEL $

(✆580432; lumbinivillagelodge@yahoo.com; dm Rs 150, s Rs 350-450, d Rs 350-750; 🛜) This charming and welcoming budget lodge has a cool central courtyard shaded by a mango tree and big, spotless rooms with fans and insect-screened windows. It's all kept bright with a fresh paint job every year. There's a peaceful rooftop setting and views looking over mustard fields. The owners run tours of the surrounding villages.

Buddha Maya Garden Hotel
HOTEL $$

(✆580220, in Kathmandu 01-4434705; www.ktmgh.com/buddha; s/d US$25/30, deluxe US$70/80; ❄🛜) Set in large grounds about 500m southeast of the site, this friendly resort offers what is possibly the best-value accommodation in Lumbini with very comfortable rooms in a tranquil village setting. There's an excellent restaurant, bicycles for hire and staff who are keen to help. Ask about discounts.

Hotel Peace Land
HOTEL $$

(✆580286; info@hotelpeaceland.com; s/d US$25/30, with air-con US$35/50; 🛜) This sparkling new hotel represents a business expansion for successful local restaurateurs. At the time we visited it was devoid of any decoration but the rooms were cool and inviting. However, the rack rate seems overly optimistic, especially considering the discount offered to locals, so do ask for a discount. The restaurant (mains Rs 180 to 320) here is the best in town.

Sunflower Travellers Lodge
HOTEL $$

(✆580338; sunflower2099py@gmail.com; r Rs1800; ❄🛜) On the eastern periphery road, this bright guesthouse has cheerful rooms and efficient Chinese management. Rooms are spotless with tubs and plenty of hot water, but there are no TVs. There's a small upstairs restaurant and a downstairs souvenir shop. The owners also run a bus service to/from Kathmandu.

Lumbini Garden Lodge
HOTEL $

(✆580146; r Rs 400-500) The other budget options in Lumbini Bazaar are nowhere near as switched on for travellers as abovementioned Lumbini Village Lodge, but if it is full then friendly, family-run Lumbini Garden Lodge has decent rooms, some with attached bath.

Hotel Lumbini Garden New Crystal
HOTEL $$$

(✆580145; www.newcrystalhotels.com; s/d incl breakfast US$80/90; ❄@) Aimed at well-heeled pilgrims, usually in tour groups, this is a comfortable three-star hotel with all the amenities, a multicuisine restaurant and plenty of religious paraphernalia available in the lobby. There are 72 mostly Western-style rooms, plus a handful of Japanese-style.

Lumbini Hokke Hotel
HOTEL $$$

(✆580136; www.theroyalresidency.net/lumbini/index.htm; s/d US$93/96; ❄) Built with real style, the Hokke looks a bit like a traditional Japanese village; rooms are Western-style (seven rooms) or Japanese-style (20 rooms), with tatami floors, paper partitions and Japanese furniture. The restaurant serves top-notch Japanese set meals as well as other cuisines. To top it off there are traditional Japanese bathhouses.

Fusian Garden
INTERNATIONAL $

(mains Rs 130-350) This is a popular little restaurant run by a bunch of keen youngsters. Ambition may still not be matched by the execution, but we think they will learn fast. The breakfasts, pancakes and *thalis* here are recommended.

THE BIRTH OF THE BUDDHA

The historical Buddha, Siddhartha Gautama, was the son of Suddhodana, ruler of Kapilavastu, and Maya Devi, a princess from the neighbouring kingdom of Devdaha. According to legend, the pregnant Maya Devi was travelling between the two states when she came upon a tranquil pond surrounded by flowering sal trees. After bathing in the cool water, she suddenly went into labour, and just had enough time to walk 25 steps and grab the branch of a Bodhi tree for support before the baby was born. The year was around 563 BC and the location has been positively identified as Lumbini.

After the birth, a seer predicted that the boy would become a great teacher or a great king. Eager to ensure the latter, King Suddhodana shielded him from all knowledge of the world outside the palace. At the age of 29, Siddhartha left the city for the first time and came face to face with an old man, a sick man, a hermit and a corpse. Shocked by this sudden exposure to human suffering, the prince abandoned his luxurious life to become a mendicant holy man, fasting and meditating on the nature of existence. After some severe austerities, the former prince realised that life as a starving pauper was no more conducive to wisdom than life as a pampered prince. Thus was born the 'Middle Way'.

Finally, after 49 days meditating under a Bodhi tree on the site of modern-day Bodhgaya in India, Siddhartha attained enlightenment – a fundamental grasp of the nature of human existence. He travelled to Sarnath, near Varanasi, to preach his first sermon and Buddhism was born. Renamed Buddha ('the enlightened one'), Siddhartha spent the next 46 years teaching the Middle Way – a path of moderation and self-knowledge through which human beings could escape the cycle of birth and rebirth and achieve nirvana, a state of eternal bliss.

The Buddha died at the age of 80 at Kushinagar, near Gorakhpur in India. Despite his rejection of divinity and materialism, all the sites associated with the Buddha's life have become centres for pilgrimage and he is worshipped as a deity across the Buddhist world.

The ruins of Kapilavastu were unearthed close to Lumbini at Tilaurakot, and devotees still cross continents to visit Bodhgaya, Sarnath and Kushinagar in India. More recently, the site of Devdaha, the home of Maya Devi, was identified on the outskirts of the Nepali town of Butwal.

❶ Information

There's a **tourist information centre** (⊙6pm-6pm) at the ticket office that displays the master plan of the complex. There are four ATMs in Lumbini Bazaar, with the Everest Bank being the most reliable for foreign cards at the time of research. For cash moneychangers, try your hotel. For internet connection **64 Cyber-Zone** (per hr Rs 60; ⊙8am-8pm) in Lumbini Bazaar has a minimum charge of Rs 20 for 15 minutes.

❶ Getting There & Away

Local buses run regularly between Lumbini and the local bus stand in Bhairawa (Rs 45, one hour). Taxis from Lumbini Bazaar charge Rs 900 to the main Bhairawa bus stand and Rs 1000 to the border at Sunauli (Belahiya). Lumbini Village Lodge helps arrange share taxis so a group of travellers can share the cost.

To reach Taulihawa from Lumbini, take a local bus to the junction with the Bhairawa road (Rs 10) and change to a bus bound for Taulihawa (Rs 110, 1½ hours).

A public bus bound for Kathmandu (Rs 500, nine to 10 hours) departs Lumbini Bazaar at 7am. Sakura Travels runs a tourist bus to Kathmandu's Kakani bus stand (Rs 900, nine hours); buy tickets at any travel agency.

❶ Getting Around

The best way to get around the compound is by bicycle – Lumbini Village Lodge in Lumbini Bazaar charges Rs 120 per day for reliable Hero-brand bikes.

Hiring a rickshaw is a good alternative. Loads of rickshaw-wallahs loiter near the entrance to the Development Zone, charging around Rs 150 per hour.

Around Lumbini

TILAURAKOT

About 29km west of Lumbini, Tilaurakot has been identified as the historical site of **Kapilavastu**, where Siddhartha Gautama spent the first 29 years of his life. The site sits in a peaceful meadow on the banks of the Banganga River. Although you can still see the foundations of a large residential compound, it takes a certain amount of imagination to visualise the city of extravagant luxury that drove the Buddha to question the nature of existence. The showy shrine nearby with several carved pachyderms is dedicated to Maya Devi.

There's a small **museum** (☑076-560128; admission Rs 20; ☉10am-4pm Wed-Mon) at the final turn-off to Tilaurakot that displays some of the artefacts found at the site.

To get here from Lumbini, catch a local bus from the Lumbini Bus Stand to the junction (Rs 10, 10 minutes) and change to a bus bound for Tilaurakot (Rs 55, 1½ hours), 3km north of Taulihawa. You can take a rickshaw to the site from Tilaurakot for Rs 100/175 one way/return. The best way to get here, though, is through Lumbini Village Lodge (see p240), which can organise a van for Rs 500 with a day's notice. Otherwise a taxi can make the return trip from Lumbini for around Rs 2000.

The Siddhartha Highway

Most travellers heading from Sunauli to Pokhara follow the Mahendra Hwy to Narayangarh, then the Prithvi Hwy from Mugling to Pokhara. A more interesting route is the dramatic Siddhartha Hwy, which weaves its way north through the dramatic Tinau Gorge towards Pokhara via the scenic mountain village of Tansen. It's a spectacular mountain road clinging to near-vertical canyon walls with views of peaks, valleys and spectacular waterfalls.

Buses run regularly on this route, and it is also regarded as one of the finest motorcycle journeys in Nepal. Landslides often block the highway during the monsoon.

BUTWAL
☑071

Flat, dry and dusty, Butwal has all the hallmarks of a typical Terai town, its bustling streets dominated by bell-ringing rickshaws. Sitting on an ancient trade route from the Indian plains towards the Himalaya, Butwal remains an important trade and transport hub at the crossroads of the north–south Siddhartha Hwy and east–west Mahendra Hwy. Nevertheless, Butwal offers no sights of interest for visitors, and hence most people choose to pass right through.

Archaeologists have recently identified a village 15km east of Butwal as the site of the kingdom of **Devdaha**, home to Maya Devi. There's a small memorial park on the site, signposted off the Mahendra Hwy towards Narayangarh.

🛏 Sleeping & Eating

Hotel Kandara
HOTEL $

(☑540175; Traffic Chowk; s/d Rs 600/800, s with air-con Rs 1500, d with air-con Rs 1700-2000; ✱) Situated on the busy highway near Traffic Chowk, Kandara is a reasonable budget choice where you can take your pick between simple rooms with attached bathrooms and deluxe rooms with bathtubs and air-con. There's a decent tandoori restaurant and off-street parking.

Hotel Greenland
HOTEL $$

(☑543411; hotelgreenland@hotmail; BP Chowk; s/d Rs 1000/1400) Greenland is a comfortable though dour place in need of natural light and some sparkle. Indeed work on a skylight had commenced when we visited. It's well removed from the madness of Traffic Chowk and relatively peaceful. It also has a quality restaurant and bar sporting mutant orange couches. Find it two blocks west of Traffic Chowk, then north for 100m.

Nanglo West
NEPALI $

(☑544455; Siddhartha Hwy; mains Rs 115-275; ☉10.30am-8.30pm) This branch of the successful chain is a bit of a poor relative and doesn't leave the same impression as the other Nanglo West. The menu features Newari dishes and there's pleasant garden seating, but if you're after a decent coffee after the drive through Tinau Gorge you may be disappointed. It's on the highway where it emerges from the hills, about 1km north of Traffic Chowk.

ℹ Information

Numerous internet centres near Traffic Chowk offer internet access for Rs 15 per hour. There are several ATMs around Traffic Chowk; the one opposite Hotel Royal takes international cards.

ℹ Getting There & Away

All long-distance buses leave from the main bus park just south of Traffic Chowk. There are buses every half-hour or so to Kathmandu (Rs 430, seven hours) and Pokhara (Rs 420, eight hours) via Mugling and the Prithvi Hwy. There are also several daily buses on the scenic route to Pokhara (Rs 360, six hours) via Tansen (Rs 95, 2½ hours). Local buses leave for Sunauli/Bhairawa (Rs 40, 45 minutes) every 10 minutes.

Along the Mahendra Hwy, there are regular buses east to Narayangarh (Rs 200, three hours), and west to Dhangadhi (Rs 645, 10 hours) and Mahendranagar (Rs 675, 12 hours) for connections to Nepalganj (get off at Kohalpur) and Bardia National Park (alight at Ambassa – blink and you'll miss it).

TANSEN (PALPA)
🎵 075 / ELEV 1372M

Tansen, 119km south of Pokhara, is far enough off the radar to make it a rewarding detour for independent travellers. Perched high above the Kali Gandaki River on the road between Butwal and Pokhara, Tansen's main attraction is both its Newari charm and distinct medieval feel. Lining Tansen's steep cobblestone streets, which are too steep for cars, are wooden Newari houses with intricately carved windows, from where the clacking of looms can be heard. On winter mornings a blanket of mist is cast over the bowl-shaped Madi Valley, earning it the moniker 'White Lake'.

Chatting to locals, you'll find they're fiercely proud of their home town, which no doubt stems from its rich history during the glory years as the capital of the Magar kingdom of Tanahun. Until the rise of the Shahs, Tanahun was one of the most powerful kingdoms in Nepal. Troops from Palpa even came close to conquering Kathmandu in the 16th century under the leadership of King Mukunda Sen. The power of the Magars waned in the 18th century and Tansen was reinvented as a Newari trading post on the trade route between India and Tibet.

Today Tansen remains the administrative headquarters of Palpa district, and many Nepalis still refer to the town as Palpa.

⊙ Sights

Sitalpati PLAZA

The main square in Tansen is dominated by (and named after) a curious octagonal pavilion, used for public functions in the days when Tansen was ruled by the governors of the Shah regime. Today it's a popular meeting spot for locals to have a chat. At the northwest corner of the square, the small, two-tiered **Bhimsen Mandir** is sacred to the Newari god of trade and commerce. Several shops on the square, and along nearby Bank Rd, sell dhaka, the fabric used for traditional Nepali jackets and *topis* (cloth hats). West of the square, **Karuwa Factory** (admission free) can make for an interesting visit to see Tansen's famed brass jugs being made.

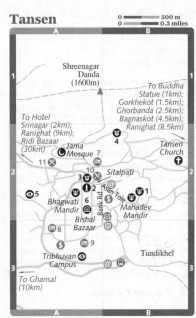

Tansen

Tansen Durbar PALACE

At the southern end of Sitalpati is the striking Tansen Durbar, which is still being restored after being razed during one of the Maoist insurgency's most violent battles. The original building was built for the provincial governor in 1927. A fan of pomp and circumstance, the governor used to ride out to greet his subjects on an elephant through the grand gateway known as **Baggi Dhoka** (or Mul Dhoka), on the south end of Sitlpati.

THE TERAI & MAHABHARAT RANGE THE SIDDHARTHA HIGHWAY

In more recent times it served as district administration headquarters, which explains why the Maoists targeted it. The reconstruction plans include a museum featuring local culture and history.

Amar Narayan Mandir
HINDU TEMPLE

At the bottom of Asan Tole (the steep road running east from Sitalpati), the Amar Narayan Mandir is a classic three-tiered, pagoda-style wooden temple. The mandir was built in 1807 by Amar Singh Thapa, the first governor of Tansen, and it's considered to be one of the most beautiful temples outside Kathmandu Valley. The carved wooden deities are exquisite; note the erotic scenes on the roof struts and the alternating skulls and animal heads on the lintel. Devotees come here every evening to light butter lamps in honour of the patron deity, Lord Vishnu. At the start of the steps to the Amar Narayan Temple is the similar but smaller **Mahadev Mandir**, sacred to Shiva.

Sleeping & Eating

City View Homestay
HOMESTAY $

(9847028885; r Rs 400) Easily the best option in town is to stay in the spotless simple rooms within the home of Man Mohan Shrestha, the energetic man behind the volunteer tourist information service known as GETUP. From the roof there are indeed great views of the city and beyond. If Mohan's rooms are full, he can find similar nearby homestays for that perfect home stay.

Hotel the White Lake
HOTEL $$

(520291; Silkhan Tole; s/d S$12/15, r without bathroom Rs 600, deluxe s/d US$25/30) The sprawling White Lake has a variety of rooms – the standard ones are pretty ordinary and overpriced but the new wing boasts more comfortable deluxe rooms. Balcony views of the 'white lake' can be vertigo inducing.

Hotel Srinagar
HOTEL $$

(520045; www.hotelsrinagar.com; s/d US$30/40; *) The most upmarket option is about 2km away on the ridge above town, a 20-minute walk west of the summit of Shreenagar Danda. Although rather isolated, the views are sensational. Rooms are comfortable but looking a little tired. Do check the plumbing before settling on a room.

Hotel Gauri Shankar Guest House HOTEL $

(9847043540; Silkhan Tole; s/d Rs 800/1200, r without bathroom Rs 400) This budget hotel is a just bearable cheapie with adequately clean rooms with TVs and Western toilets. Go for rooms on the 2nd level away from the noisy street.

Nanglo West
NEPALI $

(520184; mains Rs 80-260; 10.30am-8.30pm) You can't go without sampling the Nepali delights at this veritable oasis in the centre of Tansen. This Kathmandu chain is a class act, serving local Newari dishes like *choyla* (dried buffalo or duck meat with chilli and ginger), served with *chiura* (flattened rice) and spiced potatoes in curd. There's also a bakery out the front.

Royal Inn
NEPALI $

(522780; mains Rs 190-300; 10am-9pm;) Housed in a delightfully restored Newari house (duck your head through the doorways!) is this delightful, atmospheric venture started by young enterprising locals. In addition to the recommended Nepali *thali*, there are pizzas, *thukpa* (Tibetan noodle soup) and superb momos.

Information

Your first port of call should be **GETUP** (Group for Environmental & Tourism Upgrading Palpa; 520563, 9847028885; shrestha.manmohan@gmail.com; 9am-5pm Sun-Fri), probably the most helpful tourist information centre in the country. Led by the irrepressible Man Mohan, this NGO was set up to promote Tansen as a tourist destination. Here you can obtain excellent trekking maps (Rs 20) for all the short treks around Tansen, including the classic loop to Ranighat. GETUP can also arrange guided trips to metalwork and fabric workshops as well as organic coffee plantations.

Himalayan Bank, near Hotel the White Lake, has an ATM accepting foreign cards. For foreign exchange there are moneychangers and several banks on Bank Rd, including **Nepal Bank Limited** (10am-3pm Sun-Fri).

There are several internet cafes including **Computer Concern** (per hr Rs 30; 7am-8pm).

Getting There & Away

The bus station is at the bottom of town at the southern entrance to Tansen and the ticket office is at the east end of the stand. Buses to Pokhara (Rs 300, five hours) leave at 6am and 10am; there are also buses/microbuses to Kathmandu (Rs 450/650, 11 hours).

There are regular services south to Butwal (Rs 95, 2½ hours) from 6.30am to 5pm. Local buses for Ridi Bazaar (Rs 90, two hours) leave fairly regularly during the same hours – get an early-morning start if you want to be back the same day.

AROUND TANSEN

As well as the popular walks around Tansen, there are a few other interesting places that you can reach on foot or by bus.

RANIGHAT DURBAR

The most famous sight near Tansen is the eerie Ranighat Durbar on the east bank of the Kali Gandaki. Fancifully referred to as Nepal's Taj Mahal, this crumbling baroque palace was built in 1896 by Khadga Shamsher Rana in memory of his beloved wife, Tej Kumari. Khadga was an ambitious politician who was exiled from Kathmandu for plotting against the prime minister. Khadga followed up with another abortive attempt to seize power in 1921 and was exiled again, this time to India. After his departure, the Durbar was stripped of its valuable fittings, and the building still stands, slowly fading on the banks of the Kali Gandaki.

You can walk to Ranighat in three to four hours (return trip eight hours) along an easy-to-follow trail, beginning in Gorkhekot at the east end of Shreenagar Danda. The route down to the river is mainly downhill, through rice paddies and forest from which the ruined palace materialises. The return leg is fairly tough going, following a steeply ascending trail on the next ridge, emerging near Hotel Srinagar. It's not possible to walk here during the monsoon due to the slippery conditions. There's basic accommodation in Ranighat if you choose to stay the night.

GETUP in Tansen sells a guide and map (Rs 20). Rafting trips on the Kali Gandaki sometimes make it as far as the palace – see p299.

RIDI BAZAAR

About 28km northwest of Tansen by road (or 13km on foot), the Newari village of Ridi Bazaar sits at the sacred confluence of the Kali Gandaki and Ridi Khola rivers. Ridi is a popular destination for pilgrimages, and the site is further sanctified by the presence of saligrams – the fossils of ammonites that are revered as symbols of Vishnu.

The principal religious monument in Ridi is the **Rishikesh Mandir**, which was founded by Mukunda Sen in the 16th century. According to legend, the Vishnu idol inside was discovered fully formed in the river and miraculously aged from boy to man. The temple is on the south bank of the Ridi Khola, near the bus stand.

To reach Ridi on foot, take the trail leading northwest from the Tansen–Tamghas road near Hotel Srinagar. Buses to Ridi (Rs 90, two hours) leave from the public bus stand in Tansen.

WALKS AROUND TANSEN

Tansen is surrounded by excellent walking country. The tourist office GETUP can recommend walks, provide maps and brochures at cost price, and help organise local guides.

One of the nicest short walks is the one-hour stroll up **Shreenagar Danda**, the 1600m-high hill directly north of town. The trail starts near the small **Ganesh Mandir** (temple) above Tansen and climbs steeply through open woodland to the crest of the hill. When you reach the ridge, turn right; a 20-minute stroll will take you to a modern **Buddha statue** and a viewpoint with fabulous views over the gorge of the Kali Gandaki River to the Himalaya.

Another short and easy walk is the two-hour stroll to the **Bhairab Sthan Temple**, 9km west of Tansen. The courtyard in front of the temple contains a gigantic brass trident and inside is a silver mask of Bhairab, allegedly plundered from Kathmandu by Mukunda Sen. The walk follows the road from Tansen to Ridi Bazaar.

If you fancy something more challenging, the three-hour walk to the village of **Ghansal** passes several hilltop viewpoints, emerging on the highway about 3km south of Tansen. The walk is mainly downhill and there are spectacular valley views from Bhut Dada, about halfway along the route.

Other possible destinations for walks include **Ghorbanda**, a potters village northeast of Tansen on the way to Pokhara, and **Bagnaskot**, on the ridge east of **Gorkhekot**, which has a small Devi temple and a wonderfully exposed hilltop viewpoint. You can also follow the old **trade route** from Tansen to Butwal – GETUP has a map (Rs 20) with a detailed description of the trail. All three walks can be completed in a day if you get an early start, or there's simple homestay lodging along the way if you're not in a hurry.

The Tribhuvan Highway

From Birganj, the easiest and quickest route to Kathmandu or Pokhara is along the Mahendra Hwy to Narayangarh and then north to Mugling, but when were the best travel experiences ever easy? It's much more fun to take the winding and dramatic Tribhuvan Hwy, which leaves the Mahendra Hwy at Hetauda, east of Chitwan National Park. Landslides sometimes block the road during the monsoon, but the scenery is breathtaking and you can stop on the way at Daman for some of the best Himalayan views in Nepal. For details of the mountain-bike ride along this route, see p296.

HETAUDA
☑057

The bustling town of Hetauda marks the junction between the flat Mahendra Hwy and the steep, spectacular Tribhuvan Hwy. There isn't any great reason to stop here except to change buses or prepare your bike and legs for the steep climb to Daman. Nabil Bank has an ATM, and there are several internet cafes on the main road near Mahendra Chowk offering internet access for Rs 30 per hour.

🛏 Sleeping & Eating

Motel Avocado & Orchid Resort   HOTEL $
(☑520429; www.orchidresort.com; Tribhuvan Hwy; Nissen hut s/d Rs 350/500, s/d from Rs 600/800, deluxe from Rs 1200/1600; ❄) This welcoming resort, surrounded by rhododendron and avocado trees, is easily the best choice for travellers on all budgets. The budget rooms are in converted Nissen huts and have attached bathrooms, cold showers and bucket hot water, while the 'motel' rooms are well appointed and comfortable. The multicuisine restaurant (mains Rs 180 to 320) deserves a special mention, as do the regular garden BBQs. Decades of passing cyclists and motorcyclists contribute to the journals housed in the restaurant.

ℹ Getting There & Around

The main bus stand is just west of Mahendra Chowk. There are regular morning and afternoon buses to Pokhara (Rs 350/380, six hours) and Kathmandu (day/night Rs 350/380, six hours) via Narayangarh (Rs 110, one hour). You can also pick up services to destinations east and west along the Mahendra Hwy. Local buses and minibuses run regularly to Birganj (Rs 70 to 150, two hours).

Buses along the Tribhuvan Hwy leave from a smaller bus stand, just north of Motel Avocado. There are buses every hour or so to Kathmandu (Rs 350, eight hours) via Daman (Rs 140, four hours) until around 2pm. Microbuses destined for Palung cost Rs 220 to Daman. Rickshaws and autorickshaws can ferry you from town to the bus stand for Rs 50.

There is a more direct route to Kathmandu through Bimphedi and Pharping, but it was a rough, mostly gravel road at the time of writing, and only suitable for 4WDs. The long-term plan is for a tunnel to be built between Bimphedi and Kulekhani and to upgrade the road into the grand-sounding Kathmandu–Hetauda Tunnel Hwy, which is proposed to link Kathmandu and Hetauda via a 50km, one-hour drive. We are not holding our breath!

DAMAN
☑057

Perched 2322m above sea level, with clear views to the north, east and west, Daman boasts what is arguably *the* most spectacular outlook on the Himalaya in the whole of Nepal. There are unimpeded views of the entire range from Dhaulagiri to Mt Everest from the concrete **viewing tower** (foreigner/Nepali Rs 50/20) inside the Daman Mountain Resort.

The **Mountain Botanical Gardens** (⊙10am-5pm) comprise over 78 hectares of forest. February to March is the best time to visit, when the rhododendrons (the national flower of Nepal) are in bloom.

About 1km south of the village, a trail leads west through the forest to the tiny **Shree Rikheshwar Mahadev Mandir**, sacred to Shiva. On the way, you can drop into a gorgeous little **gompa** in a glade of trees draped with thousands of prayer flags. From the highway, it's 1km to the gompa and 1.5km to the temple.

🛏 Sleeping & Eating

There are a couple of rustic guesthouses right on the highway in the middle of the village that have very basic rooms (from Rs 300) and daal bhaat for Rs 60.

Sherpa House Daman   HOTEL $
(☑9845070584; r Rs 300) Opposite the botanical gardens, this authentic country house is the best budget choice. It's a rickety old wooden structure that sits secluded from the rest of the town, and while it's a tad spooky, that's also very much part of its appeal. Note that you'll need a torch to use the outside toilet. Make enquiries at the Sherpa Hillside & Lodge, located 75m to

CROSSING THE BORDER: NEPALGANJ TO JAMUNAHA/ RUPAIDHA BAZAAR

Border Hours

Both sides of the border are open 24 hours, but you may have trouble finding officials in the wee hours. The immigration office is about 1km from the border.

Foreign Exchange

There are several moneychangers on the Nepali side of the border, but they only exchange Indian and Nepali rupees. The Nabil and Standard Chartered banks in Nepalganj may be able to exchange other currencies.

Onward to India

For Rs 100 to 200 you can take a rickshaw from the Nepalganj bus stand to the border at Jamunaha and on to the bus stand in Rupaidha Bazaar. From here, buses and share taxis run regularly to Lucknow (seven hours). The nearest point on the Indian rail network is Nanpara, 17km from the border.

the north, where you can also get a meal of daal bhaat.

Everest Panorama Resort HOTEL $$$
(621482, in Kathmandu 01-4428500; www.everest panoramaresort.net; s/d US$96/120;) Easily the most charming place to stay in Daman, this upmarket mountain resort offers tasteful cottages with sun decks scattered across a sunny hillside facing the Himalaya. All the rooms have heaters, TVs, hot showers and mountain views, while the restaurant (mains Rs 190 to 520) provides the only Western food in Daman. Guided walks, mountain biking and pony treks can be arranged. Reception is a 200m walk from the highway along a winding forest path.

Daman Mountain Resort HOTEL $
(9847175577; www.damanresort.com; r with/ without bathroom Rs 1500/700) This ageing resort of concrete bungalows is a slightly more comfortable option than Sherpa House. It's certainly not the Savoy, but the rooms not suffering from damp are reasonable.

Getting There & Away

There are three daily buses to Kathmandu: a microbus (Rs 220, four hours) leaving at 7.30am, and two buses at 10am and 11am (Rs 180). In addition, there are numerous buses to Palung (Rs 10), from where many buses leave for Kathmandu. There are also microbuses to Hetauda (Rs 220, four hours) leaving at 6.30am and 7.30am, and buses departing at 10.30am, noon and 1pm. Alternatively, this is one of the most spectacular (and gruelling) mountain-bike routes in Nepal (see p296 for details).

WESTERN TERAI

The Mahendra Hwy runs west from Butwal to meet the Indian border at Mahendranagar, passing through one of the least developed parts of Nepal. Few travellers pass through the area, though growing numbers are visiting the spectacular Bardia National Park.

Nepalganj

081

Nepalganj is a gritty border town with a hectic Indian (in particular, Uttar Pradesh) flavour. You'll hear more Hindi spoken than Nepali. As Nepal's second city, Nepalganj is an important transport hub with mountain flights to remote airstrips in northwestern Nepal, a busy border with India, and the closest airport to Bardia National Park.

With its oppressive heat and dust, many see it as a necessary evil on the way to somewhere else, though it is also culturally rich, and home to Nepal's largest Muslim community, as well as having a sizeable expat community of foreign-aid workers.

If you find yourself spending time in Nepalganj, take a stroll through the old **bazaar** where you'll find some attractive silver Tharu jewellery. There are half a dozen small temples strung out along the main road through the bazaar, with the garish **Bageshwari Mandir**, devoted to Kali, probably the most interesting.

Nepalganj is 16km south of the Mahendra Hwy and 6km north of the Indian border. It's about 1km from the Nepali border post

Western Terai

at Jamunaha to the Indian border post at Rupaidha Bazaar – it's walkable, but easier by rickshaw.

🛏 Sleeping & Eating

Traveller's Village   GUESTHOUSE $
(☏550329; travil@wlink.com.np; Surkhet Rd; s/d Rs 800/1000, with air-con Rs 1200/800; ❄@) The hotel of choice for UN and NGO workers, it is located about 2km northeast of Birendra Chowk, almost opposite the UN compound. Traveller's Village is run by a welcoming American lady (Candy) who's lived here for 19 years. Rooms are cosy, modern and spotless, with steaming hot water in the bathrooms. Standard rooms have an air cooler and all rooms have a TV. Reservations are absolutely essential.

Kitchen Hut   HOTEL $$
(☏551231; www.kitchenhut.com.np; Surkhet Rd; s/d incl breakfast Rs 2200/3500; ❄@) The odd name of this new hotel, situated between the bazaar and the airport about 3km northeast of Birendra Chowk, is explained by the fact that this company started as one of Nepalganj's best restaurants. The spacious rooms are cool and tiled, and sport flat-screen TVs. Very good multicuisine dishes are served in the Tripti restaurant. Free pick-up from airport and bus station is on offer.

Hotel Sneha   HOTEL $$
(☏520119; Surkhet Rd; hotel@sneha.wlink.com.np; s/d US$35/45; ❄🛜) This big old-fashioned conference hotel is set in sprawling grounds, about 2km south of Birendra Chowk. The spacious rooms are set around a courtyard of royal palms and boast soft mattresses and modern amenities. The attached casino does nothing to improve the atmosphere, but the patrons usually don't interfere with the hotel guests.

Vinayak Guest House   HOTEL $
(☏522138; Surkhet Rd; r Rs 250-450, s/d Rs 550/600, with air-con Rs 1000/1200; ❄) Vinayak caters to those on a tight budget, and the overall impression is of a drab and damp hotel with basic rooms that are just adequate for travellers stuck for the night.

Candy's Place   INTERNATIONAL $
(☏550329; Surkhet Rd; mains Rs 280-400) Upstairs at Traveller's Village, Candy's Place is an unapologetic American comfort-food oasis in Nepalganj. If you've OD'd on daal bhaat, Candy serves up juicy cheese-and-bacon burgers, oven-roasted chicken with real stuffing, and tenderloin steak that can be washed down with an Australian red wine. For dessert there's banana cake, butterscotch ice cream or Candy's famous lemon meringue pie.

❶ Information

Nabil Bank (⊙10am-4.30pm Sun-Thu, 10am-2.30pm Fri) has foreign-exchange services and a 24-hour ATM.

There are numerous places on Surkhet Rd offering internet access, including **Youth Cyber Point** (per hr Rs 30; ⊙8am-6pm).

❶ Getting There & Away

Air

Nepalganj is the main air hub for western Nepal. There are several daily flights to Kathmandu (US$158, one hour) through **Yeti Airlines**

km of sal forest and grassland, and together with the new 550 sq km Banke National Park (see p348) it protects one of Asia's largest stretches of tiger habitat. That's a lot of habitat, but even though tiger numbers are increasing after their recent demise during the Maoist insurgency, you'll still need exceptionally good luck to see one here.

There are also healthy populations of wild elephants and one-horned rhinos among the 30 species of mammals living here. Bardia also has more than 250 species of birds, including the endangered Bengal florican and sarus crane. Gharial and marsh mugger crocodiles and Gangetic dolphins are occasionally spotted on rafting and canoe trips along the Geruwa River, the eastern channel of the Karnali River

Bardia National Park suffered greatly during the Maoist insurgency. Tourism dried up, lodges were mothballed and the wildlife was hit hard by poaching owing to inadequate protection. The good news is that all this is now being reversed, and while it's a long, arduous journey out here, it's well worth the effort.

(📞526556) and **Buddha Air** (📞525745). **Nepal Airlines** (📞520737) and **Sita Air** (📞692744) has morning flights to Jumla (US$74, 45 minutes), though delays and cancellations are common due to poor weather. Yeti/Tara also offers occasional flights to Dolpo for US$114. Nepal Airlines and Sita Air have flights to Simikot (US$109).

Bus

The bus stand is about 1km northeast of Birendra Chowk. Buses to Kathmandu (Rs 1150, 12 hours) and Pokhara (Rs 850, 12 hours) leave early in the morning or early in the afternoon. Kathmandu buses run via Narayangarh (Rs 950, 10 hours). Buses for Mahendranagar (Rs 360, five hours) leave hourly from 5.30am until 1pm. Buses to Butwal (Rs 430, seven hours) leave hourly.

Local buses to Thakurdwara (for Bardia National Park) leave at 11.20am and 1.30pm (Rs 200, three hours).

❶ Getting Around

Shared tempos (three-wheelers) and *tongas* (horse carriages) run between the bus stand and the border for Rs 20. A cycle-rickshaw costs around Rs 100 to the airport and about the same to Rupaidha Bazaar in India. A taxi to the airport costs Rs 500.

Bardia National Park
📞084

Bardia National Park is the largest national park and wilderness area in the Terai and has excellent wildlife-watching opportunities. Bardia is often described as what Chitwan was like 30 years ago, before being overrun by tourism. The park protects 968 sq

⊙ Sights

Crocodile Breeding Centre & Rhino Centre ZOO
(adult Rs 125; ⊙sunrise-sunset Sun-Fri) There's a small breeding centre for turtles, and marsh mugger and gharial crocodiles in the park headquarters where you can get a close look at these reptiles. And nearby is an enclosure containing Shivaram, a rhino who was injured as a baby in Chitwan. Blind in one

WORTH A TRIP

JUMLA

Hidden away in the foothills of the Sisne Himalaya, the remote village of Jumla (2730m) is the gateway to the wild northwest – the least developed and most inaccessible region of Nepal. Apart from the odd foreign-aid worker, the few visitors to Jumla are here for trekking in the remote Karnali region. Most popular is the nine-day trek to/from Rara National Park with its famous sky-blue lake, the largest in Nepal. You can also trek to Dolpo from here. For details of these treks see Lonely Planet's *Trekking in the Nepal Himalaya*.

WORTH A TRIP

GHODAGHODI TAL

This picturesque grouping of oxbow lakes is renowned for its birdwatching. Located about 40km west of Chisopani, the scene is straight out of an Impressionist painting, with its lotus flowers, water lilies and soft pastel colours. It is home to 142 different species of birds, including the grey-headed fishing eagle. You can organise a jeep and guide for Rs 5000, or catch a bus (Rs 600) from Ambassa.

eye, he wandered free around the park headquarters until he killed a man. If you have your Rs 500 park permit, the admission fee to visit these two animal exhibits is waived.

Tharu Cultural Museum MUSEUM
(adult Rs 50; ⊘noon-3pm Tue-Sat) Also located near the park headquarters is this small museum that explores the customs and rituals of the Tharu people. If you have paid Rs 125 admission to the Crocodile Breeding Centre, the admission fee to the museum is waived. You can also arrange cultural tours of the villages through most hotels; otherwise you can rent a bike and explore by yourself.

Elephant Breeding Centre ZOO
(adult Rs 50; ⊘sunrise-sunset) South of the park headquarters, the Elephant Breeding Centre is worth a visit in the morning and afternoon when the elephants have returned from grazing in the park (10am to 4pm).

🏃 Activities

You'll need to add a further Rs 500 for the cost of the park permit per day for most of the prices quoted here. For some activities there is a minimum group size to achieve these per-person costs.

Elephant Safari

An exciting way to explore the park, and the best way to spot wildlife, is on an **elephant safari** (foreigner/SAARC Rs 1000/400). These are best done early in the morning or late afternoon. Rides on the park elephants should be booked in advance at the park headquarters – your lodge will help you arrange this. If you are on a package it will already be done for you.

Fishing

The Karnali River is famous for *mahaseer,* the giant South Asian river carp that can reach 80kg in weight. Anglers can obtain **fishing permits** (foreigner/SAARC Rs 500/200) at the park headquarters. Due to their endangered status, any fish you catch will need to be released back into the water.

Guided Walks

A great way to spot wildlife in the park, and potentially the most thrilling, is on a **guided walk** (half-/full day Rs 1000/2500, birdwatching 3hr/full day Rs 650/3500). Venturing into the park on foot with your guide, however, is obviously a risk you take into your own hands (see the boxed text, p228).

4WD Safari

Jeep safaris (cost based on minimum 4 passengers half-/full day Rs 3500/4500) can be arranged directly through the lodges. These include the park permit and a guide, as well as lunch on the full-day safari. An alternative half-day trip takes you to see the blackbuck that reside outside the park. A jeep will cost Rs 5000, and can be shared by up to five passengers.

Rafting

The Geruwa River forms the western boundary of the park, and a downstream drift in an **inflatable raft** (cost based on minimum 4 passengers Rs 4500) is a relaxing way of experiencing the picturesque river and park, as well as giving you a chance of spotting a Gangetic dolphin, plus animals and birds along the riverbank. Stopping for lunch, you get to walk around the sandy bank where you can observe the heavy traffic of animal footprints. Crater marks of elephants and rhinos are criss-crossed with perfectly imprinted tiger pug marks and delicate monkey and deer prints. This is not white-water rafting, although there are some gentle dips, and there are opportunities for a brief swim in the river.

🛏 Sleeping & Eating

Most of the lodges are in close vicinity to each other near the village of Thakurdwara, on the border of the park buffer zone, about 13km from the Mahendra Hwy.

 Forest Hideaway LODGE **$$**
(☑402016, in Kathmandu 01-4225973; www.foresthideaway.com; r Rs 1000-1800, without bathroom Rs 500, safari tents Rs 650; @🖘) About 1km

north of the park headquarters, this Tharu-style resort is one of the all-round best choices at Bardia. The mud-walled budget cottages are perfectly comfortable with fans, electricity and insect netting. The safari tents on raised platforms are atmospheric, and the deluxe rooms have gas geysers to boost the hot water. All are set around a pleasant garden with hammocks and outdoor seating. It has expert guides, a good restaurant, bar and moneychanging; pick-up/drop-off transport can be arranged.

Nature's Way Bardia Wildlife Resort
LODGE $$

(☑402008; www.natureswaynepal.com; r Rs 700-1500) With a small biogas plant, large organic garden and solar water heaters, Nature's Way is leading the ecofriendly trend in Bardia. The enormous open-sided communal dining and recreational room is one of the best we've seen. Although the finishing touches were still being applied to the massive suites and comfortable junior suites, these traditionally decorated rooms will definitely raise the bar for safari accommodation.

Bardia Wildlife Resort
LODGE $

(☑402041; wildlifeparadiseresort.com; r Rs 400-800, without bathroom Rs 300) Situated in a peaceful spot along the riverbank, 1.5km south of park headquarters, this basic lodge has a true safari feel. The more expensive cottages have large rooms, though hot water is provided by bucket. There's a campfire

and a lovely garden with flowers and papaya trees.

Bardia Jungle Cottage
LODGE $

(☑402014; www.visitnepal.com/bjc; r Rs 300-1500; ☎) Right opposite the army camp entrance, this low-key, long-standing resort offers a great range of rooms from simple mud-walled singles to cement cottages with tiled bathrooms. Cross a tiny bamboo bridge to the central dining hall to hear stories from the owner, a former park warden.

Jungle Base Camp
LODGE $

(☑402007; junglehukum@gmail.com; r Rs 200-800) The budget rooms at Jungle Base Camp are rustic mud-and-thatch huts with dirt floors and lantern lighting that exude a certain jungle charm. More rupees bring a sturdy mock Tharu cottage with attached bathroom and a private verandah with table and chairs. Showers are cold with hot water arriving in a bucket.

Bardia Adventure Resort
LODGE $

(☑696335, in Kathmandu 01-4413361; www.bardia-adventure.com; r Rs 700-1400, without bathroom Rs 300) With a prime location looking out to the buffer zone, this resort has simple thatched, mud-floor huts ranging up to comfortable carpeted cottages with tiled bathrooms. The highlight here is the resort's own animal watchtower, where you can enjoy a cold beer while keeping your eyes peeled for a leopard lurking on the park's perimeter.

LOCAL KNOWLEDGE

SANTA CHAUDHARI

Santa was born in the village of Gobrella, near Tiger Tops Karnali Lodge, and has lived in Bardia all his life. He has been a wildlife guide in the national park for more than 18 years.

You spend a lot of time in the park. What is the best way to see wildlife? All ways are good. The wildlife may or may not be there. You can venture far into the forest on a 4WD safari, but the elephant can take you into the tall grass – where it is not a safe place to walk. Being on foot is also good.

How about that tiger encounter? You see the photos all over the place – a tigress and her four cubs by a river. It was 2009. I was escorting the photographer and his wife on a jungle walk when the tigress appeared across the river. It was amazing. But then the tigress must have picked up our scent. The roar and the charge will be with me forever. There wasn't a lot of time. She had crossed the river and was directly below us. One more leap was all she needed. I raised my bamboo pole and made as much noise as I could. She backed away and so did we. It could have been so different.

So tigers are the most fearsome animals here? I am most afraid of wild elephants. They are clever and strong, and waving a bamboo pole is not likely to scare an angry elephant.

Tharu Home
LODGE **$**

(☏402035; www.tharuhomeresort.com; r Rs 500-800) With a roaring campfire and youthful owners who've been working as guides since they were 11, this is one of the more social places in town. The Rs 500 rooms have attached bathrooms but a shared hot-water shower. The more expensive rooms have their own hot-water geyser. All rooms boast rather quaint curtains, bed covers and thick rugs.

Tiger Tops Karnali Lodge
LODGE **$$$**

(☏in Kathmandu 01-4361500; www.tigertops.com; packages per person per night US$250) Run by the same team as Tiger Tops in Chitwan, this top-end lodge is set on the southern edge of the buffer zone. Accommodation is in stylish Tharu-style cottages near Thakurdwara. Package rates include meals and all activities (park fees and local transfers are extra).

Tiger Tops Karnali Tented Camp
LUXURY TENTS **$$$**

(☏in Kathmandu 01-4361500; www.tigermountain.com; packages per person per night US$250) Sitting on the banks of the Geruwa River, this safari-style tented camp is the only lodging in Bardia in the park. Tents are spacious and have bamboo-fitted bathrooms. It's located in the northwest of the park, not far from Chisopani, and closes during the monsoon.

❶ Information

Park fees should be paid at the **park headquarters** (☏429719; permits foreigner/SAARC/child under 10yr Rs 500/200/free; ☉sunrise-sunset Sun-Fri) located about 13km south of the Mahendra Hwy in the village of Thakurdwara. The bumpy access road leaves the highway at Ambassa, about 500m before the Amreni army checkpost.

The park headquarters has a small **visitor information centre** (admission free; ☉10am-4pm Sun-Fri), which features informative wildlife displays. However, the best source of such information is through your lodge.

Most of the lodges are close to Thakurdwara, but because of the poor condition of the roads, visitors usually arrange to be transferred to the lodges by 4WD. Note that much of the park is inaccessible from May to September because of high river levels.

Souvenirs and **internet** (per hr Rs 40) are available at the Roadhouse Cafe.

❶ Getting There & Away

If you intend to make your own way to the park, call ahead to make sure your lodge is open and able to arrange a pick-up from Ambassa (Rs 1000 one way). The nearest airport is at Nepalganj (see p248) and your lodge will charge about Rs 5500 to pick you up or drop you off. If you're on a package, ensure this is all included.

To reach Bardia by public transport, buses leave Pokhara (Rs 1050, 14 hours) at 1pm and 1.30pm, and from Kathmandu (also Rs 1050, 14 hours) there are five buses departing between 1pm and 4.30pm. There's also a bus from Kathmandu leaving at midday that includes dinner (Rs 1250, 14 hours). There are two buses leaving from Narayangarh heading to Bardia (Rs 650, nine hours) at midnight and 4pm.

CROSSING THE BORDER: MAHENDRANAGAR TO BANBASSA

Border Hours

The Nepali side of the border is open to tourists 24 hours, but before 5am and after 8.30pm you may need to go searching for immigration officials. The Indian side of the border is open 24 hours, but is only open to vehicles from 6am to 7am, noon to 2pm and 5pm to 6pm.

Foreign Exchange

There's a small bank counter near the Nepali customs post, but it only exchanges Indian and Nepali rupees. In Mahendranagar, Nabil Bank has foreign exchange and an ATM. An autorickshaw into town costs around Rs 80.

Onward to India

From the Indian border post, take a rickshaw to the bus station in Banbassa, where you can pick up long-distance buses to Delhi (₹195, 10 hours). Local buses and shared jeeps serve Almora, Nainital and other towns in Uttaranchal. There's also a slow metre-gauge train to Bareilly, where you can pick up trains to other destinations in India.

For further information, head to shop.lonelyplanet.com to purchase a downloadable PDF of the Delhi chapter from Lonely Planet's *India* guide.

In the other direction buses depart Ambassa for Pokhara at 3pm and 4.30pm. Several buses originating in Mahendranagar and Danghadi bound for Kathmandu pass through Ambassa and your lodge should be able to help you make a connection. The *Capital Express* (Rs 1250) leaves Ambassa at 4pm.

Local buses depart Thakurdwara at 6am and 7am bound for Nepalganj (Rs 170) via Ambassa (Rs 55). Change at Ambassa for buses to Mahendranagar (Rs 300, four hours).

Sukla Phanta Wildlife Reserve

Tucked against the Indian border, **Sukla Phanta Wildlife Reserve** (☎099-521309; foreigner/SAARC per day Rs 500/200) covers 305 sq km of sal forest and *phanta* along the banks of the Bahini River. The terrain is similar to Bardia National Park and the reserve has tigers, rhinos, crocodiles, wild elephants and Nepal's largest population of swamp deer, as well as large numbers of migratory birds.

Visiting Sukla Phanta has always been difficult, and camping is the only way to stay overnight. The few visitors who make it to the park generally come on day trips from Mahendranagar with a hired car and driver (Rs 5000 per jeep). **Elephant rides** (foreigner/SAARC Rs 1000/400) can be booked at the park headquarters, but call ahead to make sure somebody will be around.

The best time to visit is November to January; the main vehicle track within the park is impassable from June to September because of monsoonal flooding.

🛏 Sleeping & Eating

Suklaphanta Nature Guides Association (☎9741060150; www.suklaphantanature.com) runs the **Suklaphanta Wildlife Camp** (2-night & 3-day packages from US$175) located about 500m from the park headquarters. Rates include meals, accommodation, park fees and jeep transfer to/from Mahendranagar. Transfer to/from Dhanghadi Airport and New Delhi can be arranged.

Mahendranagar

☎099

Mahendranagar is the most westerly border crossing into India and offers an interesting back route to Delhi and the hill towns of Uttaranchal. While it's not somewhere you'll want to spend any length of time (ie only until your bus is ready to depart), it's somewhat less chaotic than other India–Nepal border crossings. If you have time here, Mahendranagar provides a useful base to visit Sukla Phanta Wildlife Reserve and surrounding Tharu villages.

Mahendranagar is just south of the Mahendra Hwy, about 5km east of the Indian border. From the Nepali border post at Gaddachauki, it's about 1km to the Indian border post at Banbassa.

🛏 Sleeping & Eating

Hotel Sweet Dream   HOTEL $
(☎522313; Mahendra Hwy; s/d from Rs 600/750, with air-con Rs 1200/1500; ❄) On the highway about 100m east of the bus station, this conveniently located place has reasonable, carpeted rooms (that could do with a clean) as well as a multicuisine restaurant. The interior design is odd, but this is not the town to get choosy.

Hotel New Anand   HOTEL $
(☎521693; r with/without air-con Rs 1200/600; ❄) The anything but new Anand has a central location opposite the Nabil Bank with basic and tolerable rooms with a geyser, TV and a comfy chair to watch it from.

Hotel Opera   HOTEL $$
(☎522101; www.hoteloperanepal.com; r Rs 800, deluxe Rs 1500-3000; ❄) This is the 'best' hotel in town. And while the rooms are certainly spacious there is a bit to be desired in the plumbing department. It's in a reasonably quiet location but the associated casino is hardly an attraction. It probably boasts the best restaurant in town, serving hearty Nepali and Indian dishes.

❶ Information

The Nepal Tourism Board runs a small **tourist information centre** (☎523773; ◷9.30am-5pm Sun-Fri) on the Nepal side of the border. If you need to check email, there are numerous places with access for Rs 30 per hour.

A 15-minute autorickshaw ride (Rs 80) from the border, **Nabil Bank** (☎525450; ◷10am-5pm Sun-Thu, to 3pm Fri) has a foreign exchange service and an ATM.

❶ Getting There & Away

There are no longer flights departing from Mahendranagar airport. The closest airport is at Dhangadhi, 60km east of Mahendranagar, which has daily **Buddha Air** (☎091-575288) and **Yeti**

Airlines (☎091-523045) flights to Kathmandu (US$186, one hour). Buses to Dhangadhi (Rs 90) leave every 30 minutes from the main bus station. A taxi will cost Rs 3000. The bus station is about 1km from the centre on the Mahendra Hwy. Long-haul buses leave for Kathmandu (Rs 1150, 15 hours) at 5am, 11.50am, 2pm, 3pm, 3.30pm, 4pm and 4.30pm. There's a single Pokhara service (Rs 1080, 16 hours) at 2.25pm. Local buses run every 30 minutes to Nepalganj (Rs 365, five hours), passing the turn-off to Bardia National Park at Ambassa (Rs 300, four hours).

❶ Getting Around

Buses, tempos and *tongas* run regularly between the bus station and the border for Rs 15. From the border into the main town a rickshaw/taxi costs around Rs 80/100.

Taxis can be hired for trips to Sukla Phanta Wildlife Reserve for Rs 5000 per day.

EASTERN TERAI

Bound by the Indian states of Bihar, Sikkim and West Bengal, the eastern Terai is broadly a mirror image of the west. The rolling hills of the Mahabharat Range are squeezed between the dry eastern plains and the Himalaya. The Mahendra Hwy cuts east to meet the Indian border at Kakarbhitta, providing easy access to Sikkim and Darjeeling.

Birganj
☎051

There's very little in the hectic border town of Birganj to suggest that you're not in India. As the main transit point for freight between India and Nepal, the town is mobbed by trucks, deafened by car horns and jostled by rickshaws. With its oppressive heat, it's not a place you'll want to hang around too long and it is most commonly visited by travellers crossing to/from Kolkata in India.

The **clock tower** on the main road serves as a useful landmark, leading south to the town centre and Indian border, while eastwards takes you to the bus station.

🛏 Sleeping & Eating

There are a number of noisy budget places near the main bus stand, and a handful of more comfortable choices in the centre.

Hotel Makalu   HOTEL $$
(☎523054; info@hotelmakalu.com; cnr Campus & Main Rds; r with fan Rs 1350, r with air-con Rs 1800-3390; ❉@🛜) This business-class hotel is calm and relaxed – just what you need in hectic Birganj. Rooms have TVs, carpets and 24-hour hot showers, and there's a good Indian restaurant.

Hotel Bhanu Plaza   HOTEL $
(☎524034; www.bhanuplaza.com; Ghantaghar Rd; s/d/tr Rs 400/600/800) The most salubrious choice near the bus stand, Bhanu Plaza has clean rooms that get good natural light, and almost succeed in blocking out traffic noise. Room 205 is the closest thing you'll get to a view in Birganj.

Hotel Vishuwa   HOTEL $$
(☎527777; www.vishuwa.com; Bypass Rd; s/d Rs 2850/3390; ❉🛜🏊) On the outskirts of town, the three-star Vishuwa is the best

Eastern Terai

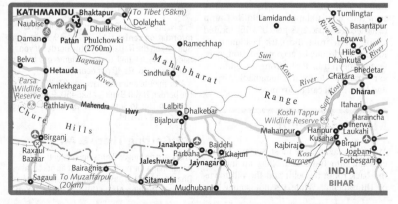

CROSSING THE BORDER: BIRGANJ TO RAXAUL BAZAAR

Border Hours

The Nepali side of the border is officially open from 6am to 7.30pm; outside these hours you'll need to find someone to stamp you through. Similarly, the Indian side is staffed from 5am to 9pm, but you can find someone at other times. Nepali visas are available on arrival from the Nepal immigration office, but payment must be in US dollars.

Foreign Exchange

There are no facilities at the border, but there are banks and moneychangers in Birganj. The Indian rupee is widely accepted in Birganj.

Onward to India

The border is 3km south of Birganj, from where it's a further 2km to the bus station in Raxaul Bazaar. Most people take a rickshaw straight through from Birganj (Rs 150).

From Raxaul, there are regular buses to Patna (₹ 125, six hours) or you can take the daily *Mithila Express* train to Kolkata's Howrah train station – it leaves Raxaul at 10am, arriving in Howrah at 5am the next morning. Seats cost ₹ 272/735/1088 for sleeper/three-tier/two-tier class (note that sleeper and two-tier class prices include air-con) and the trip takes 18 hours.

---

choice for those wanting true comfort. It also has the best restaurant in town.

Tandoor.Com NEPALI $
(meals Rs 30-220; ◎3-9pm) A slightly shabby but inviting outdoor garden eatery, it serves fantastic momos, and has a well-stocked bar good for a late-afternoon drink. Mozzies come out at night, so bring repellent.

Pooja Sweets NEPALI $
(Main Rd; mains Rs 50-100; ◎8am-8pm) On the main road, there's nothing fancy about this misthan bhandar (sweet shop and vegetarian restaurant), but its meals are reliable, cheap and tasty. The signage is in Sanskrit.

ⓘ Information

There are several banks in town with ATMs, while fast internet access (Rs 30 per hour) is available along the main road.

ⓘ Getting There & Away

Buddha Air (☑533230; Campus Rd) and **Guna Airlines** (☑526836; Adarshnagar Rd) have numerous daily flights between Simara (the airport for Birganj) and Kathmandu (US$80, 20 minutes). The airport is 22km from Birganj, and a taxi costs around Rs 1000.

Buses leave from the large, sprawling bus stand at the end of Ghantaghar Rd (New Rd). There are plenty of buses to Kathmandu (Rs 400, eight hours) from 5am until 8pm. However, the most comfortable and quickest option is to get a Tata Sumo '4WD' (Rs 500, six hours), which depart every 20 minutes, finishing up around 2pm. There are also morning buses to Pokhara (Rs 450, eight hours) via Narayangarh (Rs 200, four hours) at 5am, 6.30am and 7.30am. Regular buses head to Janakpur (Rs 200, five hours) every 20 minutes until 2pm and Hetauda (Rs 150, two hours).

ⓘ Getting Around

Rickshaws charge around Rs 150 to go from town to the Nepali border post and on to Raxaul Bazaar. Alternatively, you can take a tempo or *tonga* from the bus station to the Nepali border post for Rs 25 and then walk to the Indian side, but it's likely they'll charge more for your bag.

THE TERAI & MAHABHARAT RANGE BIRGANJ

Janakpur

🎵 041

Like the other border towns in the Terai, Janakpur's way of life is unmistakably Indian, but there's a lot more going on here than rickshaws and bustling bazaars. What makes Janakpur (also referred to as Janakpurdham) one of the most fascinating towns in the Terai is its electrifying religious atmosphere mixed with a rich historical and cultural heritage. Even though there's no architecture predating 1880, it manages to evoke an aura of grandeur not found elsewhere in the Terai.

Janakpur is known foremostly as an important pilgrimage site for Hindus all over Nepal and India, who come to pay homage to the city's connection with the Hindu epic the Ramayana. Legend has it that it's the site where Sita was born, and where she was married to Rama.

The other lure in Janakpur is its Mithila culture. Janakpur was once the capital of the ancient kingdom of Mithila, a territory now divided between Nepal and India: more than two million people in the area still speak Maithili as their native tongue. The people of Mithila are famous for their wildly colourful paintings – see the boxed text, p258.

Janakpur is actually the third city on this site. The city mythologised in the Ramayana existed around 700 BC, but it was later abandoned and sank back into the forest. Simaraungarh grew up in its place, but this city was also destroyed, this time by Muslim invaders in the 14th century.

◉ Sights

Janaki Mandir   HINDU TEMPLE

At the heart of Janakpur lies the exquisite marble Janaki Mandir, one of the finest pieces of architecture in Nepal. Built in extravagant baroque Mughal style, the Janaki Mandir is Janakpur's most important temple and is dedicated to Sita, the wife of Rama and heroine of the Ramayana. It's believed to stand on the exact spot where King Janak found the infant Sita lying in the furrow of a ploughed field. The temple only dates from 1912, but it feels much older with its white marble arches, domes, turrets and screens. It looks a little like a glorious wedding cake, designed for a maharajah.

A steady stream of pilgrims file in through the gatehouse to worship the Sita statue in the **inner sanctum** (⊙5-7am & 6-8pm). The temple is particularly popular with women, who wear their best and most colourful saris for the occasion. Early evening is the most atmospheric time to visit, as the temple is draped with colourful lights and pilgrims arrive in their masses.

Ram Sita Bibaha Mandir   HINDU TEMPLE

(admission Rs 2, camera/video Rs 5/21; ⊙5am-9pm) Almost next door to the Janaki Mandir, this rather bizarre temple marks the spot where Rama and Sita were married. The temple is topped by a modernist interpretation of a tiered pagoda roof and the walls are glass so you can peer in at the kitsch lifesized models of Sita and Rama.

Traditional Villages   VILLAGE

The sugar-cane fields and Mithila villages around Janakpur form a lush and magical mosaic. Many of the villages are built in the traditional Mithila style, with mud walls decorated with colourful paintings of people and animals.

The easiest village to reach from Janakpur is **Kuwa**, about 1km south of Murali Chowk. People are very friendly, as long as you aren't too intrusive with your camera, and you can drop in on the Janakpur Women's Development Centre (see the boxed text, p258).

If you feel like roaming further afield, **Dhanushadham**, 15km northeast of Janakpur, marks the spot where Rama allegedly drew Shiva's magic bow. Worshippers believe a fossilised fragment of the broken bow lies here.

Ram Mandir & Danush Sagar   HINDU TEMPLE

Hidden away in a stone courtyard southeast of the Janaki Mandir, the **Ram Mandir** is the oldest temple in Janakpur (constructed in 1882), built in the classic tiered pagoda style of the hills. The main temple is sacred to Rama but there are several smaller shrines to Shiva, Hanuman and Durga dotted around the compound. It's busiest in the early evening, when the courtyard is filled with incense smoke and music.

Opposite the entrance are a series of ghats (steps for ritual bathing) leading down into the **Danush Sagar**, the largest ceremonial tank at Janakpur. There are small shrines all around the perimeter and vendors in front sell flower garlands, *tika* powder, sacred threads and other ritual objects for pujas (prayers).

Nearby is the small **Janak Mandir**, sacred to the father of Sita.

If you head west from Ramanand Chowk, you'll reach two more ceremonial tanks – **Bihar Kunda** and **Ratan Saga Kunda**.

Janakpur

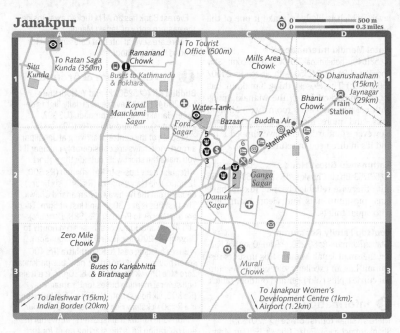

N 0 ———— 500 m
0 ———— 0.3 miles

Janakpur

✲ Festivals & Events

Sita Bibaha Panchami
HINDU

By far the most interesting time to visit Janakpur is during the fifth day of the waxing moon in November/December, when tens of thousands of pilgrims descend on the town to celebrate the re-enactment of Sita's marriage to Rama (also known as Vivaha Panchami). There are processions and performances of scenes from the Ramayana in the streets.

Rama Navami
HINDU

Celebrations for Rama's birthday in March/April are accompanied by a huge procession, which attracts many sadhus (wandering Hindu holy men).

Holi
HINDU

In March, Janakpur gets boisterous during this riotously colourful affair, but be warned: foreigners are not exempt from a ritual splattering with coloured powder and water.

Tihar
MITHILA

If you visit during in October/November, you'll see Mithila women repainting the murals on their houses.

🛏 Sleeping & Eating

Hotel Welcome
HOTEL $$

(☎520646; Station Rd; r from Rs 1000; ❄) The hotel 'where welcome never ends' was receiving a serious facelift at the time of research, with 60 new rooms set over numerous levels, which is likely to make it one of the best choices in town.

Hotel Manaki International HOTEL $$
(☎521540; hotelmanaki2010@hotmail.com; Shiv Chowk; s/d Rs 1000/1350, with air-con Rs 2000/2500; ❊☎) The closest thing Janakpur has to an 'upmarket' hotel, the Manaki International has cavernous rooms with all mod cons, and more modest standard rooms. However, standards here have slipped a bit and it's in dire need of refurbishment.

Kathmandu Guest House GUESTHOUSE $
(☎521753; Bhanu Chowk; s/d Rs 250/350) A basic but otherwise reliable cheapie. Rooms have fans, mosquito nets and clean bathrooms with squat toilets.

Rooftop Family Restaurant INDIAN $
(Station Rd; mains Rs 80-250; ⊗9am-10pm; ❊) Facing the small Janak Mandir, this upstairs restaurant has an excellent selection of vegetarian curries, plus cold beer and outdoor tables.

Information

There's a small **tourist office** (☎520755; Shankatmochan St, Pidari Chowk; ⊗10am-4pm Sun-Thu, 10am-3pm Fri), which has a few brochures but English is not a strong point.

Everest Bank has an ATM tucked away inside the eastern entry of Janaki Mandir.

There are several internet cafes in town for around Rs 20 per hour.

❶ Getting There & Around

Buddha Air (☎525022) and **Yeti Airlines** (☎520047) both have several daily flights between Janakpur and Kathmandu (US$97, 20 minutes). The airport is a Rs 100 rickshaw ride south of the centre. If arriving at Janakpur airport, rickshaws are considerably cheaper if you make the short walk outside the airport.

Regular daily buses to Kathmandu (Rs 600, 12 hours) via Narayangarh (Rs 340, six hours) depart from the highway at Ramanand Chowk. The first bus is at 5.30am and last at 5pm. There are also buses to Pokhara (Rs 588, 12 hours) at 6.40am and 3pm. Local buses run hourly to Birganj (Rs 200, five hours) until about 3pm.

Buses heading east to Kakarbhitta (Rs 400, seven hours) are at the dusty 'new' bus park near Zero Mile Chowk from 6am to 6.30pm. You'll also find several morning buses for Biratnagar (Rs 300, six hours) until 10.30am. The bus stand is a Rs 50 rickshaw ride from central Janakpur.

More one for the trainspotters, at the north end of Station Rd is the starting point for the slow metre-gauge train that runs east across the Indian border to the dusty plains town of

MITHILA ART

The vibrant artwork of the Mithila women can be traced back as far as the 7th century and is a tradition that has been passed from generation to generation. As the former capital of the kingdom of Mithila, it is appropriate that Janakpur has emerged as the centre for both preserving and promoting the ancient art of Mithila painting.

Mithila painting is part decoration, part social commentary, recording the lives of rural women in a society where reading and writing are reserved for high-caste men. Scenes in Mithila paintings colourfully record the female experience of life in the Terai – work, childbirth, marriage and the social network among village women. Today you will also see more modern subject matter, such as aeroplanes and buses, blended with traditional themes like Hindu mythology and village life.

Traditionally, Mithila paintings were used as a transient form of decoration during festivals when the mud walls of village huts were painted in white and ochre with abstract patterns or complex scenes of everyday village life. You can still see houses in the villages surrounding Janakpur with painted walls. More recently, Mithila painting has taken off as a more contemporary and collectable art form, with the women painting on canvases of rough handmade paper that is similar in texture to the mud hut walls. Not only are Mithila paintings now exhibited in galleries across the world, but more importantly the art has also opened up a whole new industry for women in impoverished rural communities.

One of the best-known social projects is the **Janakpur Women's Development Centre** (JWDC; Nare Bekas Kendra; ☎521080, 9725547633; www.maithilijanakpur.wordpress.com, info_jwdc@yahoo.com; ⊗10.30am-5pm Sun-Fri, 10.30am-4pm Nov-Feb), just south of Janakpur in the village of Kuwa. Around 40 Mithila women are employed at the centre, producing paper paintings, papier-mâché boxes and mirrors, screen-printed fabrics and hand-thrown ceramics. Money raised goes directly towards improving the lives of rural women. A rickshaw from Janakpur to the centre will cost around Rs 150.

THE BUDDHA OF BARA

At the start of 2005, nobody had heard of Ram Bahadur Banjan. By the end of the year, thousands of Nepali Buddhists were hailing the long-haired 16-year-old Tamang boy as the second incarnation of the Buddha.

Followers of the teenage guru – who is known as Om Namo Guru Buddha Gyani or Dharma Sangha – claim that he had been meditating without food or water in the forest east of Birganj for nearly 10 months. Although that sounds unlikely, the Nepali government asked the Nepal Academy of Science and Technology to investigate the claim and, if necessary, declare a miracle. Before any conclusions could be reached, Banjan mysteriously disappeared.

After reappearing on three brief occasions, in late 2008 he re-emerged from the jungle in Ratanpuri, 150km southeast of Kathmandu, to worldwide media attention. Devotees came in their hundreds of thousands to see him, with many suspecting he had attained enlightenment in Bodhgaya, just like the historical Buddha did in 592 BC.

While Dharma Sanga himself denies he's the reincarnation of Buddha, this hasn't stopped an ever-growing legion of devotees flocking to hear his talks, including many foreigners. For the latest, check www.paldendorje.com.

Jaynagar. At the time of research there were plans to upgrade the line to broad gauge. Only Indians and Nepalis can actually cross the border, but the train ride provides a delicious taste of the subcontinent. Foreigners can take the Jaynagar line as far as Khajuri (2nd/1st class Rs 20/36, three hours), about 21km southeast of Janakpur.

Koshi Tappu Wildlife Reserve

♪025

The smallest of the Terai's national parks, **Koshi Tappu Wildlife Reserve** (☏9852054105; per day foreigner/SAARC/child under 10yr Rs 500/200/free) is a birdwatcher's paradise. Consisting of 175 sq km of wet and grassland habitat, Koshi Tappu (translating to 'river islands') is home to at least 493 species of birds, as well as being the last habitat of the endangered arna (long, pointy-horned wild water buffalo). It was founded in 1976 to protect a small triangle of *phanta* and *tappu* (small islands) in the flood plain of the Sapt Kosi River – one of the three main tributaries of the Ganges.

It's a wonderfully serene spot and most travellers who visit are birdwatchers in search of rare species such as the swamp francolin, Bengal florican and sarus crane. Migratory species from Siberia and Tibet take up residence from November to February. While it lacks heavy hitters like tigers and rhinos, there's still plenty to see – including Gangetic dolphins, blue bulls, deer, golden jackals, marsh muggers, fishing cats,

mongooses, civet cats and porcupines. Wild elephants are also regular visitors, but more so to raid villagers' crops at night – and hence are seldom seen by tourists. Arna can be sighted late in the afternoon grazing on the *tappu* and sometimes crossing the river. Gangetic dolphin are best spotted from the bridge at Koshi Barrage.

Like Chitwan, the park faces a massive ecological crisis with the invasion of the fast-growing South American weed *Mikania micrantha*, which wraps itself around the park's plants, damaging local flora and food sources for wildlife.

◎ Sights & Activities

Birdwatching   BIRDWATCHING

Every lodge has a resident ornithologist who leads bird-spotting walks around the park (usually included in package rates). Both lodges also have bird hides that can be a good spot to tick a few species off your list.

River Trips   RAFTING

Exploring the park on the river via a gentle paddle in a rubber dinghy, canoe or *dunga* (wooden boat) is a great way to see wildlife, particularly arna. Rates are usually included in the lodges' package rates; otherwise the going rate for a boat and driver is Rs 1500.

Elephant Safaris   SAFARI

(foreigner/SAARC Rs 1000/400) A popular way to explore Koshi is by elephant; however, here it's more about the experience itself rather than for spotting wildlife. Rides are arranged at the park headquarters before 8am or after 4pm.

Jeep Safaris
WILDLIFE WATCHING

Another way to see the park is via a jeep in the morning or late afternoon. While you're unlikely to see a huge amount of wildlife, it's a good way of getting a feel for the park and its habitat, and is combined with a walk.

Sleeping

While rates initially appear exorbitant, keep in mind they include all meals and activities. Prebooking is essential. Both lodges close during the monsoon (June to August).

Koshi Camp
TENTED CAMP $$$

(☑9804021102, 01-4429609; www.kosicamp.com; package per person per night US$189) Located in the delightful village of Madhuban, 7km from the highway, Koshi Camp is a popular choice for birders. It has an attractive setting on the edge of the park with its own pond and bird hide. Lodging is in tents with carpet and comfy beds, with common, spotless bathrooms. The restaurant lends a safari feel, with plenty of ornithological reading material on hand. Keep an eye out for jackals in the evening. The Nepalese food here is some of the best we've eaten in the Terai, and it has its own vegie garden.

Koshi Tappu Wildlife Camp
TENTED CAMP $$$

(☑9851022162, 01-4226130; www.koshitappu.com; package per person per night US$250) This is another peaceful camp with comfortable safari tents set among tranquil jungle. A small watercourse flows through the grounds so you can watch birds from the comfort of the bar, or otherwise from the delightful bird hide overlooking a small pond. It's 4km up from Koshi Camp in the village of Prakashpur.

ⓘ Information

The information centre at the park headquarters in Kusaha has an interesting museum, with displays of elephant, deer and arna skulls, and a desiccated gharial. Here is where you arrange elephant safaris.

ⓘ Getting There & Away

Most visitors come on a package tour with a prearranged pick-up from Biratnagar airport, but it's easy enough to travel here as an independent traveller. The best way is to fly from Kathmandu to Biratnagar then take a taxi (Rs 3000, two hours) to Koshi Tappu.

By public transport, you can catch a bus along the Mahendra Hwy to Laukahi, 10km east of the Koshi Barrage. Get off at the police station, from where two daily buses (Rs 20) pass through the village road to the lodges at noon and 4pm (returning in the morning). Otherwise call ahead for one of the lodges to pick you up for around Rs 1000. For the park headquarters, get off at Jamuha, from where it's a further 2.5km walk.

Buses from Kathmandu (12 to 14 hours) are Rs 800, while from the east, you can jump on any bus heading along the Mahendra Hwy.

Itahari

Itahari is an undistinguished town at the junction of the Mahendra Hwy and the roads to Biratnagar and Hile. All long-distance buses along the Mahendra Hwy pull into the well-organised bus stand and there are fast and frequent local services to Biratnagar and places along the road to Hile.

If you get stuck overnight, the **Jay Nepal Hotel** (☑025-580113; r from Rs 700; ❄) has reasonable rooms; it is by the roundabout at the turn-off to Dharan.

Biratnagar

☑021

For what is Nepal's major industrial centre and second most-populated city (approximately 170,000 people), Biratnagar is surprisingly low-key. Sure, you'll have to dodge a rickshaw here or there in the town's centre, but it's neither as polluted nor swarming with bustling activity as you might expect.

There's nothing in terms of sights to see, and what few visitors there are in Biratnagar are en route to Koshi Tappu Wildlife Reserve, are catching a flight to Taplejung (the main trailhead for treks in the eastern hills) or are heading to/from Basantapur for white-water rafting (a further five-hour drive).

Sleeping & Eating

TOP CHOICE Hotel Eastern Star
HOTEL $$

(☑471626; easternstar_brt@wlink.com.np; r with fan Rs 1131, r with air-con from Rs 1300; ❄🛜) The best value place in town, it has a wonderful location in a quiet area. Rooms are massive and well furnished, and have comfortable beds, satellite TV and clean bathrooms. Staff are friendly, and there's a good Indian restaurant and well-stocked bar.

Dhankuta Lodge
GUESTHOUSE $

(☎522925; r with/without bathroom Rs 300/200)
Don't expect frills at this rudimentary place
opposite the bus station, but rooms are definitely tolerable for the price. Try to get one
at the back, away from the traffic noise.

Hotel Xenial
HOTEL $$$

(☎472950; www.xenialhotel.com.np; s/d from
US$68/79; ❀ 🛜 ☀) The choice of UN workers,
rooms here sparkle and feature attractive
Mithila art on the walls.

Valentine's Bakery Cafe
CAFE $

(mains from Rs 70; ⊙10am-8.30pm) Popular
with students, this modern cafe specialises
in lassis, cakes and momos.

Unique Fast Food
VEGETARIAN, INDIAN $

(Main Rd; mains Rs 65-140; ⊙9am-9pm) Fans of
the dosa will want to head to this popular
South Indian vegetarian eatery, with an im-
pressive 18 different types of dosa – includ-
ing the 'Unique special dosa' with paneer.
Up the road you'll find the modern Indian
chain-restaurant **Angan**, also vegetarian
and good for sweets.

ℹ Information

There are several banks with ATMs along or just
off Main Rd. Several internet cafes at Traffic
Chowk offer fast connections for Rs 25 per hour,
with **Digital Cyber Cafe** (⊙7.30am-9pm) a
reliable choice.

ℹ Getting There & Away

Buddha Air (☎526901) and **Yeti Airlines**
(☎536612) both have numerous daily flights
between Biratnagar and Kathmandu (US$125,
35 minutes). **Nepal Airlines** (www.nepalair
lines.com.np) also has several flights a week to
Suketar/Taplejung (US$64, 30 minutes) –
though its airport was under repair at time of
research. A rickshaw to the airport will cost
around Rs 100.

The bus stand is a Rs 20 rickshaw ride south-
west from Traffic Chowk. There are regular
buses to Kathmandu (Rs 810, 14 hours) via
Narayangarh (Rs 580, nine hours) from 4am to
4pm, and one bus to Pokhara (Rs 810, 12 hours)
at 4am. Several buses leave every morning for
Janakpur (Rs 300, six hours). There are also
regular services to Kakarbhitta (Rs 190, four
hours) from the Mahendra Hwy.

Local buses run to Dharan (Rs 60, 1½ hours)
throughout the day. There are also early morn-
ing buses to Dhankuta (Rs 170, three hours) and
Hile (Rs 300, 3½ hours).

Dharan to Hile

About 17km north of Itahari, Dharan marks
the start of yet another dramatic route into
the hills. From here, a decent tarmac road
runs north into the foothills of the Hima-
laya, providing access to a series of attractive
hill towns and trekking trailheads.

DHARAN
☑025

The sprawling town of Dharan has three dis-
tinct characters. On the western perimeter
you'll find an affluent, almost middle-class
suburban feel, with quiet streets lined with
well-maintained bungalows, neatly paved
pavements, rubbish bins and a country club
with a golf course. Up until 1990 Dharan was
the Gurkha recruiting area, and its wealth
can be largely attributed to money brought
in by these world-famous Nepali–British sol-
diers. The eastern side has steep streets and
a relaxed village feel with banana plants,
bamboo-forested hills and rustic shacks. Di-
viding the two areas is the lively Dharan Ba-
zaar, which has a more typical Terai flavour,
with its flat and dusty market.

Dharan is also one of the *shakti peeths,*
marking the spot where part of the body of
Shiva's first wife, Sati, fell after she was con-
sumed by flames. There are several impor-
tant Shaivite temples northeast of the centre
in the village of **Bijayapur**. A short walk
from here is the **Budha Subba Mandir**, set
among dense bamboo thickets down the
path, with a curious collection of rocks cov-
ered in mud – said to represent the reclining
body of Mahadev (Shiva). You're likely to en-
counter chickens being sacrificed. To reach
Bijayapur, take a right at Chata Chowk (a
10-minute walk from Dharan Bazaar), which
leads to steps at the bottom of the hill; from
here it's a 20-minute walk. An autorickshaw
costs Rs 300 return.

Several net cafes around Bhanu Chowk
(the square with the bus stand and the clock
tower across the road) offer fast net access
for Rs 20 per hour. Nabil Bank and Hima-
layan Bank have ATMs.

🛏 Sleeping & Eating

New Dreamland Hotel & Lodge
HOTEL $

(☎525024; r with/without bathroom Rs 1015/680,
with air-con Rs 1800; ❀ 🛜) Located in a peace-
ful, well-to-do part of town, Dreamland
makes for an excellent choice. Rooms here
are large, but rather bare without any

NEPAL'S BHUTANESE REFUGEES

Bhutan boasts a concept of Gross National Happiness and upholds an image as a modern-day Shangri-La, so it's surprising that in 1990, over 100,000 Lhotshampa people – an astonishing 18% of Bhutan's entire population – became refugees in Nepal.

Of Nepalese descent, the Lhotshampa people were well established in southern Bhutan after workers migrated here from Nepal in the 19th century. Yet things were to change drastically in 1988 during the nation's first census, when it was announced that anyone who couldn't provide proof of residency in Bhutan prior to 1958 was to be considered an illegal immigrant. Documentation was difficult to obtain for many Lhotshampa. Combined with an arbitrary ruling as to what exactly constituted a 'non-national', it led to rising tensions and interethnic conflict, which saw several thousand Lhotshampa imprisoned.

Laws were introduced that made it compulsory for Lhotshampa to wear traditional Bhutanese clothing, while Nepali language was banned from schools. By 1992 over 100,000 refugees had either fled or were deported from the country; many complained that they were intimidated into signing voluntary migration forms.

After 15 years of being stuck in limbo (with the Nepalese and Bhutanese governments at a stalemate over who should accept them), in 2006 it was decided to resettle the Lhotshampa refugees in Western countries. The news was hardly met with celebration, with most simply wanting to return to their homes in Bhutan. By 2011 resettlement was well under way, with half being relocated to the USA, while refugee camps had been reduced to four near Damak and another south of Itahari. Whatever the outcome, the collective cultural identity of the Lhotshampa people is at serious risk of being lost forever.

furniture except a bed. It also has a recommended restaurant with a long menu.

Hotel Nava Yug
GUESTHOUSE $

(☑524797; r Rs 500-800, without bathroom Rs 400) A respectable cheapie in the heart of the Dharan Bazaar, it's a little decrepit but the simple rooms have decent beds and Western toilet. Bucket hot water is provided, and its small restaurant does an excellent paneer mushroom curry.

TOP CHOICE Dharan Kitchen
INTERNATIONAL, INDIAN $

(mains Rs 70-280; ☺10am-10pm) Upstairs from the taxi stand (opposite the clock tower), Dharan Kitchen has a calming ambience with bamboo walls and Buddhist motifs, and serves quality Indian and Western food with cheap, cold beer.

❶ Getting There & Around

Afternoon buses leave from Bhanu Chowk for Kathmandu (from Rs 866, 14 hours) from 3pm until 7pm (there's also a 4.30am bus) and Biratnagar (Rs 67, 1½ hours). Heading north, local buses run regularly from 4am to 4pm to Bhedetar (Rs 45, 45 minutes), Dhankuta (Rs 180, two hours) and Hile (Rs 180, three hours). There are also buses east to the Indian border at Kakarbhitta (Rs 180, four hours).

BHEDETAR

Arriving from the hot dusty plains of the Terai, the cool climate of laid-back Bhedetar makes for a refreshing change. Perched at 1420m, the soaring views over Everest and Makalu are spectacular on a clear day. The best views are from **Bhedetar Charles Point** (foreigner/SAARC Rs 50/10; ☺daylight), named after Prince Charles, who visited in the 1980s.

Hotel Aruu Valley Hilltop Restaurant (☑9842055086; r Rs 600-1200, without bathroom Rs 500) makes for a pleasant place to spend the night. Set among a garden of bright flowers, its rooms are quaintly decorated with thick carpets, wicker furniture and comfortable beds with warm blankets. It also has a great restaurant with good views.

There are also several tin-roofed bhojanalayas serving simple, filling meals, *tongba* (millet beer) and *raksi* (distilled rice wine).

HILE
☑026

Hile was once the starting point for the camping trek to Makalu and the end point for the lodge trek from Lukla, but the road has advanced along the valley, reaching almost as far as Tumlingtar and Khandbari. As a result, Hile is no longer the busy trekking hub it once was. Nevertheless, the village has a bustling bazaar feel, particularly during the weekly Thursday market, and there's a good mountain viewpoint about 30 minutes' walk above town (follow the Basantapur road to the army post, then turn north along the trail to Hattikharka).

Many local inhabitants are Tibetans who resettled here after fleeing the Chinese occupation of Tibet in 1959, founding several gompas in the middle of the village.

🛏 Sleeping & Eating

Most hotels serve filling Tibetan food and warming wooden pots of *tongba*.

Gumba Hotel
GUESTHOUSE $
(📞540173; r Rs 300-400) Next to the main village gompa, this guesthouse has good-value rooms, many with views of the temple or surrounding hills. Downstairs has a popular restaurant serving up Tibetan dishes.

Kanjirowa Makalu Hotel
HOTEL $$
(📞540509; r with/without bathroom Rs 1000/800; 📶) A smart red-brick hotel on the outskirts of town, its large rooms are by far the most comfortable in town. It has a good international menu and a bar with an impressive cocktail list.

Hotel Himali
GUESTHOUSE $
(📞540140; d/tr Rs 200/300) A jumble of pot plants lends a cosy feel to this place, across from Gumba Hotel. Beds are hard, but otherwise it's good for the price. Also has a *Raiders of the Lost Ark*–style bar at the back

❶ Getting There & Away

Frequent local buses run from Dharan to Hile (Rs 180, two hours), with the last bus at 4.30pm. A few continue up the Arun Valley as far as Leguwa (Rs 310 from Dharan, five hours). Some buses from Dharan continue to Basantapur (Rs 90 from Hile, 1½ hours). Buses leave when full for the bumpy ride to Tumlingtar, stopping just before Kotlay Bhanjyang (Rs 425, six hours).

Ilam
📞027
Like its neighbour Darjeeling across the border, Ilam (pronounced 'ee-lam') is synonymous with one thing – tea. The two share an almost identical climate and topography and, while Darjeeling is a household name, Ilam quietly sets about its business in making a name for itself internationally through its quality tea.

Situated in the far east of Nepal, 90km from the border at Kakarbhitta, a walk through the small clusters of green tea plants that carpet the hills will take you to one of the most tranquil spots in the Terai. A concrete walkway leads through the tea fields up to a viewing deck on top of the hill. Otherwise there are many paths you can wander along.

On the main strip near the bus stand, **Koseli Gham** (🕐7am-7pm Sun-Fri, 10am-4pm Sat) is a small cooperative that sells Ilam tea, honey and sweets, with proceeds going to the local community. Those wanting to buy tea can head to **Ilam Tea House** (🕐7am-6.30pm) near the Green View Guest House.

🛏 Sleeping & Eating

🔺TOP CHOICE Chiyabari Cottage Ilam
GUESTHOUSE $
(📞520149; r with/without bathroom Rs 900/800; 📶) This new guesthouse is perched on the hill overlooking magical views of the tea plantations and surrounding hills. Rooms are spacious and enlivened by pot plants. It's a top spot for a meal or drink at sunset, with a choice of seating in bamboo huts, in the garden or the rooftop. There's also a swish bar indoors. Call to arrange free transport pick-up to avoid the sweaty climb up here.

Green View Guest House
GUESTHOUSE $
(📞520103; s/d Rs 550/900, without bathroom Rs 300/400; 📶) An old favourite, Green View has a prime location at the edge of a tea garden, and several rooms do indeed have a green view – of tea plantations (room 501 is the best).

Danfe Guest House
GUESTHOUSE $
(📞520048; s/d/tr Rs 300/400/600) Immersed within a tea plantation, this rustic blue-and-white cottage decorated with prayer flags has basic but otherwise sunny rooms.

Chyangba Hotel
NEPALI, TIBETAN $
(daal bhaat Rs 50, tongba Rs 50; 🕐9am-8pm) Set in a darkened back room on the main strip, the ambience is a bit grim but its momos are fantastic and it's a good spot to enjoy a tankard of *tongba*.

❶ Information

The **tourist information centre** (📞521692; ilam_2010@yahoo.com; 🕐6am-9pm) by the bus stand has some general ideas on what to see in the region, but it's not overly helpful. There's also some information available at www.mabu sandakpur.com.

There are several ATMs in the bazaar, while Bank of Asia up the road also has an ATM and can exchange foreign currency. Get online at **Unique Cyber** (per hr Rs 30; ☺7.30am-5.30pm) near Green View.

❶ Getting There & Away

The dusty bus/jeep stand is to the west of town, while the taxi stand is just off the main square.

The road to Ilam branches off at two points along the Mahendra Hwy. Buses and jeeps depart at either Charali (if arriving from Kakarbhitta) or Birtamod (if you're coming from Kathmandu). Jeeps do the journey in three hours (Rs 220, three hours).

Around Ilam

A pleasant half-day trip from Ilam is the attractive lake at **Mai Pokhari**. The 1½-hour jeep trip along a rocky track leads you to this peaceful spot, which was declared a Ramsar site in late 2008. An important pilgrimage site for Hindus and Buddhists, the lake is a striking emerald colour and is covered in water lilies and teeming with goldfish. Surrounded by cone trees and rhododendrons (which bloom in March), it makes for a beautiful stroll, and is home to 300 species of birds, plus tree frogs, leopards and jackals. The area is also known for its medicinal plants, which are claimed to cure everything from hysteria to cancer.

Your best bet to get here is to catch a jeep or taxi to Biblate, from where you can arrange onward transport to Mai Pokhari.

Otherwise it makes for an excellent eight-hour round-trip walk from Ilam.

Some other trips possible from Ilam include the **Kanyam Tea Gardens**, located 46km from Ilam, where you can visit the tea factory. If you're getting the bus here, it's about a 15-minute walk down the hill to the factory. Here you'll also find a picnic spot popular with groups of merry Nepali teenagers.

Another excellent option is a visit to **Sandakpur**, on the border with India, where you can watch an incredible sunrise over four of the world's five highest peaks; it's also a habitat for red pandas. However, it's not the easiest place to get to: it involves getting a taxi from Ilam Bazaar to Biblate (Rs 20), then another taxi for 2½ hours to Khorsanitar (Rs 200 if you're lucky to find a shared taxi, otherwise you'll be looking at around Rs 3000 for a special hire), and finally a six-hour walk. There are several basic lodges in Sandakpur, and you'll need to ensure you bring warm clothing.

Kakarbhitta
🎵 023

Kakarbhitta (Kakarvitta) is the easternmost crossing between India and Nepal, and is just a few hours' drive from Siliguri and Darjeeling in West Bengal and Gangtok in Sikkim. Like Nepal's other border towns, Kakarbhitta is hot, dusty and stressful, and there isn't any great reason to linger here other than to break up your journey. How-

---

CROSSING THE BORDER: KAKARBHITTA TO PANITANKI

Border Hours

Both sides of the border are staffed between 6am and around 9pm to 10pm. You may still be able to cross outside these times, but you'll need to go searching for immigration officials.

Foreign Exchange

Nepal Bank operates a **foreign exchange desk** (☺7am-5pm) close to the border. You can change cash and travellers cheques in US dollars, UK pounds and euros, as well as Indian and Nepali rupees.

Onward to India

It's about 100m from the Kakarbhitta bus stand to the border, and around 1km to the Indian border post at Panitanki (aka Raniganj) – around Rs 30 by rickshaw. Otherwise you can catch a shared taxi or jeep from outside the Nepali immigration office to Siliguri for Rs 80 (or Rs 800 for a special hire). From Siliguri you can head to Darjeeling by bus (₹ 90, three hours) or toy train (2nd/1st class ₹ 42/247). You can also catch a train to Kolkata (sleeper/3AC ₹ 264/695, 10 hours) departing at 8pm.

ever, 10 minutes' walk south (or a Rs 30 rick-shaw ride) is the **Satighata tea plantation**, which can be a nice way to spend time here, and is a taste of things to come on the Darjeeling side of the border.

Sleeping & Eating

Most of the hotels are crammed together in the narrow alleys leading west from the back of the bus stand. For meals, all the lodges have restaurants serving Indian, Nepali and Chinese fare.

Hotel Mechi HOTEL $
(562040; dm Rs 150, s Rs 400-900, d Rs 400-1200, r with air-con from Rs 1400; ✸) On a sleepy road near the northern edge of the bus station, Mechi has rooms to suit all budgets. Rooms are large and comfortable, and offer excellent value.

Hotel Rajat HOTEL $$
(562433; s/d Rs 300/500, r with air-con Rs 1600; ✸) The welcome here is friendly and the rooms are simple but inviting (but check whether some of the broken peepholes in the doors have been fixed...). There's a bistrolike restaurant with gingham tablecloths downstairs. It's just up the road from Hotel Mechi.

Information

The government of Nepal runs a small **tourist information centre** (562252; 10am-4pm Sun-Fri), but it's more country-wide than local information. You can check your email at **Net Point Cyber Zone** (562040; per hr Rs 40;

7am-7.30pm) on the north side of the bus station near Hotel Mechi.

Sunrise has an ATM here, but it's unreliable, so bring enough cash for onward travel.

Getting There & Away

Air

The nearest airport is at Bhadrapur, 10km southeast of Birtamod, which in turn is 13km west of Kakarbhitta. A taxi from Kakarbhitta bus stand to the airport costs Rs 600, or you can take a local bus to Birtamod, then a second bus to Bhadrapur followed by a rickshaw to the airport. **Yeti Airlines** (455232), **Buddha Air** (455218) and **Agni Air** (01-4107812) have daily flights to Kathmandu (US$154, 50 minutes) – any of the travel agents around the bus stand can issue tickets.

Bus

Travel agents in Kathmandu and Pokhara offer 'through-tickets' to Darjeeling, but you must change buses at Kakarbhitta, then again change at Siliguri – it is just as easy to do the trip in stages.

There are several daily services to Kathmandu (standard/deluxe Rs 965/1165, 17 to 21 hours) departing early morning at 4.20am and 5am, or in the afternoon at 4.30pm and 5pm. There are also buses to Pokhara (Rs 958, 17 hours) via Narayangarh (Rs 670, 12 hours).

To get to Ilam, there are plenty of buses to Birtamod (Rs 30, 25 minutes) from where you can take a bus or jeep. There are four or more daily buses to Janakpur (Rs 450, seven hours), Biratnagar (Rs 180, 3½ hours) and Birganj (Rs 610, eight hours).

Trekking Routes

Choosing a Trek

Six popular teahouse treks are described in this chapter; between them they account for 90% of all trek trips in Nepal. Easily the most popular options are the Everest Base Camp and Annapurna Circuit treks. Both offer spectacular scenery and cultural depth, as well as plenty of crowds.

Over the last few years Everest has become insanely busy in high season, while the Annapurna region has been affected by road construction along the Jomsom side. The Annapurna Circuit has the advantage of being a loop route, while Everest is an out-and-back trek, returning to Lukla via the same route.

Noticeably quieter are the Langtang and Gosainkund regions, while the Tamang Heritage Trail is quieter still and offers a good mix of traditional villages and mountain views.

If that's not enough for you, it is also possible to combine treks. The Annapurna Sanctuary Trek is easily pinned onto the end of the Annapurna Circuit to create a full month of superb trekking. Likewise the Tamang Heritage Trail is a fine way to start or end a Langtang Valley trek, which itself can be tagged onto a Gosainkund trek.

Our advice is not to rush your walk. Adding on a few days to your itinerary allows you to take in side trips, detours and monasteries, or just take a day off every now and then. These just might end up being the highlights of your trip.

Basic descriptions of the main treks are given in this chapter but these are not intended as trail guides. For full information on these routes, as well as camping treks to more remote regions, see Lonely Planet's *Trekking in the Nepal Himalaya*.

Short Treks

If you don't have time for a big trek, several shorter treks from Pokhara in the southern foothills of the Annapurnas can give you a taste of life on Nepal's trails (p282). It's also possible to cobble together a mini-trek of several days around the rim of the Kathmandu Valley (p114).

You can also throw in a couple of flights here and there to speed up the trekking process. As an example, fly in to Jomsom, overnight in Marpha (to aid acclimatisation) and take a few days to hike to the surrounding villages of Kagbeni and Muktinath before flying back to Pokhara for a four- or five-day trip.

Life on the Trail

Routes & Conditions

Most trails are clear and easy to follow, though they are often steep and taxing, with long stretches of switchbacks or stone staircases. A typical day's walk lasts from between five to seven hours and rarely spends much time on level ground. Distances on a map quickly become irrelevant with the many ups and downs and twists and turns of Nepal's trails.

A little rudimentary knowledge of the Nepali language will help to make your trek easier and more interesting, although finding your way is rarely difficult on the major trekking routes and English is fairly widely spoken. See p388 for some useful Nepali words and phrases.

Sleeping & Eating

On the Everest, Langtang and Annapurna treks it's unlikely that you will walk more than an hour or two without coming across some kind of teahouse offering food and lodging, giving you great flexibility to walk as far as you wish and avoid the crowds. These lodges range from simple extensions of a traditional wooden family home to quite luxurious places with private rooms, multi-page menus, and even attached toilets and showers. Most mattresses are foam (of varying thicknesses) and some bedding is always supplied. Nevertheless, it's still a good idea to carry a sleeping bag, especially at higher elevations and during peak season. A bucket of hot water is often available for a fee.

Food in teahouses centres on endless combinations of pasta, noodles, potato, rice and vegetables, plus momos (dumplings), rice and a half-dozen types of tea, by the cup or pot. Breakfast is normally eggs, porridge or muesli. The local staple of daal bhaat (rice, lentils and vegetables) is nutritious, available everywhere and requires minimum fuel for preparation. It's also the only meal that will truly fill you up after a day trekking.

Lodges on the main trails stock expensive Snickers bars, toilet paper etc but it's wise to carry your own emergency food supplies such as granola (muesli) bars, dried fruit or chocolate. You can save some money by bringing your own instant coffee, though most places charge a small fee for a cup of boiling water.

The lodges around Jomsom and Namche Bazaar specialise in delicious apple pie, a trekkers' staple these days, along with local versions of pizza. It's surprising how many places even have cold beer available as well; before you complain about the price (as much as Rs 350 a bottle), consider that somebody had to carry that bottle of beer all the way up there and will probably have to carry the empty bottle back again!

Organised Treks

Organised camping treks generally camp each night and all you have to do is eat and crawl into your tent. Even erecting the tent is handled by the trekking crew, who put it up for you at the site selected by your *sirdar* (group leader). The porters carry virtually all of the ingredients with them and there will be a cook with well-drilled assistants who can turn out meals with impressive ingenuity.

On an organised camping trek the day is run to a remarkably tight schedule. A typical pattern would be: up at 6am, start walking at 7am, stop for lunch at 10am, start after lunch at noon, stop walking at 3pm. Nepalis rise early, eat very little for breakfast, eat a large lunch in the late morning and a second meal before dark, then retire early – you will be best off to try and follow a similar schedule.

Some organised small groups stay in lodges and the fee you pay covers your accommodation and food costs.

Everest Base Camp Trek

Duration 14 to 20 days

Maximum elevation 5545m

Best season October to December

Start Lukla

Finish Lukla

Summary Spectacular high mountain scenery, Sherpa culture, excellent lodges and views of beautiful Mt Ama Dablam are the highs of this busy and popular trek.

LUXURY TREKKING

If you demand a bit of luxury on your trek and don't want to rough it in a tent, several companies offer deluxe lodges in the Annapurna and Everest regions. You'll get the best rates on an organised trek (as opposed to turning up on your own).

Ker & Downey (www.trekking-nepal.com) operates treks staying in its deluxe chain of lodges in Dhampus, Ghandruk, Majgaun and Birethanti on the approaches to the Annapurna Sanctuary.

There is a good selection of luxury lodges in the lower reaches of the Everest region, allowing you to make a week-long trek to Namche Bazaar and around. Priority is given to guests on these company's treks but independent trekkers can also make bookings. **Nepal Luxury Treks** (www.nepalluxurytreks.com; r US$150-225) operates the luxury Everest Summit Lodges in Lukla, Monjo, Tashinga (near Photse), Mende (near Thame) and Pangboche, as well as a lodge in Kagbeni on the Annapurna Circuit. **Yeti Mountain Home** (www.yetimountainhome.com; r US$115-185) has a chain of six attractive stone lodges in Lukla, Monjo, Phakding, Namche Bazaar, Thame, and Kongde.

On the ridge above Namche Bazaar are the **Everest Sherpa Resort** (www.everestresort.com; US$96-164) and **Syanhboche Panorama Hotel** (www.everestpanorama.com; r US$70-100), two of the highest hotels in the world.

Everybody wants to see the world's highest mountain and that's the reason why the Everest Base Camp Trek is so popular. The trek has a number of stunning attractions, not least of these is being able to say you've visited the highest mountain in the world. The trek gets you right into the high-altitude heart of the high Himalaya, more so than any other teahouse trek. There are some lovely villages and gompas (monasteries), and the friendly Sherpa people of the Solu Khumbu region make trekking through the area a joy. Most of the trek is through the Sagarmatha National Park, a Unesco World Heritage Site (Sagarmatha is the Nepali name for Everest) and a refuge for musk deer, red pandas, snow leopard, Himalayan tahr, red panda, black bear and many spectacular types of pheasant.

A return trek to Everest Base Camp from the airstrip at Lukla takes at least 14 days but you are better off budgeting a further week to take in some of the stunning and less-visited side valleys. If you have the time, one way to beat the crowds is to walk in from Shivalaya or Jiri and fly out from Lukla. If you fly straight to Lukla, be sure to schedule acclimatisation days at Namche and Pheriche to avoid altitude sickness. A shorter week-long trek from Lukla could take you on a loop through Namche Bazaar, Thame, Khumjung and Tengboche Monastery.

The trek reaches a high point of 5545m at Kala Pattar, a small peak offering views of Mt Everest and the Khumbu Icefall.

Ironically, the Everest views from base camp are actually quite unimpressive (in the words of mountain writer Ed Douglas, 'Everest is like a grossly fat man in a room full of beautiful women'). Far more stirring are the graceful lines of surrounding peaks, such as Ama Dablam, Pumori and Nuptse. Perhaps the best scenery of the trek is found in the neighbouring Gokyo Valley, off the main trail.

In the last decade the tourist crowds in the Khumbu region have swollen to record numbers, partly because of the 'Krakauer effect' – the surge in Everest-mania since the release of the bestselling Jon Krakauer book *Into Thin Air,* and the endless documentaries and publications that have followed in its wake. The scenery is still breathtaking, but don't expect to have the place to yourself. This is one trek you might consider tackling outside of October, so you won't have to share the trails with 10,000 or so other trekkers.

Facilities on the Everest trek are excellent. The upper reaches of the trek are through essentially uninhabited areas but lodges operate throughout the trekking season. These days trekking and mountaineering are the backbone of the Sherpa economy. More than half of the population in the region is now involved with tourism, and the bookstore, trek-gear shops, bakeries and internet cafes in Namche Bazaar make it look more like an alpine resort than a Sherpa village.

The walking on this trek is (surprisingly) not all that strenuous, mainly because new arrivals can only walk a few hours each day before they have to stop for the night to acclimatise. If trekkers fail to reach their goal it is usually because they failed to devote enough time to acclimatisation. It may be tempting to keep walking at the end of a three-hour day, but it's essential to take it slowly on the first 10 days of this trek. For more on mountain sickness see p382.

Emergency Facilities

There are small hospitals in Jiri, Phaplu and Khunde (just north of Namche Bazaar); the Himalayan Rescue Association (HRA) has a medical facility in Pheriche.

Access

Flights from Kathmandu to Lukla

Most Everest trekkers opt to fly to Lukla (US$120) from Kathmandu to maximise their time in the high mountains and up to 75 flights land here each day during the high season. In 2008 a Yeti Airlines plane crashed at Lukla in bad visibility, killing 14 trekkers and four Nepalis. Backlogs of hundreds of trekkers (7000 in October 2011!) can build up during spates of bad weather, so give yourself a buffer of a day or two to get back to Kathmandu.

Shivalaya Trek

While most people fly in and out of Lukla these days, it's possible to trek in or out from the trailhead at Shivalaya, just past Jiri. The trek from Shivalaya to Lukla is a hard slog and pretty sparse in the breathtaking-views department but you will at least shake the crowds. The trek doesn't follow valleys, it cuts across them, so day after day it is a tiring process of dropping down one side of a steep valley and climbing up the other. By the time you reach the base camp your ascents will total almost 9000m – the full height of Everest from sea level!

There are buses at 6am and 8am from Kathmandu's Ratna Park (City) bus station to Shivalaya (Rs 630), as well as more frequent departures to Jiri (eight hours, Rs 530 to 625, departures between 5.30am and 8.45am, with super express services at 6am and 7.30am), from where you can walk or catch bumpy local transport to Shivalaya. Keep a close eye on your luggage.

Travellers have reported being asked to buy a Gauri Shankar Conservation Area permit (Rs 2000), *if* they don't already have a

Sagarmatha National Park permit (the trek passes through the conservation area for just a few hours). Make your life easier by getting the Sagarmatha permit in Kathmandu before you leave (see p35).

The trek stages generally work out as follows; lodges are available at every night's stop.

Day 1: Shivalaya to Bhandar
Day 2: Bhandar to Sete
Day 3: Sete to Junbesi
Day 4: Junbesi to Nunthala
Day 5: Nunthala to Bupsa
Day 6: Bupsa to Lukla

The Trek

DAY ONE: LUKLA TO PHAKDING

After flying to Lukla, arranging your packs and maybe a porter, trek downhill to lodges at Cheplung (Chablung). From here the trail contours along the side of the Dudh Kosi Valley before ascending to Ghat (Lhawa; 2530m). The trail climbs again to Phakding, a collection of about 25 lodges at 2610m.

DAY TWO: PHAKDING TO NAMCHE BAZAAR

The trail crosses the river on a long, swaying bridge and then leads you along the river to climb to Benkar (2700m), a decent alternative overnight stop. A short distance beyond Benkar the trail crosses the Dudh Kosi on a suspension bridge to its east bank, and then climbs to Chumoa.

It's a short climb through forests to Monjo (2800m), where there are some good places to stay. Show your entrance ticket or buy one for Rs 1000 at the Sagarmatha National Park entrance station and register your TIMS card, then descend to cross the Dudh Kosi. On the other side it's a short distance to Jorsale (Thumbug; 2830m), the last settlement before Namche Bazaar, then the trail crosses back to the east side of the river before climbing to the high suspension bridge over the Dudh Kosi.

It's a steady two-hour climb from here to Namche Bazaar (3420m). As this is the first climb to an altitude where acute mountain sickness (AMS; see p385), also known as altitude sickness, may be a problem, take it easy and avoid rushing. There is another national park entrance station just below Namche where permits are again checked and fees collected.

Everest Base Camp Trek

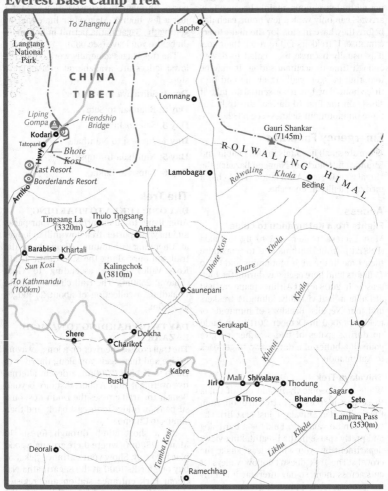

To Zhangmu

Lapche

Langtang
National
Park

CHINA
TIBET

Lomnang

Liping
Gompa

Friendship
Bridge

Gauri Shankar
(7145m)

Kodari

Tatopani

Bhote
Kosi

Last Resort

Borderlands Resort

ROLWALING HIMAL

Lamobagar

Rolwaling Khola

Beding

Tingsang La
(3320m)

Thulo Tingsang

Amatal

Barabise Khartali

Bhote Kosi

Khare Khola

Sun Kosi

Kalingchok
(3810m)

To Kathmandu
(100km)

Saunepani

Khola

Serukapti

La

Shere

Dolkha

Charikot

Khimti Khola

Kabre

Busti

Jiri Mali Shivalaya Thodung

Those

Bhandar

Sagar

Sete

Lamjura Pass
(3530m)

Deorali

Tamba Kosi

Likhu Khola

Ramechhap

DAY THREE: ACCLIMATISATION DAY IN NAMCHE BAZAAR

Namche Bazaar is the main trade and administrative centre for the entire Solu Khumbu region and has outdoor gear shops, restaurants, bakeries, pharmacies, hotels with hot showers, a pool hall, massage centre, post office, moneychanger, bank, ATM and even internet cafes. Pay a visit to the office of the **Sagarmatha Pollution Control Committee** (☺10am-5pm Mon-Fri) to find out about conservation efforts being made in the region and visit the excellent **Sagarmatha National Park Visitor**

Centre (admission free; ☺8am-4pm Sun-Fri) on the ridge above town. There is a colourful market each Saturday.

There is plenty to do around Namche Bazaar and you should spend a day here acclimatising. Remember that victims of AMS are often the fittest, healthiest people who foolishly overextend themselves. It's helpful to do a strenuous day walk to a higher altitude as part of your acclimatisation, coming back down to Namche to sleep. For this purpose, the six- to seven-hours-return day walk west to Thame is worthwhile.

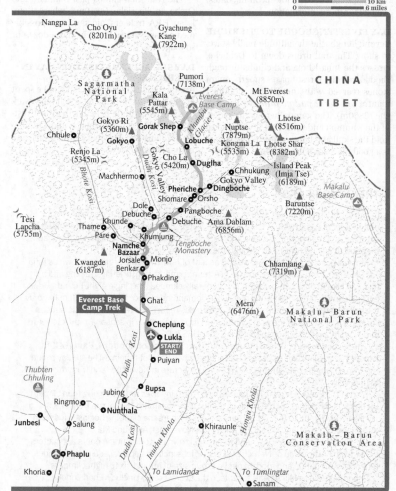

| 0 | 10 km |
| 0 | 6 miles |

DAY FOUR: NAMCHE BAZAAR TO TENGBOCHE

The slightly longer route from Namche Bazaar to Tengboche via Khumjung and Khunde is more interesting than the direct one. The route starts by climbing up to the Syangboche airstrip. Above the airstrip is the Hotel Everest View, listed in the Guinness Book of Records as the highest hotel on earth.

From the hotel or the airstrip you climb to Khunde (3840m), then Khumjung (3790m) and then rejoin the direct trail to Tengboche. The trail descends to the Dudh Kosi (3250m) where there are several small lodges and a series of picturesque water-driven prayer wheels. A steep ascent brings you to Tengboche (3870m). The famous gompa, with its background of Ama Dablam, Everest and other peaks, was burnt down in 1989 but has since risen phoenix-like from the ashes. There's a camping area and several busy lodges.

During the October/November full moon the colourful Mani Rimdu festival is held here with masked dancing and Tibetan opera in the monastery courtyard – accommodation becomes extremely difficult to find.

See www.tengboche.org for upcoming dates; see p22 for more information.

DAY FIVE: TENGBOCHE TO PHERICHE

Beyond Tengboche the altitude really starts to show. The trail drops down to Debuche, crosses the Imja Khola and climbs through rhododendron forest past superb mani stones (carved with the Tibetan Buddhist mantra *om mani padme hum*) to Pangboche (3860m). The gompa here is the oldest in the Khumbu and until 1991 it was said to hold the skull and hand of a yeti. The village is a good place for a lunch stop.

The trail then climbs past Shomare and Orsho to Pheriche (4240m), where there is an HRA trekkers' aid post and possible medical assistance. Pheriche has a dozen or so lodges.

DAY SIX: ACCLIMATISATION DAY IN PHERICHE

Another acclimatisation day should be spent at Pheriche. As at Namche, a solid day walk to a higher altitude is better than just resting; the villages of Dingboche and Chhukung (4730m) are possible destinations and both offer good views.

TREKKING PEAKS

If you want to take the next step from trekking to mountaineering, consider a short mountaineering course that takes in one of Nepal's 'trekking peaks'. Several companies organise mountaineering courses and ascents in the Solu Khumbu region and can add these on to an organised trek through the region.

Most popular is a six-day course and ascent of **Island Peak**, properly known as Imja Tse (6189m), from a base in Chhukung. After acclimatisation, briefing, training and a half-day hike to base camp, the peak is generally climbed in a single eight-hour day, departing early in the morning. It's physically demanding but not technically difficult – only the last section is on ice and snow, though guides report that retreating glaciers mean some rock climbing is increasingly required. Trips run weekly in season (mid-October to mid-November, end March to May) and cost US$700.

The second most popular option is the false summit of **Lobuche East** (6119m), a more technically difficult ascent that requires two days' of training. The six-day round trip from Dzongla costs around US$700. Trips operate in November and from mid-April to mid-May.

Also in the Everest region, **Mera Peak** (6476m) involves more trekking than climbing, though it is the highest of the trekking peaks. It's a minimum 15-day trip from Lukla and involves trekking up to the 5415m Mera La, from where the climbing begins. Trips from Kathmandu cost around US$2000 and run in November, April and May.

For all of these trips you will need to hire your own plastic climbing boots and gaiters, either from Kathmandu or Namche Bazaar. Prices include permits, equipment, guides, tent accommodation and food. Expect a group size of around six to eight climbers.

Other possible trekking peak ascents in the Everest region include Phari Lapche (6017m), Macchermo (6273m) and Kyozo/Kyajo Ri (6186m). In the Annapurna region, Pisang Peak (6091m) and Chulu East (6584m) are both five-day excursions from Manang. Companies that organise ascents include the following in Kathmandu:

» **Alternative Nepal** (☏01-4700170; www.alternativenepal.com)

» **Climb High Himalaya** (☏01-4372874; www.climbhighhimalaya.com)

» **Equator Expeditions** (☏01-4700782; www.equatorexpeditionsnepal.com, www.nepalgate.com)

» **Himalayan Ecstasy** (☏01-4700795; www.himalayanecstasy.com) Offers Island and Lobuche Peaks together in one trip for US$1000.

» **Mountain Monarch** (☏01-4361668; www.mountainmonarch.com)

» **Namaste Adventure** (☏01-4700239; www.namasteadventure.com) From trekking peaks to full-on mountaineering trips.

» **Nepal Mountain Trekking** (☏01-4700006; www.nepalmountain.com) Across from Northfield Cafe; generally a bit more expensive.

Nangkartshang Gompa, on the ridge north of Dingboche, offers good views east to Makalu (8462m), the world's fifth-highest mountain. Chhukung is a five- to six-hour return hike up the Imja Khola Valley, which offers stunning views. There is food and accommodation at Chhukung.

DAY SEVEN: PHERICHE TO DUGLHA

The trail climbs to Phulang Kala (4340m) then Duglha (4620m). It's only a two-hour trek to Duglha but the Himalayan Rescue Association (HRA) doctors at Pheriche urge everyone to stay a night here in order to aid acclimatisation.

DAY EIGHT: DUGLHA TO LOBUCHE

From Duglha the trail goes directly up the gravely terminal moraine of the Khumbu Glacier for about an hour, then bears left to a group of memorials to lost climbers and Sherpas, including Scott Fischer who died in the 1996 Everest disaster. It's a short climb past views of Pumori to the summer village of Lobuche (4930m). The altitude, cold and crowded lodges combine to ensure a fitful night's sleep.

DAY NINE: LOBUCHE TO GORAK SHEP

The return trip from Lobuche to Gorak Shep (5160m) takes just a couple of hours, leaving enough time to continue to the peak of Kala Pattar (three hours return) – or you can overnight in Gorak Shep and reach Kala Pattar early the next morning for the best chance of good weather. At 5545m this small peak offers the best view you'll get of Everest in Nepal without climbing it.

Gorak Shep was the base camp for the 1952 Swiss expedition to Everest. There is accommodation here but it's cold and the altitude makes life uncomfortable. If the altitude is getting to you, descending to Lobuche or, better, Pheriche, makes a real difference.

DAY 10: GORAK SHEP TO LOBUCHE

If you want to visit Everest Base Camp (5360m), it's a six-hour round trip from Gorak Shep. EBC is dotted with tents in the April/May climbing season but in other months there's not a great deal to see except for views of the Khumbu Icefall. There are no views of Everest from base camp. If you only have the energy for one side trip, make it Kala Pattar.

The two-hour trek back down to Lobuche seems easy after all the climbing, and some trekkers continue for another three hours down to Dingboche or Pheriche the same day.

DAY 11: LOBUCHE TO DINGBOCHE

Staying the night at Dingboche (4410m) makes an interesting alternative to Pheriche. There are good lodges, Nepal's highest internet cafe and fine views of Island Peak (Imja Tse; 6189m) and Lhotse (8516m).

DAYS 12 TO 14: DINGBOCHE TO LUKLA

The next three days retrace your steps down to Lukla via Tengboche and Namche Bazaar. If you are flying out of Lukla, get to the airline office the day before to reconfirm your seat (the airline offices are usually open from 5pm to 6pm, but sometimes it's 6pm to 7pm). If the weather has been bad, you might be vying for a flight with hundreds of other trekkers, but generally you shouldn't have a problem.

Alternative Routes & Side Trips

The side trips off the Everest Base Camp Trek rank as some of the region's highlights so it makes sense to add an extra week or so to your itinerary to explore the region more fully.

A particularly scenic side trip is the six-day detour from Namche Bazaar to the **Gokyo Valley**, culminating in the spectacular glacier and lake views from Gokyo Ri (5360m). It's important to ascend the valley slowly, overnighting in Phortse Thenga, Dole, Machhermo and Gokyo to aid acclimatisation. From Gokyo you can rejoin the main EBC trail near Khumjung or Pangboche. A loop route taking in the Gokyo Valley and Everest Base Camp via Cho La takes around 17 days.

You can combine both the Gokyo Valley and Everest Base Camp by crossing the Cho La (5420m), but you need to take this route seriously and enquire about the conditions before setting out. Some months the pass is clear of snow; at other times you'll need crampons for this high crossing.

Throw in the high crossings of the Renjo La (5345m), between Thame and Gokyo, and the Kongma La (5535m), between Lobuche and Chhukung, and you get the Three Passes Trek, a 20-day trek for experienced connoisseurs.

A shorter side trip is from Namche Bazaar to **Thame**, the gateway to the forbidden Nangpa La pass into Tibet. You can do a round trip to Thame in one very long day, but it's better to stay overnight to catch the morning views. A seven- or eight-day return itinerary from Lukla could take in Namche Bazaar, Thame, Khumjung, Khunde and

EVEREST NUTS

The world's highest peak has attracted many commendable achievements: the first ascent without oxygen (1978), first summit with an artificial leg (1998), the first ski descent (2000), the first blind ascent (2001), most ascents (21), youngest ascent (aged 13), oldest ascent (aged 78) and fastest ascent (eight hours). Sherpa Babu Chiru spent a particularly amazing 21 hours on top of Everest without oxygen in 1999.

But there have also been some admirably silly achievements. Perhaps most ambitious was the Briton Maurice Wilson, who planned to crash his Gypsy Moth airplane halfway up the mountain and then climb from there to the top, not letting his almost total lack of mountaineering or flying experience get in the way of an obviously flawed plan. He eventually froze to death at Camp III dressed in a light sweater (and, it is rumoured, women's clothing).

Maybe it's something in the national psyche (this is after all the nation that gave us Monty Python), for it was also a team of Brits who trekked all the way to Everest Base Camp to play the 'world's highest game of rugby' at 5140m. They lost.

Our personal Everest heroes are the British(!) pair who carried an ironing board up Everest to 5440m to do some extreme ironing ('part domestic chore, part extreme sport'). For anyone contemplating a repeat expedition, the duo have revealed that expedition preparation can be limited to three important factors: 'a few beers, a drunken bet and a stolen ironing board'.

Tengboche, giving you a low-altitude taste of the region.

Another recommended two-day side trip is up the Imja Khola Valley to **Chhukung**, for awesome mountain views. Chhukung is also the staging post for climbers heading to Island Peak (see p272) and the valley is well worth exploring.

As an alternative to flying back to Kathmandu you can escape the crowds on the nine-day teahouse trek southeast from **Lukla to Tumlingtar**, from where you can fly or bus back to Kathmandu. For full details see Lonely Planet's *Trekking in the Nepal Himalaya* guide.

Annapurna Circuit Trek

Duration 12 to 19 days

Maximum elevation 5416m

Best season October to November

Start Besi Sahar

Finish Jomsom or Naya Pul

Summary The sense of journey, the challenging crossing of a high pass, and excellent day trips to monasteries and mountain lakes make this a Himalayan classic.

It takes nearly three weeks to walk the entire Annapurna Circuit. For scenery and cultural diversity this has long been considered the best trek in Nepal and one of the world's classic walks. It follows the Marsyangdi Khola (Marsyangdi Valley) to the north of the main Himalayan range and crosses a 5416m pass to descend into the dramatic desertlike, Tibetan-style scenery of the upper Kali Gandaki Valley.

The walk passes picturesque villages home to Gurungs, Manangis and Thakalis, offers spectacular mountain views of the numerous 7000m-plus Annapurna peaks and boasts some of the best trekking lodges in Nepal.

Road construction is having an effect on the popularity of the Annapurna Circuit. The first half of the circuit on the Manang side is so far little affected but the former Jomsom trek, through the Kali Gandaki Valley on the west side, is now cut by a dirt road, plied by infrequent but dusty jeep and motorbike traffic. Some trekkers now end their trek in Jomsom. All is not lost though; a series of new alternative trails on the eastern side of the valley avoids the new road, the scenery is equally if not more spectacular, and the lodges are still excellent. The nature of the trail has changed from a long-distance trek to a series of day hikes from bases on the road, but in reality this trek was never a wilderness walk. There are great opportunities for adventurous mountain-biking trips along this section, though you'll have to bring your own bike (see p295).

The circuit is usually walked counter clockwise because the climb to Thorung La (5416m) from the western side is too strenuous and has too much elevation gain to consider in one day. Thorung La is often closed due to snow from mid-December to mid-March, and bad weather can move in at any time. The trail to the pass can be hard to find in fresh snow and you should be prepared to turn back due to the weather and altitude. It's essential to take your time between Manang and the pass in order to acclimatise properly. All trekkers, including porters, must be adequately equipped for severe cold and snow.

Our best tip for this trek is to remember that the side trips and excursions from places like Manang, Muktinath and Jomsom rank as some of the highlights of the trek. It's worth adding a couple of days to your itinerary and exploring some of these trails. You'll be better acclimatised for the pass and you'll manage to shake some of the crowds. This is not scenery to rush through.

Access: Kathmandu or Pokhara to Besi Sahar

Buses run to Besi Sahar between 6.30am and noon from Kathmandu (Rs 350, six hours) and there are three buses in the morning and one in the afternoon from Pokhara (Rs 200 to 250, five hours). Tourist buses are supposed to run daily from Kathmandu to Bhulbule (US$10), departing from near the International Guest House but the service is erratic so ask first at a travel agency.

From Besi Sahar (800m) buses run every hour or two to Bhulbule (Rs 60, 30 minutes to one hour), though most drivers insist on charging foreigners three or four times the local price. Cramped jeeps run as far as Syange (Rs 250), when the dirt road isn't blocked by monsoon landslides.

The Trek

DAY ONE: BESI SAHAR TO BHULBULE
If you arrive in Besi Sahar at lunchtime, it's possible to take the bus or hike along the road to Bhulbule or even Ngadi that same day. The approach to Bhulbule (840m) offers fine views of Himalchuli (to the northeast) and Ngadi Chuli (aka Manaslu II or Peak 29). You enter the Annapurna Conservation Area in Bhulbule and should register at the ACAP checkpoint. If you did not get your ACAP permit in advance (Rs 2000), you will have to pay double here.

DAY TWO: BHULBULE TO GHERMU
The trail leaves the road at Bhulbule and crosses to the east bank of the Marsyangdi, continuing to Ngadi (a good alternative first night) before reaching Bahundanda (1270m), 'Hill of the Brahmins', on a ridge. Bahundanda has several lodges, shops and restaurants.

From Bahundanda the trail drops steeply to Lili Bhir and then follows an exposed trail to Kanigaon and Ghermu (1140m), with its views of the high waterfall across the river.

DAY THREE: GHERMU TO TAL
Descend to Syange (1080m) and cross to the west bank of the Marsyangdi Khola on a suspension bridge. The trail then climbs steeply and crosses a cliff face to the stone village of Jagat, perched strategically in a steep-sided valley and looking for all the world like the toll station for the Tibetan salt trade that it was. The trail descends before climbing through forest to Chamje (1410m). You can see road construction on the cliffs above you.

The rocky trail crosses the Marsyangdi Khola again, then follows the valley steadily uphill to Tal (1700m), a former lakebed. Here the valley has been filled by ancient landslides and the river meanders through the fertile flat land before disappearing under some huge boulders. Tal is the first village in the Manang district.

DAY FOUR: TAL TO CHAME
Today is a long day, so consider breaking your walk in Timang or Koto. The trail crosses the valley floor then climbs a stone stairway before dropping down to another crossing of the Marsyangdi. The trail continues past Khotro and Karte to Dharapani (1960m), which is marked by a stone entrance chörten typical of the Tibetan-influenced villages from here northward.

Bagarchhap (2160m) is a good lunch spot. A landslide roared through the centre of this village in late 1995 and managed to wipe out much of it, including two lodges. There are more lunch spots at nearby Danaque.

The trail climbs steeply from Danaque, gaining 500m to Timang and then continues through a forest of pine and fir, past the traditional village of Thanchowk to Koto (2640m), at the junction of the Nar-Phu Valley. Nearby Chame (2710m) is the headquarters of the Manang district and it has lodges, internet cafes, trek-gear shops, a health post and a bank. At the entrance to

Annapurna Treks

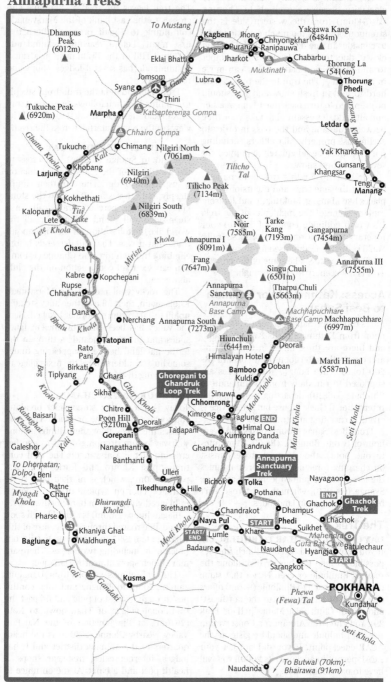

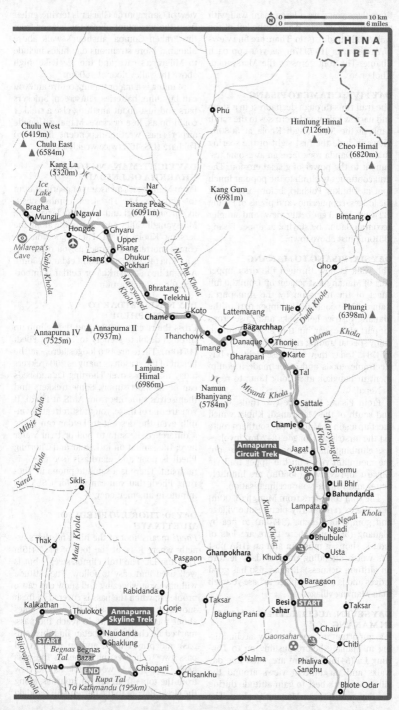

the village you pass a large mani wall with many prayer wheels. Walk to the left of the wall as all Buddhists do. There are fine views of Annapurna II (7937m) as you approach Chame. The route crosses the Marsyangdi Khola here.

DAY FIVE: CHAME TO PISANG

The trail runs through deep forest in a steep and narrow valley and recrosses to the south bank of the Marsyangdi Khola at 3080m. Views include the first sight of the soaring Paungda Danda rock face, an awesome testament to the power of glacial erosion. The trail continues to climb to the popular lunch spot at Dhukur Pokhari, before arriving at the lodges, cappuccinos and pizzas of Pisang (3240m). You'll get better views and simpler accommodation by staying at upper Pisang (3310m), just above town.

DAY SIX: PISANG TO MANANG

The walk is now through the drier upper part of Manang district, cut off from the full effect of the monsoon by the Annapurna Range. The people of the upper part of the Manang district herd yaks and raise crops for part of the year, but they also continue to enjoy special trading rights gained way back in 1784. Today they use these rights to buy electronic goods and other modern equipment in Bangkok and Hong Kong to resell in Nepal.

From Pisang there are two trails, north and south of the Marsyangdi Khola, which meet up again at Mungji. The southern route via the airstrip at Hongde (3420m) involves less climbing than the northern route, but the mountain views on the upper trail via Ghyaru and Ngawal (3660m) are infinitely better and will aid your acclimatisation.

The trail continues from Mungji (3500m) past the extraordinarily picturesque village and gompa of Bragha (3470m) to nearby Manang (3540m), where there are lots of lodges, shops, a museum and an HRA post (it's worth attending the free daily lecture on altitude sickness). Bragha also has good lodges and is a quieter place to base yourself than Manang village.

DAY SEVEN: ACCLIMATISATION DAY IN MANANG

It's important to spend a day acclimatising in Manang before pushing on to Thorung La (5416m). There are some fine day walks and magnificent views around the village, and it's best to gain altitude during the day, returning to Manang to sleep. The view of Gangapurna Glacier is terrific, either from the viewpoint above the lake or from the Praken Gompa, an hour's walk above Manang. More strenuous day hikes include to Milarepa's cave and the Ice Lake, high above the valley floor at 4600m.

Manang is a major trading centre and you can buy film, batteries, sunscreen, Snickers bars and just about anything else a trekker could break, lose or crave. Manang/Hongde airport has weather-dependent flights to Pokhara (US$107, twice weekly).

DAY EIGHT: MANANG TO YAK KHARKHA OR LETDAR

From Manang it's an ascent of nearly 2000m to Thorung La. The trail climbs steadily through Tengi and Gunsang, leaving the Marsyangdi Valley and continuing along the Jarsang Khola Valley. The vegetation becomes shorter and sparser as you reach Yak Kharkha (4020m) and then Letdar (4230m). A night in Yak Kharkha or Letdar is important for acclimatisation.

DAY NINE: LETDAR TO THORUNG PHEDI

Cross the river at 4310m and then climb up through desolate scenery to Thorung Phedi (4540m). There are two lodges here – at the height of the season as many as 200 trekkers a day may cross over Thorung La and beds can be in short supply. Some trekkers find themselves suffering from AMS at Phedi. If you are one of these, you must retreat downhill; even the descent to Letdar can make a difference. Be sure to boil or treat water here; the sanitation in Letdar and Thorung Phedi is poor and giardiasis (see p385) is rampant. There is a satellite phone in Thorung Phedi that you can use for US$5 per minute in an emergency.

DAY 10: THORUNG PHEDI TO MUKTINATH

Phedi means 'foot of the hill' and that's exactly where it is, at the foot of the 5416m Thorung La. The trail climbs steeply but is well used and easy to follow. The altitude will have you wheezing and snow can cause problems; when the pass is covered in fresh snow it is often impossible to cross. It takes about four to six hours to reach the pass, marked by chörtens (Tibetan Buddhist stupas) and prayer flags, and en route you'll pass two teahouses, plus one on the pass itself. The effort is worthwhile as the view from the top – from the Annapurnas, along the Great Barrier to the barren Kali Gandaki

THE GREAT HIMALAYAN TRAIL

If you are up for a challenge, you might want to consider the Great Himalayan Trail, a 2500km walk across the entire spine of the Nepal Himalaya, from Humla in the west to Kanchenjunga in the east. There are several logistical hurdles to overcome, mainly with coordinating a whole fistful of timed trekking permits, but at least one trekking company (World Expeditions) offers the trail as a commercial trip, lasting for 157 days and costing a cool US$30,000. Several extreme athletes have already completed the route (self-supported) in as little as 47 days.

The trail is partly a pre-existing network of trekking routes and partly a slick marketing campaign aimed at getting trekkers into regions currently not benefiting economically from tourism. Perhaps the best way to attempt the trail is to do it in segments, biting off chunks such as the Annapurna–Manaslu route or Jiri–Everest section, and doing it over several years.

For more information see the excellent The Great Himalaya Trail website (www.thegreathimalayatrail.org). And good luck.

Valley – is magnificent. From the pass you have a knee-busting and sometimes slippery 1600m descent to Muktinath (3800m).

Some people start out for the pass at 3am but this is not only unnecessary but also potentially dangerous due to the risk of frostbite and accidents in the darkness. A better starting time is 5am to 6am.

Muktinath itself has no accommodation; for that you'll have to continue for 10 minutes to nearby Ranipauwa.

DAY 11: MUKTINATH TO KAGBENI

Muktinath is a pilgrimage site for Buddhists and Hindus alike. You'll see Tibetan traders here as well as sadhus from as far away as the south of India. The shrines, in a grove of trees, include a Buddhist gompa, a Vishnu temple and the Jwalamai (Goddess of Fire) Temple, which shelters a spring and natural gas jets that provide Muktinath's famous eternal flame. It's the combination of earth, water and fire in such proximity that accounts for Muktinath's great religious significance.

From Ranipauwa the road descends through a desertlike Trans-Himalayan landscape to the dramatic village of Jharkot (3500m), with its large chörten, gompa and atmospheric animist totems. The trail continues to Khingar (3400m) and then follows the road down steeply to the medieval-looking village of Kagbeni (2840m).

If you have half a day to spare, it's worth making the short detour across the valley to the charming traditional villages of Chhyongkhar, Jhong and Purang, all traditionally part of Mustang but visitable without the need for extra permits.

DAY 12: KAGBENI TO JOMSOM

The Tibetan-influenced settlement of Kagbeni has a number of good lodges and is as close as you can get to Lo Manthang, the capital of the legendary kingdom of Mustang further to the north, without paying a US$500 permit fee.

From Kagbeni it is a dusty, rocky but mostly flat stroll along the road to Jomsom (2760m). Jomsom is the major centre in the region and it has facilities such as a hospital, an ACAP visitor centre and a police checkpost (where you must register and get your ACAP permit stamped). This is the first of the Thakali villages of the Kali Gandaki (Gandaki River). Jomsom has regular morning flights to Pokhara (US$76 to US$82) and jeep services down to Ghasa, Beni and eventually Pokhara, so this is where many travellers end their trek. For more on Jomsom see p209.

If you have some extra time, it's worth continuing south to the traditional white-washed stone village of Marpha (2680m), which has a gompa and several smaller shrines. The town boasts some of the most luxurious accommodation to be found along the trail, which makes it a good alternative to staying in Jomsom.

Try to be on the trail early in the morning in the Kali Gandaki Valley, as strong winds tend to pick up after 11am.

DAYS 13 TO 19: JOMSOM TO NAYA PUL

The Annapurna Circuit south of Jomsom follows the new road through the Kali Gandaki Valley to Naya Pul. This section of the trek has become less popular since the road was constructed but it's still a

YETI!

Along with the equally slippery notion of Shangri La, the yeti is one of Nepal's most famous cultural exports, occupying a hotly debated biological niche somewhere between zoology and folk religion.

Before you throw your arms up in the air and storm out of the room, bear in mind that the pro-yeti camp has some serious proponents. In 1938 mountaineer Bill Tilman tracked yeti footprints for over a mile, later writing that their 'existence is surely no longer a matter for conjecture'. Eric Shipton photographed a yeti print on the Menling/Menlungtse Glacier in 1951. Edmund Hillary led an expedition to Rolwaling in 1960 to track the yeti, as did Chris Bonington in 1986 and travel writer Bruce Chatwin. Reinhold Messner claimed to have seen a yeti in Tibet in 1986 and wrote a book about the subject called *My Quest for the Yeti*.

There are dozens of cases of local sightings. Villagers in the Rongbuk region of Tibet apparently discovered a drowned yeti corpse in 1958. In 1998 the official police report on the murder of a Sherpa woman near Dole on the Gokyo trek in Nepal cited 'yeti attack' as the cause of death! Japan's most celebrated yeti hunter is Yoshiteru Takahashi, who in 2003 claimed to have found a yeti cave on the slopes of Dhaulagiri (his camera froze before he could take a photo...).

The Rolwaling region seems to be the heartland of yeti sightings, followed closely by the Khumbu. Trekkers on the Everest Base Camp Trek can still see the yeti scalp at Khumjung Monastery (actually made from the skin of a serow – a type of goat/antelope). The region's 'yeti pelts' actually belong to the Himalayan blue bear.

The yeti hand of Pangboche, said to have been that of a mummified lama, mysteriously disappeared in the 1990s. One of the most bizarre stories in a field specialising in half-truths is that one of the original bones of the Pangboche hand was given to Hollywood actor James Stewart, whose wife allegedly smuggled it to the UK in her lingerie box. Weird.

The word 'yeti' comes from the Tibetan *yeh-teh*, or 'man of the rocky/snowy places'; the alternative Tibetan names are the *migyu* and *mehton kangmi*, or 'abominable snowman'. Reports from western Nepal talk of the *lamkarna*, or 'long-eared' monster. First-hand accounts of the yeti describe it as having reddish fur, a conical head, a high-pitched cry and strange body odour that smells of garlic, but a sign at Khumjung Monastery outlines the different types of yeti in more subtle and, more importantly, cultural terms. The apelike *dre-ma* and *tel-ma* are messengers of calamity, it says, while the *chu-ti* moves on all fours and preys on goats, sheep and yaks. Worst of all is the *mi-te*, a man-eater, 6ft to 8ft tall, with 'a very bad temperament'. Consider yourself warned.

rewarding walk if you take the detours on the east bank that avoid the road as much as possible. ACAP is in the process of rebuilding trails and bridges on the east bank to enable trekkers to avoid the road completely. There are excellent lodges at Marpha, Tukuche, Larjung, Lete, Kalopani, Ghasa and Tatopani. Figure on three days to Tatopani or four to five days to Gorepani.

South of Jomsom it's worth detouring down the east bank via Dhumba Lake to Katsapterenga Gompa, before returning to the road at Syang and continuing to **Marpha**.

Just south of Marpha another detour heads down the eastern bank from the Tibetan settlement around Chhairo Gompa to Chimang village, which offers superb views of Dhaulagiri, the world's sixth largest mountain.

Back on the west bank, **Tukuche** (2580m) is one of the valley's most important Thakali villages and once was a depot and customs spot for salt traders from Tibet. Several grand houses and gompas hark back to a more prosperous past.

The road continues to Khobang and Larjung (2560m), past good views of Dhaulagiri (8167m) and Nilgiri North (7061m). This section of the Kali Gandaki Valley is claimed by some to be the deepest in the world, the rationale being that in the 38km between the peaks of Annapurna I and Dhaulagiri I (both above 8000m) the valley floor drops almost 4000m. Larjung is the base for a tough excursion up to the Dhaulagiri Icefall.

Another excursion branches off the road at Kokhethati, leading to Titi Lake (2670m) for views of the eastern flank of Dhaulagiri and then down to the villages of Konjo and Taglung, with their spectacular views of Nilgiri peak. The trails eventually rejoin the road just south of conjoined Lete (2480m) and Kalopani, both of which have fine accommodation and views.

The road continues south to **Ghasa** (2000m), the last Thakali village in the valley, and then a foot trail branches down the east side of the narrowing gorge, rejoining the road after a couple of hours at the waterfall of Rupse Chhahara (1560m). The road continues down to Dana and **Tatopani** (1190m), noted for its concrete hot springs.

From Tatopani you can hop on a jeep or bus to Beni (Rs 360) and Pokhara (Rs 580) or you can continue up the steep side valley from Ghar Khola, gaining an epic 1600m past Sikha and Chitre to Ghorepani in the Annapurna foothills. This is one of the hardest days on the circuit.

An hour's climb from the ridge at upper **Ghorepani** (also known as Deorali) will take you to **Poon Hill** (3210m), one of the best Himalayan viewpoints in the lower hills. *Ghore* means 'horse' and *pani* 'water', and indeed, long caravans of pack horses were once a regular sight here.

From Ghorepani you can descend the long, stone staircases to Nangathanti (2460m), Banthanti (2250m) and Ulleri, which is a large Magar village at 1960m, before continuing steeply to Tikedhunga, Birethanti (1000m) and the nearby roadhead at Naya Pul.

A two-day trail also runs from Ghorepani to Ghandruk, where you can join up with the Annapurna Sanctuary Trek.

If you decide to take local transport between Jomsom and Pokhara, you'll have to change transport in Beni (Jomsom–Beni Rs 800, Beni–Pokhara Rs 220) and you may also have to change en route in Ghasa. Expect to stay overnight in Beni and be prepared for a bumpy ride.

NAYA PUL TO POKHARA

Catch a bus from Naya Pul to Pokhara (Rs 90, two hours) or, alternatively, you can return to Pokhara from Jomsom or Tatopani.

Annapurna Sanctuary Trek

Duration 10 to 14 days

Maximum elevation 4095m

Best season October to November

Start Phedi

Finish Naya Pul

Summary Classic walk past Gurung villages climbing to a high amphitheatre of stunning 7000m and 8000m peaks.

This trek leads right into the frozen heart of the Annapurna Range, a magnificent amphitheatre of rock and ice on a staggering scale. The trail starts in rice paddies and leads through a gorge of bamboo and forests to end among glaciers and soaring peaks – an unparalleled mountain experience. Other highlights include sublime views of fish-tailed Machhapuchhare (6997m) and one of Nepal's largest and prettiest Gurung villages at Ghandruk, which is a short detour off the main trek.

The return trek can take as little as 10 days but 14 days will give you more time to soak up the scenery. You can tack a walk to the sanctuary onto the Annapurna Circuit for an epic 25- to 30-day walk.

There are several possible routes to the sanctuary, all meeting at Chhomrong. The diversion from the Annapurna Circuit Trek branches off from Ghorepani to reach Chhomrong via Tadapani.

Access: Pokhara to Phedi

Buses leave every 40 minutes or so from Pokhara's Baglung bus stand to Phedi (Rs 45, 1½ hours), a cluster of shacks, from where the trail starts up a series of stone steps.

The Trek

DAY ONE: PHEDI TO TOLKA

From Phedi the trail climbs steeply to Dhampus (1750m), which stretches for several kilometres from 1580m to 1700m and has a number of hotels strung along the ridge. Theft is a problem in Dhampus, so take care.

The trail climbs to Pothana (1990m) and descends steeply through a forest towards Bichok. It emerges in the Modi Khola Valley and continues to drop to Tolka (1810m).

DAY TWO: TOLKA TO CHHOMRONG

From Tolka the trail descends a long stone staircase and then follows a ridge to the

AVALANCHES ON THE SANCTUARY TRAIL

There is significant danger of avalanches along the route to the Annapurna Sanctuary between Doban and Machhapuchhare Base Camp. Trekkers have died and trekking parties have been stranded in the sanctuary for days, the trail blocked by tonnes of ice and snow. Always check with the ACAP office in Chhomrong and lodges in Deorali for a report on current trail conditions, and do not proceed into the sanctuary if there has been recent heavy rain or snow.

Gurung village of Landruk (1620m). Ten minutes from here the path splits – north takes you to Chhomrong and the sanctuary, or you can detour west downhill towards Ghandruk.

The sanctuary trail turns up the Modi Khola Valley to Himal Qu (also known as Naya Pul; 1340m). It then continues up to Jhinu Danda (1750m) and its nearby hot spring before a steep climb to Taglung (2190m), where it joins the Ghandruk to Chhomrong trail.

Chhomrong, at 2210m, is the last permanent settlement in the valley. This large and sprawling Gurung village has excellent lodges, fine views and an ACAP office where you can enquire about trail conditions in the sanctuary.

DAY THREE: CHHOMRONG TO BAMBOO

The trail drops down a set of stone steps to the Chhomrong Khola, and then climbs to Sinuwa and on through rhododendron forests to Kuldi (2470m). The trek now enters the upper Modi Khola Valley, where ACAP controls the location and number of lodges and limits their size. This section of the trail is a bottleneck and you may find lodges in Bamboo are full during the high season, in which case you may have to continue for an hour to the next accommodation in Doban or sleep in the dining room. In winter it is common to find snow from this point on.

Continue on to Bamboo (2310m), which is a collection of three hotels. This stretch of the trail has leeches early and late in the trekking season.

DAY FOUR: BAMBOO TO HIMALAYAN HOTEL

The trail climbs through rhododendron forests to Doban (2540m) and on to the Himalayan Hotel at 2840m. This stretch of the trail passes several avalanche chutes. If you arrive early, it's possible to continue on to Deorali to make the following day easier.

DAY FIVE: HIMALAYAN HOTEL TO MACHHAPUCHHARE BASE CAMP

From the Himalayan Hotel it's on to Hinko (3100m) then to lodges at Deorali, at the gateway to the sanctuary. The next stretch of trail is the most subject to avalanches and you detour temporarily to the east side of the valley to avoid a dangerous chute.

At Machhapuchhare Base Camp (which isn't really a base camp since climbing the mountain is not permitted), at 3700m, there is decent accommodation available. Be alert to signs of altitude sickness before heading off to Annapurna Base Camp.

DAY SIX: MACHHAPUCHHARE BASE CAMP TO ANNAPURNA BASE CAMP

The climb to the Annapurna Base Camp at 4130m takes about two hours and is best done early in the day before clouds roll in. If there is snow, the trail may be difficult to follow. The lodges here can get very crowded at the height of the season. The frozen dawn is best observed from the glacial moraine a short stroll from your cosy lodge.

DAYS SEVEN TO 14: ANNAPURNA BASE CAMP TO NAYA PUL

On the return trip head south to Chhomrong (two days) and on to Ghandruk (one day) via the deep valley of the Khumnu Khola. From Ghandruk you can follow the valley directly down to Birethanti and Naya Pul in a day, or detour west to Ghorepani to visit Poon Hill, before descending to Birethanti (four days) and Naya Pul. Buses to Pokhara stop in Naya Pul (Rs 90, two hours).

Other Annapurna Treks

Ghachok Trek (Two Days)

This interesting two-day trek ascends the hills north of Pokhara to the traditional Gurung villages around Ghachok. It starts from Hyangja, near the Tashi Palkhel Tibetan settlement, and crosses the Mardi Khola to Lhachok before ascending to the stone-walled village of Ghachok, where you can stop overnight before turning south and returning to Pokhara via Batulechaur. With more time, you can extend this walk to visit some even more remote villages in the valley leading north from Ghachok.

Ghorepani to Ghandruk Loop (Six Days)

This triangular walk offers pleasant Gurung villages and fine views from the popular Poon Hill (3210m) viewpoint and is a good choice in winter months.

The trail starts at Naya Pul, on the road from Pokhara to Baglung, and follows the Annapurna Circuit trail in reverse for the first two days, with overnight stops in Tiked-hunga and Ghorepani. On day three, most people leave before dawn for the short 1.5km hike to Poon Hill and its fine vista of snowy peaks, including Annapurna South (7273m) and Machhapuchhare (6997m). Relax in Ghorepani for the rest of the day.

Day four involves a gentle descent to Ta-dapani, and day five continues downhill to Ghandruk, a scenic Gurung village of stone and slate houses with a colourful Buddhist monastery. The final day is an easy descent back to Naya Pul, where you can pick up buses back to Pokhara. Alternatively, head east across the valley to Landruk and stop overnight at Tolka, before continuing to Phedi on the Baglung Hwy.

Annapurna Skyline Trek (Royal Trek) (Four Days)

Following a low ridge east of Pokhara, with spine-tingling views of the Annapurna peaks, the four-day Annapurna Skyline Trek (or Royal Trek) was famously walked by Prince Charles in 1980. The path is easy to follow but because it lies off the main tourist circuit there's no teahouse accommodation en route, except at Begnas Tal. Most people bring a stove and camp at basic campsites along the route.

The trail starts near the army camp on the Prithvi Hwy, just east of the Bijayapur Khola, and crosses a flat area of rice fields before climbing the ridge to Kalikathan (1370m), which has two basic campsites with fine views.

On day two follow the forested ridge through Thulokot to teahouses at Mati Thana, before climbing to Naudanda, Lipini and finally Shaklung (1730m), with another simple camping ground.

On day three the trail descends to the valley floor, then rises to the attractive Gurung village of Chisopani (1629m) – the campsite is a short walk beyond the village near a ridge-top temple and the views are sublime. The final day involves a leisurely stroll along the ridge that separates Rupa Tal and Beg-nas Tal (see p213), emerging on the valley floor at Begnas Bazar, where buses leave regularly for Pokhara.

Langtang Valley Trek

Duration Seven to eight days

Maximum elevation 3870m

Best season September to May

Start Syabrubesi

Finish Syabrubesi

Summary A good variety of scenery, fewer crowds and accessible high alpine scenery here, though the bus trip to the trailhead is hard work.

The Langtang region is the third most popular trekking area in Nepal but receives only a fraction of the crowds that hit the Annapurna and Everest trails. Langtang has many things going for it: it's close to Kathmandu, there's a wide range of scenery, you get right into the mountains within a couple of days, the accommodation is good and there are lots of possible trek combinations.

The trek ascends the Langtang Valley from just 1470m at Syabrubesi to 3870m at Kyanjin Gompa, past ever-changing scenery and Tamang villages to a collection of high alpine pastures, glaciers and peaks on the border with Tibet. Although the trek passes through lightly populated and undeveloped areas, there are still plenty of lodges along the route. The trail offers exceptionally diverse scenery and culture. The superb day hikes from Kyanjin Gompa in particular offer spectacular close-up views of the surrounding peaks and glaciers of Langtang Lirung (7246m), Kimshung (6781m) and Langshisha Ri (6370m).

Potential add-ons to a Langtang trek include a six-day trek along the Tamang Heritage Trail or a visit to the Gosainkund lakes, after which you can either return to Dhunche (12 days total) or continue over the Laurebina La to Kathmandu (14 days total; p287).

The treks all enter the Langtang National Park (entry Rs 1000). Checkposts are at Dhunche and at Ghora Tabela. Video cameras are only allowed into the national park after paying a whopping US$1000 fee.

Emergency Facilities

The Yeti Guest House in Kyanjin Gompa has a satellite phone that can be used to summon a helicopter in an emergency.

Access: Kathmandu to Syabrubesi

The bus ride from Kathmandu to Syabrubesi is probably the worst thing about the Langtang trek. Until you actually take the journey it's hard to imagine how any bus could take nine hours to cover 120km! Buses leave Kathmandu at 6.20am, 7am and 7.30am for Syabrubesi (Rs 290, nine hours). At Dhunche you must present or pay for an entrance ticket to Langtang National Park, as well as a TIMS card.

Syabrubesi has half a dozen good lodges. **Hotel Trekkers Inn** (☏010-670050; r with/without bathroom from Rs 500/200) has clean new rooms and good food, as does **Buddha Guest House** (r with/without bathroom Rs 600/300), which serves Lavazza coffee. **Hotel Namaste** (☏010-670223; getmechheten@ yahoo.co.in; r Rs 500) has good rooms with private bathrooms and the lady who owns the hotel, Chheten Lama, is a recommended guide for female trekkers. There are several other good places.

A bus departs Syabrubesi for Kathmandu at 6.30am and 7.30am. You should book a seat in advance at the roadside ticket office. A hired vehicle from Kathmandu costs around US$110.

The Trek

DAY ONE: SYABRUBESI TO LAMA HOTEL

The trail branches off Syabrubesi's main road by a police post (you'll need to register) and crosses a suspension bridge over the Bhote Kosi. Turn right at the eastern end of the bridge and climb through the village of Old Syabru to cross a bridge to the south side of the Langtang Khola.

The trek becomes a pleasant walk through trees where langur monkeys frolic, passing a bridge, a small waterfall and *bhattis* (village inns) beside the stream at Doman (1680m). The trail then makes a steep climb over a rocky ridge to the easily missed junction where the route from Thulo Syabru joins from above.

It's then a long climb in forest past the waterfalls and two lodges of Pairo (meaning 'landslide'; 1800m) to Bamboo, a cluster of hotels at 1930m. Beyond Bamboo the trail crosses the Dangdung Khola, then climbs to a steel suspension bridge over the Langtang Khola at 2000m.

On the north bank of the Langtang Khola the route climbs alongside a series of waterfalls formed by a jumble of house-sized boulders. Climb steeply to a landslide and two sets of lodges, 15 minutes apart, at Renche (2400m), and then gently to a collection of six lodges at Changtang, popularly known as Lama Hotel, at 2480m.

DAY TWO: LAMA HOTEL TO LANGTANG

The trail continues to follow the Langtang Khola, climbing steeply through a forest of hemlocks, maples and rhododendrons, past isolated lodges at Gumanchok (Riverside) and Ghunama to the popular lunchtime spot of Ghora Tabela (2970m). There are fine views of Langtang Lirung from here, which you can admire as the army checks your national park entry permit.

From Ghora Tabela the trail climbs more gradually through a U-shaped glacial valley to the villages of Thangshyap, Ghumba and finally Langtang (3430m). The national park headquarters is here, along with a cooperative bakery, a dozen lodges and lots of yaks.

DAY THREE: LANGTANG TO KYANJIN GOMPA

It only takes the morning (passing through small villages) to climb to Kyanjin Gompa (3860m) where there is a monastery, several lodges and two cheese factories (May to December). It's worth spending two full days here to really appreciate the scenery.

DAYS FOUR TO EIGHT: LANGTANG VALLEY & RETURN TO SYABRUBESI

From Kyanjin Gompa you can climb to a viewpoint at 4300m on the glacial moraine to the north for superb views of Langtang Lirung. The most popular day hike is to the Kyanjin Ri viewpoint (4600m), while a tougher option is the climb to Tsergo Ri (4984m). Another popular long day hike leads up the valley to the pastures around Langshisha Kharka for more spectacular views.

To return to Syabrubesi, take the same path back down the valley. To connect to the Gosainkund trek, take the left branch at the junction just before Doman and climb to Thulo Syabru.

Tamang Heritage Trail

Duration Six or seven days

Maximum elevation 3700m

Best season September to May

Start Syabrubesi

Finish Syabrubesi

Summary Traditional Tamang villages, hot springs and fine views into Tibet make this little-trod cultural trek a fine add-on to the Langtang trek.

The relatively new trail is an excellent trek, either on its own or in conjunction with a Langtang trek. It attracts far fewer trekkers and is less commercialised than the other trails in this book, leading many people to compare it to trekking through Nepal thirty years ago. It's not an easy trek by any means, with plenty of steep ups and downs, but days are generally quite short. If you prefer cultural interactions over big mountain views, this might be just the trek for you.

The trail was originally set up as a community-based tourism project to give locals access to income from tourism and while there are now private lodges along the trail there are also several homestays and one community lodge.

This is one trek where a guide is particularly useful, not so much for route finding but to smooth along cultural encounters and help arrange homestays, where very little English is spoken. Many travellers have written to recommend Gotlang resident and guide Durga Tamang, who runs **Himalayan Unforgettable Adventure** (⌖01-4415525; www.nepalmountaintrekking.com).

It's possible to shorten the following itinerary by a day or two by combining days or skipping Timure, which is now linked to Syabrubesi and the Tibetan border by a new Chinese-built road completed in 2012.

DAY ONE: SYABRUBESI TO GOTLANG

From Syabrubesi look for the shortcuts heading west that avoid the huge looping switchbacks of the road. The steep trail gains 720m to two teahouses and a viewpoint (a 15-minute detour) at Bahun Danda Pass (Rongga Bhanjyang; 2180m). You can see the village of Goljung below. If the climb seems too much like hard work consider jumping on the afternoon bus that comes through Syabrubesi to Thambuchet between 3pm and 4pm.

Walk along the upper dirt road for a couple of hours to the lovely traditional village of Gotlang (2240m), the largest Tamang settlement in the area. From here you can make the 45-minute detour uphill to peaceful Parvati Kund Lake and its nearby gompa. Accommodation in Gotlang includes the private Paldor Peak and Gotlang guesthouses (r Rs 200-300), plus a good community lodge (dm Rs 150) and half a dozen homestays.

DAY TWO: GOTLANG TO TATOPANI

After a morning in Gotlang, follow the delightful line of stone chörtens down the valley, branching left after an hour to drop down and eventually cross the river before Chilime village (1760m). At the far end of Chilime cross the river on a suspension bridge and climb steeply past teahouses at Cherka and Gonggang (2230m; lodges available) to the hot-spring pools (Rs 50) and half-dozen lodges at Tatopani (2600m), an ascent of 840m.

DAY THREE: TATOPANI TO NAGTHALI GHYANG

Keep an eye on the trail (trail-finding can be tricky on this initial section) as you climb 560m via the settlement and gompa of Brimdang to the ridgetop meadow of Nagthali Ghyang (three hours; 3165m). In clear weather there are fine views of Langtang Lirung, Ganesh Himal, Paldor peak and the Saljung Himal. It's well worth making the three-hour return walk along the rhododendron-cloaked ridge to the lovely viewpoint at Tharuche (3700m). The best lodges are probably the Great Wall or Mountain View.

DAY FOUR: NAGTHALI GHYANG TO THUMAN

If you didn't do it yesterday, start off with an early morning hike to Tharuche viewpoint for the clearest views. From Nagthali descend steeply for 820m through forest to the pleasant Tamang village of Thuman (take a right 10 minutes after leaving Nagthali). Thuman (2240m) has a small gompa, half a dozen pleasant lodges and a couple of hard to find homestays and is a fine place to spend an afternoon exploring.

DAY FIVE: THUMAN TO TIMURE

Follow the ridge northeast traversing a rocky hillside then descend 640m steeply via Dalphedi to cross the Bhote Kosi River (2½ hours). From here hike north along the new road for 40 minutes to Timure (1760m), where the Peaceful Guest House offers the

Langtang Valley Trek & Tamang Heritage Trail

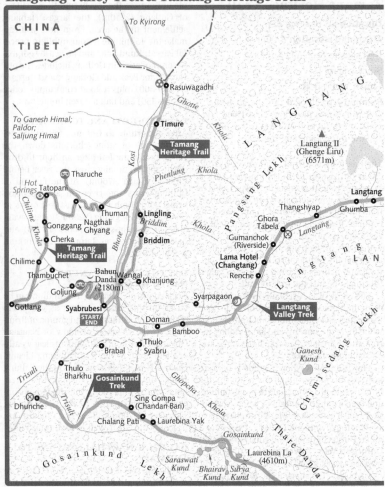

best accommodation. From Timure it's a 45-minute side trip on foot along the new Chinese-built road to the Tibetan border and the ruins of Rasuwaghadi fort, built in 1912.

If you're not bothered about making it to the border, it's possible to descend steeply from Thuman directly to the Bhote Khosi near Lingling and then ascend to Briddim from there (see Day Six).

DAY SIX: TIMURE TO BRIDDIM

From Timure follow the road downstream for an hour to an easily missed footpath branching left up to Lingling, where food and charming lodging is available at the traditional Lingling Homestay. From Lingling it's a two-hour, 400m ascent via the Pelko View Restaurant to Briddim (2230m), a scenic Tamang village, which has a gompa above the town. Briddim has 36 houses, of which 24 are homestays or lodges! The Lhasa Guest House, Tibet Homestay and Family Homestay at the top of the village are excellent.

DAY SEVEN: BRIDDIM TO SYABRUBESI

It's all downhill through pine forest to Syabrubesi (2½ hours, 770m descent), via Wangal. Alternatively link up with the Langtang

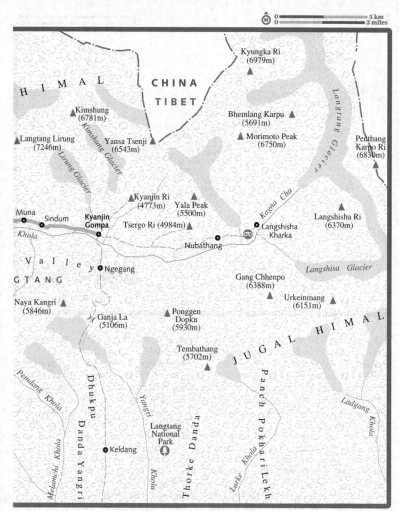

trek by taking the high northern route via Khanjung (Kyangjin) and Syarpagaon.

Gosainkund Trek

Duration Seven to eight days

Maximum elevation 4610m

Best season October to November, March to April

Start Dhunche, Syabrubesi or Thulo Syabru

Finish Sundarijal

Summary High alpine lakes and Himalayan panoramas appeal, as does the chance to continue walking all the way back to Kathmandu.

In good weather you can link the Langtang and Helambu treks via a trek to the sacred, picturesque and high-altitude Gosainkund lakes. It's also possible to hike the route as a stand-alone trek (as described here) or as a return visit from Dhunche to the lakes (seven days), though the rate of ascent in both these cases can cause acclimatisation problems (if you've already done the Langtang

Gosainkund Trek

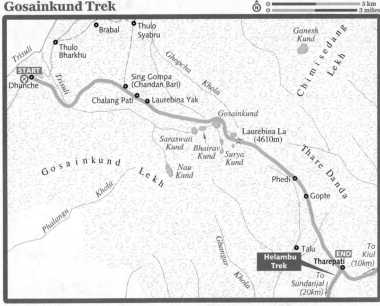

Valley trek, you'll be well acclimatised). Take particular care to acclimatise if attempting this trek in the opposite direction.

There are lodges all along the route, so finding food and accommodation is not a problem in the trekking season. This route over the Laurebina La becomes impassable during winter.

It takes four days to walk from the Tamang bazaar town of Dhunche to Tharepati in the Helambu region. The trek can also be done by turning off the Langtang trek at Thulo Syabru, and it is an excellent choice as a return route to Kathmandu. Lodge facilities are good in Thulo Syabru, Sing Gompa and Tharepati, but rooms in Phedi and Gopte are basic.

Gosainkund is the site for a great Hindu pilgrimage each August, when thousands of sadhus (holy men) trek to the sacred lakes. This is the height of the monsoon, so it's not a pleasant time for trekking.

Access: Kathmandu to Dhunche

Buses to Dhunche (Rs 250, seven hours) leave at 6.20am, 7am, 7.30am and 8.30am from Kathmandu's Machha Pokhari (Fish Pond) junction, just north of the Kathmandu Ring Rd. The direct return bus to Kathmandu leaves Dhunche at 7.15am (reserve a

seat the night before) or take a bus to Trisuli (hourly until 10am) and change.

Just before Dhunche you must present or pay for an entrance ticket to Langtang National Park, as well as a TIMS card.

Dhunche has half a dozen simple hotels. Most popular is the **Hotel Langtang View** (☑010-540141, Kathmandu 01-4355481; s/d Rs 400/500, without bathroom Rs 200/300), with a good upper floor restaurant and rooftop seating that boasts views towards Langtang Lirung and Tibet. Staff can arrange porters (Rs 900 per day) and 4WD transport to Kathmandu (Rs 8000).

Other decent places include the **Himalaya Legend** (☑010-540112; d with/without bathroom Rs 400/200), with a cosy dining hall, and **Dhunche Guest House** (r Rs 200-400) and **Hotel Tibet Mountain View** (r Rs 200-400), which are almost identical.

DAY ONE: DHUNCHE TO SING GOMPA

The first day is a strenuous one, climbing from Dhunche at 1950m to Sing Gompa (Chandan Bari) at 3330m, via Deorali. If you are coming from the Langtang trek, the route from Thulo Syabru to Sing Gompa, via Phobrang Danda, can be confusing as so directions. It's also possible to get to Sing Gompa from Syabrubesi or the Langtang trek, via Thulo Syabru.

DAY TWO: SING GOMPA TO LAUREBINA YAK

The walk climbs steeply, quickly offering fine views of the Ganesh Himal range, then emerging onto a saddle at the teahouses of Chalang Pati (3550m). The trail continues to climb to Laurebina Yak and the excellent Mount Rest Hotel. The magnificent views include the Annapurnas, Manaslu (8156m), the four peaks of the Ganesh Himal and Langtang Lirung. You should overnight in Laurebina Yak to help acclimatisation. You are now above the tree line.

DAY THREE: LAUREBINA YAK TO GOSAINKUND LAKES

The trail climbs to a pass and then continues on an exposed trail, offering views of Saraswati Kund at 4100m, the first of the Gosainkund lakes. The second lake is Bhairav (or Bhairab) Kund and the third is Gosainkund itself, at an altitude of 4380m. There are half a dozen lodges, a shrine and numerous pilgrim shelters on the northwestern side of the lake. You can walk around the lake in an hour, or climb the ridge above the lodges for fine views.

DAY FOUR: GOSAINKUND LAKES TO GOPTE

The trail climbs from the Gosainkund lakes to four more lakes near Laurebina La (4610m). It then drops steeply past a very basic seasonal lodge at Bera Goth to simple lodges at Phedi (3740m). Nearby is the site where a Thai International Airbus crashed into a mountain in 1992. Continue over side valleys to ascend Kasturee Danda (Musk Deer Ridge) before dropping to two simple, seasonal lodges at Gopte (3440m). It was in the Gopte area that an Australian trekker got lost in 1991 and was found alive after 43 days.

DAY FIVE: GOPTE TO THAREPATI

Today's walk descends to a stream and then climbs to Tharepati at 3640m, where the trail meets up with the Helambu trek. From here on you are following the Helambu trek in reverse.

DAYS SIX TO EIGHT: THAREPATI TO SUNDARIJAL

From Tharepati most people take the direct route south to Khutumsang, Chisopani and Sundarijal (two to three days). There's plenty of teahouse accommodation en route, including at Golphu (Gul) Bhanjyang, Pati Bhanjyang and Chisopani. You'll have to pay Rs 250 admission to pass through Shivapuri National Park.

SUNDARIJAL TO KATHMANDU

You can bus back to Kathmandu from Sundarijal in less than an hour (last bus 6.30pm).

Helambu Trek

Duration Six days

Maximum elevation 3640m

Best season October to April

Start Sundarijal

Finish Kiul

Summary A good taster trek and a low-altitude winter option, with few crowds.

Although it's not as well known and popular as the other treks in this book, the week-long Helambu trek is easily accessible from Kathmandu (you could leave your hotel in Kathmandu and set foot on the Helambu trail within an hour). As it stays at relatively low altitudes it also does not require bulky cold-weather equipment and clothing.

The Helambu trek starts from Sundarijal at the east end of the Kathmandu Valley, making a half-loop through the Helambu region to the northeast of Kathmandu. There is not a lot of high mountain scenery but it is a culturally interesting region. There is plenty of accommodation along the route.

Wherever you trek in the region, you will enter the Langtang National Park (admission Rs 1000). You can pay the entrance fee in advance at the national parks office in Kathmandu or pay on the spot in Khutumsang or possibly Sermathang.

Access: Kathmandu to Sundarijal

Minibuses leave from Kathmandu's Ratna Park bus station to Sundarijal (Rs 30, one hour). A taxi drop will cost Rs 800.

The Trek

Day 1: Sundarijal to Chisopani (2140m)

Day 2: Chisopani to Golphu Bhanjyang (2140m)

Day 3: Golphu Bhanjyang to Tharepati (3640m)

Day 4: Tharepati to Melamchi Ghyang (2530m)

Day 5: Melamchi Ghyang to Tarke Ghyang (2590m)

Day 6: Tarke Ghyang to Kiul (1280m)

Helambu Trek

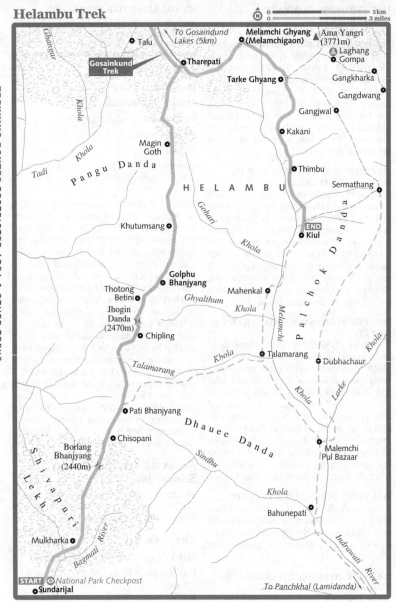

Restricted Area & Other Treks

The teahouse treks described earlier in this chapter are the ones walked by the vast majority of trekkers in Nepal. If you want to head off the beaten track, it's possible to explore remote areas like Makalu and Kanchenjunga in the east or Humla and Dolpo in the west, but you must be very self-sufficient. In these relatively untouched areas there is little surplus food for sale and the practice of catering to trekkers has not yet developed. There are no lodges on most of these treks, so you will need to make camping arrangements through a trekking company and, for most regions, pay a trekking permit fee (see p35). Throw in flights for you and your porters and it's easy to see that the remoter the trek, the more expensive it becomes.

See Lonely Planet's *Trekking in the Nepal Himalaya* for the complete story on trekking in Nepal. It has comprehensive advice on equipment selection, a dedicated health and safety section, and comprehensive route descriptions for both the popular treks (covered briefly in this book) and interesting, less heavily used routes.

Popular treks include the following:

Around Manaslu An 18-day walk around the world's eighth-tallest mountain that can now be done as a teahouse trek. The walk follows the Beri River up into the Tibetan-influenced Nupri area, before crossing the 5100m Larkya La to join the Annapurna Circuit.

Nar-Phu A seven-day add-on to the Annapurna Circuit trail that takes you to the spectacular traditional villages of Nar and Phu near the Tibetan border.

Mustang The most popular of the restricted-area treks leads to this long-forbidden Tibetan kingdom in a remote and arid land of spectacular Tibetan monasteries, canyons and cave complexes that border Tibet. Road construction is changing the region quickly.

Tarap Valley Loop Popular 12-day loop in remote Dolpo that follows the Tarap Valley to the Tibetan-style villages and monasteries around Do Tarap, then crosses the breathtaking 5000m-plus passes of the Numa La and Baga La to arrive at the turquoise Phoksumdo Lake, probably the most beautiful lake in Nepal.

Beni to Dolpo Excellent 12-day traverse from Beni, northwest of Pokhara, to Tarakot in outer Dolpo, crossing six passes and a huge swathe of midwestern Nepal in the footsteps of the book *The Snow Leopard*.

Kanchenjunga Least visited of all is the far east, where two long routes lead right to the base of the world's third-highest mountain.

Makalu Base Camp Another trek that gets you right into the heart of the mountains, following the Barun Valley up to base camp at around 5000m, offering fine views of Everest and Lhotse. The trek starts at the Tumlingtar airstrip or you can trek in from Lukla in 11 days.

Biking, Rafting & Kayaking

While Nepal may be synonymous with trekking, its world-class rapids and exhilarating mountain descents are made for white-water rafting and mountain biking. The bike trails suggested here are best suited to more experienced riders with a good level of fitness. And while most can be done on your own, you'll often need to rely on locals for directions, so hiring a guide or signing up for an organised tour will make life considerably easier. Meanwhile the rafting and kayaking routes are suitable for beginners and pros alike, and your choice is dependent on how much of a buzz you can handle.

See also the Bike Tracks & White Water chapter for general information on both activities and a recommended list of operators.

MOUNTAIN-BIKE ROUTES

The Scar Road from Kathmandu

Distance 65km

Duration Seven hours, or two days overnight in Kakani

Start/Finish Kathmandu

Summary Fine views and a challenging descent through a national park, after a tough initial climb of around 700m.

At times this can be a fairly demanding route, and is suited to more experienced riders; a guide is recommended.

Leaving Kathmandu (elevation 1337m), head towards Balaju on the Ring Rd 2km north of Thamel, and follow the sealed Trisuli Bazaar road towards Kakani, 23km away at an altitude of 2073m. You start to climb out of the valley as the road twists and turns past Nagarjun Hill (p124), which provides the road with a leafy canopy. Once you're through the initial pass and out of the valley, the road continues north-west and offers a view of endless terraced fields to your left. (If you don't fancy the climb, you can avoid cycling on the road by putting your bike on the roof of the early-morning bus to Dhunche and getting off here.) On reaching the summit of the ridge, take a turn right (at a clearly marked T-junction), instead of continuing down to Trisuli Bazaar. (If you go too far, you reach a checkpoint just 100m beyond.) At this point magnificent views of the Ganesh Himal (himal means a range with permanent snow) provide the inspiration required to complete the remaining 4km of steep and deteriorating blacktop to the crown of the hill at **Kakani** (p181) for a well-deserved rest. It's an excellent idea to overnight here at the Tara Gaon (p181) or other such guesthouse and savour the dawn views over the Himalaya.

After admiring the view, descend for just 30m beyond the gate and take the first left onto a 4WD track. This track will take you through the popular picnic grounds frequented on Saturday by Kathmandu locals. Continue in an easterly direction towards Shivapuri. The track narrows after a few kilometres near a metal gate on your left. Through the gate, you are faced with some rough stone steps and then a 10-minute push/carry up and over the hilltop to an army checkpoint. Here it's necessary for foreigners to pay a Rs 250 entry fee to the Shivapuri National Park, plus a US$5 fee for their bike. Exit the army camp, turning right where the Scar Rd is clearly visible in front of you. You are now positioned at the day's highest point – approximately 2200m.

Taking the right-hand track you start to descend dramatically along an extremely steep, rutted single trail with several water crossings. The trail is literally cut into the side of the hill, with sharp drops on the right that challenge a rider's skill and nerve. As you hurtle along, take time to admire the view of the sprawling Kathmandu Valley below – it's one of the best. In recent years the trail has become quite overgrown so you may have to carry your bike for several stretches and seek out the correct path. A guide would be useful for this section.

The trail widens, after one long gnarly climb before the saddle, then it's relatively flat through the protected Shivapuri watershed area. This beautiful mountain-biking section lasts for nearly 25km before the trail descends into the valley down a 7km spiral on a gravel road. This joins a sealed road, to the relief of jarred wrists, at **Bud**hanilkantha (p124), where you can buy refreshments. Take a moment to see the Sleeping Vishnu just up on your left at the main intersection. From here the sealed road descends gently for the remaining 15km back into the bustle of Kathmandu.

Kathmandu to Pokhara

Distance 263km

Duration Five days

Start Kathmandu

Finish Pokhara

Summary Fine views and challenging trails that take you off the beaten track and through historic Newari towns.

It's possible to ride from Kathmandu to Pokhara in 12 to 14 hours along the busy Prithvi Hwy, but unless you're in a hurry the back roads are much better suited to mountain biking. This route will take you along some fairly rural trails that see few foreigners, so a guide or an organised tour is a good idea. Otherwise you'll need to rely on villagers to point you in the right direction.

Day one sees you leaving Thamel in a northerly direction along the busy tarmac road, taking a left at the Kantipath exit. Continue along this road for 3km, past the American embassy and cross the Ring Rd at Maharajganj. From here it's a steady 6km uphill to **Budhanilkantha**, taking a break to see the Sleeping Vishnu. Continuing on, you leave the tarmac behind in a cloud of dust. The trail begins with a 3.5km climb to the army checkpoint where you pay the entry fee to **Shivapuri Nagarjun National Park**. Follow the rocky trail through the forest for 4km until you reach a clearing. Ignore the first small road on your right that has a sign pointing to Shivapuri Resort, and instead take the next right after it, leading you downhill for 18km. Ignore the crossroads and head straight. If unsure, ask locals the way to Bidur, or better yet, get a guide.

After the descent you head along a mostly flat road with the Likhu Khola on your right. After 8km you'll cross the river and then go on to a paved road where the river will be on your left for about 5km before meeting the Trisuli River. Cross the bridge on your right and take a left through the village, riding through town before taking a left at the small paved road. On reaching the main road, head right and ride 3km to

Bidur, from where you need to look out for a small turn on your right. Ask the locals for the way to Nuwakot Durbar, a steep 1.5-hour climb from Bidur. There are one or two simple teahouses in Nuwakot, but it's worth treating yourself at the Famous Farm (see p180).

Day two is an up-and-down affair that covers a distance of 65km, starting with a gradual climb along a tarmac road from Trisuli Bazaar 12km uphill to Samari. From here it's a rough trail that passes through Taksar, finishing up on a sealed road leading to Dhadhing Besi (via Ratmate), where you spend the night.

The next day starts along tarmac, taking you up to Muralibhanjyang, from where it's a dirt road past Nepal's second-largest *tar* (flatland river valley) at Tallo Rampur. Continue along the Budhi Gandaki River, which you cross, and then pass through Bunkghat. The last stretch is a gradual ascent to the Newari town of **Gorkha**, famous for its Shah palace at Gorkha Durbar. If you have time (and the energy), make the effort to explore it in the afternoon, or otherwise leave a few hours in the morning.

Day four starts with a 10km descent, crossing Daraudi River at Chhepetar. From here it's a relatively easy 35km cross-country ride passing more *tars* and jungle, finishing up the day at Sundarbazaar.

This brings you to the final day, saving the best views till last, as you whiz past towering Himalayan vistas. It's an undulating day of riding that covers around 63km, finishing up with a night out in Pokhara to celebrate the completion of your ride.

Upper Mustang – Jomsom to Lo Manthang

Distance 210km

Duration 12 days, including a rest day

Start/Finish Jomsom

Summary An epic journey through remote and stunning stretches of the country. It's a challenging and technical ride, suitable for experienced riders only.

The first obstacle is forking out the US$500 permit to visit the restricted region of Upper Mustang (applicable for 10 days). Furthermore, you'll need to be part of an organised tour – but this can be as simple as employing a guide, which in the long run is a good idea to make sure you're on the right path.

With the amount of hills you're about to tackle, a porter is highly recommended too.

Flying into Jomsom (unless you're nuts and want to ride there from Pokhara, an increasingly popular uphill assault), the journey begins with a gentle two-hour ride that'll take you to the first night's stop at the Buddhist village of Kagbeni (2801m). Day two is a mostly uphill ride along the jeep track to Muktinath, taking things slowly to get acclimatised to the altitude, while allowing you to take in stunning mountain views. The next day takes you into the restricted region of Upper Mustang, starting with an uphill climb to Gyu La (4077m). This involves carrying your bike at times, but you are rewarded with a 1000m descent along a single track. The final stage is a slight climb and river crossing to reach Chele (3050m), where you spend the night.

The next day is shorter, but no less taxing as you head up into the hills, taking on no less than four passes, all exceeding 3600m. You'll be following jeep and single tracks, with a mix of steep climbs and descents, and once again you'll have to lug your bike uphill at times. Stop for the night below Syangboche La (3800m) on the Syangboche River.

While day five begins with more climbing (sigh), once you've cleared Syangboche La and Nyi La (4010m), rest assured the remainder of the day has mostly flat tracks. It also has some of the best scenery you'll see on the trip, with great views of the Himalaya, valleys and bright-yellow mustard fields. Overnight in Charang (Tsarang), with its 400-year-old Gulpa Sect Monastery.

Day six sets out to the crowning jewel of the journey, the walled kingdom city of Lo Manthang. You'll catch your first glimpse of it as you cross the 'Windy Pass' of Lo La (3950m). Today is a bit of a climb, but riding is mostly easy along a jeep track, with a 25km total riding distance. Arrive in Lo Manthang at lunch time, and take a well-earned break. Spend a day or two here taking in the atmosphere of this amazing medieval kingdom. An option for your 'rest day' is a sidetrip up to Garphu following the Kali Gandaki River to Ghom cave.

After giving your legs a day off, it's time to leave Lo Manthang, starting with a challenging climb over Pangga (Samduling) at 4090m, a 75% rideable single track. From here it's a thrilling downhill road to Dhakmar, with dramatic landscapes. Head on to Ghami (Ghemi) for the night; it's your last stop in Mustang.

Heading back, on day nine you retrace the same trail with a single-track climb followed by a downhill to Syangboche, spending the night in Samar. Day 10 takes you over Dajori La (3735m) and Taklam La (3624m), passing sky burials en route. Next you cycle downhill to spend the night in Chhusang. From here you leave Upper Mustang and head back into the Annapurna region, a steady ride along the river taking you back to Kagbeni. You have the option to overnight or continue on down the valley to Jomsom, where you either fly to Pokhara or Kathmandu, or otherwise complete the ride through to Pokhara (see the Muktinath to Pokhara route).

There are teahouses on this route.

Muktinath to Pokhara

Distance 164km

Duration Four days (two if need to rush)

Start Kagbeni

Finish Pokhara

Summary Downhill journey that follows half the Annapurna Circuit, mostly along the jeep track from Jomsom.

While the construction of the road from Jomsom has trekkers mourning the death of the Annapurna trek, mountain-bikers are salivating at this new trail opening up to them. While most start this increasingly popular trail by flying into Jomsom, gluttons for punishment can complete the entire Annapurna Circuit, or even compete in the Yak Attack (www.yak-attack.co.uk) held annually.

Assuming you fly in, after assembling your bike enjoy a mostly flat two-hour ride to Kagbeni. Day one proper is a 1000m climb up to Muktinath, with arid desert landscape and spectacular views of Dhaulagiri and other 8000m peaks. The next day is an undulating trail taking you to Marpha via Lupra, with 30% of the day involving pushing or carrying your bike. Day four sees another downhill leg heading to Tatopani, where you can soothe those aching leg muscles in natural hotwater springs. Getting back on the bike for the final day, a descent leads you along the Kali Gandaki River to Beni. From here it's a highway ride to Nau Danda and then a jeep track to Sarangkot. Hang around for the night to see spectacular sunrise views of the Himalaya, or finish the journey via the steep narrow trail to Pokhara.

Kathmandu Valley Loop via Nagarkot & Namobuddha

Distance 110km

Duration Three days

Start/Finish Kathmandu

Summary A circular route past a classic selection of the valley's cultural sights. There are varying routes on offer, so you can tailor your trip according to tastes. Another popular option goes via Bhaktapur and Changu Narayan.

From Thamel head east past the Royal Palace, follow the road straight through Naxal and cross over the Ring Rd to visit Pashupatinath Temple. Continue along a hectic road to Bodhnath, stopping to explore this fascinating Tibetan Buddhist town. Pedal on to Jorpati, where you take a right, and traffic becomes light, passing along the edge of Gokarna Forest. Continue on to Sankhu, along the old trade route from Kathmandu to Lhasa, for another temple stop and refreshments. From here it's a jeep trail that heads mostly uphill past the Vajrayogini Temple and Lapsiphedi village en route to Jarsingpouwa. Trails from here are mostly flat until you reach Kattike, from where you'll need to suck it up for the 10km uphill to Nagarkot, where you'll spend the night.

Following the new **trekking trail** (www. netif-nepal.org/itineraries.htm) linking Nagarkot to Dhulikhel, the rough track is a one-to two-hour ride (see the boxed text p170). To access it, you'll need to follow the tarmac road heading to the viewing tower, pass by the army camp and head down to the village of Rohini Bhanjyang. From here you choose the trail on the left side; look out for the signs. After 1km, take a right down a small trail that'll lead you through to the villages of Kankre and Tanchok. From here the trail continues to Opi, passing farmhouses, from where it's a further 5km to Dhulikhel. Stop here for lunch, refreshments and mesmerising mountain views. The final leg is a two-hour up-and-down journey through gorgeous scenery to Namobuddha, home to a monumental Tibetan Buddhist monastery up on a hill. See p174 for a description of the route. Spend the night in the delightful Namobuddha Resort or in the monastery itself; reservations for both are essential.

Get an early start to explore Namobuddha Monastery, before jumping on your bike for a downhill section followed by a cross-country trail to the Newari town of Panauti. Leave at least an hour to explore the old town, before leaving town. Don't let the heavenly first 4.5km of tarmac lull you into a false sense of security. The road soon deteriorates into 3km of dirt road to the village of Kushadevi, followed by 2.5km of bone-jarring stony track to Riyale. From here the valley starts to close in and gets increasingly remote – this is definitely not the place to blow a tyre! It's amazing how remote the route is, considering how close it is to Kathmandu. If you're not an experienced mountain biker, you're probably better off considering this as a motorbike route.

The next 8.5km is on a smooth dirt road that switchbacks up the hillsides to **Lakuri Bhanjyang** (1960m). You may find some basic food stalls but the actual summit is currently occupied by the army. In the past, travel companies have set up tented camp accommodation near here but this depends on tourism numbers and the level of army presence. Figure on two to three hours to here.

From this point on it's all downhill. The first section drops down the back side of the hill, blocking the views, but you soon get great views of the Annapurna and Ganesh Himal massifs – particularly spectacular in sunset's pink glow.

A further 5km of descent, rough at times, brings you to the turn-off left to Sisneri and the first village on this side of the pass. Soon the asphalt kicks in again, shortly followed by the pleasant village of **Lubbhu**, with its impressive central three-tiered Mahalakshmi Mahadev Temple. Traffic levels pick up for the final 5km to the Kathmandu ring road near Patan; be prepared for 'civilisation' to come as a bit of a shock after such a beautiful, peaceful ride.

The Rajpath from Kathmandu

Distance 150km

Duration Two days

Start Kathmandu

Finish Hetauda

Summary Classic but gruelling on-road ride over a 2488m pass, culminating with incomparable Himalayan views at Daman.

The ride begins on the Kathmandu–Pokhara (Prithvi) Hwy, which gives the only access to the valley. After leaving the valley, the highway descends to Naubise, at the base of the Mahesh Khola Valley, 27km from Kathmandu, where the Rajpath intersects with the Prithvi Hwy. Take the Rajpath, which forks to the left and is well signposted, for Hetauda. Start a 35km climb to Tistung (2030m) past terraced fields carved into steep hillsides. On reaching the pass at Tistung you descend for 7km into the beautiful Palung Valley before the final steep 9km climb to **Daman** (p246), at a height of 2322m.

This day's ride (almost all climbing) takes between six and nine hours in the saddle. With an early start it is possible to stay in Daman, which will give you the thrill of waking up to the broadest Himalayan panorama Nepal has to offer. The following day the road climbs a further 3km to the top of the pass, at 2488m. At this point you can savour the very real prospect of an exhilarating 2300m descent in 60km!

As you descend towards the Indian plains, laid out before you to the south, notice the contrast with the side you climbed, as the south side is lush and semitropical. With innumerable switchbacks and a bit of speed you should watch out for the occasional bus and truck looming around blind corners. The road eventually flattens out after the right turn to cross a newly constructed bridge and the first main river crossing. The rest of the journey is a gently undulating route alongside a river; a further 10km brings you to **Hetauda**. (See p246 for details on accommodation; note that there are useful cyclists' notebooks in the Motel Avocado.) After a night's rest you can continue along the Rajpath towards India or turn right at the statue of the king in the centre of town and head towards Chitwan National Park.

Hetauda to Narayangarh & Mugling

Distance 91km to Narayangarh, 105km via Sauraha

Duration One to 1½ days

Start Hetauda

Finish Narayangarh or Mugling

Summary Tropical ride across the Terai plains, best during winter and combined with a visit to Chitwan.

This is a vastly different ride from the other rides described in this chapter, and in the summer months (May to September) it can be very hot and humid. From Hetauda, as you cycle along the flat, smooth road towards Narayangarh enjoying the lush subtropical scenery, watch for resort signposts on your left. The Machan Wildlife Resort (p229) turn-off is 40km from Hetauda, and the resort is reached after a further 4km of beautiful trail riding with three river crossings. Alternatively, a further 23km from the Machan turn-off brings you to the Chitwan Jungle Lodge (p229) turn-off. A further 14km brings you to Tandi Bazaar and the turn-off for Sauraha, reached by an interesting 6km-long 4WD track.

From Narayangarh (p220), on the banks of the Narayani River 20km from Sauraha, you can return to either Kathmandu or Pokhara via Mugling. Although some may say this section from Narayangarh to Mugling is best avoided on a bicycle because of heavy bus and truck traffic, it is nonetheless a very beautiful section of road to ride, and traffic during many times of the day can be light.

The alternative is to catch a bus. If you're heading to Pokhara (96km), it may be a good idea to miss the busy highway between Mugling and Pokhara by catching a bus in Mugling (p184). Here, the road is much improved and vehicles travel a lot faster in what are still quite dusty conditions.

Pokhara to Sarangkot & Naudanda

Distance 54km

Duration Seven hours, or an overnight trip

Start/Finish Pokhara

Summary Work up a sweat to two of Pokhara's best Himalayan viewpoints, followed by a great downhill coast.

Leave early and ride along Lakeside (towards the mountains) to the last main intersection and sealed road. Turn right; this is the road that returns to central Pokhara. After 2km you turn left and continue straight (north). This intersection is the zero kilometre road marker. After a further 2km there is a smaller sealed road to the left, signposted as the road to Sarangkot.

This winds its way along a ridge into **Sarangkot**, providing outstanding views of the Himalaya, which seems close enough to reach out and touch. After 6km a few tea houses make a welcome refreshment stop just where the stone steps mark the walking trail to the summit. From here it's a 4WD track that closely hugs the edge of the mountain overlooking Phewa Tal. Continue until you join a Y-intersection that doubles back sharply to the right and marks the final climb to Sarangkot point. You can turn this ride into a relaxed overnight trip by staying in lodges here (see p213).

From Sarangkot continue straight ahead, riding the narrower motorcycle trails leading to Kaski and Naudanda. After the Sarangkot turn-off the trail soon begins to climb to Kaski, towards the hill immediately in front of you. The section to Kaski takes around 30 to 60 minutes, and you may need to push your bicycle on the steeper section near the crown of the hill. Over the top you follow the trail through to **Naudanda**. You are now at around 1590m, having gained around 840m of altitude from Pokhara. The trail is rocky in parts and will test your equipment to the extreme, so do not consider riding this trail on a cheap hired bicycle.

From Naudanda it's a 32km downhill run to Pokhara along the smooth asphalt highway. The route starts with a twisting 6km descent into the Mardi Khola Valley then descends gently as it follows the river, allowing an enjoyable coast almost all the way to Pokhara.

RAFTING & KAYAKING ROUTES

Trisuli

Distance 40km

Duration One to two days

Start Baireni or Charaudi

Finish Multiple locations

Summary Popular introduction to rafting, and a wild ride during the monsoon.

With easy access just out of Kathmandu, the Trisuli is where many budget river trips operate, and is the obvious choice if you are looking for a short introduction to rafting at the cheapest possible price.

After diving into the valley west of Kathmandu, the Prithvi Hwy follows the Trisuli River. Most of the rapids along this route are class 2 to class 3, but the water can build up to class 4 in the monsoon.

The Trisuli has some good scenery but with the main busy road to Kathmandu beside the river it is not wilderness rafting. Some operators have their own fixed campsites or lodges, ranging from safari-style resorts to windblown village beaches complete with begging kids and scavenging dogs. The most established locations are the Trisuli Centre (part of Himalayan Encounter), Royal Beach Camp and Gorkha Adventure Camp (run by Equator Expeditions). All are sited in the best of the white water and have good facilities and food.

When booking, ask where the put-in point is: anything starting at Kuringhat or Mugling will mainly be a relaxing float. During the mid-monsoon months (August to early October) the Trisuli changes character completely as huge runoffs make the river swell like an immense ribbon of churning ocean, especially after its confluence with the Bhodi Gandaki. At these flows it provides a classic big-volume Himalayan river so make sure you choose a reputable company to go with.

Multiday trips continue downriver towards Narayangarh and Chitwan National Park, but the rapids below Kurintar are much more gentle.

Bhote Kosi

Distance 18km

Duration Two days

Start 95km from Kathmandu, near the Tibetan border

Finish Lamosangu

Summary Just three hours from Kathmandu, the Bhote Kosi is one of the best short raft trips to be found anywhere in the world.

The Bhote Kosi is the steepest river rafted in Nepal – technical and totally committing. With that said, beginners can still give it a go. With a gradient of 16m per kilometre, it's a full eight times as steep as the Sun Kosi, which it feeds further downstream. The rapids are steep and continuous class 4, with a lot of continuous class 3 in between.

This river is one of the most fun things you can do right out of Kathmandu and a great way to get an adrenaline fix during the low-water months, but it should only be attempted with a company that has a lot of experience on the Bhote Kosi, and is running the absolute best guides, safety equipment and safety kayakers.

The normal run is from around 95km northeast of Kathmandu to the dam at Lamosangu. The river has been kayaked above this point, but a raft trip here would not be recreational. At high flows several of the rapids become solid class 5, and the consequences of any mistakes become serious.

Most trips are two days. At higher flows the first day is normally on the easier waters of the Upper Sun Kosi, graduating to the Bhote Kosi on the second day. At lower flows both days are on the Bhote Kosi. If you are already up here then the whole Bhote Kosi River can be done as a day trip.

Camping on the Bhote Kosi is limited, with few good beaches, so most groups stay at comfortable river camps like Borderlands Resort or The Last Resort (see p178).

Rafting the Bhote Kosi out of one of these camps makes for a less hectic trip and means you can relax at the end of the day in pristine surroundings and comfort.

The environmental impact of trips is limited by staying at fixed camps, which also create local employment and business. They also offer other activities, so you can mix and match what you do.

In late 2011, plans were revealed to dam a section of the Bhote Kosi. Construction would begin from 2013 and take four years to finish – and would mean rafters would lose a vital 6km stretch of class 4 and 5 rapids. The ruling was being contested by rafting companies at the time of research.

Upper Sun Kosi

Distance 20km

Duration One day

Start Khadichour

Finish Dolalghat

Summary A great place for a short family trip or learner kayak clinics.

The top section of the Upper Sun Kosi from below the dam to near Sukute Beach is a class 3 white-water run offering an easier alternative when the Bhote Kosi is too high.

The lower section is a mellow scenic float, with forest down to the river, and it is a popular river for kayak clinics. At high flows during and just after the monsoon rains the Upper Sun Kosi is a full-on class 3 to 4 high-adrenaline day trip.

Seti Khola

Distance 32km

Duration Two days

Start Damauli

Finish Gaighat

Summary A quieter river that is perfect for beginners, birdwatchers, families and learner kayakers.

The Seti is an excellent two-day trip in an isolated area, with beautiful jungle, white sandy beaches and plenty of class 2 to 3 rapids. The warm water also makes it a popular place for winter trips and kayak clinics. During the monsoon the river changes radically as monsoon runoff creates class 3 to 4 rapids.

The logical starting point is Damauli on the Prithvi Hwy between Mugling and Pokhara. This would give you 32km of rafting to the confluence with the Trisuli River. From the take-out at Gaighat it's just a one-hour drive to Chitwan National Park.

Upper Kali Gandaki

Distance 60km

Duration Three days (two days rafting)

Start Beni or Baglung

Finish Andhi Khola

Summary Diverse trip down the holy river, through deep gorges and past waterfalls.

The Upper Kali Gandaki is an excellent alternative to the Trisuli, as there is no road alongside, and the scenery, villages and temples all combine to make it a great trip.

The rapids on the Kali Gandaki are much more technical and continuous than those on the Trisuli (at class 3 to 4 depending on the flows), and in high water it's no place to be unless you are an accomplished kayaker experienced in avoiding big holes. At medium and lower flows it's a fun and challenging river with rapids that will keep you busy.

The Kali Gandaki is one of the holiest rivers in Nepal, and every river junction is dotted with cremation sites and burial mounds. If you're wondering what's under that pile of rocks, we recommend against exploring. Because of the recent construction of a dam at the confluence with the Andhi Khola, what was once a four- to five-day trip has now become a three-day trip, starting at either Beni or Baglung (depending on the operator) and taking out at the dam site. At very high flows it will probably be possible to run the full five-day trip to Ramdhighat by just portaging the dam site. This option would add some great white water and you could visit the fantastic derelict palace at **Ranighat** (p245).

If you can raft to Ramdhighat beside the Siddhartha Hwy between Pokhara and Sunauli, you could continue on to the confluence with the Trisuli at Devghat along the **Lower Kali Gandaki**. This adds another 130km and three or four more days. The lower section below Ramdhighat doesn't have much white water, but it is seldom rafted and offers a very isolated area with lots of wildlife.

Marsyangdi

Distance 27km

Duration Four days (two days rafting)

Start Ngadi

Finish Phaliya Sanghu (Phalesangu)

Summary A magnificent blue white-water river with a spectacular mountain backdrop. Best suited to experienced rafters.

The Marsyangdi is steeper and offers more continuous white water than most other rivers in Nepal; it's not called the 'Raging River' for nothing! You can go by bus to Khudi or Bhulbule, from where it's a short walk up to the village of Ngadi, with great views of Manaslu ahead of you the whole time.

From Ngadi downstream to the dam side above Phaliya Sanghu, it's pretty much solid white water. Rapids are steep, technical and consecutive, making the Marsyangdi a serious undertaking. Successful navigation of the Marsyangdi requires companies to have previous experience on the river and to use the best guides and equipment. Rafts must be self-bailing, and should be running with a minimum of weight and gear on board. Professional safety kayakers should be considered a standard safety measure on this river.

A hydro project has severely affected this world-class rafting and kayaking river but it is still possible to have a two-day run on the rapids before reaching the dam. You could divert around the dam and continue on the lower section for another two days but at this stage it is hard to tell how much water will be released and whether it will be worth doing. Future dams are planned for the river so you might want to raft this one soon.

Karnali

Distance 180km

Duration 10 days (seven days rafting)

Start Dungeshwar

Finish Chisopani

Summary A classic trip in far western Nepal down its largest and longest river.

The Karnali is a gem, combining a short (two-hour) trek with some of the prettiest canyons and jungle scenery in Nepal. Most experienced river people who have paddled the Karnali find it one of the best all-round river trips they've ever done. In high water the Karnali is a serious commitment, combining huge, though fairly straightforward, rapids with a seriously remote location. The river flows through some steep and constricted canyons where the rapids are close together, giving little opportunity to correct for potential mistakes. Pick your company carefully.

At low water the Karnali is still a fantastic trip. The rapids become smaller when the river drops, but the steeper gradient and constricted channel keep it interesting.

The trip starts with a long, but interesting, two-day bus ride to the remote far west of Nepal. If you're allergic to bus rides, it's possible to fly to Nepalganj and cut the bus transport down to about four hours on the way over, and two hours on the way back. The new road now runs from Surkhet to Dungeshwar on the river. Once you start on the Karnali it's 180km to the next road access at Chisopani, on the northern border of the Bardia National Park.

The river section takes about seven days, giving plenty of time to explore some of the side canyons and waterfalls that come into the river valley. Better-run trips also include a layover day, where the expedition stays at the same campsite for two nights. The combination of long bus rides and trekking puts some people off, but anyone who has ever done the trip raves about it. Finish with a visit to the Bardia National Park for an unbeatable combination.

Adventurers can raft the even more remote **Seti Karnali**, a rarely run scenic stretch of river that starts at Gopghat and takes around seven days to get to Chisopani.

Sun Kosi

Distance 260km

Duration Eight to nine days (seven days rafting)

Start Dolalghat

Finish Chatara

Summary A self-sufficient expedition through central Nepal from the Himalaya to the Gangetic plain.

This is the longest river trip offered in Nepal, traversing 270km through the beautiful Mahabharat Range on its meandering way from the put-in at Dolalghat to the take-out at Chatara in the far east of the country. It's quite an experience to begin a river trip just three hours out of Kathmandu, barely 60km from the Tibetan border, and end the trip looking down the hot, dusty gun barrel of the north Indian plain just eight or nine days later. Because it's one of the easiest trips logistically, it's also one of the least expensive for the days you spend on a river.

The Sun Kosi (River of Gold) starts off fairly relaxed, with only class 2 and small class 3 rapids to warm up on during the first couple of days. Savvy guides will take this opportunity to get teams working together with precision.

The river volume increases with the air temperature as several major tributaries join the river and from the third day the rapids become more powerful and frequent. During high-water trips you may well find yourselves astonished at just how big a river wave can get.

While the lower sections of large-volume rivers are usually rather flat, the Sun Kosi reserves some of its biggest and best rapids for the last days, and the last section is non-stop class 4 before a final quiet float down the Sapt Kosi. Some companies add an extra day's rafting on the lower section of the Tamur, from Mulghat down.

At the right flow it's an incredible combination of white water, scenery, villages, and quiet and introspective evenings.

Note that a new highway is being built alongside the top 40km of the Sun Kosi; once complete (and no one knows when this will be), it'll allow shorter six-day trips on the river and will also probably halve the return time from the take-out.

Tamur

Distance 131km

Duration 11 days

Start Dobhan

Finish Chatara

Summary Remote expedition in the foothills of Kanchenjunga in the far east of the country; includes a three-day trek.

Way out in the far east, this river combines one of the best short treks in Nepal with some really challenging white-water action. The logistics of this trip make it a real expedition, and while it is a little more complicated to run than many rivers in Nepal, the rewards are worth the effort.

First you have to get to Basantapur, a 16-hour drive from Kathmandu or a one-hour flight to Biratnagar and then a six-hour drive. Most expeditions begin with a stunning three- or four-day trek from Basantapur up over the Milke Danda Range, past the alpine lake of Gupha Pokhari to Dobhan. At Dobhan three tributaries of the Tamur join forces, combining the waters of the mountains to the north (including Kanchenjunga, the world's third-largest mountain). The first 16km of rapids is intense, with rapid after rapid, and the white water just keeps coming through towering canyons until the big finale. The best time to raft is at medium flows between mid-October and mid-November.

Other Rivers

The **Upper Seti River**, just outside Pokhara, makes an excellent half-day trip when it is at high flows. Trips operate in mid-September and November (class 3+).

The **Balephi Khola** (above the Bhote Kosi) is run by a few companies from Jalbire to its confluence with the Upper Sun Kosi. Trips normally run only when the river is high from mid-September to early November and in May; it's a two-day trip that combines this river with the Upper Sun Kosi.

The **Bheri River**, which is in the west, is a great float trip with incredible jungle scenery and lots of wildlife, making it a possible family trip. This is also one of Nepal's best fishing rivers and can be combined with a visit to the Bardia National Park.

The powerful **Arun River** from Tumlingtar makes an excellent three-day wilderness trip with good class 3 rapids and pristine canyons, although the logistics of flying the start of the river and getting gear there makes it an expensive trip.

Other Rivers

Understand
Nepal

population per sq km

= 30 people

Nepal Today

Just five years ago, Nepalis were stepping out of the wreckage of a decade-long civil war; today Nepal is a quite different country, literally. An elected prime minister instead of a hereditary monarch now rules as head of state, reflecting the change from traditional Hindu kingdom to Communist-led federal republic. Security is much improved across the country, the once omnipresent roadblocks are a thing of the past and the crippling strikes that defined so much of the 2000s are a receding memory.

There have been other less obvious benefits to the end of Nepal's civil war. Soldiers have been pulled back from active duty to patrol the boundaries of Nepal's national parks – good news for wildlife, bad news for the poachers who reduced Nepal's rhino population by more than 30% during the armed conflict.

Tourism generates around US$335 million each year in foreign earnings for Nepal and it is estimated that the money spent by each tourist supports 10 or 11 Nepalis.

For the first time in years Nepal's trekking lodges, hotels and restaurants are once again crammed to capacity and funds are being poured into infrastructure and construction. The government has also turned its attention to improving living conditions for Nepal's workers, something that was rarely a priority under the autocratic rule of the Shah kings.

This is only the start of a long process of recovery, but locals are already breathing a sigh of relief.

The Hard Work Begins

The initial optimism engendered by the end of the armed conflict has been tempered somewhat by the fundamental infrastructure problems that make daily life a struggle for most Nepalis. Electricity shortages are a fact of life, despite a huge potential for hydropower. Kathmandu's population boomed during the decade of civil war and the city is now close to

Greetings

» Nepalis rarely shake hands – the *namaste* greeting (placing your palms together in a prayer position) is a better choice.

» If you are introduced to a lama (Tibetan Buddhist monk or priest), it is customary to offer a khata (white scarf).

Body Language

» A sideways tilt or wobble of the head conveys agreement in Nepal, not a 'no'.

» Don't sit with the soles of your feet pointing towards a person or a Buddha image.

» Avoid touching children on the head, particularly young monks.

» When giving or receiving money, use your right hand and touch your right elbow with your left hand, as a gesture of respect.

belief systems
(% of population)

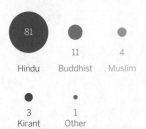

81 — Hindu

11 — Buddhist

4 — Muslim

3 — Kirant

1 — Other

if Nepal were 100 people

16 would be Chhetri
13 would be Brahman-Hill
7 would be Magar
7 would be Tharu
57 would be Other

breaking point. Petrol stations run dry with monotonous regularity and prices for food and cooking kerosene are soaring.

There is no doubt that political tensions remain. Integrating the more than 19,000 Maoist soldiers into civilian life or the national army has created significant political tensions and this political infighting has repeatedly delayed the writing of a new constitution, to the growing frustration of many Nepalis. Calls for greater representation by groups such as the Madhesi of the Terai have added to the political instability.

The wounds of the People's War will doubtless take a long time to heal. Over 1000 Nepalis remain unaccounted for, victims of political 'disappearance' or simple murder, and finding justice for these crimes may prove elusive.

Looking to the Future

Despite the problems, for most Nepalis the election of a stable government and the end of armed conflict has been a massive cause for optimism. A key aim for the future is to complete a new, more inclusive Nepali constitution. For decades government in Nepal has been dominated by a narrow band of castes and ethnicities – Newars, Chhetris and Bahuns – with little regional representation. Ethnic minorities, lower castes and women's groups are clamouring for their voices to be heard in the new political environment. The challenge for Nepal's politicians is to avoid the power struggles and political myopia that has characterised so much of the past and to move all of the country forward, away from the darkness of recent years.

» Population: 29.4 million (2011 estimate)

» Surface area: 147,181 sq km

» UN Human Development Index: 157, out of 187 countries

» Life expectancy: 66 years

» Adult literacy rate: 49%

» Gross national income: US$240 per capita

» Average age: 21 years

Top Books

The Snow Leopard (Peter Matthiessen) Classic and profound account of a trek to Dolpo.
Arresting God in Kathmandu (Samrat Upadhyay) Nine short stories from the first Nepali writer to be published in English.

Snake Lake (Jeff Greenwald) Memoir of family loss set against Nepal's political revolution.
Little Princes (Connor Grennan) Moving and inspiring account of volunteering in a Nepali orphanage.

Top Films

Himalaya (1999; Eric Valli) Stunningly shot in Dolpo; also released as *Caravan*.
Everest (1998; David Breashears) Imax film shot during the disastrous 1997 climbing season.

History

Nepal's history began in, and centres on, the Kathmandu Valley. Over the centuries Nepal's boundaries have extended to include huge tracts of neighbouring India, and contracted to little more than the Kathmandu Valley and a handful of nearby city-states, but the valley remained the crucible of political power and cultural sophistication. Though it has ancient roots, the modern state of Nepal emerged only in the 18th century and is in many ways still forging itself as a modern nation state.

Squeezed between the Tibetan plateau and the plains of the subcontinent – the modern-day giants of China and India – Nepal has long prospered from its location as a resting place for traders, travellers and pilgrims. An ethnic melting pot, it has bridged cultures and absorbed elements of its neighbours, yet has retained a unique character.

After travelling through India and Nepal for a while, many travellers notice both the similarities and differences. 'Same, same', they say, '...but different'.

> Nepal is said to get its name from Nepa, the name given to the Newari kingdom of the Kathmandu Valley; the word Nepa is derived from the name of a mythological Hindu sage, Ne, who once lived in the valley.

The Kiratis & Buddhist Beginnings

Nepal's recorded history emerges from the fog of antiquity with the Hindu Kiratis. Arriving from the east around the 7th or 8th century BC, these Mongoloid people are the first known rulers of the Kathmandu Valley. King Yalambar, the first of their 29 kings, is mentioned in the Mahabharata, the Hindu epic, but little more is known about the Kiratis.

In the 6th century BC, Prince Siddhartha Gautama was born into the Sakya royal family of Kapilavastu, near Lumbini, later embarking on a path of meditation and thought that led him to enlightenment as the Buddha, or 'Enlightened One'. The religion that grew up around him continues to shape the face of Asia.

Around the 3rd century BC, the great Indian Buddhist emperor Ashoka visited Lumbini and erected a pillar at the birthplace of the Buddha. Popular legend recounts how he then visited the Kathmandu

TIMELINE

60 million BC	100,000 BC	c 563 BC
The Himalaya rise as the Indo-Australian tectonic plate crashes into the Eurasian plate. The Tethys Sea is pushed up, resulting in sea shells atop Mt Everest and fossilised ammonites in the Kali Gandaki Valley.	Kathmandu Valley is created as a former lake bed dries. Legend relates how the Buddhist Bodhisattva Manjushri created the valley by cutting the Chobar Gorge and draining the lake's waters.	Siddhartha Gautama is born in Lumbini into royalty and lives as both prince and ascetic in Nepal before gaining enlightenment, as the Buddha, under a Bodhi (pipal) tree.

Valley and erected four stupas around Patan, but there is no evidence that he actually made it there in person. Either way, his Mauryan empire (321–184 BC) played a major role in popularising Buddhism in the region, a role continued by the north Indian Buddhist Kushan empire, which spanned the 1st to 3rd centuries AD.

Over the centuries a resurgent Hinduism came to eclipse Buddhism across the subcontinent and by the time the Chinese Buddhist pilgrims Fa Xian (Fa Hsien) and Xuan Zang (Hsuan Tsang) passed through the region in the 5th and 7th centuries the site of Lumbini was already in ruins.

Licchavis, Thakuris, then Darkness

Buddhism faded and Hinduism reasserted itself with the arrival from northern India of the Licchavis. In AD 300 they overthrew the Kiratis, who resettled in the east to become the ancestors of today's Rai and Limbu people.

Between the 4th and 9th centuries the Licchavis ushered in a golden age of cultural brilliance. Their strategic position allowed them to prosper from trade between India and China. The chaityas (a particular style of stupa) and monuments of this era can still be seen at the Changu Narayan Temple, north of Bhaktapur, and in the backstreets of Kathmandu's old town. It's believed that the original stupas at Chabahil, Bodhnath and Swayambhunath date from the Licchavi era.

You can visit the archaeological site of Kapilavastu, at Tilaurakot, where Siddhartha Gautama (the Buddha) lived for first 29 years of his life.

HISTORY LICCHAVIS, THAKURIS, THEN DARKNESS

A WARNING ABOUT FACTS & FIGURES

References for most things in Nepal are inconsistent. For example, we've seen several different figures for Nepal's total area. The dates given for when temples were built is also a matter of speculation: some sources give a date of construction for a certain temple and the period when the king who built it reigned, and the two only sometimes coincide.

Many temples in Nepal have alternative names. For example, Vishnu Temple in Patan's Durbar Sq is referred to as Jagannarayan or Char Narayan Temple. Where possible we have provided alternative names that are commonly used.

Further confusion results from different systems of transliteration from Sanskrit – the letter 'h', or the use of the double 'hh' appears inconsistently, so you may see Machhendranath and Machendranath (and no-one really knows how to spell Machhapuchhare!). This difference only occurs during transliteration, of course – the Nepali script is always consistent. The letters 'b' and 'v' are also used interchangeably in different systems – Shiva's fearsome manifestation is Bhairab or Bhairav.

Finally, texts differ in their use of the words Nepali and Nepalese. In this book we use Nepali for the language and for other terms relating to the country and the people.

c 250 BC	57 BC	AD 464	629
Mauryan Emperor Ashoka (r 268–231 BC) visits Lumbini, embraces Buddhism and reputedly builds four stupas on the outskirts of Patan, ushering in a golden age for Buddhism.	Nepal's official Vikram (Bikram) Samwat calendar starts, in spring. Thus to Nepalis the year 2013 is 2070.	Nepal's earliest surviving inscription is carved into the beautiful Changu Narayan Temple in the Kathmandu Valley on the orders of King Manadeva.	The Chinese Buddhist pilgrim Xuan Zang (Hsuan Tsang) visits Lumbini and describes the Ashoka pillar marking the Buddha's birthplace. His text helps archaeologists relocate and excavate the lost site in 1895.

Amsuvarman, the first Thakuri king, came to power in 602, succeeding his Licchavi father-in-law. He consolidated his power to the north and south by marrying his sister to an Indian prince and his daughter Bhrikuti to the great Tibetan king Songsten Gompo. Together with the Tibetan king's Chinese wife Wencheng, Bhrikuti managed to convert the king to Buddhism around 640, changing the face of both Tibet and, later, Nepal.

The mid-13th century saw the de facto rule of Queen Deva-ladevi, the most powerful woman in Nepal's history.

From the late 7th century until the 13th century, Nepal slipped into its 'dark ages', of which little is known. Tibet invaded in 705 and Kashmir invaded in 782. The Kathmandu Valley's strategic location and fertile soil, however, ensured the kingdom's growth and survival. King Gunaka-madeva is credited with founding Kantipur, today's Kathmandu, around the 10th century.

The Golden Age of the Mallas

The first of the Malla kings came to power in the Kathmandu Valley around 1200. The Mallas (literally 'wrestlers' in Sanskrit) had been forced out of India and their name can be found in the Mahabharata and in Buddhist literature. This period was a golden one that stretched over 550 years, though it was peppered with fighting over the valuable trade routes to Tibet.

The first Malla rulers had to cope with several disasters. A huge earthquake in 1255 killed around one-third of Nepal's population. A devastating Muslim invasion by Sultan Shams-ud-din of Bengal less than a century later left plundered Hindu and Buddhist shrines in its wake, though the invasion did not leave a lasting cultural effect (unlike the invasion of the Kashmir Valley, which remains Muslim to this day). In India the damage was more widespread and many Hindus were driven into the hills and mountains of Nepal, where they established small Rajput principalities.

Apart from this, the earlier Malla years (1220–1482) were largely stable, reaching a high point under the third Malla dynasty of Jayasthithi Malla (r 1382–95), who united the valley and codified its laws, including the caste system.

After the death of Jayasthithi Malla's grandson Yaksha Malla in 1482, the Kathmandu Valley was divided up among his sons into the three kingdoms of Bhaktapur (Bhadgaon), Kathmandu (Kantipur) and Patan (Lalitpur). The rest of what we today call Nepal consisted of a fragmented patchwork of almost 50 independent states, stretching from Palpa and Jumla in the west to the semi-independent states of Banepa and Pharping, most of them minting their own coins and maintaining standing armies.

879	c 1260	13th to 15th centuries	1349
The Newari lunar calendar, the Nepal Samvat, is introduced as the national calendar and used officially until the late 18th century. It is still used for Newari festivals in the Kathmandu Valley.	Nepali architect Arniko travels to Lhasa and Kublai Khan's capital Dadu (Beijing), bringing with him the design of the pagoda and changing the face of religious temples across Asia.	The Khasa empire of the western Mallas reaches its peak in the far western Karnali basin around Jumla. Its lasting contribution is Nepali – the national language spoken today.	Muslim armies of Sultan Shams-ud-din plunder the Kathmandu Valley, destroying the stupa at Swayambhunath and carrying off cartloads of booty.

The rivalry between the three kingdoms of the Kathmandu Valley found its expression not only in warfare but also in the arts and culture, which flourished in the competitive climate. The outstanding collections of exquisite temples and buildings in each city's Durbar Sq are testament to the huge amounts of money spent by rulers desperate to outdo each other.

The building boom was financed by trade, in everything from musk and wool to salt, Chinese silk and even yak tails. The Kathmandu Valley stood at the departure point for two separate routes into Tibet, via Banepa to the northeast and via the Kyirong Valley near Langtang to the northwest. Traders would cross the jungle-infested Terai during winter to avoid the virulent malaria and then wait in Kathmandu for the mountain passes to open later that summer. Kathmandu grew rich and its rulers converted their wealth into gilded pagodas and ornately carved royal palaces. In the mid-17th century Nepal gained the right to mint Tibet's coins using Tibetan silver, further enriching the kingdom's coffers.

For an online history of Nepal visit www.infoclub.com.np/nepal/history.

In Kathmandu King Pratap Malla (1641–74) oversaw that city's cultural high point with the construction of the Hanuman Dhoka palace, the Rani Pokhari pond and the first of several subsequent pillars that featured a statue of the king facing the protective temple of Taleju, who the Mallas had by that point adopted as their protective deity. The mid-17th century also saw a high point of building in Patan.

The Malla era shaped the religious as well as the artistic landscape, introducing the dramatic chariot festivals of Indra Jatra and Machhendranath. The Malla kings shored up their position by claiming to be reincarnations of the Hindu god Vishnu and establishing the cult of the Kumari, a living goddess whose role it was to bless the Malla's rule during an annual celebration.

The cosmopolitan Mallas also absorbed foreign influences. The Indian Mughal court influenced Malla dress and painting, presented the Nepalis with firearms and introduced the system of land grants for military service, a system that would have a profound effect in later years. In the early 18th century Capuchin missionaries passed through Nepal to Tibet, and when they returned home they gave the West its first descriptions of exotic Kathmandu.

Visit the birthplace and launching pad of Nepal's unifier, Prithvi Narayan Shah, at Gorkha and see his second royal palace at Nuwakot.

But change didn't only come from abroad. A storm was brewing inside Nepal, just 100km to the east of Kathmandu.

Unification under the Shahs

In 1768 Prithvi Narayan Shah, ruler of the tiny hilltop kingdom of Gorkha (halfway between Pokhara and Kathmandu), stood poised on the edge of the Kathmandu Valley, ready to realise his dream of a unified Nepal. It

1380	1428–82	1531–34	1641–74
Ame Pal founds the kingdom of Lo (Mustang). The present king of Mustang, Jigme Palbar Bista, traces his family back 25 generations to this king. Mustang remains an independent kingdom until 1951.	The rule of Yaksha Malla, the high point of the Malla reign, ends in the fracture of the Kathmandu Valley into the three rival kingdoms of Kathmandu, Patan and Bhaktapur.	Sherpas (literally 'easterners') settle in the Solu-Khumbu region near Mt Everest. The Nangpa La remains the most important Sherpa trade route with Tibet.	Rule of Malla king Pratap Malla, a dancer, poet and great supporter of arts, who shapes the face of Kathmandu, building large parts of Hanuman Dhoka palace.

had taken more than a quarter of a century of conquest and consolidation to get here but Shah was about to redraw the political landscape of the Himalaya.

Shah had taken the strategic hilltop fort of Nuwakot as early as 1744, blockading the valley after fighting off reinforcements from the British East India Company, but it took him until 1768 to take Kathmandu, sneaking in while everyone was drunk during the Indra Jatra festival. A year later he finally took Kirtipur, after three lengthy failed attempts. In terrible retribution his troops hacked over 50kg of noses and lips off Kirtipur's residents; unsurprisingly, resistance throughout the valley quickly crumbled. In 1769 he advanced on the three cowering Malla kings and ended the Malla rule, thus unifying Nepal.

Shah moved his capital from Gorkha to Kathmandu, establishing the Shah dynasty, whose line continues to this day. Shah died just six years later in Nuwakot but is still revered as the founder of the nation.

Shah had built his empire on conquest, and his insatiable army needed ever more booty and land to keep it satisfied. Within six years the Gurkhas had conquered eastern Nepal and Sikkim. The expansion then turned westwards into Kumaon and Garhwal, only halted on the borders of the Punjab by the armies of the powerful one-eyed ruler Ranjit Singh.

CARS

The first cars were transported to the Kathmandu Valley in parts, on the backs of porters, before there were even any roads or petrol in the kingdom.

The expanding boundaries of 'Greater Nepal' by this time stretched from Kashmir to Sikkim, eventually putting it on a collision course with the world's most powerful empire, the British Raj. Despite early treaties with the British, disputes over the Terai led to the first Anglo-Nepali War, which the British won after a two-year fight. The British were so impressed by their enemy that they decided to incorporate Gurkha mercenaries into their own army, a practice that continues to this day (Gurkha troops served recently in Iraq and Afghanistan).

The 1816 Sugauli treaty called a screeching halt to Nepal's expansion and laid down its modern boundaries. Nepal lost Sikkim, Kumaon, Garhwal and much of the Terai, though some of this land was restored to Nepal in 1858 in return for support given to the British during the Indian Mutiny (Indian War of Independence). A British resident was sent to Kathmandu to keep an eye on things but the British knew that it would be too difficult to colonise the impossible hill terrain and were content to keep Nepal as a buffer state. Nepalis to this day are proud that their country was never colonised by the British, unlike the neighbouring hill states of India.

Following its humiliating defeat, Nepal cut itself off from all foreign contact from 1816 until 1951. The British residents in Kathmandu were the only Westerners to set eyes on Nepal for more than a century.

On the cultural front, temple construction continued apace, though perhaps of more import to ordinary people was the revolutionary introduction, via India, of chillies, potatoes, tobacco and other New World crops.

1729	1750	1768–69	1790–92
The three kingdoms of the Kathmandu Valley send presents to the Qing court in Beijing, which from then on views Nepal as a tributary state.	King Jaya Prakash Malla builds Kathmandu's Kumari Temple. Not long afterwards comes the Nyatapola Temple in Bhaktapur, the literal high point of stupa-style architecture in Nepal.	Nepal is unified under Prithvi Narayan Shah (1723–75), known as the father of the Nepali nation, to form the Shah dynasty. Kathmandu becomes the capital.	Nepal invades Tibet and sacks Shigatse. Avenging Chinese troops advance down the Kyirong Valley as far as Nuwakot. As part of the ensuing treaty the Nepalis pay tribute to the Chinese emperor until 1912.

The Shah rulers, meanwhile, swung from ineffectual to sadistic. At one point the kingdom was governed by a 12-year-old female regent, in charge of a nine-year-old king, while Crown Prince Surendra (r 1847–81) expanded the horizons of human suffering by ordering subjects to jump down wells or ride off cliffs, just to see whether they would survive.

The Ranocracy

The death of Prithvi Narayan Shah in 1775 set in motion a string of succession struggles, infighting, assassinations, backstabbing and intrigue that culminated in the Kot Massacre in 1846. This bloody night was engineered by the young Chhetri noble Jung Bahadur and it catapulted his family into power, just as it sidelined the Shah dynasty.

Ambitious and ruthless, Jung Bahadur organised (with the queen's consent) for his soldiers to massacre 55 of the most important noblemen in the kingdom while they were assembled in the Kot courtyard adjoining Kathmandu's Durbar Sq. He then exiled 6000 members of their families to prevent revenge attacks.

Jung Bahadur took the title of prime minister and changed his family name to the more prestigious 'Rana'. He later extended his title to *maharajah* (king) and decreed it hereditary. The Ranas became a parallel 'royal family' within the kingdom and held the reins of power – the Shah

Nepal's flag is like no other, consisting of two overlapping red triangles, bearing a white moon and a white 12-pointed sun (the first mythological kings of Nepal are said to be descendents of the sun and moon).

HISTORY THE RANOCRACY

TRANS-HIMALAYAN TRADE

For centuries, hardy caravans of yaks and goats criss-crossed the high Himalaya, bringing salt harvested from Tibet's great salt lakes to barter for rice and barley carried up from the Middle Hills of Nepal. Wool, livestock and butter were exchanged for sugar, tea, spices, tobacco and Indian manufactured goods. Twelve major passes linked Nepal and Tibet, the easiest of which were in Mustang, ensuring that the Kali Gandaki Valley became the main entrepôt for transferring, storing and taxing the trade.

Over the last half-century much of the traditional border trade has dried up. The arrival of the Indian railway line at the Nepali border greatly aided the transportation of cheap Indian salt, sounding a death knell for the caravan trade. The real nail in the coffin came in the 1960s, when the Chinese closed the borders to local trade.

Ironically the Chinese are currently leading a resurgence of trade and road construction. Chinese truckers now drive over the passes to Lo Manthang in Mustang and in 2012 another road border crossing opened at Rasuwaghadi, linking the Tibetan Kyirong Valley with Nepal's Langtang region along a route long used for trade and invasion. You'll see the occasional yak caravan headed for the Tibetan border, as well as telltale cans of Lhasa Beer on trekking routes in the Manaslu, Everest and Mustang regions.

1814–16
Anglo-Nepali War ends in victory for Britain. The ensuing Treaty of Sugauli establishes Nepal's boundaries and gives Britain the right to recruit Gurkha soldiers in Nepal and maintain a residency in Kathmandu.

1815
5000 Nepali soldiers begin serving as troops in the East India Company after impressing the British with their valour and loyalty.

RICHARD I'ANSON/LONELY PLANET IMAGES ©

» Gurkha soldiers

Nepal's founding father, Prithvi Narayan Shah, referred to Nepal as 'a yam between two boulders' – namely China and India – a metaphor that is as true geologically as it is historically.

kings became listless figureheads, requiring permission even to leave their palace.

The family line of Rana prime ministers held power for more than a century, eventually intermarrying with the Shahs. Development in Nepal stagnated, although the country did at least manage to preserve its independence.

Jung Bahadur Rana travelled to Europe in 1850, attending the opera and the races at Epsom, and brought back a taste for neoclassical architecture that can be seen in Kathmandu today. Under the Ranas, *sati* (the Hindu practice of casting a widow on her husband's funeral pyre) was abolished, 60,000 slaves were released from bondage, and a school and college were established in the capital. But while the Ranas and their relatives lived lives of opulent luxury, the peasants in the hills were locked in a medieval existence.

Modernisation began to dawn on Kathmandu with the opening of the Bir Hospital, Nepal's first, in 1889. Over the next 15 years Kathmandu also saw its first piped water system, limited electricity and the construction of the Singh Durbar, at one time considered the largest palace in Asia. The 29-year reign (1901–29) of Prime Minister Chandra Shumsher in particular brought some sweeping changes, including the introduction of electricity and the outlawing of slavery. In 1923 Britain formally acknowledged Nepal's independence and in 1930 the kingdom of Gorkha was renamed the kingdom of Nepal, reflecting a growing sense of national consciousness.

Elsewhere in the region dramatic changes were taking place. The Nepalis supplied logistical help during Britain's invasion of Tibet in 1903, and over 300,000 Nepalis fought in WWI and WWII, garnering a total of 13 Victoria Crosses – Britain's highest military honour – for their efforts.

After WWII, India gained its independence and the communist revolution took place in China. Tibetan refugees fled into Nepal in the first of several waves when the new People's Republic of China tightened its grip on Tibet, and Nepal became a buffer zone between the two rival Asian giants. At the same time King Tribhuvan, forgotten in his palace, was being primed to overthrow the Ranas.

Restoration of the Shahs

In late 1950 King Tribhuvan was driving himself to a hunting trip at Nagarjun when he suddenly swerved James Bond–style into the Indian embassy, claimed political immunity and was flown to Delhi in an Indian Air Force jet. Meanwhile, the recently formed Nepali Congress Party, led by BP Koirala, managed to take most of the Terai by force from the Ranas and established a provisional government that ruled from the border town of Birganj. India exerted its considerable influence and negotiated

1846	1850	1854	1856
The Kot Massacre ends in the killing of the cream of the court aristocracy, ushering in the Rana era (1846–1951) and sidelining the Shah kings to puppet status.	Jung Bahadur Rana travels to Europe, becoming the first Nepali ruler to cross the *kalo pani* (black water, or ocean) and thus temporarily losing his caste.	The *Muluki Ain* legal code formalises the Nepali caste system, defining diet, legal and sexual codes and enshrining state discrimination against lower castes. The law is revised only in 1963.	Peak XV is declared the world's highest peak. It is later renamed Everest after the head of Trigonometric Survey, George Everest (who actually pronounced his name *eve*-rest).

a solution to Nepal's turmoil, and King Tribhuvan returned in glory to Nepal in 1951 to set up a new government composed of demoted Ranas and members of the Nepali Congress Party.

Although Nepal gradually reopened its long-closed doors and established relations with other nations, dreams of a new democratic system were not permanently realised. Tribhuvan died in 1955 and was succeeded by his cautious son Mahendra. A new constitution provided for a parliamentary system of government and in 1959 Nepal held its first general election. The Nepali Congress Party won a clear victory and BP Koirala became the new prime minister. In late 1960, however, the king decided the government wasn't to his taste after all, and he had the cabinet arrested and swapped his ceremonial role for real control (much as King Gyanendra would do 46 years later).

In 1962 Mahendra decided that a partyless, indirect *panchayat* (council) system of government was more appropriate to Nepal. The real power remained with the king, who chose 16 members of the 35-member National Panchayat, and appointed the prime minister and his cabinet. Political parties were banned.

Mahendra died in 1972 and was succeeded by his 27-year-old British-educated son Birendra. Nepal's hippie community was unceremoniously booted out of the country when visa laws were tightened in the run-up to Birendra's spectacular coronation in 1975. Simmering discontent with corruption, the slow rate of development and the rising cost of living erupted into violent riots in Kathmandu in 1979. King Birendra announced a referendum to choose between the *panchayat* system and one that would permit political parties to operate. The result was 55% to 45% in favour of the *panchayat* system; democracy had been outvoted.

Nepal's military and police apparatus were among the least publicly accountable in the world and strict censorship was enforced. Mass arrests, torture and beatings of suspected activists were well documented, and the leaders of the main opposition, the Nepali Congress, spent the years between 1960 and 1990 in and out of prison.

During this time over one million hill people moved to the Terai in search of land and several million crossed the border to seek work in India (Nepalis are able to cross the border and work freely in India), creating a major demographic shift in favour of the now malaria-free Terai.

People Power

In 1989, as communist states across Europe crumbled and pro-democracy demonstrations occupied China's Tiananmen Sq, Nepali opposition parties formed a coalition to fight for a multiparty democracy with the king

A History of Nepal by John Whelpton is one of the few available titles on the subject. It concentrates on the last 250 years and explains not only political events but also the changes in people's lives. It's cheaper to buy in Nepal than abroad.

1911	1914–18	1923	1934
King George V visits the Terai on a hunting trip as a guest of the maharajah of Nepal, bagging 39 tigers and 18 rhinos, travelling with a small army of beaters.	Around 100,000 Nepalis fight and 10,000 lose their lives in WWI. Thirty years later 200,000 Gorkha and army forces serve in WWII, mostly in Myanmar (Burma).	Britain affirms Nepal's sovereignty and independence in a treaty of friendship, redefining Nepal's status from that of a British protectorate.	A massive earthquake destroys much of the Kathmandu Valley, killing over 8000 people in under a minute, injuring 16,000 and destroying a quarter of all homes in Nepal.

as constitutional head; the upsurge of protest was called the Jana Ando-lan, or People's Movement.

In early 1990 the government responded to a nonviolent gathering of over 200,000 people with bullets, tear gas and thousands of arrests. After several months of intermittent rioting, curfews, a successful strike and pressure from various foreign-aid donors, the government was forced to back down. The people's victory did not come cheaply; it is estimated that more than 300 people lost their lives.

On 9 April King Birendra announced he was lifting the ban on polit-ical parties and was ready to accept the role of constitutional monarch. Nepal became a democracy.

In May 1991, 20 parties contested a general election for a 205-seat parliament, which was won by the Nepali Congress Party, but the polit-ical atmosphere remained uneasy. In April 1992 a general strike degener-ated into street violence between protesters and police, and resulted in a number of deaths. Two years later a midterm election resulted in a coalition government led by the Communist Party. This was one of the few times in the world that a communist government had come to power by popular vote.

Political stability did not last long, and the late 1990s were littered with dozens of broken coalitions, dissolved governments and sacked politicians. After a decade of democracy it seemed an increasing number of people, particularly young Nepalis and those living in the countryside, were utterly disillusioned.

Forget Kath-mandu: An Elegy for Democracy, by Manjushree Thapa, starts with Nepal's royal massacre, moves to a political history of the last 200 years, then ends with a description of a trek through Maoist-held areas in 2003.

The People's War

In 1996 the Maoists, a Communist-party splinter group, fed up with gov-ernment corruption, the failure of democracy to deliver improvements to the people, and the dissolution of the communist government, declared a 'people's war'. The Maoists presented the then prime minister with a 40-point charter of demands that ranged from preferential state policies towards backward communities to an assertive Nepali identity, an end to privately funded schools and better governance.

The insurgency began in the Rolpa district of midwestern Nepal and gathered momentum, but it was initially ignored by Kathmandu's poli-ticians, even when Maoists stole Rs 50 million from a bank in Dolpo in September 2000. The repercussions of this nonchalance finally came to a head in November 2001 when the Maoists broke their ceasefire and an army barracks was attacked west of Kathmandu. The initial Maoist forces were armed with little more than ancient muskets and *khukuris* (Ghurkha knives) but they quickly obtained guns looted from police sta-tions, homemade explosives and automatic weapons, all bankrolled by robbery and extortion and aided by an open border with India.

1949	1951	1953	1954
Bill Tilman gets permission from King Tribhuvan to trek in Nepal, includ-ing around the Kali Gandaki, Helambu and Solu-Khumbu regions. He is the first foreigner to trek to Everest Base Camp in 1950.	King Tribhuvan and the Nepali Congress Party, with Indian support, overthrow the Rana regime and establish a new coalition government. Nepal opens its doors to the outside world.	Everest is summited for the first time by New Zealander Edmund Hillary and Tibetan Sherpa Tenz-ing Norgay on 29 May, just in time for the coronation of Queen Elizabeth II.	Boris Lissanevitch establishes Nepal's first hotel, the Royal, in the Bahadur Bhawan palace. Its Yak and Yeti Bar becomes the expat hub for mountaineers and diplomats until its closure in 1971.

Initial police heavy-handedness fuelled a cycle of violence and retribution that only succeeded in alienating the local people. Political disenfranchisement, rural poverty, resentment against the caste system, issues of land reform and a lack of faith in the squabbling and self-interested politicians of distant Kathmandu swelled the ranks of the Maoists, who at their peak numbered 15,000 fighters, with a further militia of 50,000. Attacks spread to almost every one of Nepal's 75 districts, including Kathmandu. At their peak Maoists effectively controlled around 40% of the country, including two protected areas in the far west and several of Nepal's main trekking routes (for years trekkers in the Annapurna region were forced to hand over 'donations' to Maoist gangs).

The political temperature rose after the king brought in the army and armed militias loyal to the government in 2001. The USA labelled Nepal's Maoists a terrorist group and handed over millions of dollars to help fight Nepal's own 'war on terror'. Although they were self-declared Maoists, the group owed more to Peru's Sendero Luminoso (Shining Path) than to any Chinese connection. Ironically the 'people's' armed struggle was led by two high-caste intellectuals: Pushpa Kamal Dahal (known by his *nom de guerre* Prachanda, which means 'the fierce') and Baburam Bhattarai, who is currently serving as Nepal's prime minister.

One early victim of the war was the freedom of the Nepali press. Between 2002 and 2005 more journalists were arrested in Nepal than in any other country and in 2005 Reporters Sans Frontiers described Nepal's media as the world's most censored.

Several Maoist truces, notably in 2003 and 2005, offered some respite, though these reflected as much a need to regroup and rearm as they did any move towards a lasting peace. By 2005 nearly 13,000 people, including many civilians, had been killed in the insurgency, more than half of them following the royal order to send in the army. Amnesty International accused both sides of horrific human-rights abuses, including summary executions, abductions, torture and child conscription. Dark days had come to Nepal.

> For background on the Maoist rebellion read *Himalayan People's War: Nepal's Maoist Rebellion*, edited by Michael Hutt.

Stalled Development & the Failure of Aid

During the second half of the 20th century Nepal saw impressive movements towards development, namely in education and road construction, with the number of schools increasing from 300 in 1950 to over 40,000 by 2000. But the relentless population growth (Nepal's population grew from 8.4 million in 1954 to 26 million in 2004) simply cancelled out many of these advances, turning Nepal from a food exporter to a net importer within a generation.

The Maoist insurgency only worsened the plight of the rural poor by bombing bridges and telephone lines, halting road construction, diverting

HISTORY STALLED DEVELOPMENT & THE FAILURE OF AID

MAOISTS

1955–72
The rule of King Mahendra sees the introduction of elections, which are then voided as the king seizes direct power, introducing the *panchayat* system of government.

1959
Nepal's first general election is held. The Dalai Lama flees Tibet and China closes the Tibet–Nepal border, seriously affecting the trade of salt for grain and creating great social change in the Himalaya.

1960
Eradication of malaria opens the Terai to rapid population growth. Today the Terai contains around half of Nepal's population and most of its industry and agricultural land.

» Dalai Lama

JOHN SONES / LONELY PLANET IMAGES ©

much-needed government funds away from development and causing aid programs to suspend activity due to security concerns. It is estimated that during the decade-long conflict the Maoists destroyed Rs 30 billion of government infrastructure, while the government blew US$108 billion on military spending. Meanwhile, an entire generation of rural Nepali children missed out on their education.

After a half-century of outside assistance and over US$4 billion in aid (60% of its development budget), Nepal remains one of the world's 10 poorest countries, with the highest income disparity in Asia and one of its lowest health-spending levels. Seven million Nepalis lack adequate food or basic health care and education.

Royal Troubles & Political Change

On 1 June 2001 the Nepali psyche was dealt a huge blow when Crown Prince Dipendra gunned down almost every member of the royal family during a get-together in Kathmandu. Dipendra did not die straight away and, despite being in a coma, he was pronounced the king of Nepal. His rule ended two days later, when he too was declared dead. King Birendra's brother Gyanendra was then crowned in what may have been a moment of déjà vu – he had already been crowned once before, aged three, and ruled as king for three months, after his grandfather Tribhuvan fled to India in 1950.

In the days that followed the massacre, a tide of emotions washed over the Nepali people – shock, grief, horror, disbelief and denial. A 13-day period of mourning was declared and in Kathmandu impromptu shrines were set up for people to pray for their king and queen. About 400 shaven-headed men roamed the streets around the palace on motorbikes, carrying pictures of the monarch. Half a million stunned Nepalis lined the streets during the funeral procession. When the shock of this loss subsided the uncertainty of what lay ahead hit home.

The beginning of the 21st century saw the political situation in the country turn from bad to worse. Prime ministers were sacked and re-placed six times between 2000 and 2005, making a total of nine governments in 10 years. The fragile position of Nepali politicians is well illustrated by Sher Bahadur Deuba, who was appointed prime minister for the second time in 2001, before being dismissed in 2002, reinstated in 2004, sacked again in 2005, thrown in jail on corruption charges and then released.

Nepal's disappointing experiment with democracy faced a major setback in February 2005 when King Gyanendra dissolved the government, amid a state of emergency, promising a return to democracy within three years. Freedom of the press was curtailed and telephone

Confusingly, three Koirala brothers have all served as prime ministers of Nepal; BP Koirala in 1959, MP Koirala in 1951 and 1953 and GP Koirala, four times, most recently in 2006.

Massacre at the Palace: The Doomed Royal Dynasty of Nepal, by Jonathan Gregson, takes a wider look at Nepal's royal family and reveals that assassination and murder have been part of royal life for centuries; it also examines the recent massacre. Also published as *Blood Against the Snows.*

1965	1975	1990	1991
Colonel James 'Jimmy' Roberts founds Mountain Travel, Nepal's first trekking company, and leads a group of women up the Kali Gandaki Valley, laying the path for Nepal's trekking industry.	Birendra is crowned king in Kathmandu's Hanuman Dhoka, three years after the death of his father Mahendra. The king wears the traditional jewel-encrusted and feathered headdress of the Shah kings.	The mass demonstrations of the People's Movement force King Birendra to accept a new constitution, restoring democracy and relegating the king to the role of constitutional Hindu monarch.	The Nepali Congress Party wins the general election, with the Communist Party of Nepal-Unified Marxist-Leninist (CPN-UML) the next largest party. The political atmosphere remains tense.

lines were cut periodically to prevent demonstrations. Tourism levels slumped and a mood of pessimism descended over the country.

Everything changed in April 2006, when days of mass demonstrations, curfews and the deaths of 16 protestors forced the king to restore parliamentary democracy. The following month the newly restored parliament voted to reduce the king to a figurehead, ending powers that the royal Shah lineage had enjoyed for over 200 years. The removal of the king was the price required to bring the Maoists to the negotiating table, and a peace accord was signed later that year, drawing a close to the bloody decade-long insurgency.

The pace of political change in Nepal was remarkable. The Maoists achieved a majority in the elections of 10 April 2008 and a month later

THE ROYAL MASSACRE

The night of 1 June 2001 has entered the annals of history as one of Nepal's greatest tragedies, a bloodbath that could have been lifted straight from the pages of Shakespeare.

That night, in a hail of bullets, 10 members of Nepal's royal family, including King Birendra and Queen Aishwarya, were gunned down during a gathering at the Narayanhiti Palace by a deranged, drunken Crown Prince Dipendra, who eventually turned a weapon on himself. The real motive behind the massacre will never be known, but many believe Dipendra's rage was prompted by his parents' disapproval of the woman he wanted to marry.

The initial disbelief and shock gave way to suspicion and a host of conspiracy theories, many concerning the new king, Gyanendra (who was in Pokhara at the time of the massacre), and his son Paras (who emerged unscathed from the attack). None of this was helped by an official inquiry that initially suggested the automatic weapon had been discharged by accident, or the fact that the victims were quickly cremated without full post-mortems and the palace building then razed to the ground. Other theories included that old chestnut – a CIA or Indian secret-service plot.

A surreal royal exorcism followed on the 11th day of mourning, as a high-caste priest, dressed in the gold suit, shoes and black-rimmed glasses of King Birendra and donning a paper crown, climbed onto an elephant and slowly lumbered out of the valley, taking with him the ghost of the dead king. The same scapegoat ritual (known as a *katto* ceremony) was performed for Dipendra, except that a pregnant woman dashed underneath his elephant en route, believing this would ensure she give birth to a boy. She was trampled by the elephant and died, adding a further twist to the tragedy.

Doubtless, the truth of what really happened that night will never be known. In the words of Nepali journalist Manjushree Thapa: 'We lost the truth; we lost our history. We are left to recount anecdotes and stories, to content ourselves with myth.'

1994	1996–2006	May 1996	1999
Midterm elections result in a coalition of the Communist Party of Nepal (CPN-UML) and the Rastriya Prajatantra Party (RPP), the old *panchayats*, with the support of the Nepali Congress.	A decade-long Maoist insurgency brings the country to its knees and results in the death of 13,000 Nepalis. Development projects stall and tourism levels plummet.	Eight climbers die on a single day, May 11, on Everest, making this the single worst year for Everest fatalities. An Imax film and Jon Krakauer's book *Into Thin Air* chronicle the disaster.	The body of British climber George Mallory is discovered near the summit of Everest, reigniting conjecture that he made it to the top of the world a good 30 years before Hillary.

Following the 2008 abolition of the monarchy, the king's face was removed from the Rs 10 note, the prefix 'Royal' disappeared from the name of the national airline as well as national parks, and the king's birthday was dumped as a national holiday.

parliament abolished the monarchy completely by a margin of 560 votes to four, ending 240 years of royal rule. The new government saw former guerrilla leader Pushpa Kamal Dahal as prime minister and Dr Baburam Bhattarai as finance minister. In 2009 Pushpa Kamal Dahal resigned due to infighting, hinting at turmoil to come.

Former Maoist 'terrorists' became cabinet ministers, members of the People's Liberation Army joined the national army and a new constitution was commissioned (though four years later it had still to be written), all as part of a process to bind the former guerrillas into the political mainstream. After a decade of darkness, violence and social upheaval, a renewed optimism in the political process was palpable throughout Nepal.

June 2001	February 2005	2006	2007
Prince Dipendra massacres 10 members of the royal family in the Narayanhiti Palace, including his father, King Birendra, before shooting himself. The king's brother, Gyanendra, is crowned king of Nepal.	King Gyanendra dismisses the government and assumes direct control of the country in a state of emergency, citing the need to crush the Maoist rebels.	After weeks of protests, King Gyanendra reinstates parliament, which votes to curtail his emergency powers. Maoists and government officials sign a peace agreement and the Maoist rebels enter an interim government.	Nepal becomes the fifth-largest remittance-receiving country in the world, with Nepali workers abroad sending home an estimated US$1.6 billion a year.

Religion

From the simple, early morning offerings of a Kathmandu housewife at a local Hindu temple, to the chanting of Buddhist monks in a village monastery, religion is a cornerstone of Nepali life. In Nepal, Hinduism and Buddhism have mingled wonderfully into a complex, syncretic blend. Nowhere is this more evident than in Kathmandu, where Tibetan Buddhists and Nepali Hindus often worship at the same temples.

The Buddha was born in Nepal over 25 centuries ago but the Buddhist religion first arrived in the country later, around 250 BC, thanks to the great Indian-Buddhist emperor Ashoka. Buddhism eventually lost ground to Hinduism, although the Tantric form of Tibetan Buddhism made its way full circle back into Nepal in the 8th century AD. Today, Buddhism is practised mainly by the people of the high Himalaya, such as the Sherpas and Tamangs, and by Tibetan refugees.

Take the concepts of Hinduism and Buddhism, add some Indian and Tibetan influences and blend this with elements of animism, faith healing and a pinch of Tantric practice and you get a taste of Nepal's fabulous spiritual stew. Thanks to the tendency towards assimilation and synthesis there is little religious tension in Nepal and religion has long played little part in the country's politics.

> It is joked that Nepal has three religions – Hinduism, Buddhism and Tourism.

Hinduism

Hinduism is a polytheistic religion that has its origins in the Aryan tribes of central India dating back about 3500 years ago. Hindus believe in a cycle of life, death and rebirth with the aim being to achieve *moksha* (release) from this cycle. With each rebirth you can move closer to, or further from, eventual *moksha;* the deciding factor is karma, which is literally a law of cause and effect. Bad actions during your life result in bad karma, which ends in a lower reincarnation. Conversely, if your deeds and actions have been good you will reincarnate on a higher level and be a step closer to eventual freedom from rebirth. Buddhism later adapted this concept into one of its core principles.

TIKA

A visit to Nepal is not complete without being offered a *tika* by one of the country's many sadhus (wandering Hindu holy men; see p321) or Hindu priests. The ubiquitous *tika* is a symbol of blessing from the gods and is worn by both women and men. It can range from a small dot to a full-on mixture of yoghurt, rice and sindur (a red powder and mustard-oil mixture) smeared on the forehead. The *tika* represents the all-seeing, all-knowing third eye, as well as being an important energy point, and receiving this blessing is a common part of most Hindu ceremonies. It is an acknowledgment of a divine presence at the occasion and a sign of protection for those receiving it. Shops these days carry a huge range of tiny plastic *tikas*, known as *bindi,* that women have turned into an iconic fashion statement.

Hinduism has a number of holy books, the most important being the four Vedas, the 'divine knowledge' that is the foundation of Hindu philosophy. The Upanishads are contained within the Vedas and delve into the metaphysical nature of the universe and soul. The Mahabharata is an epic 220,000-line poem that contains the story of Rama. The Ramayana, the famous Hindu epic, is based on this.

The Hindu religion has three basic practices: puja (religious offering or prayer), the cremation of the dead, and the rules and regulations of the caste system.

There are four main Hindu castes: Brahmin (Brahman ethnic group; priest caste); Kshatriya (Chhetri in Nepali; soldiers and governors); Vaisya (tradespeople and farmers); and Sudra (menial workers and craftspeople). These castes are then subdivided, although this is not taken to the same extreme in Nepal as it is in India. Beneath all the castes are the Harijans, or 'untouchables' – the lowest, casteless class for whom the most menial and degrading tasks are reserved.

Despite common misconceptions, it is possible to become a Hindu, although Hinduism itself is not a proselytising religion. Once you are a Hindu you cannot change your caste – you're born into it and are stuck with your lot in life for the rest of that lifetime.

Hindu Gods

Westerners often have trouble coming to grips with Hinduism, principally because of its vast pantheon of gods. The best way to look upon the dozens of different Hindu gods is simply as pictorial representations of the many attributes of the divine. The one omnipresent god usually has three physical representations: Shiva the destroyer and reproducer, Vishnu the preserver and Brahma the creator.

Most temples are dedicated to one of these gods, but most Hindus profess to be either Vaishnavites (followers of Vishnu) or Shaivites (followers of Shiva).

The oldest deities are the elemental Indo-European Vedic gods, such as Indra (the god of war, storms and rain), Suriya (the sun), Chandra (the moon) and Agni (fire). Added to this is a range of ancient local mountain spirits, which Hinduism quickly co-opted. The Annapurna and the Ganesh Himal massifs are named after Hindu deities, and Gauri Shankar

COWS

The cow is the holy animal of Hinduism, and killing a cow in Nepal brings a jail term.

PUJA & SACRIFICE

Every morning, Hindu women all over Nepal can be seen walking through the streets carrying a plate, usually copper, filled with an assortment of goodies. These women are not delivering breakfast but are taking part in an important daily ritual called *puja*. The plate might contain flower petals, rice, yoghurt, fruit or sweets, and is an offering to the gods made at the local temple. Each of the items is sprinkled onto a temple deity in a set order and a bell is rung to let the gods know an offering is being made. Once an offering is made it is transformed into a sacred object and a small portion (referred to as *prasad*) is returned to the giver as a blessing from the deity. Upon returning home from her morning trip, the woman will give a small part of the blessed offerings to each member of the household.

Marigolds and sweets don't cut it with Nepal's more terrifying gods, notably Kali and Bhairab, who require a little extra appeasement in the form of bloody animal sacrifices. You can witness the gory executions, from chickens to water buffalo, at Dakshinkali (p164) in the Kathmandu Valley, Manakamana Temple (p184) and the Kalika Temple at Gorkha (p187), or during the annual Dasain festival in October (p20), when these temples are literally awash with blood offerings.

SADHUS

Sadhus are Hindu ascetics who have left their homes, jobs and families and embarked upon a spiritual search. They're an easily recognised group, usually wandering around half-naked, smeared in dust with their hair matted, and carrying nothing except a *trisul* (trident) and a begging bowl.

Sadhus wander all over the subcontinent, occasionally coming together at great religious gatherings such as the Maha Shivaratri festival at Pashupatinath in Kathmandu and the Janai Purnima festival at the sacred Hindu lakes of Gosainkund. You may also see sadhus wandering around Thamel and posing for photos in Kathmandu's Durbar Sq.

A few sadhus are simply beggars using a more sophisticated approach to gathering donations, but most are genuine in their search. Remember that if you take a picture of a sadhu, or accept a *tika* blessing from him, you will be expected to pay some *baksheesh* (tip), so negotiate your photo fee in advance to avoid any unpleasantness.

and Mt Kailash in Tibet are said to be the residences of Shiva and Parvati (Shiva's shakti, or female energy).

The definitions that follow include the most interesting and frequently encountered 'big names', plus associated consorts, manifestations, re-incarnations, vehicles and religious terminology.

SHIVA

As reproducer and destroyer, Shiva is probably the most important god in Nepal – so it's important to keep on his good side! Shiva is often represented by the phallic lingam, symbolic of his creative role. His *vahana* (vehicle) is the bull Nandi, which you'll often see outside Shiva temples. The symbol most often seen in Shiva's hand is the trident.

Shiva is also known as Nataraja, whose dance shook the cosmos and created the world. Shiva's home is Mt Kailash in the Himalaya and he's supposed to be keen on smoking hashish. In the Kathmandu Valley, Shiva is most popularly worshipped as Pashupati, the lord of the beasts. As the keeper of all living things, Pashupati is Shiva in a good mood. The temple of Pashupatinath, outside Kathmandu, is the most important Hindu temple in the country.

Shiva appears as bushy-eyebrowed Bhairab when he is in his fearful or terrible manifestation. Bhairab can appear in 64 different ways, but none of them is pretty. Typical of Tantric deities, he has multiple arms (each clutching a weapon), he dances on a corpse and wears a headdress of skulls and earrings of snakes. More skulls dangle from his belt, and his staring eyes and bared fangs complete the picture. Usually Bhairab is black, carries a cup made from a human skull and is attended by a dog.

The gruesome figure near the Hanuman Dhoka palace entrance in Kathmandu is a good example of this fearsome god at his worst. Bhairab's female counterparts are the Joginis, wrathful goddesses whose shrines can be found near Sankhu at the eastern end of the Kathmandu Valley, at Guhyeshwari near Pashupatinath and at Pharping.

Outside of the Kathmandu Valley, Shiva is most commonly worshipped as Mahadeva (Great God), the supreme deity.

The kings of Nepal long enjoyed added legitimacy because they were considered to be incarnations of Vishnu.

VISHNU

Vishnu is the preserver in Hindu belief, although in Nepal (where he often appears as Narayan) he also is seen to have played a role in the creation of the universe. Narayan is the reclining Vishnu, sleeping on the cosmic ocean, and from his navel appears Brahma, who creates the universe.

Vishnu has four arms and can often be identified by the symbols he holds: the sankha (conch shell); the disc-like weapon known as a chakra

(chakra means 'wheel', though in this sense it relates to Vishnu's weapon); the stick-like weapon known as a gada; and a padma (lotus flower). Vishnu's vehicle is the faithful man-bird Garuda; a winged Garuda will often be seen kneeling reverently in front of a Vishnu temple. Garuda has an intense hatred of snakes and is often seen destroying them. Vishnu's shakti is Lakshmi, the goddess of wealth and prosperity, whose vehicle is a tortoise.

BRAHMA

Sita is believed to have been born in Janakpur, and a temple there marks the site where she and Rama married. A great festival takes place there in November/December.

Despite his supreme position, Brahma appears much less often than Shiva or Vishnu. Like those gods, Brahma has four arms, but he also has four heads, to represent his all-seeing presence. The four Vedas are supposed to have emanated from his mouths.

PARVATI

Shiva's shakti is Parvati the beautiful and she is the dynamic element in their relationship. Just as Shiva is also known as Mahadeva (the Great God), Parvati is Mahadevi (or just Devi), the Great Goddess. Shiva is often symbolised by the phallic lingam, so his shakti's symbol is the yoni, representing the female sex organ. Their relationship is a sexual one and it is often Parvati who is the energetic and dominant partner.

Shiva's shakti has as many forms as Shiva himself. She may be peaceful Parvati, Uma or Gauri, but she may also be fearsome Kali, the black goddess, or Durga, the terrible. In these fearsome forms she holds a variety of weapons in her hands, struggles with demons and rides a lion or tiger. As skeletal Kali, she demands blood sacrifices and wears a garland of skulls.

THE LIVES OF VISHNU

Vishnu has 10 incarnations, appearing in the following sequence:

Matsya The fish.

Kurma The tortoise, on which the universe was built.

Varaha The boar, who bravely destroyed a demon that would have drowned the world.

Narsingha (or Narsimha) More demon destruction in incarnation four; half-man and half-lion (see p162 for an explanation of the legend behind this incarnation).

Vamana (or Vikrantha) The dwarf, who reclaimed the world from the demon-king Bali. The dwarf asked the demon for a patch of ground upon which to meditate, saying that the patch need only be big enough that he, the dwarf, could walk across it in three paces. The demon agreed, only to see the dwarf swell into a giant who strode across the universe in three gigantic steps.

Parasurama A warlike, axe-wielding Brahmin who fought the warrior-caste Chhetris after they killed his father.

Rama The hero of the Ramayana who, with help from Hanuman the monkey god, rescued his beautiful wife Sita from the clutches of Rawana, the evil king of Lanka.

Krishna The fun-loving, gentle and much-loved cowherd, who dallied with his beloved gopis (milkmaids), danced, played his flute and still managed to remain devoted to his wife Radha.

Buddha The teacher. Needless to say, Buddhists don't accept that the Buddha was just an incarnation of another religion's god.

Kalki We haven't seen incarnation number 10 yet, but it will be as Kalki the destroyer, when Vishnu wields the sword that will destroy the world at the end of the Kaliyuga, the age we are currently in.

GANESH

Ganesh, with his elephant head, is probably the most easily recognised and popular of the gods. He is the god of prosperity and wisdom, and there are thousands of Ganesh shrines and temples across Nepal. His parents are Shiva and Parvati and he has his father's temper to thank for his elephant head. Returning from a long trip, Shiva discovered Parvati in bed with a young man. Not pausing to think that their son might have grown up a little during his absence, Shiva lopped his head off! Parvati then forced Shiva to bring their son back to life, but he could only do so by giving him the head of the first living thing he saw – which happened to be an elephant.

Chubby Ganesh has a super-sweet tooth and is often depicted with his trunk in a mound of sweets and with one broken tusk; one story tells how he broke it off and threw it at the moon for making fun of his weight, another tale states that Ganesh used the tusk to write the Mahabharata.

Unlike in neighbouring India, Nepal's Hindu and Muslim communities coexist remarkably peacefully.

HANUMAN

The monkey god Hanuman is an important character from the Ramayana who came to the aid of Rama to help defeat the evil Rawana and release Sita from his grasp. Hanuman's trustworthy and alert nature is commemorated by the many statues of the god that guard palace entrances, most famously the Hanuman Dhoka in Kathmandu's Durbar Sq.

MACHHENDRANATH

A strictly Nepali Hindu god, Machhendranath (also known as Bunga Dyo) has power over the rains and the monsoon and is regarded as protector of the Kathmandu Valley. Typical of the intermingling of Hindu and Buddhist beliefs in Nepal, in the Kathmandu Valley at least, Machhendranath has come to be thought of as an incarnation of Avalokiteshvara, the Buddhist's Bodhisattva of Compassion.

There are two forms of Machhendranath based on colour and features: Seto (White) Machhendranath of Kathmandu, and Rato (Red) Machhendranath of Patan. Some scholars say that they are the same god, others say they are distinct. Both deities feature in the Kathmandu Valley's spectacular chariot festivals – for Kathmandu's festival see p70 and for Patan's see p135.

TARA

The goddess Tara is another deity who appears in both the Hindu and Buddhist pantheons. There are 108 different Taras but the best known are Green Tara and White Tara. Tara is generally depicted sitting with her right leg hanging down and her left hand in a *mudra* (hand gesture).

Actress Uma Thurman is named after the beautiful Hindu goddess Uma, a manifestation of Parvati. Uma forms half of the Uma-Maheshwar image, a common representation of Shiva and Parvati.

SARASWATI

The goddess of learning and the consort of Brahma, Saraswati rides upon a white swan and holds the stringed musical instrument known as a *veena*. Students, in particular, honour Saraswati during the spring festival of Basanta Panchami, when locals flock to the Saraswati shrine at the top of Swayambhunath outside Kathmandu.

Buddhism

Strictly speaking, Buddhism is not a religion, as it is centred not on a god but on a system of philosophy and a code of morality. Buddhism was founded in northern India in the 6th century BC when prince Siddhartha Gautama achieved enlightenment. According to some believers, Gautama Buddha was not the first Buddha but the fourth and he is not expected to be the last 'enlightened one'.

The Buddha never wrote down his dharma (teachings) and a schism that developed later means that today there are two major Buddhist schools: Hinayana and Mahayana.

The Buddha renounced material life to search for enlightenment but unlike other prophets found that starvation did not lead to discovery. He developed his rule of the Middle Way (moderation in all things). The Buddha taught that all life is suffering, and that suffering comes from our desires and the illusion of their importance. By following the 'eight-fold path' these desires can be extinguished and a state of nirvana, where we are free from their delusions, can be reached. Following this process requires going through a series of rebirths until the goal is reached and no more rebirths into the world of suffering are necessary. The path that takes you through this cycle of births is karma, but this is not simply fate. Karma is a law of cause and effect; your actions in one life determine what you will have to experience in your next life.

The first images of the Buddha date from the 5th century AD, 1000 years after his death (stupas were the symbol of Buddhism previous to this). The Buddha didn't want idols made of himself but a pantheon of Buddhist gods grew up regardless, with strong iconographical influence from Hinduism. As in Hinduism, the many Buddhist deities reflect various aspects of the divine, or 'Buddha-nature'. Multiple heads convey multiple personalities, *mudras* convey coded messages, and everything from eyebrows to stances indicate the nature of the deity.

There are many different types of Buddha images, though the most common are those of the past (Dipamkara), present (Sakyamuni) and future (Maitreya) Buddhas. The Buddha is recognised by 32 physical marks, including a bump on the top of his head, his third eye and the images of the Wheel of Law on the soles of his feet. In his left hand he holds a begging bowl and his right hand touches the earth in the witness *mudra*. He is often flanked by his two disciples.

Bodhisattvas are beings who have achieved enlightenment but decide to help everyone else gain enlightenment before entering nirvana. The Bodhisattva Manjushri has strong connections to the Kathmandu Valley. The Dalai Lama is considered a reincarnation of Avalokiteshvara (Chenresig in Tibetan), the Bodhisattva of Compassion. Tibetan Buddhism also has a host of fierce protector gods, called *dharmapalas*.

The pipal tree, under which the Buddha gained enlightenment, is also known by its highly appropriate Latin name, *ficus religious*.

Bön is Tibet's pre-Buddhist animist faith, now largely considered a fifth school of Tibetan Buddhism. Nepal has small pockets of Bön followers.

Tibetan Buddhism

There are four major schools of Tibetan (Vajrayana) Buddhism, all represented in the Kathmandu Valley: Nyingmapa, Kagyupa, Sakyapa and Gelugpa. The Nyingmapa order is the oldest and most dominant in the

MAIN SCHOOLS OF BUDDHISM

BUDDHIST SCHOOL	COUNTRIES PRACTISED	DESCRIPTION
Hinayana (Theravada, or Doctrine of the Elders)	Sri Lanka, Myanmar (Burma) and Thailand	Holds that the path to nirvana is essentially an individual pursuit.
Mahayana	Vietnam, Japan and China	Holds that the combined belief of its followers will eventually be great enough to encompass all of humanity and bear it to salvation. Less austere and ascetic than Hinayana.
Vajrayana (Tibetan Buddhism)	Tibet, Nepal, Ladakh	A more esoteric, Tantric version of Mahayana.

A BUBBLE IN A STREAM

The core Buddhist vision of impermanence is summed up perfectly in these lines from the *Diamond Sutra:*
> Thus shall you think of all this fleeting world,
> A star at dawn, a bubble in a stream,
> A flash of lightning in a summer cloud,
> A flickering lamp, a phantom, and a dream

Nepal Himalaya. Its origins come from the Indian sage Padmasambhava (Guru Rinpoche), who is credited with the establishment of Buddhism in Tibet in the 8th century.

The Dalai Lama is the head of the Gelugpa school and the spiritual leader of Tibetan Buddhists. In some texts the Gelugpa are known as the Yellow Hats, while the other schools are sometimes collectively identified as the Red Hats.

Islam

Nepal's small population of Muslims (about 4% of the total population) is mainly found close to the border with India, with a large population in Nepalganj. The first Muslims, who were mostly Kashmiri traders, arrived in the Kathmandu Valley in the 15th century. A second group arrived in the 17th century from northern India and they primarily manufactured armaments for the small hill states. The largest Muslim group are the Terai Muslims, many of whom still have strong ties with the Muslim communities in the Indian states of Bihar and Uttar Pradesh.

Padmasam-bhava (Guru Rinpoche) is a common image in Nyingmapa monasteries and is recognisable by his *khatvanga* staff of human heads and his fabulously curly moustache.

Shamanism

Shamanism is practised by many mountain peoples throughout the Himalaya and dates back some 50,000 years. Its ancient healing traditions are based on a cosmology that divides the world into three main levels: the Upper World where the sun, moon, stars, planets, deities and spirits important to the shaman's healing work abide; the Middle World of human life; and the Lower World, where more malevolent deities and spirits exist.

Faith healers protect against a wide range of spirits, including headless *mulkattas,* who have eyes in their chest and signify imminent death; *pret,* the ghosts of the recently deceased that loiter at crossroads; and *kichikinni,* the ghost of a beautiful and sexually insatiable siren who is recognisable by her sagging breasts and the fact that her feet are on backwards.

During ceremonies, the *dhami* or *jhankri* (shaman or faith healer) uses techniques of drumming, divination, trances and sacrifices to invoke deities and spirits that he or she wishes to assist in the ritual. The shaman essentially acts as a broker between the human and spirit worlds.

The People of Nepal

The National Psyche

Nepal's location between India and Tibet, the diversity of its 60 or more ethnic and caste groups, its isolating geography and myriad (up to 100) languages have resulted in a complex mosaic of customs and beliefs that make it hard to generalise about a 'Nepali people'.

Perhaps the dominant Nepali cultural concepts are those of caste and status, both of which contribute to a strictly defined system of hierarchy and deference. Caste determines not only a person's status, but also their career and marriage partner, how that person interacts with other Nepalis and how others react back. This system of hierarchy extends even to the family, where everyone has a clearly defined rank. The Nepali language has half a dozen words for 'you', each of which conveys varying shades of respect.

When it comes to their religious beliefs, Nepalis are admirably flexible, pragmatic and, above all, tolerant – there is almost no religious or ethnic tension in Nepal. Nepalis are generally good humoured and patient, quick to smile and slow to anger, though they also have a reputation as fierce fighters (see the boxed text on p194 about the famous Gurkha forces).

The Nepali view of the world is dominated by prayer and ritual and a knowledge that the gods are not remote, abstract concepts but living, present beings who can influence human affairs in very direct ways. Nepalis perceive the divine everywhere, from the greeting *namaste*, which literally means 'I greet the divine inside of you', to the spirits and gods present in trees, passes, sacred river confluences and mountain peaks.

The notions of karma and caste, when combined with a tangled bureaucracy and deep-rooted corruption, tend to create an endemic sense of fatalism in Nepal. Confronted with problems, many Nepalis will simply respond with a shrug of the shoulders and the phrase *khe garne?*, or 'what is there to do?', which Westerners often find frustrating yet oddly addictive.

Traditional Lifestyle

The cornerstones of Nepali life are the demands (as well as the rewards) of one's family, ethnic group and caste. To break these time-honoured traditions is to risk being ostracised from family and community. While young Nepali people, especially in urban areas, are increasingly influenced by Western values and lifestyle, the vast majority of people live by traditional customs and principles. The biggest modernising influences in Nepal are probably satellite TV, roads and tourism – in that order.

Both Magars and Gurungs have made up large numbers of Gurkha regiments, and army incomes have contributed greatly to the economy of their regions.

The website www.mountainvoices.org/nepal.asp.html has an interesting collection of interviews with Nepali mountain folk on a wide variety of topics.

In most ethnic groups, joint and extended families live in the same house, even in Kathmandu. In some smaller villages extended clans make up the entire community. Traditional family life has been dislocated by the large number (over one million) of Nepali men forced to seek work away from home, whether in Kathmandu or the Terai, or abroad in India, Malaysia or the Gulf States.

Arranged marriages remain the norm in Nepali Hindu society and are generally between members of the same caste or ethnic group, although there is a growing number of 'love marriages'. Child marriages have been illegal since 1963 and today the average age of marriage for girls is just under 19. The family connections generated by a marriage are as much a social contract as a personal affair, and most families consult matchmakers and astrologers when making such an important decision.

To decide not to have children is almost unheard of and Nepali women will often pity you if you are childless. Having a son is important, especially for Hindu families, as some religious rites (such as lighting the funeral pyre to ensure a peaceful passage into the next life) can only be performed by the eldest son. Girls are regarded by many groups as a financial burden whose honour needs to be protected until she is married.

Children stay at school for up to 12 years; 70% of children will begin school but only 7% will reach their 10th school year, when they sit their School Leaving Certificate (SLC) board examination. Many villages only have a primary school, which means children either have to walk long distances each day or board in a bigger town to attend secondary school. The ratio of boys to girls at both primary and secondary schools is almost 2:1 in favour of boys.

Despite what you may see in Kathmandu and Pokhara, Nepal is overwhelmingly rural and poor; 85% of people live in the countryside. Farming is still the main occupation and debt is a factor in most people's lives. Large areas of land are still owned by *zamindars* (absent landlords) and up to 50% of a landless farmer's production will go to the landowner as rent. It remains to be seen whether the Maoist government will be able to make a dent into this imbalance.

Most rural Nepali families are remarkably self-sufficient in their food supply, raising all of it themselves and selling any excess in the nearest town, where they'll stock up on things such as sugar, soap, cigarettes, tea, salt, cloth and jewellery. Throughout Nepal this exchange of goods has created a dense network of trails trodden by everyone from traders and porters to mule caravans and trekking groups.

The rhythms of village life are determined by the seasons and marked by festivals – New Year, harvest and religious festivals being the most important. Dasain remains the biggest event of the calendar in the Middle Hills and is a time when most Nepali families get together.

Older people are respected members of the community and are cared for by their children. Old age is a time for relaxation, prayer and meditation. The dead are generally cremated and the deceased's sons will shave their heads and wear white for an entire year following the death.

For a guide to some cultural dos and don'ts when visiting Nepal, see p354.

Population

Nepal currently has a population of around 29.4 million (2011 estimate), a number that is increasing at the rapid rate of 2.1% annually. Over 2.5 million people live in the Kathmandu Valley and perhaps one million in Kathmandu. Four million Nepalis reside in India. Around half of Nepal's population lives in the flat fertile lands of the Terai, which also acts as the nation's industrial base, and the population here is increasing rapidly.

Traditional prejudice against daughters is reflected in the bitter Nepali proverb: 'Raising a girl is like watering your neighbour's garden.'

THE PEOPLE OF NEPAL POPULATION

There are around 130,000 refugees, some Tibetan, but most expelled from Bhutan.

People

Up to half a million Nepali men seek seasonal work in Indian cities; in 2010 they and other Nepali workers overseas sent home US$3.35 billion, making this Nepal's largest single source of foreign currency.

The human geography of Nepal is a remarkable cultural mosaic of peoples who have not so much assimilated as learned to coexist. The ethnic divisions are complex and numerous; you'll have to do your homework to be able to differentiate between a Limbu, Lepcha, Lhopa and Lhomi – and that's just the Ls!

Simplistically, Nepal is the meeting place of the Indo-Aryan people of India and the Mongoloid peoples of the Himalaya. There are three main cultural zones running east to west: the north, including the high Himalaya; the Middle Hills; and the Terai. Each group has adapted its lifestyle and farming practices to its environment but, thanks largely to Nepal's tortured topography, has retained its own traditions. Social taboos, especially among caste Hindus, have limited further assimilation between groups.

Nepal's diverse ethnic groups speak somewhere between 24 and 100 different languages and dialects, depending on how finely the distinctions are made. Nepali functions as the unifying language, though less than half of Nepal's people speak Nepali as their first language.

Himalayan Zone

The hardy Tibetan peoples who inhabit the high Himalaya are known in Nepal as Bhotias (Bhotiyas), a slightly derogatory term among caste Hindus. Each group remains distinct but their languages are all Tibetan-based and, with a few exceptions, they are Tibetan Buddhists.

The Bhotiyas' names combine the region they came from with the suffix 'pa' and include the Sherpas (literally 'easterners') of the Everest region, the Dolpopas of the west and the Lopas, or Lobas (literally 'southerners'), of the Mustang region.

The withering of Trans-Himalayan trade routes and the difficulty of farming and herding at high altitude drive these people to lower elevations during winter, either to graze their animals or to trade in India and the Terai. Yak herding and the barley harvest remain the economic bedrocks of the high Himalaya.

Thakalis

Originating along the Kali Gandaki Valley in central Nepal, the Thakalis have emerged as the entrepreneurs of Nepal. They once played an important part in the salt trade between the subcontinent and Tibet, and travellers will meet them most frequently in their adopted roles as ho-

NEPALI NAMES

You can tell a lot about a Nepali person from their name, including often their caste, profession, ethnic group and where they live. Gurung and Sherpa are ethnic groups as well as surnames. The surname Bista or Pant indicates that the person is a Brahman, originally from western Nepal; Devkota indicates an eastern origin. Thapa, Pande and Bhasnet are names related to the former Rana ruling family. Shrestha is a high-caste Newari name. The initials KC often stand for Khatri Chhetri, a mixed-caste name. The surname Kami is the Nepali equivalent of Smith.

Sherpa names even reveal which day of the week the person was born: Dawa (Monday), Mingmar (Tuesday), Lhakpa (Wednesday), Phurba (Thursday), Pasang (Friday), Pemba (Saturday) and Nyima (Sunday). The one thing you can't tell from a Sherpa name is their sex – Lhakpa Sherpa could be a man or a woman!

teliers and lodge owners, especially on the Annapurna Circuit. Originally Buddhist, many pragmatic Thakalis have now adopted Hinduism.

Tamangs

The Tamangs make up one of the largest groups in the country. They live mainly in the hills north of Kathmandu and have a noticeably strong Tibetan influence, from their monasteries, known as *ghyang*, to the mani walls that mark the entrance to their villages. You can stay in traditional Tamang villages on the Tamang Heritage Trail walk.

According to some accounts, ancestors of the Tamang were horse traders and cavalrymen from an invading Tibetan army who settled in Nepal. They are well known for their independence and suspicion of authority, probably caused by the fact that in the 19th century they were relegated to a low status, with much of their land distributed to Bahuns and Chhetris. As bonded labourers they were dependent upon menial work such as portering. Many of the 'Tibetan' souvenirs, carpets and thangkas (religious paintings) you see in Kathmandu are made by Tamangs.

Tibetans

About 12,000 of the 120,000 Tibetans in exile around the world live in Nepal. Although their numbers are small, Tibetans have a high profile, partly because of the important roles they play in tourism and the Tibetan carpet industry.

Tibetans are devout Buddhists and their arrival in the valley has rejuvenated a number of important religious sites, most notably the stupas at Swayambhunath and Bodhnath.

Sherpas

The Sherpas who live high in the mountains of eastern and central Nepal are probably the best-known Nepali ethnic group. These nomadic Tibetan herders moved to the Solu Khumbu region of Nepal 500 years ago from eastern Tibet, bringing with them their Tibetan Buddhist religion and building the beautiful gompas (monasteries) that dot the steep hillsides. They are strongly associated with the Khumbu region around Mt Everest, although only 3000 of the total 35,000 Sherpas actually live in the Khumbu; the rest live in the lower valleys of the Solu region.

Tourism stepped in after the collapse of trade over the Nangpa La pass in 1959, after the Chinese sent thousands of troops to enforce their claim on Tibet, and these days the Sherpa name is synonymous with mountaineering and trekking. Potatoes were introduced to the region in the late 19th century and are now the main Sherpa crop.

Middle Hills Zone

The Middle Hills of Nepal are the best places to witness village life at its most rustic. In the east are the Kirati, who are divided into the Rai and Limbu groups. The Newari people dominate the central hills around the Kathmandu Valley, while the Magars and Gurungs inhabit the hills of the Kali Gandaki northwest of Pokhara.

Moving west, the Bahun and Chhetri are the dominant groups, although the lines between castes have become blurred over time.

Rais & Limbus

The Rais and Limbus are thought to have ruled the Kathmandu Valley in the 7th century BC until they were defeated around AD 300. They then moved into the steep hill country of eastern Nepal, from the Arun Valley to the Sikkim border, where many remain today. Others have moved to

THE PEOPLE OF NEPAL PEOPLE

Changes in trading patterns and traditional culture among Nepal's Himalayan people are examined in *Himalayan Traders*, by Christoph von Fürer-Haimendorf.

Despite associations in the West, Sherpas actually do very little portering, focusing mostly on high-altitude expedition work. Most of the porters you meet on the trails are Tamang or Rai, or from other groups.

the Terai or India as economic migrants. Many Rai work as porters in the Middle Hills.

Describing themselves as Kirati, these tribes are easily distinguishable by their Mongolian features. They are of Tibeto-Burmese descent and their traditional religion is distinct from Buddhism and Hinduism, although the latter is exerting a growing influence. Himalayan hunterwarriors, they are still excellent soldiers and are well represented in the Gurkha regiments.

Many of the men still carry a large khukuri (traditional curved knife) tucked into their belt and wear a *topi* (traditional Nepali cap). Some communities in upper Arun live in bamboo houses.

Newars

Sherpas: Reflections on Change in Himalayan Nepal, by James F Fisher, offers an anthropological snapshot of how tourism and modernisation have affected Sherpa religious and cultural life. Fisher worked with Edmund Hillary in the Khumbu in the 1960s, bringing the first schools and airstrip to the region.

The Newars of the Kathmandu Valley number about 1.1 million and make up 6% of the population. Their language, Newari, is distinct from Tibetan, Nepali or Hindi, and is one of the world's most difficult languages to learn. The Newars are excellent farmers and merchants, as well as skilled artists, famed across Asia. The Kathmandu Valley is filled with spectacular examples of their artistic work, and their aesthetic influence was felt as far away as Lo Manthang and Lhasa.

Their origins are shrouded in mystery: most Newars have both Mongoloid and Caucasian physical characteristics. It's generally accepted that their ancestors were migrants of varied ethnicity who settled in the Kathmandu Valley over centuries – possibly originating with the Kiratis, or an even earlier group.

Newars lead a communal way of life and have developed several unique customs, including the worship of the Kumari, a girl believed to be a living god (see the boxed text, p66), and the annual chariot festivals that provide the high point of the valley's cultural life. Living so close to the centre of power has also meant there are many Newars in the bureaucracies of Kathmandu.

Newari men wear *surwal* (trousers with a baggy seat that are tighter around the calves, like jodhpurs), a *daura* (thigh-length double-breasted shirt), a vest or coat and the traditional *topi* hat. Newari castes include the Sakyas (priests), Tamrakar (metal casters) and the Jyapu (farmers). Jyapu women wear a black sari with a red border, while the men often wear the traditional trousers and shirt with a long piece of cotton wrapped around the waist.

Gurungs

The Gurungs, a Tibeto-Burmese people, live mainly in the central midlands, from Gorkha and Baglung up to Manang and the southern slopes of the Annapurnas, around Pokhara. One of the biggest Gurung settlements is Ghandruk, with its sweeping views of the Annapurnas and

MOVING TIGERS

Nepal's national board game is *bagh chal,* which literally means 'move the tigers'. The game is played on a lined board with 25 intersecting points. One player has four tigers, the other has 20 goats, and the aim is for the tiger player to 'eat' five goats by jumping over them before the goat player can encircle the tigers and prevent them moving. You can buy attractive brass *bagh chal* sets in Kathmandu and Patan, where they are made.

Nepal's other popular game is *carom,* which looks like finger snooker. Players use discs that glide over a chalked-up board to pot other discs into the corner pockets.

Machhapuchhare. Gurung women wear nose rings, known as *phuli,* and coral necklaces.

The Gurungs (who call themselves Tamu, or highlanders) originally migrated from western Tibet, bringing with them their animist Bön faith. One distinctive aspect of village life is the *rodi,* a cross between a town hall and a youth centre, where teenagers hang out and cooperative village tasks are planned.

Magars

The Magars, a large group (around 8% of the total population), are a Tibeto-Burmese people who live in many parts of the midlands zone of western and central Nepal. With such a large physical spread there are considerable regional variations.

The Magars are excellent soldiers and fought with Prithvi Narayan Shah to help unify Nepal. Their kingdom of Palpa (based at Tansen) was one of the last to be incorporated into a unified Nepal.

The Magars generally live in two-storey, rectangular or square thatched houses washed in red clay. They have been heavily influenced by Hinduism, and in terms of religion, farming practices, housing and dress, they are hard to distinguish from Chhetris.

Bahuns & Chhetris

The Hindu caste groups of Bahuns and Chhetris are dominant in the Middle Hills, making up 30% of the country's population.

Even though the caste system was formally abolished in 1963, these two groups remain the top cats of the caste hierarchy. Although there is no formal relationship in Hinduism between caste and ethnicity, Nepal's Bahuns and Chhetris (Brahmin priests and Kshatriya warriors, respectively) are considered ethnic groups as well as the two highest castes.

Bahuns and Chhetris played an important role in the court and armies of Prithvi Narayan Shah and after unification they were rewarded with tracts of land. Their language, Khas Kura, then became the national language of Nepal and their high-caste position was religiously, culturally and legally enforced. Ever since, Bahuns and Chhetris have dominated the government in Kathmandu, making up over 80% of the civil service.

A number of Bahuns and Chhetris had roles as tax collectors under the Shah and Rana regimes and to this day many are moneylenders with a great deal of power. Outside the Kathmandu Valley, the majority of these groups are simple farmers, indistinguishable in most respects from their neighbours.

The Bahuns tend to be more caste-conscious and orthodox than other Nepali Hindus, which sometimes leads to difficulties in relationships with 'untouchable' Westerners. Many are vegetarians and do not drink alcohol; marriages are arranged within the caste.

Terai Zone

Until the eradication of malaria in the 1950s, the only people to live in the valleys of the inner Terai and along much of the length of the Terai proper were Tharus and a few small associated groups, who enjoyed a natural immunity to the disease. After the Terai opened for development, large numbers of people from the midlands settled here – every group is represented and around 50% of Nepali people live in the region.

A number of large groups straddle the India–Nepal border. In the eastern Terai, Mithila people dominate; in the central Terai, there are many Bhojpuri-speaking people; and in the western Terai, Abadhi-speaking people are significant. All are basically cultures of the Gangetic plain and Hindu caste structure is strictly upheld.

THE PEOPLE OF NEPAL PEOPLE

JANAI

Bahun and Chhetri men can be recognised by their sacred thread – the janai, worn over the right shoulder and under the right arm – which is changed once a year during the Janai Purnima festival.

Tharus

One of the most visible groups is the Tharus, who are thought to be the earliest inhabitants of the Terai and descended from either Rajasthani Rajputs or the royal clan of Sakya, the Buddha's family. About one million Tharu speakers inhabit the length of the Terai, including the inner Terai around Chitwan, although they mainly live in the west.

Tharu clans have traditionally lived in thatched huts with wattle walls or in traditional long houses. Their beliefs are largely animistic, involving the worship of forest spirits and ancestral deities, but they are increasingly influenced by Hinduism.

Over generations many Tharus have been exploited by *zamindars* and fallen into debt or entered into bonded labour. In 2000 the *kamaiyas* (bonded labourers) were freed by government legislation, but little has been done to help these people who are now without land and work. Consequently, in most Terai towns in western Nepal you will see squatter settlements of former *kamaiyas*.

The lives and roles of Nepali women are examined in the insightful *The Violet Shyness of their Eyes: Notes from Nepal*, by Barbara J Scot, and *Nepali Aama*, by Broughton Coburn, which details the life of a remarkable Gurung woman.

Women in Nepal

Women have a hard time of it in Nepal. Female mortality rates are higher than men's, literacy rates are lower and women generally work harder and longer than men, for less reward. Women only truly gain status in traditional society when they bear their husband a son. Bearing children is so important that a man can legally take a second wife if the first has not had a child after 10 years.

Nepal has a strongly patriarchal society, though this is less the case among Himalayan communities such as the Sherpa, where women often run the show (and the lodge). Boys are strongly favoured over girls, who are often the last to eat and the first to be pulled from school during financial difficulties. Nepal has a national literacy rate of 49%, with the rate among women at 35%.

The traditional practice of *sati,* where a woman was expected to throw herself on her husband's funeral pyre, was outlawed in the 1920s. Nepal legalised abortion in 2002. In 2005 landmark rulings gave women under the age of 35 the right, for the first time, to apply for a passport without their husband's or parent's permission, and safeguarded their right to inherited property. The rural custom of exiling women to cowsheds for four days during their period was made illegal in 2005.

HUMAN TRAFFICKING IN NEPAL

Trafficking of girls is a major problem in Nepal's most impoverished rural areas. Some 10,000 to 15,000 girls are tricked or sold every year into servitude, either as domestic, factory or sex workers. Brokers called *dalals* sell Nepali girls for around US$2500 into the brothels of Mumbai. It is believed that over 100,000 Nepali women work in Indian brothels, often in conditions resembling slavery, and around half of these women are thought to be HIV positive. When obvious AIDS symptoms force these women out of work, some manage to return to Nepal. However, they are shunned by their families and there is virtually no assistance available for them or their children.

Particularly common in the Tharu areas of Dang and Bardia is the tradition of selling young daughters, aged seven to 10, to work as *kamlaris*, or indentured slaves, in the families of wealthy high-caste households. One organisation, the **Nepal Youth Foundation** (www.nepalyouthfoundation.org), has come up with an ingenious way of persuading families to hold on to their daughters: it gives them a piglet and kerosene stocks for every girl they keep at home and pays to send the child to school. So far the organisation has steered 10,000 girls away from slavery.

On the death of her husband, a widow is often expected to marry the brother of the deceased and property is turned over to her sons, on whom she is then financially dependent. In the far western hills the traditional system of polyandry (one woman married to two brothers) emerged over centuries in response to limited amounts of land and the annual trading trips that required husbands to leave their families for months at a time. The practice kept population levels down and stopped family land being broken up between brothers. All children born into the family are considered the elder brother's. In recent years the system has started to break down.

The annual festival of Teej is the biggest festival for women, though ironically it honours their husbands. The activities include feasting, fasting, ritual bathing (in the red and gold saris they were married in) and ritual offerings.

Arts & Architecture

Wander around the towns of the Kathmandu Valley and you'll come across priceless wood carvings and stone sculptures at every turn, in surprisingly accessible places. Nepal's artistic masterpieces are not hidden away in dusty museums but are part of a living culture, to be touched, worshipped, feared or simply paid no heed.

Architecture & Sculpture

Kathmandu Valley's Unesco World Heritage Sites

» Durbar Sq, Kathmandu

» Durbar Sq, Patan

» Durbar Sq, Bhaktapur

» Swayambhunath Stupa

» Bodhnath Stupa

» Pashupatinath

» Changu Narayan

Architecture and the sculpting arts in Nepal are inextricably intermingled. The finest woodcarvings and stone sculptures are often part of a building. Indeed a temple is simply not a temple without its deity statue and its finely carved adornments.

The earliest architecture in the Kathmandu Valley has faded with history. Grassy mounds are all that remain where Patan's four Ashoka stupas once stood (p131), and the impressive stupas of Swayambhunath (p108) and Bodhnath (p160) have been rebuilt many times over the centuries.

The Licchavi period from the 4th to 9th centuries AD was a golden age for Nepal, and while the temples may have disappeared, magnificent stone sculptures have withstood the ravages of time and can still be found. Beautiful pieces lie scattered around temples of the Kathmandu Valley. The Licchavi sculptures at the temple of Changu Narayan near Bhaktapur (p156) are particularly good examples, as is the statue of Vishnu asleep on a bed of serpents at Budhanilkantha (p124).

No wooden buildings and carvings are known to have survived in Nepal from that period, or indeed before the 12th century. However, within Lhasa's Jokhang Temple there are carved wooden beams and columns dating from before the 9th century that are clearly the work of Newari artisans.

It was in the Malla period that Nepali artistry with wood really came into its own, as the famed skills of the valley's Newari people reached their zenith, particularly between the 15th and 17th centuries. Squabbling and one-upmanship between the city states of Kathmandu, Patan and Bhaktapur fuelled a competitive building boom as each tried to outdo the other with even more magnificent palaces and temples.

The great age of Nepali architecture came to a dramatic end when Prithvi Narayan Shah invaded the valley in 1769. These days traditional building skills are still evidenced in the periodically ongoing restoration projects in Kathmandu, Patan and Bhaktapur. Moreover, today's architects will often incorporate traditional features into their buildings, particularly hotels.

Newari Pagoda Temples

The Nepali architect Arniko can be said to be the father of the Asian pagoda. He kick-started the introduction and reinterpretation of the pagoda in China and eastern Asia when he brought the multiroofed Nepali pagoda design to the court of Kublai Khan in the late 13th century.

The distinctive Newari pagoda temples are a major feature of the Kathmandu Valley skyline, echoing, and possibly inspired by, the horizon's pyramid-shaped mountain peaks. While strictly speaking they are neither wholly Newari nor pagodas, the term has been widely adopted to describe the temples of the valley.

The temples are generally square in design, and may be either Hindu or Buddhist (or both, as is the nature of Nepali religion). On occasion, temples are rectangular or octagonal; Krishna can occupy an octagonal temple, but Ganesh, Shiva and Vishnu can only inhabit square temples.

The major feature of the temples is the tiered roof, which may have one to five tiers, with two or three being the most common. In the Kathmandu Valley there are two temples with four roofs and another two with five (Kumbeshwar at Patan and Nyatapola at Bhaktapur). The sloping roofs are usually covered with distinctive *jhingati* (baked clay tiles), although richer temples will often have one roof of gilded copper. The bell-shaped *gajur* (pinnacle) is made of baked clay or gilded copper.

The temples are usually built on a stepped plinth, which may be as high as or even higher than the temple itself. In many cases the number of steps on the plinth corresponds with the number of roofs on the temple.

The temple building itself has a small sanctum, known as a *garbha-griha* (literally 'womb room'), housing the deity. Worshippers practise individually, with devotees standing outside the door to make their supplications. The only people permitted to actually enter the sanctum are pujari (temple priests).

Perhaps the most interesting feature of the temples is the detailed decoration, which is only evident close up. Under each roof there are often brass or other metal decorations, such as *kinkinimala* (rows of small bells) or embossed metal banners. The metal streamer that often hangs from above the uppermost roof to below the level of the lowest roof (such as on the Golden Temple in Patan) is called a *pataka*. Its function is to give the deity a way to descend to earth.

The other major decorative elements are the wooden *tunala* (struts) that support the roofs. The intricate carvings are usually of deities associated with the temple or of the *vahana* (deity's vehicle) but quite

The cultural organisation Spiny Babbler (www.spiny babbler.org) has an online Nepali art museum and articles on Nepali art. It is named after Nepal's only endemic species of bird.

Get a great overview of Buddhist and Nepali art at the Patan Museum (p129) and at Kathmandu's National Museum (p111), both of which explain the concepts behind Buddhist and Hindu art and iconography in an insightful and accessible way.

NEPAL'S STOLEN HERITAGE

In recent decades Nepal has had a staggering amount of its artistic heritage spirited out of the country by art thieves – 120 statues were stolen in the 1980s alone. Much of the stolen art languishes in museums or private collections in European nations and in the US, while in Nepal the remaining temple statues are increasingly kept under lock and key.

One of the reasons photography is banned in some temples in Nepal is that international thieves often put photos of temple artefacts in their underground 'shopping catalogues'. Pieces are then stolen to order, often with the aid of corrupt officials, to fetch high prices on the lucrative Himalayan art market. UN conventions against the trade exist but are weakly enforced.

Catalogues of stolen Nepali art have been produced in an attempt to locate these treasures, and several pieces have been given back to Kathmandu's National Museum, including a Buddha statue stolen from Patan that was returned after a dealer tried to sell it to a museum in Austria for a cool US$200,000.

REPOUSSÉ METALWORK

Many of the richly decorated objects used for religious rituals in Nepal make use of the ancient technique of repoussé – where a design is hammered into the metal from the back using hammers and punches. First the metal shape is set into a bed of *jhau* (a mixture of resin and brick dust), then the design is painstakingly applied and the resin is melted away, allowing finishing touches to be added from the front using engraving tools. This style of metalwork has been produced since at least the 2nd millennium BC and the technique is still practised today in alleyways across the Kathmandu Valley.

a few depict explicit sexual acts (see the boxed text, p68, for more on Nepali erotic art).

Shikhara Temples

The second-most common temples are the shikhara temples, which have a heavy Indian influence. The temples are so named because their tapering towers resemble a shikhara (mountain peak, in Sanskrit). Although the style developed in India in the 6th century, it first appeared in Nepal in the late Licchavi period.

The tapering, pyramidal tower is the main feature, and is often surrounded by four similar but smaller towers. These may be located on porches over the shrine's entrances.

The Krishna Mandir and the octagonal Krishna Temple, both in Patan's Durbar Sq, and the spire of the Mahabouddha Temple in Patan are all excellent examples.

The Art of God Making

Newari art and craft skills extend far beyond the woodwork for which they are so well known and include ceramics, brickwork, stone sculptures and intricate metalwork. The finest metalwork includes the stunning images of the two Tara goddesses at Swayambhunath (p109) and the Golden Gate (Sun Dhoka) in Bhaktapur (p144).

Statues are created through two main techniques – the repoussé method of hammering thin sheets of metal and the 'lost wax' method. In the latter, the statue is carved in wax, which is then encased in clay and left to dry. The wax is then melted, metal is poured into the clay mould and the mould is then broken, revealing the statue. Finishing touches include grinding, polishing and painting before the statue is ready to be sanctified.

Nepal, by Michael Hutt, is an excellent guide to the art and architecture of the Kathmandu Valley. It outlines the main forms of art and architecture and describes specific sites within the valley, often with layout plans. It has great colour plates and black-and-white photos.

Painting

Chinese, Tibetan, Indian and Mughal influences can all be seen in Nepali painting styles. The earliest Newari paintings were illuminated manuscripts dating from the 11th century. Newari *paubha* paintings are iconic religious paintings similar to Tibetan thangkas. Notable to both is a lack of perspective, symbolic use of colour and strict iconographic rules.

Modern Nepali artists struggle to make a living, although there are a few galleries in Kathmandu that feature local artists. Some artists are fortunate enough to get a sponsored overseas exhibition or a posting at an art college outside the country to teach their skills. Commissioning a painting by a local artist is a way to support the arts and take home a unique souvenir of your trip.

The eastern Terai has its own distinct form of colourful mural painting called Mithila art – see the boxed text, p258.

Music & Dance

The last few years have seen a revival in Nepali music and songs, both folk and 'Nepali modern'. The staple Hindi film songs have been supplanted by a vibrant local music scene thanks to advances made in FM radio.

In the countryside most villagers supply their own entertainment. Dancing and traditional music enliven festivals and family celebrations, when villages erupt with the energetic sounds of *bansari* (flutes), *madal* (drums) and cymbals, or sway to the moving soulful sounds of devotional singing and the gentle twang of the four-stringed *sarang*. Singing is one important way that girls and boys in the hills can interact and flirt, showing their grace and wit through dances and improvised songs.

There are several musician castes, including the *gaine,* a dwindling caste of travelling minstrels, the *ghandarba,* whose music you can hear in Kathmandu, and the *damai,* who often perform in wedding bands. Women generally do not perform music in public.

Nepali dance styles are as numerous and varied as Nepal's ethnic groups. They range from the stick dances of the Tharu in the Terai, to the line-dancing style of the mountain Sherpas. Joining in with an enthusiastic group of porters from different parts of the country at the end of a trekking day is a great way to learn some of the moves. Masked dances are also common, from the Cham dances performed by Tibetan Buddhist monks to the masked Hindu dances of Nava Durga in Bhaktapur (p155).

A good introduction to popular Nepali folk music is the trio (flute, sitar and tabla) of Sur Sudha, Nepal's de facto musical ambassadors, whose evocative recordings will take you back to the region long after you've tasted your last daal bhaat. Try their *Festivals of Nepal* and *Images of Nepal* recordings. You can listen to track excerpts at www.amazon.com and check out the band on their website (www.sursudha.com).

You can see 'for-tourist' versions of Nepal's major dances at Newari restaurants in Kathmandu (see p96 for more information).

Himalayan Voices: an Introduction to Modern Nepali Literature, by Michael Hutt, includes work by contemporary poets and short-story writers.

ARTS & ARCHITECTURE MUSIC & DANCE

TIBETAN CARPETS

One of the most amazing success stories of the last few decades is the local Tibetan carpet industry. Although carpet production has long been a cottage industry inside Tibet, in 1960 the Nepal International Tibetan Refugee Relief Committee, with the support of renowned Swiss geologist Toni Hagen and the Swiss government, began encouraging Tibetan refugees in Patan to make and sell carpets.

Tibetan and New Zealand wool is used to make the carpets. The exuberant colours and lively designs of traditional carpets have been toned down for the international market, but the old ways of producing carpets remain the same. The intricacies of the senna loop method are hard to pick out in the blur of hands that is usually seen at a carpet workshop; each thread is looped around a gauge rod that will determine the height of the carpet pile, then each row is hammered down and the loops of thread split to release the rod. To finish it off the pile is clipped to bring out the design.

The carpet industry has declined somewhat over recent years, largely because of political instability and negative publicity about the exploitative use of child labour and the use of carcinogenic dye. Still, today Nepal exports more than 700,000 sq metres of rugs annually, valued at around US$60 million. The industry accounts for around 50% of the country's exports of manufactured goods to countries other than India, and employs over 200,000 workers directly, and up to a million indirectly. Groups such as **Rugmark** (www.rugmark.org) work to reduce child labour in Nepal's carpet production, which has dropped to less than 3% today.

One of Nepal's most famous singers is the Tibetan nun Choying Drolma, who is based in Pharping in the Kathmandu Valley and who can count Tracy Chapman among her fans. Her CDs *Cho* and *Selwa,* recorded with guitarist Steve Tibbetts, are transcendentally beautiful and highly recommended.

The folk song that you hear everywhere in Nepal (you'll know which one we mean when you get there) is '*Resham Pheeree Ree*' ('My Heart is Fluttering Like Silk in the Wind').

Film

The Nepali film industry has come a long way since the 1980s and early '90s, when only four or five films were produced annually. In the late '90s the Kathmandu film industry ('Kollywood') was making up to 70 films per year, although this bubble burst in 2001 when government-imposed curfews caused audience numbers to plummet and finances to dry up.

According to John Whelpton in his *History of Nepal,* the first film shown in Kathmandu depicted the wedding of the Hindu god Ram. The audience threw petals and offerings at the screen as they would do at a temple or if the god himself were present.

The Oscar-nominated Nepali-French film *Caravan,* directed by Eric Valli, is the most famous 'Nepali' film and played to packed houses in Kathmandu. It features magnificent footage of the Upper Dolpo district of western Nepal as it tells the tale of yak caravaners during a change of generations. It was renamed for distribution abroad as *Himalaya.*

Basantpur by Neer Shah, the coproducer of *Caravan,* is a Nepali film depicting the intrigues and conspiracies of life at the Rana court. In 2011, Shah directed *Masan,* a film based on the eponymous book by Gopal Prasad Rimal, a noted playwright who ushered in a new era in Nepali literature. Another Nepali film to watch is *Mukundo* (Mask of Desire), directed by Tsering Rita Sherpa, which explores secular and spiritual desires in Kathmandu. Tulsi Ghimire is another popular Nepali director. Perhaps the best-known film shot in Nepal is Bernado Bertolucci's *Little Buddha,* which was partly filmed at Bhaktapur's Durbar Sq and the Gokarna Forest.

The website www.mountain musicproject. blogspot.com has links to radio and video clips of several Nepali musicians, including Rubin Gandharba – the 'Nepali Bob Dylan'.

Kagbeni, by Bhu-san Dahal, is Ne-pal's first ever HD movie. A creepy supernatural tale adapted from the short story *The Monkey's Paw,* by WW Jacobs, it is set in the foothills around Annapurna.

ARTS & ARCHITECTURE FILM

NEPALI NOVELS

The last few years have seen a bounty of novels written by Nepali writers. Pack one of them in your backpack for added insights into the country.

Arresting God in Kathmandu, by Samrat Upadhyay, is an engaging and readable series of short stories set in Kathmandu by an author billed as the first Nepali writer writing in English (he is now living in the US). His follow-ups include the novel *Guru of Love* and *The Royal Ghosts,* a series of short stories set against the backdrop of the Maoist uprising.

Mountains Painted With Turmeric, by Lil Bahadur Chettri, is a classic 1958 short novel, translated into English by Michael Hutt. The novel realistically portrays the struggles of a farming family trapped in a cycle of poverty and social conservatism in eastern Nepal.

Several novels have tried to make sense of the political chaos in Nepal's recent history. *Palpasa Café,* by Narayan Wagle, tells the story of an artist, an expat Nepali and a guerrilla, set against the backdrop of the war, revolution and political violence that has dominated life in rural Nepal for the past 10 years. The author is the editor of the *Kantipur* newspaper.

The Tutor of History, by Manjushree Thapa, is a portrait of a rural Nepali village in western Nepal during the run-up to elections. It's worth a read for its insights into modern Nepal. Thapa is also the author of *Tilled Earth,* a collection of short stories.

Literature

Nepal's literary history is brief, dating back to just the 19th century. The written language was little used before then, although religious verse, folklore, songs and translations of Sanskrit and Urdu dating back to the 13th century have been found.

One of the first authors to establish Nepali as a literary language was Bhanubhakta Acharya (1814–68), who broke away from the influence of Indian literature and recorded the Ramayana in Nepali; this was not simply a translation but a Nepali-ised version of the Hindu epic. Motiram Bhatta (1866–96) also played a major role in 19th-century literature, as did Lakshmi Prasad Devkota (1909–59) in the 20th century.

In a country where literacy levels are extremely low, Nepal's literary community has always struggled. However, today a vibrant and enthusiastic literary community exists, meeting in teashops and bookstalls in Kathmandu and other urban centres. Kathmandu Literary Jatra (www.litjatra.com) had its inaugural event in Patan in 2011, with readings and talks by regional and international authors, including Narayan Wagle and William Dalrymple. The plan is for it to continue as Nepal's premier annual literary gathering each September.

The Kathmandu International Mountain Film Festival (www.kimff.org) screens over 60 Nepali and international films every December. Film South Asia (www.filmsouthasia.org) is a biennial (odd years) festival of South Asian documentaries.

Environment & Wildlife

Nepal is both blessed and burdened by its incredible environment. Its economy, history, resources and culture are all intrinsically tied to the string of magnificent mountains that represent a continental collision zone. This often-daunting landscape has played a role in setting back development because of the logistical problems of bringing roads, electricity, health care and education to remote communities in mountainous areas. However, as the human population continues to rise, and technology aids development of once-remote ecosystems, the Himalaya and plains are faced with enormous environmental threats.

For ways in which you can minimise your environmental impact while travelling in Nepal see the Responsible Travel chapter (p352).

> Nepalis divide the year into six, not four, seasons: Basanta (spring), Grisma (pre-monsoon heat), Barkha (monsoon), Sharad (postmonsoon), Hemanta (autumn) and Sheet (winter).

The Lay of the Land

Nepal is a small, landlocked strip of land, 800km long and 200km wide. However, it fits a lot of terrain into just 147,181 sq km. Heading north from the Indian border, the landscape rises from just 70m above sea level to 8848m at the tip of Mt Everest. This dramatic landscape provides an outstanding variety of habitats for an incredible array of plants and animals.

Colliding Continents

> The Kali Gandaki Valley between the Annapurna and Dhaulagiri massifs is considered the world's deepest gorge, with a vertical gain of 7km.

Imagine the space currently occupied by Nepal as an open expanse of water, and the Tibetan plateau as the coast. This was the situation until 60 million years ago when the Indo-Australian plate collided with the Eurasian continent, bucking the earth's crust up into mighty ridges and forming the mountains we now call the Himalaya.

The upheaval of mountains caused the temporary obstruction of rivers that once flowed unimpeded from Eurasia to the sea. Simultaneously, new rivers arose on the southern slopes of these young mountains as moist winds from the tropical seas to the south rose and precipitated. For the next 60 million years, the mountains moved up, and rivers and glaciers cut downwards, creating the peaks and valleys seen across Nepal today.

The modern landscape of Nepal – a grid of four major mountain systems, incised by the north–south gorges of rivers – is not the final story. The Indo-Australian plate is still sliding under the Eurasian Himalaya at a rate of 27mm per year and pushing the Himalaya even higher. As fast as the mountains rise, they are being eroded by glaciers, rivers and landslides, and chipped away by earthquakes and the effects of cold and heat.

Nepal is still an active seismic zone. A huge earthquake caused devastation around the country in 1934 and a similar-sized quake today would undoubtedly cause massive damage to the densely packed and poorly constructed buildings that dominate the Kathmandu Valley.

Valley Low & Mountain High

Nepal's concertina topography consists of several physiographic regions, or natural zones: the southern plains, the four mountain ranges, and the valleys and hills in between. Most people live in the fertile lowlands or on the sunny southern slopes of mountains. Above 4000m the only residents are yak herders, who retreat into the valleys with the onset of winter.

The Terai & Chure Hills

The only truly flat land in Nepal is the Terai (or Tarai), a patchwork of paddy fields, sal forests, tiny thatched villages and sprawling industrial cities. The vast expanse of the Gangetic plain extends for 40km into Nepal before the land rises to create the Chure Hills. With an average height of 1000m, this minor ridge runs the length of the country, separating the Terai from a second low-lying area called the inner Terai, or the Dun.

Mahabharat Range

North of the inner Terai, the land rises again to form the Mahabharat Range, or the 'Middle Hills'. These vary between 1500m and 2700m in height and form the heartland of the inhabited highlands of Nepal. Locals cultivate rice, barley, millet, wheat, maize and other crops on spectacular terraced fields set among patches of subtropical and temperate forest. These hills are cut by three major river systems: the Karnali, the Narayani and the Sapt Kosi.

Pahar Zone

Between the Mahabharat Range and the Himalaya lies a broad, extensively cultivated belt called the Pahar zone. This includes the fertile valleys of Kathmandu, Banepa and Pokhara, which were once the beds of lakes, formed by trapped rivers. After the Terai this is the most inhabited part of Nepal, and the expanding human population is putting a massive

The Terai makes up only 17% of Nepal's area but holds 50% of its population and 70% of its agricultural land.

Saligrams (fossilised ammonites) are found throughout the Himalaya and are regarded as symbols of Vishnu – they also provide clear proof that the Himalaya used to lie beneath the ancient Tethys Sea.

ENVIRONMENT & WILDLIFE THE LAY OF THE LAND

MT EVEREST

Everest has gone by a number of different names over the years. The Survey of India christened the mountain 'Peak XV', but it was renamed Everest after Sir George Everest (pronounced *Eve*-rest), the surveyor general of India in 1865. It was later discovered that the mountain already had a name – Sherpas call the peak Chomolungma, after the female guardian deity of the mountain, who rides a red tiger and is one of the five sisters of long life. There was no Nepali name for the mountain until 1956 when the historian Babu Ram Acharya invented the name Sagarmatha, meaning 'head of the sky'.

Using triangulation from the plains of India, the Survey of India established the elevation of the summit of Everest at 8839m. In 1954 this was revised to 8848m using data from 12 different survey stations around the mountain. In 1999, a team sponsored by National Geographic used GPS data to produce a new elevation of 8850m, but in 2002 a Chinese team made measurements from the summit using ice radar and GPS systems and produced a height of 8844.43m.

So is Everest shrinking? No; the Chinese calculated the height of the bedrock of the mountain, without the accumulated snow and ice. In fact, Everest is still growing at a rate of 6mm a year as plate tectonics drives the Indian subcontinent underneath Eurasia. In 2011 the Chinese agreed with the Nepalis that the official height is 8848m.

strain on natural resources. Only a few areas of forest have escaped the ravages of firewood collectors.

The stunningly located Pokhara area, right at the foot of the Annapurna massif, is unique because there is no major barrier to the south to block the path of spring and monsoon rain clouds. As a result Pokhara receives an exceptionally high level of rainfall, limiting cultivation to below 2000m.

The Himalaya

The Sanskrit word Himalaya means abode *(alaya)* of the snows *(himal)*. There is no such thing as the Himalayas. To pronounce it correctly, as they do in the corridors of the Royal Geographical Society, emphasise the second syllable – him-*aaar*-liya, old chap...

One-third of the total length of the Himalaya lies inside Nepal's borders, and the country claims 10 of the world's 14 tallest mountains. The Himalayan range is broken into groups of massifs divided by glaciers and rivers draining down from the Tibetan plateau.

Because of the southerly latitude (similar to that of Florida), along with the reliable rainfall, the mountains are cloaked in vegetation to a height of 3500m to 4000m. Humans mainly inhabit the areas below 2700m. The range is crossed by passes that have been used for centuries by Himalayan traders and migrating peoples, and, most recently, Tibetan refugees.

The Trans-Himalaya

North of the first ridge of the Himalaya is a high-altitude desert, similar to the Tibetan plateau. This area encompasses the arid valleys of Mustang, Manang and Dolpo, as well as the minor peaks of the Tibetan marginals (the fourth range of mountains that sweep from central to northwestern Nepal). The moisture-laden clouds of the monsoon drop all their rain on the south side of the mountains, leaving the Trans-Himalaya in permanent rain shadow. Surreal crags, spires and badlands eroded by the scouring action of the wind are characteristic of this stark landscape.

Soul of the Rhino, by Hemanta R Mishra, is an intriguing peek into the world of the one-horned Indian rhinoceros and the humans who share its habitat.

Wildlife

Nepal is a region of exceptional biodiversity, with a rare concentration of varied landscapes and climatic conditions. The following is a guide to the species that travellers are likely to see – or would like to see. If you're a nature buff, it's worth carrying a spotters' guide; see the sidebars in this chapter for some suggestions.

Mammals & Birds

The diverse environments of the Himalaya and the Middle Hills provide a home for a remarkable array of birds, reptiles, amphibians and mammals. However, poaching and hunting threaten many mammal and bird species. Your best chances for spotting wildlife are in national parks and conservation areas, or high in the mountains far away from human habitation.

DINNER AT THE ROTTING CARCASS

Three of Nepal's nine species of vultures are critically endangered and thousands more birds die every year after scavenging dead cows that have been treated with the anti-inflammatory drug diclofenac. A new scheme to feed vultures with uncontaminated meat has yielded remarkable results. Nicknamed the 'vulture restaurant', the project has doubled the vulture population of Nawalparasi district in the western Terai in just two years. Plans are now afoot to open vulture bistros across the country to save these magnificent birds from extinction.

MONKEY MAYHEM

Because of Hanuman, the monkey god from the Ramayana, monkeys are considered holy and are well protected, if not pampered, in Nepal. You will often see troops of muscular red-rumped rhesus macaques harassing tourists and pilgrims for food scraps at Kathmandu's monuments and temples. These monkeys can be openly aggressive and they carry rabies, so appreciate them from a distance (and if that doesn't work, carry a stick).

You may also spot the slender common langur, with its short grey fur and black face, in forested areas up to 3700m. This species is more gentle than the thuggish macaque but again, keep your bananas out of sight and out of reach.

Signature Species

Nepal has a number of 'signature species' that every visitor wants to see. Unfortunately, these also tend to be the species most threatened by poaching and habitat loss. Opportunities to view the following animals are usually restricted to national parks, reserves and sparsely populated areas of western Nepal. For more on signature species see the boxed text, p225.

At the top of the jungle food chain is the royal Bengal tiger (*bagh* in Nepali), which is solitary and territorial. Chitwan, Bardia and Banke National Parks in the Terai protect sufficient habitat to sustain viable breeding populations. In addition to loss of habitat, a major threat to tigers is poaching to supply skins for Tibetan traditional clothing and body parts for Chinese medicine.

The spotted leopard (*chituwa*) is more common than the tiger and is a significant threat to livestock. Like the tiger, this nocturnal creature has been known to target humans when it is unable, through old age or illness, to hunt for its normal prey species. The endangered snow leopard is so rare and shy that it is almost a legend, but there are thought to be 350 to 500 snow leopards surviving in the high Himalaya, particularly around Dolpo. Snow leopards are so elusive that many locals believe the animals have the power to vanish at will.

Found in the grass plains (*phanta*) of the Terai region, the one-horned rhinoceros (*gaida*) is the largest of the three Asian rhino species. Rhino populations plummeted due to poaching during the Maoist insurgency but they have gradually recovered since 2005 – today there are around 500 rhinos in Chitwan and smaller populations in Bardia National Park and Sukla Phanta Wildlife Reserve.

The only wild Asian elephants (*hathi*) in Nepal are in the western part of the Terai and Chure Hills. However, herds of domesticated elephants are found at all the national parks in the Terai, where they are used for antipoaching patrols and carrying tourists on safaris.

The predator most commonly seen in the hills is the Himalayan black bear. This large omnivore frequently raids crops on the edge of mountain villages. In the rare event of an attack by a bear, the best defence is to lie face down on the ground. All of Nepal's bears are threatened by the trade in animal parts for Chinese medicine.

Perhaps the rarest animal of all is the endangered Ganges River dolphin. This mammalian predator lacks lenses in its eyes and is almost blind. It hunts its way through the silty waters of lowland rivers using sonar. There are thought to be fewer than 100 dolphins left in Nepal, with most living in the Karnali River.

Bis Hajaar Tal (literally '20,000 lakes') in Chitwan National Park and the Koshi Tappu Wildlife Reserve are both Ramsar sites (www.ramsar.org), designated as wetlands of international importance.

Nepal's national parks and conservation areas are described in detail at www.visitnepal.com/nepal_in formation/nepal parks.php.

BIRDWATCHING

Smaller Mammals

Deer are abundant in the lowland national parks, providing a vital food source for tigers and leopards. Prominent species include the sambar and the spotted deer. In forests up to 2400m, you may hear the scream-like call of the barking deer *(muntjac)*, the oldest species of deer on earth. At higher altitudes, watch for the pocked-sized musk deer, which stands just 50cm high at the shoulder. Unfortunately these animals have been severely depleted by hunting to obtain the musk gland found in the abdomen of male deer.

At high altitudes, look out for the Himalayan tahr, a shaggy mountain goat, and the blue sheep *(naur* in Tibetan, *bharal* in Nepali), which is genetically stranded somewhere between goats and sheep. The boulder fields and stunted forests of the high Himalaya also provide shelter for several small rodents. The mouse-hare *(pika)* is commonly spotted scurrying nervously between rocks on trekking trails. You must climb even higher to the Trans-Himalayan zone in western Nepal to see the Himalayan marmot, related to the American groundhog.

Birds

More than 850 bird species are known in Nepal and almost half of these can be spotted in the Kathmandu Valley. The main breeding season and the best time to spot birds is March to May. Resident bird numbers are augmented by migratory species, which arrive in the Terai in February and March en route from Siberia. The best places in Nepal for birdwatching are Koshi Tappu Wildlife Reserve (p259) and Chitwan National Park (p221). The best spots in the Kathmandu Valley are Pulchowki Mountain (p167), Nagarjun Hill (p124) and Shivapuri Nagarjun National Park (p125).

Eight species of stork have been identified along the watercourses of the Terai, and demoiselle cranes fly down the Kali Gandaki and Dudh Kosi for the winter, before returning in spring to their Tibetan nesting grounds. The endangered sarus crane can be spotted in Bardia National Park and the Lumbini Crane Sanctuary (p238).

Raptors and birds of prey of all sizes are found in Nepal. In the Kathmandu Valley and Terai, keep an eye out for the sweeping silhouettes of vultures and fork-tailed pariah kites circling ominously in the haze. In the mountains, watch for golden eagles and the huge Himalayan griffon and lammergeier.

There are six species of pheasant in Nepal, including the national bird, the *danphe,* also known as the Himalayan monal or impeyan pheasant. Females are a dull brown, while males are an iridescent rainbow of colours. In areas frequented by trekkers, these birds are often quite tame, though they will launch themselves downhill in a falling, erratic flight if disturbed.

Bird Conservation Nepal (www.birdlifenepal.org) is an excellent Nepali organisation based in Kathmandu that organises birdwatching trips and publishes books, birding checklists and a good quarterly newsletter.

CROCODILES

Nepal is home to two species of crocodile. The endangered and striking-looking gharial inhabits rivers, hunting for fish with its elongated snout lined with sharp teeth. Fossils of similar crocodiles have been found that date back 100 million years, attesting to the effectiveness of its odd-looking design. The gharial was hunted to the brink of extinction, but populations have recovered since the establishment of hatcheries.

The stocky marsh mugger prefers stagnant water and is omnivorous, feeding on anything within reach, including people. In fact, the Western word 'mugger' comes from the Hindi/Nepali name for this skulking predator.

Nepal hosts 17 species of cuckoo, which arrive in March, heralding the coming of spring. The call of the Indian cuckoo is likened to the Nepali phrase *kaphal pakyo*, meaning 'the fruit of the box myrtle is ripe'. The call of the common hawk cuckoo sounds like the words 'brain fever' – or so it was described by British *sahibs* (gentlemen) as they lay sweating with malarial fevers.

While trekking through forests, keep an eye out for members of the timalid family. The spiny babbler is Nepal's only endemic species, and the black-capped sibia, with its constant prattle and ringing song, is frequently heard in wet temperate forests. In the Pokhara region, the Indian roller is conspicuous when it takes flight, flashing iridescent turquoise on its wings. Local superstition has it that if someone about to embark on a journey sees a roller going their way it is a good omen.

Another colourful character is the hoopoe, which has a retractable crest, a long curved bill, eye-catching orange plumage, and black-and-white stripes on its wings. Nepal is also home to 30 species of flycatchers and 60 species of warblers, as well as bee-eaters, drongos, minivets, parakeets and sunbirds.

Around watercourses, look out for thrushes, such as the handsome white-capped river chat and the delightfully named plumbeous redstart. Scan the surrounding trees for the black-and-white pied kingfisher and the white-breasted kingfisher with its iridescent turquoise jacket.

Different species of crows have adapted to different altitudes. The yellow-billed blue magpie and Himalayan tree pie are commonly seen in the temperate zone. Above the tree line, red- and yellow-billed choughs gather in flocks, particularly in areas frequented by humans. In the Trans-Himalayan region you will also see the menacing black raven, which scours the valleys looking for scavenging opportunities.

> Nepal covers only 0.1% of the world's surface area but is home to nearly 10% of the world's species of birds, including 72 critically endangered species.

Plants

And the Wildest dreams of Kew are but the facts of Kathmandu.

Rudyard Kipling

There are about 6500 known species of trees, shrubs and wildflowers in Nepal, but perhaps the most famous is *Rhododendron arboreum* (*lali gurans* in Nepali), the national flower of Nepal. It might better be described as a tree, reaching heights of 18m and forming whole forests in the Himalaya region. More than 30 other species of rhododendrons are found in the foothills of the Himalaya. The rhododendron forests burst into flower in March and April, painting the landscape in swathes of white, pink and red.

The best time to see the other wildflowers of the Himalaya in bloom is during the monsoon, when the trails are muddy and the skies overcast. The views may be obscured but the ground underfoot will be a carpet of mints, scrophs, buttercups, cinquefoils, polygonums, ephedras, cotoneasters, saxifrages and primulas.

Many of the alpine species found above the tree line bear flowers in autumn, including irises, gentians, anemones and the downy-petalled edelweiss. In subtropical and lower temperate areas, look for aree pink luculia, mauve osbeckia and yellow St John's wort, as well as flowering cherry trees. Marigolds are grown in gardens and plantations across Nepal to provide the garlands offered at Hindu temples. In the Kathmandu Valley, silky oak, with its spring golden inflorescence, bottlebrush and eucalyptus are planted as ornamentals.

In the foothills of the Himalaya, as well as in the plains, look for the magnificent mushrooming canopies of banyan and pipal trees, which often

> *Birds of Nepal*, by Robert Fleming Sr, Robert Fleming Jr and Lain Singh Bangdel, is a field guide to Nepal's many hundreds of bird species. *Birds of Nepal*, by Richard Grimmett and Carol Inskipp, is a comprehensive paperback with line drawings.

NATIONAL PARKS & CONSERVATION AREAS

CA = Conservation Area, HR = Hunting Reserve, NP = National Park, WR = Wildlife Reserve

NAME	LOCATION	FEATURES	BEST TIME TO VISIT	ENTRY FEE (RS)
Annapurna CA (p274)	north of Pokhara	most popular trekking area in Nepal, high peaks, diverse landscapes, varied culture	Oct-Apr, May	2000
Banke NP (p348)	far western Terai	sal forest, tigers, one-horned rhinoceros	Oct-early Apr	500
Bardia NP (p249)	far western Terai	Geruwa River, tigers, rhinoceros, over 250 bird species	Oct-early Apr	500
Chitwan NP (p221)	central Terai	sal forest, rhinoceros, tigers, gharials, 450 bird species, World Heritage site	Oct-Feb	500
Dhorpatan HR	west-central Nepal	Nepal's only hunting reserve (access is difficult), blue sheep	Mar-Apr	500
Kanchenjunga CA	far eastern Nepal	third-highest mountain in the world, blue sheep & snow leopards	Mar-Apr, Oct-Nov	1000
Khaptad NP	far western Nepal	core area is important religious site	Mar-Apr	1000
Koshi Tappu WR (p259)	eastern Nepal	Sapt Kosi River, grasslands, 439 bird species	Mar-Apr, Oct-Nov	500
Langtang NP (p283)	northeast of Kathmandu	varied topography, culture, migratory birds	Mar-Apr	1000

form the focal point of villages. The pipal tree has a special religious significance in Nepal – the Buddha gained enlightenment under a pipal tree and Hindus revere various species of pipal as symbols of Vishnu and Hanuman.

Sal, a broad-leaved, semideciduous hardwood, dominates the low-lying forests of the Terai. Sal leaves are used as disposable plates and the heavy wood is used for construction and boat building. On the flat plains, many areas are covered by *phanta* – this grass can grow to 2.5m high and is used by villagers for thatching and by elephants for a snack on the run.

FLORA

Himalayan Flowers & Trees, by Dorothy Mierow and Tirtha Bahadur Shrestha, is the best available field guide to the plants of Nepal.

National Parks & Reserves

Nepal's first national park was established in 1973 at Chitwan National Park in the Terai. There are now 10 national parks, three wildlife reserves, three conservation areas and, somewhat incongruously, one hunting reserve, protecting 18% of the land in Nepal. Entry fees apply for all the national parks and reserves, including conserved areas on trekking routes in the mountains.

The main agency overseeing national parks and conservation areas is the **Department of National Parks and Wildlife Conservation** (www. dnpwc.gov.np). However, the last few years have seen a shift in the management to international nongovernmental organisations (NGOs) and

NAME	LOCATION	FEATURES	BEST TIME TO VISIT	ENTRY FEE (RS)
Makalu-Barun NP & CA (p290)	eastern Nepal	bordering Sagarmatha NP, protecting diverse mountain landscapes	Oct-May	1000
Manaslu CA (p290)	west-central Nepal	rugged terrain, 11 types of forest, bordering Annapurna CA	Mar-Apr, Oct-Nov	2000
Parsa WR	central Terai	bordering Chitwan NP, sal forests, wild elephants, 300 bird species	Oct-Apr	500
Rara NP	northwestern Nepal	Nepal's biggest lake, little visited, migratory birds	Mar-May, Oct-Dec	1000
Sagarmatha NP (p267)	Everest region	highest mountains on the planet, World Heritage site, monasteries, Sherpa culture	Oct-May	1000
Shey Phoksumdo NP	Dolpo, western Nepal	Trans-Himalayan ecosystem, alpine flowers, snow leopards, blue sheep	Jun-Sep	1000
Shivapuri Nagarjun NP (p125)	northeast of Kathmandu	close to Kathmandu, many bird & butterfly species, good hiking & cycling	Oct-May	250
Sukla Phanta WR (p253)	southwestern Nepal	riverine flood plain, grasslands, endangered swamp deer, wild elephants	Oct-Apr	500

not-for-profit organisations with a degree of autonomy from the government of Nepal. The **National Trust for Nature Conservation** (www.ntnc.org.np), formerly the King Mahendra Trust for Nature Conservation, runs the Annapurna Conservation Area Project and Manaslu Conservation Area. The **Mountain Institute** (www.mountain.org) runs a number of conservation projects in the Himalaya.

The government imposed the first protected areas with little partnership with locals and initially without their cooperation. Recent initiatives have concentrated on educating local people and accommodating their needs, rather than evicting them completely from the land.

The community forest model has been particularly successful in Nepal – many protected areas are surrounded by buffer zones of community-owned forests, whose owners harvest natural resources and thus have a stake in their continued existence. See the website of the **Federation of Community Forest Users** (www.fecofun.org) for more information.

Nepal's Terai national parks are under threat from an alien invader – the South American creeper *Mikania micrantha*, which is dubbed 'mile a minute' owing to its prodigous growth rate.

Environmental Challenges

The environment of Nepal is fragile and a rapidly growing population is constantly adding to environmental pressures. Much of the land between the Himalaya and the Terai has been vigorously modified to provide space for crops, animals and houses. Forests have been cleared and wildlife

BANKE NATIONAL PARK

With the creation of the 550-sq-km Banke National Park in 2010, Nepal gained its 10th national park and was able to boast one of the largest stretches of tiger habitat in Asia. Banke adjoins Suhela Wildlife Sanctuary in India and is connected to Bardia National Park through community forests and buffer zones. Along with India's Katerniaghat Wildlife Sanctuary these reserves provide an important corridor for wild elephants and rhinos, and, it is hoped, a significant boost to tiger conservation. This increase in officially protected tiger habitat was part of Nepal's 2010 pledge to double the country's tiger population by 2022 (the next Chinese zodiac Year of the Tiger).

populations depleted, and roads have eaten into valleys that were previously accessible only on foot. As a result, Shangri La is not immune from the environmental challenges that confront a shrinking planet.

Population growth is the biggest issue facing the environment in Nepal. More people need more land for agriculture and more natural resources for building, heating and cooking. The population of Nepal is increasing at a rate of 1.8% every year (as of 2011), and food security and growth is providing the economic incentive for the settlement of previously uninhabited areas.

There have also been some environmental successes in Nepal. Foreign and Nepali NGOs have provided solar panels, biogas and kerosene-powered stoves, and parabolic solar cookers for thousands of farms, trekking lodges, schools and monasteries across Nepal.

Contact the following organisations for more information on environmental issues in Nepal:

Bird Conservation Nepal (www.birdlifenepal.org)

Himalayan Nature (www.himalayannature.org)

International Centre for Integrated Mountain Development (www.icimod.org)

National Trust for Nature Conservation (www.ntnc.org.np)

Resources Himalaya (www.resourceshimalaya.org)

Wildlife Conservation Nepal (www.wcn.org.np)

World Conservation Union (www.iucnepal.org)

World Wildlife Fund Nepal (www.wwfnepal.org)

Nature Treks (www.nature-treks.com) offers organised walks with expert naturalists at Shivapuri Nagarjun National Park, Chitwan National Park, Bardia National Park and in the Langtang area.

Deforestation

Almost 80% of Nepali citizens rely on firewood for heating and cooking, particularly in the mountains, leading to massive problems with deforestation. Nepal has lost more than 70% of its forest cover in modern times and travellers are contributing to the problem by increasing the demand for firewood in mountain areas.

As well as robbing native species of their natural habitat, deforestation drives animals directly into conflict with human beings. The loss of tree cover is a major contributing factor to the landslides that scar the valleys of the Himalaya after every monsoon.

It's not all doom and gloom though – in recent years, a number of community forests have been established on the boundaries of national parks. The forests are communally owned and the sustainable harvest of timber and other natural resources provides an economic alternative to poaching and resource gathering inside the parks. See the website of the Federation of Community Forest Users (www.fecofun.org) for more information.

Wildlife Poaching

Nepal's 10-year Maoist insurgency did not only affect human beings. Soldiers were withdrawn from national-park checkpoints, leading to a massive upsurge in poaching. Nepal's rhino population fell by 30% between 2000 and 2005; elephants, tigers, leopards and other endangered species were also targeted.

The main engines driving poaching are the trade in animal parts for Chinese medicine and the trade in animal pelts to Tibet for the manufacture of traditional costumes known as *chubas*. Travellers can avoid contributing to the problem by rejecting souvenirs made from animal products – see p352 for more information.

Hydroelectricity

On the face of things, harnessing the power of Nepal's rivers to create electricity sounds like a win-win situation, but the environmental impact of building new hydroelectric plants can be devastating. Entire valleys may be flooded to create new reservoirs and most of the energy is diverted to the overpopulated Kathmandu Valley or exported to China and India.

As well as displacing local people and damaging the local environment, large hydro schemes affect the flow of water downstream, disrupting the passage of nutrient-rich silt to agricultural land in the plains. Recent floods have exacerbated concerns about the new hydroelectric plant on the Kali Gandaki and the proposed plant on the West Seti River. The latter is notably generating interest from the China Three Gorges Corporation.

Tourism

Tourism has brought health care, education, electricity and wealth to some of the most remote, isolated communities on earth, but it has also had a massive impact on the local environment.

Forests are cleared to provide timber for the construction of new lodges and fuel for cooking and heating, and trekkers contribute massively to the build-up of litter and the erosion of mountain trails.

Even the apparent benefits of tourism can have environmental implications – the wealth that tourism has brought to villages in the Himalaya has allowed many farmers to increase the size of their herds of goats, cows and yaks, leading to yet more deforestation as woodland is cleared to provide temporary pastures.

For information on alternative energy projects in Nepal, visit the websites of the Centre for Rural Technology (www.crtnepal.org), the Foundation for Sustainable Technologies (www.fost-nepal.org) and Drokpa (www.drokpa.org).

CLIMATE CHANGE IN THE HIMALAYA

Every year, the Terai faces severe flooding problems because of increased drainage from the mountains caused by the monsoon rains. In recent years, these problems have been exacerbated by deforestation, which increases run-off from mountain slopes, and by higher than average rainfall, linked to climate change.

In the mountains, the flood risk comes from a different source. Rising global temperatures are melting the glaciers that snake down from the Himalaya, swelling glacial lakes to dangerous levels.

In 1985 a natural dam collapsed in the Thame Valley, releasing the trapped waters of the Dig Tsho lake and sending devastating floods roaring along the Dudh Kosi Valley.

Scientists are now watching the Imja Tsho in the Chhukung Valley with alarm. Since 1960 the lake has grown by over 35 million cu metres – when it ruptures, experts are predicting a 'vertical tsunami' that will affect one of the most heavily populated and trekked parts of the Himalaya.

Water Supplies

Despite the natural abundance of water, water shortages are another chronic problem in Nepal, particularly in the Kathmandu Valley. Where water is available, it is often contaminated with heavy metals, industrial chemicals, bacteria and human waste. In Kathmandu, the holy Bagmati River has become one of the most polluted rivers on earth; see www.friendsofthebagmati.org.np for more on this sorry story.

In the Terai, one of the biggest problems is arsenic poisoning from contaminated drinking water. Up to 1.4 million people are thought to be at risk from this deadly toxin, which is drawn into wells and reservoirs from contaminated aquifers.

Responsible Travel

In the 50 years since Nepal opened its borders to outsiders, tourism has brought many benefits, in terms of wealth generation, employment opportunities, infrastructure, health care, education and transport, creating a level of social mobility that would have been unthinkable in the past. Many of the Nepalis who own trekking companies today worked as porters themselves 20 years ago.

Sadly, the negative effects of tourism are also clear to see. Begging is widespread and litter chokes mountain trails. New hotels and lodges are being built at an unprecedented rate, and forests are vanishing as lodge owners collect ever more firewood to keep trekkers supplied with warm showers and hot meals.

There is endless discussion among travellers about the most environmentally and culturally sensitive way to travel. What is certain is that making a positive contribution is as much about the way you behave as the money you spend. Independent travellers may spend less money, but they have a much greater impact on poverty alleviation by contributing directly to the local economy.

The following sections cover some of the issues you will need to think about, but drop into the Kathmandu office of Kathmandu Environmental Education Project (KEEP; p33) for more advice.

For tips on responsible trekking in Nepal, see p35.

> For more on the general issues of responsible travel, check out Tourism Concern (www.tourism concern.org.uk).

Economic Choices

Don't underestimate your power as an informed consumer. You can maximise the impact of the money you spend by frequenting locally owned restaurants and lodges, and by shopping at fair-trade craft stores. By choosing local trekking agencies, tour companies and lodges that have a policy of reducing their environmental and cultural impact, you are providing an example to other travellers and an incentive for other companies to adopt the same practices.

Many trekking and travel companies now donate part of their profits to local charities. Himalayan Encounters supports a school for the deaf near its Famous Farm guesthouse, Borderlands supports schools around its resort and the Butterfly Lodge in Pokhara contributes funds from its guesthouse to an orphanage.

Entry fees to historical sights contribute to their preservation, and the growth of 'ecotourism' in Nepal's national parks and conservation areas has encouraged the government to make environmental protection a priority. Hiring guides on treks also helps; as well as improving your cultural understanding, it provides employment for local people, infusing money into the hill economy.

> The Sagarmatha Pollution Control Committee was set up to combat the growing problem of pollution in the Everest region – drop into its office in Lukla or Namche Bazaar for information on current issues and campaigns.

Ethical Shopping

Many species in Nepal are being driven towards extinction by the trade in animal parts. Although most products made from endangered species are sent to China or Tibet for use in traditional medicine, travellers also contribute to the problem by buying souvenirs made from wild animals.

In particular, avoid anything made from fur, and the metal-inlaid animal skulls and tortoise shells sold as cultural souvenirs. Another item to avoid is the *shahtoosh* shawl, a form of pashmina that comes from (and results in the death of) the endangered *chiru* (Tibetan antelope). *Shahtoosh* is illegal in Nepal.

NGOS WORKING IN NEPAL

The following worthwhile organisations are just some of hundreds in Nepal that accept donations.

Development Organisations

Community Action Nepal (www.canepal.org.uk) Charity founded by mountaineer Doug Scott, working in porter villages in the Middle Hills.

Ford Foundation Nepal (www.fordnepal.org) Runs education, development and cultural projects across Nepal.

Global Action Nepal (www.gannepal.org) Sponsors various development projects in Nepal, and has run volunteer programs in the past.

Himalayan Light Foundation (www.hlf.org.np) Provides solar power and renewable energy to villages across Nepal.

Himalayan Projects (www.himalayanprojects.org) Belgian organisation that supports education and health projects in the Annapurna region.

Nepal Trust (www.nepaltrust.org) Runs integrated development programs in northwestern Nepal.

Room to Read (www.roomtoread.org) Establishes libraries and other educational facilities around Nepal.

Children's Organisations

APC Nepal (www.pommecannelle.org) Operates a home for street kids in Basantapur, Kathmandu.

Educate the Children Nepal (www.etc-nepal.org) Provides education and training opportunities for children and women in rural areas.

Just One (www.just-one.org) Provides family-focused rehabilitation support and educational opportunities to disadvantaged children in Nepal, including Kathmandu's street kids.

Read Nepal (www.readglobal.org) Provides education at village level across Nepal.

Health Organisations

Britain-Nepal Medical Trust (www.britainnepalmedicaltrust.org.uk) Joint venture providing health care in Nepal since 1968.

Fred Hollows Foundation (www.hollows.com.au) Australian organisation treating cataract blindness in Nepal.

Himalayan Cataract Project (www.cureblindness.org) Works to cure blindness caused by cataracts.

Himalayan Rescue Association (www.himalayanrescue.org) Provides emergency medicine to villagers and trekkers at high altitude.

Also be aware of the threat posed to Nepal's cultural heritage by the illegal trade in antiquities (see the boxed text, p335). The export of real antiques is banned but local artisans still use traditional techniques, so you can avoid any problems by buying modern reproductions.

Fair Trade

Fair-trade principles can make a genuine difference in Nepal, a nation where 90% of the population live in underdeveloped rural areas. A number of nonprofit organisations support local cooperatives that pay artisans a fair wage to produce traditional crafts in safe working conditions, using sustainable materials, without child labour. Many of these organisations provide work, training and education for workers from neglected economic groups, including women, the disabled and members of the 'untouchable' castes.

Established by the Nepali philanthropist Tulsi Mehar, Mahaguthi (www.mahaguthi.org) provides support, employment and rehabilitation for destitute women, funded through the sale of quality handicrafts at its fair-trade shops in Patan and Lazimpat (in Kathmandu). See p139 for information on Mahaguthi and other fair-trade stores in Patan.

The workshops run by Tibetan refugees at Jawalakhel in Patan also contribute directly to the welfare of disadvantaged people – see p139 for details.

See also the boxed text on p258 about the crafts produced by the Janakpur Women's Development Centre.

More information on fair trade can be found on the websites of the Fair Trade Group Nepal (www.fairtradegroup nepal.org) and the World Fair Trade Organisation (www.ifat.org).

Begging

Hinduism and Buddhism have a long tradition of giving alms to the needy. However, begging in Nepal today is also fuelled by the perception that foreigners will hand out money on demand. In areas frequented by tourists, some groups of beggars work specific street corners using tried-and-tested scams to separate tourists from their money. Among all this, there are also many people who are genuinely in need.

At many religious sites you will see long lines of beggars, and pilgrims customarily give a coin to everyone in the line (there are special money-changers nearby who will change notes for loose change). Sadhus (holy men) are also dependent on alms, though there are plenty of con artists among their ranks.

In tourist areas, you can expect to be hit with requests for 'one pen, one bonbon, one rupee' by children and even sometimes by adults. Don't encourage this behaviour. Most Nepalis find it offensive and demeaning (as do most visitors), and it encourages a whole range of unhealthy attitudes.

If you want to make a difference, you'd do best to work through an NGO that is trying to improve the situation. See p85 for one perspective on how to help street children.

Haggling is a way of life in Nepal (see p365), but getting the balance right is tricky. Wrangling over the last Rs 10 may lead to the vendor making a loss to save face, while paying over the odds will drive up local inflation (especially for the next traveller).

Ways to Help

You only need to look at the standards of dentistry in Nepal to realise that handing out sweets to children is neither appropriate nor responsible. If you want to give something to local people, make the donation to an adult, preferably someone in authority, such as a teacher or a lama (Tibetan Buddhist monk or priest) at a local monastery. Appropriate gifts include toothbrushes and toothpaste, pens and paper, biodegradable soap, and school books, preferably with lessons in Nepali or other local languages.

Donations to local or international NGOs working in the area are always gratefully accepted. Sir Edmund Hillary's **Himalayan Trust** (☎01-4412168; www.himalayan-trust.org; Dilli Bazaar, Kathmandu) supports education, health care, cultural projects and afforestation across the Himalaya, and similar work is carried out by the **Sir Edmund Hillary Foundation** (www.thesiredmundhillaryfoundation.ca) in Canada and the **American Himalayan Foundation** (www.himalayan-foundation.org) in the USA. The American Himalayan Foundation also runs various social and cultural projects to benefit Sherpas and Tibetan refugees.

If you have any clothes or medicines left at the end of your trip, don't haul them home. Instead, donate them to the porter's clothing bank at KEEP (p33).

Cultural Considerations

Travellers may find the traditional lifestyle of people in Nepal to be picturesque, but in many places it is a meagre, subsistence-level existence that could be improved in numerous ways. The challenge faced by many charitable organisations working in Nepal is how to bring a

NEPALI CUSTOMS & ETIQUETTE

» When visiting monasteries or temples, avoid smoking and remove your shoes and hat before you enter.

» Always walk clockwise around Buddhist stupas (bell-shaped religious structures), chörtens (Tibetan-style stupas) and mani (stone carved with a Tibetan Buddhist chant) walls, even if this involves detouring off the trail.

» Some Hindu temples are closed to non-Hindus (this is normally indicated by a sign) and others will not allow you to enter with any leather items (mainly shoes and belts).

» Locals always leave a donation in a gompa or temple and you should follow their example.

» If you are introduced to a Buddhist lama it is customary to give them a *kata* (white scarf). Place it in the lama's hands, not around their neck.

» Short shorts, sleeveless tops and other revealing items of clothing are unsuitable for women or men; nudity is unacceptable anywhere. Women should carry a sarong with them if they will be bathing at local water taps.

» Public displays of affection between men and women are frowned upon, so tone down the public intimacy.

» Nepali men often walk around hand in hand, but this does not carry any sexual overtones.

» Never point at someone, or beckon them with a single finger. If you do need to beckon someone over to you, use your whole hand instead of one finger, and be careful to keep your palm facing downwards.

» Never step over someone's legs – politely ask them to move their legs so you can get past.

» Always remove your shoes before you enter a private house.

» Food becomes ritually *jhuto* (polluted) if touched by someone else's hand, plate or utensils, so only eat off your own plate and never use your own fork or spoon to serve food off a communal plate.

» When using water from a communal jug or cup, pour it straight into your mouth without touching the sides (and without pouring it all over your shirt!).

» Don't use your left hand for eating or passing food to others as this hand is used for personal ablutions. Wash your hands and mouth before dining.

» In general, when eating in a group, no one gets up until everyone has finished their food. If you have to leave early, make your apologies by saying *bistaai khaanus* (please eat slowly).

» Do not throw rubbish onto any fire used for cooking – fire is considered sacred.

modern standard of living without destroying the traditional culture of the mountains.

You can do your bit by showing respect for local traditions – this will also demonstrate to local people that the relationship between locals and foreigners is one of equals. Many of the problems experienced by travellers in Nepal have been caused by past travellers who have treated locals as second-class citizens.

Nepalis do not like to give negative answers and will always try to give some answer, even if they do not know the answer to your question. If you are given incorrect information, this may be through fear of disappointing you. Raising your voice or shouting shows extremely bad manners and will not solve your problem, whatever it might be. Always try to remain cool, calm and collected.

Hindus have strict rules about keeping food and drink ritually pure and unpolluted. For example, a high-caste Brahmin cannot eat food prepared or touched by a lower-caste individual.

The behaviour of some photographers at places such as Pashupatinath (the most holy cremation site in Nepal) is shameful – imagine the outrage if a busload of scantily clad, camera-toting tourists invaded a family funeral in the West. Do not intrude with a camera, unless it is clearly OK with the people you are photographing. Ask first, and respect the wishes of local people. Photography is prohibited at many temples and monasteries, and it is plainly inappropriate at cremations or where people are washing in public at riverbanks or cisterns. If you attend any religious ritual, get explicit permission from senior participants before you start clicking.

World Expeditions (www.worldexpeditions.com) has a useful online booklet on responsible tourism – follow the 'Responsible Travel' links.

Survival Guide

Directory A–Z

Accommodation

In Kathmandu and Pokhara there is a wide variety of accommodation, from rock-bottom fleapits to five-star international hotels. Prices are rising, especially in Kathmandu, but it's still possible to find a place with pleasant gardens and decent rooms for less than Rs 1500 (US$18.50) a night, including private bathroom and hot water.

Some of Nepal's best deals are now to be found in its stylish midrange and top-end accommodation.

Most hotels have a wide range of rooms under one roof, including larger (often top-floor) deluxe rooms that are good for families and small groups. Budget rooms are often on the darker, lower floors and have solar-heated hot-water showers,

which won't be hot in the mornings or on cloudy days. Midrange rooms have better mattresses, satellite TV and a tub. Almost all places offer wi-fi these days.

The main towns of the Terai have hotels of a reasonable standard, with rooms with fans and mosquito nets costing around Rs 400 (US$5); grimy, basic places catering to local demand start at around Rs 50 (less than US$1). Some of the cheap places have tattered mosquito nets, if any at all.

Elsewhere in the country the choice of hotels can be very limited, but you will find places to stay along most of the major trekking trails, making Nepal one of the few places in the world where you can trek for three weeks without needing a tent. On lesser-trekked trails, places may be spartan – the ac-

commodation may be dorm-style or simply an open room in which to unroll your sleeping bag – but the Annapurna and Everest treks have excellent lodges and guesthouses every couple of hours.

All midrange and top-end hotels charge a value added tax (VAT) of 13% and a service charge of 10%. Most midrange and top-end places quote their prices in US dollars (though you pay in rupees). Budget places quote prices in rupees and sometimes include or quietly forget about tax.

Most hotels have different rates for single and double occupancy, but the 'single room' may be much smaller than the double. The best deal for a solo traveller is to get a double room for a single price.

Discounts

Nepal's hotel prices are highly seasonal, with peak season running from October to November and March to April, but even beyond this room rates fluctuate according to tourist demand. In this book we have generally given the hotel's advertised high-season room rates and, as a guide, also mentioned any discount we were offered during high-season

BOOK YOUR STAY ONLINE

For more accommodation reviews by Lonely Planet authors, check out http://hotels.lonelyplanet.com. You'll find independent reviews, as well as recommendations on the best places to stay. Best of all, you can book online.

research. You will find that rates drop even lower during the monsoon season (June to September).

The exact room rate you will be quoted depends on the season and current numbers of tourists. At many hotels the printed tariffs are pure fiction, published to fulfil government star-rating requirements and in the hope that you might be silly enough to pay them. Some midrange hotels offer discounts for booking online (and a free airport transfer), but you'll get at least this much on the spot, if not more.

If business is slow you can often negotiate a deluxe room for a standard-room rate or inclusive of tax. When business picks up (as is currently the case), you may just have to take what's on offer.

You can also negotiate cheaper rates for longer stays. In the cool of autumn and spring you can get a further discount on rooms that are air-conditioned simply by agreeing to turn off the air-con.

Activities

Nepal is the world's greatest trekking destination, even (and perhaps especially) if the only camping you do at home is lip-syncing to Kylie Minogue and Queen songs.

There are also plenty of great day hikes around Nepal, particularly in the Kathmandu Valley and around Bandipur, Tansen and Pokhara. We have detailed many of these in the relevant chapters.

Many adventure travel companies offer combination activity trips that include some rafting, kayaking and canyoning using a fixed riverside camp. Nepal is a great place to spend three or four days learning the basics of kayaking, rock climbing or mountaineering.

Business Hours

Reviews in this book mention business hours only if they're different from the standards listed in the following table.

	OPENING HOURS
airline offices	9am-1pm & 2-6pm Sun-Fri, 9am-1pm Sat
banks	9am-noon & 2-4pm Sun-Fri, 10am-noon Sat
bars & clubs	generally close by 11pm or midnight, even in Kathmandu
embassies	9am-1pm & 2-5pm Mon-Fri
government offices	10am-1pm & 2-5pm (to 4pm in winter) Mon-Thu, 10am-3pm Fri (also 10am-5pm Sun outside the Kathmandu Valley)
museums	generally closed Tue
restaurants	8am-10pm
shops	10am-8pm (some shops closed on Sat)

Children

Increasing numbers of people are travelling with their children in Nepal, and with a bit of planning it can be remarkably hassle-free. Check out Lonely Planet's *Travel with Children* for handy hints and advice about the pros and cons of travelling with kids.

» In the main tourist centres (Kathmandu and Pokhara), most hotels have triple rooms and quite often a suite with four beds, which are ideal for families with young children. Finding a room with a bathtub can be a problem at the bottom end of the market.

» Many Kathmandu hotels have a garden or roof garden, which can be good play areas. Check them thoroughly, however, as some are definitely not safe for young children.

» Walking the crowded, narrow and pavement-less streets of Kathmandu and other towns can be a hassle with young kids unless you can get them up off the ground – a backpack or sling is ideal. A pusher or stroller is more trouble than it's worth unless you bring one with oversized wheels, suitable for rough pavements.

» Keep mealtimes stress-free by eating breakfast at your hotel, having lunch at a place with a garden (there are plenty of these) and going to restaurants armed with colouring books, stories and other distractions.

» Disposable nappies are available in Kathmandu and Pokhara, but for a price – better to bring them with you if possible. Cloth nappies can be a headache, but remember that disposable nappies are almost indestructible, and waste disposal in Nepal is already a major problem.

» Cots are generally not available in budget or midrange hotels; similarly, nappy-changing facilities and high chairs are a rarity.

Customs Regulations

All baggage is X-rayed on arrival and departure, though it's a pretty haphazard process. In addition to the import and export of drugs, customs is concerned with the illegal export of antiques.

» You may not import Nepali rupees, and only nationals of Nepal and India may import Indian currency.

» There are no other restrictions on bringing in either cash or travellers cheques, but the amount taken out at departure should not exceed the amount brought in.

» Officially you should declare cash or travellers cheques in excess of US$2000, or the equivalent, but no one seems to bother with this.

Antiques

Customs' main concern is preventing the export of antique works of art, and with good reason: Nepal has been a particular victim of international art theft over the last 20 years.

It is very unlikely that souvenirs sold to travellers will be antique (despite the claims of the vendors), but if there is any doubt, they should be cleared and a certificate obtained from the **Department of Archaeology** (☎01-4250683; Ramshah Path, Kathmandu) in central Kathmandu's National Archives building. If you visit the department between 10am and 1pm, you should be able to pick up a certificate by 5pm the same day. These controls also apply to the export of precious and semi-precious stones.

Electricity

Electricity is 220V/50 cycles; 120V appliances from the USA will need a transformer. Sockets usually take plugs with three round pins, sometimes the small variety, sometimes the large. Some sockets take plugs with two round pins. Local electrical shops sell cheap adapters.

Blackouts ('load shedding') are a fact of life across Nepal, especially in Kathmandu; these peak in February with up to 16 hours a day of cuts. Power surges are also likely, so bring a voltage guard with spike suppressor (automatic cut-off switch) for your laptop.

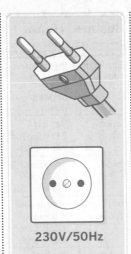

230V/50Hz

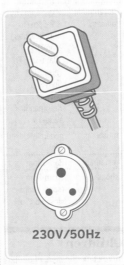

230V/50Hz

Embassies & Consulates

Travellers continuing beyond Nepal may need visas for Bangladesh, China, India, Myanmar (Burma) and Thailand.

The only visas dished out in Kathmandu for Tibet (actually there's no such thing as a 'visa for Tibet'; it's just a Chinese group visa and a travel permit for Tibet)

are for organised groups. Individuals wishing to travel directly to China (not Tibet) will need to show an air ticket to Chengdu, Beijing, Shanghai or Guangzhou to prove that they aren't going to Tibet. See p376 for advice about travelling to Tibet.

To find Nepali embassies and consulates in other countries, check out the websites of Nepal's **Ministry of Foreign Affairs** (www.mofa.gov.np) or **Department of Immigration** (www.immi.gov.np).

Foreign embassies and consulates include the following:

Australia (off Map p56; ☎01-4371678; www.nepal.embassy.gov.au; Bansbari, Kathmandu)

Bangladesh (Map p56; ☎01-4372843; bdootktm@wlink.com.np; Maharajganj, Kathmandu) Tourist visas are not issued here, but are available on arrival in Dhaka, Bangladesh.

Canada (Map p60; ☎01-4415193; www.cconepal.org.np; Lazimpat, Kathmandu)

China (Map p56; ☎01-4440286; www.chinaembassy.org.np; Hattisar, Kathmandu; ⏲9.30-11am & 2.30-4pm Mon-Fri) Visa applications are accepted on Monday, Wednesday and Friday from 9.30am to 11.30am; passports are generally returned the next working day at around 4pm, though same-day express services are also possible. The visa section is located in Hattisar; the main embassy is in Baluwatar (see Map p60).

France (Map p60; ☎01-4412332; www.ambafrance-np.org; Lazimpat, Kathmandu; ⏲9am-11.30am Mon, Tue, Thu & Fri) Plans to relocate to the nearby ambassador's residence.

Germany (Map p56; ☎01-4412786; www.kathmandu.diplo.de; Gyaneshwar, Kathmandu)

India (Map p60; ☎01-4410900; www.indianembassy.org.np; Lainchhaur)

HOW MUCH TIME DO YOU HAVE?

So much fun to have in Nepal, so little time! This table helps you match up the time you have at your disposal with a selection of some of the adventures available.

DURATION	ACTIVITY
One day	Bungee jump at the Last Resort (p178)
	Paraglide at Sarangkot (p198)
	Take a mountain flight (p76)
Two days	Go canyoning at Borderlands or the Last Resort (p178)
	Raft the Bhote Kosi (p298) or Trisuli Rivers (p297)
	Trek from Nagarkot to Sundarijal (p170)
	Combine an afternoon of rock climbing with a 70m morning abseil down into Siddha Gufa cave, near Bandipur (p189)
Three days	Mountain bike the Kathmandu–Nagarkot–Dhulikhel–Namobuddha–Lakuri Bhanjyang route (p295)
	Raft the Upper Kali Gandaki (p299)
Four days	Learn to kayak at a kayak clinic (p44)
	Do a canyoning and Bhote Kosi rafting combo (p178)
	Raft the Marsyangdi (p299)
	Travel to Chitwan from Kathmandu and take a safari excursion in the national park (p228)
	Experience the views on the Annapurna Skyline Trek (p283)
Six days	Hike the Tamang Heritage Trail near Langtang (p285)
	Complete the Ghorepani to Ghandruk Loop Trek (p283)
Seven days	Fly in to Lukla, then trek to Thame, Namche Bazaar and Tengboche on the first four days of the Everest Base Camp Trek (p273)
	Walk the Langtang Valley Trek (p283)
Eight days	Walk the Helambu Trek (p289)
Nine days	Raft the Sun Kosi (p300)
10 days	Do a Karnali River trip (p300)
15 days	Trek up to Everest Base Camp, with flights in and out of Lukla (p267)
19 days	Complete the Annapurna Circuit Trek (p274)
21 days	Combine the Everest Base Camp and Gokyo treks (p273)

Israel (Map p60; ☑01-4411811; http://kathmandu.mfa.gov.il; Lazimpat, Kathmandu; ☺9am-noon Mon-Fri)

Japan (Map p56; ☑01-4426680; www.np.emb-japan.go.jp; Pani Pokhari, Kathmandu)

Myanmar (Burma; off Map p128; ☑01-5592811, 01-5592774; Nakkhu Height, Char Ghare, Sainbu Bhaisepati,

Ward 4; ☺visa applications 10am-noon) Recently moved to an inconvenient location on the road to Bungamati, south of Patan. Three photos required.

Netherlands (Map p128; ☑01-5523444; www.netherlandsconsulate.org.np; Bakhundol, Patan; ☺10am-noon Mon & Wed-Fri, to 11am Tue)

Pakistan (Map p56; ☑01-4374024; www.pakemb.org.np; Narayan Gopal Chowk, Ring Rd, Maharajganj, Kathmandu)

Thailand (off Map p56; ☑01-4371410; www.thaiembassy.org/kathmandu; Bansbari, Kathmandu; ☺9.30am-noon & 2-4pm Mon-Fri) Most nationalities don't need a visa for stays of less than

PRACTICALITIES

» Nepal's main English-language papers are the daily *Kathmandu Post* (www.kantipuronline.com), *Himalayan Times* (www.thehimalayantimes.com) and *Republica* (www.myrepublica.com); the latter is produced in conjunction with the *International Herald Tribune*. The *Nepali Times* (www.nepalitimes.com) is weekly.

» *ECS* (www.ecs.com.np; Rs 100) is a glossy, expat-orientated monthly magazine with interesting articles on travel and culture, plus apartment listings. *Himal* magazine (www.himalmag.com) is also good.

» There aren't any noticeable discounts for holders of student or senior cards. Those under 30 can sometimes get discounts on flights to India without a student card.

» Most hotel rooms offer satellite TV, which generally includes Star TV, BBC World and CNN.

» Nepal has adopted the metric system of weights, alongside traditional measures used mainly in rural areas.

» In the Kathmandu Valley you can tune in to the BBC World Service on FM radio at 103 MHz.

30 days. Three photos are required, there's a 48-hour turnaround and visas cost US$25 (paid into the Bank of Kathmandu).

UK (Map p60; ☑01-4410583; www.ukinnepal.fco.gov.uk; Lainchhaur, Kathmandu; ⊙8.15am-12.30pm & 1.30-5pm Mon-Thu, 8.15am-1.15pm Fri)

USA (Map p56; ☑01-4007200, after-hr emergency 01-4007266; http://nepal.usembassy.gov; Maharajganj, Kathmandu; ⊙US citizen services 1.30-4pm Mon-Fri)

Food

You can eat like a king in Kathmandu and Pokhara, where restaurants offer a world map of cuisines, with dishes from Tibet, China, India, Japan, Thailand, Mexico, Italy, France and the Middle East. Take advantage of these offerings – once you start trekking it's rice and vegetables, all day, every day...

Interestingly, the Nepali word for eating is *khanu*, which is also used for the verbs 'to drink' and 'to smoke'.

Staples & Specialities

The staple meal of Nepal is *daal bhaat tarkari* – literally lentil soup, rice and curried vegetables. If you are lucky it will be spiced up with *achar* (pickles) and maybe some *chapati* (unleavened Indian bread), *dahi* (curd or yoghurt) or *papad* (pappadam – crispy fried lentil-flour pancake). To eat daal bhaat the local way, pour the soupy daal onto the rice, mix it into balls with your fingers, add a pinch of pickle and vegetables and shovel it into your mouth with your right hand. If you order daal bhaat, someone will come around offering free extra helpings of rice, daal or *tarkari*. Only very occasionally does it come with *masu* (meat).

Most Hindu Nepalis are vegetarians, some out of choice and some out of necessity. However, the Newars of the Kathmandu Valley are great meat eaters – buff (water buffalo) is the meat of choice, but goat is also common. Cows are sacred to Hindus and are never eaten. Some Kathmandu restaurants import real beef from India and you can also get yak steaks at some trekking lodges.

Spices feature heavily in Newari food, especially chilli, and Newari dishes are usually served with *chiura* (dry, beaten rice).

Many Newari dishes are only eaten at celebrations or family events, but several upmarket restaurants in Kathmandu now offer good Newari cuisine. Nepal is also one of the best places to try Tibetan cuisine, though most dishes are simple variations on momos (dumplings) or *thuk* noodle stews (*thukpa* are long noodles, whereas *thenthuk* is more like torn pasta).

WE DARE YOU!

In Newari eateries you can find dishes made from just about every imaginable part of an animal. Dishes for the brave include *jan-la* (raw steak with the skin attached), *bul-la* (dregs of rice wine with diced spleen and pieces of bone), *ti-syah* (fried spinal bone marrow) and *swan-puka* (lung filled through the windpipe with spicy batter and then boiled, sliced and fried) topped off with some *cho-hi* (steamed blood pudding). Still hungry?

One cheap and cheerful dish you'll find everywhere is chow mein (thin noodles fried with vegetables or meat).

Most Nepalis round off a meal with a *digestif* of *pan* (betel nut and leaf mixture). Those little spots of red on the pavement that look like little pools of blood are (generally) *pan*.

Food Nepal (www.food-nepal.com) offers an excellent introduction to Nepali food and ingredients, with recipes from mango *lassi* to chicken chilli. *The Nepal Cookbook,* by the Association of Nepalis in the Americas, is a good collection of home recipes, or try *Taste of Nepal,* by Jyoti Pathak.

Desserts

Like their Indian neighbours, Nepalis enjoy a huge range of sticky sweets, mostly based on milk curd, *jaggery* (palm sugar) and nuts. Top treats include *barfi* (milk fudge), *rasbari* (milk balls), *lal mohan* (deep-fried milky dough balls), *kheer* (rice pudding) and *julebi* (orange-coloured, syrupy, fried dough swirls).

Anyone who visits Bhaktapur should try the *juju dhau* (king of curds), wonderfully creamy thick yoghurt. *Sikarni* is a popular traditional dessert of whipped yoghurt with cinnamon, nuts and dried fruit. Because of the vagaries of refrigeration, avoid ice cream except in upmarket tourist restaurants.

Where to Eat & Drink

In 1955 Kathmandu had only one restaurant. These days, every other building in Kathmandu is a restaurant, serving food from across the globe. However, travel outside Kathmandu and Pokhara and you'll find that menus quickly shrink to chow mein, fried rice, fried potatoes and daal bhaat.

At local restaurants, known as bhojanalayas, the custom is to eat with your right hand. Also look out for the vegetarian restaurants known as misthan bhandar, which serve Indian sweets and *dosas* (fried lentil-flour pancakes).

Nepali towns have a range of snack foods, from muffins in bakeries to grilled corn cobs on the street. A couple of *samsa* (samosas – potato curry, fried in a lentil-dough parcel) or *papad* make a great snack. Newari beer snacks are legendary – try a plate of *sekuwa* (spiced, barbecued meat) or 'masala peanuts' (with chilli and spices) when you have a beer.

Drinks
NONALCOHOLIC

The golden rule in Nepal is *don't drink the water* (see p387). Cheap bottled water is available everywhere but every bottle contributes to Nepal's mountain of waste plastic. You can purify your own water if you carry a water bottle and iodine drops or tablets.

Tea is almost always safe. Tourist restaurants often serve the world's weakest tea – typically an ineffectual Mechi tea bag dunked into a glass of sweet, hot milk. For proper Nepali *chiya* (sometimes called masala tea), the leaves are boiled with milk, sugar and spices. If you want Western-style tea, ask for 'milk separate'. Kathmandu and Pokhara now have dozens of places to get proper espresso coffee.

In Tibetan-influenced areas the drink of choice is black tea churned with salt and butter – providing useful metabolites for dealing with high altitude and cold weather. It's an acquired taste – locals often pour it over their *tsampa* (roasted barley flour).

In Indian-influenced areas, look out for *lassi* – a refreshing drink of curd (yoghurt) mixed with sugar and what may be untreated water (proceed with caution).

ALCOHOLIC

Nepali beer is pretty good, especially after a hard day's trek. Tuborg (Danish), Carlsberg (Danish) and San Miguel (Spanish) are brewed under licence in Nepal; local brands include Gorkha, Everest and Kathmandu Beer. Nepal Distilleries produces a variety of bottled spirits that claim to be rum, whisky, brandy and gin. Most are pretty grim, but Khukri Rum goes down well with mixers.

Officially, alcohol is not sold by retailers on the first two days (full-moon days) and the last two Saturdays of the Nepali month, but this rarely affects tourist restaurants.

Gay & Lesbian Travellers

Nepal is the only country in South Asia that does not criminalise same-sex relations. A landmark Supreme Court hearing in December 2007 ordered the government to end discrimination against sexual minorities and to ensure equal rights. That said, there's not a big open gay scene in Nepal and gay Nepalis are vulnerable to police harassment and blackmail. Gay couples holding hands in public will experience no difficulties, as this is socially acceptable, but public displays of intimacy by anyone are frowned upon.

Aashanepal Travel & Tours (☎01-4266189; www.aashanepal.com.np) A gay-friendly tour company in Kathmandu.

THE LOCAL FIREWATER

On trekking routes, look out for the traditional home-brews of the hills. One drink you'll find everywhere is *chang*, a mildly alcoholic Tibetan concoction made from fermented barley or millet and water. It can be drunk hot or cold – local connoisseurs take it hot with a raw egg in it...

In eastern Nepal, look out for *tongba*, a Himalayan brew made by pouring boiling water into a wooden (or metal) pot full of fermented millet. The liquid is slurped through a bamboo straw and more hot water is added periodically to seep extra alcohol from the mash.

Harder spirits include *arak*, fermented from potatoes or grain, and *raksi*, a distilled rice wine that runs the gamut from smooth-sipping schnapps to headache-inducing paint stripper.

Blue Diamond Society
(☎01-4443350; www.bds.org.np) The first gay organisation in Kathmandu. It provides education, support and advice to Nepal's gay and transgender community, and runs the country's only AIDS/HIV prevention program. Its founder became the country's first openly gay member of parliament.

Insurance

A travel-insurance policy to cover theft, loss and medical problems is an excellent idea for travel in Nepal. There is a wide variety of policies available, so check the small print carefully. Some policies exclude 'dangerous activities', which may include riding a motorbike and trekking (and definitely bungee jumping and rafting).

Choose a policy that covers medical and emergency repatriation, including helicopter evacuation for trekkers and general medical evacuation to Bangkok or Delhi, which alone can cost a cool US$40,000.

You may prefer a policy that pays doctors or hospitals directly rather than you having to pay on the spot and claim later. In Nepal, most medical treatment must be paid for at the point

of delivery. If your insurance company does not provide upfront payment, be sure to obtain a receipt so you can reclaim later. Some policies ask you to call back (reverse charges) to a centre in your home country where an immediate assessment of your problem is made.

Bear in mind that many insurance policies do not cover 'acts of terrorism', civil war or regions that your country's government advises against travel to, so double-check how your insurance company defines these notions and Nepal's political situation.

Worldwide traveller insurance is available at www.lonelyplanet.com/travel_services. You can buy, extend and claim online anytime – even if you are already on the road.

Internet Access

Email and internet services are offered in dozens of places in Kathmandu and Pokhara and are generally cheap at around Rs 50 per hour. Internet access is also available in most other towns – you can even send email from Namche Bazaar on the Everest trek – but connections are usually slow and relatively expensive, as

they may involve a dial-up call to Kathmandu.

Most hotels, restaurants and cafes in Kathmandu and Pokhara offer wi-fi if you have your own laptop. It is often free but midrange and top-end hotels can charge anywhere from Rs 200 to 700 for 24-hour access.

Language Courses

Nepali is not a difficult language to learn, and you will see notices around Kathmandu advertising language courses. Most schools offer courses or individual tuition. Expect to pay about US$50 for a two-week course or around US$3 to US$5 per hour for private tuition.

There are often flyers around Bodhnath advertising Tibetan-language tuition and apartments to rent, as well as opportunities to volunteer-teach Tibetan refugees.

Language centres in Kathmandu and Pokhara include the following:

Centre for Buddhist Studies (☎01-4483575; www.cbs.edu.np; Kathmandu) Based at the Rangjung Yeshe Institute, this affiliate of Kathmandu University offers a two-month Tibetan-language course (US$2250) from mid-June, with accommodation provided by local Tibetan families. It also offers longer, university-accredited courses.

Cosmic Brontosaurus Language School (Map p201; ☎9846069834; prem knwr@gmail.com; Pokhara; per hr Rs 250-450; ☺noon-4pm) Offering individual or group lessons from beginner to advanced, the rather primitive classroom in a wooden shack along the lake is surrounded by banana plants and is the perfect spot to learn Nepali. Prem, who runs the school, is a lovely guy, and has seven years' experience working with the UN as a translator.

Intercultural Training & Research Centre (ITC; ☎01-4412793; www.itcnepal. com; Kathmandu) This well-respected language centre works with many NGOs, including the UK's Voluntary Service Overseas (VSO). It offers crash courses (three hours), 60-hour beginner courses and six-week intermediate courses. Tuition is one-on-one and costs around Rs 350 to 400 per hour. Contact Parbati Shrestha.

Kathmandu Environmental Education Project (KEEP; Map p80; ☎01-4410952; www.keepnepal.org; Thamel, Kathmandu; ☺10am-5pm Sun-Fri) Offers Nepali-language classes between April and June.

Kathmandu Institute of Nepali Language (Map p80; ☎01-4437454; www.ktmnepali language.com; Bhagwan Bahal, Kathmandu) Offers a week's course (12 hours) for US$60.

Legal Matters

Hashish has been illegal since 1973, but it's still readily available in Nepal. Thamel is full of shifty, whispering dealers. In practice, Nepali police aren't very interested in people with a small amount of marijuana on them (they're more focused on smuggling), but the technical penalty for drug possession is around five years in prison, so potential smokers should keep the less-than-salubrious condition of Nepali jails firmly in mind. Don't try taking any out of the country, either – travellers have been arrested at the airport on departure.

If you get caught smuggling something serious – drugs or gold – chances are you'll end up in jail, without trial, and will remain there until someone pays for you to get out. Jail conditions in Nepal are reportedly horrific. Bribery is sometimes used to avoid jail. This is illegal and can land the perpetrator in deeper strife. Deniability that a bribe was offered – where the accused believed it was a legitimate fee – is the only defence.

A handful of foreigners currently languish in jails in Kathmandu, mostly for drug offences. If you want to pay a humanitarian visit you can contact your embassy for a list of names and their locations. Take along items of practical use, such as reading matter, blankets and fresh fruit.

Killing a cow is illegal in Nepal and carries a punishment of two years in prison.

Money

The Nepali rupee (Rs) is divided into 100 paisa (p). There are coins for denominations of one, two, five and 10 rupees, and banknotes in denominations of one, two, five, 10, 20, 25, 50, 100, 500 and 1000 rupees. Since the abolition of the monarchy in 2008, images of Mt Everest have replaced the king on all banknotes.

Away from major centres, changing a Rs 1000 note can be difficult, so it is always a good idea to keep a stash of small-denomination notes. Even in Kathmandu, many small businesses – especially rickshaw and taxi drivers – simply don't have sufficient spare money to allow them the luxury of carrying a wad of change.

ATMs

Standard Chartered Bank has 24-hour ATMs in Kathmandu and Pokhara. Other banks, such as Himalaya Bank and Nabil Bank, also have ATMs but some only accept local cards.

Frequent power outages can limit the machines' working hours, so use one when you see it's working. Using an ATM attached to a bank during business hours will minimise hassle in the rare event that the machine eats your card.

It's not a bad idea to inform your bank that you'll be using your card abroad, otherwise they might suspect fraud and freeze your card.

Changing Money

Official exchange rates are set by the government's Nepal Rastra Bank and listed in the daily newspapers. Rates at the private banks vary, but are generally not far from the official rate.

There are exchange counters at the international terminal at Kathmandu's Tribhuvan Airport and banks and/or moneychangers at the various border crossings. Pokhara and the major border towns also have official money-changing facilities, but changing travellers cheques can be time consuming elsewhere in the country, even in some quite large towns. If you are trekking, take enough cash in small-denomination rupees to last the whole trek.

BARGAINING

Haggling is regarded as an integral part of most commercial transactions in Nepal, especially when dealing with souvenir shops, hotels and guides. Ideally, it should be an enjoyable social exchange, rather than a conflict of egos. A good deal is reached when both parties are happy, so keep things light; Nepalis do not appreciate aggressive behaviour. Remember that Rs 10 might make quite a difference to the seller, but in real terms it amounts to very little (less than US$0.15).

TAXING TAXES

Most midrange and top-end hotels and restaurants add a 13% value added tax (VAT), as well as a 10% service charge. The service charge is craftily calculated from the total *after* VAT, resulting in a whopping 24.3% surcharge to your bill. You'll have to mentally figure in the taxes to avoid a nasty shock when your bill comes, though on the plus side it does do away with the dilemma of how much to tip! Some budget places charge only VAT or service, especially restaurants. Where hotels quote their rates including tax we mention this in the review.

The best private banks are Himalaya Bank, Nepal Bank and Standard Chartered Bank. Some hotels and resorts are licensed to change money but their rates are lower. Travellers cheques from the main companies are easily exchanged in banks in Kathmandu and Pokhara for a 2% surcharge.

When you change money officially, you are required to show your passport, and you are issued with a foreign exchange encashment receipt showing your identity and the amount of currency you have changed. Hang onto the receipts as you need them to change excess rupees back into foreign currency at banks. You can change rupees back into foreign currency at most moneychangers without a receipt.

If you leave Nepal via Kathmandu's Tribhuvan Airport, the downstairs exchange counter will change rupees back to foreign currency to the amount covered by your exchange receipts. Official re-exchange is not possible at any bank branches at the border crossings.

Many upmarket hotels and businesses are obliged by the government to demand payment in hard currency (euros or US dollars); they will also accept rupees, but only if you can show a foreign exchange encashment receipt that covers the amount you owe

them. In practice this regulation seems to be widely disregarded. Airlines are also required to charge tourists in hard currency, either in cash US dollars, travellers cheques or credit cards, and this rule is generally followed.

In addition to the banks, there are licensed moneychangers in Kathmandu, Pokhara, Birganj, Kakarbhitta and Sunauli/Bhairawa. The rates are often marginally lower than the banks, but there are no commissions, they have much longer opening hours (typically from 9am to 7pm daily) and they are also much quicker, the whole process often taking no more than a few minutes.

Most licensed moneychangers will provide an exchange receipt; if they don't you may be able to negotiate better rates than those posted on their boards.

Credit Cards

Major credit cards are widely accepted at midrange and better hotels, restaurants and fancy shops in the Kathmandu Valley and Pokhara only. Most places levy a 3% to 4% surcharge to counter the credit card company's fees to the vendor.

Branches of Standard Chartered Bank and some other banks such as Nabil Bank and Himalaya Bank give cash advances against Visa and MasterCard in Nepali rupees only (no com-

mission is charged), and will also sell you foreign-currency travellers cheques against the cards with a 2% commission.

International Transfers

In general, it's easiest to send money through companies such as **Western Union** (www.westernunion.com) or **Moneygram** (www.visitnepal.com/moneygram), which can arrange transfers within minutes. To pick up funds at a Western Union branch you'll need your passport and 10-digit transfer code.

Note that money can often only be received in Nepali rupees, rather than US dollars.

Tax & Tipping

It is possible for tourists to get the value added tax (VAT) refunded on consumer goods but it's an ordeal and is probably only relevant if you've made a major purchase. For more information, see the website of Tribhuvan International Airport (www.tiairport.com.np/regulation/vat-refund.html).

Round up the fare for taxi drivers. Trekking guides and porters generally expect a tip of 15% to 20% for a job well done.

Photography

Bringing a video camera to Nepal poses no real problem and there are no video fees to worry about. The exception to this is in the upper Mustang and Langtang border regions, where an astonishing US$1000 fee is levied.

Film & Equipment

» Almost all flavours of memory stick, flash card etc and batteries are available in Kathmandu. Note that travellers have reported buying cards in Kathmandu that do not have as much memory as the packet claims.

» A panoramic camera can be very useful if you're trekking; it's the only way to do justice to those jaw-dropping views. Some digital cameras have a panoramic feature built in.

Photographing People

» Most Nepalis are content to have their photograph taken, but always ask permission first. Sherpa people are an exception and can be very camera-shy.

» Bear in mind that if a sadhu (holy man) poses for you, they will probably insist on being given *baksheesh* (a tip).

» For advice and general rules for photographing people and events in Nepal, see p354.

Restrictions

» It is not uncommon for temple guardians to not allow photos of their temple, and these wishes should be respected.

» Don't photograph army camps, checkpoints or bridges.

Technical Tips

» To photograph Nepal's diverse attractions you need a variety of lenses, from a wide-angle lens for compact temple compounds to a long telephoto lens for mountain shots or close-ups of wildlife.

» A polarising filter is useful to increase contrast and bring out the blue of the sky.

» Remember to allow for the intensity of mountain light when setting exposures at high altitude.

» A flash is often necessary for shots inside temples or to 'fill in' shots of sculptures and reliefs.

Post

The postal service to and from Nepal is, at best, erratic but can occasionally be amazingly efficient. Most articles do arrive at their destination...eventually.

Couriers

For a 500g package of documents, **FedEx** (www.fedex.com/np) and **DHL** (www.dhl.com/np) charge around US$40/50 to the US/UK, and slightly less to Australia. FedEx offers a 25% discount if you drop documents directly to their office. Packages other than documents cost up to 50% more for the same weight.

Parcel Post

Having stocked up on gifts and souvenirs in Nepal, many people send them home from Kathmandu. Parcel post is not cheap or quick, but the service is reliable. Sea mail is much cheaper than airmail, but it is also much slower (packages take about 3½ months) and less reliable.

As an idea, a 2kg package to the UK/US/India costs Rs 1785/2185/600 via airmail, 25% less at 'book post' rate (a special rate for books only).

The contents of a parcel must be inspected by officials *before* it is wrapped. There are packers at the Kathmandu foreign post office who will wrap it for a small fee. The maximum weight for sea mail is 20kg; for airmail it's 10kg, or 5kg for book post.

Some specialised shipping companies, such as Diki Continental Exports (p104) in Kathmandu, offer considerably cheaper rates than airmail and are not much more expensive than sea mail. Parcels still go by air, but the catch is that they have to be picked up at an international airport and you'll have to deal with customs' paperwork and fees there.

If an object is shipped out to you in Nepal, you may find that customs' charges for clearance and collection at your end add up to more than the initial cost of sending it. Often it's worth paying extra to take it with you on the plane in the first place.

Postal Rates

Airmail rates for a 20g letter/postcard in Nepal are Rs 2/1; in India and surrounding countries Rs 18/15; in Europe and the UK Rs 35/25; and in the US and Australia Rs 40/30.

DASAIN STOPPAGES

Dasain (15 days in September or October) is the most important of all Nepali celebrations. Tens of thousands of Nepalis hit the road to return home to celebrate with their families. This means that while villages are full of life if you are trekking, buses and planes are fully booked and overflowing, porters may be hard to find (or more expensive than usual) and cars are difficult to hire. Many hotels and restaurants in regional towns close down completely, and doing business in Kathmandu (outside Thamel) becomes almost impossible.

The most important days, when everything comes to a total halt, are the ninth day (when thousands of animals are sacrificed) and the 10th day (when blessings are received from elder relatives and superiors). Banks and government offices are generally closed from the eighth day of the festival to the 12th day. For more information on the festival, see p20.

Public Holidays

A remarkable number of holidays and festivals affect the working hours of Nepal's government offices and banks, which seem to close every other day and certainly for the following public holidays and some or all of the festival days mentioned in the Month by Month chapter. This list is not exhaustive and the exact festival timings (and thus their public holiday dates) change annually according to Nepal's lunar calendar.

Prithvi Narayan Shah's Birthday 10 January

Basanta Panchami (start of Spring) January/February

Maha Shivaratri (Shiva's Birthday) February/March

Bisket Jatra (Nepali New Year) 14 April

Janai Purnima July/August

Teej (Festival of Women) August/September

Indra Jatra (Indra Festival) September

Dasain September/October

Tihar (Divali) October/November

Constitution Day 9 November

Safe Travel

Kathmandu is currently enjoying a much-needed period of political stability and public optimism. The strikes, demonstrations and turmoil that defined much of the last decade have reduced greatly in number and length. Don't count your chickens yet, though. The political situation remains somewhat tense, and political agitation could return to the capital at any moment.

You can minimise the chances of bumping into trouble by heeding the following general advice:

» Register with your embassy in Kathmandu, especially if trekking (see p28).

» Be flexible with your travel arrangements in case your transport is affected by a bandh (strike) or security situation.

» Don't trek alone. Lone women should avoid travelling alone with a male guide.

» Be familiar with the symptoms of altitude sickness when trekking and observe sensible acclimatisation; see p385.

» Avoid travelling on night buses.

» Keep photocopies of your passport, visa, air ticket and travellers cheques separate from the originals.

Demonstrations & Strikes

For the last decade Nepal has been wracked by frequent demonstrations and strikes – some called by politicians, some by students, some by Maoists, and some by all three! The political situation has greatly improved but occasionally demonstrations still occur.

A normal demonstration is a julus. If things escalate there may be a chakka jam ('jam the wheels'), when all vehicles stay off the street, or a bandh, when all shops, schools and offices are closed. In the event of a strike the best thing to do is hole up in your hotel with a good book. In this case you'll likely have to dine at your hotel.

If political instability returns, it pays to heed the following points:

» Keep an eye on the local press and news websites to find out about impending strikes, demonstrations and curfews – follow websites such as www.ekantipur.com, www.thehimalayantimes.com and www.nepalitimes.com.np.

» Don't ever break curfews and don't travel during bandhs or blockades. Get very nervous if you notice that your car is the only one on the streets of Kathmandu!

» Avoid marches, demonstrations and disturbances, as they can quickly turn violent.

NEPALI CALENDARS

Nepali holidays and festivals are principally dated by the lunar calendar, falling on days relating to new or full moons. The lunar calendar is divided into bright and dark fortnights. The bright fortnight is the two weeks of the waxing moon, as it grows to become *purnima* (the full moon). The dark fortnight is the two weeks of the waning moon, as the full moon shrinks to become *aunsi* (the new moon).

The Nepali New Year starts on 14 April with the month of Baisakh. The Nepali calendar is 57 years ahead of the Gregorian calendar used in the West, thus the year 2013 in the West is 2070 in Nepal. You can convert between Nepali and Gregorian dates at www.rajan.com/calendar.

The Newars of the Kathmandu Valley, on the other hand, start their New Year from the day after Deepawali (the third day of Tihar), which falls on the night of the new moon in late October or early November. Their calendar is 880 years behind the Gregorian calendar, so 2013 in the West is 1133 to the Newars.

» The website www.nepal bandh.com warns of any upcoming strikes.

» When roads are closed the government generally runs buses with armed police from the airport to major hotels, returning to the airport from Tridevi Marg at the east end of Thamel.

Load Shedding

Electricity cuts ('load shedding') are a fact of life in Kathmandu and Pokhara, especially in winter, when water and thus hydro power levels are at their lowest.

Electricity is currently rationed across Kathmandu, shifting from district to district every eight hours or so. Most hotels post a schedule of planned electricity cuts, which can last up to 16 hours a day in both Kathmandu and Pokhara. Try to choose a hotel with a generator and make sure your room is far away from it.

Scams

Some Nepalis are impressively inventive in their range of imaginative scams. Watch out for the following:

» Deals offered by gem dealers that involve you buying stones to sell for a 'vast profit' at home. The dealers normally claim they are not able to export the stones without paying heavy taxes, so you take them and meet another dealer when you get home, who will sell them to a local contact and you both share the profit. Except they don't. And you don't.

» Children or young mothers asking for milk. You buy the milk at a designated store at an inflated price, the child then returns the milk and pockets some of the mark-up.

» Be wary of kids who seem to know the capital of any country you can think of; they are charming but a request for money will arrive at some point.

» 'Holy men' who do their best to plant a *tika* (a red

paste denoting a blessing) on your forehead, only to then demand significant payment.

» Credit card scams are not unheard of; travellers have bought souvenirs and then found thousands of dollars worth of internet porn subscriptions chalked up on their bill.

Theft

While petty theft is not on the scale that exists in many countries, reports of theft from hotel rooms in tourist areas (including along trekking routes) do occasionally reach us, and theft with violence is not unheard of. Never store valuables or money in your hotel room.

One of the most common forms of theft is when backpacks are rifled through when they're left on the roof of a bus. Try to make your pack as theft-proof as possible – small padlocks and cover bags are a good deterrent.

There's little chance of ever retrieving your gear if it is stolen, and even getting a police report for an insurance claim can be difficult. Try the tourist police, or, if there aren't any, the local police station. If you're not getting anywhere, go to **Interpol** (☑01-4412602) at the Police Headquarters in Naxal, Kathmandu.

Telephone

The phone system in Nepal works pretty well (as long as the electricity is working) and making local, STD and international calls is easy. Reverse-charge (collect) calls can only be made to the UK, USA, Canada and Japan.

Private call centres offer the cheapest and most convenient way to make a call. Look for signs advertising STD/ISD services. Many hotels offer international direct-dial facilities but always check their charges before making a call.

Private call centres charge around Rs 10 to 40 per minute to most countries. Internet phone calls are cheaper, costing around Rs 10 per minute (calls to mobile phones are often more expensive), but these are only available in Kathmandu and Pokhara.

Most internet cafes offer internet phone calls through Skype (www.skype.com) for a couple of rupees per minute on top of their normal internet rates.

Local phone calls cost around Rs 5 per minute, with long-distance domestic calls costing around Rs 10 per minute. Out in rural areas you may find yourself using someone's mobile phone at a public call centre.

Mobile Phones

Ncell (☑9809005000; www.
ncell.com.np) is the most
popular and convenient pro-
vider. To get a SIM card take
a copy of your passport and
one photo to an Ncell office.
A SIM card costs Rs 99, with
local calls around Rs 2 per
minute and incoming calls
free. International calls cost
from Rs 2 (the US) to Rs 15
(UK) per minute. It's easy to
buy a scratch card to top up
your balance, in denominations from Rs 50 to 1000.
You can normally get a SIM
card on arrival at Tribhuvan
Airport.

For 3G internet access,
you can buy a USB data
card and SIM card package
for Rs 2400, with which you
can even get internet access
on the Everest Base Camp
Trek! (The first tweet from
the summit of Everest was
sent in May 2011...) Surfing
costs Rs 0.40 to 2 per MB,
depending on the package.
Check out the website for
details.

Nepal Telecom (www.ntc.
net.np) operates the Namaste
Mobile network and has
roaming agreements with
companies such as Vodafone
and Cingular, but signing up
for a SIM card is a more labor-
ious process than for Ncell.

You will need an unlocked
GSM 900 compatible phone
to use local networks.

Unlike using a landline,
you need to dial the local
area code when making a
local call on a mobile.

Time

Nepal is five hours and 45
minutes ahead of GMT; this
curious time differential is
intended to make it very
clear that Nepal is a separate
place to India, where the time
is five hours and 30 minutes
ahead of GMT. There is no
daylight-saving time in Nepal.

When it's noon in Nepal
it's 1.15am in New York,
6.15am in London, 1.15pm
in Bangkok, 2.15pm in Ti-
bet, 4.15pm in Sydney and
10.15pm the previous day in
Los Angeles, not allowing for
daylight saving or other local
variations.

Toilets

» Outside of Kathmandu and
Pokhara, the 'squat toilet' is
the norm, except in hotels
and guesthouses geared
towards tourists.

» Next to a squat toilet
(*charpi* in Nepali) is a bucket
and/or tap, which has a two-
fold function: flushing the
toilet and cleaning the nether
regions (with the left hand
only) while still squatting
over the toilet.

» In tourist areas you'll find
Western toilets and probably
toilet paper (depending on
how classy the place is). In
general, put used toilet paper
in the separate bin; don't
flush it down the toilet.

» Most rural places don't
supply toilet paper, so always
carry an emergency stash if
you don't want to rely on the
bucket/tap procedure.

» More rustic toilets in rural
areas may consist of a few
planks precariously posi-
tioned over a pit in the ground.

Tourist Information

The **Nepal Tourism Board**
(☑01-4256909, 24hr tour-
ism hotline 01-4225709; www.
welcomenepal.com) operates
an office in Kathmandu's
Tribhuvan Airport and a more
substantial office at the Tourist
Service Centre in central Kathmandu, both of which have
simple brochures and maps.

The other tourist offices in
Pokhara, Bhairawa, Birganj,
Janakpur and Kakarbhitta
are virtually useless unless
you have a specific inquiry.

Travellers with Disabilities

Wheelchair facilities, ramps
and lifts (and even pave-
ments!) are virtually nonexistent throughout Nepal and
getting around the packed,
twisting streets of traditional
towns can be a real challenge
if you are in a wheelchair. It
is common for hotels to be
multilevel, with most rooms
on the upper floors. Many
places – even midrange es-
tablishments – do not have
lifts. Bathrooms equipped
with grips and railings are
not found anywhere, except
perhaps in some of the top-
end hotels.

There is no reason why a
visit and even a trek could
not be customised through a
reliable agent for those with
reasonable mobility. As an inspiration, consider Erik Wei-
henmayer, who became the
first blind climber to summit
Everest in 2001 (and wrote a
book called *Touch the Top of
the World*), or Thomas Whit-
taker, who summited in 1998
with an artificial leg, at the
age of 50.

Useful resources:

**Access-Able Travel
Source** (www.access-able.
com) General website.

Accessible Journeys
(☑800-846-4537; www.
disabilitytravel.com) US company that has experience in
arranging private tours for
travellers with disabilities.

**International Disabled
Traveller** (www.disabledtrave
ler.blogspot.com) Well-written
and witty blog from a
wheelchair-bound American
woman who volunteered and
even trekked in Nepal.

Navyo Nepal (☑01-
4239436; www.navyonepal.
com) In Nepal; has some
experience in running cultural
tours and treks for people
with disabilities.

Visas

All foreigners, except Indians,
must have a visa. Nepali
embassies and consulates
overseas issue visas with no
fuss. You can also get one on
the spot when you arrive in
Nepal, either at Kathmandu's

Tribhuvan Airport or at road borders: Nepalganj, Birganj/Raxaul Bazaar, Sunauli, Kakarbhitta, Mahendranagar, Dhangadhi and even the funky Kodari checkpoint on the road to Tibet.

A Nepali visa is valid for entry for three to six months from the date of issue. Children under 10 require a visa but are not charged a visa fee. Your passport must have at least six months of validity. Citizens of South Asian countries and China need visas, but these are free.

You can download a visa application form from the websites of the Nepali embassy in Washington, DC (www.nepalembassyusa.org) or London (www.nepembassy.org.uk).

To obtain a visa upon arrival by air in Nepal you must fill in an application form and provide a passport photograph. Visa application forms are available on a table in the arrivals hall, though some airlines (like Thai and Qatar) provide this form on the flight. The process can take up to an hour, depending on the numbers. To get a jump on the immigration queue, you can download the visa-on-arrival form from www.treks.com.np/visa. A single-

entry visa valid for 15/30/90 days costs US$25/40/100. At Kathmandu's Tribhuvan Airport the fee is payable in any major currency, but at land borders officials require payment in cash US dollars; bring small bills.

Multiple-entry visas are useful if you are planning a side trip to Tibet, Bhutan or India. You can change your single-entry visa to a multiple-entry visa at Kathmandu's Central Immigration Office (see p104) for US$20.

If you are just planning a lightning visit to Kathmandu then it's possible to get a nonextendable one-day transit visa at Kathmandu's airport for US$5, as long as you have an air ticket out of the country. Transit visas are nonextendable.

Don't overstay a visa. You can pay a fine of US$3 per day at the airport if you have overstayed less than 30 days (plus a US$2 per day visa extension fee), but it's far better to get it all sorted out in advance at Kathmandu's Central Immigration Office, as a delay could cause you to miss your flight.

It's a good idea to keep a number of passport photos with your passport so they are immediately handy for

trekking permits, visa applications and other official documents.

Visa Extensions

Visa extensions are available from immigration offices in Kathmandu and Pokhara only and cost a minimum US$30 (payable in rupees only) for a 15-day extension, plus US$2 per day after that. To extend a multiple-entry visa add on US$20. If you'll be in Nepal for more than 60 days you are better off getting a 90-day visa on arrival, rather than a 60-day visa plus an extension.

Every visa extension requires your passport, money, one photo and an application form. Collect all these before you join the queue. Plenty of photo shops in Kathmandu and Pokhara can make a set of eight digital passport photos for around Rs 250.

Visa extensions are available the same day, normally within two hours, though some travellers have paid an extra Rs 300 fee to get their extensions within 10 minutes. For a fee, trekking and travel agencies can assist with the visa-extension process and save you the time and tedium of queuing.

INDIAN VISAS & RE-ENTRY ENDORSEMENTS IN NEPAL

Many travellers get an Indian visa in Nepal but it's not a straightforward process. Visa applications must be made at the **India Visa Service Centre** (Map p60; ✆4001516; www.nepalsbi.com.np/indian_passport/; ⊙9am-noon Mon-Fri), at the State Bank of India to the right of the embassy, not at the embassy itself. Get to the gates before 8.45am and get a number or you won't be seen before noon. After filling in a telex form (take a black pen) and paying Rs 300, you need to return on a specified date (generally three working days later) with a visa form and one photo. Visas are then issued between 4.30pm and 5.30pm the same day. A six-month tourist visa costs Rs 3250 and a 15-day transit visa costs Rs 1700, plus a Rs 250 service fee. US citizens can get a 10-year tourist visa for Rs 11,500. Transit visas are issued the same day (no telex required), but start from the date of issue and are nonextendable.

Travellers theoretically need a re-entry endorsement to re-enter India within two months of their last visit, even with a multiple-entry visa. If you are flying to Nepal via India you should be able to get a waiver from Indian immigration on first arrival if you show your itinerary. The safest thing is to get an endorsement from an Indian embassy, though this involves another layer of bureaucracy and a fee (Rs 700 at the Indian embassy in Kathmandu). It's generally easier to arrange all this in your home country.

You can extend a tourist visa up to a total stay of 150 days within a calendar year, though as you get close to that maximum you'll have to provide an air ticket to show you're leaving the country.

You can get up-to-date visa information at the website of the **Department of Immigration** (www.immi.gov.np).

Women Travellers

Generally speaking, Nepal is a safe country for women travellers. However, women should still be cautious. Some Nepali men may have peculiar ideas about the morality of Western women, given their exposure to Western films portraying women wearing 'immodest' clothing. Dress modestly, which means wearing clothes that cover the shoulders and thighs – take your cue from the locals to gauge what's acceptable in the area. Several women have written to say that a long skirt is very useful for impromptu toilet trips, especially when trekking.

Sexual harassment is low-key but does exist. Trekking guides have been known to take advantage of their position of trust and responsibility and some lone women trekkers who hire a guide have had to put up with repeated sexual pestering. The best advice is to never trek alone with a local male guide. **Chhetri Sisters Trekking** (☑061-462066; www.3sistersadventure.com) in Pokhara is run by women and specialises in providing female staff for treks.

We've had reports of attacks on women near trance parties, notably outside Pokhara, so we suggest sticking with friends and avoiding wandering off alone.

The best chance of making contact with local women is to go trekking, as it is really only in hiking areas that Nepali women have a role that brings them into contact with foreign tourists – often the man of the house is a trekking guide or porter, or is away working elsewhere, which leaves women to run lodges and teahouses along the routes.

Transport

GETTING THERE & AWAY

Considering the enduring popularity of Nepal as a travel destination, there are surprisingly few direct international flight connections into Kathmandu. If you are coming during the prime travel and trekking months of October and November, book your long-haul and domestic flights well in advance.

Overland and air-travel connections to India are particularly good, so it's easy to combine a dream trip to both Nepal and India, with possible add-ons to Bhutan and Tibet.

Flights, tours and even treks can be booked online at lonelyplanet.com/bookings.

Entering the Country

Nepal makes things easy for foreign travellers. Visas are available on arrival at the international airport in Kathmandu and at all land border crossings that are open to foreigners, as long as you have passport photos to hand and can pay the visa fee in foreign currency (some crossings insist on payment in US dollars). Your passport must be valid for at least six months and you will need a whole free page for your visa.

Air

Airports

Nepal has one international airport, **Tribhuvan International Airport** (☎01-4472256; www.tiairport.com.np), just east of Kathmandu. Little has changed here since the 1980s and dusty signboards still warn travellers not to import more than the prescribed number of tricycles, disk records and perambulators. There are no direct long-distance flights to Nepal – getting here from Europe, the Americas or Australasia will always involve a stop in the Middle East or Asia.

Facilities at the airport are limited – there are foreign exchange booths before and after immigration, and there is a dusty tourist information counter by the terminal exit. Fill out the forms for your visa on arrival before you go to the immigration counter, as queues can be long here. A small stand provides instant passport photos, but bring some from home to be safe.

On departure, all baggage must go through the X-ray machine as you enter the terminal. Make sure that custom officials stamp all the baggage labels for your carry-on luggage.

Always ask your hotel if there is a bandh (strike) planned for the day you intend to fly. Taxi drivers may refuse to carry passengers during a strike, but the government may run special bus services. Even on a bandh day, you should be safe if you arrange a taxi to the airport before 8am.

There are plans to transform Bhairawa airport into an international airport, but this has been dragging on for years.

Airlines

Because Nepal does not lie on any major transit routes, flights to Kathmandu are expensive, particularly during the peak trekking season (October to November). Budget travellers fly to India first, and then pick up a cheap transfer to Kathmandu, though this incurs its own visa hassles.

Nepal's flagship carrier **Nepal Airlines** (code RA; Map p60; ☎01-4220757; www.nepalairlines.com.np; Kantipath) is a shoestring operation, with only two leased planes for its entire international operations. Delays and even cancellations are common; Hong Kong–Kathmandu passengers were delayed for two full days in 2011 when a rogue mouse was spotted onboard. However, its safety record is comparable with other regional carriers. There are flights to Delhi, Dubai, Doha, Hong Kong, Bangkok and Kuala Lumpur.

Following are other airlines serving Nepal:
Air China (☎01-4440650; www.airchina.com; Dhobi Dhara)
Air India (☎01-4410906; www.airindia.in; Hattisar)

CLIMATE CHANGE & TRAVEL

Every form of transport that relies on carbon-based fuel generates CO_2, the main cause of human-induced climate change. Modern travel is dependent on aeroplanes, which might use less fuel per kilometre per person than most cars but travel much greater distances. The altitude at which aircraft emit gases (including CO_2) and particles also contributes to their climate change impact. Many websites offer 'carbon calculators' that allow people to estimate the carbon emissions generated by their journey and, for those who wish to do so, to offset the impact of the greenhouse gases emitted with contributions to portfolios of climate-friendly initiatives throughout the world. Lonely Planet offsets the carbon footprint of all staff and author travel.

Arkefly (☑01-4410635; www.arkefly.nl; Malla Treks, Lekhnath Marg)

Biman Bangladesh Airlines (☑01-4434869; www.biman-airlines.com; Nag Pokhari, Naxal)

China Eastern (☑01-4411666; http://en.ceair.com; Hattisar)

China Southern Airlines (☑01-4427262; www.flychinasouthern.com; Marcopolo Business Hotel, Kamal Pokhari)

Dragonair (☑01-4444820; www.dragonair.com; Narayan Chaur, Naxal)

Druk Air (☑01-4239988; www.drukair.com.bt; Woodlands Complex, Durbar Marg)

Etihad (☑01-4233533; www.etihadairways.com; near Yak & Yeti Hotel, Lal Durbar)

GMG Airlines (☑01-4420252; www.gmgairlines.com)

Gulf Air (☑01-4435322; www.gulfair.com; Hattisar)

Jet Airways (☑01-4446375; www.jetairways.com; Sundar Bhawan, Hattisar)

Jetlite (☑01-4446375; www.jetlite.com; Sundar Bhawan, Hattisar)

Korean Airlines (☑01-4252048; www.koreanair.com; Ratna Bhawan Bldg, Hattisar)

Oman Air (☑01-4444381; www.omanair.com; Saakha Centre, Hattisar)

Pakistan International Airways (☑01-4439234; www.piac.com.pk; Hattisar)

Qatar Airways (☑01-4440467; www.qatarairways.com; Sundar Bhawan, Hattisar)

Silk Air (☑01-4226582; www.silkair.com; Kamaladi)

Thai Airways (☑01-4223565; www.thaiair.com; Durbar Marg)

Budget Indian airlines flying to Nepal include **SpiceJet** (www.spicejet.com), **IndiGo** (www.goindigo.in) and **Kingfisher** (www.flykingfisher.com).

Regional airlines connecting Kathmandu to the Gulf States include **Air Arabia** (www.airarabia.com) and **Fly Dubai** (www.flydubai.com).

Tickets

During the autumn trekking season, from October to November, every flight into and out of Kathmandu can be booked solid, and travellers sometimes have to resort to travelling overland to India to get a flight out of the region. To beat the rush, book well in advance and give yourself plenty of time between the end of your trek and your international flight home. If you are booking a flight in Kathmandu, book at the start of your trip, not at the end.

The other golden rule when flying out of Kathmandu is *reconfirm your booking*, especially when travelling on Nepal Airlines.

If you are connecting through Delhi on two separate tickets, you will likely need to collect your luggage and check in separately for the connecting flight, for which you will need to have arranged a transit or tourist visa in advance. Sometimes an airline representative can collect and check in the bags on your behalf but you should check this. Some

airlines have refused to fly passengers to Delhi to connect with other flights if they don't have an Indian visa.

Asia

The most popular route between Asia and Kathmandu is the daily Thai Airways flight to/from Bangkok (US$360), though Nepal Airlines also covers this connection (US$221), as does Jet Airways on a much longer connection via Delhi.

There are also convenient flights to Hong Kong (Dragon Air), Kuala Lumpur (Nepal Airlines), Singapore (Silk Air) and Seoul (Korean Airlines). There are no direct flights to Japan; most people change in Bangkok, Singapore, Hong Kong or Seoul.

For China there are flights to Beijing, Chengdu and Lhasa (Air China), as well as Kunming (China Eastern) and Guangzhou (China Southern Airlines). Flights are insanely priced, costing around US$415 to Lhasa, US$400 to Chengdu (via Lhasa!) and around US$420 to Beijing.

You can only buy tickets to Lhasa as part of a tour group package. You must also join an organised tour of Bhutan to fly to Paro on Druk Air (US$229).

Australia & New Zealand

There are easy connections from Australia and New Zealand through Bangkok, Seoul, Singapore, Guangzhou or Hong Kong.

Canada

Flying from Canada, you can go east or west around the globe. Fares from Vancouver through Asia tend to be slightly cheaper than flights from Toronto via Europe or the Gulf. Jet Airways offers a convenient single-airline route from Toronto through Brussels to Delhi and on to Kathmandu.

Continental Europe

The Dutch budget airline Arkefly has the only direct flights from Europe to Kathmandu, from Amsterdam. Etihad, Qatar Airways and Gulf Air all offer smooth connections through the Gulf to Paris, Frankfurt and other European cities. Jet Airways offers a useful connection from Brussels to Kathmandu via Delhi, or alternatively, you can take any flight to Delhi and change.

India, Pakistan & Bangladesh

Seats between Kathmandu and Delhi can be found for as little as US$100, especially if you book in advance online. Jet and Jetlite are the best carriers flying the Delhi–Kathmandu route, though budget Indian airlines like IndiGo and Spicejet offer the cheapest fares. All fly daily. Fares are best booked online, though you may have trouble using a non-Indian credit card on some sites.

Indian Airlines flies from Kathmanda to Delhi, Kolkata and Varanasi; Nepal Airlines also flies between Kathmandu and Delhi twice a week. Buddha Air flies twice a week to Lucknow.

You can get to Dhaka with Biman Bangladesh Airlines and GMG Airlines, and to Karachi with Pakistan International Airlines (PIA).

One reliable agent in India is **STIC Travels** (☑11-237 37 135; www.stictravel.com).

Good online Indian travel agencies include **Cleartrip** (www.cleartrip.com), **Make My Trip** (www.makemytrip.com) and **Yatra** (www.yatra.com).

UK & Ireland

There are easy connections to Kathmandu from London and Dublin with Etihad, Gulf Air and Qatar Airways, changing in the Gulf. All three airlines also fly from Manchester, Edinburgh and other regional UK airports. The fastest connection from London to Kathmandu is with Jet Airways, with one smooth change in Delhi. Cheaper Jet connections via Mumbai require an overnight stay.

USA

North America is halfway around the world from Nepal, so you can go east or west around the globe. Flying west involves a change in Asia – Korean Airlines offers good connections through Seoul, but you could also change in Bangkok, Hong Kong or Singapore. Flying east normally involves a stop in Europe and again in the Gulf or in India. Jet Airways has a convenient route from New York with stops in Brussels and Delhi.

For reasonably priced fares to Nepal, start with specialist travel agencies like **Third Eye Travel** (☑1-800 456 393; www.thirdeyetravel. com), **Angel Travel** (☑1-800 922 1092; www.angeltravel. com) and **USA Asia** (☑1-800 872 2742; www.usaasiatravel. com).

Land

Depending on the political situation and the condition of the roads, you can enter Nepal overland at six border crossings – five from India and one from Tibet.

Border Crossings
INDIA

All of the land borders between India and Nepal are in the Terai. The most popular crossing point is Sunauli, near Bhairawa, which provides easy access to Delhi and Varanasi in India.

Be suspicious of travel agents in India or Nepal who offer 'through tickets' between the two countries: everyone has to change buses at the border.

Indian domestic train tickets can now be booked in advance online at **Cleartrip** (www.cleartrip.com) or **IRCTC** (www.irctc.co.in). Get timetables and fares at **Indian Railways** (www.trainenquiry. com; www.indianrail.gov.in). **The Man in Seat 61** (www. seat61.com/India.htm) is a good general resource.

Sunauli/Bhairawa

The crossing at Sunauli is by far the most popular route between India and Nepal. The easiest way is to travel between Delhi and Gorakhpur by train (Vaishali Exp; 22 hours). You can then pick up a bus to Sunauli (three hours). There are also direct buses to Sunauli from Varanasi (10 hours).

Once across the border, you can visit the Buddhist pilgrimage centre of Lumbini before you continue your journey. From Bhairawa buses run regularly to Kathmandu (eight hours) and Pokhara (eight hours), usually passing through Narayangarh, where you can change for Chitwan National Park. Buddha Air and Yeti Airlines fly daily from Bhairawa to Kathmandu (US$116).

Mahendranagar

The western border crossing at Mahendranagar is also reasonably convenient for

Delhi. There are daily buses from Delhi's Anand Vihar bus stand to Banbassa, the nearest Indian village to the border (10 hours). Banbassa is also connected by bus with most towns in Uttaranchal.

From Mahendranagar there are slow overnight bus services to Kathmandu (15 hours) but it's better to do the trip in daylight and break the journey at Bardia National Park, Nepalganj or Narayangarh. Check that the road is open and make sure there are no security problems before you travel.

Kakarbhitta

The eastern border crossing at Kakarbhitta offers easy onward connections to Darjeeling, Sikkim, Kolkata and India's northeast states. Travel agencies in Kathmandu and Darjeeling offer 'through buses' across the border, but these all involve a change of vehicle at the border. It's just as easy to do the journey in stages.

From Darjeeling, take a morning bus/jeep to Siliguri (two hours) then a bus (one hour) to Panitanki on the Indian side of the border. Jeeps also run to the border from Kalimpong (three hours) and Gangtok (4½ hours) in Sikkim. Coming from Kolkata, you can take the overnight *Darjeeling Mail*, *Kanchankaya* or *Padatik* expresses from Sealdah sta-

tion to New Jalpaiguri (NJP) near Siliguri, then a bus to the border (₹259/673/911 in sleeper class/air-con three-tier/air-con two-tier).

From Kakarbhitta there are overnight buses to Kathmandu (17 hours) or Pokhara (17 hours) but it's more interesting to break the journey at Janakpur (five hours) or at Chitwan National Park (accessible from Sauraha Chowk on the Mahendra Hwy).

Birganj/Raxaul Bazaar

The border crossing from Birganj to Raxaul Bazaar is handy for Patna and Kolkata. Buses run from the bus station in Patna straight to Raxaul Bazaar (eight hours). From Kolkata, take the daily *Mithila Express* – it leaves Kolkata's Howrah station at 3.45pm, arriving in Raxaul at 8.30am the next morning (₹272/735/1008 in sleeper class/air-con three-tier/air-con two-tier).

From Birganj, there are regular day/night buses to Kathmandu (eight hours) and Pokhara (seven hours), via Narayangarh (three hours). There are also regular services to most other towns around the Terai.

Nepalganj

Few people use the crossing at Nepalganj in western Nepal as it's not particularly convenient for anywhere else. The nearest town in

India is Lucknow, where you can pick up slow buses to Rupaidha Bazaar (seven hours), near the border post at Jamunaha. You might also consider taking a train to Nanpara, 17km from the border.

Over the border in Nepalganj, there are regular day/night buses to Kathmandu (12 hours) and buses to Pokhara (12 hours), passing through Narayangarh (eight hours). Yeti Airlines and Buddha Air have flights from Nepalganj to Kathmandu (US$158).

TIBET

Officially only organised 'groups' are allowed into Tibet from Nepal. The good news is that travel agencies in Kathmandu are experts in assembling overland groups to get around this restriction. In general, travellers face fewer restrictions entering Tibet through China, so it makes more sense to visit Nepal after a trip through Tibet, not before.

Travelling overland to Tibet from Nepal is not an easy option. Altitude sickness is a real danger: the maximum altitude along the road is 5140m and tours do not always allow sufficient time to acclimatise safely. The road is often closed by landslides during the monsoon months (May to August) and there are often additional restrictions on travel at times of political tension.

The vast majority of travellers enter Tibet at Kodari/Zhangmu on the Friendship Highway, though organised groups can trek from Simikot through far-western Nepal to Mt Kailash. Other road connections, including the road from Tibet to Mustang and the new (2012) road between Kyirong and Langtang, are not open to foreigners.

Travel Restrictions

At the time of research, it was only possible to cross into Tibet with a Tibet Tourism Permit, which can only

NEPAL–INDIA BORDER CROSSINGS

BORDER CROSSING (NEPAL TO INDIA)	NEAREST INDIAN TOWNS
Belahiya to Sunauli (p235)	Varanasi, Agra & Delhi
Mahendranagar to Banbassa (p252)	Delhi & hill towns in Uttaranchal
Kakarbhitta to Panitanki (p264)	Darjeeling, Sikkim & Kolkata
Birganj to Raxaul Bazaar (p255)	Patna & Kolkata
Nepalganj to Jamunaha/ Rupaidha Bazaar (p247)	Lucknow

be arranged through a travel agency when you book a package tour to Lhasa. If you turn up at the border at Kodari with just a Chinese visa you'll be turned away, and Air China won't sell you an air ticket to Lhasa without this permit.

At the time of research, when people booked this tour they were put on a group visa and any existing Chinese visas in their passports were cancelled. Splitting from this group visa in Lhasa is almost impossible, but it is apparently possible (but a headache) to fly out of Tibet to Chengdu and then continue through China on a standard Chinese tourist visa. Visiting Tibet from China entails far fewer visa hassles.

Tour Options
The easiest way to visit Tibet from Nepal is to join a drive-in, fly-out overland jeep tour from Kathmandu to Lhasa, overnighting in Nyalam, Dingri/Lhatse, Shigatse, Gyantse and Lhasa. Several agencies offer eight-day trips for as little as US$350, including permit fees, transport by cramped Land Cruiser or minibus, accommodation in dorms and shared twin rooms and sightseeing (but not meals). Trips normally leave on Tuesday and Saturday from April to October and weekly at other times. Don't expect too much from these budget tours. A private trip for four people in a Land Cruiser costs around US$600 per person.

Add on to this around US$85 for a group visa and transport out of Tibet, which currently costs around US$415 for a flight back to Kathmandu or US$190/260 for a hard/soft sleeper on to Beijing (48 hours).

Some agencies also offer pricey trips that include a detour to Mt Everest Base Camp (on the Tibetan side). There are also very expensive trekking trips from Simikot in far-western Nepal to Purang in far-western Tibet, and then on to Mt Kailash. Land Cruiser trips to Mt Kailash are also possible. Rates increase from July to September, and there are fewer tours from December to February.

The agency will need one week to get your visa and permits. You can normally get a maximum of between 15 and 20 days on a group visa. If you are heading on to China you will need to get your own separate 'group' visa. For more details see Lonely Planet's *Tibet* and *China* guides.

Most of the companies advertising Tibet trips in Kathmandu are agencies for other companies – the following agencies run their own trips.

Ecotrek (Map p80; ☎01-4423207; www.ecotrek.com.np; Thamel)

Green Hill Tours (Map p80; ☎01-4700968; Thamel)

Royal Mount Trekking (Map p60; ☎01-4241452; www.royaltibet.com; Durbar Marg)

Tashi Delek Nepal Treks & Expeditions (Map p80; ☎01-4410746; www.tashidelektreks.com.np; Thamel)

Other travel companies in Thamel offering customised tours to Tibet include the following:

Adventure Silk Road (www.silkroadgroup.com)

Dharma Adventures (www.dharmaadventures.com)

Earthbound Expeditions (www.trektibet.com)

Explore Himalaya (www.explorehimalaya.com)

Car & Motorcycle

A steady trickle of people drive their own motorbikes or vehicles overland from Europe, for which an international carnet is required. If you want to abandon your transport in Nepal, you must either pay a prohibitive import duty or surrender it to customs. It is not possible to import cars more than five years old. Make sure you bring an international driving permit.

GETTING AROUND

Getting around in Nepal can be a challenging business. Because of the terrain, the weather conditions and the condition of vehicles, few trips go exactly according to plan. Nepali ingenuity will usually get you to your destination in the end, but build plenty of time into your itinerary and treat the delays and mishaps as part of the rich tapestry that is Nepal. Oh, and bring snacks, lots of snacks.

Walking is still the most common method of getting from A to B in Nepal, particularly in the mountains where there are no roads and few airstrips. Elsewhere, people get around on buses, jeeps, motorcycles, trains and planes that seem to be held together more by faith than mechanical integrity.

The wise traveller avoids going anywhere during major festivals (see the boxed text Dasain Stoppages, p367), when buses, flights and hotels are booked solid.

Air

Considering the nature of the landscape, Nepal has an excellent network of domestic flights. Engineers have created runways deep in the jungle and high in the mountains, clinging to the sides of Himalayan peaks. However, pilots must still find their way to these airstrips using visual navigation and few years pass without some kind of air disaster in the mountains.

Because flights are dependent on clear weather, services rarely leave on time and many flights are cancelled at the last minute because of poor visibility. It is essential to build extra time into your itinerary. Even if you take off on time, you may not be able to land at your intended destination because of fog. It would be unwise to book a flight back

Domestic Air Routes

CHINA
TIBET

Only the most popular flight connections are shown
Mountain flight — — — —

Simikot
Jumla
Dunai
Jomsom
Dhangadhi
Manang
Pokhara
Nepalganj
KATHMANDU
Lukla
Mountain Flight
Meghauli
Bhairawa
Bharatpur
Phaplu
Taplejung
Tumlingtar
Birganj/Simara
Janakpur
Bhadrapur
Biratnagar
INDIA

to Kathmandu within three days of your international flight out of the country.

In the event of a cancellation, airlines will try to find you a seat on the next available flight (some airlines run extra flights to clear the backlog once the weather clears). If you decide not to wait, you will be able to cancel the ticket without penalty, though it can take a long time to arrange a refund.

Airlines in Nepal

The largest domestic airline is the notoriously unreliable **Nepal Airlines** (Map p60; ☑01-4220757; www.royalnepal-airlines.com; Kantipath), formerly Royal Nepal Airlines (RNAC). All things considered, Nepal Airlines has a comparable safety record to other domestic airlines, but if your destination is served by a private airline, this will almost always be the better option. Nepal Airlines currently has services to Biratnagar, Pokhara, Lukla, Phaplu, Bhojpur, Lamidanda, Tumlingtar, Suketar, Dolpo, Manang, Jumla and Simikot, among other airstrips.

Services are more reliable on Nepal's private airlines, though fares are slightly higher. Most flights operate out of Kathmandu, but there are minor air hubs at Pokhara,

Nepalganj and Surkhet in the southwest and Biratnagar in the southeast. Most airlines also offer scenic 'mountain flights' in the morning – if you're flying from Kathmandu you will probably have to wait until the airline finishes its morning quota of mountain flights before domestic services begin.

The following domestic airlines have offices in Kathmandu:

Agni Air (☑01-4107812; www.agniair.com; Shantinagar) Serves Lukla, Pokhara, Tumlingtar, Phaplu, Bhadrapur, Biratnagar and Jomsom.

Buddha Air (☑01-5542494; www.buddhaair.com; Hattisar) Destinations include Pokhara, Bhadrapur, Janakpur, Bharatpur, Bhairawa, Biratnagar, Simara and Nepalganj.

Guna Airlines (☑01-4106691; www.gunaairlines.com) Serves Pokhara, Biratnagar, Bhairava and Simara.

Sita Air (☑01-4490103; www.sitaair.com.np; Sinamangal) Destinations include Lukla, Tumlingtar, Pokhara and Jomsom.

Tara Air (☑01-4213002; www.taraair.com; Thamel Chowk) Subsidiary of Yeti Airlines. Kathmandu to Lukla, Lamidanda, Phaplu, Meghauli, Syangboche; Pokhara to Jomsom and

Manang; and Lukla to Syangboche in the Everest region.

Yeti Airlines (☑01-4213002; www.yetiairlines.com; Thamel Chowk) Sherpa-owned and the largest private airline; destinations include Pokhara, Biratnagar, Nepalganj, Lukla, Bhadrapur, Janakpur, Bhairawa, Tumlingtar and Bharatpur.

Air Safety

Air safety is something you should bear in mind when deciding to fly internally in Nepal, but this has to be weighed up against the risks of travelling by road and the time that is saved by flying. Given the choice between a 45-minute flight and a 17-hour bus ride on poorly maintained mountain roads, most people prefer to fly.

Recent accidents have included the following:

October 2008 Yeti Airlines flight carrying European trekkers crashes beside the runway at Lukla, killing 18 people.

August 2010 Agni Air flight en route to Lukla crashes, killing all 14.

December 2010 Tara Air flight crashes en route from Lamidanda to Kathmandu, killing 22.

September 2011 Buddha Air mountain flight crashes

in bad weather at Godawari, killing 19.

Tickets

Airlines come and go and schedules change, so it's best to make reservations through a travel agent, a trekking agency or your hotel. Foreign visitors must pay for airfares in hard currency, typically US dollars. Residents and Nepali citizens pay approximately 40% of the tourist price, which helps if you are flying your guide or porter out to Lukla for the Everest trek. There is a 10% to 15% penalty for cancellations before departure. If you fail to show up for the flight, you generally forfeit the ticket.

All travellers are charged an insurance surcharge of US$2 per leg, as well as a fuel surcharge. Fares quoted in this book include all these surcharges. Tickets are not exchangeable between airlines. However, airlines have been known to swap passengers at the last minute! Always reconfirm your flight the day before you fly. If you 'drop off' the reservation list, it could be days before you get back on.

Note that domestic airlines have a 15kg allowance for hold baggage – and on some flights you cannot pay to carry excess baggage. Knives, cigarette lighters, gas cylinders and trekking poles are not permitted in carry-on luggage.

Bicycle

There are plenty of bicycle-rental shops in Kathmandu and Pokhara, and this is a cheap and convenient way of getting around. Generic Indian- and Chinese-made bicycles cost around Rs 350 per day to rent, but the clunky gears make even a downhill stretch seem like hard work. Several cycling agencies in Kathmandu rent out imported mountain bikes for around US$8 to US$12

per day. Children's bicycles can also be hired.

See p38 for detailed information on mountain biking in Nepal.

Bus

Buses are the main form of public transport in Nepal and they're incredibly cheap. Often they're also incredibly uncomfortable. Buses run pretty much everywhere and will stop for anyone, but you'll find it much easier to get a seat if you catch a bus at its source rather than mid-run. For longer-distance buses it's best to book a couple of days in advance.

Public Buses

Most towns in lowland Nepal are accessible by bus from Kathmandu or Pokhara, but Nepali buses are slow, noisy and uncomfortable, and breakdowns are almost guaranteed. Fortunately, services are frequent enough that you can always hop onto another bus if your first bus dies on a lonely stretch of highway.

On longer journeys, buses stop regularly for refreshments, but travel after dark is not recommended – drivers take advantage of the quiet roads to do some crazy speeding, and accidents and fatalities are depressingly common. In fact, you are 30 times more likely to die in a road accident in Nepal than in any developed country. Some night buses stop for a few hours' sleep, en route, but others keep blazing through the night with the music blaring at full volume. The single best thing you can do to stay safe is to avoid travelling by road at night.

Myriad private companies run 'ordinary buses' and faster, more expensive 'express buses' that offer seats with more padding and luxuries such as curtains to keep out the sun. Tickets can be purchased in advance at the relevant counter (ask locals where to go as signs are often in Nepali) or on board from the driver.

Large pieces of baggage go on the roof – the conductor will take your bag up for a tip or you can do it yourself. Theft from luggage is not uncommon so padlock your bags shut and tie the straps to the railings. Always keep an eye on your belongings at rest stops – backpacks are extremely easy for thieves to walk off with.

The fast, frequent and phenomenally crowded 'local buses' that run between smaller towns are handy for day trips, but

---

AIR-CONDITIONING OF THE GODS

With the cramped conditions inside Nepal's buses, many locals and foreigners prefer to ride up on the roof. For legal reasons, we are required to say this is probably not a good idea – but the truth is that it is probably not significantly more dangerous than riding inside. You'll also get the sense of being surrounded by the environment you are passing through, rather than viewing it through a murky window.

If you do ride on the roof, make sure you are well wedged in, so you don't catapult off when the bus swerves, brakes or lurches. It's also best to sit facing forwards – that way you can see low-hanging wires and branches before you get swatted. Make sure you have sunscreen and appropriate clothing too, as it can be surprisingly cold up there.

you'll have your work cut out getting on board with a backpack. Prices for foreigners are often bumped up by unscrupulous conductors on these buses.

Note that road travel in the far east and west of Nepal can be impossible after the monsoon. Every year the rains lead to floods that destroy stretches of road and wash away bridges. The Mahendra Hwy between Mohanpur and Itahari was blocked for weeks following devastating floods on the Sapt Kosi in 2008. Where roads are blocked, it may be possible to get around the blockage on foot or by local transport – ask locals for advice.

Tourist Buses

Travel agencies run a number of useful bus services to popular tourist destinations, leaving from the Tourist Bus Park in Pokhara and the Thamel end of Kantipath in Kathmandu. These are more comfortable and less crowded than local buses but cost a little more.

Greenline (☑4257544; www.greenline.com.np; Tridevi Marg) has deluxe buses between Kathmandu, Pokhara and Sauraha (for Chitwan National Park).

Car & Motorcycle

Hire

There are no drive-yourself rental cars available in Nepal, but you can easily hire a car or jeep with a driver through a travel agency. Expect to pay between US$60 and US$100 per day, including fuel. Taxis are cheaper but you must negotiate a fare directly with the driver. Remember that you'll have to pay for the driver's return trip whether or not you return, as well as their food and accommodation for overnight trips.

Motorcycles can be rented in Kathmandu and Pokhara for around Rs 500 to 700 per day. You'll need an international driving permit or a licence from your own country that shows you are licensed to ride a motorcycle – a car drivers' licence won't cut it. You must also leave your passport as a deposit. It's not a bad idea to take some digital photographs of the bike in case operators complain of damages that existed before you ever set foot on the bike. See p107 and p212 for details.

Note that there are major fuel shortages in Nepal. Petrol stations can be dry for days at a time and the only option for motorists is to queue for hours at the few stations that have fuel or to buy fuel in reused bottles from local shops.

Insurance

If you are planning to drive a motorbike in Nepal you should double-check to see if you are covered by your travel insurance. Rental companies rarely offer insurance and you will be fully liable for the vehicle and damage to other vehicles in the event of an accident.

Road Rules

If you do drive, be aware that you drive on the left-hand side of the road, left turns are allowed without stopping, and that traffic entering a roundabout has priority over traffic already on the roundabout. Locals rarely signal and other vehicles will pull out regardless of whether or not anyone is coming – drive defensively. Try to avoid any dealings with traffic police; locals are routinely stung for bribes and foreigners are increasingly being targeted.

Finally, our best advice is to trust nothing and nobody. Expect kids, chickens, ducks, women, old men, babies, cows, dogs and almost anything else that can move to jump in front of you at any moment, without any kind of warning. Good luck.

Tours

The winding roads of Nepal are glorious for mountain riding and several companies run fully supported motorcycle tours. Contact the following companies for more information:

Asia-Bike-Tours (www.asiabiketours.com)

Blazing Trails (www.blazingtrailstours.com)

Enfielders (www.enfielders.com)

Hearts and Tears (www.heartsandtears.com; see p212)

Himalayan Enfielders (www.himalayanenfielders.com)

Himalayan Offroad (www.himalayanoffroad.com)

Himalayan Roadrunners (www.ridehigh.com)

Hitching

It is possible to hitch rides on trucks and private vehicles but you will be expected to pay for your ride. The usual rules apply – never hitch alone and don't ride with drunken drivers.

Local Transport

Autorickshaw & Cycle-Rickshaw

Cycle-rickshaws are common in the old part of Kathmandu and in towns in the Terai, and they provide an atmospheric way to explore the crowded and narrow streets. Prices are highly negotiable.

Nepal's two-stroke, three-wheeled autorickshaws are being phased out everywhere, but a few are still hanging on in a couple of Terai towns.

Taxi

Metered taxis are found in larger towns such as Kathmandu and Pokhara, and these can be hired for both local and long-distance journeys. Metered taxis have black licence plates; private cars that operate as taxis for long-distance routes have red plates.

Taxis can be flagged down anywhere, and they loiter at

official stops in tourist destinations such as Bhaktapur and Patan. On some routes, taxi drivers may refuse to use the meter – this is often an attempt to overcharge tourists, but it may also reflect rising fuel costs and traffic delays. If a driver refuses to use the meter, try another taxi. If no taxis are willing to use the meter, haggle down to reach a reasonable price.

Tempo

Tempos are outsized autorickshaws that run on fixed routes in larger cities. Kathmandu's archaic, polluting diesel tempos have been replaced by electric and gas-powered *safa* (clean) tempos and petrol minibuses, dramatically reducing the smog in the Kathmandu Valley. Drivers pick up and drop off anywhere along the route; tap on the roof with a coin when you want to stop.

Tours

Organised treks are the most common kind of tour in Nepal (see p266 for details), but there are also wildlife-spotting tours at many of Nepal's national parks and some interesting sightseeing tours around the Kathmandu Valley. Pretty much any travel agent in Nepal can organise a bespoke tour to match your interests, budget and timeframe.

For organised mountain-biking and rafting tours see p39 and p42. For other adventure sports see p77.

Best of Asia (BOA) Overland Trips (www.boa -overland.com) offers overland truck tours to and across Nepal, including a 14-day trip to India and 26-day trip to Kailash and Tibet, with an office in the Kathmandu Guest House.

Train

Trains run from Janakpur to Jaynagar over the Indian border but only locals can cross there. Nevertheless, these narrow-gauge locos offer a slow but atmospheric method of seeing the countryside of the Terai. See p258 for more details.

Health

Kathmandu has the best health facilities in the country, but standards at clinics and hospitals decline the further you get from the capital. In mountainous areas, there may be no health facilities at all. Trekkers who become unwell in the mountains are generally evacuated to Kathmandu, or overseas in the event of something really serious. Always take out travel insurance to cover the costs of hospital treatment and emergency evacuations.

Many of the most popular areas for visitors are remote and inaccessible, so you should read up on the possible health risks. While trekking, it makes sense to carry an emergency medical kit so that you can treat any symptoms until you reach medical care.

BEFORE YOU GO

Insurance

Considering the terrain, potential health risks and high cost of medical evacuation, it is unwise to travel to Nepal without adequate health insurance. See p364 for details.

Recommended Vaccinations

You do not officially require any immunisations to enter the country, unless you have come from an area where yellow fever is present – in which case, you must show proof of immunisation.

It is best to seek medical advice at least six weeks before travelling, since some vaccinations require multiple injections over a period of time.

Note that some vaccinations should not be given during pregnancy or to people with allergies.

Vaccinations you might consider:

Diphtheria and tetanus Vaccinations for these two diseases are usually combined and are recommended for everyone. After an initial course of three injections (usually given in childhood), boosters are necessary every 10 years.

Hepatitis A The vaccine for hepatitis A (eg Avaxim, Havrix 1440 or VAQTA) provides long-term immunity (possibly lifelong) after an initial injection and a booster at six to 12 months.

Hepatitis B Vaccination involves three injections, the quickest course being over three weeks with a booster at 12 months.

Influenza 'Flu' is considered by many to be the most common vaccine-preventable illness in travellers. This vaccine is annual.

Japanese B encephalitis (JBE) This is a mosquito-borne viral encephalitis that occurs in the Terai and occasionally in the Kathmandu Valley, particularly during the monsoon. JBE vaccine is given as three injections over three to four weeks and is usually boosted at three years. Recommended for prolonged stays.

Meningococcal meningitis A single-dose vaccine boosted every three to five years is recommended for individuals at high risk and for extended stays.

Polio This serious, easily transmitted disease is still found in Nepal. Everyone should keep up to date with this vaccination, which is normally given in childhood. A booster every 10 years maintains immunity.

Rabies Vaccination should be considered for long-term visitors, particularly if you plan to travel to remote areas. In Nepal the disease is carried by street dogs and monkeys. Vaccination is strongly recommended for children, who may not report a bite. Pretravel rabies vaccination involves having three injections over 21 to 28 days. If someone who has been vaccinated is bitten or scratched by an animal they will require two vaccine booster injections, while those not vaccinated will require more. The booster for rabies vaccination is usually given after three years.

Tuberculosis (TB) This disease is highly endemic in Nepal, though cases are extremely rare among travellers. Most people in the West are vaccinated during childhood.

Typhoid Drug-resistant typhoid fever is a growing problem in Nepal, particularly in the Terai. If you are travelling in Nepal for long periods, you should consider vaccination. The vaccine is available as an injection or oral capsules – ask your doctor for advice.

Yellow fever This disease is not endemic in Nepal and a vaccine for yellow fever is required only if you are coming from an infected area. The record of this vaccine should be provided in a World Health Organization (WHO) Yellow Vaccination Booklet and is valid for 10 years.

Medical Checklist

Following is a list of items you should consider including in your medical kit – consult your pharmacist for brands available in your country.

» aspirin or paracetamol (acetaminophen in the USA) for pain or fever

» anti-inflammatory (ibuprofen) for muscle and joint pain, headache and fever

» antibiotics, particularly if travelling off the beaten track; in Nepal, antibiotics are sold without prescription, which has led to widespread resistance to some common antibiotics

» promethazine (Phenergan) for relief of severe nausea

» rehydration mixture to prevent dehydration during bouts of diarrhoea; particularly important when travelling with children

» antihistamine for allergies, eg hay fever; for skin conditions, carry hydrocortisone 1% cream

» cold and flu tablets, throat lozenges and nasal decongestant

» multivitamins for long trips

» antifungal cream such as clotrimazole 1% for fungal skin infections and thrush

» antiseptic (such as povidone-iodine) for cuts and grazes

» bandages, crêpe wraps, Band-Aids (plasters) and other wound dressings

» water purification tablets or iodine

» scissors, tweezers and an electric thermometer (mercury thermometers are prohibited by airlines)

» sterile kit in case you need injections; discuss with your doctor

» motion-sickness tablets, such as Dramamine, for long bus rides

Other Preparations

Visiting Nepal may take you to some very remote areas, so it makes sense to visit the doctor before you travel for a general check-up. If you have any pre-existing medical conditions, bring any medication you need from home. Ask your physician to give you a written description of your condition and your medications with their generic names in case you have to visit a doctor in Nepal.

It pays to get a dental check-up well before embarking on a trek. A previous author of this guide cracked a molar on a particularly tough piece of dried beef while on a research trek and had to walk for five days to reach a dentist who performed an emergency root canal operation without anaesthetic! Be warned.

Contact-lens wearers should bring plenty of solution and take extra care with hygiene to avoid eye infections. Carry backup prescription glasses and sunglasses in case you can't wear your lenses at some point.

Websites

Medex (www.medex.org.uk) offers a free download of the useful booklet *Travel At High Altitude*, aimed at laypeople and full of good advice for staying healthy in the mountains. A Nepali translation of the booklet is also available on the website.

Other useful sites:

Centers for Disease Control and Prevention (www.cdc.gov)

Fit for Travel (www.fitfortravel.scot.nhs.uk)

International Society for Mountain Medicine (www.ismmed.org)

Kathmandu CIWEC Clinic (www.ciwec-clinic.com)

MASTA (www.masta-travel-health.com)

Nepal International Clinic (www.nepalinternationalclinic.com)

Further Reading

Lonely Planet's *Healthy Travel Asia & India* is packed with information such as pre-trip planning, emergency first aid, immunisation and disease information, and what to do if you get sick on the road. *Travel with Children* from Lonely Planet includes advice on travel health for younger children. A useful health-care overview for travel in remote areas is David Werner's *Where There Is No Doctor*.

Specific titles covering trekking and health:

Medicine for Mountaineering & Other Wilderness Activities (James A Wilkerson) covers many medical problems typically encountered in Nepal.

Mountain Medicine (Michael Ward) has good background info on cold and high-altitude problems.

Altitude Illness: Prevention & Treatment (Stephen Bezruchka) is essential reading for high-altitude trekking, written by an experienced Nepal trekker.

Wilderness First Aid & Wilderness Medicine (Dr Jim Duff and Peter Gormly) is an excellent portable companion, available in Nepal at the Kathmandu Environmental Education Project (KEEP) or published abroad by Cicerone.

IN NEPAL

Availability & Cost of Health Care

Kathmandu has several excellent clinics, including the CIWEC Clinic Travel Medicine Center and Nepal International Clinic (see p102). While trekking, your only option may be small, local health posts, and even these are few and far between. In remote areas, you should carry an appropriate medical kit and be prepared to treat yourself until you can reach a health professional.

Infectious Diseases

Hepatitis

There are several different viruses that cause hepatitis (inflammation of the liver). The symptoms are similar in all forms of the illness and include fever, chills, headache, fatigue, feelings of weakness as well as aches and pains, followed by loss of appetite, nausea, vomiting, abdominal pain, dark urine, light-coloured faeces, jaundiced (yellow) skin and yellowing of the whites of the eyes.

Hepatitis A and E are transmitted by contaminated drinking water and food. Hepatitis A is virtually 100% preventable by using any of the current hepatitis A vaccines. Hepatitis E causes an illness very similar to hepatitis A and there is at present no way to immunise against this virus.

Hepatitis B is only spread by blood (unsterilised needles and blood transfusions) or sexual contact. Risky situations include having a shave, tattoo or body piercing with contaminated equipment.

HIV & AIDS

HIV and AIDS are growing problems in Nepal, with an estimated 75,000 Nepalis infected with the virus, so insist on brand-new disposable needles and syringes for injections. Blood used for transfusions is usually screened for HIV/AIDS but this cannot always be done in an emergency. Try to avoid a blood transfusion unless it seems certain you will die without it.

Malaria

Antimalarial tablets are only recommended if you will be spending long periods in the Terai, particularly during the monsoon. There is no risk in Kathmandu or Pokhara, or on typical Himalayan trekking routes.

It makes sense to take measures to avoid being bitten by mosquitoes, as dengue fever, another mosquito-borne illness, has been sporadically documented in the lowlands. Use insect repellent if travelling to the Terai, particularly if staying overnight in jungle areas or in cheap hotels. Plug-in mosquito killers are more effective than combustible mosquito coils, which can cause respiratory problems.

Rabies

The rabies virus causes a severe brain infection that is almost always fatal. Feral dogs and monkeys are the main carriers of the disease in Nepal. Rabies is different from other infectious diseases in that a person can be immunised after having been exposed. Human rabies immune globulin (HRIG) is stocked at the CIWEC clinic and the Nepal International Clinic in Kathmandu (see p102).

In addition to the HRIG, five injections of rabies vaccine are needed over a one-month period. Travellers who have taken a preimmunisation series only need two rabies shots, three days apart, if they are bitten by a possibly rabid animal.

If you receive a bite or a scratch from an animal in Nepal, wash the wound with soap and water, then a disinfectant, such as povidone-iodine, then seek rabies immunisations. Considering the risk, it makes sense to keep your distance from animals in Nepal, particularly street dogs and monkeys.

Respiratory Infections

Upper respiratory tract infections (such as the common cold) are common ailments in Nepal, especially in polluted Kathmandu. Respiratory infections are aggravated by high altitude, cold weather, pollution, smoking and over-

EMERGENCY TREATMENTS FOR TREKKING

While trekking it may be impossible to reach medical treatment, so consider carrying the following drugs for emergencies (the concentrations in which these drugs are sold in Nepal are noted next to the drug):

» azithromycin 250mg – a broad-spectrum antibiotic, useful for traveller's diarrhoea; take the equivalent of 500mg per day for three consecutive days

» norfloxacin 400mg or ciprofloxacin 500mg – for traveller's diarrhoea; the usual treatment is two tablets daily for one week

» tinidazole 500mg – the recommended treatment for giardiasis is four pills all at once for two days; for amoebiasis, take four pills at once for three days, then diloxanide furoate 500mg three times a day for 10 days

crowded conditions, which increase the opportunities for infection.

Most upper respiratory tract infections go away without treatment, but any infection can lead to complications such as bronchitis, ear infections and pneumonia, which may need to be treated with antibiotics.

Fever

If you have a sustained fever (over 38°C) for more than two days while trekking and you cannot get to a doctor, an emergency treatment is a course of the broad-spectrum antibiotic azithromycin (500mg twice a day for seven days), but seek professional medical help as soon as possible.

Traveller's Diarrhoea

Even veteran travellers to South Asia seem to come down with the trots in Nepal. It's just one of those things. The main cause of infection is contaminated water and food, due to low standards of hygiene. However, diarrhoea is usually self-limiting and most people recover within a few days.

Dehydration is the main danger with diarrhoea, particularly in children, pregnant women or the elderly. Soda water, weak black tea with a little sugar, or soft drinks allowed to go flat and half-diluted with clean water will help you replace lost liquids. In severe cases, take oral rehydration salts made up with boiled or purified water. In an emergency you can make up a solution of six teaspoons of sugar and half a teaspoon of salt to a litre of boiled or bottled water. Stick to a bland diet as you recover.

Loperamide (Imodium) or diphenoxylate (Lomotil) can be used to bring temporary relief from the symptoms, but they do not cure the problem.

In the case of diarrhoea with blood or mucus (dysentery), any diarrhoea with fever, profuse watery diarrhoea and persistent diarrhoea not improving after 48 hours, you should visit a doctor for a stool test. If you cannot reach a doctor, the recommended treatment is norfloxacin 400mg or ciprofloxacin 500mg twice daily for three days.

These drugs are not recommended for children or pregnant women. The preferred treatment for children is azithromycin in a dose of 10mg per kilogram of body weight per day (as a single dose each day for three days).

Amoebic Dysentery

Caused by the protozoan *Entamoeba histolytica*, amoebic dysentery is characterised by a gradual onset of low-grade diarrhoea, often with blood and mucus. Infection persists until treated. If medical treatment is not available, tinidazole or metronidazole are the recommended drugs. Treatment is a 2g single dose of tinidazole daily or 250mg of metronidazole three times daily for five to 10 days. Alcohol should not be consumed while taking these medications.

Cyclospora

This waterborne intestinal parasite infects the upper intestine, causing diarrhoea, fatigue and loss of appetite lasting up to 12 weeks. Fortunately, the illness is a risk in Nepal mainly during the monsoon, when few tourists visit. Iodine is not sufficient to kill the parasite but it can be removed by water filters and it is easily killed by boiling.

The treatment for *Cyclospora* diarrhoea is trimethoprim and sulfamethoxazole (sold commonly as Bactrim) twice a day for seven days. This drug cannot be taken by people who are allergic to sulphur.

Giardiasis

Also known as giardia, giardiasis accounts for around 12% of the diarrhoea among travellers in Nepal. The disease is caused by a parasite, *Giardia Lamblia*, found in water that has been contaminated by waste from animals.

Symptoms include stomach cramps, nausea, a bloated stomach, watery and foul-smelling diarrhoea, and frequent sulphurous burps and farts but no fever. The best treatment is four 500mg tablets of tinidazole taken as a single dose each day for two consecutive days. Tinidazole cannot be taken with alcohol.

Environmental Hazards

Acute Mountain Sickness (AMS)

Above 2500m, the concentration of oxygen in the air you breathe starts to drop off markedly, reducing the amount of oxygen that reaches your brain and other organs. Decreasing air pressure at altitude has the additional effect of causing liquid to leak from the capillaries into the lungs and brain, which can be fatal. The human body has the ability to adjust to the changes in pressure and oxygen concentration as you gain altitude, but this is a gradual process.

The health conditions caused by the effects of

altitude are known collectively as altitude sickness or acute mountain sickness (AMS). If allowed to develop unchecked, AMS can lead to coma and death. However, you can avoid this potentially deadly condition by limiting your rate of ascent, which will allow your body to adjust to the altitude. There is also a 100% effective treatment if you do experience serious symptoms: descend immediately.

If you go trekking, it is important to read up on the causes, effects and treatment of altitude sickness before you start walking. Attend one of the free lectures on altitude sickness given by the Himalayan Rescue Association in Kathmandu (p33).

The onset of symptoms of AMS is usually gradual, so there is time to adjust your trekking schedule or retreat off the mountain if you start to feel unwell. Most people who suffer severe effects of AMS have ignored obvious warning signs.

ACCLIMATISATION

The process of acclimatisation is still not fully understood, but it is known to involve modifications in breathing patterns and heart rate and an increase in the oxygen-carrying capacity of the blood. Some people have a faster rate of acclimatisation than others, but almost anyone can trek to high altitudes as long as the rate of ascent does not exceed the rate at which their body can adjust.

AMS is a notoriously fickle affliction and it can affect trekkers and walkers who are accustomed to walking at high altitudes as well as people who have never been to altitude before. AMS has been fatal at 3000m, although 3500m to 4500m is the usual range.

SYMPTOMS

On treks above 4000m, almost everyone experiences some symptoms of mild altitude sickness – breathlessness and fatigue linked to reduced oxygen in the blood being the most common.

Mild symptoms usually pass if you stop ascending and give your body time to 'catch up' with the increase in altitude. Once you have acclimatised at the altitude where you first developed symptoms, you should be able to slowly continue your ascent. Serious symptoms are a different matter – if you develop any of the symptoms described here, you should descend immediately.

Mild Symptoms

Mild symptoms of AMS are experienced by many travellers above 2800m. Symptoms tend to be worse at night and include headache, dizziness, lethargy, loss of appetite, nausea, breathlessness, irritability and difficulty sleeping.

Never ignore mild symptoms of AMS – this is your body giving you an alarm call. You may develop more serious symptoms if you continue to ascend without giving your body time to adjust.

Serious Symptoms

AMS can become more serious without warning and it can be fatal. Serious symptoms are caused by the accumulation of fluid in the lungs and brain, and include breathlessness at rest, a dry, irritative cough (which may progress to the production of pink, frothy sputum), severe headache, lack of coordination (typically leading to a 'drunken walk'), confusion, irrational behaviour, vomiting and eventually unconsciousness and death.

PREVENTION

If you trek above 2500m, observe the following rules:

» **Ascend slowly** Where possible, do not sleep more than 300m higher than the elevation where you spent the previous night. If any stage on a trek exceeds this increase in elevation, take at least one rest day to acclimatise before you start the ascent. If you or anyone else in your party seems to be struggling, take a rest day as a precaution.

» **Climb high, sleep low** It is always wise to sleep at a lower altitude than the greatest height reached during the day. If you need to cross a high pass, take an extra acclimatisation day before you cross. Be aware that descending to the altitude where you slept the previous night may not be enough to compensate for a very large increase in altitude during the day.

» **Trek healthy** You are more likely to develop AMS if you are tired, dehydrated or malnourished. Drink extra fluids while trekking. Avoid sedatives or sleeping pills and don't smoke – this will further reduce the amount of oxygen reaching your lungs.

» **If you feel unwell, stop** If you start to display mild symptoms of AMS, stop climbing. Take an acclimatisation day and see if things improve. If your symptoms stay the same or get worse, descend immediately.

» **If you show serious symptoms, descend** If you show any serious symptoms of AMS, descend immediately to a lower altitude. Ideally this should be below the altitude where you slept the night before you first developed symptoms. Most lodges can arrange an emergency porter to help you descend quickly to a safe altitude.

TREATMENT

Treat mild symptoms by resting at the same altitude until recovery. Take paracetamol or aspirin for headaches. Diamox (acetazolamide) can be used to reduce mild symptoms of AMS. However, it is not a cure and it will not stop you from developing serious symptoms. The usual dosage of Diamox is 125mg to 250mg twice daily. The medication is a diuretic so you should drink extra liquid to avoid dehydration. Diamox may also cause disturbances to vision and the sense of taste and it can cause a harmless tingling sensation in the fingers.

If symptoms persist or become worse, descend immediately – even 500m can help. If the victim cannot walk without support, they may need to be carried down. Any delay could be fatal; if you have to descend in the dark, seek local assistance.

In the event of severe symptoms, the victim may need to be flown to a lower altitude by helicopter. Getting the victim to a lower altitude is the priority – get someone else from the group to call for helicopter rescue and start the descent to the pick-up point. Note that a helicopter rescue can cost US$2500 to US$10,000.

Emergency treatments for serious symptoms of AMS include supplementary oxygen, nifedipine, dexamethasone and repressurisation using a device known as a Gamow bag (this should only be administered by health professionals), but these only reduce the symptoms and they are not a 'cure'. They should never be used to avoid descent or to enable further ascent.

The only effective treatment for sufferers of severe AMS is to descend rapidly to a lower altitude.

Water

Don't drink the water in Nepal. Ice should be avoided except in upmarket tourist-oriented restaurants. While trekking, purify your own water rather than buying purified water in polluting plastic bottles.

WATER PURIFICATION

The easiest way to purify water is to boil it thoroughly. Most trekkers prefer to purify water using iodine drops or tablets. Chlorine tablets (eg Puritabs or Steritabs) kill many pathogens but are not effective against giardia and amoebic cysts. Follow the directions carefully – filter water through a cloth before adding the chemicals and be sure to wet the thread on the lid to your water bottle. Once the water is purified, vitamin C can be added to remove the chemical taste.

Trekking filters take out all parasites, bacteria and viruses, and make water safe to drink. However, it is very important to read the specifications so that you know exactly what the filter removes from the water. Another option is a UV light–based treatment such as a Steripen.

Language

Nepali belongs to the Indo-European language family and has about 35 million speakers. It's closely related to Hindi and is written in the Devanagari script (also used for Hindi). Although Nepali is the national language and is used as a lingua franca between Nepal's ethnic groups, many other languages are also spoken in the country. The Newars of the Kathmandu Valley speak Newari. Other languages are spoken by the Tamangs, Sherpas, Rais, Limbus, Magars, Gurungs and other groups. In the Terai (bordering India), Hindi and Maithili are often spoken.

It's quite easy to get by with English in Nepal. Most people visitors have to deal with in the Kathmandu Valley and in Pokhara will speak some English. Along the main trekking trails, particularly the Annapurna Circuit, English is also widely understood.

Most Nepali consonant sounds are quite similar to their English counterparts. The exceptions are the so-called retroflex consonants and the aspirated consonants. Retroflex sounds are made by curling the tongue tip back to touch the roof of the mouth as you make the sound – they are indicated in this chapter by a dot below the letter, eg ṭ or ḍ as in Kaṭhmanḍu. Aspirated consonants are pronounced more forcefully than in English and are made with a short puff of air – they are indicated in this chapter by adding h after the consonant, eg ph is pronounced as the 'p' in 'pit', and th is pronounced as the 't' in 'time'.

As for the vowels, a is pronounced as the 'u' in 'hut', ā as the 'ar' in 'garden' (no 'r' sound), e as in 'best' but longer, i as in 'sister' but longer, o as in 'sold', u as in 'put', ai as in 'aisle' and au as the 'ow' in 'cow'. The stressed syllables are indicated with italics.

WANT MORE?

For in-depth language information and handy phrases, check out Lonely Planet's *Nepali Phrasebook*. You'll find it at **shop .lonelyplanet.com**, or you can buy Lonely Planet's iPhone phrasebooks at the Apple App Store.

BASICS

Even if you learn no other Nepali, there is one word every visitor soon picks up – *namaste* (pronounced na·ma·ste). Strictly translated it means 'I salute the god in you', but it's used as an everyday greeting that encompasses everything from 'Hello' to 'How are you?' and even 'See you again soon'. It should be accompanied with the hands held in a prayer-like position, the Nepali gesture equivalent to Westerners shaking hands.

Hello./Goodbye.	na·ma·ste
How are you?	ta·pāi·lai kas·to chha
Excuse me.	ha·jur
Please (give me).	di·nu·hos
Please (you have).	khā·nu·hos
Thank you.	dhan·ya·bad

Unlike in many other countries, verbal expressions of thanks are not the cultural norm in Nepal. Although neglecting to say 'Thank you' may make you feel a little uncomfortable, it is rarely necessary in simple commercial transactions – foreigners saying *dhanyabad* all the time sound distinctly odd to Nepalis.

Yes. (I have)	chā
No. (I don't have)	chhai·na
I	ma
OK.	theek·cha
Wait a minute.	ek chhin par·kha·nos
good/pretty	ram·ro

LANGUAGES OF NEPAL

Language	Estimated % of the Population
Nepali	47.8
Maithili	12.1
Bhojpuri	7.4
Tharu	5.8
Tamang	5.1
Newari	3.6
Magar	3.3
Rai	2.7
Awadhi	2.4
Limbu	1.4
Gurung	1.2
Sherpa	0.7
Other	6.5

I don't need it.	ma·lai cha·hi·na
I don't have it.	ma san·ga chhai·na
Do you speak English?	ta·pāi an·gre·ji bol·na sak·nu hun·chha
I only speak a little Nepali.	ma a·li a·li ne·pā·li bol·chhu
I understand.	ma bujh·chu
I don't understand.	mai·le bu·jhi·na
Please say it again.	phe·ri bha·nu·hos
Please speak more slowly.	ta·pāi bi·stā·rai bol·nu·hos

ACCOMMODATION

Where is a ...?	... ka·hā chha
campsite	shi·vir
guesthouse	pā·hu·na ghar
hotel	ho·ṭel
lodge	laj

Can I get a place to stay here?	ya·hā bās paun·chha
Can I look at the room?	ko·thā her·na sak·chhu
How much is it per night?	ek rāt·ko ka·ti pai·sā ho
Does it include breakfast?	bi·hā·na·ko khā·na sa·met ho

clean	sa·fā
dirty	mai·lo
fan	pan·khā
hot water	tā·to pā·ni
room	ko·thā

EATING & DRINKING

I'm a vegetarian.	ma sāh·kā·ha·ri hun
I don't eat spicy food.	ma pi·ro khan·di·na
Please bring me a spoon.	ma·lai cham·chah lyau·nu·hos
Can I have the bill?	bil pau·na sak·chhu

banana	ke·rah
bread	ro·ṭi
cauliflower	go·bi
chicken	ku·kha·ra/murgh
egg	phul
eggplant	bhaṇ·ṭa
fish	mā·chha
lentils	daal
meat	ma·su
mutton	kha·si
okra	ram·to·ri·ya
peanut	ba·dam
potato	a·lu
(cooked) rice	bhāt
spinach	sag

cold beer	chi·so bi·yar
boiled water	u·māh·le·ko pa·ni
hot lemon	ta·to pa·ni·mah ka·ga·ti
lemon soda	so·ḍa·mah ka·ga·ti
milk	dudh
sugar	chi·ni
tea	chi·ya
yoghurt	da·hi

EMERGENCIES

Help!	gu·hār
It's an emergency!	ā·paṭ par·yo
There's been an accident!	dur·gha·ṭa·nā bha·yo
Please call a doctor.	dāk·ṭar·lai bo·lāu·nu·hos
Where is the (public) toilet?	shau·chā·la·ya ka·hā chha
I'm lost.	ma ha·rā·ye

HEALTH

Where can I find a good doctor?	rām·ro dāk·ṭar ka·hā pāin·cha
Where is the nearest hospital?	ya·hā as·pa·tāl ka·hā chha
I don't feel well.	ma·lāi san·cho chhai·na

I'm having trouble breathing.	sās pher·na sak·di·na
I have altitude sickness.	lekh lāg·yo
I have a fever.	jo·ro ā·yo
I have diarrhoea.	di·shā lāg·yo
medicine	au·sa·dhi
pharmacy/chemist	au·sa·dhi pa·sal
I have ...	ma·lāi ... lāg·yo
asthma	dam·ko bya·thā
diabetes	ma·dhu·me·ha
epilepsy	chā·re rog

SHOPPING & SERVICES

Where's the market?	ba·zār ka·hā chha
What is it made of?	ke·le ba·ne·ko
How much?	ka·ti
That's enough.	pugyo
I like this.	ma·lai yo ram·ro lag·yo
I don't like this.	ma·lai yo ram·ro lag·en·a

cheap	sas·to
envelope	kham
expensive	ma·han·go
less	kam
little bit	a·li·ka·ti
money	pai·sa
more	ba·dhi
stamp	ti·ka

bank	baink
... embassy	... rāj·du·tā·vas
museum	sam·grā·hā·la·ya
police	pra·ha·ri
post office	post a·fis
tourist office	tu·rist a·fis

What time does it open/close?	ka·ti ba·je khol·chha/ ban·da gar·chha
I want to change some money.	pai·sā sāt·nu man·lāg·chha
Is there a local internet cafe?	ya·hā in·tar·net kyah·phe chha
I'd like to get internet access.	ma·lai in·tar·net cha·hi·yo
I'd like to check my email.	i·mel chek gar·nu·par·yo
I'd like to send an email.	i·mel pa·thau·nu·par·yo

TIME & DATES

What time is it?	ka·ti ba·jyo
It's one o'clock.	ek ba·jyo

minute	mi·nat
hour	ghan·tā
day	din
week	hap·tā
month	ma·hi·nā

yesterday	hi·jo
today	ā·ja
now	a·hi·le
tomorrow	bho·li

What day is it today?	ā·ja ke bār
Today is ...	ā·ja ... ho

Monday	som·bār
Tuesday	man·gal bār
Wednesday	budh·bār
Thursday	bi·hi·bār
Friday	su·kra·bār
Saturday	sa·ni·bār
Sunday	āi·ta·bār

TRANSPORT & DIRECTIONS

Where?	ka·hā
here	ya·hā
there	tya·hā

Signs	
खुला	Open
बन्द	Closed
प्रवेश	Entrance
निकास	Exit
प्रवेश निषेध	No Entry
धूम्रपान मनाही छ	No Smoking
मनाही/निषेध	Prohibited
शाचालय	Toilets
तातो	Hot
चिसो	Cold
खतरा	Danger
रोक्नुहोस	Stop
बाटो बन्द	Road Closed

Numbers

0	sun·ya	शून्य
1	ek	एक
2	du·i	दुइ
3	tin	तीन
4	chār	चार
5	panch	पाँच
6	chha	छ
7	sāt	सात
8	āṭh	आठ
9	nau	नौ
10	das	दस
11	e·ghār·a	एघार
12	bā·hra	बाह्र
13	te·hra	तेह्र
14	chau·dha	चौध
15	pan·dhra	पन्ध्र
16	so·hra	सोह्र
17	sa·tra	सत्र
18	a·ṭhā·ra	अठार
19	un·nais	उन्नाईस
20	bis	बीस
21	ek kais	एककाईस
22	bais	बाईस
23	teis	तेईस
24	chau·bis	चौबीस
25	pach·chis	पच्चीस
26	chhab·bis	छब्बीस
27	sat·tais	सत्ताईस
28	aṭ·ṭhais	अट्ठाईस
29	u·nan·tis	उनन्तीस
30	tis	तीस
40	chā·lis	चालीस
50	pa·chās	पचास
60	sā·ṭhi	साठी
70	sat·ta·ri	सत्तरी
80	a·si	असी
90	nab·be	नब्बे
100	ek say	एक सय
1000	ek ha·jār	एक हजार
10,000	das ha·jār	दस हजार
100,000	ek lākh	एक लाख
200,000	du·i lākh	दुइ लाख
1,000,000	das lākh	दस लाख

What is the address? — the·gā·nā ke ho

Please write down the address. — the·gā·nā lekh·nu·hos

How can I get to ...? — ... ko·lā·gi ka·ti pai·sā lāg·chha

Is it far from here? — ya·hā·ba·ta ke tā·dhā chha

Can I walk there? — hi·ḍe·ra jā·na sa·kin·chhu

boat — nāu

bus — bus

taxi — tyakh·si

ticket — ti·kaṭ

I want to go to ... — ma ...·mā jān·chhu

Where does this bus go? — yo bus ka·hā jān·chha

I want a one-way ticket. — jā·ne ti·kaṭ di·nu·hos

I want a return ticket. — jā·ne·āu·ne ti·kaṭ di·nu·hos

How much is it to go to ...? — ... jā·na ka·ti par·chha

Does your taxi have a meter? — ta·pāi ko tyakh·si mā me·ter chha

TREKKING

Which way is ...? — ... jā·ne ba·to ka·ta par·chha

Is there a village nearby? — na·ji·kai gaun par·chha

How many hours to ...? — ... ka·ti ghan·ṭā

How many days to ...? — ... ka·ti din

Where is the porter? — bha·ri·ya ka·ta ga·yo

I want to sleep. — ma·lai sut·na man lag·yo

I'm cold. — ma·lai jā·ḍo lag·yo

Please give me (water). — ma·lai (pa·ni) di·nu·hos

bridge — pul

cold — jā·ḍo

downhill — o·rā·lo

left — bā·yā

right — dā·yā

teahouse — bhaṭ·ti

uphill — u·kā·lo

way/trail — sā·no bā·ṭo

GLOSSARY

Beware of the different methods of transliterating Nepali and the other languages spoken in Nepal. There are many and varied ways of spelling Nepali words. In particular, the letters 'b' and 'v' are often interchanged.

ACAP – Annapurna Conservation Area Project

Aditya – ancient *Vedic* sun god, also known as Suriya

Agni – ancient *Vedic* god of the hearth and fire

Agnipura – Buddhist symbol for fire

AMS – acute mountain sickness, also known as altitude sickness

Annapurna – the goddess of abundance and an incarnation of *Mahadevi*

Ashoka – Indian Buddhist emperor who spread Buddhism throughout the subcontinent

Ashta Matrikas – the eight multi-armed mother goddesses

Avalokiteshvara – as *Gautama Buddha* is the *Buddha* of our era, so Avalokiteshvara is the *bodhisattva* of our era

bagh chal – traditional Nepali game

bahal – Buddhist monastery courtyard

ban – forest or jungle

bandh – strike; see also *julus* and *chakka jam*

Bhadrakali – Tantric goddess who is also a consort of *Bhairab*

Bhagwati – a form of *Durga*, and thus a form of the goddess *Parvati*

Bhairab – the 'terrific' or fearsome Tantric form of *Shiva* with 64 manifestations

bhanjyang – mountain pass

Bhimsen – one of the Pandava brothers, from the *Mahabharata*, seen as a god of tradesmen

bhojanalaya – basic Nepali restaurant or canteen

Bhote – Nepali term for a Tibetan, used in the names of rivers flowing from Tibet

Bodhi tree – a pipal tree under which the *Buddha* was sitting when he attained enlightenment; also known as 'bo tree'

bodhisattva – a near-*Buddha* who renounces the opportunity to attain *nirvana* in order to aid humankind

Bön – the pre-Buddhist animist religion of Tibet

Brahma – the creator god in the Hindu triad, which also includes *Vishnu* and *Shiva*

Brahmin – the highest Hindu caste, said to originate from *Brahma's* head

Buddha – the 'Awakened One'; the originator of Buddhism

chaitya – small *stupa*, which usually contains a *mantra* rather than a Buddhist relic

chakka jam – literally 'jam the wheels', in which all vehicles stay off the street during a strike; see also *bandh* and *julus*

chakra – *Vishnu's* disc-like weapon; one of the four symbols he holds

Chandra – moon god

chautara – stone platforms around trees, which serve as shady places for porters to rest

Chhetri – the second caste of Nepali Hindus, said to originate from *Brahma's* arms

chörten – Tibetan Buddhist *stupa*

chowk – historically a courtyard or marketplace; these days used more to refer to an intersection or crossroads

daal – lentil soup; the main source of protein in the Nepali diet

Dalai Lama – spiritual leader of Tibetan Buddhist people

danda – hill

deval – temple

Devi – the short form of *Mahadevi*, the *shakti* to *Shiva*

dhaka – hand-woven cotton cloth

dharma – Buddhist teachings

dhoka – door or gate

Dhyani Buddha – the original Adi *Buddha* created five Dhyani Buddhas, who in turn create the universe of each human era

doko – basket carried by porters

dorje – Tibetan word for the 'thunderbolt' symbol of Buddhist power; *vajra* in Nepali

durbar – palace

Durga – fearsome manifestation of *Parvati*, *Shiva's* consort

gaida – rhinoceros

Ganesh – son of *Shiva* and *Parvati*, instantly recognisable by his elephant head

Ganga – goddess of the Ganges

Garuda – the man-bird *vehicle* of *Vishnu*

Gautama Buddha – the *Buddha* of our era

Gelugpa – one of the four major schools of Tibetan Buddhism

ghat – steps beside a river; a 'burning ghat' is used for cremations

gompa – Tibetan Buddhist monastery

gopi – milkmaids; companions of *Krishna*

gufa – cave

Gurkhas – Nepali soldiers who have long formed a part of the British army; the name comes from the region of Gorkha

Gurung – western hill people from around Gorkha and Pokhara

Hanuman – monkey god

harmika – square base on top of a *stupa's* dome, upon which the eyes of the *Buddha* are painted

hathi – elephant

himal – range or massif with permanent snow

hiti – water conduit or tank with waterspouts

hookah – water pipe for smoking

howdah – riding platform for passengers on an elephant

Indra – king of the *Vedic* gods; god of rain

Jagannath – *Krishna* as Lord of the Universe

janai – sacred thread, which high-caste Hindu men wear looped over their left shoulder

jatra – festival

jayanti – birthday

jhankri – faith healers who perform in a trance while beating drums

Jogini – mystical goddesses and counterparts to the 64 manifestations of *Bhairab*

julus – a procession or demonstration; see also *bandh* and *chakka jam*

Kali – the most terrifying manifestation of *Parvati*

Kalki – *Vishnu's* tenth and as yet unseen incarnation during which he will come riding a white horse and wielding a sword to destroy the world

Kam Dev – *Shiva's* companion

karma – Buddhist and Hindu law of cause and effect, which continues from one life to another

KEEP – Kathmandu Environmental Education Project

Khas – Hindu hill people

khat – see *palanquin*

khata – Tibetan prayer scarf, presented to an honoured guest or Buddhist *lama*

khola – stream or tributary

khukuri – traditional curved knife of the *Gurkhas*

kosi – river

kot – fort

Krishna – fun-loving eighth incarnation of *Vishnu*

Kumari – living goddess; a peaceful incarnation of *Kali*

kunda – water tank fed by springs

la – mountain pass

lama – Tibetan Buddhist monk or priest

lingam – phallic symbol signifying *Shiva's* creative powers

Machhendranath – patron god of the Kathmandu Valley and an incarnation of *Avalokiteshvara*

Mahabharata – one of the major Hindu epics

Mahadeva – literally 'Great God'; *Shiva*

Mahadevi – literally 'Great Goddess', sometimes known as *Devi*; the *shakti* to *Shiva*

Mahayana – the 'greater vehicle' of Buddhism; a later adaptation of the teaching, which lays emphasis on the *bodhisattva* ideal

makara – mythical crocodile-like beast

Malla – royal dynasty of the Kathmandu Valley responsible for most of the important temples and palaces of the valley towns

mandala – geometrical and astrological representation of the path to enlightenment

mandir – temple

mani – stone carved with the Tibetan Buddhist chant *om mani padme hum*

Manjushri – Buddhist *bodhisattva*

mantra – prayer formula or chant

Mara – Buddhist god of death; has three eyes and holds the *wheel of life*

math – Hindu priest's house

mela – country fair

misthan bhandar – Indian-style sweet house and snack bar

naga – serpent deity

Nagpura – Buddhist symbol for water

namaste – traditional Hindu greeting (hello or goodbye), with the hands brought together at chest or head level, as a sign of respect

Nandi – *Shiva's vehicle*, the bull

Narayan – *Vishnu* as the sleeping figure on the cosmic ocean; from his navel *Brahma* appeared and went on to create the universe

Narsingha – man-lion incarnation of *Vishnu*

Newari – people of the Kathmandu Valley

nirvana – ultimate peace and cessation of rebirth (Buddhism)

om mani padme hum – sacred Buddhist *mantra*, which means 'hail to the jewel in the lotus'

padma – lotus flower

pagoda – multistoreyed Nepali temple, whose design was exported across Asia

palanquin – portable covered bed usually shouldered by four men; also called a *khat*

Parvati – *Shiva's* consort

pashmina – goat-wool blanket or shawl

Pashupati – *Shiva* as Lord of the Animals

path – small, raised platform to shelter pilgrims

phanta – grass plains

pipal tree – see *Bodhi tree*

pokhari – large water tank, or small lake

prasad – food offering

prayer flag – square of cloth printed with a *mantra* and hung in a string as a prayer offering

prayer wheel – cylindrical wheel inscribed with a Buddhist prayer or *mantra* that is 'said' when the wheel spins

Prithvi – *Vedic* earth goddess

puja – religious offering or prayer

pujari – priest

purnima – full moon

rajpath – road or highway, literally 'king's road'

Ramayana – Hindu epic

Rana – a hereditary line of prime ministers who ruled Nepal from 1846 to 1951

rath – temple chariot in which the idol is conveyed in processions

rudraksha – dried seeds worn in necklaces by *sadhu*s

SAARC – South Asian Association for Regional Cooperation; includes India, Nepal, Pakistan, Bangladesh and Sri Lanka

sadhu – wandering Hindu holy man

Sagarmatha – Nepali name for Mt Everest

sal – tree of the lower Himalayan foothills

saligram – a black ammonite fossil of a Jurassic-period sea creature that is also a symbol of *Shiva*

sankha – conch shell, one of *Vishnu's* four symbols

Saraswati – goddess of learning and creative arts, and consort of *Brahma*; carries a lute-like instrument

seto – white

Shaivite – follower of *Shiva*

shakti – dynamic female element in male/female relationships; also a goddess

Sherpa – Buddhist hill people of Tibetan ancestry famed for work with mountaineering expeditions; with a lower-case 's' it refers to a trek leader

shikhara – Indian-style temple with a tall, corn-cob-like spire

Shiva – the most powerful Hindu god, the creator and destroyer; part of the Hindu triad with *Vishnu* and *Brahma*

sindur – red vermilion powder and mustard-oil mixture used for offerings

sirdar – leader/organiser of a trekking party

stupa – bell-shaped Buddhist religious structure, originally designed to hold the relics of the *Buddha*

Sudra – the lowest Nepali caste, said to originate from *Brahma's* feet

sundhara – fountain with golden spout

tabla – hand drum

tahr – wild mountain goat

tal – lake

Taleju Bhawani – Nepali goddess, an aspect of *Mahadevi* and the family deity of the *Malla* kings of the Kathmandu Valley

tappu – island

Tara – White Tara is the consort of the *Dhyani Buddha* Vairocana; Green Tara is associated with Amoghasiddhi

teahouse trek – independent trekking between village inns (ie no camping)

tempo – three-wheeled, automated minivan commonly used in Nepal

Thakali – people of the Kali Gandaki Valley who specialise in running hotels

thali – literally a plate with compartments for different dishes; an all-you-can-eat set meal

thangka – Tibetan religious painting

third eye – symbolic eye on *Buddha* figures, used to indicate the *Buddha's* all-seeing wisdom and perception

thukpa – noodle soup

tika – red sandalwood-paste spot marked on the forehead, particularly for religious occasions

tole – street or quarter of a town; sometimes used to refer to a square

tonga – horse carriage

topi – traditional Nepali cap

torana – carved pediment above temple doors

Tribhuvan – the king who in 1951 ended the *Rana* period and Nepal's long seclusion

trisul – trident weapon that is a symbol of *Shiva*

tunala – carved temple struts

tundikhel – parade ground

Uma Maheshwar – *Shiva* and *Parvati* in a pose where *Shiva* sits cross-legged and *Parvati* sits on his thigh and leans against him

Upanishads – ancient *Vedic* scripts; the last part of the *Vedas*

vahana – a god's animal mount or *vehicle*

Vaishnavite – follower of *Vishnu*

Vaisya – caste of merchants and farmers, said to originate from *Brahma's* thighs

vajra – the 'thunderbolt' symbol of Buddhist power in Nepal; *dorje* in Tibetan

Vedas – ancient orthodox Hindu scriptures

Vedic gods – ancient Hindu gods described in the *Vedas*

vehicle – the animal with which a Hindu god is associated

vihara – Buddhist religious buildings and pilgrim accommodation

Vishnu – the preserver; one of the three main Hindu gods, along with *Brahma* and *Shiva*

wheel of life – Buddhist representation of how humans are chained by desire to a life of suffering

yak – cow-like Nepali beast of burden (only pure-blood animals of the genus *Bos grunniens* can properly be called yaks; cross-breeds have other names)

yaksha – attendant deity or nymph

Yama – *Vedic* god of death; his messenger is the crow

Yellow Hats – name sometimes given to adherents of the *Gelugpa* school of Tibetan Buddhism

yeti – abominable snowman; mythical hairy mountain man of the Himalaya

yogi – yoga master

yoni – female sexual symbol, equivalent of a *lingam*

zamindar – absentee landlord and/or moneylender

behind the scenes

SEND US YOUR FEEDBACK

We love to hear from travellers – your comments keep us on our toes and help make our books better. Our well-travelled team reads every word on what you loved or loathed about this book. Although we cannot reply individually to postal submissions, we always guarantee that your feedback goes straight to the appropriate authors, in time for the next edition. Each person who sends us information is thanked in the next edition – the most useful submissions are rewarded with a selection of digital PDF chapters.

Visit **lonelyplanet.com/contact** to submit your updates and suggestions or to ask for help. Our award-winning website also features inspirational travel stories, news and discussions.

Note: We may edit, reproduce and incorporate your comments in Lonely Planet products such as guidebooks, websites and digital products, so let us know if you don't want your comments reproduced or your name acknowledged. For a copy of our privacy policy visit lonelyplanet.com/privacy.

OUR READERS

Many thanks to the travellers who used the last edition and wrote to us with helpful hints, useful advice and interesting anecdotes:

Craig Alsup, Jan Ardesch, Anne-Karin Atwood, Trin Au, Christy Auer, Leonie Bartlett, Buddhi Bhatta, Liz Bissett, Carl Bloch, Stina Bostrom, Sally Brodziak, Jeroen Buijs, Mark Buzinkay, Richard Carroll, Kathryn Cehrs, Alice Chan, Jian Chen, Nelson Chen, David Childress, Benjamin Chisholme, Nickie Clare, Suzie Coad, Gerald Cohen, Margaret Collins, James Cooper, Louis Corbeil, Henry Coulter, Yoav Dan, Mark Davis, Gary Dawson Smith, Theo de Bray, Lian de Graaf, Alexandra de Groote, Nadine Delannoy, Ben Demarco, Caron Dhoju, Kyaron Dhoju, Chad Dibble, Joanne Divine, Kay Dunlevy, Ricardo Egana, Daniel Ek, Navyo Eller, Bronwyn Ellis, Claire Faugeras, Sarah Ferris, Brett Gamon, Dave Garwood, Macartan Gaughan, Hilde Geels, Daniel Gerster, Ben Goldsmisth, Sheila Gooden, Doug Grant, Laura Grant, Thomas Grindrod, James Gurd, Martine Hamlet, Martin Harris, Sonja Hilbrand, David and Sally Hillebrandt, Maziar Hosseinzadeh, Greg Hoyt, Dr Gisela Huber, Duane Hybertson, Petros Isaakidis, Monique Jochman, Sandy Jordan, Sushma Joshi, Basia Jozwiak, Pascal Kaufmann, Andrea Ketcham, Berend Klompsma, Natalie Klötzer, Kristin Kudebeh, Michael Lange, Stone Leung, Benjamin Linder, Amanda Marr, David Martin, Mark Mascarenhas, Scott Mason, Anna Matyasfalvi, Anne Mawdsley, Solveig Mitt, Nabiha Mohammed, Michael Moldoveanu, Sarah Montagu, Steve Morgan, Robert Morton, Anson Moxness, Caroline Murray, Stefania Nardin, Augustus Nasmith Jr, Ross Neal, Alexis Negre, Don Pagett, Amalia Peloc, Xavi Pérez, Mareike Pergher, Mikael Persson, Matt Piercy, Jodi Polak, Olivia Pollock, Jiri Preclik, Bill Prime, Raaz the Secret, Karen Rae, Jose Ramon Infante, Muna Rana, Therese Ranerup, Laurel Redding, Jack Richeson, Suzanne Rigg, Theresa Rooney, Gladys Rousseau, Sourav Roy, Alexandra Rudorff, Michal Rudziecki, Claudia Ruepp, Lauren Ruff, Kerstin Rusch, Elena Rybiakova, Harjinder Samra, Bradley Schultz, Raymond Schweichert, Markus Schweitzer, Howard Sercombe, Dan Seymour-Davies, Rahul Sharma, Deborah Sherman, Gyanu Shrestha, Neil Small, Carter Smith, Martina Specht, Lucien Staarink, Belinda Stein, Tracy Stevens, Scott Swensen, Howard Tarpey, Sam Tarshis, Binod Thapa, Myriam Thomachot, Joe Thurgoof, Richard Tigran Gazarian, Franciska Tillema, Melissa Umphress, Steve Umphress, Sarah van den Bos, Wilfred van der Pluijm, Maaike van Dooren, Jack van Doren, Berry van Welzen, Robbert Veern, Mike Vingoe, Mark Volmer, Andrea Votavova, Andrew Whitmarsh, David Wilken, Chris Williamson, Kwa Yiqian

AUTHOR THANKS

Bradley Mayhew

Thanks to Michelle and Puchun, Jehan Seirafi, Ruth at Global Vision International, Niraj Shrestha, Rajeev Shrestha, Rajan Simkhada, porter Gompu Sherpa, phantom trekking partner Carol Davis, Durga Tamang and Megh Ale. Cheers as always to Trent and Lindsay.

Lindsay Brown

I am very grateful for the assistance of Stan Armington in Pokhara, Durga Bhandari in Kathmandu, Ram Prasad Rijal in Sauraha, Man Mohan Shrestha in Tansen, Lila Mani Sharma in Lumbini and Mohan Arayal, Santa Chaudhari and Khageshwor Gautam in Bardia. Thanks also to co-authors Bradley and Trent, and to Jenny, Pat and Sinead at home.

Trent Holden

A huge thanks to everyone that I met along the road who helped out with invaluable tips and feedback. In no particular order I'd like to thank Tony Jones, Niraj Shrestha, Jenny and Santosh, Chimi Gurung, Sarita Bhatta, Erin McEvoy, Dmytro Dmytrenko and Megh Ale. I'd also like to thank my co-authors Bradley and Lindsay. Finally, all my love to my family and my girlfriend, Kate.

ACKNOWLEDGMENTS

Cover photograph: Bodhnath Stupa, Bodhnath. Felix Hug/Lonely Planet Images.

Many of the images in this guide are available for licensing from Lonely Planet Images: www.lonelyplanetimages.com.

THIS BOOK

This 9th edition of Lonely Planet's Nepal guidebook was researched and written by Bradley Mayhew (coordinating author), Lindsay Brown and Trent Holden. Bradley and Trent also worked on the previous edition along with coordinating author Joe Bindloss. This guidebook was commissioned in Lonely Planet's Melbourne office, and produced by the following:

Commissioning Editors Kate Morgan, Maryanne Netto, Kalya Ryan, Glenn van der Knijff

Coordinating Editors Michelle Bennett, Carolyn Boicos, Rebecca Chau

Coordinating Cartographer Peter Shields

Coordinating Layout Designer Mazzy Prinsep

Managing Editors Brigitte Ellemor, Angela Tinson

Senior Editors Susan Paterson, Martine Power

Managing Cartographers David Connolly, Corey Hutchison, Adrian Persoglia

Managing Layout Designers Chris Girdler, Jane Hart

Assisting Editors Janet Austin, Pete Cruttenden, Andi Jones, Kate Kiely, Kellie Langdon, Luna Soo

Assisting Cartographers Karusha Ganga, Rachel Ime-son, Valentina Kremenchutskaya, Jacqueline Nguyen, Sophie Reed, Andy Rojas

Cover Research Naomi Parker

Internal Image Research Aude Vauconsant

Language Content Branislava Vladisavljevic

Thanks to Ryan Evans, Briohny Hooper, Yvonne Kirk, Shawn Low, Wayne Murphy, Trent Paton, Kirsten Rawlings, Alison Ridgway, Gerard Walker

index

how to use this book

These symbols will help you find the listings you want:

- 👁 Sights
- 🏃 Beaches
- 🏃 Activities
- 🛶 Courses
- 👆 Tours
- 🎊 Festivals & Events
- 🛏 Sleeping
- 🍴 Eating
- 🍷 Drinking
- ⭐ Entertainment
- 🛍 Shopping
- ℹ️ Information/ Transport

These symbols give you the vital information for each listing:

- 🕿 Telephone Numbers
- 🕐 Opening Hours
- 🅿 Parking
- ⊖ Nonsmoking
- ❄ Air-Conditioning
- @ Internet Access
- 📶 Wi-Fi Access
- 🏊 Swimming Pool
- 🥗 Vegetarian Selection
- 📖 English-Language Menu
- 👪 Family-Friendly
- 🐾 Pet-Friendly
- 🚌 Bus
- ⛴ Ferry
- Ⓜ Metro
- Ⓢ Subway
- 🚊 Tram
- 🚆 Train

Reviews are organised by author preference.

Look out for these icons:

- **TOP CHOICE** Our author's recommendation
- **FREE** No payment required
- 🍃 A green or sustainable option

Our authors have nominated these places as demonstrating a strong commitment to sustainability – for example by supporting local communities and producers, operating in an environmentally friendly way, or supporting conservation projects.

Map Legend

Sights
- 🏖 Beach
- Buddhist
- 🏰 Castle
- ✝ Christian
- Hindu
- ☪ Islamic
- ✡ Jewish
- Monument
- 🏛 Museum/Gallery
- Ruin
- Winery/Vineyard
- 🦁 Zoo
- 👁 Other Sight

Activities, Courses & Tours
- Diving/Snorkelling
- Canoeing/Kayaking
- Skiing
- Surfing
- Swimming/Pool
- Walking
- Windsurfing
- Other Activity/ Course/Tour

Sleeping
- Sleeping
- Camping

Eating
- 🍴 Eating

Drinking
- Drinking
- Cafe

Entertainment
- 🎭 Entertainment

Shopping
- 🛍 Shopping

Information
- 💲 Bank
- Embassy/ Consulate
- ➕ Hospital/Medical
- @ Internet
- Police
- Post Office
- Telephone
- Toilet
- ℹ️ Tourist Information
- • Other Information

Transport
- ✈ Airport
- Border Crossing
- Bus
- Cable Car/ Funicular
- Cycling
- Ferry
- Ⓜ Metro
- Monorail
- 🅿 Parking
- Petrol Station
- Taxi
- Train/Railway
- Tram
- • Other Transport

Routes
- Tollway
- Freeway
- Primary
- Secondary
- Tertiary
- Lane
- Unsealed Road
- Plaza/Mall
- Steps
- Tunnel
- Pedestrian Overpass
- Walking Tour
- Walking Tour Detour
- Path

Geographic
- Hut/Shelter
- Lighthouse
- Lookout
- ▲ Mountain/Volcano
- Oasis
- Park
-)(Pass
- Picnic Area
- Waterfall

Population
- Capital (National)
- ◉ Capital (State/Province)
- City/Large Town
- Town/Village

Boundaries
- International
- State/Province
- Disputed
- Regional/Suburb
- Marine Park
- Cliff
- Wall

Hydrography
- River, Creek
- Intermittent River
- Swamp/Mangrove
- Reef
- Canal
- Water
- Dry/Salt/ Intermittent Lake
- Glacier

Areas
- Beach/Desert
- + + + Cemetery (Christian)
- × × × Cemetery (Other)
- Park/Forest
- Sportsground
- Sight (Building)
- Top Sight (Building)

OUR STORY

A beat-up old car, a few dollars in the pocket and a sense of adventure. In 1972 that's all Tony and Maureen Wheeler needed for the trip of a lifetime – across Europe and Asia overland to Australia. It took several months, and at the end – broke but inspired – they sat at their kitchen table writing and stapling together their first travel guide, *Across Asia on the Cheap*. Within a week they'd sold 1500 copies. Lonely Planet was born. Today, Lonely Planet has offices in Melbourne, London and Oakland, with more than 600 staff and writers. We share Tony's belief that 'a great guidebook should do three things: inform, educate and amuse'.

OUR WRITERS

Bradley Mayhew

Coordinating Author, Kathmandu, Around the Kathmandu Valley, Trekking Routes A self-professed mountain junkie, Bradley has been travelling to Nepal and the Himalaya for almost 20 years, including several months each in Pakistan, Ladakh, Tibet, Bhutan and Sikkim. Bradley has coordinated several editions of this guide and is also the coordinating author of Lonely Planet guides to *Tibet, Bhutan, Central Asia* and *Trekking in the Nepal Himalaya*. For this edition he focused on the Kathmandu area but still managed to sneak off for treks around Manaslu and the Tamang Heritage Trail. He was most recently seen starring in a five-part Arte TV documentary retracing the route of Marco Polo.

Read more about Bradley Mayhew at:
lonelyplanet.com/members/nepalibrad

Lindsay Brown

Pokhara, The Terai & Mahabharat Range (Central and Western), Arts & Architecture, Environment & Wildlife Nepal is a favourite destination for Lindsay, a former conservation biologist and Publishing Manager at Lonely Planet, who is as much at home on a mountain trail as on the back of an elephant swaying through the jungle. Lindsay has trekked, jeeped, ridden and stumbled across many a mountain pass, and has contributed to Lonely Planet's *Bhutan; South India & Kerala; India; Rajasthan, Delhi & Agra;* and *Pakistan & the Karakoram Highway* guides, among others.

Trent Holden

Around the Kathmandu Valley, Kathmandu to Pokhara, The Terai & Mahabharat Range (Eastern), Biking, Rafting & Kayaking During his travels, Trent has found that nowhere quite compares to the craziness and serendipity of the subcontinent, so it was with great delight that he returned to Nepal to update another edition of this title. His first trip here was in 2001, which coincided with the tragedy of the royal-family massacre. Despite that shocking event, Nepal is a place that never fails to impress him more upon each visit. A freelance writer from Melbourne, Trent is currently based in Laos. This is his seventh assignment for Lonely Planet; other titles he's co-authored include *India* and *East Africa*.

Published by Lonely Planet Publications Pty Ltd
ABN 36 005 607 983
9th edition – July 2012
ISBN 978 1 74179 723 7
© Lonely Planet 2012   Photographs © as indicated 2012
10 9 8 7 6 5 4 3 2 1
Printed in Singapore